NORTH CAROLINA
TAXPAYERS

1701–1786

North Carolina Taxpayers

1701-1786

Compiled by
CLARENCE E. RATCLIFF

Dedicated to
My Wife

LOIS A. RATCLIFF

NOTE

THIS WORK lists the names of the taxpayers resident in about half of the North Carolina counties formed before 1786. A second volume, it is hoped, will deal with the remaining counties. The object of this present volume is to set down in writing, while research is fresh, a list of those persons paying poll taxes or property taxes sometime between the years 1701 and 1786. For genealogical purposes, of course, the intent is to identify individuals in relation to a specific time and place, and to make public a class of records likely to assist in the advancement of research.

The majority of the names given here were copied from tax lists microfilmed at the North Carolina State Archives in Raleigh (roll numbers 155.108 and 115.49). Supplementing this basic list, and integrated throughout the text, are names which have been extracted from *The North Carolinian*, afterwards called the *Journal of North Carolina Genealogy* and then simply *North Carolina Genealogy*, from which journal have also been taken names of persons owning headrights and landrights.

For ease of reference the names of taxpayers are given in a single alphabetical sequence. In all cases taxpayers are listed by county of residence and date, and in some cases additional data is supplied. The combined lists, with repeat entries for those people who appear in more than one tax list, contain approximately 28,000 names.

TABLE 1

County	Tax List Dates	Abbreviation
Anson	1763	Anso
Beaufort	1717, 1755, 1764	Beau
Bertie	1757, 1769	Bert
Bladen	1763, 1781	Blad
Brunswick	1769, 1772	Brun
Bute	1771	Bute
Caswell	1777	Casw
Chowan	1717, 1721, 1753	Chow
Craven	1719, 1720, 1769	Crav
Cumberland	1755, 1767	Cumb
Currituck	1715, 1755	Curr
Dobbs	1769, 1779	Dobb
Edgecombe	1734	Edge
Franklin-Warren-Vance	1771	FWV
Gates	1786	Gate
Granville	1755, 1769, 1784	Gran
Hyde	1764	Hyde
New Hanover	1755, 1762, 1763, 1765, 1767	NewH
Northampton	1762	NorH
N.C. Headrights, Landrights	1701, 1741	N.C.
Onslow	1769, 1770	Onsl
Orange	1755	Oran
Pasquotank	1754, 1769	Pasq
Perquimans	1720, 1740	Perq
Pitt	1762, 1763, 1764, 1775	Pitt
Randolph	1779	Rand
Roanoke River	1720	Roan
Rowan	1758, 1759	Rowa
Surry	1771, 1772	Surr
Tryon	1776	Tryo
Tyrrell	1755	Tyrr

TABLE 2

Sources

Date	County	Source
1763	Anson	NCSA 155.108
1717	Beaufort	JNCG 9:1124
1755	Beaufort	NCSA 115.49
1764	Beaufort	NCSA 155.108
1757	Bertie	NC 4:487-501
1769	Bertie	NCSA 115.49
1763	Bladen	NCSA 155.108
1781	Bladen	NCSA 115.49
1769	Brunswick	NCSA 155.108
1772	Brunswick	NCSA 155.108
1771	Bute	JNCG 7:899-907
1777	Caswell	NCSA 155.108
1717	Chowan	NC 6:741-745
1721	Chowan	JNCG 16:2553-2559
1753	Chowan	JNCG 13:1816-1819
1719	Craven	JNCG 19:2835-2836
1720	Craven	NCSA 155.108
1769	Craven	NCSA 155.108
1755	Cumberland	NCSA 115.49
1767	Cumberland	NCSA 115.49
1715	Currituck	JNCG 10:1279-1283
1755	Currituck	NCSA 115.49
1769	Dobbs	NCSA 155.108
1779	Dobbs	JNCG 12:1789-1793
1734	Edgecombe	JNCG 14:2099-2100
1771	Franklin-Warren-Vance	JNCG 11:1499-1515
1786	Gates	NCSA 115.49
1755	Granville	NCSA 115.49
1769	Granville	NCSA 155.108
1784	Granville	NCSA 115.49
1764	Hyde	NCSA 155.108
1755	New Hanover	NCSA 115.49
1762	New Hanover	NCSA 155.108

1763	New Hanover	NCSA 155.108
1765	New Hanover	NCSA 155.108
1767	New Hanover	NCSA 155.108
1701	N.C. Headrights	CRONC I:393-396
1741	N.C. Landrights	JNCG 12:1759-1769
1741	N.C. Landrights	JNCG 13:1824-1834
1762	Northampton	NCSA 155.108
1769	Onslow	NCSA 155.108
1770	Onslow	NCSA 155.108
1755	Orange	NCSA 115.49
1754	Pasquotank	NCSA 155.108
1769	Pasquotank	NCSA 155.108
1720	Perquimans	JNCG 16:2484-2489
1740	Perquimans	NC 1:117-119
1762	Pitt	NCSA 155.108
1763	Pitt	NCSA 155.108
1764	Pitt	NCSA 155.108
1775	Pitt	NCSA 155.108
1779	Randolph	NCSA 155.108
1758	Rowan	JNCG 10:1383
1759	Rowan	JNCG 13:1883-1890
1720	Roanoke River	JNCG 19:2837-2838
1771	Surry	NC 3:340-344
1772	Surry	NC 4:396-401
1776	Tryon	JNCG 14:2104-2105
1755	Tyrrell	NCSA 115.49

References

NCSA North Carolina State Archives, microfilm rolls 155.108 and 115.49.

NC *The North Carolinian* (1955-1961), edited by William Perry Johnson, continued as

JNCG *Journal of North Carolina Genealogy* (1962 – 1966) and *North Carolina Genealogy* (1967 – 1975), edited by William Perry Johnson.

CRONC *Colonial Records of North Carolina,* edited by William L. Saunders.

AARON, Jacob	Rowa	1759	ADAMS, Ezekiel	Crav	1769
John	Rowa	1759	George	Oran	1755
Wm	Rowa	1759	Isaac	Beau	1764
ABBOT, Caleb	Pasq	1769	Isaac	Oran	1755
Henry	Beau	1755	Jacob	Cumb	1767
Henry	Pasq	1769	James	Anso	1763
James	FWV	1771	James	Beau	1743
John	Oran	1755	James	Beau	1755
Thomas	Dobb	1769	James	Beau	1764
Waddington	Bute	1771	James	FWV	1771
Waddington & s.			Jesse	Cumb	1767
Joseph & Wm	FWV	1771	John	Anso	1763
ABENATHY, Robert	Gran	1755	John	Beau	1755
Robert s. Robert	Gran	1755	John	Casw	1777
ABERCROMBIE, Robert	Oran	1755	John	Cumb	1767
ABINGTON, James	Bert	1757	John	FWV	1771
James	Bert	1769	John	Oran	1755
ACKERSON, Wm	Pitt	1764	John	Rowa	1759
ACKISS, Aaron	Crav	1769	John	Surr	1771
John	Crav	1742	Joseph	Beau	1755
John	Crav	1769	Joseph	Beau	1764
ACKLAND, John	Pasq	1769	Joseph	Cumb	1755
ACOCK, James	Oran	1755	Levey	Pitt	1762
Mary	Bute	1771	Levey	Pitt	1763
Mary s. Robert	FWV	1771	Levi	Pitt	1762
Richard	Bute	1771	Levi	Pitt	1763
Richard & s.			Margaret	Crav	1769
Abner & John	FWV	1771	Matthew	Chow	1721
Richard	Edge	1743	Matthew	Tyrr	1755
Wm	Bute	1771	Peter	Chow	1744
Wm	FWV	1771	Richard	Anso	1763
Wm	Norh	1743	Samuel	Gran	1784
ACON, Thomas	Chow	1753	Thomas	Cumb	1767
ACRE, Isaac	Bute	1771	Thomas	Pitt	1762
Isaac Constable	FWV	1771	Thomas	Pitt	1763
Wm	Bute	1771	Trion	Rand	1779
Wm	FWV	1771	Wm	Anso	1763
ACRED, John	Bert	1769	Wm	Beau	1742
ACRY, Isaac	Gran	1755	Wm	Beau	1755
ADAIR, James	Dobb	1769	Wm	Beau	1764
James	John	1752	Wm	Casw	1777
James	Tryo	1776	Wm	Rand	1779
ADAMAN, Thomas	Gran	1755	Wm	Surr	1771
ADAMS, Aaron	Rand	1779	Wm Sr.	Surr	1771
Abraham	Beau	1755	Wm Sr.	Surr	1772
Abraham	Pitt	1775	Willoughby	Beau	1744
Andrew & wife			Willoughby Jr.	Crav	1769
Eleanor	Bert	1757	Willoughby Sr.	Crav	1769
Ann	Beau	1755	ADAMSON, Alexander	NewH	1762
Archibald	Pitt	1762	ADCOCK, Bolin	Gran	1769
Archibald	Pitt	1763	Bolling	Gran	1784
Archibald	Pitt	1775	Edmond	Bute	1771
Charles	Oran	1755	Edmond	FWV	1771
Charles	Surr	1771	Edmond	Gran	1755
Charles	Surr	1772	Edward	Gran	1784
Daniel	Casw	1777	Henry	Bute	1771
Daniel	Oran	1755	Henry	FWV	1771

ADCOCK, Henry	Gran	1755		ALBERTSON, Joshua	Perq	1740
John	Gran	1769		Nathan	Perq	1720
John	Gran	1784		Nathaniel	Perq	1740
Leonard	Gran	1755		Peter	Perq	1720
Leonard	Gran	1769		ALBRITTON, George	Pitt	1762
Leonard	Gran	1784		George	Pitt	1763
Robert	Gran	1784		George	Pitt	1764
Solomon	Gran	1769		James	Pitt	1762
ADDAMS, Andrew	Dobb	1769		James 3 slaves	Pitt	1762
George	Pasq	1769		James	Pitt	1763
ADDELOT, Francis	Pasq	1769		James Jr.	Pitt	1763
ADDERLY, John	Chow	1721		James Sr.	Pitt	1764
ADDERSON, Christoph	Brun	1769		James	Pitt	1764
Chrostopher	Brun	1772		Matthew	Pitt	1762
Thomas	Gran	1769		Matthew	Pitt	1763
ADDISON, Elijah	Pasq	1769		Matthew	Pitt	1764
Thomas	Rand	1779		Peter	Pitt	1763
Wm	NewH	1762		Peter	Pitt	1764
ADDLEMAN, Peter	Surr	1771		Richard	Pitt	1775
Peter	Surr	1772		Thomas	Pitt	1762
ADIMAN, Thomas	Surr	1772		Thomas	Pitt	1764
ADIN, Robert	Bert	1757		Thomas	Pitt	1775
ADKIN, Moses	NewH	1767		ALCOCK, John	Crav	1769
ADKINS, Archibald	Pitt	1775		ALDERMAN, Daniel	NewH	1762
Arthur	Bute	1771		Daniel	NewH	1763
Arthur	FWV	1771		ALDERSON, Ann		
David	Gran	1784		(widow)	Beau	1764
Eleazer	Brun	1769		John	Beau	1755
Eleazer	Brun	1772		Sarah	Beau	1755
James	Pitt	1762		Simon	N.C.	1701
James Jr.	Gran	1784		ALDRIDGE, Drury	Dobb	1779
Wm	Casw	1777		Nathaniel	Rand	1779
Wm	Gran	1769		Wm	Dobb	1779
AERES, Robert	Dobb	1779		Wm	Oran	1755
AGENDER, Jacob	Rowa	1759		ALEN, Cuin	NewH	1755
AHAIR, Wm	Onsl	1769		ALEXANDER, Anguish	Surr	1771
Wm	Onsl	1770		Anthony	Chow	1717
AIKEN, Aaron	Crav	1769		Anthony Sr.	Chow	1721
Anthony	Casw	1777		Anthony Sr.	Tyrr	1755
John	Crav	1769		Benjamin	Onsl	1769
Thomas	Crav	1769		Benjamin	Rand	1779
AIKING, James	Cumb	1767		Benjamin Jr.	Tyrr	1755
AKERMAN, Frederick	Crav	1769		Benjamin Sr.	Tyrr	1755
AKGOE, David	Onsl	1770		Benjamin	Tyrr	1755
AKINS, Isham	Gran	1784		David	Rand	1779
James	Casw	1777		Ezekiel	NewH	1755
James	Gran	1784		Ezekiel	NewH	1762
John	Casw	1777		Ezekiel	NewH	1763
Joseph	Gran	1784		Ezek.	NewH	1767
Wm	Casw	1777		Francis	NewH	1744
ALBAN, Ed	Chow	1717		Francis	NewH	1755
ALBERRY, Frederick	Surr	1772		Francis	NewH	1763
ALBERTSON, Aaron	Pesq	1740		George	Rand	1779
Albert	Perq	1720		Gideon	Tyrr	1755
Albert Jr.	Perq	1720		Isaac Jr.	Tyrr	1755
Albert	Perq	1740		Isaac Sr.	Tyrr	1755
Arthur	Chow	1753		James	Rand	1779
Arthur	Perq	1740		Jesse	Surr	1771
Elias	Pasq	1754		John	Tyrr	1755
Esau	Perq	1720		John alegator	Tyrr	1755
Isaac	Pasq	1754		Joseph	NewH	1755
John	Beau	1755		Joseph	NewH	1762
John	Pitt	1763		Joseph	NewH	1763
John	Pitt	1764		Joseph	NewH	1767
Joseph	Beau	1755		Joseph	Rand	1779

ALEXANDER, Joseph			ALLEN, Drury		
Esq.	Tyrr	1755	Constable	Brun	1769
Joshua Sr.	Tyrr	1755	Drury 6 slaves	Brun	1769
Josiah	Tyrr	1755	Drury	Gran	1769
Lemuel	Tyrr	1755	Drury	NewH	1762
Levy	Onsl	1769	Drury	NewH	1763
Levy	Onsl	1770	Drury	Brun	1772
Mary	NewH	1762	Eleanor	Brun	1772
Mary	NewH	1763	Elear	NewH	1741
Mary	NewH	1767	Elizabeth	Pasq	1754
Mickell	Tyrr	1755	Elkanah	NewH	1762
Nicholas	Cray	1720	George	Bute	1771
Sims	Rand	1779	George	FWV	1771
Stephen	Rand	1779	George	Gate	1786
Thomas	Oran	1755	Gershom	Surr	1771
Wm	Rand	1779	Gideon	Cumb	1755
Wm	Tyrr	1755	Grant	Gran	1784
ALFORD, Benjamin	Dobb	1769	Grisham	Surr	1772
Benjamin	Dobb	1779	James	Rand	1779
Goodrich	FWV	1771	Joel	Brun	1769
Goodrick	Bute	1771	Joel	Brun	1772
Jacob s. of			John	Beau	1755
Lodwick	Gran	1755	John	Bert	1757
John			John	Bert	1769
Julius	Bute	1771	John	FWV	1771
Julius	Gran	1755	John	Crav	1769
Julius & son			John 4 slaves	Crav	1769
John	FWV	1771	John	NewH	1762
Lodwick	Bute	1771	John	Surr	1771
Lodwick Jr.	Bute	1771	John	Surr	1772
Lodwick s. Julius			Jones	FWV	1771
& Warren	FWV	1771	Joseph	Bute	1771
Lodwick Jr.	FWV	1771	Joseph Jr.	Crav	1769
Lodwick	Gran	1755	Joseph	FWV	1771
Wm	Dobb	1769	Mary	Casw	1777
Wm	Dobb	1779	Merriman	Pitt	1762
Wm	Pitt	1762	Paul	Pitt	1775
ALING, Samuel	Perq	1740	Peter	NewH	1762
ALKIN, James	Onsl	1743	Peter	Pitt	1762
ALKINS, James	Onsl	1769	Peter	Pitt	1763
Samuel	Cumb	1755	Priscilla	Pitt	1762
ALL, Edmund	Gran	1769	Richard	Beau	1755
ALLDRAY, Thomas	Surr	1772	Richard	NorH	1762
ALLDRIDGE, Joseph	Casw	1777	Richard	Pitt	1762
Nathaniel	Rand	1779	Richard	Pitt	1763
Wm	Oran	1755	Richard	Pitt	1764
Wm	Rand	1779	Richard	Pitt	1775
ALLEGOOD, Hillery	Pitt	1762	Richard	Surr	1771
ALLEN, Adoniram	Surr	1771	Robert	Bert	1757
Adoniram	Surr	1772	Robert	Bert	1769
Ananias	Gran	1755	Robert Jr.	Bute	1771
Arthur	Chow	1753	Robert Sr.	Bute	1771
Benjamin	Pasq	1769	Robert	Dobb	1769
Benjamin	Pitt	1775	Robert Jr.	FWV	1771
Cain	NewH	1755	Robert Sr.	FWV	1771
Charles	Bute	1771	Robert	Gran	1755
Charles s. Wm	FWV	1771	Robert	Gran	1784
Clifton	Casw	1777	Roger	Pitt	1762
Daniel	Rowa	1759	Roger	Pitt	1763
David	Surr	1771	Roger	Pitt	1764
Dempsey	Pitt	1762	Roger	Pitt	1775
Dempsey	Pitt	1763	Roper	Bute	1771
Dempsey	Pitt	1764	Rosser	FWV	1771
Drury	Bute	1771	Samuel	Beau	1755
Drury	FWV	1771	Samuel	Gran	1784

ALLEN, Samuel	Oran 1755	ALPHIN, Hezekiah	Gate 1786
Samuel	Rand 1779	Joseph	Chow 1753
Shadrack	Crav 1769	Joseph	Gate 1786
Thomas	Bert 1769	Solomon	Gate 1786
Thomas	Curr 1755	Wm	Onsl 1769
Thomas	Pitt 1762	Wm	Onsl 1770
Thomas	Pitt 1763	ALSTON, George	Gran 1769
Thomas	Pitt 1764	George	Gran 1784
Thomas	Pitt 1775	James	Bert 1757
Wm	Blad 1763	James	Chow 1753
Wm	Casw 1777	James	FWV 1771
Wm	Crav 1769	John Esq.	Chow 1721
Wm	Gran 1769	John Esq.	Chow 1753
Wm	Gran 1784	John	Bute 1771
Wm	NewH 1762	John	Chow 1717
Wm Constable	NewH 1762	John	Edge 1743
Wm	NorH 1741	John	Edge 1744
Wm	NorH 1762	John	FWV 1771
Zachariah	Pitt 1775	Joseph	Brun 1769
ALLEY, Edmund	Casw 1777	Joseph	Brun 1772
ALLICE, Katharine	Bert 1769	Joseph	Bute 1771
ALLIGOOD, Hillary	Crav 1769	Joseph	Edge 1743
Hillary	Pitt 1762	Joseph	Edge 1744
Hillary	Pitt 1763	Joseph	FWV 1771
Hillary	Pitt 1764	Joseph	Gran 1769
ALLIN, David	Gran 1769	Peter	Brun 1769
Edmond	Gran 1769	Peter	Brun 1772
Wm	Gran 1769	Philip	Bute 1771
ALLING, David	Surr 1772	Philip s. Thomas	FWV 1771
Richard	Surr 1772	Philip	Gran 1755
ALLISON, Adam	Rowa 1759	Samuel	Gran 1784
Andrew	Rowa 1759	Solomon	Bute 1771
James	Gran 1784	Solomon	FWV 1771
James	Gran 1755	Solomon	Gran 1755
John	Casw 1777	Solomon	Gran 1784
John	Gran 1784	Wm	Bute 1771
John	Oran 1755	Wm	FWV 1771
Richard	Rowa 1759	Wm	Gran 1784
Robert	Oran 1755	ALTMAN, James	Anso 1763
Robert	Gran 1769	ALWAYS, Henry	Crav 1769
Robert	Gran 1784	Obadiah	Crav 1769
Robert Jr.	Gran 1784	ALWICK, John	Crav 1769
Robert	Casw 1777	AMAN, Dennis	Onsl 1769
Robert	Rowa 1759	Dennis	Onsl 1770
Thomas	Rowa 1759	Jacob	Onsl 1769
ALLMAN, James	Anso 1763	Jacob	Onsl 1770
ALLOM, Jeremiah	Bert 1769	Philip	Onsl 1769
John	Bert 1757	Philip	Onsl 1770
John	Crav 1769	AMBLER, Wm	Perq 1740
ALLRED, Elias	Rand 1779	AMBROSE, Daniel	Onsl 1769
James	Rand 1779	Daniel	Onsl 1770
John	Oran 1755	Jesse	Chow 1753
John Jr.	Rand 1779	John	Onsl 1769
John Sr.	Rand 1779	Wm	Onsl 1741
Solomon	Oran 1755	Wm	Onsl 1769
Thomas	Oran 1755	Wm	Onsl 1770
Thomas	Rand 1779	Zachariah	Onsl 1769
Wm	Oran 1755	Zachariah	Onsl 1770
Wm Jr.	Rand 1779	AMBROSS, David	Chow 1717
Wm Sr.	Rand 1779	David	Chow 1721
ALLSOE, John	Beau 1755	AMES, John	Chow 1717
ALLSQUIRE, Abraham	Tyrr 1755	Lewis	Gran 1784
ALLY, John	Chow 1721	Thomas	Tyrr 1755
ALMON, Garrett	Oran 1755	Wm	Gran 1769
ALMOND, Moses	Crav 1769	AMIETT, Peter	Crav 1769

AMIETT, Vincent	Crav	1769	ANDERSON, Robert	Tyrr	1755
AMOS, Charles	Gran	1755	Sam	Rowa	1759
John	NowH	1762	Samuel	Blad	1763
John	Chow	1717	Shadrack s. of		
Wm	Gran	1784	Lewis	Gran	1755
ANALIN, Wm	Casw	1777	Stephen	Blad	1763
ANDERS, Joseph	Blad	1781	Susannah	Edge	1744
Stephen	Blad	1781	Tamer d. of		
ANDERSON, Alexander			Lewis	Gran	1755
	Bute	1771	Wm	Blad	1763
Alexander	Cumb	1755	Wm	Blad	1781
Alexander	FWV	1771	Wm	Casw	1777
Alexander	Gran	1755	Wm	Cumb	1767
Carolus	Edge	1743	Wm	Pitt	1763
Catherine d. of			ANDRESS, Wm	Pasq	1754
George	Gran	1755	Lee	Pitt	1775
David	Cumb	1767	ANDREWS, Abner	Bert	1757
Dennis	Gran	1769	Adam	Crav	1769
Edmond	Onsl	1743	Adam	Rand	1779
Edmund	Onsl	1770	Coored	Rand	1779
Elmore	Onsl	1769	Edmund	Pitt	1764
George	Casw	1777	Gray	Bute	1771
George	Gran	1755	Gray	FWV	1771
George	Gran	1769	John	Beau	1755
Henry	Pitt	1762	John	Crav	1769
Henry	Pitt	1763	John	Dobb	1769
Henry	Pitt	1764	John	Dobb	1779
Isaac	Rand	1779	John	Pitt	1763
James	Casw	1777	Joseph	Bute	1771
James	Cumb	1767	Joseph	FWV	1771
James	Gran	1784	Micajah	Crav	1769
James	Perq	1720	Peter	Crav	1769
James	Rand	1779	Richard	Casw	1777
James	Roan	1720	Solomon	Pitt	1762
James	Tryo	1776	Solomon	Pitt	1763
Jerry s. of Geo	Gran	1755	Solomon	Pitt	1764
John	Blad	1763	Thomas	Crav	1769
John	Blad	1744	Thomas	Dobb	1769
John	Brun	1772	Walter	Perq	1740
John Jr.	Brun	1769	Warren	Tyrr	1742
John	Casw	1777	Warren	Tyrr	1755
John	Cumb	1755	Wm	Beau	1755
John Jr.	Cumb	1755	Wm	Bert	1757
John	Cumb	1767	Wm	Crav	1769
John	Curr	1755	Wm	Dobb	1769
John Jr.	Curr	1755	Wm	Dobb	1779
John	Dobb	1779	Wm	Edge	1744
John	Gran	1755	Wm	FWV	1771
John	NewH	1752	ANERUM, John	NewH	1767
John	Oran	1755	ANESLEY, John	N.C.	1701
John	Perq	1720	ANGEL, Benjamin	Surr	1772
John	Pitt	1762	Charles	Rowa	1759
John	Rand	1779	Charles	Surr	1771
John	Tyrr	1755	John	Crav	1720
Joseph	Blad	1763	John	Surr	1771
Joseph	Chow	1742	John	Surr	1772
Joseph	Chow	1742	Nicholas	Surr	1771
Lewis	Gran	1755	ANGLAN, James	Oran	1755
Lewis	Gran	1784	ANGUS, John	Casw	1777
Mary d. Lewis	Gran	1755	ANKROM, John	Brun	1772
Robert Jr.	Beau	1755	ANSELL, John	Curr	1755
Robert	Chow	1717	Mary	Curr	1755
Robert	Chow	1721	Nathan	Curr	1755
Robert	Rowa	1758	ANTHONY, David	Bute	1771
Robert	Rowa	1759	David	FWV	1771

ANTHONY, John	Casw	1777	ARMOUR, Wm	Pasq	1769
Thomas	Casw	1777	ARMSTRONG, Assiah	Curr	1755
APPERSON, John	Bert	1769	Christopher	Cumb	1755
Wm	Bert	1769	Clement	NewH	1762
APPEL, John	Dobb	1769	George	Cumb	1755
APPLEWAITE, Wm	Casw	1777	George	Cumb	1767
ARABIA, Jethro	Tyrr	1755	James	Pitt	1764
ARANDAL, Wm	Dobb	1769	John	Cumb	1755
ARCHBELLE, John	Beau	1764	John Jr.	Cumb	1767
Nathan Jr.	Beau	1764	John Sr.	Cumb	1767
ARCHDEACON, James	Casw	1777	John	Surr	1771
Wm	Beau	1755	John	Surr	1772
Wm	Chow	1721	Martin	Surr	1771
Wm	Pitt	1762	Martin	Surr	1772
Wm	Pitt	1764	Thomas	Cumb	1755
ARCHEBALD, John	Beau	1764	Walter	Dobb	1769
Nathan	Beau	1755	Wm	Cumb	1755
Nathan Jr.	Beau	1764	Wm	Cumb	1767
ARCHER, Armstrong	Bert	1757	Wm	Oran	1755
Baker & wife			ARNAL, Joshua	Pasq	1769
Elizabeth	Bert	1757	ARNALL, Edward	Chow	1742
George	Rand	1779	ARNELL, John	Chow	1753
Hancock	Bert	1757	Richard	Chow	1753
Jacob	Bert	1757	ARNETT, Philemon	Dobb	1779
John w. Frances,			Wm	Pitt	1762
d. Ann, s.			ARNOLD, Aaron	FWV	1771
Jeremiah	Bert	1757	Abraham	Crav	1769
John	Bert	1769	Ambrose	Casw	1777
Thomas & w. Mary	Bert	1757	Edward	Gate	1786
Thomas Jr. w.			Francis	Rand	1779
Elizabeth	Bert	1757	James	Bute	1771
Wm	Rand	1779	James	Beau	1764
ARD, James 2 slaves			James	FWV	1771
	Blad	1763	John	Bute	1771
ARELINE, John	Chow	1721	John	Casw	1777
ARES, David	Tyrr	1755	John	FWV	1771
John Jr.	Tyrr	1755	John	Gate	1786
John Sr.	Tyrr	1755	John	Perq	1720
ARGO, John	Dobb	1769	John	Rand	1779
Wm	Rand	1779	Joseph	Perq	1740
ARINTON, Thomas	Chow	1721	Moses	Crav	1769
Thomas	Roan	1720	Peter	Onsl	1769
ARIRET, James	Pitt	1775	Peter	Onsl	1770
ARKILL, Wm	Chow	1721	Thomas	Beau	1764
ARLEGE, Thomas	Rand	1779	Thomas	Bute	1771
ARLEW, James	NewH	1755	Thomas	FWV	1771
ARLINE, James (Cpt.)			Wm	Crav	1769
	Gate	1786	Wm	Gate	1786
James	Gate	1786	Wm	Perq	1740
John	Chow	1721	Wm	Beau	1764
ARLOW, Bridgett	NewH	1762	AROOK, Richard	Gran	1755
Bridgett	NewH	1763	ARRINGTON, Christop	Perq	1740
ARMFIELD, Isaac	Rowa	1759	Thomas	Anso	1763
Wm	Rowa	1759	Thomas	Chow	1721
ARMISTEAD, Anthony	Bert	1757	Thomas	Roan	1720
Anthony	Bert	1763	Wm	Anso	1763
Mors	Bert	1763	ARTHUR, James	Crav	1769
Moss	Bert	1757	John	Chow	1717
Wm	Bert	1757	John	Chow	1721
Wm	Bert	1763	ARTORS, John	Perq	1740
ARMOUR, Argent	Pasq	1769	ARUNDALE, Benjamin	Gran	1755
David	Pasq	1769	ARUNDELL, Ed	Chow	1717
Robert	Pasq	1754	ASBELL, Emanuel	Rand	1779
Thomas Sr.	Pasq	1754	Martin	Pasq	1720
Wm Sr.	Pasq	1769	Martin	Pasq	1740

ASBELL, Pierce	Casw	1777	ATHERLY, Joseph	Crav	1769
ASH, Abigail w.			Joseph Jr.	Crav	1769
Thos	Gran	1755	Sarah	Crav	1769
John	NewH	1755	ATKINS, David	Chow	1717
Thomas	Gran	1755	David	Chow	1721
ASHBIMAN, Lewis	Rand	1779	Elisha	Crav	1769
ASHBURN, Anderson	Casw	1777	Silas	Blad	1781
Canard	Bert	1757	ATKINSON, Amos	Beau	1755
Edward	Bert	1757	Amos	Pitt	1762
John	Casw	1777	Amos	Pitt	1763
Nicholas	Bert	1757	Azzio	Pitt	1764
Thomas	Bert	1757	Carlton	Cumb	1767
Thomas	Bert	1769	Charleton	Blad	1763
ASHBURY, Joseph	Crav	1769	Daniel	NewH	1767
ASHE, John	NewH	1762	Daniel	NorH	1762
John	NewH	1763	Henry	Blad	1763
John	NewH	1767	Henry	Cumb	1767
Samuel	NewH	1762	John	Dobb	1769
Samuel	NewH	1763	John	Casw	1777
Samuel	NewH	1767	John	NewH	1767
ASHLEY, Grover	Casw	1777	Ransom	Casw	1777
Groves	Gran	1784	Robert	Casw	1777
John	Anso	1763	Roger	Casw	1777
Joseph	Perq	174	Samuel Esq.	Casw	1777
Robert	Anso	1763	Thomas	Cumb	1767
Solomon	Curr	1755	ATTOM, John	Bert	1769
Thomas	Chow	1717	ATWATER, Titus	Crav	1769
Thomas	Chow	1721	ATWOOD, Thomas	Crav	1769
Wm	Bert	1769	AUGHTERY, Obadiah	Bert	1757
Wm	Bute	1771	AUSTIN, Daniel	Onsl	1741
Wm	Casw	1777	David	Surr	1772
Wm	Chow	1753	John	Bute	1771
Wm	FWV	1771	John	FWV	1771
ASHMORE, Walter	Rand	1779	John	Casw	1777
ASKERT, Wm	Gran	1769	John Jr.	Surr	1772
ASKEW, Aaron	Bert	1757	John Sr.	Surr	1772
Amos	Bert	1757	Richard	Gate	1786
Godfrey	Bert	1757	Thomas	Cart	1743
James	Bert	1757	Thomas	Curr	1755
John	Bert	1742	Wm	Casw	1777
John	Bert	1757	Wm	Surr	1771
Nicholas	Bert	1757	Wm	Surr	1772
Sarah	Bert	1757	AUTREY, James	Pitt	1762
Thomas Constable	Bert	1757	John	Beau	1755
Thomas	Crav	1769	John Sr.	Pitt	1762
Wm	Bert	1757	John	Pitt	1763
ASKIE, Wm	Gran	1784	Wm	Pitt	1762
ASKINS, Aaron	Bert	1769	AVANT, Benjamin	Bute	1771
David	Bert	1769	Benjamin	FWV	1771
John	Bert	1769	AVARY, Jesse	Pitt	1775
John	Crav	1769	John	Pitt	1775
Joshua	Onsl	1769	King	Pitt	1775
Thomas	Casw	1777	Wm	Pitt	1775
ASLEW, James	NewH	1755	AVERA, Alexander	Cumb	1767
ASMONT, Francis	Gate	1786	Henry	Bert	1757
ASPIN, Thomas	Casw	1777	Thomas	Crav	1743
ASQUE, Charles	Bute	1771	Wm	Cumb	1767
Charles	FWV	1771	AVERARD, Charles		
John	Bute	1771	Sr.	Bert	1769
John s. Philemon			Charles	Bert	1769
Wm	FWV	1771	Charles of Tatro	Bert	1769
Serug	Bute	1771	Henry Sr.	Bert	1769
ASTEEN, Thomas	Oran	1755	Henry	Bert	1769
ASTON, James	Rowa	1759	AVERITT, Charles		
ATHERLY, Jonathan	Crav	1769	Sr.	Bert	1757

AVERITT, Charles s.		BADGETT, John	Gran 1784
Charles	Bert 1757	John	Bute 1771
Charles	Pitt 1763	John	FWV 1771
David	Pitt 1762	Roger	Gran 1755
David	Pitt 1764	Thomas	Casw 1777
Elizabeth	NewH 1762	Wm	Casw 1777
George	Pitt 1764	BADHAM, Wm	Chow 1721
Henry	Bert 1742	BADJET, James	Surr 1772
James	Pitt 1763	BAGG, James	Pitt 1764
James	Pitt 1764	BAGGE, Lorenzo	Surr 1771
John	Beau 1755	Traugot	Surr 1771
Thomas	Blad 1781	BAGGETT, Barnaby	Bert 1769
Thomas	Pitt 1762	BAGGITT, Everett	Dobb 1779
Wm	Pitt 1764	Hardy	Bert 1757
AVERS, John	Beau 1755	Thomas	Bert 1757
AVERY, Charles	Onsl 1769	BAGLEY, Henry	Gran 1784
Charles	Onsl 1770	Nathan	Pasq 1769
George	Pitt 1763	Thomas	Perq 1740
James	Beau 1755	Wm	Bute 1771
John	Crav 1769	Wm	FWV 1771
Thomas	Onsl 1769	BAGWELL, John	Tryo 1776
AVIRETT, Arthur	Onsl 1769	BAILER, Adam	Casw 1777
Arthur	Onsl 1770	Peter	Casw 1777
Benjamin	Onsl 1769	BAILES, John	Curr 1715
Benjamin	Onsl 1770	BAILEY, Abraham	Onsl 1769
John	Onsl 1769	Abraham	Onsl 1770
AVIS, Ambrose'		David	Beau 1764
estate	Dobb 1769	David	Pasq 1754
John	Dobb 1769	David	Pasq 1769
Thomas	Bert 1769	David	Rand 1779
Thomas	Tyrr 1755	Henry	Beau 1764
AVORY, George	Pitt 1762	James	Bute 1771
George	Pitt 1763	James & s. Wm	FWV 1771
George	Pitt 1764	James	Blad 1769
James	Pitt 1762	James	Gran 1769
James	Pitt 1763	Jeremiah	Gran 1769
AVRIT, Thomas	Blad 1781	Jeremiah Jr.	Gran 1769
Wm	Blad 1781	Jeremiah	Gran 1784
AWTRY, John	Rand 1779	John	Anso 1763
AXDALE, Eleanor	Beau 1755	John	Blad 1769
AYCOCK, Charles	Dobb 1769	John	Bute 1771
Thomas	Dobb 1769	John	Crav 1763
Wm	Dobb 1769	John	FWV 1771
AYLER, Wm	Dobb 1769	John	Gran 1784
AYLOS, James	Casw 1777	John S. of	
AYMES, John	Chow 1721	Philip	Onsl 1769
AYRES, David	Tyrr 1755	John s. of	
John Jr.	Tyrr 1755	Philip	Onsl 1770
John Sr.	Tyrr 1755	John Sr.	Pasq 1754
		John	Pasq 1754
		John Jr.	Pasq 1769
		John Sr.	Pasq 1769
BABB, Christopher	FWV 1771	John	Rand 1779
Mary, widow	Crav 1769	Matthew	Anso 1763
Moses	Bute 1771	Patrick	Pasq 1754
Moses	FWV 1771	Phillip	Onsl 1769
Thomas	Bute 1771	Phillip	Onsl 1770
Thomas	FWV 1771	Richard	Gran 1784
BACCOT, Samuel	Brun 1772	Richard Jr.	Pasq 1754
BACCUS, John	Chow 1753	Robert	Gran 1769
BACH, Wm	Beau 1755	Sarah	Blad 1781
BACHELDER, Wm	Onsl 1769	Thomas	Anso 1763
BADDIE, Willis	NorH 1762	Thomas s.	
BADGETT, John	Gran 1755	Abraham	Onsl 1769
John	Gran 1769		

BAILEY, Thomas s.			BAKER, Wm	Gate	1786
Abra	Onsl	1770	Wm	Gran	1755
Wm	Gran	1784	Wm	Oran	1755
BAIN, James	Rand	1779	BAKY, Joseph	Gran	1784
John	Gran	1755	BALCH, Joseph	Crav	1742
BAIRD, James	Blad	1781	BALCOMB, Jacobod	Beau	1764
James	Bute	1771	BALDERES, Wm	Pitt	1763
James	FWV	1771	BALDRY, Wm	Beau	1755
John	Bute	1771	BALDWIN, Elisha	Rowa	1759
John	Casw	1777	Henry	Casw	1777
John	FWV	1771	John 5 slaves	Blad	1763
BAKER, Abraham s.			Joseph	Blad	1763
John Sr.	Dobb	1769	Wm	Pitt	1763
Absalom	Gran	1755	Wm Jr.	Pitt	1763
Absalom	Gran	1769	Wm	Pitt	1764
Benjamin	Bert	1757	Wm Jr.	Pitt	1764
Benjamin Jr.	Gate	1786	Wm	Pitt	1775
Elijah	Dobb	1769	Wm	Rowa	1759
Elijah	Dobb	1779	Wm	Beau	1755
Finley	FWV	1771	BALE, David	Gran	1784
Gissa	Bert	1757	James	Dobb	1769
Henry	Bute	1771	BALES, Andrew	Cumb	1767
Henry	Chow	1753	Barter	Surr	1772
Henry	Curr	1755	David	Edge	1744
Henry	FWV	1771	John	Rowa	1759
Henry	Rowa	1759	John	Surr	1772
James	Bert	1757	Robert	Rowa	1759
James	Bert	1769	Thomas	Surr	1772
Jesse	Bert	1757	Wm	Surr	1772
John	Bert	1757	BALFOUR, Andrew	Rand	1779
John	Chow	1721	BALKUM, Baruck	Beau	1755
John Sr.	Dobb	1769	Jacob	Beau	1755
John	Dobb	1779	BALL, Daniel	Bute	1771
John	Gate	1786	Daniel s. Daniel		
John	NewH	1762	& Mark	FWV	1771
John	NewH	1763	George	Tryo	1776
John	Surr	1771	Henry 2 slaves	Dobb	1769
John	Surr	1772	James	Beau	1755
Jonathan	Bert	1769	John	Beau	1755
Lawrence	Chow	1753	John	Blad	1763
Lawrence	Gate	1786	John	Pitt	1763
Mary	NewH	1767	Joshua	Curr	1755
Michael	Surr	1771	Mark	Dobb	1769
Michael	Surr	1772	Moses	Dobb	1769
Moses	Bert	1757	Thomas	Chow	1717
Moses	Chow	1717	Wm	Bute	1771
Nicholas	Surr	1772	Wm	FWV	1771
Philip	FWV	1771	BALLANCE, Benjamin	Pasq	1769
Richard	Chow	1753	John	Curr	1742
Robert	Bert	1769	John	Curr	1755
Robert	Blad	1763	BALLARD, Benjamin	Onsl	1769
Rubin	Dobb	1769	David	Surr	1772
Samson	Crav	1769	Elias	Dobb	1769
Samuel	Blad	1743	Eliph	Perq	1740
Samuel	Gate	1786	Elisha	Tyrr	1755
Solomon	Bert	1757	Honor	Chow	1743
Solomon	Bert	1769	Humphrey	Bute	1771
Thomas	Bert	1757	Humphrey	FWV	1771
Thomas s. James	Bert	1757	Humphrey	Gran	1755
Thomas	Surr	1771	James s. John	Onsl	1770
Wm	Bert	1757	Jesse	Onsl	1769
Wm	Bute	1771	Jethro	Gate	1786
Wm	Chow	1717	John	Bute	1771
Wm Sr.	Chow	1721	John	Chow	1721
Wm	FWV	1771	John	Dobb	1769

BALLARD, John Jr.	Dobb	1769	BANKS, Thomas	Gran	1769
John	Edge	1741	Wm 12 slaves	Crav	1769
John	FWV	1771	BANKSON, Laurence	Edge	1744
John & s. John	FWV	1771	Laurence	Oran	1755
John	Gran	1755	BANN, Ennis	Dobb	1769
John	Onsl	1769	BANNER, Henry	Rowa	1759
John	Tyrr	1755	Henry	Surr	1771
Joseph	Beau	1755	Henry	Surr	1772
Joseph	Bute	1771	Joseph	Surr	1771
Joseph & s.			Joseph	Surr	1772
Kellis &			BANNERMAN, Robert	Cumb	1767
Mourning	FWV	1771	BANNISTER, Henry	Surr	1772
Joseph	Gate	1786	BAPTISS, Benjamin	Perq	1740
Joseph	Onsl	1769	BARADLE, Joseph	Bert	1743
Joseph	Tyrr	1755	BARAN, Wm	Casw	1777
Kedar	Gate	1786	BARAY, Robert	Oran	1755
Lewis	Bute	1771	BARBER, Aaron	Oran	1755
Lewis & s. James	FWV	1771	Andrew	Crav	1769
Reuben	Crav	1769	Cha.	Chow	1717
Richard	Gran	1755	Charles	Bert	1757
Stephen	Surr	1771	Charles	Chow	1721
Thomas	Bert	1769	Charles	Curr	1715
Thomas	Cumb	1767	John	Bert	1757
Thomas	Gran	1755	John	Curr	1715
Thomas	Surr	1771	John s. Richard	Onsl	1769
Thomas	Surr	1772	John s. Richard	Onsl	1770
Wm	Bute	1771	John	Pitt	1762
Wm	Crav	1769	John	Pitt	1763
Wm	FWV	1771	John	Pitt	1764
Wm	Gran	1755	Joseph	Beau	1755
BALLENCE, Richard	Curr	1715	Joseph	Onsl	1769
Samuel	Curr	1715	Joseph	Onsl	1770
BALLENGER, Henry	Rowa	1759	Joseph	Pitt	1762
BALLENTINE, James	Cumb	1767	Joseph	Pitt	1763
Peter	Curr	1755	Joseph	Pitt	1764
BALLIN, John	Anso	1763	Mitchell	Onsl	1769
Wm	Anso	1763	Mitchell	Onsl	1770
BALLOONE, Michael	Brun	1769	Richard	Onsl	1769
Michael	Brun	1772	Richard	Onsl	1770
BALLSTON, John	Crav	1720	Richard	Perq	1740
BALTHROP, Sharp	FWV	1771	Thomas	Onsl	1770
BANBURY, Wm	Chow	1721	Thomas	Pitt	1764
BANDY, James	Gran	1755	Wm	Crav	1769
BANE, Hugh	Cumb	1767	Wm	Onsl	1744
BANES, Richard	Beau	1764	Wm	Oran	1755
BANGO, Octiller	Bert	1757	Wm	Pitt	1762
BANGS, Jonathan	Crav	1742	Wm	Pitt	1763
BANICKS, John	NewH	1763	Wm	Pitt	1764
BANISTER, John			BARBIE, Joseph	Oran	1755
(Cpt.)	Casw	1777	BARBREE, Abraham	Bert	1757
BANK, Charles	Pitt	1763	BARBYBACK, Ramsey	Crav	1720
BANKS, Henry	Curr	1755	BARCLIFF, John Jr.	Perq	1740
Henry	Perq	1740	John Sr.	Perq	1740
James	Perq	1740	Joseph	Perq	1740
John	Perq	1720	Wm	Perq	1740
John	Perq	1740	BARCO, Anna	Pasq	1754
John	Rowa	1759	Coston	Pasq	1769
John	Surr	1771	Jane	Pasq	1754
John	Surr	1772	John	Pasq	1754
Jonathan 4			Joseph	Pasq	1754
slaves	Pasq	1769	Joseph	Pasq	1769
Littleton	Bute	1771	Peter	Pasq	1754
Littleton	FWV	1771	Peter	Pasq	1769
Richard	Curr	1755	Wm 2 slaves	Pasq	1769
Stephen	Curr	1755	BARD, James	Rowa	1759

BARD, James 1 slave	Dobb 1769		James	Casw 1777
BARDEN, Hugh	Onsl 1769		John	Casw 1777
Hugh	Onsl 1770		John	Rand 1779
James	Dobb 1779		Nicholas	Rand 1779
Jesse	Dobb 1779		Robert	Rand 1779
John	Chow 1721		Samuel	Rand 1779
BARDIN, Bores	Dobb 1769		Thomas	Chow 1753
George	Dobb 1769		Thomas	Surr 1772
Jacob	Dobb 1769		Wm	Oran 1755
James	Dobb 1769		Wm	Perq 1740
Jesse	Dobb 1769		BARKLEY, Thomas	Oran 1755
Thomas	Gran 1769		BARLEY, John	Dobb 1769
BARDLIFF, John	Pasq 1769		Thomas s. John	Dobb 1769
BARDON, Wm	Tyrr 1755		BARLOW, George	Bert 1757
BAREFIELD, Blake	Dobb 1779		Thomas	NewH 1767
David	Blad 1763		BARNARD, Persilla	Pasq 1769
Henry	Chow 1721		Rebecca	Pasq 1769
James	Dobb 1769		Samuel	Curr 1755
John	Chow 1717		Wm	Pasq 1754
John	Chow 1721		BARNELL, Joseph	Gran 1769
John	Dobb 1769		Thomas	Gran 1769
Joshua	Blad 1763		BARNES, Abram	Blad 1763
Josiah	Blad 1763		Barnet	Anso 1763
Miles	Beau 1764		Benjamin	Gate 1786
Moses	Onsl 1769		Charles	Anso 1763
Moses	Onsl 1770		Dempsey	Gate 1786
Nathan	Blad 1763		George	Rand 1779
Richard	Blad 1763		James	Cumb 1755
Richard	Chow 1717		James	NorH 1741
Richard Sr.	Chow 1721		Jeremiah	Perq 1720
Richard	Dobb 1769		Jeremiah	Perq 1740
Richard s. Rich	Dobb 1769		John	Anso 1763
Roger	Blad 1763		John Jr.	Bert 1757
Samuel	Bert 1757		John Sr.	Bert 1757
Samuel	Bert 1769		John	Bert 1769
Sarah	Dobb 1769		John Jr.	Bert 1769
Thomas	Bert 1744		John	Brun 1769
Thomas	Bert 1757		John	Brun 1772
Thomas	Bert 1769		John	Dobb 1769
Thomas	Dobb 1769		Joseph	Chow 1753
Thomas	Dobb 1779		Joseph	Perq 1740
Thomas	Pitt 1762		Merriman	Gran 1769
Thomas	Tyrr 1755		Nathan	NorH 1742
Wm	Dobb 1769		Robert	Perq 1720
Wm s. Richard	Dobb 1769		Samuel	Dobb 1769
BAREFOOT, John			Simon	Dobb 1769
5 slaves	Dobb 1769		Thomas	Chow 1753
John	Dobb 1779		Thomas	Gate 1786
Mills	Dobb 1769		Wm	Anso 1763
BARGAMON, Elias	Crav 1744		BARNETT, Catherine	Gran 1769
Elias	Dobb 1769		Hugh	Casw 1777
Elisha s. Elias	Dobb 1769		Hugh Jr.	Casw 1777
BARGE, Lewis	Cumb 1767		Hugh	Oran 1755
BARGER, James	Rand 1779		Humphrey	Oran 1755
BARGONEER, John	Cumb 1767		James	Beau 1755
BARHAM, Wm	Blad 1750		James	Dobb 1769
BARKER, Ambrose	Gran 1784		James	Gran 1755
Barton	Casw 1777		James	Pitt 1762
Davis	Casw 1777		Jesse	Gran 1784
Edward	Brun 1769		John	Casw 1777
Edward	Brun 1772		John	Pitt 1762
George	Casw 1777		John	Pitt 1763
George	Surr 1771		John	Pitt 1764
George	Surr 1772		Joseph	Anso 1763
BARKER, Israel	Casw 1777		Joseph	Gran 1769

BARNETT, Joseph	Pitt 1762	BARRON, Francis	Dobb 1779
Lewis	NewH 1755	Wm	Crav 1744
Richard	Oran 1755	Wm	Crav 1769
Robert	Oran 1755	Wm	Dobb 1769
Samuel	NewH 1755	BARROTT, Jonathan	Gran 1755
Samuel	Oran 1755	Wm	Tyrr 1755
Sarah	Casw 1777	BARROW, Abraham	Beau 1755
Sarah	Gran 1784	Abraham	Onsl 1769
Thomas Jr.	Casw 1777	Abraham	Pitt 1762
Thomas Sr.	Casw 1777	Abraham	Pitt 1763
Thomas	Gran 1784	Abraham	Pitt 1764
Thomas	NorH 1762	Benjamin	Beau 1755
Wm	Beau 1755	Benjamin	Pitt 1762
Wm	Dobb 1769	Benjamin	Pitt 1763
Wm	Oran 1755	Benjamin	Pitt 1764
BARNHILL, Alex	Pitt 1763	Benjamin	Pitt 1775
Alex	Pitt 1764	Benton	Pitt 1763
Alexander	Pitt 1762	Daniel	Bute 1771
Henry	Pitt 1762	Daniel	FWV 1771
Henry	Pitt 1763	David	Dobb 1769
James	Oran 1755	Ellis	Onsl 1769
John	Pitt 1762	Hosea	Onsl 1769
John	Pitt 1763	Hosea	Onsl 1770
John	Pitt 1764	Isom	Pitt 1763
BARNS, Abraham	Blad 1763	James	Beau 1755
Elias Esq.	Blad 1781	James	Chow 1717
Jacob	Cumb 1755	James	FWV 1771
James	Cumb 1755	James	Pitt 1762
John	Curr 1755	James	Pitt 1763
Wm	NewH 1755	James	Pitt 1764
Wm	Tyrr 1755	Jane	Beau 1755
Wm (Cpt.)	Tyrr 1755	Jane widow	Pitt 1764
BARNUM, John	Bert 1757	John	Beau 1741
BARQUIN, John	NewH 1767	John	Beau 1755
BARR, James	Crav 1769	John	Beau 1764
James	Dobb 1769	John s. John	Beau 1764
Robert	Crav 1769	Joseph	Beau 1741
Wm	Gate 1786	Joseph	Perq 1720
BARRADAILL, Joseph	Bert 1757	Joseph	Perq 1740
BARRADIAL, Joseph	Bert 1741	Joseph	Pitt 1762
BARRAN, Wm	Crav 1720	Joseph	Pitt 1763
BARRATT, Richard	Curr 1755	Joseph	Pitt 1764
BARRELL, John	Bert 1757	Rachel	Perq 1720
BARRENTON, Isaac	Crav 1769	Richard	Beau 1741
James	Crav 1769	Richard	Beau 1755
Wm	Crav 1769	Richard	Pitt 1762
BARRETT, Henry	Rand 1779	Richard	Pitt 1763
John	Beau 1755	Richard	Pitt 1764
John	Bert 1757	Rubin	Pitt 1762
Joshua	Beau 1755	Rubin	Pitt 1764
Joshua	Dobb 1769	Samuel	Beau 1764
Margaret	Rand 1779	Samuel	Pitt 1762
Nathaniel	Surr 1771	Samuel	Pitt 1763
Thomas	NorH 1762	Samuel	Pitt 1764
Wm	Brun 1772	Sherod	Dobb 1779
Wm	FWV 1771	Simon	Blad 1763
Wm	Onsl 1769	Simon	Dobb 1779
BARRINGER, Jacob	Rowa 1759	Simon	Pitt 1775
BARRINGTON,		Taylor	Blad 1763
Benjamin	N.C. 1701	Taylor	Dobb 1779
Elizabeth	N.C. 1701	Taylor s. Simon	Dobb 1769
Mary	N.C. 1701	Thomas	Pitt 1762
BARRINO, Arthur	Crav 1769	WM & s. Wm	FWV 1771
BARRON, Arthur	Crav 1769	Wm	Pitt 1762
David	Dobb 1769	Wm	Pitt 1763

BARRS, John	Dobb	1769	BASS, Edward	Dobb	1779
John	Dobb	1779	Edward	Edge	1744
BARRY, Comfort	Casw	1777	Edward	Gran	1769
Rebecca	Cumb	1755	Edward	Gran	1784
BARTHOLOMEW, Adam	Beau	1764	Isaac	Bert	1757
Charles	Bute	1771	Jacob	Bute	1771
Charles	FWV	1771	Jacob & s.		
Charles	Gran	1755	Theoph	FWV	1771
BARTLETT, Darby	Curr	1715	John	Dobb	1769
Samuel	Dobb	1779	John	Dobb	1779
Thomas	Perq	1720	John	Gran	1769
Thomas	Pitt	1764	John	NorH	1742
Wm	Perq	1720	Matthew	Dobb	1769
Wm s. Wm Andrew	Perq	1720	Moses	Cumb	1755
Willoughby	Curr	1755	Moses	Dobb	1779
BARTLEY, John	Bert	1757	Reuben	Gran	1769
BARTON, Benjamin	Casw	1777	Reuben	Gran	1784
Benjamin	Rowa	1759	Richard 10 slaves		
Burr	Oran	1755		Dobb	1769
Charles	Casw	1777	Richard	Dobb	1779
Charles	Cumb	1755	Samuel	NorH	1762
Indith	Casw	1777	Simon	Bute	1771
John	Bert	1757	Simon s. Elijah &		
John	Rand	1779	James (blacks)		
John	Rowa	1759		FWV	1771
Margaret	Anso	1763	Thomas	Bert	1757
Neal	Casw	1777	Thomas	Bert	1769
Richard	Cumb	1767	Thomas	FWV	1771
Robert	Casw	1777	Wm s. Ben John & dau		
Samuel	Onsl	1770	Honor (blacks)		
Thomas	Casw	1777		FWV	1771
Thomas	Oran	1755	Wm	Gran	1755
Wm	Bert	1757	Wright	Dobb	1769
Wm Jr.	Bert	1757	BASSETT, Abraham	Crav	1744
Wm	Gran	1784	David	Brun	1772
Wm	Oran	1755	Richard	Beau	1744
Wm	Rand	1779	Samuel	Brun	1771
Wm	Surr	1771	BASSFORD, James	Brun	1769
BARTRAM, W. Esq.	Blad	1763	BASSMETH, John	Pasq	1754
BARWICK, John	Dobb	1779	John	Pasq	1769
Joshua s. Wm	Dobb	1769	Joseph	Pasq	1754
Wm	Dobb	1769	Wm	Pasq	1754
Wm shoemaker	Dobb	1769	BASSWOOD, James	Brun	1772
BARY, Robert	NewH	1755	BASTABLE, Wm	Perq	1720
BASCER, Thomas	Bert	1769	BASTIN, John	Rowa	1759
BASDEN, Hugh	Onsl	1769	BASTON, Wm	Rand	1779
BASHAM, John	Rand	1779	BATCHELOR, Mary	Dobb	1769
Wm	Casw	1777	Richard	Chow	1717
BASIL, James	Dobb	1769	Wm s. of Mary	Dobb	1769
BASINDINE, Charles	Oran	1755	BATCHER, Woody	Dobb	1769
BASKET, Elizabeth	FWV	1771	BATE, Augustine	Bert	1757
James	Bute	1771	James	Chow	1721
James	FWV	1771	Nancy	Bert	1769
James s. of Wm	Gran	1755	Sarah	Bert	1769
Wm	Gran	1755	BATEMAN, Claburn	Dobb	1779
Wm s. Wm	Gran	1755	John	Perq	1740
BASMAN, James	Bert	1743	Jonathan	Chow	1717
BASS, Aaron	Dobb	1769	Jonathan	Chow	1721
Andrew	Crav	1752	Joseph	Curr	1715
Andrew 8 slaves	Dobb	1769	Thomas	Chow	1717
Andrew	Dobb	1779	Thomas	Chow	1721
Arthur	Dobb	1779	Thomas	Crav	1769
Benjamin	Gran	1769	BATES, Daniel	Dobb	1769
Benjamin Jr.	Gran	1784	Humphrey Esq.	Tyrr	1755
Benjamin Sr.	Gran	1784	John	Rand	1779

BATHEY, Jenny	Bert	1757	BEARD, Lewis	Rowa	1759
BATHY, John	Chow	1753	Neil	Blad	1763
Tristram	Chow	1753	Robert	Crav	1743
BATMAN, John	Tyrr	1755	BEARDEN, Ambrose	Gran	1755
Nathan	Tyrr	1755	Benjamin	Gran	1769
Thomas	Perq	1740	Benjamin	Gran	1784
Thomas	Tyrr	1755	Humphrey	Casw	1777
BATSON, Peter	Onsl	1743	Richard	Bute	1771
BATTARS, John	Pitt	1764	Richard	FWV	1771
Wm	Pitt	1764	BEARFIELD, Miles	Brun	1772
BATTEY, John	Anso	1750	Richard	Edge	1744
BATTLE, Mary	Onsl	1769	BEASIE, James	Oran	1755
Mary	Onsl	1770	BEASLEY, Abraham	Crav	1769
Nathaniel	Bert	1769	Benjamin	Blad	1763
Thomas s. of			Benjamin	Cumb	1767
Mary	Onsl	1770	Benjamin	Curr	1715
BAUCOM, Nicholas	Crav	1742	Benjamin	Tyrr	1755
BAULTHROP, John	FWV	1771	Isaac	Curr	1755
Sharp	FWV	1771	Isaac	Rand	1779
BAUM, Abraham	Curr	1715	Jacob	Curr	1755
Adam	Curr	1755	James	Chow	1717
John	Curr	1755	James s. of		
Morris	Curr	1755	Francis	Chow	1721
BASTER, John	Bute	1771	James s. of		
John	FWV	1771	James	Chow	1721
Nathaniel	Bute	1771	John	Chow	1753
Nathaniel	FWV	1771	John	Crav	1769
BAWL, John	Pitt	1764	John	Curr	1755
BAXLEY, Edmond	Blad	1781	Major	Rowa	1758
John	Blad	1763	Mary	Chow	1721
Thomas	Blad	1763	Robert	Chow	1753
BAXTER, Israel	Pitt	1763	Robert	Gran	1784
John	Bute	1771	Simon	Crav	1769
John	FWV	1771	Solomon	Crav	1769
Nathaniel	Bute	1771	Solomon Jr.	Crav	1769
Nathaniel	FWV	1771	Thomas	Beau	1755
Peter	Casw	1777	Thomas	Beau	1764
BAXTON, James	Gran	1769	Thomas	Onsl	1769
BAYLEY, Ambrose	Crav	1769	Thomas Jr.	Onsl	1769
BAYLONG, Wm	NewH	1762	Thomas	Onsl	1770
BAYNES, John	Gran	1769	Wm	Cumb	1767
BAZEL, Francis	Dobb	1769	Wm	Curr	1755
BAZEMORE, Jesse	Bert	1757	BEASON, Richard	Rowa	1759
Jesse	Bert	1769	Samuel	Anso	1750
John	Bert	1757	Wm	Surr	1772
John	Bert	1769	Wm	Surr	1771
John Jr.	Bert	1769	BEATTY, Francis	Rowa	1759
BAZIN, Charles	NewH	1767	James	Rowa	1759
BEA, Wm	Cumb	1767	Thomas	Rowa	1759
BEACKLE, Jacob	Oran	1755	BEAVER, Jeremiah	Gran	1784
BEAL, James	Pasq	1769	John	Gran	1784
BEALE, John	Bute	1771	Wm	Gran	1784
John & s. Wm	FWV	1771	BEAZEY, Elijah	Gran	1784
BEAMAN, Wm	Pitt	1762	BECATS, Mathias	Surr	1771
Edmond	Bert	1757	BECK, Caleb	Dobb	1779
Ozias	Bert	1757	Frederick	Gran	1784
Wm	Pitt	1762	Gideon	NewH	1762
BEAN, John	Rand	1779	Jeffrey	Rand	1779
Joseph	Crav	1720	Matthew	Bert	1757
Richard	Rand	1779	Valentine	Surr	1771
BEARD, Daniel	Blad	1763	Widow	Rand	1779
Daniel	Blad	1781	BECKHAM, James	FWV	1771
John	Anso	1763	John	Bute	1771
John	Rowa	1759	John	FWV	1771

BECKHAM, Stephen	Bute	1771	BELL, Benjamin		Pasq	1769
Stephen Jr.	Bute	1771	Burrell		Bert	1757
Stephen & s. Wm			Caleb		Curr	1755
Stephen	FWV	1771	Francis		FWV	1771
Stephen Jr.	FWV	1771	Francis Jr.		Rand	1779
Wm s. James			Francis Sr.		Rand	1779
Simon	Bute	1771	Francis		Rowa	1759
Wm Jr.	FWV	1771	George Jr.		Cart	1745
BECKLEY, Joseph	Curr	1715	George	1 slave	Dobb	1769
BECKMAN, Wm	Bute	1771	George		Dupl	1752
BECKNALL, Samuel	Surr	1771	James		Brun	1769
Samuel	Surr	1772	James		Brun	1772
Thomas	Surr	1772	James Jr.		Brun	1772
BECKUM, John s.			James		Cart	1741
of Wm	Gran	1755	James		Crav	1769
Malcomb	Surr	1771	James		NewH	1762
Simon s. of Wm	Gran	1755	James		NewH	1763
Thomas	Gran	1755	Jesse		Bute	1771
Wm	Gran	1755	Jesse		FWV	1771
Wm Jr.	Gran	1755	John		Beau	1764
BECTON, Frederick	Crav	1769	John		Brun	1769
George	Crav	1769	John		Brun	1772
John	Crav	1741	John		Dobb	1769
John	Crav	1745	John		FWV	1771
Michael	Crav	1769	John		Pasq	1754
Richard	Beau	1755	John		Rand	1779
BEDSCOTT, John	Crav	1769	Joseph		Bute	1771
BEDWELL, Robert	Surr	1772	Joseph		FWV	1771
BEECHOM, Edmond	Curr	1755	Joseph		Gran	1755
BEECHUM, Wm	Curr	1755	Joseph		Pasq	1754
BEECK, Jeffrey	Oran	1755	Joseph Jr.			
BEEFLE, Felty	Rowa	1759	2 slaves		Pasq	1769
Paul	Rowa	1759	Joseph Sr.			
BEELER, Jacob	Rowa	1759	4 slaves		Pasq	1769
BEEM, Jeremiah	Oran	1755	Joshua		Gran	1784
BEEMAN, Edmond	Bert	1757	Lancelot		Bert	1757
Israel	Gate	1786	Lancelot			
Ozias	Bert	1757	3 slaves		Pasq	1769
Ozias	Dobb	1779	Linsey		FWV	1771
Wm	Pitt	1762	Moses		Beau	1755
BEESLEY, Henry	Oran	1755	Nathan		Pasq	1769
Thomas	Beau	1755	Richard		Bert	1757
BEESON, Alexander	Rowa	1759	Robert		Curr	1755
Benjamin Jr.	Rand	1779	Robert		Rand	1779
Benjamin Sr.	Rand	1779	Samson		Pasq	1769
Ebenezer	Rand	1779	Samuel		Bute	1771
Edward	Rand	1779	Samuel		FWV	1771
Isaac	Rand	1779	Samuel s. of			
Isaac	Rowa	1759	Thos.		Gran	1755
John	Rand	1779	Starkey		Pitt	1775
Richard	Rand	1779	Thomas		Bute	1771
Richard	Rowa	1759	Thomas		FWV	1771
Wm	Rand	1779	Thomas		Gran	1755
Wm	Rowa	1759	Thomas s. of			
BEGLEY, Jacob	Gate	1786	Thos.		Gran	1755
BEHOE, Moses	Bute	1771	Wm		Bute	1771
Moses	FWV	1771	Wm		Curr	1715
BEILS, John	Pasq	1754	Wm		Curr	1755
BELCHER, Woode	Dobb	1779	Wm		Dobb	1769
BELER, Lewis	Bert	1769	Wm Jr.		Dobb	1769
BELFARE, Wm	Dobb	1769	Wm		Dobb	1779
BELIEU, Isaac	Casw	1777	Wm		Edge	1743
BELL, Aaron	Dobb	1779	Wm		Gran	1769
Augustine	Pasq	1769	Wm		Pasq	1754
Benjamin	Pasq	1754	Wm Jr.		Pasq	1754

BELL, Wm	Pitt 1775	BENNETT, Thomas	Chow 1753
Wm	Rand 1779	Thomas	Cumb 1755
BELLIS, Elijah	Cumb 1767	Thomas	Cumb 1767
Francis	Cumb 1767	Thomas	Dobb 1769
BELLONE, Michael	Brun 1772	Thomas Jr.	Tyrr 1755
BELMAN, John	Perq 1740	Thomas Sr.	Tyrr 1755
Peter	Crav 1720	Timothy	Rand 1779
BELMONT, Doloz	Crav 1720	Wm	Chow 1721
BELOTE, John	Bert 1757	Wm	Dobb 1769
Wm	Bert 1757	Wm	Gran 1769
BEN, George	Bute 1771	Wm	Gran 1784
George	FWV 1771	Wm	NewH 1763
BENBERRY, Wm	N.C. 1701	Wm	NorH 1748
BENBOW, Charles	Blad 1763	Wm	Onsl 1769
Powell	Cumb 1767	BENNING, John	Crav 1769
BENBURY, Jane	Chow 1753	BENNY, Joseph	Crav 1720
John Esq.	Chow 1753	BENSON, John	Beau 1755
John Jr.	Chow 1753	John	Bute 1771
Wm	Chow 1753	John	Crav 1745
Wm Jr.	Chow 1753	John	Crav 1769
BENDER, John	Rowa 1759	John	FWV 1771
BENGAL, Alexander	Chow 1717	Marlin	Dobb 1769
Wm	Cumb 1755	Nathan	NewH 1762
BENGUMELTON, Obadiah		Nathan	NewH 1763
	N.C. 1701	BENTLEY, Caleb	Oran 1755
BENN, Wm	Bert 1757	James	Bert 1769
BENNERMAN, Charles	NewH 1762	James	NewH 1763
BENNERS, John		James s. of John	Onsl 1769
25 slaves	Crav 1769	James s. of John	Onsl 1770
BENNETT, Ann	Bute 1771	Jesse	NewH 1763
Anne	FWV 1771	John	Chow 1717
Benjamin	Curr 1715	John	Onsl 1769
Dan	NewH 1762	John	Onsl 1770
Daniel	NewH 1763	John	Tyrr 1755
Hamed	Dobb 1779	Wm	Bert 1757
James	Crav 1743	Wm	Dobb 1769
James	Surr 1771	Wm	NewH 1763
James	Surr 1772	Wm	Onsl 1769
Jesse orphan of		Wm s. of John	Onsl 1769
Jno	Curr 1715	Wm s. of John	Onsl 1770
John	Anso 1763	BENTON, Aaron	Dobb 1769
John	Bute 1771	Elijah	Chow 1753
John	Curr 1715	Elijah	
John	Dobb 1769	Elizabeth	Gate 1786
John	Dobb 1779	Elizabeth	Pasq 1754
John	FWV 1771	Epaphroditus	Chow 1717
Joseph	Curr 1715	Epaphroditus	Chow 1753
Joseph	Dobb 1779	Francis	Chow 1721
Joseph	Onsl 1769	Francis	Dobb 1769
Lewis	Gran 1784	Francis Jr.	Dobb 1769
Libenon	NewH 1762	Isaac	Gate 1784
Mark	Bute 1771	James	Casw 1777
Mark	FWV 1771	James	Pitt 1762
Nehemiah	Onsl 1770	Jesse Esq.	Casw 1777
Peter	Gran 1784	Jesse	Gate 1784
Reuben	Bute 1771	Jesse	Surr 1771
Reuben & s.		Jethro	Chow 1753
James	FWV 1771	Jethro	Gate 1784
Richard	Bute 1771	Job	Brun 1772
Richard	FWV 1771	John	Bert 1769
Richard	Gran 1755	John	Chow 1753
Richard	Gran 1784	John	Pasq 1754
Richard	Surr 1771	Jonathan	Dobb 1779
Richard	Surr 1772	Joseph	Dobb 1769
Stephen	Bert 1769	Josiah	Gate 1786

BENTON, Kedar	Gate 1786		BEVIL, Wm	NewH 1762
Margaret	Anso 1763		Wm	NewH 1763
Mary	Gate 1786		Zechariah	Gran 1784
Miles	Gate 1786		BEVIN, Joseph	NewH 1762
Moses	Brun 1772		Joseph	NewH 1763
Moses	Chow 1753		Thomas	NewH 1762
Moses	Gate 1786		Thomas	NewH 1763
Samuel	Gate 1786		BEXLEY, Simon	Beau 1755
Samuel	Gran 1755		Simon	Crav 1769
Samuel	Gran 1769		Wm Constable	Beau 1755
Samuel	Pasq 1754		Wm Jr.	Beau 1755
Vincent	Gran 1769		BEYER, Benjamin	Bert 1769
Vincent	Pasq 1754		BEYNER, Richard	Beau 1755
BERAYER, Charles	Rowa 1759		BIBBA, Edmon (black)	
BERNARD, John	Pasq 1754			FWV 1771
BEROTH, Johannes	Surr 1772		Mary (black)	FWV 1771
John	Surr 1771		BIBBE, John	Rand 1779
BERRY, Hudson	Casw 1777		BIBEN, Morris	Blad 1763
John	Bert 1757		BIBLIGHAUS, George	Surr 1771
John	Bert 1769		BICKERDITE, John	Rand 1779
John	Casw 1777		BIDDLE, Jacob	Onsl 1741
John	Pasq 1769		Jacob	Onsl 1769
Lancelot	Crav 1769		BIGGFORD, Jeremiah	Blad 1763
Samuel	Crav 1769		Jeremiah	NewH 1743
Thomas	Anso 1763		BIGGS, James	Durr 1755
Thomas	Crav 1769		John	Crav 1769
Thomas	Oran 1755		Joseph	Tyrr 1755
Wm	Gran 1755		Wm	Crav 1769
BERRYDON, John	Dobb 1769		BILLENSLEY, John	N.C. 1701
BERRYMAN, Benjamin	Chow 1753		BILLING, Wm	Rand 1779
Benjamin	Gate 1786		BILLINGHAM, John	Rand 1779
Charles	NewH 1767		BILLINGSLEA, Elizabeth	
Edward	Chow 1753			Rand 1779
Edward	Gate 1786		John	Rand 1779
Joseph	Onsl 1769		BILLIPS, John	Bert 1769
Richard	Chow 1721		Zerubabel	Bert 1757
Wm	Gate 1786		BILOK, John	Bert 1769
BEST, Benjamin	Dobb 1769		BINCLE, Peter	Surr 1772
Benjamin	Dobb 1779		BINFORD, Daniel	FWV 1771
Brian	Blad 1781		BINKS, James	FWV 1771
Henry & wife			BINKSON, Andrew	Casw 1777
Mary	Bert 1757		BINUM, Amy	Bert 1757
Henry	Crav 1743		George	Surr 1771
Humphrey	Surr 1771		Gray	Surr 1771
Humphrey	Surr 1772		Luke	Oran 1755
John	Tyrr 1755		Margaret	Bert 1757
Joseph	Tyrr 1755		BIRAM, Peter	Bert 1757
Kedar	Bute 1771		BIRCH, John	Gran 1755
Kedar	FWV 1771		BIRD, Charles	NorH 1762
Thomas	Bert 1757		Edmond	Bert 1757
Thomas	Tyrr 1755		Edward	Bert 1757
BETHEY, James	Gate 1786		Edward	Bert 1769
John	Gate 1786		Edward	Chow 1721
BETT, Benjamin	Dobb 1769		Edward	Chow 1753
Brian	Blad 1781		Elijah	Chow 1753
Wm Sr.	Dobb 1769		Jesse	Bert 1757
BETTERLEY, Thomas	Chow 1717		Jesse	Bute 1771
Thomas	Chow 1721		Jesse	FWV 1771
BETTIS, Francis	Cumb 1755		John	Bute 1771
George	FWV 1771		John	Chow 1721
James	Bute 1771		John	Dobb 1769
James	FWV 1771		John	FWV 1771
BEVERET, Benjamin	NewH 1742		John & s. Enos	FWV 1771
BEVERLY, John	Chow 1721		John	Gran 1755
John	Oran 1755		Joshua	Dobb 1769
			Moses	Bert 1757

BIRD, Nathaniel	Dobb	1769	BLACK, Archibald	Cumb	1755
Needom	Bute	1757	Betty	Crav	1769
Needom	FWV	1771	Edward	Anso	1763
Richard	Dobb	1769	George	Casw	1777
Richard s. of			George	Rand	1779
Wm	Dobb	1769	Henry	Casw	1777
Thomas	Bert	1757	Henry	Crav	1769
Thomas	Bute	1771	Hugh	Cumb	1767
Wm	Bert	1757	Isaiah	NewH	1762
Wm	Bute	1117	John	Casw	1777
Wm	Dobb	1769	John	FWV	1771
Wm	FWV	1771	Kenith	Cumb	1767
Wm	Gran	1769	Martin	Crav	1769
BIRDSONG, James	NewH	1767	Matthew	Blad	1763
BIRELY, John	Rowa	1759	Nancy d. of		
BIRKETT, Benjamin	Pitt	1763	Henry	Curr	1715
Benjamin	Pitt	1764	Samuel	Bert	1769
John	Chow	1717	Thomas	Casw	1777
Joseph	Pitt	1764	Wm	Bute	1771
BIRKINHEAD, George	N.C.	1701	Wm	Cumb	1767
Thomas	Chow	1721	Wm	FWV	1771
Thomas	N.C.	1701	Wm	Oran	1755
BIRNS, Wm	Cumb	1755	BLACKALL, Sarah	Chow	1753
BISHOP, Abner Const	Anso	1763	BLACKBURN, Ambrose	Surr	1771
Charles	NewH	1762	Ambrose Younger	Surr	1772
Charles	NewH	1763	Augustine	Surr	1772
Drury	Bute	1771	Newman	Surr	1771
Drury	FWV		BLACKELAND,		
George	Bute	1771	Christop	NewH	1755
George	FWV	1771	BLACKLEDGE,		
George s. of			Richard	Crav	1769
Henry	Gran	1755	BLACKLEY, James	Gran	1755
Grace	NewH	1767	BLACKMAN, Daniel	Gran	1755
Greer	NewH	1763	John	Crav	1743
Henry	Gran	1755	John	Gran	1755
Jacob	NewH	1755	John	Gran	1784
James	Gran	1784	John	Roan	1720
John Jr. 5 slaves			John s. of John	Gran	1755
	Crav	1769	Solomon	Gran	1755
John Sr.	Crav	1769	Stephen	Dobb	1769
John	Edge	1744	Thomas	Chow	1721
John	Gran	1755	BLACKNEY, John	Gran	1755
John	Perq	1740	BLACKSHEAR, Alexander		
Joseph	Bute	1771		Crav	1769
Joseph	FWV	1740	Elisha	Crav	1769
Joseph	FWV	1771	James	Crav	1769
Joseph	Gran	1755	BLACKSTOCK, Wm	Pasq	1754
Littleton	NewH	1763	BLACKSTONE, James	Pitt	1762
Littleton	NewH	1767	James	Pitt	1764
Littleton	Onsl	1770	John	Pitt	1764
Stockley	Newh	1763	BLACKWELL, Isaiah	Casw	1777
Stockley	NewH	1767	James	Pitt	1764
Wm	Bute	1771	John	Gran	1784
Wm	FWV	1771	Micajah	Bert	1769
Wm	NewH	1763	Robert	Casw	1777
BISSELL, John	Dobb	1779	BLACKWOOD, Wm	Oran	1755
BITLER, Peter	Surr	1772	BLAIR, Enos	Rand	1779
BIVEN, Morris	Blad	1763	John	Beau	1764
Thomas	NewH	1755	BLAKE, Archibald	Anso	1763
BIZBEE, Ira	Rand	1779	Benjamin	Oran	1755
Stockley	NewH	1762	John	Casw	1777
Wm	NewH	1762	Joseph	NewH	1744
BIZZELL, John	Dobb	1769	Joseph	NewH	1755
Thomas s. of			Joseph	NewH	1762
John	Dobb	1769	Joseph	NewH	1763

BLAKE, Joshua	Crav	1769	BLANGO, Betty	Beau	1755
Martin	Crav	1769	Dinah (black)	Beau	1755
Samuel	Pitt	1764	Sarah (black)	Beau	1755
Wm	Gran	1755	Sarah (black)	Beau	1764
Wm	NewH	1763	Sarah Jr.		
Wm	NewH	1767	(black)	Beau	1755
Wm	Oran	1755	Tom (black)	Beau	1755
BLAKEY, John	Casw	1777	BLANING, Hugh	NewH	1743
Lawrence	Crav	1769	BLANKETPICKER, John		
BLALOCK, David	Gran	1784		Rowa	1759
James	Rand	1779	BLANKS, Joseph	Gran	1784
Jeremiah	Gran	1784	BLANN, James'		
John	Edge	1743	estate	NewH	1767
John	Gran	1769	BLANSHARD, Abner	Gate	1786
Mittenton	Casw	1777	Demsey	Gate	1786
Richard Jr.	Cumb	1767	Elizabeth	Gate	1786
Richard Sr.	Cumb	1767	Keziah	Gate	1786
Thomas	Casw	1777	Moses	Gate	1786
Wm Sr.	Casw	1777	BLASSINGHAM, John		
Wm	Casw	1777		Gran	1755
Wm	Rand	1779	Thomas	Anso	1763
BLAN, Wm	NewH	1767	Thomas	Gran	1755
BLANCHARD, Aaron	Chow	1717	BLASTON, James	Pitt	1763
Aaron	Chow	1753	James	Pitt	1764
Aaron	Gate	1786	John	Pitt	1764
Amaziah	Chow	1753	BLEACHER, Jacob	Oran	1755
Amerias	Gate	1786	BLEDSOE, Aaron	Surr	1771
Amos	Chow	1753	Barnabas	Surr	1771
Benjamin	Chow	1717	George	Bute	1771
Benjamin	Chow	1753	George s. Rush		
Eph.	Chow	1717	Abram	FWV	1771
Ephraim	Chow	1753	George Jr.	FWV	1771
James	Bert	1769	George	Gran	1755
Keziah	Gate	1786	John	Surr	1771
Mary	Chow	1753	John	Surr	1772
Mecager	Chow	1753	Moses	Surr	1771
Michael	NewH	1762	Wm	Gran	1755
Michael	Newh	1763	BLEER, Sarah	Pasq	1754
Michael	NewH	1767	BLENNING, Elizabeth	Blad	1763
BLANCHETT, John	Cumb	1767	BLETCHENDEN, Abraham		
Peter	Bute	1771		Bert	1757
Peter	FWV	1771	John	Perq	1740
Thomas	Bute	1771	Thomas	Perq	1720
Thomas s. of			Thomas	Perq	1740
Hudson	FWV	1771	BLEW, Malcomb	Rowa	1759
Thomas	Gran	1755	BLEWET, Wm	Anso	1763
BLANCHFIELD, Else	Cumb	1767	BLEWLETT, Abraham	Chow	1717
BLANCHFORD, Aaron	Chow	1721	Abraham	Chow	1721
Ephraim	Chow	1721	BLEY, Elizabeth	Chow	1753
Ka.	Chow	1721	BLIN, Mourning	Beau	1755
Michael	NewH	1755	Peter	Beau	1764
BLAND, George	Beau	1755	BLIRGER, Wm	Pasq	1754
George	Pitt	1762	BLITH, Samuel	Dobb	1779
George	Pitt	1763	BLOCKER, Elizabeth	Blad	1763
George	Pitt	1764	Jacob	Cumb	1755
George	Pitt	1775	Jacob	Cumb	1767
James	NewH	1762	Mary	Blad	1763
James	NewH	1763	Michael	Crav	1743
James	HewH	1764	BLOODWORTH, David		
Jesse	NewH	1763		NewH	1762
Moses	Rand	1779	David Constable	NewH	1763
Thomas	Blad	1763	David	NewH	1767
Wm	Cumb	1767	Robert	NewH	1767
Wm	NewH	1763	Timothy	NewH	1742
Wm	Rand	1779	Timothy	NewH	1762

BLOODWORTH, Timothy			BOATMAN, Waterman	Bute	1771
.	NewH	1763	Waterman	FWV	1771
Timothy	NewH	1767	BOATWRIGHT, Daniel	NewH	1767
BLOUNT, Ann	Chow	1717	BOBETT, Drury	Bute	1771
Ben	Chow	1717	Drury	FWV	1771
Benj.	Chow	1721	John	Bute	1771
Benjamin	Pitt	1762	John s. Isham		
Benjamin	Pitt	1763	Stephn	FWV	1771
Benjamin	Pitt	1764	John	Edge	1743
Benjamin	Tyrr	1755	John	Gran	1755
Charles	Chow	1753	John	Roan	1720
Francis	Crav	1769	Lewis Jr.	Bute	1771
Frederick			Lewis Jr.	FWV	1771
21 slaves	Pasq	1769	Lewis	Gran	1755
Gershom	Tyrr	1755	Miles	Bute	1771
Jacob	Chow	1717	Miles	FWV	1771
Jacob 12 slaves	Crav	1769	Miles	Gran	1755
Jacob	Pitt	1762	Wm	Bute	1771
Jacob	Pitt	1763	Wm	FWV	1771
Jacob	Pitt	1764	Wm	Gran	1784
Jacob	Tyrr	1755	BOBO, Samson	Bute	1771
James Jr.	Chow	1717	Samson	FWV	1771
James	Curr	1674	BOCOS, Wm	Hyde	1742
James	NewH	1744	BODDID, Willis	NorH	1762
James	Pitt	1764	BODDIE, David	Onsl	1770
James	Roan	1720	Jacob	Onsl	1770
John	Beau	1764	John	Gran	1769
John Esq.	Chow	1717	BODINE, Vincent	Gran	1769
John Sr.	Chow	1717	BOGAN, Patrick	Oran	1755
John	Chow	1717	Wm	Oran	1755
John	Chow	1753	BOGET, Moses	Dobb	1769
John	NewH	1743	BOGEY, Alexander		
John	N.C.	1701	Con	Crav	1769
John	Roan	1720	BOGGS, Elizabeth	Surr	1771
John Jr.	Tyrr	1755	BOGUE, Josiah	Perq	1740
John Sr.	Tyrr	1755	Wm	Perq	1720
Joseph	Chow	1753	Wm s. of Wm	Perq	1720
Reading	Beau	1764	BOHANNON, Andrew	Surr	1771
Reading	Tyrr	1755	Duncan	Oran	1755
Reuben	Pasq	1769	John	Oran	1755
Richard	Beau	1764	Wm Constable	Crav	1769
BLUE, Duncan	Cumb	1767	BOHEN, Robert	Crav	1769
John	Cumb	1767	BOILEAU, Wm	Edge	1742
Malcomb	Cumb	1755	BOIRDSTON, Thomas	Bert	1769
Malcomb	Rowa	1759	BOLDIN, Thomas	Anso	1763
BLUM, Jacob	Surr	1771	BOLES, David	Pasq	1769
Jacob	Surr	1772	John	Dobb	1779
BLUNT, Jacob	Beau	1755	Wm	Surr	1771
Jacob	Blad	1781	BOLIN, Isaac	Anso	1763
James	Beau	1755	John	Rand	1779
James	Blad	1763	BOLLIN, Mitchell	Rand	1779
James	Dobb	1769	Wm	Rand	1779
John	Beau	1755	BOLLING, James	Gran	1755
John	Blad	1763	John	Anso	1763
John	Blad	1781	John s. of Wm	Gran	1755
Joseph	Beau	1755	John	Gran	1784
Joseph	Pasq	1754	Wm	Anso	1763
Thomas	Beau	1755	Wm	Gran	1755
Wm	Curr	1755	BOLLINGER, Wm	Curr	1674
BLYN, James	NewH	1767	BOLOM, Thomas	Gran	1769
BLYTH, James	NewH	1763	BOLTON, Aaron	Bert	1757
BLYTHE, James	NewH	1762	Charles	Casw	1777
BOAN, John	Anso	1763	David	FWV	1771
BOASMAN, Ralph	Perq	1720	Richard	Beau	1755
Widow	Chow	1721	Thomas	Bert	1757

BOMP, Jesse	Surr	1772	BONNER, Thomas	Chow	1753
BOND, Charles	Surr	1772	Thomas	FWV	1771
Dempsey	Gate	1786	Thomas	Gran	1784
Edward	Gran	1769	Thomas	Hyde	1752
Francis	Crav	1769	Wm	Bert	1757
George	Rand	1779	Wm	Chow	1717
Jacob	Surr	1771	Wm	Chow	1721
Jacob	Surr	1772	Wm	Chow	1753
Jake	Perq	1740	Wm	Tyrr	1755
James	Beau	1755	BONNEY, Edward	Curr	1715
James	Beau	1764	BOOKER, John	Gran	1755
James	Bert	1769	Richard	Pitt	1775
Jesse	Surr	1771	Sampson	Crav	1769
Jesse	Surr	1772	BOOKOUT, Joseph	Rand	1779
John	Beau	1764	BOOKS, Henry	NewH	1763
John	Bert	1769	BOOLEY, Peter	Crav	1769
John	Onsl	1770	BOOM, Peter	Curr	1755
Lewis	Bert	1769	BOOMER, Henry	Pitt	1764
Nicholas	Anso	1763	BOONE, Cornelius	Dobb	1769
Richard	Beau	1755	Edward	Rowa	1759
Richard	Beau	1764	Edward	Surr	1771
Richard	Chow	1753	James	Bert	1757
Richard	Gate	1786	James	Bert	1769
Robert	Beau	1755	James	Chow	1717
Robert	Beau	1764	James	Gate	1786
Samuel	Onsl	1769	John	Surr	1772
Samuel	Onsl	1770	Joseph	Chow	1721
Samuel	Perq	1720	Joseph	Dobb	1779
Samuel	Perq	1740	Joseph	Edge	1744
Sarah	Beau	1764	Nicholas	NorH	1742
Thomas	Bert	1769	Stephen	NewH	1763
Thomas	Gran	1784	Stephen	NewH	1767
Wm	Beau	1755	Thomas	Blad	1763
Wm	Crav	1743	Thomas	Brun	1769
Wm	Dobb	1769	Thomas	Brun	1772
Wm	Dobb	1779	Thomas		
Wm	Gate	1786	(Virginian)	Chow	1721
BONDES, James	Casw	1777	Thomas	Dobb	1769
BONDICE, Elisha	Casw	1777	Wm	Chow	1721
BONES, Alexander	Casw	1777	Wm	Norh	1762
BONHAM, Hezekiah	NewH	1763	BOOTEY, Peter	Crav	1769
Hezekiah	NewH	1767	BOOTH, Wm	Gate	1786
Samuel	NewH	1762	BORAN, Wm	Casw	1777
Samuel	NewH	1763	BORDEN, Lott	Blad	1763
BONNER, Benjamin	Gran	1769	BORDIN, Bores	Dobb	1769
Henry	Beau	1755	BORDMAN, John	Surr	1772
Henry	Beau	1764	BORFIELD, John	Dobb	1769
Henry	Bert	1757	BORING, Charles	Oran	1755
Henry	Chow	1717	Wm	Oran	1755
Henry	Chow	1721	BORK, James Jr.	Surr	1771
Henry	Chow	1753	BORTON, James	Onsl	1770
James	Beau	1755	John	Onsl	1770
James	Beau	1764	BOSAFFS, James	Pitt	1775
James	Bert	1757	BOSMAN, Ralph	Perq	1740
James	Bert	1769	BOSSELL, Thomas	Bert	1757
John	Chow	1753	Thomas	Perq	1720
Moses	Bert	1757	BOSSWILL, Henry	Blad	1763
Moses	Gran	1769	BOSSWORTH, Joseph	Blad	1763
Thomas	Beau	1741	BOSTER, Joseph	Gran	1784
Thomas H.	Beau	1755	BOSTICK, Charles	Casw	1777
Thomas Jr.	Beau	1755	Charles	Onsl	1770
Thomas	Beau	1764	Wm	Surr	1772
Thomas	Bert	1757	BOSTON, James	Onsl	1770
Thomas	Bute	1771	John	Onsl	1770
Thomas	Chow	1721	John	Rowa	1759

BOSWELL, Amos	Pasq	1769	BOWERS, Benjamin	Beau	1755
George	Perq	1740	Benjamin Esq.	Pitt	1762
James	Casw	1777	Benjamin	Pitt	1763
John	Perq	1740	Benjamin	Pitt	1764
Ransom	Gran	1769	Christian	Crav	1769
Thomas	Bert	1769	David	Pitt	1775
Thomas	Perq	1720	Giles	Bute	1771
Wm s. of Thomas	Perq	1720	Giles s. Jesse	FWV	1771
BOTSFORD, James	Rand	1779	Philemon	Gran	1784
BOTTOM, John			BOWIE, John	Gran	1755
Overseer	FWV	1771	BOWING, John	Pitt	1775
BOUCUS, Daniel	Curr	1755	Silas	NewH	1755
Wm	Curr	1755	BOWLES, John	Casw	1777
BOUGE, Robert	Perq	1740	BOWLIN, Martin	Curr	1715
Wm	Perq	1740	BOWLING, John	Casw	1777
BOULTON, John	Blad	1763	Wm	Casw	1777
BOUNDS, Abigail	Perq	1720	BOWMAN, Peter	Surr	1771
James	Anso	1763	Ralph	Dobb	1769
James Jr.	Anso	1763	Robert	Surr	1771
John	Anso	1763	BOWN, John	Dumb	1767
Samuel	Perq	1740	BOWRING, Edmund	Curr	1755
Thomas	Bert	1757	BOWZER, James	Dodd	1769
BOURN, James	Beau	1741	BOX, Francis	Tyrr	1755
Samuel			BOYCE, Arthur	Dobb	1769
BOUS, John	Surr	1772	Christopher	Chow	1753
BOUSHER, Henry	NewH	1742	Epaphroditus	Chow	1753
BOUTINELL, John	N.C.	1701	John	Perq	1740
Samuel	N.C.	1701	Moses	Chow	1753
Wm	N.C.	1701	Moses	Gate	1786
BOUTWELL, Samuel	Beau	1741	Wm	Gate	1786
Samuel	Beau	1755	BOYD, Amos	Dobb	1779
Samuel	Beau	1764	Daniel	Bert	1769
BOW, Frank	Pasq	1769	Ethelred	Dobb	1779
Robert	Pasq	1769	James	Dobb	1779
BOWDEN, Avery	Crav	1769	James	Gran	1755
Nicholas	Crav	1769	James	Gran	1769
BOWDIN, Thomas	NewH	1762	John	Beau	1755
Thomas	NewH	1763	John	Beau	1764
Thomas	NewH	1767	John	Blad	1743
BOWDOWN, John	Bute	1771	John	Blad	1763
John	FWV	1771	John	Crav	1769
Thomas	Gran	1784	John	Gran	1769
Travis	Gran	1769	John	Gran	1784
Wm	Bute	1771	Joseph	Beau	1755
Wm	FWV	1771	Joseph	Pitt	1762
Wm	Gran	1769	Joseph	Pitt	1763
Wm	Gran	1784	Joseph	Pitt	1764
BOWDRIE, Elisha	Rand	1779	Moses	Dobb	1779
BOWEN, Benjamin	Bert	1769	Patrick	FWV	1771
Clifton	NewH	1755	Reuben	Pasq	1769
Daniel	Bert	1757	Robert	Beau	1741
David	Bert	1769	Robert	Beau	1755
David	NewH	1762	Robert Jr.	Beau	1755
David	NewH	1767	Robert	Beau	1764
Giles	Gran	1755	Robert Jr.	Beau	1764
John	Beau	1764	Robert	Gran	1755
John	Bert	1757	Robert	Gran	1769
John	Bert	1769	Robert	Gran	1784
Luke	NewH	1755	Robert	Pitt	1762
Luke	NewH	1762	Samuel	Cumb	1767
Luke	NewH	1763	Samuel	Gran	1769
Nathan	Bert	1769	Thomas	Beau	1755
Richard	Pitt	1762	Thomas	Beau	1764
Richard	Pitt	1763	Thomas	Dobb	1779
Richard	Pitt	1764	Thomas 15 slaves	Pasq	1769

BOYD, Wm	Beau	1755		BRADEY, Wm	Beau	1755
Wm	Beau	1764		BRADFIELD, George	Gran	1769
Wm	Chow	1753		BRADFORD, David	Gran	1755
Wm	Crav	1743		David	Oran	1755
Wm	Pasq	1754		John	Gran	1784
Wm 6 slaves	Pasq	1769		John	Oran	1755
BOYER, George	Gran	1769		Mary	Gran	1784
John	Gran	1769		Philemon	Gran	1755
Richard	Casw	1777		Pilemon s.		
Wm	Bert	1769		Philemon	Gran	1755
Wm	Dobb	1769		Philem on	Gran	1769
BOYIT, Dred s.				Philip	Gran	1784
Edward	Dobb	1769		Richard of		
Edward	Dobb	1769		Philem	Gran	1755
Edward s. of				Richard	Gran	1769
Edward	Dobb	1769		Richard	Gran	1784
George	Dobb	1769		Shadrack	Dobb	1769
James s. of				Thomas	Gran	1755
Thomas Sr.	Dobb	1769		Thomas	Gran	1769
Joseph s. of				Thomas	Gran	1784
George	Dobb	1769		Thomas	Oran	1755
Josiah s. of				BRADHAM, John	Onsl	1741
Geo.	Dobb	1769		BRADLEY, Daniel	FWV	1771
Thomas Jr.	Dobb	1769		Dennis	Bute	1771
Thomas Sr.	Dobb	1769		Francis	Bute	1771
BOYKIN, Benjamin	Dobb	1769		Francis s.		
Christopher	N.C.	1701		Francis James	FWV	1771
Drury	Dobb	1769		Henry	Chow	1717
Thomas	Dobb	1769		Henry	Chow	1721
Thomas Sr.	Dobb	1779		Henry Jr.	Chow	1721
Thomas	Dobb	1779		Hugh	Oran	1755
BOYLES, Charles	Rowa	1759		James	Casw	1777
Daniel	Rowa	1759		Jerry	Surr	1771
John	Rowa	1759		John	Bute	1771
Robert	Rowa	1759		John	Crav	1752
Wm	Surr	1771		John	Dobb	1769
Wm	Surr	1772		John	FWV	1771
BOYTON, Moses	Onsl	1769		John	Pasq	1769
Moses s. of				John	Tryo	1776
Moses	Onsl	1769		Joseph	Edge	1743
BOYSTER, Bales	Surr	1771		Richard	Curr	1755
Thomas	Surr	1771		Richard	FWV	1771
BOZAN, Wm	Crav	1720		Richard	NewH	1763
BOZMAN, Samuel	Pitt	1764		Terry	Surr	1772
BOZWELL, John	Gran	1784		Thomas	Bute	1771
Ransom	Gran	1784		Thomas	FWV	1771
Richard	Onsl	1770		Thomas	Rowa	1759
Wm	Onsl	1770		Thomas	Tryo	1776
BRABLE, Wm	Curr	1755		Wm	Curr	1755
BRACK, Eleazer	Onsl	1770		Wm	NewH	1763
George	Onsl	1770		BRADLY, Francis	Gran	1755
Richard	Onsl	1770		John	Gran	1755
Wm	Onsl	1770		Wm	Beau	1755
BRACKER, Thomas	Dobb	1769		Wm cooper	Crav	1769
BRACKING, Samuel	Casw	1777		BRADSHAW, Hugh	Crav	1769
BRADBURY, George	Dobb	1779		John	Casw	1777
James	Dobb	1769		Moses	Casw	1777
James	Surr	1771		Samuel	Crav	1769
James	Surr	1772		Thomas	Crav	1769
BRADDY, James	Chow	1753		BRADY, James	Gate	1786
Joseph	Chow	1753		James Jr.	Gate	1786
BRADEN, James	Gate	1786		John	Curr	1755
BRADEY, John	Beau	1755		Joseph	Gate	1786
Joshua	Beau	1755		Joseph	Onsl	1769
Owen	Blad	1763		Wm	Pitt	1762

BRAMLET, Ambrose	Surr	1771
Ambrose	Surr	1772
BRAMS, James	Gran	1784
BRANCH, Arthur	Dobb	1769
Fra.	Chow	1717
Francis	Chow	1721
John	Dobb	1769
Margaret	Chow	1721
Randall	Dobb	1769
Thomas of Arthur	Dobb	1769
Wm	Chow	1717
Wm	Dobb	1769
BRAND, Edmund	Dobb	1779
John Jr	Dobb	1769
John	Dobb	1779
BRANDON, Edward	Oran	1755
James Sr.	Rowa	1759
James Esq.	Rowa	1759
Richard	Rowa	1759
Thomas	Rowa	1759
BRANHAM, John	Surr	1772
Spenor	Surr	1772
BRANNUM, John	Surr	1771
BRANSON, Thomas	Oran	1755
BRANSTON, Abraham	Cumb	1767
BRANTLEY, James	Gran	1755
John	Gran	1755
Joseph	Gran	1755
Joseph s of John	Gran	1755
Lewis	Gran	1755
Thomas	Blad	1763
Thomas	Tryo	1776
BRANTON, John	Blad	1763
Samuel	Crav	1769
Wm	Oran	1755
BRANWELL, Richard Sr.		
	Dobb	1769
Richard Jr.	Dobb	1769
Valentine	Cumb	1767
Wm	Dobb	1769
BRASFIELD, Caleb	Gran	1784
Elizabeth	Gran	1784
BRASHEAR, Bazel	Oran	1755
Jesse	Oran	1755
Robert Sr.	Oran	1755
BRASSELL, Jacob	Roan	1720
John		
Richard	Dobb	1779
Val	Roan	1720
BRASSWELL, George	Surr	1771
Mary	Chow	1721
Richard	Oran	1755
Robert	Chow	1721
Samson	Surr	1771
Wm	Chow	1717
BRATCHER, Roger	Crav	1769
Thomas	Crav	1769
BRATON, Benjamin Jr	Dobb	1769
Thomas	Casw	1777
BRATTON, John	Rand	1779
Robert	Rand	1779
BRAVEBOY, David	Blad	1763
John	Chow	1717
John	Tyrr	1755
BRAVOY, Irby	Gran	1755

BRAWLEY, Hugh	Rowa	1759
John	Rowa	1759
BRAXTON, Wm	NewH	1763
Wm	NewH	1767
BRAY, Capt.	Chow	1721
Christopher	Onsl	1770
Christopher	Pasq	1754
Cornelius s Henry		
	Pasq	1769
Daniel	Pasq	1754
Daneil	Pasq	1769
Edward	Oran	1755
Elizabeth orphan	Curr	1715
Henry Sr.	Pasq	1754
Henry Sr.	Pasq	1769
Jacob	Pasq	1769
James orphan of Wm		
	Curr	1715
John orphan of Wm		
	Curr	1715
Joseph	Onsl	1769
Joseph	Onsl	1770
BRAY, Joshua	Pasq	1754
Joshua	Pasq	1769
Sarah orphan of Wm		
	Curr	1715
Thomas	Chow	1717
Wallace	Curr	1715
Wallis	Curr	1755
Wm	Curr	1755
Wm Jr.	Pasq	1769
Wm Sr.	Pasq	1754
Wm Sr.	Pasq	1769
BRAYFORD,	Blad	1763
BRAZIEL, Samson	Surr	1772
BRAZIL, Wm	Dobb	1769
BREED, Joseph	Oran	1755
BREEDLOVE, Charles	Casw	1777
John	Gran	1784
BREELER, Abraham	Beau	1755
Abraham	Pitt	1762
Abraham	Pitt	1763
Abraham	Pitt	1764
BREES, Henry	Beau	1755
BREETON, Wm	Dobb	1769
BRENT, Thomas	Pasq	1754
BRENTON,Benjamin Sr	Dobb	1769
BRETT, Benjamin	Bute	1771
BREWER, Henry	Oran	1755
Howell	Oran	1755
John	Dobb	1769
John	Tyrr	1755
Joseph	Bute	1771
Joseph s Hezekiah		
	FWV	1771
Moses	Dobb	1779
Nehemiah	Cumb	1767
Reas	FWV	1771
Sarah	Bert	1757
Thomas	Bute	1771
Thomas	FWV	1771
Wm	Gran	1755
Wm	Tyrr	1755
Zechariah	FWV	1771
Zinience	Cumb	1767

BRIAN, Darby	Perq	1720	BRIGHT, ANN guardian			
Ed	Chow	1717	Silas	Curr	1715
James	Chow	1717	Charles orphan	Curr	1715
John s. òf Ed	Chow	1717	Charles guardian		
Lewis	Chow	1717	Silas	Curr	1715
Mat.	Chow	1717	Charles	Pasq	1769
Mr.	Curr	1674	Ephraim	Pasq	1754
Thomas	Onsl	1770	Henry Jr.	Curr	1715
BRICE, Francis	Cart	1741	Henry Sr.	Curr	1715
Francis	Crav	1720	Henry orphan of		
Francis	Onsl	1742	Henry	Curr	1715
John	N.C.	1701	Henry	Curr	1755
Robert	N.C.	1701	Hezekiah	Pasq	1769
Wm	Crav	1720	Isaac	Pasq	1769
Wm	Crav	1741	James s. of		
BRICKELL, John	Bert	1757	Simon Sr.	Dobb	1769
Mathias	Bert	1757	James	Pasq	1769
BRICKHOUSE, Benjamin			John orphan	Curr	1755
	Curr	1715	Keziah	Curr	1715
Benjamin	Curr	1755	Malachi s. of		
Peter	Tyrr	1755	Hezekiah	Pasq	1769
BRICKLE, James	Beau	1764	Nathan	Pasq	1769
James	NewH	1767	Richard Jr.	Curr	1715
BRIDGERS, Athrel	Dobb	1779	Richard Sr.	Curr	1715
Henry	NorH	1762	Richard s. of		
Jacob	Edge	1734	Henry	Curr	1715
Joseph	NorH	1762	Richard	Pasq	1769
Samuel	Blad	1781	Robert	Pasq	1769
Wm Jr.	Chow	1721	Samuel	Curr	1755
Wm	Roan	1720	Silas	Curr	1755
BRIDGES, James	Gran	1769	Simon	Blad	1763
John	Gran	1769	Simon	Crav	1742
John	Gran	1784	Simon 2 slaves	Dobb	1769
Joseph	Bute	1771	Simon Sr. 6		
Joseph	FWV	1771	slaves	Dobb	1769
Joseph	Gran	1755	Stockwell	Crav	1769
Joseph	Gran	1784	Wm bro of		
Joshua	FWV	1771	Robert	Pasq	1769
Moses	Casw	1777	Willis	Curr	1755
Richard	Chow	1753	Willis	Pasq	1769
Robert	Bert	1769	BRILE, Adam	Rand	1779
Thomas	Bute	1771	Coatley	Rand	1779
Thomas & s. Ben	FWV	1771	George	Rand	1779
Thomas	Gran	1755	BRIMER, Benjamin	Rowa	1759
Thomas	Gran	1784	BRIN, David	Rand	1779
Wm	Bute	1771	John	Chow	1753
Wm	Chow	1721	BRINEGAR, Adam	Rowa	1759
Wm	Cumb	1755	BRINK, Frederick	Casw	1777
Wm	FWV	1771	Jonas	Casw	1777
Wm	Gran	1755	BRINKLEY, Daniel	Crav	1769
Wm	Gran	1784	Francis	Gate	1786
BRIDGETT, Andrew	Oran	1755	James	Gran	1784
BRIERLY, Wm	Beau	1755	John	Pitt	1764
BRIGGS, Benjamin	Dobb	1779	Joseph	Crav	1769
Jacob	Gate	1786	Joseph	Edge	1750
John	Dobb	1779	Joseph	Gate	1786
Margaret	Surr	1771	Josiah	Gate	1786
Margaret	Surr	1772	Michael	Bert	1757
Moses	Gate	1786	Michael	Chow	1717
Richard	Gate	1786	Michael	Gran	1769
Solomon	Gate	1786	Michael	Perq	1740
BRIGHT, Aaron	Pasq	1769	Peter	Gran	1769
Albert	Anso	1763	Peter	Gran	1784
BRIGHT, ANN orphan	Curr	1715	Peter	Perq	1740

BRINKLEY, Rachel	Gate	1786	BROCK, Horatio	Beau	1755
BRINSON, Aaron	Onsl	1770	Isaac	Casw	1777
Adam	Onsl	1749	James	Casw	1777
Carson Jr.	Crav	1752	Joseph 2 slaves	Dobb	1769
Carson	Onsl	1741	Reuben	Casw	1777
George	Dobb	1769	Samuel	Edge	1742
George	Onsl	1769	Samuel	Gran	1784
George	Onsl	1770	Wm	Bute	1771
Isaac	NewH	1762	Wm	FWV	1771
Isaac	Onsl	1769	BROCKETT, Benjamin	Crav	1743
Isaac	Onsl	1770	Joel 2 slaves	Pasq	1754
James 3 slaves	Crav	1769	Joel	Pasq	1769
John Esq.	Onsl	1769	John 1 slave	Pasq	1769
John Sr.	Onsl	1769	BROCKMAN, John	Casw	1777
John Esq.	Onsl	1770	BRODIE, John	Gran	1784
John Sr.	Onsl	1770	BRODWAY, John	Casw	1777
John	Pitt	1762	BROGDON, David	Bert	1757
John	Pitt	1763	George	Bute	1771
John	Pitt	1764	George s. Maridy	FWV	1771
Lester	Onsl	1769	James	Roan	1720
Matthew	Onsl	1769	John	Bert	1757
Matthew	Onsl	1770	John Jr.	Bert	1757
Sarah	Onsl	1769	John Sr.	Bert	1757
Sarah	Onsl	1770	John	Bert	1769
Stiron	Onsl	1769	John	Dobb	1779
BRISCOE, Edward Jr.	Chow	1753	Mary	Bert	1769
Edward	Gate	1786	Peterson	Bert	1757
BRISLER, George	Gran	1769	Thomas	Gran	1755
BRISON, Robert	NewH	1762	Wm	Bute	1771
BRISSEY, Francis	Gran	1784	Wm	FWV	1771
BRISTON, James	Gate	1786	BROMAT, Nimrod	Gran	1784
BRISTOW, Elizabeth	Gran	1784	BRON, Pat	Cumb	1755
George	Gran	1784	BROOKINS, Bridgeman	Dobb	1769
James	Gran	1784	BROOKS, Arthur	Casw	1777
John	Gran	1784	Christopher	Onsl	1770
Philip	Gran	1784	David	Casw	1777
BRITT, Benjamin	Bute	1771	Isaac	Cumb	1755
Benjamin	FWV	1771	Isaac	Pitt	1775
Jesse	Dobb	1779	Jacob	Oran	1755
Joseph	Blad	1763	James	Beau	1755
Richard	Cumb	1755	James	Pitt	1762
Simon	Dobb	1769	James	Pitt	1763
BRITTLE, John	NorH	1762	James	Pitt	1764
BRITTON, Bennett	Pitt	1762	James	Rand	1779
Charles	Pasq	1754	Jesse s. of John	Dobb	1769
Charles	Pasq	1769	Joab	Cumb	1755
Francis	NewH	1755	John	Anso	1763
James	Rowa	1759	John Jr.	Anso	1763
John	Bert	1757	John	Beau	1755
BROADAWAY, James	Dobb	1769	John	Beau	1764
Nicholas	Anso	1763	John	Blad	1741
Nicholas		1748	John	Casw	1777
Robert	Anso	1763	John	Cumb	1755
BROADSHOOT, John	NorH	1762	John	Dobb	1769
BROADWELL, David	Bert	1757	John s. of John	Dobb	1769
David	Bert	1769	John	Oran	1755
BROCK, Charles	Surr	1771	John	Pitt	1762
Elias	Rowa	1759	John	Pitt	1763
Elias	Surr	1771	John	Pitt	1764
Elias Constable	Surr	1772	John	Pitt	1775
Frederick	Oran	1755	Joseph	Beau	1769
George	Casw	1777	Joseph	Crav	1769
George	Gran	1769	Joseph	Onsl	1769
George	Gran	1784	Joseph	Onsl	1770
George		1744	Mark	Cumb	1755

BROOKS, Robert	Curr	1755	BROWN, Augustine	FWV	1771
Thomas	Blad	1741	Beal	Chow	1721
Thomas	Casw	1777	Benjamin	Beau	1755
Thomas	Oran	1755	Benjamin	Bert	1757
Wm	Anso	1763	Benjamin	Chow	1753
Wm	Beau	1755	Benjamin	Pitt	1762
Wm	Beau	1764	Benjamin	Pitt	1763
Wm	Crav	1769	Benjamin	Pitt	1764
Wm	Curr	1744	Charles	Cumb	1767
Wm	Gate	1786	Daniel	Pasq	1769
BROOKSHIRE, Jesse	Rand	1779	Daniel	Rand	1779
Mannering Jr.	Rand	1779	David	NewH	1755
Mannering Sr.	Rand	1779	David	Surr	1771
Mary	Rand	1779	Dorothy, widow	Beau	1755
Swift	Rand	1779	Dorothy, widow	Beau	1764
Wm Manin	Rowa	1759	Edward	Crav	1769
BROOM, Augustine	Bute	1771	Edward	NewH	1763
Benjamin	Crav	1769	Francis	Bert	1757
John	Bute	1771	Francis	Casw	1777
John	FWV	1771	Francis		
John	Roan	1720	Constable	Chow	1721
Josiah	Bert	1757	George	Blad	1763
BROOSE, John	Roan	1720	George Esq.	Blad	1781
Walter	FWV	1771	George Jr.	Blad	1781
BROSIER, John	Pasq	1769	George	Crav	1769
Michael	Pasq	1769	Henry	FWV	1771
Simon	Pasq	1769	Hugh	Cumb	1755
BROTBURY, George	Dobb	1769	Hugh	Cumb	1767
BROTHERS, Benjamin	Pasq	1769	Jacob	Beau	1755
Covington	Pasq	1769	Jacob	Beau	1764
Drew 1 slave	Pasq	1769	James	Anso	1763
John	Casw	1777	James	Beau	1755
John	Pasq	1754	James	Bert	1757
John	Pasq	1769	James	Bert	1769
Joseph	Pasq	1754	James	Blad	1763
Joseph 1 slave	Pasq	1769	James	Casw	1777
Malachi	Pasq	1769	James Jr.	Chow	1753
Michael	Pasq	1769	James Sr.	Chow	1753
Richard	Pasq	1769	James	Curr	1715
Richard s. of			James	Dobb	1769
John	Pasq	1769	James	Gate	1786
Robert	Pasq	1769	James	NewH	1741
Samuel	Pasq	1754	James	Pitt	1762
Thomas	Pasq	1769	James	Pitt	1763
Wm	Pasq	1754	James	Pitt	1764
Wm	Pasq	1769	James	Rand	1779
BROUGHTON, Adam	Pasq	1769	James	Rowa	1759
Willoughby	Surr	1771	James	Surr	1771
Willoughby	Surr	1772	James	Surr	1772
BROWDER, John	Blad	1763	Janson	Dobb	1769
John	FWV	1771	Jeremiah	Dobb	1769
John	N.C.	1701	Jeremiah	Rand	1779
BROWER, John	Rand	1779	Jesse	Gate	1786
BROWMAN, Robert	Surr	1772	Jesse	Pitt	1764
Wm	Surr	1772	Jesse	Surr	1771
BROWN, Abraham	Casw	1777	Jesse Jr.	Surr	1771
Andrew	Beau	1755	Jesse Jr.	Surr	1772
Andrew	Pitt	1762	Jesse Sr.	Surr	1772
Andrew	Pitt	1763	John	Beau	1742
Andrew	Pitt	1764	John	Beau	1755
Arthur	Beau	1755	John	Beau	1764
Arthur	Bert	1757	John	Bert	1743
Arthur	Bert	1769	John Esq.	Bert	1757
Arthur	Pitt	1763	John	Blad	1763
Augustine	Bute	1771	John	Blad	1781

BROWN, John	Brun	1769	BROWN, Tom	Beau	1755
John	Brun	1772	Tom	Blad	1781
John	Bute	1771	Walton	Onsl	1769
John	Casw	1777	Wm	Anso	1763
John	Chow	1721	Wm	Bert	1757
John Jr.	Chow	1721	Wm	Bert	1769
John	Cumb	1755	Wm	Bute	1771
John Jr.	Cumb	1755	Wm	Casw	1777
John	Dobb	1769	Wm cooper	Casw	1777
John	Dobb	1779	Wm	Crav	1769
John	Edge	1743	Wm	Cumb	1767
John	FWV	1771	Wm	FWV	1771
John	Gran	1769	Wm	Gran	1769
John	NewH	1755	Wm	NewH	1762
John	Onsl	1741	Wm	Onsl	1769
John	Oran	1755	Wm	Onsl	1770
John Sr. 4			Wm	Oran	1755
slaves	Pasq	1754	Wm s. of John	Pasq	1769
John Jr.	Pasq	1769	Wm	Surr	1771
John Sr.	Pasq	1769	Wm	Surr	1772
John	Pitt	1764	Willis	Gate	1786
John	Pitt	1775	Wilson	Tyrr	1755
John	Rand	1779	BROWNEY, John Sr.	Chow	1721
John	Roan	1720	BROWNING, Carrigan	Crav	1769
John	Surr	1771	David	FWV	1771
John	Surr	1772	Enos	Casw	1777
Jon	Beau	1755	Francis	Casw	1777
Jon	Beau	1764	George	Crav	1769
Jonas	Pitt	1775	Isham	Casw	1777
Joseph	Gate	1786	John	Casw	1777
Joseph	Rand	1779	John	Crav	1769
Joseph	Rowa	1759	John Jr.	Crav	1769
Josiah	Bert	1757	John Jr.	Tyrr	1755
Leonard	Casw	1777	Perrigan	Crav	1769
Malachi s. of			Wm	Crav	1769
John	Pasq	1769	Wm	Gran	1755
Mark	Casw	1777	Wm	NewH	1762
Matthew	Cumb	1755	Wm	Oran	1755
Michael	Rand	1779	BROWNLEE, John	Cumb	1767
Micham	Onsl	1770	BRUCE, George	Gran	1755
Morgan	Anso	1763	George	Gran	1769
Peter	Cumb	1767	James	Anso	1763
Peter	Pasq	1754	John	Roan	1720
Peter	Pasq	1769	Thomas	Gran	1755
Ph.	Chow	1717	Walter	Bute	1771
Phil.	Chow	1721	Walter	FWV	1771
Randle	Surr	1771	Wm	Casw	1777
Randle	Surr	1772	BRUCKS, Wm	Curr	1755
Richard	Bert	1757	BRUCKSHEAR, Manen	Rowa	1758
Richard	Chow	1721	Mahen	Rowa	1759
Robert	Rand	1779	Wm	Rowa	1758
Samuel	Gate	1786	Wm	Rowa	1759
Susannah	Casw	1777	BRUFFET, John	Crav	1769
Thomas	Beau	1755	BRUMBLE, Wm	Blad	1763
Thomas	Beau	1764	BRUMMIT, John	Gran	1769
Thomas	Blad	1741	Samuel	Gran	1769
Thomas	Blad	1781	Thomas	Gran	1769
Thomas	Cumb	1767	BRUNER, George	Rowa	1759
Thomas	Dobb	1769	Henry	Rowa	1759
Thomas	Dobb	1779	BRUNT, Charles	Curr	1715
Thomas	Edge	1743	John	Curr	1715
Thomas	Gran	1769	Thomas	Curr	1715
Thomas	Gran	1784	Thomas	Pasq	1769
Thomas	NewH	1767	BRUTAIN, David	Anso	1763
Thomas	Onsl	1769	BRUTON, John	Dobb	1769

BRUTON, Joseph	Dobb	1779		BRYAN, Thomas	Onsl	1769
Joseph	Crav	1769		Thomas	Onsl	1770
Samuel	Anso	1763		Thomas	Ro	1759
BRYAN, Absalom	Tyrr	1755		Will	Roan	1720
Ann Cady	Crav	1769		Wm	Bert	1757
Anne 7 slaves	Crav	1769		Wm	Bert	1769
Barnaby	Bert	1769		Wm 3 slaves	Blad	1763
Baxton	NewH	1767		Wm	Crav	1769
Blake	Dobb	1779		Wm 9 slaves	Crav	1769
Darby	Tyrr	1755		Wm	Pitt	1762
David	Bert	1757		Wm	Pitt	1763
David	Dobb	1769		Wm	Pitt	1764
Edward	Bert	1757		BRYANT, Alice	NorH	1742
Edward	Blad	1763		Bryant	Gran	1784
Edward	Chow	1721		Charles	NorH	1762
George	Bert	1769		David	Gran	1755
Hardy 2 slaves	Crav	1769		David	Surr	1771
Isaac 2 slaves	Crav	1769		Edward	Casw	1777
James	Chow	1721		James	Chow	1721
James Sr.	Chow	1721		James	NorH	1744
James	NewH	1762		John	Casw	1777
Jesse	Crav	1769		John Jr.	Rand	1779
Jethro	Bert	1769		John Sr.	Rand	1779
John	Bert	1757		John	Surr	1772
John	Blad	1763		Joseph	Onsl	1769
John Esq.	Chow	1721		Nathan	Onls	1769
John s. of Ed.	Chow	1721		Nathan	Onsl	1770
John	Chow	1721		Rowland	Gran	1784
John	Crav	1742		Thomas	Perq	1720
John	Crav	1745		Wm	Casw	1777
John	Crav	1769		Wm	Gran	1769
John of Trent	Crav	1769		Wm	Surr	1771
John of Council	Crav	1769		BRYLEY, Joseph	Pitt	1762
John	Dobb	1769		Joseph	Pitt	1763
John	NewH	1762		Joseph	Pitt	1764
John	NewH	1763		Ruth	Pitt	1762
John	Roan	1720		Ruth, widow	Pitt	1762
John	Rowa	1758		Richard	Pitt	1762
John	Rowa	1759		Richard	Pitt	1763
John Constable	Rowa	1759		Wm	Pitt	1763
Joseph	Crav	1745		Wm	Pitt	1764
Joseph 16 slaves				BRYNTT, Wm	Casw	1777
	Crav	1769		BUCHANNON,		
Joseph	Rowa	1759		Alexander	Cumb	1767
Lewis	Chow	1721		Andrew	Casw	1777
Lewis	Crav	1741		Andrew	Surr	1772
Lewis	Crav	1769		Crawford	Gran	1755
Lewis Jr.	Crav	1769		James	Gran	1769
Martha	Bert	1769		Wm	Crav	1769
Matthew	Chow	1721		Wm	Gran	1784
Michael	Bert	1757		BUCK, Ebenezer	Pasq	1769
Morgan Jr.	Rowa	1759		Edward	Pitt	1762
Nathan 3 slaves	Crav	1769		Edward	Pitt	1763
Needham	Bert	1742		Francis		
Needham	Bert	1743		Constable	Pitt	1762
Needham	Bert	1757		Francis		
Needham	Bert	1769		Constable	Pitt	1763
Needham	Crav	1742		Francis		
Philemon	Blad	1763		Constable	Pitt	1764
Philemon	Crav	1769		Henry	Pitt	1764
Shelley	Blad	1763		Isaac	Beau	1743
Stephen	Blad	1763		Isaac	Beau	1744
Thad	Pitt	1775		Isaac	Beau	1752
Thomas Sr. 4				Isaac	Beau	1755
slaves	Blad	1763		Isaac Jr.	Beau	1755

BUCK, Isaac	Pitt	1762	BUMPASS, Samuel	Oran	1755
Isaac	Pitt	1763	Sarah	Casw	1777
Isaac	Pitt	1775	BUNCH, Embree	Bert	1757
John	Brun	1769	BUNCH, Embry	Bert	1769
Samuel	Dobb	1769	Gideon	Oran	1755
BUCKINGHAM, Joseph	Oran	1755	Henry	Bert	1757
BUCKLEY, Edward	Casw	1777	Jeremiah	Bert	1757
BUCKNER, Benjamin	Rand	1779	Jeremiah	Bert	1769
Henry	Rand	1779	Jeremiah Jr.	Bert	1769
Wm	Bert	1757	Lovick	Bert	1769
BUCKSTON, Jarvis	Crav	1769	Micajah	Chow	1753
BUDGER, Wm	Dobb	1769	Micajah	Oran	1755
BUFFALO, Wm	NorH	1762	Nancy	Bert	1769
BUFFALONE, Wm	NorH	1762	Nehemiah	Bert	1769
BUFFEL, Wm	Curr	1755	BUNDY, Benjamin	Pasq	1754
BUFFELO, Wm	NorH	1762	Caleb 1 slave	Pasq	1769
BUFFERD, Wm	Gran	1769	Christopher	Rand	1779
BUFFKIN, Ralph	Perq	1720	Dempsey s. of		
BUGG, James	Onsl	1770	Caleb	Pasq	1769
BUIE, Archibald	Cumb	1767	Jehu s. of		
Archibald	Cumb	1767	Samuel	Pasq	1769
Daniel	Cumb	1767	Josiah	Perq	1740
Duncan	Cumb	1767	Moses	Pasq	1754
Gilbert	Cumb	1767	Ruth	Pasq	1769
John	Cumb	1767	Samuel 1 slave	Pasq	1769
Malcomb	Cumb	1767	Samuel	Rand	1779
BUIES, Wm	Rowa	1759	Wm	Perq	1740
BULLARD, John	Blad	1763	BUNN, James	Dobb	1769
John	Blad	1781	James	Dobb	1779
BULLEN, Wm	Cumb	1755	John	NorH	1762
BULLER, James	Gran	1769	Wm		1743
BULLOCK, Charles	Gran	1784	Wm	Dobb	1779
Edward	Gran	1769	Wm Jr.	NorH	1762
George	Onsl	1769	Wm Sr.	NorH	1762
George	Onsl	1770	BUNNELL, Moses	Curr	1755
Henry Sr.	Gran	1784	BUNNEY, Robert	Crav	1769
Isaiah	Pitt	1763	BUNSDALE, Abraham	Bert	1769
Isaiah	Pitt	1764	BUNT, Ben	Anso	1763
James	Beau	1755	BUNTEN, Ebenezer	NewH	1755
James	Pitt	1762	BUNTIN, Daniel	Pitt	1775
James	Pitt	1763	BUNTING, Ebenezer	NewH	1755
James	Pitt	1764	Ebenezer	NewH	1762
John	Gran	1755	Ebenezer	NewH	1763
John	Gran	1769	Ebenezer	NewH	1767
Joshua	Beau	1755	Francis 1 slave	Pasq	1769
Len	Gran	1769	BUNTON, Ebenezer	Rand	1779
Micajah	Gran	1784	BUOY, Archibald	Cumb	1755
Nathaniel	Bute	1771	Daniel	Cumb	1755
Nathaniel	FWV	1771	Duncan	Cumb	1755
Nathaniel s.			Gilbert	Cumb	1755
Richard	Gran	1755	Zechariah	Blad	1742
Richard	Gran	1755	BURCH, Charles	Bert	1769
Samuel	Casw	1777	Cimburton	Gran	1769
Samuel	Pitt	1775	Henry	Surr	1771
Thomas	Pitt	1762	James	Bert	1769
Thomas	Pitt	1763	John	Bute	1771
Thomas	Pitt	1764	John	FWV	1771
Wm	Gran	1769	John	Surr	1771
Wm	Gran	1784	Joseph	Bert	1757
BULTSCHECK, Joseph	Surr	1772	Joseph	Pitt	1763
BUMMER, Matthew	Tyrr	1755	Nicholas	Gran	1769
BUMPASS, John	Casw	1777	Nicholas Jr.	Gran	1769
John	Oran	1755	Nicholas	Gran	1784
L & E	Casw	1777	Wm	NewH	1755
Robert	Oran	1755	Wm	Surr	1771

BURCH, Wm	Surr	1772	James	Bute	1771
BURCHAM, James	Rowa	1759	James	FWV	1771
Joseph	Rowa	1759	James Jr.	Surr	1771
BURCHET, James	Gran	1784	James	Surr	1772
Joseph	Bute	1771	John	Surr	1772
Joseph s. James	FWV	1771	John Jr.	Surr	1772
Joseph	Gran	1784	Joseph	Surr	1771
BURCK, Wm	Dobb	1769	Joseph	Surr	1772
BURD, John	Oran	1755	Martin	Surr	1771
Nathaniel	Dobb	1779	Theophilis	FWV	1771
BURDEAUX, Anthony	NewH	1762	Thomas	Dobb	1769
Anthony	NewH	1763	Thomas	Dobb	1779
Anthony	NewH	1767	Wm	NorH	1762
BURDEN, Joseph	Pasq	1754	Wm	Pitt	1764
Susannah	Pasq	1754	BURKETT, John	Pitt	1762
Thomas	Gran	1755	Joseph Sr.	Pitt	1762
Thomas	Gran	1784	Joseph	Pitt	1762
BURDINE, Vincent	Bute	1771	Mary	Pitt	1762
Vinson	FWV	1771	Moses	Pitt	1762
BURFORD, Daniel	Bute	1771	Thomas	Chow	1753
Daniel	Gran	1784	BURKS, Record	Oran	1755
John	Gran	1755	BURLEY, John	Dobb	1769
Phil. (Cpt.)	FWV	1771	Robert	NewH	1755
Robert	Pasq	1769	BURN, Andrew	Bert	1769
Wm Jr.	Gran	1784	Bartholomew	NewH	1763
BURGAW, Estate	NewH	1763	John	Bert	1757
BURGER, John	Brun	1769	John	Bert	1769
John	Brun	1772	Lawrence	Blad	1781
Philip	Pitt	1764	BURNALL, Ann w. Wm	Gran	1755
BURGESS, Asa s. of			Wm	Gran	1755
Stephen	Pasq	1769	BURNAM, Alexander	Gran	1755
Jacob	Bert	1757	BURNE, Matthew	Blad	1763
James	Rand	1779	BURNETT, Abraham s.		
John	Pasq	1754	of John	Onsl	1770
John	Pasq	1769	Alexander Sr.	Curr	1755
Joseph	Pitt	1762	Alexander	Gran	1755
Joseph	Pitt	1763	Alexander	NewH	1762
Joseph	Pitt	1764	David	Bute	1771
Malachi	Blad	1781	David	FWV	1771
Philip	Beau	1755	Isaac Jr.	Onsl	1769
Richard	Cumb	1755	Isaac Sr.	Onsl	1769
Richard	FWV	1771	Isaac Jr.	Onsl	1770
Samuel	Curr	1715	Isaac Sr.	Onsl	1770
Solomon	Pitt	1763	John	Crav	1769
Solomon	Pitt	1764	John	Onsl	1742
Stephen	Pasq	1754	John	Onsl	1744
Stephen	Pasq	1769	John	Onsl	1769
Thomas	Curr	1755	John	Onsl	1770
Thomas	Casw	1777	John	Rowa	1742
Thomas	Pasq	1754	Joseph	Curr	1755
Thomas Jr.	Pasq	1769	Joshua	Surr	1772
Timothy	Casw	1777	Lebanon	Curr	1755
Widow	Casw	1777	Leven	NewH	1755
Wm	Anso	1763	Leven	Onsl	1769
Wm	Pasq	1754	Samuel	NewH	1755
Wm Jr.	Pasq	1754	Samuel	Onsl	1769
Wm	Pasq	1769	Samuel	Onsl	1770
BURGHARD, George	Rowa	1759	Solomon	Onsl	1769
BURK, Benjamin	Pitt	1764	Solomon	Onsl	1770
Benjamin	Surr	1771	Wm	Gran	1784
Benjamin	Surr	1772	BURNEY, James	Oran	1755
Charles	Bute	1771	Robert	Crav	1769
Charles	FWV	1771	Simon	Beau	1745
Edward	Onsl	1769	Simon	Beau	1755
BURK, Edward	Pitt	1764	Simon 5 slaves	Pitt	1762

BURNEY, Simon	Pitt	1763
Simon	Pitt	1764
Simon	Pitt	1775
Wm 2 slaves	Blad	1763
Wm (Cpt.)	Pitt	1763
Wm	Pitt	1764
Wm (Cpt.)	Pitt	1775
BURNHAM, Alexander	Bute	1771
Alexander	FWV	1771
Alexander	Gran	1784
Benjamin 2 slaves		
	Pasq	1769
Caleb	Pasq	1769
David 4 slaves	Pasq	1769
Gabriel	Pasq	1769
James	Curr	1755
John	Bert	1769
John	Pasq	1769
Joshua	Pasq	1754
Joshua 1 slave	Pasq	1769
Wm	Bert	1769
BURNS, Andrew	Bert	1757
Bartholomew	NewH	1755
Bartholomew	NewH	1767
Charles	Oran	1755
Francis	Onsl	1769
Francis	Onsl	1770
Frederick	Onsl	1769
Frederick	Onsl	1770
James	Gran	1769
James	Onsl	1769
James	Onsl	1770
James s. of James		
	Onsl	1769
James s. of James		
	Onsl	1770
John	Curr	1755
Otway	Onsl	1770
BURNSIDE, James	Cumb	1767
BURRINGTON, Estate	NewH	1762
George	NewH	1755
BURRIS, James	Bert	1769
John	Curr	1755
John	Surr	1771
Joshua	Bert	1757
Joshua	Bert	1769
Sarah	Curr	1755
Wm	Surr	1772
BURROWS, Robert	Curr	1715
Wm	Bute	1771
Wm	Gran	1755
BURSLEY, Thomas	Edge	1734
BURT, John	Oran	1755
Wm	Chow	1717
Wm	Chow	1721
Wm	Cumb	1767
BURTENSHALL, Richard		
	Chow	1717
Richard	Chow	1721
BURTON, Charles	Casw	1777
David	Casw	1777
John	Casw	1777
John	Curr	1755
Richard	Oran	1755
Robert	Gran	1784

BURTON, Samuel	Beau	1741
Thomas	NewH	1767
Wm	Crav	1744
BUSBEY, Tho.	Roan	1720
BUSH, Abraham	Dobb	1769
Abram	Dobb	1779
Benjamin	Crav	1769
Bib	Dobb	1769
Bibby	Dobb	1769
Bibby	Dobb	1779
Crawford	Rowa	1759
David	Chow	1753
Jeremiah	Bute	1771
Jeremiah	FWV	1771
John	Bute	1771
John	Chow	1717
John	Chow	1721
John	FWV	1771
John	Perq	1740
Joseph	Casw	1777
Richard	Dobb	1769
Wm	Chow	1717
Wm	Chow	1721
Wm	Crav	1769
BUSICK, James	Crav	1769
Wm	Crav	1769
BUSSETT, Abraham	Crav	1750
BUSTIAN, Christopher		
	Curr	1715
BUSTONHEAD, Richard	Beau	1764
BUSWELL, Barker	Casw	1777
BUT, Stannop	Curr	1755
BUTCHER, Thomas	Dobb	1769
Thomas	Dobb	1779
BUTCHMAN, Henry	Cumb	1767
John	Cumb	1767
BUTLER, Ann	Bert	1769
Ann	Gran	1784
Christopher	Chow	1753
Elisha	Dobb	1769
Isaac	Gran	1784
Jacob	Chow	1753
James	Bute	1771
James	FWV	1771
James	NorH	1762
Job	Chow	1753
John	Onsl	1744
John	Onsl	1769
John	Onsl	1770
John	Pitt	1763
Joseph	Blad	1781
Joseph	Casw	1777
Martha	Bert	1769
Robert	Bert	1757
Robert	Edge	1743
Someral	Blad	1781
Thomas	Gran	1784
Walter	Casw	1777
Wm	Onsl	1744
Wm	Pitt	1762
Wm Sr.	Pitt	1763
Wm	Pitt	1763
Wm	Pitt	1764
BUTTEN, Frederick	Crav	1769
George	Crav	1769

BUTTEN, Joseph	Crav 1769		CABLE, Wm	Surr 1772
Michael	Crav 1769		CADER, Stephen	Pitt 1775
BUTTER, James	Gran 1784		CADLE, Andrew	Casw 1777
Wm	Pitt 1764		Andrew	Oran 1755
Wm	Rowa 1759		Benjamin	Oran 1755
BUTTERTON, Joseph	Bert 1757		James	Cumb 1767
Joseph s. of			Mark	Surr 1772
Joseph	Bert 1757		Zechariah	Oran 1755
Robert	Bert 1757		Zechariah Jr.	Oran 1755
Robert	Bert 1769		CAHAN, James	Edge 1734
Sarah	Bert 1769		CAHOON, Dudley	Onsl 1770
BUTTREY, Christopher			James	Dobb 1769
	Tyrr 1755		John	Onsl 1770
BUTTS, James	Dobb 1769		Micajah	Brun 1772
Nicholas	Oran 1755		Wm of Aligator	Tyrr 1755
BUXEL, James	NewH 1762		Wm	Tyrr 1755
BUXTON, Bryan	NewH 1762		CAIGOR, Adam	Surr 1771
BUZBEE, John	Gran 1769		CAIL, Jane	Beau 1755
Miles	Gran 1769		John	Dobb 1779
BYARD, Nathan	Casw 1777		Peter	Beau 1764
Wm	Gran 1769		Robert	Perq 1720
BYERS, George	Gran 1784		Wm	Oran 1755
Jack	Crav 1720		CAIN, Chambers	NewH 1742
Lewis	Dobb 1769		Christopher	Brun 1769
Matthew	Crav 1720		Christopher	Brun 1772
Nathan	Casw 1777		Christopher	NewH 1762
Wm	Gran 1784		Christopher	NewH 1763
BYNOM, Gray	Surr 1772		Daniel	Oran 1755
BYNUS, Margaret	Bert 1757		James	Blad 1781
BYRD, John & s.			John	Blad 1781
Isaac	FWV 1771		John	Brun 1772
Thomas	Bert 1742		Joseph	Blad 1763
Thomas	Chow 1717		Joseph	Blad 1781
Thomas	FWV 1771		Nathaniel	Curr 1755
Wm	FWV 1771		Nathaniel	Pasq 1769
Wo. (widow)	Chow 1717		Richard	Brun 1772
BYRNE, Bartholomew	NewH 1762		Samuel s. of Wm	Blad 1763
Lawrence	Blad 1763		Samuel	Blad 1781
Margaret	Blad 1781		Widow	Blad 1781
Matthew	Blad 1763		Wm 4 slaves	Blad 1763
Peter	Blad 1781		Wm Jr.	Blad 1763
BYRNEY, Wm	Blad 1763		Wm	Blad 1781
BYRUM, Bryan	Chow 1753		Wm 2 slaves	Brun 1769
Henry	Bert 1757		Wm	Brun 1772
Jacob	Gran 1784		Wm	Chow 1721
John	Bert 1769		Wm	Edge 1742
John	Perq 1740		CAIRNS, Wm	Oran 1755
Peter	Bert 1757		CAKE, John Jr.	Bert 1757
Wm	Bute 1771		John	Chow 1721
Wm	FWV 1771		Robert	Bert 1757
Wm	Gran 1784		Robert	Bert 1769
BYUS, James s. of			Stephen	Bert 1769
John	Gran 1755		CALBIN, Wm	Cumb 1767
John	Gran 1755		CALDWELL, Andrew	Oran 1755
Wm s. of John	Gran 1755		Charles	Casw 1777
			James	Casw 1777
			Spencer	Dobb 1779
			CALE, Rice	Chow 1753
CAALL, Edward	Pitt 1763		Wm	Bert 1757
CABLE, John	Rand 1779		CALEF, James	Beau 1750
Nicholas	Rand 1779		James	Beau 1755
CADE, Godfrey	Surr 1772		CALEO, Thomas	Crav 1720
John	Blad 1781		CALER, Wm	NorH 1762
Stephen	Dobb 1769		CALESTE, James	Dobb 1769
Waddell	Dobb 1769		CALLAHAN, John	Beau 1755

CALLAHAN, John	Pitt	1762	CAMPBELL, John	NewH	1762
Wm	Surr	1772	John	NewH	1763
CALLER, Robert	Bute	1771	John	NewH	1767
CALLIOM, Wm	Rowa	1759	John	Rand	1779
CALLOWAY, Caleb	Perq	1740	Jonathan	Rand	1779
Edward	Onsl	1769	Joshua	Curr	1755
Isaac	Onsl	1770	Joshua	Perq	1769
John	Onsl	1770	Keziah	Curr	1755
Joshua	Perq	1720	Laughlin	Oran	1755
Joshua	Perq	1740	Leven	Onsl	1769
Thomas	Perq	1740	Leven	Onsl	1770
CALLUM, Edward	Bert	1757	Lothlan	Rand	1779
Edward	Bert	1769	Malk	Rand	1779
CALMER, Alexander	NewH	1755	Margaret	Casw	1777
CALOR, George	Dobb	1769	Mary	Blad	1781
John s. of			Matthew	Cumb	1767
George	Dobb	1769	Micajah	Dobb	1779
CALPER, Joseph	Edge	1734	Patrick	Cumb	1767
CALVERT, Joseph	Bute	1771	Richard	Casw	1777
Joseph	FWV	1771	Richard	Curr	1755
CALVIN, Alexander	NewH	1755	Robert	Casw	1777
James	Cumb	1755	Shadrack	Dobb	1779
CAM, Dan	Cumb	1755	Thomas	Chow	1753
CAMBER, Thomas	NewH	1755	Thomas	Gran	1755
CAMERON, Daniel	Cumb	1767	Thomas	Pasq	1769
John	Cumb	1767	Thomas	Pitt	1764
CAMMER, Henry	Oran	1755	Wm	Cumb	1767
CAMP, John	Casw	1777	Wm	Gran	1755
Joseph	Casw	1777	Wm	NewH	1762
Nathan	Casw	1777	Wm	NewH	1763
Richard	Oran	1755	Wm	NewH	1767
CAMPBELL, Abiah	Curr	1755	CAMPEN, Benjamin	Beau	1755
Alexander	Bert	1743	Ed	Beau	1755
Alexander	Chow	1721	James	Beau	1742
Alexander	Cumb	1767	James	Beau	1755
Alexander	Dobb	1779	James	Beau	1764
Archibald	Beau	1745	John	Beau	1755
Archibald	Pitt	1762	John	Beau	1764
Archibald	Pitt	1763	Joram	Beau	1755
Archibald	Pitt	1764	Joram	Beau	1764
Charles	Cumb	1755	Joseph	Beau	1755
Charles	Cumb	1767	Joseph	Beau	1764
Daniel	Cumb	1767	Robert	Beau	1742
Fuguhard	Cumb	1767	Robert	Beau	1755
Henry	Onsl	1769	Sarah (widow)	Beau	1764
Henry	Onsl	1770	Thomas	Beau	1742
Hugh	NewH	1763	Thomas	Beau	1755
Hugh	NewH	1767	Thomas	Beau	1764
James	Beau	1755	CAMPERLIN, Jacob	Surr	1771
James	Beau	1764	CAMPLACE, John	NewH	1763
James Esq.	Bert	1769	CANCER, Thomas	NewH	1762
James	Chow	1753	CANDELTON, Joseph	Pasq	1754
James	Cumb	1767	CANE, Cornelius	Rowa	1758
James	NewH	1755	CANNADAY, Alexander	Pasq	1769
James	Oran	1755	Daniel	Crav	1769
John		1743	Edmund	Pitt	1763
John	Bert	1757	Edward	Crav	1769
John Esq.	Bert	1757	Francis	Gran	1769
John	Bert	1769	James	Bert	1769
John	Cumb	1755	James	Pasq	1769
John	Cumb	1767	John	Beau	1755
John	Gran	1755	John	Bert	1757
John s. of			John	Pitt	1775
Thomas	Gran	1755	John Sr.	Rand	1779
John	NewH	1755	John	Tyrr	1755

CANNADAY, Joshua	Crav	1769	CAPLE, Marmaduke	Curr	1715
Mary	Bert	1757	CAPPER, George	Onsl	1770
Nagdaff	Gran	1769	CAPPS, Francis	Bute	1771
Patrick	Chow	1717	Francis	FWV	1771
Richard	Chow	1717	Horatio	Bute	1771
Richard	Chow	1721	Horatio	FWV	1771
Thomas	Rand	1779	James	Beau	1755
Wm	Chow	1721	John	Beau	1764
Wm	Crav	1769	John	Bute	1771
Wm	Edge	1734	John	FWV	1771
Wm Jr.	Oran	1755	Joshua	Bute	1771
Wm Sr.	Oran	1755	Joshua	FWV	1771
Wm	Tyrr	1741	Matthew	Chow	1717
CANNEL, Moses	Gran	1755	Richard s. of		
CANNON, Charles	Gran	1755	Thos	Beau	1764
David	Beau	1755	Thomas	Beau	1755
Dennis	Pitt	1762	Thomas	Beau	1764
Dennis	Pitt	1763	Will	N.C.	1701
Dennis	Pitt	1764	Wm s. of Thomas	Beau	1764
Edward	Crav	1769	Wm	Dobb	1769
Elizabeth 11 slaves			CARDEN, Wm	Oran	1755
	Crav	1769	CAREY, Andrew	Beau	1755
George	Beau	1755	CARGILE, James	Casw	1777
George	Pitt	1763	John	Casw	1777
George	Pitt	1764	Wm	Casw	1777
Henry	Beau	1755	CARKEET, Wm	Tyrr	1755
Henry 1 slave	Crav	1769	CARLEEN, John	Crav	1769
James	Beau	1755	Richard	Crav	1769
James	Dobb	1769	Richard Jr.	Crav	1769
Jer.	Chow	1753	Thomas	Crav	1769
Jeremiah	Cumb	1767	CARLISLE, Edward	Bute	1771
John	Onsl	1769	Edward	FWV	1771
John	Onsl	1770	Edward	Gran	1755
John	Pitt	1762	Richard	Bute	1771
John	Pitt	1763	Richard	FWV	1771
John	Pitt	1764	Samuel	Gran	1755
John Jr.	Pitt	1764	Wm	Casw	1777
John	Pitt	1775	CARMACK, James	Crav	1769
Joseph	Anso	1763	John	Crav	1769
Joseph	Blad	1763	John Constable	Crav	1769
Robert	Casw	1777	Solomon	Crav	1769
Samuel	Pitt	1762	CARMAN, Wm	Perq	1720
Samuel	Pitt	1763	CARMICHAEL, Archibald		
Samuel	Pitt	1764		Casw	1777
Samuel	Pitt	1775	Duncan	Casw	1777
Wm	Beau	1742	Jeremiah	Casw	1777
Wm	Beau	1755	Wm	Surr	1771
Wm Jr.	Beau	1755	Wm	Surr	1772
Wm	Pitt	1763	CARMAN, Caleb	Casw	1777
Wm	Pitt	1764	John	Casw	1777
Wm	Pitt	1775	John Sr.	Casw	1777
CANTON, Isaac	NewH	1767	Wm	Perq	1720
CANTRELL, John	Oran	1755	CARNE, Francis	Oran	1755
Joseph	Casw	1777	John	Rand	1779
Joseph	Rowa	1759	Joseph	Rand	1779
Thomas	Casw	1777	CARNEY, Barnaby	Bert	1769
CAPE, John	Gran	1769	Joseph	Casw	1777
Williamson	Gran	1755	Joshua	Casw	1777
CAPEHART, George	Bert	1743	CARNS, Edmond	Gran	1784
George	Bert	1757	Joseph	Gran	1784
George	Bert	1769	CARON, Alice	Curr	1755
John	Bert	1757	CARPENTER, George	Crav	1769
John	Bert	1769	James	Bute	1771
Michael	Bert	1757	James	FWV	1771
Richard	Bert	1769	John	Anso	1763

CARPENTER, John Jr.	Anso	1763
Owen	Cumb	1767
Philip	Bute	1771
Philip	FWV	1771
CARR, James	Surr	1772
Job	Curr	1755
John	Bute	1771
John	FWV	1771
Jonathan	Bert	1769
Thomas	Oran	1755
Thomas	Surr	1772
CARRAWAY, Adam	Dobb	1769
Adam	Dobb	1779
Arthur	Crav	1769
Barret	Dobb	1769
Elijah	Dobb	1769
Henry	Dobb	1769
Henry	Dobb	1779
James 4 slaves	Crav	1769
John	Crav	1743
John	Crav	1769
John	Cumb	1767
John 5 slaves	Dobb	1769
John Jr.	Dobb	1769
Joshua	Dobb	1769
Joshua	Dobb	1779
Thomas Sr. 4 slaves	Crav	1769
Thomas	Crav	1769
Thomas 3 slaves	Dobb	1769
Thomas	Dobb	1779
Wm	Beau	1755
Wm	Beau	1764
Wm	Crav	1769
Wm 5 slaves	Crav	1769
CARROLL, Benjamin	Bute	1771
Benjamin	FWV	1771
Benjamin	Gran	1755
Charles	FWV	1771
Daniel	Bert	1757
John	Bute	1771
John	Cumb	1755
John	Cumb	1767
John	FWV	1771
John	Gran	1784
John	NorH	1742
Richard	Casw	1777
Sterling	Cumb	1767
Thomas	Bute	1771
Wm	Bute	1771
Wm s. John Thos		
Wm	FWV	1771
Wm	Gran	1755
Wm	Gran	1784
CARRON, George	Tyrr	1755
James Jr.	Curr	1715
James Sr.	Curr	1715
James	Curr	1715
James Sr.	FWV	1771
John	Curr	1715
CARRUTH, Adam	Rowa	1759
James	Rowa	1759
Robert	Rowa	1759
Walter	Rowa	1759
CARRUTHERS, Eunice	Crav	1769
James	Chow	1753
John	Crav	1745
John 5 slaves	Crav	1769
Nathaniel	Perq	1740
Wm Sr.	Brau	1750
Wm	Beau	1752
Wm Jr.	Beau	1755
Wm Sr.	Beau	1755
Wm	Crav	1741
Wm 2 slaves	Crav	1769
CARRY, James	Casw	1777
John	Casw	1777
Joseph	Casw	1777
Samson	Anso	1763
CARSON, James	Rand	1779
James	Rowa	1759
Thomas	Pitt	1775
Thomas	Surr	1772
Uriah	Surr	1772
Wm	Casw	1777
Wm	Rand	1779
CARTER, Abel 5 slaves	Crav	1769
Alexander	Chow	1753
Ann	Gate	1786
Benjamin	Bert	1757
Benjamin Jr.	Bert	1757
Benjamin	Bert	1769
Benjamin	Oran	1755
Daniel	Pasq	1769
Daniel	Tyrr	1755
Edward	Brun	1769
Edward	Brun	1772
Edward	Dobb	1769
Edward	Tyrr	1755
Elizabeth	Dobb	1769
Finch	Rand	1779
George	Anso	1763
Isaac	Gate	1786
James	Anso	1750
James	Blad	1763
James	Dobb	1769
James	Gate	1786
James	NewH	1762
John w. Ann s. Edward Isaac	Bert	1757
John	Dobb	1769
John	Gate	1786
John	Oran	1755
Joseph	Chow	1721
Joseph	Rand	1779
Moor	Gate	1786
Moses	Surr	1772
Robbert	Bert	1757
Robert	Bert	1769
Robert	Brun	1769
Robert	Brun	1772
Robert	Cumb	1767
Samuel	Rand	1779
Samuel	Surr	1771
Samuel	Surr	1772
Thinch	Oran	1755
Thomas	Gran	1769
Thomas Jr.	Gran	1784

CARTER, Walter	Curr	1755	CASH, Peter	Gran	1784
Wm	Bert	1757	Sarah	Gran	1784
Wm	Bert	1769	CASNER, Anton	Surr	1771
Wm	Rand	1779	CASON, Henry	Pitt	1762
CARTESTIN, John	Rand	1779	Henry	Pitt	1763
CARTWRIGHT, Abraham	Pasq	1754	Henry	Pitt	1764
Ahaz s. of			Hillery	Pitt	1762
Hezekiah	Pasq	1769	Hillery	Pitt	1763
Asey s. of Isaac	Pasq	1769	Hillery	Pitt	1764
Benjamin	Pasq	1754	James	Beau	1755
Benjamin	Pasq	1769	James	Pitt	1762
Caleb	Pasq	1769	James	Pitt	1763
Caleb s. of			John	Beau	1755
Isaac	Pasq	1769	John	Pitt	1762
Christopher	Pasq	1754	John	Pitt	1764
David	Pasq	1754	Wm	Beau	1745
Dempsey s. of			Wm	Beau	1755
Isaac	Pasq	1769	Wm	Pitt	1762
Hezekiah 1 slave			CASTELLO, James	Bert	1744
	Pasq	1769	James	Cart	1741
Isaac	Pasq	1754	James	Chow	1721
Isaac Sr.	Pasq	1769	James	Tyrr	1743
Isaac	Pasq	1769	John	Bert	1757
Jacob	Pasq	1769	John	Bert	1769
Jesse	Pasq	1769	CASTER, Henry	Crav	1748
Job	Pasq	1754	Michael	Bert	1769
Job	Pasq	1769	CASTLE, John	Gran	1755
John	Pasq	1754	CASWELL, Benjamin	Dobb	1769
John	Pasq	1769	Martin 2 slaves	Dobb	1769
John s. of John	Pasq	1769	Martin	Dobb	1779
John 1 slave	Pasq	1769	Matthew	Chow	1721
Joseph	Surr	1771	Matthew	Tyrr	1755
Josiah	Pasq	1754	Richard 25 slaves		
Mathias 1 slave	Pasq	1769		Dobb	1769
Moses	Pasq	1769	Richard	Dobb	1769
Peter	Pasq	1769	Richard Esq.	Dobb	1779
Robert	Pasq	1754	Richard	John	1750
Robert Jr.	Pasq	1754	Samuel	Dobb	1779
Robert Sr. 3			Wm	Curr	1715
slaves	Pasq	1769	CATAPHET, James	Pitt	1775
Robert Jr.	Pasq	1769	CATCHEM, Jacob	Oran	1755
Thomas Sr.	Pasq	1754	Jacob	Gran	1769
Thomas	Pasq	1754	CATE, Abraham	Pasq	1754
Thomas	Pasq	1769	Benjamin		
Wm	Pasq	1769	John	Casw	1777
CARTY, John	Surr	1771	John	Oran	1755
CARVER, Wm	Blad	1763	Robert	Casw	1777
Wm	Casw	1777	Robert Sr.	Oran	1755
CARY, Andrew	Beau	1764	Thomas Jr.	Oran	1755
Edward	Gran	1755	Thomas Sr.	Oran	1755
Wm	Gran	1755	CATER, Edward	Oran	1755
CASE, Caleb	Pasq	1769	CATES, Charles	Surr	1771
James	Pasq	1769	Charles	Surr	1772
Jeremiah	Dobb	1779	John	Surr	1771
John	Gran	1769	John	Surr	1772
John	Pasq	1754	Josiah	Casw	1777
John	Pasq	1769	Thomas	Casw	1777
Roger	Chow	1721	CATHEY, Alexander	Rowa	1759
Roger	Roan	1720	Andrew	Rowa	1759
Thomas	Pasq	1754	James	Rowa	1759
Thomas	Pasq	1769	John	Rowa	1759
Wm	Curr	1755	CATHOLIC, Daniel	Onsl	1769
CASEY, Micajah	Dobb	1769	Daniel	Onsl	1770
CASH, Howard	Gran	1784	CATLIN, Samuel	Crav	1769
Joseph	Gran	1784	CATO, Francis	Bert	1757

CATO, George	Bert 1757	Henry	Surr 1772
John	Pitt 1764	CHAMBERS, John	Beau 1755
CATON, John	Crav 1769	John	Casw 1777
Moses	Crav 1769	John	Oran 1755
Solomon	Crav 1769	Richard	Oran 1755
Wm	Crav 1769	Thomas	Pasq 1769
CATTLETT, Hazelwood	Bute 1771	Wm	Blad 1763
Hazelwood	FWV 1771	Wm	Casw 1777
John	Rand 1779	Wm Jr.	Casw 1777
CAUDLE, James	Gran 1769	Wm	Oran 1755
James	Gran 1784	CHAMBLES, Joel	Gran 1784
CAULKINS, Elias	Brun 1772	CHAMLEY, John	Bert 1757
Jonathan	NewH 1763	CHAMNESS, Anthony	Oran 1755
Wm	Brun 1769	Joseph	Rand 1779
Wm	Brun 1772	CHAMPION, Allen	Gran 1784
Wm	NewH 1763	Charles	Gran 1784
CAUSEY, John	Crav 1769	Henry	NewH 1767
CAUSON, Wm Sr.	Pitt 1763	John Jr.	Gran 1769
CAUTHORN, James	Bute 1771	John Sr.	Gran 1769
CAVANAUGH, Charles	Bert 1742	John	Gran 1784
CAVANES, George	Gran 1784	John Jr.	Gran 1784
CAVEN, Robert	Blad 1763	John	NewH 1767
CAVENDER, James	Casw 1777	Joseph	Chow 1753
CAVITS, Wm	Chow 1753	Orlando	Chow 1717
CAWLEY, Elisha	Cumb 1755	Orlando	Chow 1721
John	Bute 1771	Wm	Gran 1769
John	Bute 1771	Wm	Gran 1784
John s. Cattlet,		CHANCE, Benjamin	Crav 1769
John Richard	FWV 1771	Bright	Dobb 1779
CAWTHON, Wm	Gran 1784	John	Crav 1769
CAYLOR, Simond	Crav 1720	John	Pasq 1754
CAZE, John	Rand 1779	CHANCEY, Edmond Sr.	Pasq 1769
CEALE, Joseph	Bert 1757	Edmond Jr.	Pasw 1769
CELEY, Chils	Rand 1779	Francis	Oran 1755
CELLARS, Judith s.		Hannah	Perq 1740
Thomas	FWV 1771	Hosea	Perq 1740
CEMP, Joseph	Blad 1781	James	Oran 1755
Zebulon	Pasq 1754	John	Blad 1763
CERBLEY, Lawrence	Pitt 1764	Thomas	Perq 1740
CERMEAN, James	Pitt 1762	Wm Commander	Pasq 1769
James	Pitt 1764	Zachariah	Perq 1740
CHADWICK, David	Pitt 1762	Zachariah	Perq 1742
David	Pitt 1763	CHANDLER, James	Gran 1769
David	Pitt 1764	Joel	Gran 1769
John	Beau 1764	Joel	Gran 1784
John	Gran 1784	John	Blad 1763
Jonathan	Crav 1769	John	Cumb 1767
Samuel	Cart 1742	John	Gran 1769
CHALCRAFT, James	Pitt 1764	John	Gran 1784
Samuel	Pitt 1764	Joseph	Gran 1769
CHALKHILL, John	NewH 1755	Joseph	Gran 1784
CHALWELL, John	NewH 1763	Thomas	Pasq 1769
CHAMBERLAIN, Jeremiah		Wm	Gran 1769
	Pasq 1769	Wm	Pasq 1769
John	Pasq 1769	CHANT, John	Curr 1715
Katharine	Pasq 1754	CHAPMAN, Charles	NorH 1762
Robert	Pasq 1754	George	Gran 1784
Wm	Crav 1742	Giles	Oran 1755
Wm	Crav 1743	Henry	NorH 1762
Wm	Pasq 1769	Henry	Pitt 1775
CHAMBERS, Edmond	Oran 1755	John	Crav 1769
Edmond	Rand 1779	Richard	Tyrr 1755
Francis	Onsl 1770	Samuel	Oran 1755
George	Beau 1755	Wm	Gran 1784
Henry	Surr 1771		

CHAPPEL, Christopher		
	Bute	1771
Christopher	FWV	1771
Moses	Bert	1757
Richard	Chow	1753
Wm	Curr	1755
CHARLES, James	Surr	1771
James	Surr	1772
Samuel	Perq	1720
CHARLESCRAFT, Anthony		
	Onsl	1769
Anthony	Onsl	1770
Jacob	Onsl	1770
James	Beau	1755
James	Onsl	1769
James	Onsl	1770
James	Pitt	1762
John	Pitt	1762
CHARLTON, George	Crav	1749
Job	Chow	1753
John	Chow	1753
Joseph	Crav	1769
Wm	Chow	1721
Wm	Crav	1769
CHARON, Wm	Beau	1743
CHASON, Joseph	Cumb	1767
Richard	Onsl	1744
Richard	Onsl	1769
Richard	Onsl	1770
CHATWIN, Joseph	Onsl	1769
Joseph	Onsl	1770
CHAUNCEY, Jemimah		
Wo	Beau	1764
Willey	Beau	1755
CHAVERS, Ann	Gran	1784
Gibea	Gran	1769
Gordon	FWV	1771
Lurana	Gran	1769
Shadrack	Gran	1769
Wm	Edge	1742
Wm overseer	FWV	1771
Wm	Gran	1769
Wm Jr.	Gran	1769
CHAVES, Batt	Roan	1720
Gilbert	Gran	1755
Wm	Gran	1755
Wm s. of Wm	Gran	1755
CHEASLEY, Samuel	Casw	1777
CHEASTON, Richard	Perq	1740
CHEATHAM, James	Bute	1771
James	FWV	1771
CHEAVERS, Thomas	FWV	1771
CHEEK, Charles	Cumb	1755
Eleazer	Pitt	1762
John	Anso	1763
John	Blad	1745
John	FWV	1771
Richard	Gran	1755
Robert	Bute	1771
Robert	Cumb	1767
Robert	FWV	1771
Wm	Bute	1771
Wm & s. John	FWV	1771
Wm	Gran	1755
CHEERS, John	Brun	1772

CHEESEBOROUGH, John	Brun	1772
CHENEY, Francis Sr.	Rand	1779
Francis Jr.	Rand	1779
Frank	Onsl	1769
Philip	Onsl	1770
Solomon	Pitt	1775
CHENLERAFT, James	Pitt	1763
Samuel	Pitt	1763
CHERRIT, John	Pitt	1763
CHERRY, Aaron	Bert	1757
Aaron	Bert	1769
Cader	Bert	1769
Charles	Pitt	1764
Eleazer	Pitt	1762
Eleazer	Pitt	1763
Faithful	Tyrr	1755
George	Pitt	1764
Job	Tyrr	1755
John	Beau	1755
John	Beau	1764
John	Tyrr	1755
Lazarus	Pitt	1764
Lemuel	Pitt	1775
Nathan	Pitt	1764
Samuel	Beau	1742
Samuel	Pitt	1764
Solomon	Bert	1757
Solomon	Bert	1760
Bert	Pitt	1764
CHERRYHOLMES, John		
	Chow	1721
CHESHIRE, John	Chow	1717
Joseph	Chow	1721
Richard	Blad	1763
Richard	Blad	1781
Wm	Blad	1781
CHESSON, James	Perq	1720
James	Tyrr	1755
John	Tyrr	1755
Richard 560 acres		
	Perq	1720
CHESTER, John	Beau	1755
John	Beau	1764
CHEVERS, Joel	Anso	1763
CHEVIN, N.	N.C.	1701
CHILDERS, Abraham	Casw	1777
Joseph	FWV	1771
Robert	Bute	1771
Robert s. John	FWV	1771
CHILES, Hezekiah	Gran	1769
Hezekiah	Gran	1784
John	Gran	1784
Moses	Dobb	1769
Nathan	Gran	1769
Nathaniel Jr.	Gran	1784
Nathaniel Sr.	Gran	1784
Thomas	NewH	1755
CHILLEY, Joseph	Crav	1769
CHITTOM, James	Curr	1755
John	Curr	1755
Wm	Curr	1755
CHIVIS, Frederick	Cumb	1755
Jacob	Cumb	1755
John	Cumb	1755
Richard	Cumb	1755

CHRISP, Wm	Tyrr	1755	CLARK, Annie	Perq	1720
CHRIST, Rudolph	Surr	1771	Archibald	Cumb	1767
CHRISTIAN, Drury	Bute	1771	Baptist	Rand	1779
Drury	FWV	1771	Benjamin	Blad	1763
Turner	Bute	1771	Benjamin	Blad	1781
Turner	FWV	1771	Benjamin	Gran	1784
CHRISTMAS, John (Cpt.)			Charles	NorH	1762
	Bute	1771	Christopher	Anso	1763
John Jr.	Bute	1771	Christopher	Bert	1769
John & s. Richard			Christopher	Gran	1755
	FWV	1771	Daniel	Cumb	1755
John Jr.	FWV	1771	Daniel	Cumb	1767
Moses	Gran	1755	David	Blad	1763
Thomas	Bute	1771	David	Onsl	1769
Thomas	FWV	1771	Edward	Beau	1764
CHRISTOPHER, Charles			Edward	Rand	1779
	Beau	1764	Eli	Beau	1764
CHUMNEY, Wm	Gran	1769	Francis	Anso	1763
CHURCH, Abner	Brun	1769	Francis	Gran	1755
Abner	Brun	1772	Francis	Onsl	1747
Caleb	Curr	1755	George	Bute	1771
Cornelius	Pitt	1762	George	FWV	1771
Cornelius	Pitt	1764	George	Rand	1779
Elizabeth s. Isaa			Gilbert	Cumb	1767
	Beau	1755	Gilbert	Gran	1784
Francis	Pitt	1775	Henry	Curr	1755
Isaac s. of Eliza.			Henry	N.C.	1701
	Beau	1755	James	Crav	1769
Isaac	Pitt	1763	James	Dobb	1769
Isaac	Pitt	1764	James	FWV	1771
Jacob	Beau	1764	James	NorH	1762
James	Pitt	1764	James	Oran	1755
Jane	Chow	1721	James	Pasq	1754
Jesse	Pitt	1762	Jeremiah	Anso	1763
John	Beau	1755	John	Beau	1755
John	Pitt	1762	John	Beau	1764
Joseph	Curr	1715	John s. of		
Richard	Chow	1721	Joseph	Beau	1764
Thomas	Oran	1755	John s. of John	Bert	1757
CHURCHWELL, Richard	Surr	1771	John	Blad	1743
CHURTON, Wm	Oran	1755	John	Blad	1744
CICAMIN, James	Pitt	1764	John	Blad	1745
CILBURN, Amos	Surr	1771	John	Crav	1744
CIRKMAN, Wm	Beau	1764	John	Crav	1769
CIRVIN, Laurence	Pitt	1762	John	Cumb	1755
CITER, Charles	Pasq	1754	John tailor	Cumb	1767
CITTERLIN, Jonathan	Chow	1721	John	Dobb	1769
CLANSEY, Timothy	Onsl	1741	John	Gran	1755
CLANTON, Edward	Bute	1771	John	Pasq	1754
Edward	FWV	1771	John	Rand	1779
Reuben	FWV	1771	Joseph	Beau	1764
Wm Jr.	Bute	1771	Joseph 2 slaves		
Wm Sr.	FWV	1771		Blad	1763
Wm Jr.	FWV	1771	Joseph 8 slaves		
Wm	NorH	1742		Blad	1763
CLAPP, Barnett	Oran	1755	Joseph	NewH	1742
George	Oran	1755	Joseph	Rand	1779
Lodwick	Oran	1755	Major	Beau	1755
CLAPTON, Richard	Bute	1771	Nathaniel	Casw	1777
Richard	FWV	1771	Neil	Cumb	1755
CLAREY, Robert	Edge	1744	Patrick	Bert	1769
Timothy	Perq	1720	Penny	Onsl	1769
CLARK, Alexander	Blad	1742	Randel	Gran	1755
Alexander	Cumb	1755	Rebecca	Chow	1717
Andrew	Roan	1720	Richard	Gran	1755

CLARK, Robert	Gran	1755	CLEMENT, Wm	Gran	1784
Samuel	Chow	1721	CLEMENTS, George	Bert	1757
Samuel	NorH	1762	George	Bert	1769
Samuel Jr.	Rand	1779	Giles	Beau	1750
Samuel Sr.	Rand	1779	Giles	Crav	1769
Samuel	Rowa	1758	Peyton	Gran	1769
Sherrod	Onsl	1769	Samuel	FWV	1771
Sylvanus	Pasq	1769	Thomas	Beau	1755
Tho.	Chow	1717	Wm	FWV	1771
Thomas	Beau	1755	CLEMMON, Robert	Dobb	1769
Thomas	Bute	1771	CLEMMONS, Benjamin	Cumb	1767
Thomas	FWV	1771	Cowzins 8 slaves	Dobb	1769
Thomas	NewH	1742	CLEMONDS, Edward	Brun	1769
Thomas	Pitt	1762	Edward	Brun	1772
Thomas	Pitt	1763	CLEMONS, Peyton	Gran	1755
Thomas	Pitt	1764	Peyton	Gran	1769
Thomas	Rand	1779	Richard	Gran	1755
Waller	Gran	1769	CLENTON, Stephen		
Wm	Beau	1755	Sr.	Surr	1771
Wm	Beau	1764	Stephen Jr.	Surr	1771
Wm	Casw	1777	CLERK, Gilbert	Cumb	1755
Wm	Crav	1769	Kenith	Cumb	1755
Wm	Dobb	1769	CLETHERAL, John	Crav	1769
Wm	Onsl	1769	CLETON, Stephen	Surr	1771
Wm	Onsl	1770	CLEVELAND, Benjamin	Surr	1771
Wm	Pitt	1762	CLIDLEY, John	Casw	1777
Wm	Pitt	1763	CLIFFORD, James	Beau	1764
Wm	Pitt	1764	CLIFT, Jonathan	Chow	1721
Wm	Rand	1779	Joseph	Oran	1755
Wm	Rowa	1758	Peter	NewH	1742
CLARKSTON, James	Gran	1769	CLIFTON, Covington	Gran	1769
CLARRAGE, Jacob	Pasq	1754	Ezekiel	Onsl	1769
CLASH, Nicholas	Beau	1755	Ezekiel	Onsl	1770
CLAXTON, James	Gran	1769	John	Brun	1772
Richard	Gran	1769	John	NewH	1762
CLAY, Jno.	Chow	1717	John	Onsl	1769
John	Chow	1721	John	Onsl	1770
Samuel	Gran	1784	Peter	Bert	1769
CLAYTON, Benone	Blad	1763	Richard	Onsl	1769
Daniel	Gran	1769	Thomas	Bert	1757
Francis	NewH	1767	Thomas	Bute	1771
Henry	Perq	1720	Thomas	FWV	1771
James 5 slaves	Crav	1769	CLINGMAN, Alexander	Rowa	1759
Janes	Curr	1744	CLITHERAL, John	NewH	1741
John	Blad	1741	CLOSE, Thomas	Rand	1779
John	Blad	1743	CLOTHAM, Wm	Surr	1771
John	Casw	1777	CLOUD, John Jr.	Surr	1771
Richard	Gran	1769	Joseph	Surr	1771
Stephen	Crav	1744	Wm	Surr	1771
Stephen Jr.	Surr	1771	CLYBURN, John	Blad	1781
Stephen Sr.	Surr	1771	COADY, John	Rand	1779
Susannah	Casw	1777	COALMAN, John	Gran	1755
Thomas	Casw	1777	COAR, Arthur	Dobb	1779
CLEAR, Timothy	Crav	1769	Thomas	Dobb	1779
CLEARWATER, Jacob	Rand	1779	COART, John	Dobb	1779
CLEAVES, Wm	Gate	1786	Joseph	Crav	1769
CLELAND, John	Chow	1753	COATS, Benjamin	FWV	1771
CLEMENT, Jeptha	Gran	1784	George	Pasq	1769
John	Gran	1784	Henry	Rowa	1759
Obadiah	Gran	1784	James	Pasq	1769
Samuel	Gran	1784	James	Rowa	1759
Simon	Gran	1784	John	Pasq	1769
Stephen	Gran	1784	Malachi	Pasq	1769
Thomas	Beau	1764	Wm	Pasq	1769
Thomas	Gran	1784	Wm	Rowa	1759

COAY, James	Bert	1757
Mack	Bert	1757
COBB, Abel	Surr	1771
Abel	Surr	1772
Benjamin	Dobb	1779
Edward	Beau	1755
Edward Jr.	Beau	1755
Edward	Pitt	1762
Edward Jr.	Pitt	1762
Edward	Pitt	1763
Edward Jr.	Pitt	1763
Edward	Pitt	1764
Edward Jr.	Pitt	1764
Henry	Bert	1757
Henry	Casw	1777
Henry	Oran	1755
James	Beau	1755
James	Bert	1769
James	Dobb	1779
James Jr.	Pitt	1762
James Sr.	Pitt	1762
James Jr.	Pitt	1763
James Sr.	Pitt	1763
James	Pitt	1764
Jesse	Dobb	1769
Jesse	Dobb	1779
John	Casw	1777
Joseph	NorH	1742
Nancy	Bert	1769
Noah	Casw	1777
Stephen	Dobb	1769
Stephen	Dobb	1779
Thomas	Bert	1769
Wm	Bert	1769
COBHAM, Thomas	Brun	1769
Thomas 29 slaves		
	Brun	1772
COBLE, James	Pitt	1764
John	Rand	1779
Nicholas	Rand	1779
COBURN, Samuel	Anso	1750
COCHETREES, Tabolt.		
	Gran	1769
COCHRAN, David	Casw	1777
Hannah	N.C.	1701
John	Casw	1777
John	NewH	1743
Joseph	N.C.	1701
Katharine	Bert	1769
Lydia	N.C.	1701
Mary	N.C.	1701
Moses	Surr	1771
Moses	Surr	1772
Nathan	N.C.	1701
Robert	Cumb	1767
Thomas	Blad	1763
Wm	Blad	1750
COCK, Drury s. of		
Tho	Gran	1755
Thomas s. Drury	Gran	1755
COCKBURN, George	Chow	1721
George	Tyrr	1755
George Jr.	Tyrr	1755
Henry	Casw	1777
Mary	Casw	1777

COCKE, Wm	Gran	1784
COCKERHAM, Jacob	Anso	1763
Thomas	Anso	1763
COCKRAM, Moses	Surr	1771
Moses	Surr	1772
COCKRELL, Ed.	Chow	1717
Edward	Chow	1721
Wm	Chow	1721
COCKS, Benjamin	NewH	1755
CODY, Godfrey	Surr	1771
Percy	Rowa	1759
Thomas	Rowa	1759
Thomas	Surr	1772
Wm	Surr	1771
COE, Timothy	Oran	1755
COEN, Daniel	Pasq	1754
COFFIELD, James	Bert	1757
COGDILL, Charles	Crav	1720
David s. of		
Margare	Dobb	1769
David s. of		
Margare	Dobb	1779
Francis		
2 slaves	Dobb	1769
Francis	Dobb	1779
George	Crav	1720
Margaret s.		
David	Dobb	1769
Richard		
11 slaves	Crav	1769
COGDON, John	NewH	1755
COGGIN, John	Bute	1771
John s. Matthew		
Wm	FWV	1771
Thomas	Bert	1757
COGSDELL, Charles	Crav	1720
COGSWELL, John	Surr	1771
John	Surr	1772
CAHOON, James	Dobb	1769
COKE, Wm	Gran	1769
COKER, Caleb	Rowa	1758
Joseph	Surr	1771
Joseph	Surr	1772
Nathaniel s.		
of Ro	Dobb	1769
Robert s.		
NaSoTho	Dobb	1769
Robert	Surr	1771
Robert	Surr	1772
Solomon s. of		
Rob	Dobb	1769
Solomon	Surr	1772
Thomas s. of		
Rober	Dodd	1769
Wm	Surr	1771
Wm	Surr	1772
COLANCE, Rowling	Cumb	1755
COLBERT, Joseph	Blad	1763
Thomas	NewH	1767
COLBERTSON,		
Nicholas	Oran	1755
COLBREATH, Anguish		
	Cumb	1767
Duncan, Constable		
	Cumb	1767

COLBREATH, Nevil	Cumb	1767
Nevin	Blad	1763
Nevin	Cumb	1767
Peter	Blad	1763
Peter	Cumb	1767
COLCLOUGH, Alexander		
	FWV	1771
John	FWV	1771
Wm Jr.	FWV	1771
Wm Sr.	FWV	1771
COLE, Abraham	Surr	1771
Anthony	Gran	1784
Edward	Beau	1755
Guy	Onsl	1770
Isaiah	Casw	1777
James	Dobb	1779
John	Anso	1763
John	Bute	1771
John	Casw	1777
John	Dobb	1769
John	Gran	1755
John	Gran	1784
Mark	Anso	1763
Rhodam	Gran	1784
Stephen	Anso	1763
Stephen	Cumb	1767
Stephen	Rand	1779
Thomas	Crav	1720
Thomas	FWV	1771
Wm	Anso	1763
Wm	Bute	1771
Wm	Dobb	1769
Wm s. of John	FWV	1771
Wm	Gran	1784
Wm	Rand	1779
COLEBREATH, Daniel	Blad	1763
COLEMAN, Daniel	Bute	1771
Daniel	FWV	1771
Elias	Dobb	1779
John (deceased)	Anso	1763
John	Bute	1771
John (deceased)	Casw	1777
John s. Richard		
John	FWV	1771
John	NewH	1763
Richard	Bute	1771
Richard	Casw	1777
Richard s. Richard		
	Gran	1755
Richard	Gran	1755
Robert	Crav	1720
Robert	Gran	1784
Thomas	Crav	1769
W.	Beau	1755
Warner	Cumb	1767
Wm	Anso	1763
COLENS, Thomas	Oran	1755
Thomas Jr.	Oran	1755
COLER, Wm	Rand	1779
COLES, Wm	Crav	1748
COLESON, Thomas	Perq	1720
Wm	Perq	1720
Wm	Perq	1740
COLEY, Christe	Rand	1779
COLINGS, Richard	Pasq	1754

CALKINS, Jonathan	NewH	1755
COLLAR, John	Dobb	1779
Robert (Cottar?)	FWV	1771
COLLEY, Robert	Blad	1742
Robert	Cumb	1755
COLLIER, John	Dobb	1769
John	NorH	1744
John	Rand	1779
Joseph	Pasq	1769
Samuel	NewH	1763
Samuel	NewH	1767
Samuel	Pasq	1769
Thomas	Crav	1769
COLLINS, Charles	Casw	1777
Dennis	Oran	1755
Edward & bro		
Thos	Bert	1757
George	Beau	1755
Henry	Gran	1755
Hezekiah	Oran	1755
Isaac	Oran	1755
James	Beau	1755
James Sr.	Crav	1744
James	Cumb	1767
James	Dobb	1769
James	Oran	1755
Jesse	Bert	1769
Job	Rand	1779
John	Beau	1755
John	Bert	1742
John	Casw	1777
John	Crav	1769
John	Gran	1784
John	Oran	1755
John	Tyrr	1755
Joseph	Bert	1757
Joseph	Bert	1769
Joseph	Oran	1755
Joshua, Constable		
	Crav	1769
Joshua	Curr	1755
Josiah	Bert	1769
Lewis	Gran	1769
Lewis	Gran	1784
Luke	Bert	1769
Martin	Casw	1777
Michael	Bert	1757
Michael	Bute	1771
Michael	FWV	1771
Middleson	Casw	1777
Obadiah	Casw	1777
Paul	Casw	1777
Samuel	Crav	1769
Samuel	Gate	1786
Samuel	Oran	1755
Thomas	Bert	1769
Thomas	Crav	1769
Thomas	Cumb	1755
Thomas	Gate	1786
Thomas	Perq	1720
Wm	Bert	1757
Wm	Bute	1771
Wm	Chow	1753
Wm	FWV	1771
Wm	Gran	1755

COLLINS, Wm	Onsl	1742	CONGLETON, David	Beau	1764
Wm	Tyrr	1755	James	Beau	1764
COLLOCK, Richard	Anso	1763	Sarah	Beau	1755
COLLOM, Francis	Blad	1781	Wm	Beau	1741
COLLOUGH, John	Bute	1771	Wm	Pitt	1762
Wm Sr.	Bute	1771	Wm	Pitt	1763
COLLSON, John	Anso	1763	Wm	Pitt	1764
John	Casw	1777	CONLEY, David	Casw	1777
COLLUM, John	Gran	1769	Henry	Cumb	1767
COLOHON, John	Pitt	1762	Michael	Cumb	1755
COLPER, Coniciman	Edge	1734	Michael Sr.	Cumb	1767
COLSON, Abraham	Surr	1771	Michael	Cumb	1767
Daniel	Bute	1771	CONNER, Cader	Pasq	1769
Daniel	FWV	1771	Daniel	Dobb	1769
James	Surr	1771	David	Oran	1755
James	Surr	1772	Edward	Cumb	1755
John	Chow	1721	Francis	Dobb	1769
COLTHREAD, Wm	Bute	1757	Isaac	Beau	1764
COLTON, John	Roan	1720	James 2 slaves	Crav	1769
COLTRAINE, Wm	Rowa	1759	James	Tyrr	1742
COLVET, John	Crav	1769	John	Oran	1755
COLVIN, Alexander	Blad	1741	John	Pasq	1769
Alexander	NewH	1762	John	Rand	1779
Alexander	NewH	1763	Lewis	Crav	1769
Alexander	NewH	1767	Lewis	Dobb	1769
John	NewH	1763	Lewis	Surr	1771
John	NewH	1767	Lewis	Surr	1772
Wm	Cumb	1755	Mark	Crav	1769
Wm	Cumb	1767	Morris	Brun	1772
Wm	Gran	1755	Morris	Crav	1769
COLWELL, Henry	Surr	1772	Richard	Bute	1771
COMBER, James	NewH	1755	Richard s. Demsey		
Jesse	Rand	1779		FWV	1771
Joseph	Rand	1779	Wm	Bute	1771
Thomas	NewH	1755	Wm	FWV	1771
COMBOE, Wm	Cumb	1755	Wm	Pitt	1762
Wm	NewH	1755	CONNERLY, Wm	Brun	1769
COMBOW, Solomon	NewH	1762	CONNWAY, James	Casw	1777
Stephen	NewH	1762	Thomas	Casw	1777
COMBS, James	Crav	1769	CONOOR, Thomas	NewH	1763
John	Tyrr	1755	CONRAD, Christian	Surr	1771
Robert	Tyrr	1755	Christian	Surr	1772
Wm	Oran	1755	John	Gran	1784
COMES, Mason Sr.	Surr	1771	CONSALE, Andrew	Curr	1715
Mason Jr.	Surr	1772	CONSTANT, Wm	Anso	1763
Mason Sr.	Surr	1772	Wm	Rand	1779
Wm	Surr	1771	CONWAY, John Jr.	Rand	1779
Wm	Surr	1772	Wm	Onsl	1769
COMINGS, David	Roan	1720	CONWELL, Daniel	Surr	1771
COMMANDER, John	Pasq	1754	Daniel	Surr	1772
John 5 slaves	Pasq	1769	John	Surr	1771
Joseph	Pasq	1754	John	Surr	1772
Joseph 3 slaves	Pasq	1769	COOK, Abel	Surr	1771
Wm 2 slaves	Pasq	1769	Abraham	Anso	1763
CONANT, John	Surr	1772	Abraham	Gran	1755
CONDALL, John	Anso	1763	Abraham	Gran	1769
CONE, John s. of			Abraham	Rowa	1759
Peter	Beau	1764	Arthur	Oran	1755
Joseph	Beau	1764	Benjamin	Bute	1771
Neal	Tyrr	1755	Benjamin	Dobb	1769
Peter	Beau	1755	Benjamin	FWV	1771
Peter & s. John	Beau	1764	Burghart	Rowa	1759
Wm	Cumb	1767	Charles	Bute	1771
CONGER, John	Rowa	1759	Charles	FWV	1771
Jonathan	Rowa	1759	Cornelius	Rowa	1759

COOK, Cornelius	Surr 1771	COOK, Wm	Gran 1769
Cornelius	Surr 1772	Wm	Gran 1784
David	Pasq 1754	Wm	Pitt 1763
Demsey	Bert 1769	Wm	Pitt 1764
Drury	Bute 1771	COOKE, Richard	Gran 1784
Drury	FWV 1771	Richard D.	Gran 1784
Elemuell	Pasq 1754	Shem	Gran 1784
Elimelech	Dobb 1769	Stephen	Crav 1769
Henry	Bute 1771	Wm	Gran 1784
Henry	FWV 1771	COOKSON, Lemuel	Beau 1755
Henry	Surr 1771	COOLEY, John	Rowa 1758
Henry	Surr 1772	John Const.	Surr 1771
Jacob	Bute 1771	John Constable	Surr 1772
Jacob	FWV 1771	COOMBS, Thomas	Pitt 1762
James	Bute 1771	Thomas	Pitt 1763
James	Crav 1743	COONS, Francis	Surr 1771
James	Crav 1748	Michael	Rowa 1759
James	FWV 1771	COONSE, Casper	Rand 1779
James	NewH 1755	George	Rand 1779
James	NewH 1767	COOPER, Alexander	Casw 1777
James	Onsl 1769	Benjamin	Blad 1763
James	Rand 1779	Benjamin	Bute 1771
John	Beau 1755	Benjamin	Crav 1742
John	Bute 1771	Benjamin	FWV 1771
John	Chow 1717	Benjamin	Pasq 1754
John	Crav 1769	Benjamin	Pasq 1769
John	FWV 1771	Benjamin	Pitt 1775
John	NewH 1750	Cannon	Gran 1769
John	NewH 1755	Cannon	Gran 1784
John Jr.	NewH 1755	Cornelius	Gran 1769
John	Onsl 1769	Cornelius	Gran 1784
John	Pitt 1762	Edward	Tyrr 1755
John	Pitt 1763	George	Blad 1763
John	Pitt 1764	George	Cumb 1767
John Jr.	Pitt 1764	George	Onsl 1769
John	Pitt 1775	Henry	Beau 1755
John	Roan 1720	Henry	Bute 1771
John	Rowa 1759	Henry	Casw 1777
John	Tyrr 1741	Henry	FWV 1771
Jonas	Dobb 1769	Henry	Pitt 1762
Joshua	Surr 1771	Henry	Pitt 1763
Martin	Bert 1757	Isaac	Blad 1763
Mary	Bert 1769	Isaac	Cumb 1767
Matthias	Beau 1755	Isles	Curr 1755
Nicholas	Surr 1772	Jacob	Gran 1784
Peter	Bute 1771	James	Beau 1755
Nicholas	FWV 1771	James	Beau 1764
Reuben	Bert 1769	John	Bert 1757
Robert	Surr 1772	John	Casw 1777
Samuel	Beau 1764	John	Curr 1755
Samuel	Bert 1769	John	Onsl 1769
Thomas	Bute 1771	John Jr.	Onsl 1769
Thomas 1 slave	Crav 1769	John	Onsl 1770
Thomas Jr.	Crav 1769	John Jr.	Onsl 1770
Thomas Jr.	Crav 1769	John	Pasq 1769
Thomas	FWV 1771	John	Pitt 1762
Thomas & s. Wm	FWV 1771	John	Pitt 1763
Thomas	NewH 1755	Joseph	Blad 1763
Thomas	Pitt 1775	Joseph	Curr 1755
Thomas	Rowa 1759	Joseph	Gran 1769
Wm & s. Dennis	Bert 1757	Nathaniel	Tyrr 1755
Wm Jr.	Bert 1769	Robert	Bute 1771
Wm Sr.	Bert 1769	Robert	Crav 1769
Wm	Dobb 1769	Robert s. Thomas	
Wm	Gran 1755		FWV 1771

COOPER, Samuel	Pasq	1754	CORBYN, John	NewH	1755
Samuel	Surr	1771	John	NewH	1762
Thomas	Bert	1769	John	NewH	1763
Thomas	Gran	1755	CORDELL, Absalom	Blad	1781
Thomas 300 acres			George	Gran	1769
	N.C.	1701	Joseph	Surr	1771
Thomas	Pitt	1764	CORDEN, Benjamin	Pitt	1762
Wm	Beau	1744	Benjamin	Pitt	1763
Wm	Bute	1771	John	Casw	1777
Wm s. Jacob			John	Gran	1769
John	FWV	1771	Joseph	Casw	1777
Wm	Gran	1755	Joseph	Gran	1784
Wm	Gran	1755	Wm	Casw	1777
Wm	Gran	1784	CORDWELL, Paren	Surr	1772
COOR, James	Crav	1769	Spencer 2 slaves		
COOS, Henry	Pitt	1763		Dobb	1769
COPE, Wm	Oran	1755	CORENNENKET, Wm	Surr	1771
COPELAND, Charles	Chow	1753	COREY, John	Pasq	1754
Henry	Bert	1757	CORIE, John	Pasq	1769
James	Chow	1742	CORLEW, John	NewH	1750
James	Chow	1743	CORNELIUS, Robert	Surr	1771
John	Bert	1757	Roland	Surr	1771
John	Cumb	1755	West	Surr	1771
John	Cumb	1767	CORNELL, Samuel	Crav	1769
John's estate	Gate	1786	CORPHEW, Jonathan	Tyrr	1755
Peter	Cumb	1767	CORPREW, Matthew	Beau	1755
Richard	Oran	1755	Samuel	Beau	1755
Wm	Chow	1717	CORRY, Malcomb	Surr	1771
Wm	Chow	1721	CORSON, Thomas	Surr	1771
Wm	Chow	1753	Uriah	Surr	1771
Wm's estate	Gate	1786	CORTIS, James s.		
COPES, Jacob	Crav	1769	Rich	Beau	1764
COPKINS, Wm	Pitt	1764	Richard s. James		
COPLAND, Joseph	Oran	1755		Beau	1764
Nicholas Jr.	Oran	1755	Samuel	Rowa	1759
Nicholas Sr.	Oran	1755	CORTNEY, John	Onsl	1750
COPPEDGE, James	Bute	1771	John	Roan	1720
James	FWV	1771	Robert	Onsl	1744
COPPOCK, Moses	Gran	1755	CORY, Benjamin	Pitt	1764
CORAH, Thomas	Pasq	1769	Benjamin	Pitt	1775
CORAM, Robert	Casw	1777	Jeremiah	Pitt	1764
CORBETT, James	Brun	1769	John	Pasq	1754
James	Brun	1772	Thomas	Pasq	1754
John	Bert	1757	COSAND, Gabriel	Chow	1721
John	Pitt	1775	COSLIN, Christian	Gate	1786
Joseph	NewH	1742	COSO, Solomon	Beau	1764
Meredith	Pitt	1775	COSSTON, James	Chow	1753
Thomas	Brun	1769	Peter	NewH	1767
Thomas	NewH	1742	COST, Thomas	Rand	1779
Thomas	NewH	1762	COSTIN, Demsey's		
Thomas	NewH	1763	estate	Gate	1786
Wm	NorH	1762	James	Gate	1786
CORBEY, Ediram	Surr	1772	John	NewH	1762
CORBIN, David	Gran	1769	John	NewH	1767
Edmund	NewH	1767	COTANCH, Wm	Pasq	1754
Francis	NewH	1762	COTHERN, James s.		
Francis	NewH	1763	Thomas	FWV	1771
Francis	NewH	1767	COTTERELL, Wm	Casw	1777
CORBIT, John	Beau	1755	Wm	Chow	1753
John	Pitt	1762	COTTON, Alexander	Bert	1757
John	Pitt	1763	Arthur	Bert	1757
John Jr.	Pitt	1763	Benjamin	Bert	1757
John	Pitt	1764	Benjamin	Dobb	1769
John Jr.	Pitt	1764	Ephraim	Dobb	1769
Thomas	NewH	1755	Ephraim	Dobb	1779

COTTON, James	Bert	1757
John Esq. 1040		
acres	Chow	1721
John 850 acres	Chow	1721
John	Dobb	1769
COUCH, James	Oran	1755
Matthew	Oran	1755
Wm	Oran	1755
COULAHAN, Robert	Crav	1743
COULSON, Jacob	N.C.	1701
John	N.C.	1701
Mary	N.C.	1701
Mary Jr.	N.C.	1701
Wm	Onsl	1769
COULSTRAIN, Wm	Rand	1779
COULTER, Alex.	Tryo	1776
COUNCILL, Hardee	Blad	1763
Hardy	Cumb	1767
Hardy	Tyrr	1755
James	Blad	1781
John	Blad	1781
COUNSEL, Charles	NorH	1762
COUPER, Henry	Beau	1755
COUPLES, Wm	Brun	1769
Wm	Brun	1772
COURT, John	Dobb	1769
COURTIER, Caleb	Rand	1779
John	Rand	1779
COURTNEY, John	Cumb	1755
COUTANCH, Michael	Beau	1755
Michael Jr.	Beau	1755
Wm	Pasq	1754
COVERNESS, Frederick		
	Gran	1784
COVINGTON, Clifton	Gran	1769
Francis	Dobb	1769
Francis	Dobb	1779
Nehemiah	Onsl	1770
Philemon 2 slaves		
	Crav	1769
COWAN, Andrew	NewH	1763
Ann	NewH	1762
Ann	NewH	1775
Duncan	NewH	1755
Edward	Rand	1779
Isabella	NewH	1762
Isabella	NewH	1763
John	NewH	1743
John	Rand	1779
John	Rowa	1759
Magnus	NewH	1755
Magnus	NewH	1762
Wm	Gran	1784
Wm	Rowa	1759
Wm	Tyrr	1755
COWAND, Wm	Bert	1757
COWARD, Benjamin	Gran	1755
Carl	Pitt	1764
Coble	Pitt	1764
Edward	Dobb	1769
Edward Jr.	Dobb	1769
Edward s. of		
James	Dobb	1769
Elisha	Dobb	1769
Ezekiel	Dobb	1769

COWARD, James	Bute	1771
James	Dobb	1769
James	FWV	1771
John	Dobb	1769
Lewis	Crav	1769
Nathaniel	Dobb	1769
Needham	Dobb	1769
Wm	Anso	1763
Wm	Bert	1757
Wm	Chow	1721
Wm	Dobb	1769
Wm	Pitt	1762
Zachariah	Dobb	1779
COWELL, Benjamin	Curr	1755
Solomon	Curr	1755
Wm	Tyrr	1755
COWINGS, James	Chow	1753
COWLET, Wm	Rand	1779
COX, Aaron	Crav	1769
Aaron	Onsl	1769
Aaron	Onsl	1770
Abia	Pitt	1762
Abia	Pitt	1764
Absalom	Curr	1755
Amos	Rand	1779
Andrew s. of		
Moses	Dobb	1769
Anthony	Curr	1744
Arthur	Dobb	1769
Arthur	Oran	1755
Benjamin	Bert	1769
Benjamin	Dobb	1779
Benjamin	Pitt	1762
Benjamin	Pitt	1763
Benjamin Sr.	Rand	1779
Benjamin	Rand	1779
Benjamin	Surr	1771
Charles	NewH	1741
Charles	Onsl	1741
Charles	Onsl	1769
Charles	Pitt	1762
Charles	Pitt	1763
Daniel	Crav	1744
David	Tryo	1776
Duke	Curr	1755
Edward	Crav	1769
Edward	Cumb	1767
Edward	Curr	1715
Elender	Gran	1769
Elijah	Pitt	1775
Elizabeth	Pitt	1775
Enoch	Rand	1779
Ephraim	Rowa	1759
Ephraim	Surr	1771
Frederick	Surr	1771
Frederick	Surr	1772
George	Cumb	1767
George	Tryo	1776
Gilbert	Blad	1763
Harmon	Rand	1779
Harmon Jr.	Rand	1779
Henry	Rand	1779
Herman	Oran	1755
Isaac	Rand	1779
Jacob	Surr	1771

COX, Jacob	Surr	1772
Jasper	Onsl	1769
Jerry, cousin of		
Robert	Perq	1720
John	Dobb	1769
John Jr. 2 slave	Dobb	1769
John	Onsl	1741
John	Onsl	1770
John	Oran	1755
John	Pasq	1754
John	Rand	1779
Joseph	Crav	1769
Longfield	Crav	1769
Marmin	Dobb	1769
Micajah	Dobb	1769
Moses	Dobb	1769
Moses	Onsl	1769
Moses Jr.	Onsl	1769
Peter	Bute	1771
Peter	FWV	1771
Peter	Gran	1784
Richard	Dobb	1769
Richard	Surr	1771
Richard	Surr	1772
Robert, cousin of		
Jerry	Perq	1720
Robert	Perq	1740
Robert	Perq	1744
Samuel	Rand	1779
Samuel	Surr	1772
Simon	Blad	1763
Solomon s. of		
Moses	Dobb	1769
Solomon s. of		
John	Onsl	1770
Solomon	Pasq	1754
Spencer	Onsl	1769
Thomas	Crav	1769
Thomas	Curr	1715
Thomas Jr.	Curr	1715
Thomas 2 slaves	Dobb	1769
Thomas s. of		
John	Dobb	1769
Thomas Jr.	Dobb	1769
Vincent	Bute	1771
Vincent	FWV	1771
Vincent	Gran	1769
Wm	Anso	1763
Wm	Oran	1755
Wm	Rand	1779
Zachariah	Oran	1755
Zachariah	Rowa	1759
COYG, Adam	Surr	1772
COYLE, James	Surr	1771
Patrick	Gran	1755
Patrick	Rowa	1759
COZART, Amos	Gran	1784
Anthony	Gran	1769
David	Gran	1784
Jacob	Gran	1769
Jacob	Gran	1784
John	Casw	1777
Peter	Casw	1777
CRABB, John	Bute	1771
John	FWV	1771
CRABB, John	Bute	1771
Thomas s. Thomas	FWV	1771
Thomas	Gran	1755
CRABTREE, Benjamin	Rand	1779
James	Rand	1779
John	Rand	1779
John Jr.	Rand	1779
Samuel	Rand	1779
CRADUCK, Walter	N.C.	1701
CRAFORD, James	Oran	1755
CRAFT, David	Dobb	1779
Elizabeth	Crav	1720
James	Bert	1757
James	Rand	1779
John	Gran	1769
Levi	Dobb	1779
Samuel	Onsl	1769
Thomas	Gran	1769
CRAFTCHANS, John		
Esq.	Dobb	1769
CRAIG, John	Gran	1769
John	Gran	1784
Wm	Oran	1755
CRAMBIC, Hannah	Pasq	1754
CRANDELL, Elijah	Brun	1772
George	NewH	1762
George	NewH	1763
CRANDELL, George	NewH	1767
James	Beau	1755
James Jr.	Beau	1755
James	Pitt	1762
James Jr.	Pitt	1762
James	Pitt	1763
James	Pitt	1764
James Jr.	Pitt	1764
Samuel	Pitt	1764
CRANE, Ambrose	Gran	1755
John	Cumb	1755
John	Surr	1771
Lewis	Cumb	1755
Philip	Surr	1771
Thomas	Cumb	1755
Wm	Cumb	1755
CRANFIELD, Wm	Chow	1717
CRANFORD, James	Onsl	1747
Wm	Chow	1717
Wm	Chow	1721
CRANK, Thomas	Chow	1717
Thomas	Tyrr	1755
CRARR, Philip	Surr	1771
CRAVEN, James	Chow	1743
James Esq.	Chow	1753
Joseph	Rand	1779
Peter	Rand	1779
Thomas	Rand	1779
CRAVEY, Owen	Chow	1721
CRAWFORD, Charles	Crav	1769
David	Dobb	1779
Hardy	Dobb	1769
James	Gran	1755
James	Onsl	1769
James	Onsl	1770
James	Oran	1755
James	Pitt	1762
James	Pitt	1763

CRAWFORD, James	Rand	1779	CRISONBERRY, Aaron	Casw	1777
John	Anso	1763	Nicholas	Casw	1777
John	Dobb	1779	CRISP, Nicholas	Chow	1717
John	Onsl	1769	Nicholas	Chow	1721
John	Onsl	1770	Rudolph	Surr	1771
John	Tryo	1776	CRISPIN, Joseph	Crav	1769
Lazarus	Dobb	1779	CRISTA, Robert	Dobb	1779
Leonard	Rand	1779	CRISTIE, David	Bert	1769
Neil	Blad	1763	CRISWELL, James	Cran	1769
Peter	Rand	1779	CRISWICK, Wm	Bute	1771
Philip	Rand	1779	Wm	FWV	1771
Richard	Cumb	1755	CRIT, Ben	Edge	1734
Robert	Dobb	1769	CRITCHER, Esther	Gran	1784
Robert	Dobb	1779	Thomas	Gran	1784
Samuel	Rand	1779	CRITCHFIELD, John	Surr	1772
Wm	Dobb	1769	CRITTENDEN, Henry	NorH	1762
Wm	Dobb	1779	Wm	Anso	1763
CRAWLEY, David	Chow	1721	CROCKER, Arthur	Gran	1755
CRAY, Wm	Onsl	1769	Jacob	Gran	1755
Wm	Onsl	1770	John	N.C.	1701
CREACH, James	Pasq	1754	Joseph	NewH	1762
Joshua	Dobb	1779	CROFFORD, James	Gate	1786
CREAGER, Nicholas	Surr	1771	Wm	Gate	1786
Nicholas	Surr	1772	CROFT, John	Gran	1784
CREAL, John	Dobb	1769	Thomas	Gran	1784
CRECEY, Levi	Chow	1753	CROFTS, Christopher	NewH	1742
CREECH, Benjamin			CROFTON, Ambrose	Beau	1764
Jr.	Dobb	1769	Samuel	Gran	1784
Charles	Cumb	1767	Theophilus	Beau	1764
Ezekiel	Dobb	1779	Thomas	Beau	1764
Jeremiah	Bert	1757	Wm	Beau	1764
John	Dobb	1769	CROFUS, Samuel	Beau	1764
John	Dobb	1779	CROMARTEE, Wm	Blad	1763
Samuel	Pasq	1769	CROMPTON, Thomas	Oran	1755
CREEKMORE, Wm	Crav	1769	CROMWELL, George	Bert	1757
CREEL, Charles	Cumb	1767	John	Pasq	1769
John	Crav	1742	CROOM, Jesse	Dobb	1769
Lazarus	Cumb	1755	Jesse	Dobb	1779
CREES, John	Edge	1734	Major 15 slaves	Dobb	1769
CREF, John	Curr	1715	CROPLEY, Vines	Chow	1717
CREMER, Adam	Surr	1772	Wm	N.C.	1701
CREMSHAW, Abraham	Gran	1755	CROSBY, John	Chow	1721
Gideon	Gran	1755	Richard	Cumb	1755
Gideon	Gran	1769	CROSLEY, John	Beau	1764
Gideon	Gran	1784	John	Chow	1721
CREOL, Thomas	Anso	1763	Robert	Gran	1784
CRESEY, John	Perq	1740	CROSS, Abel	Gate	1786
CRESON, Abraham	Rowa	1759	Cyprian	Gate	1786
Peter	Rowa	1759	David	Gate	1786
Peter	Surr	1772	Elisha	Gate	1786
CRETCH, Richard	Cumb	1755	Hardy	Gate	1786
CREWS, Caleb	Gran	1784	Henry	Pitt	1762
Gideon	Gran	1784	Isaac	Blad	1763
Hardy	Casw	1777	Jacob	Rowa	1759
James	Gran	1784	Peter	Rowa	1759
Thomas	Bert	1744	Sarah	Gate	1786
Thomas	Bert	1757	Thomas	Pitt	1762
Thomas overseer	FWV	1771	CROUCHFIELD, Edmond		
Thomas	Gran	1784		Oran	1755
Wm	Bert	1757	CROW, Isaac	Dobb	1769
CRICKETT, John	Bert	1757	John	Dobb	1779
Thomas	Bert	1742	Samuel	Roan	1720
CRIEF, John	Casw	1777	Wm s. of Isaac	Dobb	1769
CRIM, Sarah's			Wm	Dobb	1779
estate	NewH	1762	CROWLER, Wm	Tyrr	1755

CROX, Charles	Pitt	1764		CUMMINS, Robert	Onsl	1769
Henry	Pitt	1764		Robert	Onsl	1770
CROXTON, Arthurm	Perq	1740		Stephen	Onsl	1769
CRUICKSHANKS, John				Thomas	Onsl	1769
	Edge	1743		Thomas	Onsl	1770
CRUMMELL, Alexander	Pitt	1762		W. S.	Onsl	1769
Alexander Jr.	Pitt	1762		Wm	Casw	1777
Elisha	Pitt	1762		CUMP, Jesse	Surr	1772
CRUMMY, John	Chow	1721		CUNILY, David	Casw	1777
CRUMPTON, James	Casw	1777		CUNNEFFE, Michael	Pasq	1769
CRUNK, Richard	Rowa	1758		CUNNING, Cloud	Blad	1763
CRUSE, John	Blad	1763		CUNNINGHAM, James	Brun	1769
CRUTCHER, Thomas	Gran	1769		James	Brun	1772
CRUTCHFIELD, Edmond				James	NorH	1762
	Blad	1763		John	Rowa	1759
Richard	Bute	1771		Jonathan	Bute	1771
Richard & s. Wm	FWV	1771		Jonathan	FWV	1771
Richard	Gran	1755		Thomas	NewH	1741
CRUTHER, John	Rand	1779		Thomas	NewH	1755
CUBBAGE, George	Blad	1743		Thomas	NewH	1763
CUFFANE, Toney	Dobb	1769		Thomas	NewH	1767
CUFFORD, Tone	Dobb	1769		Wm	Crav	1742
CULBERT, Anthony	Crav	1743		Wm	Gran	1769
Nicholas	Crav	1743		Wm	N.C.	1701
CULBERSON, James	Casw	1777		Wm	Pasq	1769
Robert	Casw	1777		CUP, Christopher	Oran	1755
Wm	Casw	1777		CUPPER, John	Chow	1753
CULL, Edward	Bert	1757		Joseph	Curr	1715
CULLAM, Dennis	Blad	1763		CUPPLIES, Chas.		
CULLEN, Ebenezer	Crav	1769		(Rev.)	Bute	1771
Edmund	Crav	1749		Charles (Rev.)	FWV	1771
Jonathan	Crav	1749		CURL, Benjamin	Dobb	1769
Nehemiah	Crav	1769		CURLEE, James	Gate	1786
Southey	Crav	1769		Nathan	Pasq	1754
Thomas	Crav	1769		Wm	Chow	1717
CULLIFER, Andrew	Bert	1757		Wm	Chow	1721
John	Bert	1769		Wm	Crav	1741
Nathaniel	Bert	1769		Wm	Dobb	1769
Wm	Bert	1757		CURLING, Jacob	Pasq	1769
CULLINS, Jonathan	Gate	1786		Lemuel	Pasq	1769
CULLIVER, Nathaniel	Chow	1721		Walter	Pasq	1769
CULPEPPER, Benjamin	Edge	1741		CURRELL, Wm	Tyrr	1755
John	Anso	1763		CURRIE, David	Bert	1769
Joseph	Anso	1763		James	Oran	1755
Robert	Anso	1763		Thomas	Gran	1769
Sampson	Anso	1763		CURRIN, Elizabeth	Gran	1784
Wm	Anso	1763		Hugh	Gran	1784
CULS, Joseph	Pitt	1764		Wm	Gran	1784
CULVERHOUSE, Thomas	Gran	1784		CURRIOR, James	Casw	1777
Wilmore	Gran	1784		CURRY, Daniel	Blad	1763
CUMBO, David	Brun	1772		Ezekiel	Rand	1779
Solomon	NewH	1763		James	Chow	1721
Solomon	NewH	1767		Thompson	FWV	1771
Stephen 1 slave	Brun	1769		CURSLEY, Wm	Edge	1734
Stephen	Brun	1772		CURSTON, Richard	Gran	1755
CUMMINGS, David	Crav	1769		CURTIS, Benjamin	Rand	1779
James	Crav	1769		Caleb	Rand	1779
John	Crav	1769		James	Rand	1779
Thomas	Crav	1769		John	FWV	1771
Thomas	NewH	1741		John	Rand	1779
CUMMINGS, Edward	Crav	1743		Joseph	Rand	1779
CUMMINS, George	Onsl	1769		Moses	Bute	1771
George	Onsl	1770		Moses	FWV	1771
John	Casw	1777		Richard	Beau	1755
Moses	Onsl	1770		Russell	FWV	1771

CURTIS, Samuel	Rand	1779	DANIEL, John	Dobb	1779
Samuel	Rowa	1758	John	Gran	1769
Thomas	Rand	1779	John Sr.	NewH	1763
CURWIN, James	Gran	1769	Joseph	Gran	1755
CUSEY, James	Casw	1777	Josiah	Pitt	1762
CUSHION, Katharine	Bert	1769	Josiah	Pitt	1764
CUSICK, Wm	Rowa	1759	Leffly	Gran	1769
CUSTIS, Hancock	Beau	1764	Matthew	Casw	1777
CUTHRILL, Joshua	Crav	1769	Nathaniel	Dobb	1769
Thomas	Crav	1769	Nathaniel	Dobb	1779
Thomas Jr.	Crav	1769	Owen	Chow	1721
CUTLER, Robert	Beau	1755	Robert	Beau	1755
Robert	Beau	1764	Robert 28 slaves	Brun	1769
Robert s. Robert			Robert	Brun	1772
	Beau	1764	Robert Esq.		
CUTNALL, Joshua	Pitt	1775	4 slaves	Pitt	1762
CUTREY, Wm	Oran	1755	Robert	Pitt	1763
CUTS, Joseph	Pitt	1762	Robert	Pitt	1764
CYLES, John	Oran	1755	Robert	Tyrr	1755
CYTISON, James	Perq	1720	Sarah	Brun	1772
			Seleh	Gran	1784
			Stephen	Brun	1772
			Thomas	Dobb	1769
DABBS, Wm	Chow	1753	Thomas	Gran	1755
DABINGS, Hugh	Oran	1755	Thomas	Pitt	1762
DADIS, Thomas	Rand	1779	Thomas	Pitt	1764
DAFRON, Michael	Rand	1779	Thomas	Rowa	1759
DAIL, Wm	Dobb	1779	Thomas		1745
DAILEY, Mary	Bert	1769	Wm	Beau	1755
Patrick	Beau	1755	Wm	Bert	1769
DAINS, Thomas	Perq	1740	Wm 9 slaves	Brun	1769
DALE, Thomas	Dobb	1769	Wm	Brun	1772
Wm	Crav	1744	Wm	Chow	1753
Wm s. of Thomas	Dobb	1769	Wm	Curr	1755
DALEY, Joshua	Pasq	1769	DANIELL, Alexander	Pitt	1775
DALRYMPLE, John	NewH	1762	George 8 slaves	Brun	1769
John	NewH	1763	John	Brun	1769
John	NewH	1767	Robert 10 slaves	Tyrr	1755
Martha 16 slaves	Brun	1769	DANIELS, John	NewH	1762
Martha	Brun	1772	DANFORD, John	NewH	1763
DALY, John	Bert	1757	DANFORTH, John	NewH	1762
John	Tyrr	1755	DANN, Daniel	Pasq	1754
DAMRON, John	Surr	1771	DANSBY, Jacob	Gran	1755
DANBY, Daniel	NorH	1743	DANSEY, Joseph	Gran	1755
Hestor	N.C.	1701	DARBY, George	Casw	1777
Southerd	Curr	1715	DARDEN, James	Bute	1771
DANCY, James	NorH	1762	James	FWV	1771
DANE, Moses	Beau	1755	Joseph	Chow	1721
DANIEL, Aaron	Beau	1755	DARK, Samuel	Anso	1763
Chesley	Gran	1769	DARNELL, Charles	FWV	1771
Chisley	Gran	1784	Isaac	Surr	1771
Daniel	FWV	1771	John	Surr	1771
Daniel	Pitt	1764	John	Surr	1772
Eustice	Gran	1755	Joseph	Bute	1771
George	Brun	1772	Joseph	FWV	1771
Isaac	Dobb	1769	Ward	Bute	1771
James	Dobb	1769	Ward s. Ward -		
James Sr.	Dobb	1779	Wm	FWV	1771
James	Gran	1755	DARRAH, Archibald	Blad	1763
James Constable	Gran	1769	DARSONS, John	Perq	1740
James	Gran	1784	DARWIN, John	Gate	1786
John	Brun	1769	DAUGE, Benjamin	Curr	1755
John	Brun	1772	Caleb	Pasq	1769
John	Cumb	1767	Fetter	Curr	1715
John s. Thomas	Dobb	1769	James	Curr	1715

DAUGE, James	Pasq 1769		DAVIS, Benjamin	Crav 1769
John 7 slaves	Pasq 1769		Benjamin	Dobb 1769
Peter	Curr 1715		Benjamin	Rand 1779
Peter	Curr 1755		Boster	Gran 1784
Peter Jr. 3			Charles	Oran 1755
slaves	Pasq 1769		Cornelius	Casw 1777
Richard	Curr 1715		David	Pasq 1754
DAUGHERTY, Jesse	Onsl 1769		David Jr.	Pasq 1754
Michael	Onsl 1769		David Jr.	
DAUGHITY, Absalom	Crav 1769		1 slave	Pasq 1769
Daniel 1 slave	Crav 1769		David Sr.	
Owen 2 slaves	Gate 1786		4 slaves	Pasq 1769
DAUGHTER, Edward	Gate 1786		David	Rowa 1759
John	Gate 1786		David	Surr 1771
Wm	Gate 1786		David	Surr 1772
DAVAN, John	NewH 1755		Devotion	
DAVENPORT, Elias	Bert 1757		5 slaves	Pasq 1769
Francis	Gran 1755		Edward	Blad 1763
Francis	Gran 1769		Edward	Chow 1721
Isaac	Rowa 1758		Edward	NewH 1762
Isaac	Tyrr 1755		Edward	NewH 1763
James	Tyrr 1755		Edward	NewH 1765
John	Chow 1721		Edward	NewH 1767
John	Rand 1779		Edward	N.C. 1701
John	Tyrr 1755		Elisha	Dobb 1779
John Jr.	Tyrr 1755		Elizabeth	
Joseph	Tyrr 1755		5 slaves	Brun 1769
Richard	Tyrr 1755		Elizabeth	Brun 1772
Wm	Rowa 1759		Elizabeth	NewH 1763
DAVEY, Gabriel	Casw 1777		Elizabeth	N.C. 1701
Thomas	Casw 1777		Elliott	N.C. 1701
DAVID, Aaron	Bert 1769		Enoch	Rand 1779
David	NewH 1762		Francis	Chow 1721
David	NewH 1763		Francis	Cumb 1755
David	NewH 1765		Francis	Onsl 1769
David	NewH 1767		Francis	Onsl 1770
David	Oran 1755		Frederick	Bute 1771
Thomas	Pitt 1763		Frederick	FWV 1771
Thomas Jr.	Pitt 1763		Frederick	Gran 1769
DAVIDSON, Alexander	Casw 1777		Frederick	Pasq 1769
Robert	NewH 1763		Gabriel	Anso 1763
Robert	NewH 1767		Garrett	Chow 1753
Wm	Gate 1786		George	Bert 1769
Wm	Rand 1779		George	Casw 1777
DAVIES, Evin	Oran 1755		George	Curr 1755
John	Oran 1755		Henry	Casw 1777
DAVIS, Abraham	Pasq 1754		Henry	Crav 1743
Abraham 2			Herman	Oran 1755
slaves	Pasq 1769		Hezekiah	Casw 1777
Absalom	Gran 1769		Howell	Rowa 1759
Absalom	Gran 1784		Hugh 200 acres	Perq 1720
Adam	Rowa 1758		Hugh	Rowa 1759
Alice	N.C. 1701		Ichabod	Dobb 1779
Allen	Casw 1777		Isaac	Surr 1772
Ann 1 slave	Pasq 1769		Iwl	Crav 1720
Anthony s. of			Jacob	Casw 1777
Abraham	Pasq 1769		James	Crav 1769
Arthur	Chow 1721		James s. of	
Arthur	NorH 1762		James	Dobb 1769
Arthur	Pasq 1769		James	Dobb 1769
Arthur	Roan 1720		James Sr.	Dobb 1779
Augustine	Gran 1769		James	Gate 1786
Augustine	Gran 1784		James	Pasq 1769
Bassel	Casw 1777		James	Rand 1779
Benjamin Const.	Blad 1763		James	Rowa 1759

DAVIS, Jane	Brun 1772	DAVIS, Roger	
Jane widow	Bute 1771	15 slaves	Brun 1769
Jane & s. Lewis	FWV 1771	Roger	Brun 1772
Jean	Brun 1769	Roger	NewH 1762
Jean	Brun 1772	Roger	NewH 1763
Jehu	NewH 1762	Samson	Dobb 1769
Jehu's estate	NewH 1762	Samuel	Anso 1751
Jesse	Rand 1779	Samuel	Anso 1763
John	Anso 1763	Samuel	Beau 1742
John Jr.	Anso 1763	Samuel	Beau 1764
John 27 slaves	Brun 1769	Samuel	NorH 1762
John	Brun 1772	Samuel	Onsl 1769
John	Bute 1771	Samuel	Onsl 1770
John Jr.	Casw 1777	Samuel	Pasq 1754
John Sr.	Casw 1777	Samuel 1 slave	Pasq 1769
John	Chow 1721	Samuel	Pitt 1763
John	Chow 1753	Samuel	Pitt 1764
John 2 slaves	Crav 1769	Samuel	Surr 1771
John	Dobb 1769	Samuel	Surr 1772
John	Dobb 1779	Scrias	FWV 1771
John	FWV 1771	Shadrack	Pasq 1769
John s. John		Shepherd	FWV 1771
Thomas	FWV 1771	Solomon 1 slave	
John 2 slaves	Gate 1786		Gran 1769
John	Gran 1755	Solomon 1 slave	
John	Gran 1769		Pasq 1769
John Jr.	NewH 1755	Thomas	Anso 1763
John Sr.	NewH 1762	Thomas	Beau 1743
John Jr.	NewH 1763	Thomas	Beau 1755
John Sr.	NewH 1763	Thomas 1 slave	Blad 1763
John	NorH 1762	Thomas tanner	Blad 1763
John	Pasq 1769	Thomas 5 slaves	Blad 1763
John	Rowa 1759	Thomas 37 slaves	Brun 1769
John	Surr 1772	Thomas	Brun 1772
Jonathan	FWV 1771	Thomas	Chow 1753
Jonathan	NorH 1762	Thomas	Chow 1721
Joseph	Dobb 1769	Thomas	Crav 1743
Joseph	Gran 1784	Thomas	Cumb 1755
Joseph	Pasq 1754	Thomas	Cumb 1767
Joseph 1 slave	Pasq 1769	Thomas	Curr 1715
Joseph	Rand 1779	Thomas	Curr 1755
Joshua	Pasq 1754	Thomas	Dobb 1769
Josiah	Dobb 1769	Thomas	Dobb 1779
Lewis	Gran 1769	Thomas	Gran 1755
Lewis	Rowa 1759	Thomas	Hyde 1743
Lewis	Tyrr 1755	Thomas	NewH 1763
Littleton	Crav 1769	Thomas	Onsl 1769
Mary	Dobb 1769	Thomas	Onsl 1770
Matthew	Chow 1753	Thomas	Oran 1755
Merrick	Rowa 1759	Thomas	Pasq 1769
Morgan	Surr 1771	Thomas 200 acres	Perq 1720
Morgan	Surr 1772	Thomas	Perq 1740
Moses	Gate 1786	Thomas	Pitt 1762
Peter	Bute 1771	Thomas Jr.	Pitt 1762
Peter & s. Thomas,		Thomas	Pitt 1763
Wm & Richard	FWV 1771	Thomas Jr.	Pitt 1763
Peter & s. Giles		Thomas	Pitt 1764
& Matthew	FWV 1771	Thomas Jr.	Pitt 1764
Peter	Gran 1755	Thomas	Pitt 1775
Philip	Surr 1771	Thomas Jr.	Pitt 1775
Philip	Surr 1772	Wm	Beau 1745
Ralph	Dobb 1769	Wm	Beau 1755
Richard	Brun 1772	Wm Esq. 11 slaves	
Robert	Gran 1769		Blad 1763
Robert	Oran 1755	Wm	Blad 1763

DAVIS, Wm 20 slaves		
	Brun	1769
Wm	Brun	1772
Wm	Bute	1771
Wm 4 slaves	Crav	1769
Wm	Curr	1715
Wm	FWV	1771
Wm & s. John		
& Wm	FWV	1771
Wm	Gran	1755
Wm	N.C.	1701
Wm	Pasq	1754
Wm patroller	Pasq	1769
Wm	Rowa	1759
Wm	Surr	1771
Wm	Surr	1772
Wm	Tryo	1776
DAVISSON, James Sr.		
	Rand	1779
James	Rand	1779
John	Bert	1757
John Jr.	Bert	1757
John	Bert	1769
John	Chow	1753
John	Rand	1779
DAW, Dinah	Beau	1755
Dinah widow	Beau	1764
John	Beau	1764
Nicholas	Beau	1764
Wm	Beau	1764
DAWLEY, Edward	Cumb	1767
DAWS, Abijah	Bert	1757
Wm	Chow	1721
DAWSON, Britton	NorH	1762
Christopher		
7 slaves	Crav	1769
Francis 7 slaves		
	Crav	1769
Hezekiah	NorH	1762
Hinds, s. of Wm	Dobb	1769
James		1744
Joel	Dobb	1769
Joel	Dobb	1779
John Esq.	Bert	1769
John	FWV	1771
John 5 whites		
18 b	NorH	1743
John	Rowa	1759
Joseph	Dobb	1769
Joshua	Bute	1771
Joshua	FWV	1771
Levi 10 slaves	Crav	1769
Mary 4 slaves	Crav	1769
Thomas	Dobb	1779
Wm	Cumb	1755
Wm	Dobb	1769
Wm	Dobb	1779
DAY, Bishelham	Casw	1777
Edmond	FWV	1771
Francis	Oran	1755
Henry	Oran	1755
John	Casw	1777
John	Gran	1755
John	NorH	1743
Peter	Gran	1755

DAY, Wm	Casw	1777
DEAL, Abel 1 slave		
	Crav	1769
Adam	Pitt	1762
Adam	Pitt	1763
Edward	Crav	1769
Edward	Pitt	1763
Harbound	Pitt	1763
Henry	Pitt	1764
John	Beau	1755
John	NewH	1767
John	Pasq	1769
John	Pitt	1762
John	Pitt	1763
Joshua	Perq	1740
Richard	Pasq	1769
Thomas	Pasq	1769
Wm	Pitt	1763
Wm	Pitt	1764
DEAN, Anthony	Roan	1720
Daniel	Chow	1717
Henry	Cumb	1767
John	Oran	1755
Joseph	Oran	1755
Moses	Pitt	1763
Moury	Pitt	1762
Richard	Dobb	1769
Thomas	Crav	1769
DEARDEN, Charles	Onsl	1769
DEARHAM, Annie	N.C.	1701
Elizabeth Jr.	N.C.	1701
Ellis	N.C.	1701
Francis	N.C.	1701
Joseph	N.C.	1701
Mary	N.C.	1701
Richard	N.C.	1701
Thomas Jr.	N.C.	1701
DEAS, Arthur	Anso	1763
James	Anso	1763
DEATHERIDGE, George	Surr	1772
John	Surr	1771
DEBO, Hannah	Casw	1777
John	Oran	1755
Lodowick	Casw	1777
Solomon	Oran	1755
DEBOISE, Anthony	NewH	1744
John	NewH	1755
DEBORD, John	Gran	1755
John Constable	Gran	1755
DEBOW, Anthony	NewH	1767
DEBUSH,	NewH	1755
DECKER, James	Tryo	1776
Jos.	Tryo	1776
DEEL, Adam	Beau	1764
John	Beau	1764
DEFNEL, Wm	Crav	1769
DEGG, James	Pitt	1763
James	Pitt	1764
Michael	Surr	1772
DEKEFORT, John	NewH	1767
Moses	NewH	1767
DELAMAR, Francis	Crav	1769
Thomas 2 slaves	Crav	1769
DELANEY, Wm	Pasq	1754
DELOACH, Francis	NorH	1762

DELOACH, James	Beau	1755		DENTON, Benjamin	Gran	1784
James	Pitt	1762		Edward	Gran	1755
James	Pitt	1764		Edward	NewH	1767
DELON, Henry	Bert	1743		Isaac	Casw	1777
DELWELL, Francis	Cumb	1767		James	Chow	1717
Henry	Pasq	1754		Samuel	Gran	1769
DEMINT, Charles	Bert	1769		Thomas	Anso	1763
Charles	Brun	1772		Thomas	Gran	1769
John	Bert	1769		Thomas	Surr	1771
John Sr.	Bert	1769		DEROSSET, Armand	NewH	1741
John	Brun	1772		Elizabeth	NewH	1762
John	FWV	1771		Elizabeth	NewH	1767
DEMORY, John	NorH	1762		Lewis	NewH	1762
DEMSEY, George	Bert	1769		Lewis	NewH	1765
James	Bert	1769		Lewis	NewH	1767
Joseph	Bert	1769		Moses	NewH	1762
Joshua	Bert	1769		Nathan	NewH	1767
Thoroughgood	Bert	1769		DESMIT, Joseph	Gran	1784
Zechariah	Dobb	1779		DEVANE, John	NewH	1762
DENBY, Eliza	Curr	1755		John	NewH	1763
James	Bute	1771		John	NewH	1765
James	FWV	1771		John	NewH	1767
John	Curr	1755		Thomas	NewH	1755
DENHAM, Isaac	Casw	1777		Thomas Jr.	NewH	1762
Wm	Beau	1755		Thomas Sr.	NewH	1762
DENMAN, Charles	Perq	1720		Thomas Jr.	NewH	1763
Christopher	Perq	1740		Thomas Sr.	NewH	1763
Wm	FWV	1771		Thomas Jr.	NewH	1765
DENMARK, Wm	Pitt	1762		Thomas Sr.	NewH	1765
DENNARD, John	Tryo	1776		Thomas Jr.	NewH	1767
Thomas	Tryo	1776		Thomas Sr.	NewH	1767
DENNEY, Ascryer	Surr	1771		DEVINE, Jenkins	Bute	1771
Asery	Surr	1772		Jenkins	FWV	1771
Edmond	Surr	1771		DEVOLL, Wm	Onsl	1769
Edmund	Surr	1772		Wm	Onsl	1770
Henry	Surr	1771		DEW, John 1,030 acre		
Henry	Surr	1772			Chow	1717
John	Surr	1771		John	Chow	1717
John	Surr	1772		DEWEY, Stephen	Crav	1769
Lazarus	Surr	1772		DIAMOND, John	Edge	1743
Samuel	Surr	1771		DIARS, John	Surr	1772
Samuel	Surr	1772		DIAS, John	Beau	1755
Wm	Rowa	1759		DICK, Thomas	Brun	1769
DENNIS, Daniel	Dobb	1779		Thomas	Brun	1772
John	Oran	1755		Thomas	NewH	1762
Nathaniel	Anso	1763		Thomas	NewH	1763
Rachel	Rand	1779		DICKENS, Charles	Pitt	1762
Samuel	Oran	1755		Charles	Pitt	1764
Thomas	Rand	1779		John	Curr	1755
DENNY, Benjamin	Gran	1784		Robert	Gran	1769
David	Dobb	1769		Wm	Curr	1755
James	Oran	1755		DICKENSON, Leven	Crav	1769
DENSON, Edmond	Bute	1771		DICKERS, Mary	Cumb	1767
Edmond	FWV	1771		DICKERSON, Griffith	Bute	1771
Shadrack	Anso	1763		Griffith	FWV	1771
Wm	Bute	1771		John	Gran	1755
Wm	FWV	1771		John Jr.	Gran	1755
Wm's estate	Gran	1784		John	Gran	1769
DENT, John	Bute	1771		Malachi	Gran	1769
John	FWV	1771		Martin	Bute	1771
Michael	Bute	1771		Martin	FWV	1771
Michael	FWV	1771		Wm	Gran	1755
Wm	Bute	1771		Wm	Gran	1769
DENTON, Abraham	Casw	1777		Zachariah	Bute	1771
Arthur	Surr	1772		Zachariah	FWV	1771

DICKEY, Edward	Rowa 1759		DILLON, Peter	Rowa 1759
James Esq.	Oran 1755		DIMENT, Wm	Bert 1757
James	Oran 1755		DIMOCK, Catherine	Crav 1742
James Jr.	Rand 1779		DIMSEY, George	Crav 1742
James Sr.	Rand 1779		DINKINS, Charles	Pitt 1763
John	Rand 1779		James	Dobb 1769
Matthew	Rand 1779		John	Bute 1771
DICKINGS, Josiah	Chow 1753		John	FWV 1771
DICKINGS, Robert			John	Surr 1772
Esq.	Casw 1777		Thomas	Anso 1763
DICKINSON, Daniel	Dobb 1779		Wm	Anso 1763
Ezekiel	Beau 1755		Wm	Surr 1771
Francis	Crav 1743		Wm	Surr 1772
Joel	Dobb 1769		DINSON, James	Anso 1763
Joel	Dobb 1779		Shadrack	Anso 1763
John	Beau 1755		DINWIDDIE, John	Casw 1777
John	Chow 1721		DIONE, Richard	Beau 1764
John	Dobb 1779		DISMOND, Jeremiah s.
Malachi	Rand 1779		of John	Dobb 1769
Nathaniel	Casw 1777		John	Crav 1743
Shadrack	Dobb 1769		John	Dobb 1769
Winburn	Dobb 1779		DIX, Boater	Rowa 1759
DICKONS, Charles	Pitt 1762		DIXON, Ann	Pitt 1775
DICKS, John	Anso 1763		Benjamin	Beau 1764
Wm	Hyde 1742		Chosewell	Beau 1755
DICKSON, Isaiah	Casw 1777		Chosewell	Beau 1764
John	Chow 1717		Chosewell	Crav 1769
John	Curr 1755		Draper s. of
John	Dupl 1751		Wm Sr.	Beau 1755
John	Dupl 1752		Draper s. of
Josiah	Oran 1755		Wm Sr.	Beau 1764
Michael	Casw 1777		Henry (Cpt.)	Casw 1777
Michael Jr.	Casw 1777		Henry Sr.	Casw 1777
Michael	Oran 1755		Jacob	Beau 1764
Simon	Oran 1755		Jacob	Casw 1777
Thomas	Anso 1763		James	Beau 1764
Thomas	Cumb 1767		John	Beau 1755
Thomas	Pasq 1754		John Jr.	Beau 1755
Wm	Cumb 1767		John	Beau 1764
DIFFEE, Wm	Rowa 1758		John	Casw 1777
Wm	Rowa 1759		John Jr.	NewH 1748
DIFFEY, Wm	Rand 1779		Jonathan	NewH 1762
Wm Jr.	Rand 1779		Jonathan	NewH 1763
DIGGS, Marshall	Anso 1763		Jonathan	NewH 1767
DIKES, George	Beau 1755		Murphy	Dobb 1769
George Jr.	Pitt 1762		Rightson	Onsl 1769
George Sr.	Pitt 1762		Rightson	Onsl 1770
George	Pitt 1762		Thomas	Beau 1755
George	Pitt 1763		Thomas	Beau 1764
George Sr.	Pitt 1763		Thomas Jr.	Beau 1764
George	Pitt 1764		Thomas	Onsl 1769
George	Pitt 1775		Thomas	Onsl 1770
DILDAY, Charles	Gate 1786		Walter	Beau 1755
Henry Sr.	Gate 1786		Walter Jr.	Beau 1755
John	Chow 1753		Walter	Beau 1764
Joseph	Gate 1786		Wm	Beau 1755
DILL, Archibald	Casw 1777		Wm Jr.	Beau 1755
James	Oran 1755		Wm	Beau 1764
Job	Bert 1757		Wm Jr.	Beau 1764
John	Casw 1777		DIXSON, Edward	Pitt 1762
Philip	Anso 1763		Edward	Pitt 1763
Richard	Casw 1777		Edward	Pitt 1764
DILLARD, George	Bert 1769		Jacob	Casw 1777
Joseph	Gran 1755		John	Curr 1715
DILLON, John	Gran 1784		John	Pitt 1762

DIXSON, John	Pitt	1763	DOKE, James	Surr	1772
John	Pitt	1764	DOKES, John	Rowa	1759
Rightson	Onsl	1770	DOLAND, Henry	Rowa	1759
Robert	Cumb	1755	DOLLAR, Wm	NewH	1767
Roland	Pitt	1762	DOLLARHIDE, Ezekiel	Rand	1779
Roland	Pitt	1763	Francis	Oran	1755
Thomas	Onsl	1770	Francis	Rand	1779
Walter	Pitt	1762	Francis	Rowa	1759
Walter	Pitt	1763	DOLLARSHIELD, Ezekiel		
Walter	Pitt	1764		Casw	1777
Wm	Pitt	1762	DOLREE, Jacob	Dobb	1769
Wm	Pitt	1763	Thomas	Dobb	1769
Wm	Pitt	1764	DONAGAN, John	Surr	1771
DOAK, James	Surr	1771	Joseph	Surr	1771
James	Surr	1772	Thomas	Surr	1771
DOANE, Hezekiah	Brun	1769	DONALD, Thomas	Rowa	1759
Hezekiah	Brun	1722	DONALDSON, Hannah	Casw	1777
Hezekiah	NewH	1763	Humphrey	Casw	1777
Hezekiah	NewH	1767	Isaac	Surr	1772
Jeremiah	NewH	1767	Robert	Casw	1777
Moses	Pitt	1764	Robert	Oran	1755
Nehemiah	NewH	1763	DONAM, Hugh	Surr	1771
Sarah	Blad	1763	DONAWAY, Abraham	Casw	1777
Wm	NewH	1769	DONE, Richard	Cumb	1767
DOATY, Benjamin	Brun	1769	Zekiah	NewH	1755
Benjamin	Brun	1772	DONEFIN, John	Pitt	1762
Edward	NewH	1765	John	Pitt	1764
DOBBINS, Alexander	Casw	1777	DONENT, Wm	Bert	1769
Alexander	Rowa	1759	DONNALLY, Arthur	Cumb	1767
Hugh	Casw	1777	DONOHOE, Summers	Blad	1763
Hugh Jr.	Casw	1777	DOO, George	Curr	1755
James	Rowa	1759	DOOLEN, Henry	Tryo	1776
John Jr.	Cumb	1755	DOOLITTLE, Joseph	Oran	1755
John Sr.	Cumb	1755	DOPIUS, Wm	Crav	1720
John	Cumb	1755	DORAM, John	NewH	1755
John Jr.	Cumb	1767	Travis	NewH	1762
John Sr.	Cumb	1767	Travis	NewH	1767
John	Cumb	1767	DORCEY, Elias	Bute	1771
Mad	Casw	1777	Elias	FWV	1771
Rachel	Casw	1777	Solomon	Bute	1771
DOBBS, Arthur			Solomon	FWV	1771
(Gov.)	NewH	1762	DORDAN, John	Pitt	1763
Arthur (Gov.)	NewH	1763	DORE, Frederick	NewH	1762
DOCHESTER, James	Oran	1755	DORK, Henry	Crav	1720
DOCK, Barefoot	Dobb	1769	DORMAN, Benjamin	Cumb	1767
John	Dobb	1769	DORMANT, Michael	Edge	1743
DOCTON, Jacob	Perq	1740	DOSHIRE, Timothy	Oran	1755
James s. of			DORTON, Wm	Surr	1771
Thomas	Perq	1720	Wm	Surr	1772
Thomas 275 acres	Perq	1720	DORTSCH, Walter	Dobb	1779
Thomas	Perq	1740	DOSSIE, Wm	Bute	1771
DODD, Richard	Gran	1769	Wm	FWV	1771
DODSON, Charles	Gran	1755	DOTEY, Edward	NewH	1763
Charles	Gran	1784	DOTSON, Charles	Surr	1771
Charles	Surr	1771	Charles	Surr	1772
Charles	Surr	1772	Isaac	Oran	1755
Reuben	Surr	1771	John	Surr	1771
Reuben	Surr	1772	Reuben	Surr	1772
Wm	Gran	1769	Rolley	Casw	1777
Wm	Gran	1784	DOTY, Benjamin	Onsl	1769
DOE, Edward	Beau	1755	Benjamin	Onsl	1770
Peter	Curr	1742	Peter s. of		
Ralph	Curr	1715	Benjam	Onsl	1770
Ralph	Perq	1720	DOUBLY, Edward	NewH	1755
DOKE, James	Surr	1771	DOUBTY, Edward	NewH	1755

DOUD, Conner	Cumb	1767
David	NewH	1755
Emmanuel	Beau	1755
John Jr.	NewH	1755
Wm	Beau	1755
Wm	Cumb	1767
DOUDING, John	Beau	1755
DOUGGAN, James	Rand	1779
Thomas	Rand	1779
DOUGHDY, John	Curr	1755
DOUGHERTY, John	Dobb	1769
Doughtie, Francis	Chow	1753
Jethro	Bert	1757
Wm	Chow	1753
DOUGLAS, Alexander s.		
of John	FWV	1771
Alexander	Gran	1769
Andrew	Surr	1771
Elizabeth & s.		
Casiah	Bert	1757
James	Curr	1715
James	Curr	1755
Jesse	Casw	1777
John	Bute	1771
John	Casw	1777
John s. Alexander		
Samuel	FWV	1771
John	Oran	1755
Joseph	Rand	1779
Thomas	Casw	1777
Wm	FWV	1771
DOUGLIN, John	Pasq	1754
DOUTHER, George	Oran	1755
DOUTHIT, John	Rowa	1759
DOUTY, Edward	NewH	1762
DOVE, Benjamin	Oran	1755
John	Oran	1755
Peter	Perq	1720
DOW, Nicholas	Beau	1755
Wm	Beau	1755
DOWD, Conner	Cumb	1767
DOWDIN, Benjamin	Beau	1755
John	Pitt	1764
Wm	Beau	1755
DOWELL, John	Casw	1777
DOWEN, John	Pitt	1764
DOWEY, James	Blad	1763
John	Blad	1763
Robert	Blad	1741
DOWING, John	Rand	1779
DOWLASS, John	Blad	1763
DOWLEY, Elisha	Beau	1764
DOWLING, Benjamin	Crav	1769
James	Cumb	1755
DOWNER, John	Anso	1763
Thomas	Anso	1763
DOWNEY, James	Gran	1755
James	Gran	1769
James	Gran	1784
James Jr.	Gran	1784
John	Gran	1784
Robert	Gran	1755
Robert	Gran	1769
DOWNING, Elisha	Dobb	1769
George	Dobb	1769

DOWNING, George	NorH	1741
Joseph	Dobb	1769
Richard	Onsl	1770
Robert	Gran	1755
Wm 2530 acres	Chow	1721
Wm	Chow	1721
Wm	Onsl	1770
DOWNINGS, James	Oran	1755
Downs, Elias	Oran	1755
Richard	Anso	1763
DOYLE, Daniel	Cumb	1767
John	Edge	1742
DOZER, James	Bute	1771
James	FWV	1771
DOZIER, John	Gran	1755
Leonard s. of		
John	Gran	1755
DRAKE, Aaron	Chow	1721
Edward	Gate	1786
Thomas	Edge	1734
Thomas	Pitt	1763
THOMAS	Pitt	1764
DRAPER, Nathaniel	Beau	1755
Nathaniel	Crav	1769
Richard	Tyrr	1755
Wm	Brun	1772
Wm	Gate	1786
Wm	Rand	1779
DRAUGHAN, James	Bert	1769
John	Bert	1757
John	Bert	1769
Robert	Bert	1757
Thomas	Bert	1769
DRENON, Robert	Surr	1772
DREW, John	Brun	1772
John	Dobb	1769
DREWRY, Amey	Gran	1784
John	Chow	1721
DRIGGAS, Betty	Crav	1769
Eleanor	Crav	1769
DRIGGOTT, John	Beau	1764
DRINKWATER, Powder	Chow	1717
DRISCOLL, Dennis	Chow	1753
Dennis	Gran	1784
Timothy	Gran	1784
DRIVER, Byrd	Gran	1784
DRIZALMOSES, John	NewH	1755
DROMGOLD, Francis	NewH	1765
DRUGALMOURS, John	NewH	1755
DRUGGAN, James	Rand	1779
Thomad	Rand	1779
DRULARD, Peter	NewH	1755
DRY, Wm	Brun	1769
Wm	Brun	1772
Wm Sr.	NewH	1755
Wm	NewH	1755
Wm	NewH	1762
Wm Sr.	NewH	1763
DUBBERLY, John	Crav	1769
Wm	Crav	1769
DUBERRY, Giles	Bute	1771
Giles	FWV	1771
DUBOIS, Anthony	NewH	1762
Anthony	NewH	1763
Anthony	NewH	1765

DUBOIS, John	NewH 1762	DUKE, James	Crav 1769
John	NewH 1763	James 1 slave	Pasq 1769
John	NewH 1767	Joel	Bute 1771
DUBUSK, John	Blad 1763	Joel	FWV 1771
DUCAMP, John	Blad 1763	John	Bute 1771
DUCK, Jacob	Dobb 1769	John	Chow 1753
Joseph	Cumb 1767	John	FWV 1771
DUCKENFIELD, Wm	N.C. 1701	John	Gate 1786
Wm Esq.	Chow 1721	John	NorH 1762
Wm J. P.	Chow 1717	Joseph	Bute 1771
DUCKMANCER, John	Cumb 1767	Joseph & s. Wm	FWV 1771
DUDLEY, Bishop	NewH 1763	Joseph	NewH 1743
Bishop	NewH 1765	Major	Bute 1771
Bishop	NewH 1767	Major	FWV 1771
Chr.	Chow 1717	Mary	Gran 1755
Christopher	NewH 1755	Matthew	Bute 1771
Christopher	NewH 1762	Matthew	FWV 1771
Christopher	NewH 1763	Melvin	Chow 1753
Christopher	Onsl 1743	Men	Blad 1763
Elizabeth	Onsl 1769	Nehemiah	Crav 1769
Elizabeth	Onsl 1770	Peter	Crav 1769
James	Beau 1743	Robert	Gran 1755
James	Beau 1755	Samuel	Bute 1771
James	Pitt 1762	Samuel	Edge 1743
James	Pitt 1763	Samuel s. Britian	
James	Pitt 1764	Burwell Sterling	
Joseph	Beau 1755		FWV 1771
Margaret	NewH 1765	Samuel	Gran 1755
Margaret	Onsl 1769	Wm (Cpt.)	Bute 1771
Margaret	Onsl 1770	Wm (Cpt.)	FWV 1771
Richard	Beau 1755	Wm & s. Green	FWV 1771
Richard	Cumb 1767	Wm	Gran 1755
Robert	Bert 1757	DUKEYSAR, Schansiew	
Thomas	Cart 1742		NewH 1767
Thomas	Curr 1741	DULAN, James	FWV 1771
Thomas Jr.	Curr 1755	DULANEY, Ben, s.	
Thomas Sr.	Curr 1755	Thos	Onsl 1770
Wm	Beau 1755	Patrick	Blad 1763
Wm	Onsl 1769	Thomas	Onsl 1769
Wm	Onsl 1770	Thomas	Onsl 1770
DUERS, James	Bert 1757	Thomas Jr.	Onsl 1770
James	Bert 1769	DULING, Thomas	Crav 1769
DUFF, Thomas	NewH 1765	DULY, Richard	Gran 1769
Thomas	NewH 1767	DUMAS, Benjamin	Anso 1763
DUFFEE,	Pitt 1775	Benjamin Jr.	Anso 1763
DUFFIE, Samuel	Bute 1771	David	Anso 1763
Samuel	FWV 1771	DUNAGAN, John	Oran 1755
DUFFIELD, Richard	Pitt 1763	Thomas	Oran 1755
Thomas	Pitt 1762	DUNAHO, Thomas	Cumb 1767
Thomas	Pitt 1763	DUNBAR, Elizabeth	
Thomas	Pitt 1764	wo.	Beau 1764
DUFFY, Hugh	Pasq 1769	John	Anso 1763
DUGALL, Artr.	Chow 1717	Robert	Edge 1743
Arthur	Chow 1721	Samuel	Beau 1755
DUGER, Benjamin	Surr 1772	Samuel	Beau 1764
Wm	Surr 1771	Wm	Beau 1742
Wm	Surr 1772	Wm	Beau 1751
DUGGAR, John	Gran 1769	Wm	Beau 1755
Wm	Gran 1755	DUNBIBIN, Daniel's	
DUGGER, John	Gran 1784	Estate	NewH 1762
DUKE, Benjamin	Bute 1771	Daniel's Estate	NewH 1763
Benjamin	FWV 1771	Daniel's Estate	NewH 1767
Daniel	Curr 1755	DUNCAN, Abraham	1743
Green	Bute 1771	Agnes	Casw 1777
Green	FWV 1771	Agnes	NewH 1762

DUNCAN, Alexander	Cumb	1755	DUNN, Samuel s.		
Alexander	NewH	1762	Susannah	Dobb	1769
Alexander	NewH	1763	Spence	Onsl	1770
Alexander	NewH	1767	Susannah	Dobb	1769
Charles	Surr	1771	Walter	Dobb	1779
Charles	Surr	1772	Wm	Blad	1763
Daniel	Casw	1777	Wm	Crav	1769
Daniel	NewH	1762	DUNNING, Jesse	Bert	1757
David	Rowa	1759	Jesse	Bert	1769
George	Beau	1755	John	Bert	1757
George	Gran	1784	John	Bert	1769
James	NewH	1743	Samuel	Bert	1757
John	FWV	1771	DUNOVIN, John	Casw	1777
John	Gran	1755	DUNS, Samuel	Beau	1769
John Jr.	Gran	1784	DUNSCOMB, Samuel	Chow	1753
John Sr.	Gran	1784	DUNSTAN, Richard	Crav	1769
John	Rand	1779	DUNSTON, Barnabus	Bert	1757
John	Surr	1771	Richard	Beau	1755
John	Surr	1772	DUPREE, Benjamin	Pitt	1775
Joseph	Oran	1755	Gardner	NewH	1763
Joseph	Surr	1772	Garnet	Brun	1769
Marshall	Surr	1771	Garnet	Brun	1772
Marshall	Surr	1772	James	Blad	1763
Miles	Casw	1777	James	Blad	1781
Miles	NewH	1762	James	Brun	1769
Peter	Tyrr	1755	James	Brun	1772
Rice	FWV	1771	Josa.	Brun	1769
Robert	Bute	1771	Joseph	Brun	1772
Robert	FWV	1771	Josiah	NewH	1763
Robert	Surr	1772	Lewis	Blad	1781
Thomas	Casw	1777	Lewis	Brun	1769
Wm	Gran	1784	Lewis	Brun	1772
Wm	Surr	1771	Samuel	Brun	1769
DUNEFIN, John	Pitt	1763	Samuel	Brun	1772
DUNFIELD, Edward	Cumb	1767	Sterling	Pitt	1775
DUNFORD, Wm	Gate	1786	Wm Jr.	Crav	1746
DUNHAM, Hugh	Surr	1772	DURANT, George		
Wm	Cumb	1755	1050 acres	Perq	1720
DUNKIN, John	Gran	1755	Thomas 816 acres		
DUNLAP, James	Rowa	1759		Perq	1720
James	Surr	1771	DURDAN, John	Dobb	1779
James	Surr	1772	Wm	Dobb	1779
John	Surr	1771	DURDINS, John	Dobb	1769
John	Surr	1772	John s. of		
Samuel	Surr	1771	John	Dobb	1769
Samuel	Surr	1772	Richard	Dobb	1769
DUNLOP, John	Pasq	1769	Wm	Dobb	1769
DUNN, Benjamin	Cumb	1767	DURHAM, Isaac	Oran	1755
David	Crav	1742	James	Crav	1744
Francis	Crav	1769	John	Bute	1771
Jacob	Cumb	1767	John	FWV	1771
Jacob	Dobb	1769	Joseph	Casw	1777
James	Onsl	1769	Matthew	Oran	1755
James	Onsl	1770	Samuel	FWV	1771
John	Blad	1763	Thomas	Casw	1777
John	Crav	1750	Thomas	Oran	1755
John	Crav	1769	Wm	FWV	1771
John Jr.	Crav	1769	Wm Sr.	FWV	1771
John, Brice's			DURNAL, Wm	Rand	1779
Ck	Crav	1769	Wm	Tryo	1776
John	Cumb	1767	DURSKIN, Sarah	Rand	1779
John	Rowa	1759	DUTCHESS, Wm	Surr	1771
Joseph 2 slaves	Blad	1763	DWIGHT, Samuel	Brun	1769
Joseph	Cumb	1767	Samuel	Brun	1772
Robert	Blad	1752	DWITE, Joseph	Tyrr	1755

DYAR, James	Gran 1784	Eason, George	Perq 1740
DYAS, Thomas	Crav 1769	Isaac	Gate 1786
DYE, Martin	Bute 1771	Isaac	Pitt 1762
Martin	FWV 1771	Isaac	Pitt 1763
DYER, James	Cumb 1767	Isaac	Pitt 1764
John	Surr 1771	Jacob	Gate 1786
Samuel	Gran 1769	James	Chow 1753
DUTY, Matthew	Bute 1771	Jesse	Gate 1786
Matthew	FWV 1771	Lewis	Gate 1786
Richard	Gran 1784	Mary 300 acres	Perq 1720
Wm	Bute 1771	Mary	Perq 1740
Wm	FWV 1771	Moses	Gate 1786
DYNES, Wm	Surr 1771	OBED	Pitt 1764
DYSON, James	Onsl 1769	Seth	Gate 1786
		Thomas	Bert 1757
		Thomas 130 acres	
			Perq 1720
EADY, John	Curr 1755	Thomas	Perq 1740
EAGAN, Darby	Brun 1769	Thomas	Surr 1772
Darby	Brun 1772	EASTER, Abraham	Hyde 1745
Elizabeth	Brun 1772	John	Gran 1784
EAGLE, Frederick	Dobb 1779	Easterling, Wm	Crav 1769
Richard's estate	Brun 1769	EASTERWOOD, Laurence	
Richard	Brun 1772		Anso 1763
Richard	NewH 1755	Thomas	Tyrr 1755
Richard	NewH 1762	Eastwood, Alexander	Casw 1777
Richard	NewH 1763	Israel	Casw 1777
EAKES, Zachariah	Gran 1769	Israel	Gran 1769
EARLE, Gamaliel	Gran 1769	Israel	Gran 1784
John	Gran 1769	Joseph	Beau 1755
John	NewH 1755	Joseph	Pitt 1762
John	NewH 1762	Joseph	Pitt 1763
John	NewH 1765	Joseph	Pitt 1764
John	NewH 1767	EATON, Charles	Gran 1769
John	Pasq 1769	Charles	Gran 1784
Joseph	Brun 1769	Thomas (Col.)	Bute 1771
Joseph	Brun 1772	Thomas (Col.)	FWV 1771
Richard	NewH 1755	Thomas n of	
Richard	NewH 1762	Roan	FWV 1771
Richard	NewH 1763	Wm 11 whites	
Richard	NewH 1765	23 b	Edge 1743
Richard	NewH 1767	EAVER, Wm	Gran 1755
Thomas	Gran 1784	EAVES, Benjamin	Bute 1771
Wm	FWV 1771	Benjamin	FWV 1771
EARLEY, Benjamin	Bert 1757	Wm	Edge 1743
James	Bert 1757	Wm	Tryo 1776
James	Bert 1769	EBURN, Elisha	Beau 1764
John	Bert 1757	ECCOLS, James	Beau 1764
John	Chow 1717	John	Beau 1742
John	Chow 1721	John	Beau 1755
Widow	Chow 1721	Jones	Beau 1755
Wm	Bert 1757	ECKLIN, Charles	Beau 1764
Wm	Chow 1717	EDEMAN, Thomas	Surr 1771
EARLS, John	Gran 1784	EDENS, John	Onsl 1769
John Jr.	Gran 1784	Wm	NorH 1742
EARY, Peter	Rowa 1759	EDGARTON, John	Edge 1741
EASLEY, Byron	Gran 1769	EDGE, John	Blad 1763
Millington	Gran 1769	EDGINSTON, Scrupe	Ruth 1782
Wm	Gran 1784	Scrupe	Tryo 1776
Willington	Gran 1784	EDMON, Wm	Blad 1763
EASON, Abner	Chow 1753	EDMOND, James	Cumb 1767
Abraham	Gate 1786	EDMONDS, Henry	Dobb 1769
Alexander	Gate 1786	James	Gran 1784
George	Gate 1786	EDMONDSON, Bryan	Onsl 1769
George	Perq 1720	James	Dobb 1779

EDMONDSON, James	Pitt	1762	EDWARDS, John s. of		
James	Pitt	1763	Grace	Onsl	1769
James	Pitt	1764	John	Onsl	1770
James	Pitt	1775	John	Perq	1720
John	Crav	1720	John	Pitt	1762
John	Crav	1769	John	Pitt	1763
John	Dobb	1779	Joseph	Beau	1764
Joseph	Crav	1742	Joseph	Bute	1771
Joseph	Crav	1769	Joseph & s.		
EDMONS, James	Blad	1763	Charles	Fwv	1771
EDNEY, Newton	Pasq	1769	Joseph	Pitt	1764
Robert	Pasq	1743	Joseph	Rand	1779
Samuel	Pasq	1769	Joseph	Surr	1772
EDWARDS, Ambrose	Beau	1764	Joshua	Onsl	1769
Ambrose	Pitt	1763	Josiah	Onsl	1769
Anowel	Rowa	1759	Josiah	Onsl	1770
Anthony	Bute	1771	Morgan	Rand	1779
Anthony	FWV	1771	Nathaniel		
Benjamin	Beau	1764	6 slaves	Pasq	1769
Benjamin	Dobb	1769	Obadiah	Pitt	1764
Benjamin	Dobb	1779	Peter	Rand	1779
Cader	Surr	1771	Philemon	Bute	1771
Cader	Surr	1772	Philemon	FWV	1771
Charles	Gran	1755	Pomfret	Gran	1784
Charles	Gran	1769	Pomfrey	Gran	1769
Charles	Gran	1784	Robert	Blad	1763
Charles	Pitt	1762	Reuben	Onsl	1770
Charles	Pitt	1763	Samuel	Pitt	1762
Charles	Pitt	1764	Samuel	Pitt	1763
Christopher	Pitt	1762	Samuel	Pitt	1764
Daniel	Pitt	1762	Simon	Crav	1769
Elijah	FWV	1771	Solomon	Pitt	1763
Grace	Onsl	1769	Thomas	Bert	1769
Grace	Onsl	1770	Thomas	Dobb	1769
Isaac	Beau	1755	Thomas s. Thomas	Dobb	1769
Isaac	NorH	1741	Thomas	Onsl	1769
Isaac	Onsl	1770	Thomas	Onsl	1770
Isaac	Pitt	1763	Titus	Bert	1757
James	Beau	1764	Titus	Bert	1769
James	Pitt	1762	Walker	Pitt	1762
James Jr.	Pitt	1762	Walker	Pitt	1763
James Sr.	Pitt	1763	Walker	Pitt	1764
James Jr.	Pitt	1763	Wm	Beau	1755
James	Pitt	1764	Wm	Beau	1764
Joel	Bute	1771	Wm	Bert	1757
Joel	FWV	1771	Wm	Blad	1763
John	Anso	1763	Wm	Bute	1771
John	Blad	1743	Wm & s. Benjamin	FWV	1771
John	Bute	1771	Wm	Gran	1755
John Sr.	Chow	1717	Wm	NewH	1765
John	Chow	1717	Wm	Onsl	1769
John 570 acres	Chow	1721	Wm	Onsl	1770
John Jr.	Chow	1721	Wm	Pitt	1762
John	Dobb	1769	Wm	Pitt	1763
John s. of			Wm	Pitt	1764
Thomas	Dobb	1769	EFLAND, Peter	Oran	1755
John	Dobb	1779	EGAN, Darby	NewH	1762
John	Edge	1742	Darby	NewH	1763
John	FWV	1771	John	NewH	1762
John	Gran	1755	John	NewH	1763
John	Gran	1784	EGGERTON, Benjamin	Bute	1771
John	NorH	1762	Benjamin	FWV	1771
John Jr.	NorH	1762	Benjamin	Gran	1755
John	Onsl	1741	James Constable	Bute	1771
John	Onsl	1769	John	Gran	1755

EGGERTON, Pat.	Chow	1717	ELLIOTT, Wm		Bute	1771
Patrick	Chow	1721	Wm		FWV	1771
Scrup	FWV	1771	Wm & s Wm		FWV	1771
Scrup	Tryo	1776	Wm		Perq	1740
Wm 300 acres	Perq	1720	Wm		Pitt	1762
Willmot	Bute	1771	Wm		Pitt	1763
Willmot	FWV	1771	Wm		Rand	1779
EGGLESTON, David	Rand	1779	Wm		Surr	1771
John	Brun	1772	Wm		Surr	1772
EIVA, Robert	Dobb	1769	ELLIS, Aaron		Bert	1757
ELDER, John	Rand	1779	Aaron		Gate	1786
ELDRIDGE, Wm	NorH	1742	Absalom		Dobb	1769
ELEY, Samuel	FWV	1771	Benjamin		Beau	1755
ELKINS, John	Cumb	1767	Benjamin		Brun	1772
Joseph	Cumb	1755	Benjamin		Bute	1771
Joshua	Cumb	1767	Benjamin		FWV	1771
Samuel	Cumb	1755	Benjamin		Pitt	1762
Samuel Sr.	Cumb	1767	Benjamin Jr.		Pitt	1762
ELLEGOOD, Elisha	Beau	1755	Benjamin Jr.		Pitt	1763
Francis	Beau	1764	Benjamin Sr.		Pitt	1763
Hillary	Beau	1755	Benjamin Jr.		Pitt	1764
Jacob	Beau	1764	Benjamin Sr.		Pitt	1764
John	Beau	1764	Daniel		Gate	1786
Mathias	Pasq	1769	Edward		Bute	1771
ELLER, LEeonard	Rand	1779	Edward Jr.		Bute	1771
Michael	Brun	1772	Edward		FWV	1771
ELLERBEE, Edward	Anso	1763	Edward Jr.		FWV	1771
John	Anso	1763	Elisha		Gate	1786
John	Blad	1741	Ephraim		FWV	1771
Thomas	Anso	1763	Evan		Blad	1750
ELLINGTON, Daniel	Gran	1784	Evan		Blad	1763
ELLIOTT, Aaron	Perq	1720	Evan		Blad	1781
Abraham	Perq	1740	Evan		Brun	1772
Abraham	Rand	1779	Francis		Chow	1721
Alexander	Rand	1779	Grissom		Chow	1753
Caleb	Perq	1740	Henry		Pitt	1762
Eric	Perq	1740	Henry		Pitt	1763
George	Bute	1771	Henry		Pitt	1764
George	Casw	1777	Henry		Pitt	1775
George Sr.	FWV	1771	Isham		FWV	1771
George	Gran	1784	Jacob		Chow	1753
Jacob	Dobb	1769	James		Blad	1763
Jacob	Gran	1784	James		Blad	1781
Jacob	Pasq	1769	James		Brun	1772
Jacob	Perq	1740	James Jr.		Brun	1772
Jacob	Rand	1779	James Jr.		Chow	1753
Jacob Jr.	Rand	1779	James Sr.		Chow	1753
James	Bute	1771	James		Rand	1779
James	FWV	1771	Jesse		Bute	1771
James	Oran	1755	Jesse		FWV	1771
Job	Onsl	1770	Joel		Dobb	1769
John	Dobb	1769	John Jr.		Blad	1763
John	Onsl	1769	John Sr. 4			
John	Onsl	1770	slaves		Blad	1763
John	Rand	1779	John		Brun	1772
Joseph	Rand	1779	John Jr.		Brun	1772
Joshua	Perq	1740	John Sr.		Bute	1771
Michael	Casw	1777	John Jr. s.			
Moses	Perq	1740	Joshua		Bute	1771
Peter	Beau	1755	John		Bute	1771
Peter	Beau	1764	John		Chow	1753
Thomas	Perq	1720	John Jr. s.			
Thomas Jr.	Perq	1720	Joshua		FWV	1771
Thomas	Perq	1740	John Sr.		FWV	1771
Wm	Beau	1755				

ELLIS, John	FWV	1771
John	Gate	1786
John	NorH	1762
John	Onsl	1770
John s. John	Onsl	1770
Joshua	Bute	1771
Joshua	FWV	1771
Leonard	Rand	1779
Marcus	Gran	1755
Mary	Pitt	1775
Michael	Curr	1755
Michael	Pitt	1762
Michael	Pitt	1764
Moses	Chow	1753
Nimrod	Gran	1769
Reuben	FWV	1771
Richard 5 slaves		
	Crav	1769
Richard	FWV	1771
Robert 13 slaves		
	Brun	1769
Robert	Brun	1772
Robert	NewH	1762
Robert	NorH	1762
Shadrack	Gate	1786
Thomas	Surr	1771
Walter	Casw	1777
Wm	Blad	1763
Wm	Blad	1781
Wm	Brun	1772
Wm	Bute	1771
Wm	Dobb	1769
Wm	FWV	1771
Wm	Gate	1786
Wm	Gran	1755
Wm	Perq	1720
Wm	Pitt	1775
Wm	Rowa	1758
Willis	Brun	1772
ELLISON, Alonso	Beau	1764
James	Beau	1742
James	Beau	1755
Wm	Surr	1771
Wm	Surr	1772
ELLOSON, Wm	Pasq	1754
ELLWELL, Benjamin	Blad	1763
Elizabeth	Blad	1781
John	Blad	1763
ELMORE, George	Bute	1771
George	FWV	1771
George	Surr	1771
George	Surr	1772
Peter	Casw	1777
Thomas	Surr	1771
Travis	Casw	1777
ELMS, John	FWV	1771
ELROD, Christopher	Brun	1772
Robert	Brun	1772
ELSEY, Jacob	Surr	1771
ELSON, John	Rand	1779
ELSTON, Zachariah	Perq	1740
ELTON, Robert	Tyrr	1755
ELVINSTON, Hardy	Dobb	1779
ELWEL, Benjamin	Cumb	1767
ELWICK, Darwin	Gran	1755

ELY, Samuel	Bute	1771
Samuel	FWV	1771
EMBRAY, John	Oran	1755
Moses	Oran	1755
EMERY, Waitman	Beau	1755
EMMERY, Ephraim	Gran	1784
EMMIT, John	Pasq	1769
EMPSON, John	Pasq	1769
ENGELS, Charles	Surr	1772
Dolar	Crav	1720
Peter	Crav	1720
ENGLAND, John	NewH	1755
John	Surr	1771
John	Surr	1772
Joseph	Surr	1772
ENGLISH, James	Bert	1757
James	Pitt	1763
James	Pitt	1764
James	Pitt	1775
Joseph	Dobb	1769
Thomas	Anso	1763
Thomas	Pitt	1763
Thomas Jr.	Pitt	1763
Thomas	Pitt	1764
Thomas	Pitt	1775
Wm	Pitt	1763
Wm	Pitt	1764
ENGRAM, Jacob	Dobb	1779
ENNIS, Wm	Rand	1779
ENITT, Edmond	Crav	1720
ENLESS, Abraham	Chow	1753
ENLOES, Abraham	Beau	1755
ENLOW, John	Pitt	1775
ENNET, Raymond	Cumb	1767
ENNETT, Joseph	Onsl	1769
ENOCH, David	Brun	1772
Edward	Surr	1772
Enoch	Brun	1772
John	Brun	1772
ENSLEY, John	Cumb	1767
ENYARD, Abraham	Surr	1772
John	Surr	1772
ENYART, Silas	Brun	1772
EPLEY, Jacob	Cumb	1767
EPPERSON, Wm	Bert	1757
EPSLEY, Brozey	Blad	1763
Jacob	Blad	1763
ERBE, Henry	NewH	1755
ERBY, Jer.	Onsl	1769
Wm	Anso	1763
ERICKSON, Andrew	Onsl	1769
ERNSTT, Jacob	Surr	1771
Jacob	Surr	1772
ERNY, Robert	Casw	1777
ERTS, Henry	NewH	1755
ERVIN, Francis s.		
Rob	Dobb	1769
James	Blad	1781
Jared	Blad	1781
John	Dobb	1769
Richard	Dobb	1769
Robert	Dobb	1769
Robert	Oran	1755
ERWIN, David Sr.	Rand	1779
John	Casw	1777

ERWIN, John	Rand 1779		EVANS, Benjamin		NewH 1762
Joseph	Rowa 1759		Benjamin		NewH 1763
Robert	Rowa 1759		Benjamin		Pitt 1762
Wm	Rand 1779		Benjamin		Pitt 1764
ESDEL, Argyle	Curr 1755		Benjamin		Rowa 1759
ESKRIDGE, Richard	Casw 1777		Black Robin		Chow 1721
ESPY, Usher	NewH 1762		Burrell (Negro)		FWV 1771
ESTES, Abraham	Gran 1755		Burwell		Gran 1784
Elisha	Oran 1755		Charles		Pitt 1762
Reuben	Casw 1777		Charles		Pitt 1763
Richard	Casw 1777		Charles		Pitt 1764
Thomas	Rand 1779		David		Anso 1763
Wm	Gran 1784		David		Dobb 1769
ESTRIDGE, Abraham	Gran 1769		David		Dobb 1779
Ephraim	Gran 1755		David		NewH 1741
ETHERIDGE, Abraham	Pasq 1769		David		NewH 1755
Adam	Curr 1755		David Sr.		NewH 1767
Amos	Curr 1755		David		Rowa 1759
Andrew	Curr 1715		David		Surr 1771
Eleanor	Curr 1755		Edward		NorH 1762
Henry	Curr 1715		Elizabeth		Blad 1781
Henry	Curr 1755		George		Blad 1763
John	Brun 1772		George		Cumb 1755
John	Curr 1743		George		Cumb 1767
Joshua	Pasq 1769		George		Pitt 1764
Marmaduke	Curr 1715		Isaac		Curr 1755
Mathias	Curr 1755		Isaac		Onsl 1769
Matthew	Pasq 1769		Isaac		Onsl 1770
Richard	Curr 1715		Isham		Dobb 1769
Richard	Curr 1755		Isom		Dobb 1769
Samuel	Blad 1763		Isom		Dobb 1779
Samuel	Brun 1772		Isom		Surr 1771
Samuel Jr.	Curr 1755		Jacob		Beau 1755
Samuel Sr.	Curr 1755		James		Bert 1757
Sarah	Curr 1755		James	2 slaves	Crav 1755
Thomas	Pasq 1769		James		Onsl 1769
Timothy	Curr 1755		James		Onsl 1770
Wm	Curr 1755		James		Pitt 1762
Willis Jr.	Curr 1755		Jane		Bute 1771
Willis Sr.	Curr 1755		Jane		Chow 1753
Willis	Pasq 1769		Jane		FWV 1771
ETHERINGTON, Francis			Joan		Onsl 1770
	Anso 1763		Joel		Dobb 1779
ETHRADY, Joshua	Pasq 1754		John		Beau 1755
Matthew	Pasq 1754		John		Chow 1717
EURE, Benjamin	Gate 1786		John		Chow 1721
Charles	Gate 1786		John		Chow 1753
Daniel	Gate 1786		John		Cumb 1767
James	Chow 1753		John		Curr 1715
James Jr.	Chow 1753		John		Dobb 1769
James	Gate 1786		John		Dobb 1779
John	Gate 1786		John		NewH 1750
Mills	Gate 1786		John		Onsl 1770
Samuel	Chow 1753		John		Pasq 1769
Samuel	Gate 1786		John		Pitt 1762
Stephen	Chow 1753		John		Pitt 1763
Stephen	Gate 1786		John		Pitt 1764
Uriah	Gate 1786		Jonathan		Cumb 1755
EUSTACE, Judith	Blad 1781		Jonathan		Cumb 1767
EVANS, Asa s. of			Jonathan		NewH 1755
John	Pasq 1769		Jonathan		NewH 1762
Benjamin	Beau 1755		Jonathan		NewH 1763
Ben.	Chow 1717		Jonathan		NewH 1765
Benjamin	Curr 1755		Jonathan		NewH 1767
Benjamin	NewH 1755				

EVANS, Jonathan		
419 acres	Perq	1720
Josa	Cumb	1755
Joseph	Bert	1757
Joseph	Curr	1755
Josdph	Pitt	1762
Joseph	Pitt	1763
Joshua	Bert	1769
Josiah Constable	Blad	1763
Major (negro)	Bute	1771
Major (negro)	FWV	1771
Major	Gran	1769
Major	Gran	1784
Margaret	NewH	1765
Margaret	NewH	1767
Mary	Perq	1720
Nathan	Casw	1777
Nicholas	Rowa	1759
Richard	Beau	1755
Richard	Gran	1784
Richard	Onsl	1770
Richard	Pitt	1762
Richard	Pitt	1763
Richard	Pitt	1764
Robert	Bert	1757
Robert	Chow	1721
Robert	NewH	1767
Rt.	Chow	1717
Sarah	Cumb	1755
Simon	Cumb	1755
Solomon	Rand	1779
Thomas	Beau	1755
Thomas	Bert	1757
Thomas	Blad	1763
Thomas	Casw	1777
Thomas Jr.	Casw	1777
Thomas	Chow	1721
Thomas	Crav	1751
Thomas	Curr	1755
Thomas	NewH	1743
Thomas	Rowa	1759
Thomas	Surr	1771
Thomas	Surr	1772
Walker	Pitt	1763
Wm	Cumb	1767
Wm	NewH	1763
Wm	NewH	1767
EVERAGE, Abner	Surr	1771
Abner	Surr	1772
Edward	Cumb	1767
EVERETT, Arthur	NewH	1765
Athaliah	Crav	1769
Henry	Beau	1741
Henry	Beau	1742
Henry	Beau	1755
Henry	Beau	1764
Henry s. Henry	Beau	1764
James	Beau	1764
James s. of		
Henry	Beau	1764
James	Tyrr	1755
Joseph	Dobb	1769
Joseph	Dobb	1779
Joshua	Tyrr	1755
Nat.	Chow	1717

EVERETT, Nathaniel	Chow	1721
Nathaniel	Tyrr	1755
Nathaniel Jr.	Tyrr	1755
Robert s. of		
Henry	Beau	1764
Thomas	Beau	1755
Thomas	Onsl	1742
Thomas	Onsl	1770
Thomas	Tyrr	1755
Wm	Tyrr	1755
EVERHARDT, Jacob	Rowa	1759
Philip	Rowa	1759
EVERLY, George	Rand	1779
EVERS, James	Blad	1781
EVERTON, Daniel	Onsl	1769
Daniel	Onsl	1770
Daniel	Pasq	1754
Jeremiah	Pasq	1769
Thomas	Curr	1755
Wm	Pasq	1769
EVERY, Abner	Surr	1771
Abner	Surr	1772
EVETT, Tomm	Crav	1720
EVITT, Walter	Beau	1755
Walter	Beau	1764
EVRIT, John	Rand	1779
EWBANKS, John	Crav	1769
Thomas	Crav	1769
EWELL, Thomas	Pitt	1764
EWILL, Thomas	Pitt	1762
FAGAN, Bedford	Tyrr	1755
Edward	Cumb	1767
George	Cumb	1755
George	Cumb	1767
Henry	Gran	1755
Richard	Tyrr	1755
Richard, overseer		
	Tyrr	1755
FAINE, Joel	Bute	1771
Joel	FWV	1771
FAIRCHILD, James	Chow	1717
James	Chow	1721
FAIRCLOOF, Jesse	Pasq	1769
Thomas	Pasq	1769
FAIRCLOTH, Frederick		
	Dobb	1779
John	Cumb	1755
John	Dobb	1779
Wm Jr.	Dobb	1779
FAIRCLUF, Thomas	Pasq	1769
FAIRFAX, Peter	Dobb	1769
FAIRLESS, Robert	Bert	1757
Wm	Bert	1757
FAIRLY, Wm	Bert	1757
FAISON, Dixon	NorH	1762
Henry	NorH	1762
James	NorH	1762
FALAW, James	Chow	1753
FALCON, John	Bute	1771
John	FWV	1771
FALCONER, George	Pitt	1775
John	Chow	1717

FALCONER, John	Chow	1721	FARMER, Wm	Cumb	1767
Thomas	Chow	1753	Wm	Rowa	1759
FALKINBURG, Andrew	Anso	1763	FARNELL, Benjamin	Onsl	1769
Henry	Anso	1763	Benjamin	Onsl	1770
Isaac	Anso	1763	Thomas	Onsl	1769
FALKNER, Charles	Cumb	1767	Thomas	Onsl	1770
Francis Jr.	Cumb	1767	FARR, John	Onsl	1744
Francis Sr.	Cumb	1767	FARRAR, Wm	Gran	1769
Jacob	Cumb	1767	FARREL, John	Dobb	1769
James	Anso	1763	John	Gran	1755
James	Dobb	1769	Joseph	Gran	1755
Wm	Cumb	1767	FARRER, Andrew	NorH	1762
FANNING, Hezekiah	Casw	1777	John	Chow	1753
John	Dobb	1769	Samuel	NorH	1762
John	Dobb	1779	Tanre	NorH	1762
John	Rand	1779	Thomas	NorH	1762
Thomas	Rand	1779	Wm	Gran	1769
Thomas	Rowa	1758	Wm	Gran	1784
FANSHAW, John	Curr	1715	FARRIS, Absalom	Tryo	1776
Moses	Curr	1755	John	Blad	1763
Richard	Curr	1755	Wm	NewH	1744
Thomas Jr.	Curr	1715	FARROW, Abram	FWV	1771
Thomas Sr.	Curr	1715	Frederick	Gate	1786
FARDISHAR, James			Hezekiah	Curr	1755
(Cpt.)	Casw	1777	Isaac	Curr	1755
FAREBOUGH, Jacob	Gran	1784	Jacob	Curr	1755
FARGISON, John	Beau	1755	Jacob Jr.	Curr	1755
FARGUS, James	NewH	1762	FATCH, John	NewH	1762
John	NewH	1762	Onesimus	NewH	1762
John	HewH	1763	FATHERNE, Benjamin	Beau	1764
FARICE, James	Casw	1777	Hillary	Beau	1764
James Jr.	Casw	1777	Wm	Beau	1764
FARIS, Sarah	NewH	1762	FAULK, John	Dobb	1769
Sarah	NewH	1763	John	Edge	1743
Sarah	NewH	1765	Wm	Dobb	1769
Sarah	NewH	1767	Wm	Tyrr	1755
Wm	NewH	1755	FAULKNER, Emanuel	Bute	1771
FARLEY, James	Casw	1777	Emanuel s. Moses		
FARLOW, George	Rand	1779	Aaron	FWV	1771
James	Chow	1717	Emanuel	Gran	1755
James	Chow	1721	Francis	Gran	1755
John	Rowa	1759	James	Anso	1763
Nathan	Rand	1779	James	Dobb	1779
Rachel	Chow	1753	John	Crav	1742
Wm	Rand	1779	Nathan	Bute	1771
FARMER, Asahel	Pitt	1775	Nathan s. Emanuel		
Benjamin	Surr	1771		FWV	1771
Benjamin	Surr	1772	Thomas s. Emanuel		
Conrad	Gran	1769		FWV	1771
Daniel	Casw	1777	Wm	Brun	1769
Gregory	Casw	1777	Wm	Brun	1772
Isaac	Edge	1743	Wm	Bute	1771
John	Gran	1769	Wm	FWV	1771
John	Gran	1784	FAULKS, Moses	Dobb	1769
Joseph	Bert	1757	Richard	Dobb	1769
Joseph	Bert	1769	Wm	Tyrr	1743
Josiah	Gran	1784	FEAL, Thomas	Crav	1743
Mary	Rand	1779	FEALDIN, Wm		
Samuel	Casw	1777	Constable	Anso	1763
Samuel	Oran	1755	FEAR, Barnabus	Surr	1771
Samuel	Rowa	1759	Barnabus	Surr	1772
Thomas	Beau	1744	FEBIN, John	Onsl	1743
Thomas	Casw	1777	FEBRINTON, Nathaniel		
Wm	Blad	1763		Surr	1771
Wm	Cumb	1755	FEE, James	Anso	1763

FEEZER, Jacob	Rowa	1759
FEGIN, George	Cumb	1755
FEIZER, Peter	Surr	1771
FELL, Edward	Bert	1757
FELLOW, Wm	Dobb	1769
FELLOWS, John	Dobb	1769
John	Dobb	1779
Wm	Dobb	1769
FELLS, John	Dobb	1769
FELPS, Aaron	Dobb	1769
James	Chow	1753
Wm	Dobb	1769
FELTON, Job	Surr	1772
John	Gate	1786
Richard	Chow	1753
Richard	Gate	1786
Sarah	Gate	1786
Thomas	Gate	1786
Wm	Chow	1753
FELTS, Francis	Bute	1771
Francis	FWV	1771
Frederick	FWV	1771
Humphrey 50 acres	Perq	1720
John	Perq	1740
Nathaniel	Bute	1771
Nathaniel & s. Roland	FWV	1771
Wm	Perq	1720
FENLEY, Rt. (Robert)	Chow	1717
FENLOW, John	Cumb	1767
FENN, Elisha	Bute	1771
Elisha & s. Wm John	FWV	1771
FENNELL, John	Chow	1753
Nicholas	NewH	1767
FENSINGER, Wm	Onsl	1769
FENTON, Richard	Curr	1755
FERE, Barnabus	Surr	1771
Barnabus	Surr	1772
⟋FERGUS, John	Brun	1769
John	Brun	1772
⟋FERGUSON, Adam 1 slave	Crav	1769
Alexander	Oran	1755
Andrew	Casw	1777
Andrew	Oran	1755
James	Dobb	1769
James	Gran	1755
John	Beau	1755
John	Casw	1777
John	Oran	1755
Joseph	Dobb	1769
Joseph	Gran	1755
Mary	Chow	1721
Slocum 1 slave	Crav	1769
Wm	Gran	1755
Wm	Surr	1772
FERN, Thomas	Crav	1769
FERREBEE, James	Pasq	1769
FERREBY, Jane	Curr	1755
John	Curr	1755
Joseph	Curr	1755
Wm	Curr	1755

FERRELL, Benjamin	Pasq	1769
Bryan	Bute	1771
Bryant	FWV	1771
Charles	Casw	1777
George 1 slave	Pasq	1769
Humphrey	NorH	1762
John	Bute	1771
John	Dobb	1779
John s. John Fred Pullie	FWV	1771
John	Pasq	1754
Joseph	Pasq	1754
Joseph	Pasq	1769
Nicholas	Chow	1717
Nicholas	Chow	1753
Nicholas	Perq	1740
Wm	Bute	1771
Wm	Casw	1777
Wm	Dobb	1779
Wm	FWV	1771
Wm	Pasq	1769
FERRIS, Isaac	NewH	1755
Wm	NewH	1743
Wm	NewH	1744
FERRISTER, Matthew	Cumb	1755
FESQUE, Samuel	Pasq	1769
FERVE, Jacob	Surr	1772
FEWOX, Robert	Chow	1717
Robert	Chow	1721
FFULFORD, John	Crav	1720
John	Pitt	1763
FIDLER, James	Surr	1771
James	Surr	1772
John	Surr	1771
John	Surr	1772
FIELDS, Abigail	Onsl	1769
Abigail	Onsl	1770
Brittle	Dobb	1769
Brittle	Dobb	1779
Davis	Surr	1771
Davis	Surr	1772
James	Perq	1740
Job	Onsl	1769
John Jr.	Rand	1779
John	Rowa	1759
Luke	Surr	1772
Lydia	Rand	1779
Reuben	Bert	1757
Robert	Rowa	1758
Robert	Rowa	1759
Samuel	Onsl	1769
Samuel	Onsl	1770
Smith	Cumb	1767
Widow	Onsl	1770
Zechariah s. of Abigail	Onsl	1769
Zechariah	Onsl	1742
Zechariah	Onsl	1743
Zechariah	Onsl	1750
FIFE, David	Dobb	1769
Thomas	Pitt	1763
FIGG, James	Gate	1786
Joseph	Gate	1786
FIGURDS, Wm	NorH	1762
FIGURES, James	Onsl	1770

FIGURES, Joseph	Onsl	1769	FIVEASHE, Francis	Roan	1720
FIKE, John	Gran	1755	John	Blad	1781
Malachi s. of			John Sr.	Blad	1781
John	Gran	1755	FLAKE, Arthur	Beau	1755
FILGO, Anthony	Bert	1769	Arthur	Pitt	1762
FILLEAU, John	Crav	1742	Arthur	Pitt	1763
FILMAN, Moses	Crav	1741	John	Pitt	1763
FINAKEN, Charles	Pitt	1763	Mary	Pitt	1762
Charles	Pitt	1764	Robert	Beau	1755
FINCH, Edmond	Gran	1784	Robert	Pitt	1762
John	Gran	1769	Samuel	Anso	1763
John	Gran	1784	Samuel	Gran	1755
John Jr.	Gran	1784	Wm	Beau	1755
Wm	Gran	1769	FLANAGAN, John	Gran	1755
Williamson	Gran	1769	FLANIKIN, Edward	Beau	1755
FINCHER, Benjamin	Rand	1779	Richard	Beau	1755
Jonathan	Rand	1779	Richard	Beau	1764
FINCKEN, Charles	Pitt	1762	Wm	Beau	1755
FINLEY, George	Oran	1755	FLANNERY, Thomas	Surr	1771
James	Surr	1771	Thomas	Surr	1772
James	Surr	1772	FLANNIGAN, James	Bert	1742
Robert	Pasq	1769	FLEEMAN, Henry	Gran	1784
FINNEY, John	Onsl	1769	Thomas	Gran	1784
Thomas	Blad	1763	FLEETWOOD, Francis	N.C.	1701
Thomas	NewH	1742	Henry	N.C.	1701
Wm	NorH	1762	Henry Jr.	N.C.	1701
FINSINGER, Wm	Onsl	1770	John	Bert	1769
FIPS, Thomas	Pitt	1764	John	Dobb	1779
FISCUS, Frederick	Surr	1772	Mary	N.C.	1701
FISH, Thomas	Crav	1769	Wm	Bert	1742
Wm	Bute	1771	Wm	Bert	1769
Wm	Edge	1743	FLEMING, Bailey	Gran	1769
Wm	FWV	1771	George	Pitt	1762
FISHER, Adam	Curr	1755	George	Pitt	1763
Andrew	Surr	1771	George	Pitt	1764
Andrew	Surr	1772	James	Chow	1717
George	Crav	1769	John	Bert	1757
George 12			John	Gran	1769
slaves	Curr	1755	John Sr.	Gran	1784
James	Onsl	1770	John	Pitt	1762
James	Surr	1771	John Jr.	Pitt	1762
James	Surr	1772	John	Pitt	1763
John	Chow	1721	John	Pitt	1764
Joseph	Onsl	1770	John Jr.	Pitt	1764
Nathaniel	NewH	1755	Peter	Gran	1769
Randel Constable			Peter	Gran	1784
	Crav	1720	Thomas	Gran	1784
Thomas	Crav	1742	Wm	Gran	1784
FITCH, Thomas	Casw	1777	FLENTON, Job	Surr	1771
Thomas	NewH	1755	FLETCHER, Ambrose	Surr	1771
FITZGERALD, Michael	NewH	1762	Ambrose	Surr	1772
Michael	NewH	1763	Francis	Pasq	1769
Michael	NewH	1765	James	Casw	1777
Michael	NewH	1767	James	Surr	1771
Wm	Surr	1755	James	Surr	1772
Wm	Surr	1771	Ralph 160		
FITZPATRICK, Andrew	Surr	1772	acres	Perq	1720
Edward	Crav	1742	Ralph	Perq	1740
Samuel	Surr	1772	Robert	Curr	1755
FITZRANDOLPH, Benjamin			Wm	Casw	1777
	Blad	1763	FLIAMONDS, John	Bert	1757
Benjamin	Blad	1781	FLING, Daniel	Blad	1763
Chancey	Blad	1763	Daniel	NewH	1755
Gayton	Blad	1763	FLINN, George	Gran	1755
FIVEASHE, Dempsey	Blad	1781	George	Surr	1772

FLINN, Lenn	Surr	1771	FONDRAN, John	Gran	1755
Lenn	Surr	1772	FONVIELLE, David		
Michael	Cumb	1767	7 slaves	Crav	1769
Thomas	Surr	1771	Francis 4 slaves	Crav	1769
Thomas	Surr	1772	Frederick		
FLOOD, Absalom			2 slaves	Crav	1769
w. Mary	Bert	1757	Isaac 6 slaves	Crav	1769
Enoch	Bert	1757	John 7 whites		
Wm	Crav	1769	18 b	Crav	1742
FLOWERS, Edward	Blad	1763	John 12 slaves	Crav	1769
Hardy	Dobb	1769	John Jr.		
John	Anso	1763	12 slaves	Crav	1769
John	Dobb	1779	Wm (Brice		
John Jr.	Perq	1720	7 slaves)	Crav	1769
John Sr.	Perq	1720	FONVILLE, John		
Laurence	Pitt	1775	Const	Onsl	1769
Ransford	NorH	1762	John Constable	Onsl	1770
Simon	Dobb	1769	Stephen	Onsl	1769
Wm	Dobb	1779	FOORD, Alexander	Bert	1769
Wm Jr.	Dobb	1769	Thomas	Cumb	1767
FLOWRAN, Lazarus	Curr	1755	FOOTE, Abner	Dobb	1769
FLOYD, Charles	Gran	1769	George Esq.	Casw	1777
Enoch	Anso	1763	Henry	Bute	1771
Griffin	Beau	1755	Henry	FWV	1771
Griffin	Pitt	1762	Thomas	Dobb	1769
Griffin	Pitt	1763	FORAN, Thomas	Pitt	1762
Griffin	Pitt	1764	Absalom	Gran	1784
James	Casw	1777	Ann	Beau	1755
James	Dobb	1769	Ann	Pitt	1775
John	Beau	1755	Arthur	Pitt	1764
John	Dobb	1769	Arthur	Pitt	1775
John	Pitt	1762	Bailey Sr.	Pasq	1754
John	Pitt	1763	Bailey Jr.	Pasq	1769
John	Pitt	1764	Bailey Sr.	Pasq	1769
Peter	Beau	1755	Charles		
Peter	Beau	1764	Constable	Pitt	1762
Samuel	Dobb	1769	Charles	Pitt	1763
Sandry	NorH	1762	Charles	Pitt	1764
Thomas	Bute	1771	David	Pasq	1769
Thomas	Dobb	1769	Edward	Pasq	1754
Thomas & s.			Henry 1 slave	Pasq	1769
Amos	FWV	1771	Isaac 2 slaves	Pasq	1754
Valentine	Bute	1771	Isaac	Pasq	1769
Wm	Gran	1769	Jacob	Pasq	1754
Wm	Gran	1784	Jacob	Pasq	1769
FLUKER, David	Bute	1771	James	Pasq	1754
David	FWV	1771	John	Beau	1755
FLUQUINION, Daniel	Gran	1755	John (Col.)	NewH	1744
FLYNN, Patrick	Casw	1777	John	Pasq	1754
FOAMHIDE, Moses	Dobb	1769	Joseph	Pitt	1762
FOCKLE, Gottleib	Surr	1771	Joseph	Pitt	1763
Gottlieb	Surr	1772	Joseph	Pitt	1764
FOGGATEE, Edmund	Blad	1763	Joseph	Pitt	1775
FOLD, Richard	Onsl	1741	Luke	Pasq	1769
FOLES, David	Surr	1771	Moses	Pasq	1754
FOLEY, Mason	Casw	1777	Thomas	Pasq	1769
FOLKNER, Wm	Dobb	1769	Wm	Anso	1750
FOLKS, Andrew	Surr	1771	Wm	NewH	1741
John	Beau	1755	FORBIS, David	Surr	1771
John	NewH	1763	FORBUS, George Jr.	Rowa	1759
John	NewH	1765	FORBUSH, David	Surr	1772
Solomon	Dobb	1779	FORCECLOTH, Wm	Dobb	1769
Wm	Dobb	1779	Wm s. of Wm	Dobb	1769
FOLSOM, Ebenezer	Beau	1755	FORD, Absalom	Gran	1784
Nathaniel	Beau	1755	Alexander	Bert	1757

FORD, Benjamin	Gran	1755
Daniel	Crav	1769
David	Casw	1777
Henry	Casw	1777
John	Oran	1755
Marcus Constable	NewH	1767
Nath	Beau	1755
Simeon	Gran	1769
Simon	Casw	1777
Simon	NorH	1762
Thomas	Gran	1755
Wm s. of Thomas	Gran	1755
FORDHAM, Benjamin	Crav	1744
Benjamin Jr.	Crav	1769
Benjamin Sr.	Crav	1769
FORDICE, George	N.C.	1701
FORE, Daniel	Pitt	1762
FOREHAM, James	Dobb	1769
FOREHAND, Anthony	Pasq	1769
Boswell	Pasq	1769
Daniel s.		
Thomas	Pasq	1769
David	Pasq	1769
James	Dobb	1769
James	Pasq	1769
Jarvis s. Thomas	Pasq	1769
Lemuel	Pasq	1769
Thomas	Pasq	1769
FOREMAN, Ben.	Chow	1717
Benj.	Roan	1720
Benjamin	Edge	1741
Caleb	Hyde	1764
Elizabeth	N.C.	1701
George	NewH	1755
John	N.C.	1701
Wm	Edge	1734
FORESETT, Francis	Onsl	1770
FORKNER, Lewis	Surr	1771
Lewis	Surr	1772
Robert	Dobb	1779
Wm Jr.	Surr	1771
Wm Sr.	Surr	1771
Wm Jr.	Surr	1772
Wm Sr.	Surr	1772
FORKSEY, Benjamin	Pasq	1754
Ezekiel	Pasq	1754
Philip	Pasq	1754
FORN, Thomas	Bert	1757
FORNAM, John Jr.	Bert	1769
FORREST, Henry	Gate	1786
FORRISTER, Francis	Brun	1772
James	Beau	1755
James Jr.	Oran	1755
James Sr.	Oran	1755
James	Perq	1740
James	Surr	1771
John	Brun	1772
Mary, Executor	NewH	1767
Richard	Gran	1769
Thomas	Oran	1755
Wm	Blad	1763
Wm	Oran	1755
FORSET, Francis	Bert	1757
FORSYTHE, John	Gran	1784
Thomas	Gran	1769

FORT, Benjamin	Dobb	1769
Benjamin	Dobb	1779
Elias	Anso	1750
John	Edge	1742
Wm	Dobb	1769
FORTESKUE, Luke	Hyde	1744
FOSCUE, Benjamin	Crav	1769
Richard	Crav	1769
FOSQUE, Simon	Crav	1769
FOSTER, Christopher	Bute	1771
Christopher	FWV	1771
Francis	Perq	1720
Francis	Perq	1740
James	Rand	1779
John	Bute	1771
John	FWV	1771
Kim	Onsl	1770
Kimmy	Onsl	1769
Robert	FWV	1771
Samuel	Brun	1772
Wm	Crav	1769
Wm (Sheppard)	Crav	1769
Wm (N. W.)	Onsl	1769
Wm	Onsl	1770
FOULKS, John	NewH	1765
FOUNTAIN, Francis		
Sr.	Dobb	1769
Francis Jr.	Dobb	1769
Peter	Dobb	1769
FOUSE, Jacob	Rand	1779
FOUTS, Andrew	Rand	1779
David	Rand	1779
David Jr.	Rand	1779
Jacob	Rand	1779
John (Michl.)	Rand	1779
John Jr.	Rand	1779
John Sr.	Rand	1779
Michael	Rand	1779
FOWLER, Ann	Brun	1772
Arthur	Rand	1779
Edward	Blad	1781
Edward	Gran	1755
Elisha	Oran	1755
John	Bute	1771
John & s. James	FWV	1771
John	Gran	1769
John	Gran	1784
John	Rand	1779
Richard	Gran	1769
Richard Jr.	Gran	1769
Richard	Gran	1784
Samuel	Gran	1755
Thomas	Gran	1769
Wm	Gran	1769
Wm	Gran	1784
FOX, Aaron	Onsl	1769
Aaron	Onsl	1770
John	Pasq	1769
Laurence	FWV	1771
Moses	Onsl	1769
Moses	Onsl	1770
Thomas	Gran	1755
Thomas	Onsl	1769
Thomas	Onsl	1770
FOXWORTH, Moses	Chow	1717

FOXWORTH, Moses	Chow	1721
Joseph	Perq	1740
Wm	Perq	1740
FOY, Francis	Chow	1753
James 2 slaves	Crav	1769
James	Onsl	1770
Job	Crav	1769
John 7 slaves	Crav	1769
Thomas 10 slaves	Crav	1769
FOYLES, James	Onsl	1769
James	Onsl	1770
Rose	Onsl	1770
Sam	Onsl	1770
FRANCIS, Edward	Surr	1772
Joseph	N.C.	1701
Matthew	Surr	1771
Matthew	Surr	1772
Richard	Dobb	1779
FRANCK, Edward	Crav	1769
Eliner 4 slaves	Crav	1769
FRANCKS, John	Crav	1750
FRANK, Martin	Crav	1742
Wm	Rowa	1759
FRANKLIN, Bentley	Anso	1763
Edward	Rand	1779
Laurence	Anso	1763
Thomas	Crav	1769
FRANKS, Jacob	Cumb	1767
FRANKUM, Joshua	Brun	1769
Joshua	Brun	1772
FRAYSHEAR, Wm	Anso	1763
FRAZIER, Caleb	Rand	1779
Daniel	Bert	1757
Daniel	Bert	1769
Daniel	Crav	1769
Daniel	Gran	1769
Ephraim	Gran	1784
George	Rand	1779
Jacob	Onsl	1769
Jacob	Onsl	1770
James	Onsl	1769
Jeremiah	Gran	1769
Jeremiah	Gran	1784
John	Bert	1757
John	Rand	1770
John	Rowa	1759
Malachi	Bert	1769
Samuel	Crav	1769
Sarah	Gran	1784
Thomas	Chow	1753
Thomas	Crav	1769
Thomas	Rand	1779
Wm	Bert	1757
Wm	Gran	1769
Wm	Gran	1784
FREDERICK, Felix	FWV	1771
John	Anso	1763
Thomas	Cumb	1755
FREE, Christian	Onsl	1769
Jonathan	Onsl	1770
Moses	Rand	1779
FREEMAN, Bridges	Bute	1771
Bridges	FWV	1771
David	Bert	1769
Demsey	Gate	1786

FREEMAN, Edward	Bute	1771
Edward	FWV	1771
Elizabeth	Bute	1771
Elizabeth s. Henry		
John & Joseph	FWV	1771
Gabriel	Rand	1779
James	Bert	1757
James	Gate	1786
John	Beau	1764
John	Bert	1757
John Jr.	Bert	1757
John (Cpt.)	Bert	1769
John	Chow	1753
John	Dobb	1769
John s. of John	Dobb	1769
John	Rowa	1759
Jonathan	Rowa	1759
Joshua	Bert	1769
King	Bert	1769
Mapes	Bert	1769
Michael	Bert	1779
Richard	Chow	1753
Richard	Gate	1786
Samuel	Gran	1755
Samuel	Rowa	1759
Samuel	Surr	1771
Samuel	Surr	1772
Solomon	Bert	1769
Stephen	Blad	1763
Thomas	Blad	1763
Thomas	Chow	1753
Wm	Bute	1771
Wm 150 acres	Chow	1721
Wm	Chow	1753
Wm & s. Robert		
Wm	FWV	1771
FRENCH, Elizabeth	Perq	1720
James	Anso	1763
John	Crav	1750
Joseph	Onsl	1770
Joshua	Onsl	1769
Michael	Crav	1744
Samuel	Anso	1763
Vouchier	Onsl	1769
FRESHWATER, Thaddius		
	Pasq	1769
Wm 3 slaves	Pasq	1769
FREYSER, Josiah	Edge	1734
FRIAR, George	Cumb	1767
FRIZELL, John	Pitt	1764
FROHOCK, John	Rowa	1759
FRONE, Peter	N.C.	1701
FROST, Edward	Dobb	1769
Joshua	Surr	1771
Wm	Chow	1717
FRYE, Christian	Rowa	1759
John	Beau	1755
Michael	Surr	1771
Michael	Surr	1772
Peter	Rowa	1759
Peter Jr.	Surr	1771
Peter	Surr	1772
FRYER, Isaac	Gate	1786
James	Chow	1753
Richard	Chow	1721

FRYER, Thomas	Gate	1786	FULP, George	Surr	1771
Wm	Chow	1753	George	Surr	1772
Wm	Gate	1786	FULREL, Thomas	NorH	1762
FRYLEY, Frederick	Rowa	1759	FULSHER, Jacob	Crav	1769
Wm	Chow	1717	Jesse 2 slaves	Crav	1769
Wm 1,854 acres	Chow	1721	Joshua	Crav	1769
FUDGE, Jacob	Crav	1742	Wm r slaves	Crav	1769
FULCAR, John	Curr	1755	FULTCH, George	Cumb	1755
FULCHER, James	Casw	1777	FULTON, John	Pitt	1764
Wm	Casw	1777	Joseph	Gran	1755
Wm	Crav	1744	Thomas	Cumb	1767
FULFORD, John	Pitt	1763	FUNCANNON, Peter	Rand	1779
FULGHAM, John	Dobb	1779	FUNTON, Wm	Pitt	1775
FULGUM, John	Dobb	1769	FUR, Joseph	Gran	1755
Michael	Dobb	1769	FURBUSH,	Pasq	1754
Rayford	Dobb	1769	FURNELL, Algernon	NewH	1762
FULKERSON, Abraham	Casw	1777	Algernon	NewH	1763
Abraham	Surr	1771	FURREL, Wm	Casw	1777
Abraham	Surr	1772	FUSSELL, Aaron	FWV	1771
James	Surr	1771	Aaron Jr.	FWV	1771
FULLAM, Barnet	Gran	1784	Aaron	Gran	1755
FULLELOVE, John	Gran	1769	Benjamin	NewH	1741
FULLER, Alexander	Onsl	1769	Benjamin	NewH	1744
Alexander	Onsl	1770	Moses	FWV	1771
Arthur	Gran	1755	Thomas s. of Aaron		
Brittain	Rand	1779		Gran	1755
David	Gran	1784	FUTCH, John	NewH	1763
Elijah	Casw	1777	John	NewH	1765
Elizabeth	Bute	1771	John	NewH	1767
Elizabeth s. David			Neeimus	NewH	1755
	FWV	1771	Onesimus	NewH	1763
Ezekiel	Gran	1769	Onesimus	NewH	1765
Ezekiel	Gran	1784	Onesimus	NewH	1767
Henry	Casw	1777	Wm	NewH	1763
Henry	Gran	1755	Wm	NewH	1765
Henry	Gran	1769	FUTICAL, Thomas	Pitt	1764
Henry Sr. Constable			FUTRELL, Thomas	Chow	1721
	Gran	1784	Thomas	NorH	1762
Henry Jr.	Gran	1784	Thomas	Roan	1720
Israel	Gran	1769	FUZZELL, Aaron	Bute	1771
James	Casw	1777	Aaron Jr.	Bute	1771
John	Casw	1777	Moses	Bute	1771
John T.	Casw	1777			
Jones	Gran	1784			
Joseph	Gran	1784			
Nehemiah	Casw	1777	GABRIEL, Nathaniel	Crav	1769
Peter	Casw	1777	GADDIS, Isaac	Oran	1755
Samuel	Gran	1755	James	Rand	1779
Samuel	Gran	1769	John	Surr	1772
Samuel Esq.	Gran	1784	GAFF, Henry	Cumb	1755
Settleton	Gran	1784	GAINER, Arthur	Tyrr	1755
Solomon Jr.	Gran	1769	GAINES, Michael	Rand	1779
Solomon	NorH	1741	Wm	Bert	1757
Timothy	Gran	1755	Wm	Bert	1769
Wm	Casw	1777	GAINEY, Wm	Chow	1717
FULLERTON, Andrew	Beau	1764	Wm Jr.	Chow	1717
Mathias	Chow	1753	Wm 1,100 acres	Chow	1721
Robert	Chow	1721	GAIRNS, John	NewH	1762
FULLINGTON, Judith	Gate	1786	GALBREATH, John	FWV	1771
Thomas	Chow	1753	Wm & s. Wm	FWV	1771
FULLS, George	Oran	1755	GALE, Christopher	Beau	1717
FULLWOOD, Andrew	Onsl	1769	Miles	Chow	1753
Andrew	Onsl	1770	GALLIMORE, John	Gran	1755
Mary	Onsl	1750	John	Gran	1769
FULMORE, John	Crav	1769	GALLIN, John	Crav	1741

GALLOP, Abel	Pasq	1754
John	Pasq	1754
John	Pasq	1769
John 1 slave	Pasq	1769
Jonas	Pasq	1754
Jonas	Pasq	1769
Jonas Jr.	Pasq	1769
Mark Sr.	Pasq	1754
Mark Jr.	Pasq	1769
Mark Sr.	Pasq	1769
GALLOWAY, Benjamin	Blad	1763
Caleb	Blad	1763
John	Brun	1769
John	Brun	1772
John	Dobb	1779
Mary	Chow	1753
Thomas	Brun	1769
Thomas	Brun	1772
Thomas	NewH	1755
Wm	Brun	1769
Wm	Brun	1772
GAMALIEL, Christian	Dobb	1769
Henry	Dobb	1769
GAMBLE, David	Surr	1772
James	Surr	1772
Martin	Surr	1772
GAMBLING, James	Pasq	1769
Jesse	Pasq	1769
Joshua & s.		
James	Pasq	1769
Joshua s. Joshua	Pasq	1769
GAMISE, Elwood	Casw	1777
GAMWELL, James	Pasq	1769
GANER, James	Tyrr	1755
GANN, Henry		
GANT, Isham	Bute	1771
Isham s. of John	Gran	1755
John	Gran	1755
John s. of John	Gran	1755
GARDINER, Isaac	Tyrr	1755
Samuel	Tyrr	1755
Thomas	Tyrr	1755
GARDNER, Alvin	Dobb	1779
Conway	Gran	1769
Henry	Rand	1779
James	Bert	1769
James	Bute	1771
James	Cumb	1767
James	Dobb	1769
James	FWV	1771
John	Bert	1769
John 150 acres	Chow	1721
John 500 acres	Chow	1721
John	Rowa	1759
Joseph	Cumb	1767
Josiah	NewH	1762
Lewis	Dobb	1769
Mart. 1,400 acres		
	Chow	1721
Martin	Bert	1743
Martin	Bert	1769
Needham	Dobb	1779
Wm	Bert	1742
Wm	Chow	1721
Wm Esq.	Cumb	1767

GARGANUS, James	Onsl	1769
James	Onsl	1741
James	Onsl	1770
Jesse	Onsl	1770
John	Onsl	1769
John	Onsl	1770
Nicholas	Onsl	1769
Nicholas	Onsl	1770
Zachariah	Onsl	1769
Zachariah	Onsl	1770
GARLAND, John	Dobb	1769
John	Dobb	1779
Samuel	Surr	1771
Samuel	Surr	1772
GARLINGTON, John	Crav	1769
John	NewH	1767
GARNER, Henry	Rowa	1759
James	Rand	1779
John	Bert	1757
John	Cumb	1767
John	Gran	1784
John	Oran	1755
John (Foushar)	Rand	1779
Joseph	Pitt	1762
Joseph	Pitt	1763
Lewis	Dobb	1779
Martin Jr.	Bert	1757
Martin Sr.	Bert	1757
Vincent	Rand	1779
GARNES, Elijah	Rand	1779
Jacob	Rand	1779
GARNETT, Anthony	Gran	1755
GARRALD, James	Pitt	1762
Wm	Pitt	1762
GARREL, Jesse	Bert	1769
GARRETT, Benjamin	Surr	1771
Benjamin	Surr	1772
Daniel	Chow	1717
Daniel	Chow	1721
Daniel (or David)		
	Rowa	1759
Daniel Jr.	Tyrr	1755
Daniel Sr.	Tyrr	1755
Everett	Chow	1753
James	Curr	1755
James	Pitt	1763
James	Pitt	1764
Jesse	Gran	1784
John	Beau	1755
John	Casw	1777
John	Chow	1753
John	Curr	1755
John	Surr	1771
Joseph	Surr	1771
Joseph	Surr	1772
Matthew	FWV	1771
Mr.	N.C.	1701
Mrs.	Beau	1755
Nathaniel	Bute	1771
Nathaniel	FWV	1771
Richard	Chow	1753
Thomas	Beau	1755
Thomas Jr.	Beau	1755
Thomas Jr.	Chow	1717
Thomas Sr.	Chow	1717

GARRETT, Thomas Jr.		GATLIN, Lazarus	Crav 1769
	Chow 1721	Thomas	Crav 1769
Thomas Sr.	Chow 1721	Thomas	NewH 1741
Thomas Jr.	Chow 1753	GATLING, George	Gate 1786
Thomas Sr.	Chow 1753	Wm	Chow 1753
Thomas	FWV 1771	Wm	Gate 1786
Thomas	Pitt 1764	Wm Jr.	Gate 1786
Truman	Curr 1755	GATTES, Isham	Casw 1777
Wm	Bute 1771	GAUNT, Andrew	FWV 1771
Wm overseer	FWV 1771	Edward	Bute 1771
Wm	Pitt 1763	Edward	FWV 1771
Wm	Pitt 1764	Isham	Bute 1771
GARREY, Thomas	Edge 1741	Isham	FWV 1771
GARRIS, Benjamin	Dobb 1779	John	Bute 1771
John	Dobb 1779	John & s.	
John	NorH 1762	Charles	FWV 1771
John	NorH 1762	GAVIN, Charles	Chow 1717
GARRISON, Isaac		Widow 780 acres	Chow 1721
Sr.	Surr 1771	GAVINS, Charles	
Isaac Jr.	Surr 1772	3 w 2 b	Dupl 1752
Isaac Sr.	Surr 1772	Charles 10 black	
GARRON, Jacob	Rand 1779		Dupl 1752
GARROSS, Benjamin	Onsl 1769	GAWSE, Needham	
GARROTT, Daniel	Beau 1764	5 bla	Brun 1769
John	Beau 1764	Wm 7 slaves	Brun 1769
John Jr.	Beau 1764	Wm	Brun 1772
John	Pasq 1769	GAY, Jesse	Onsl 1769
Thomas	Pitt 1762	Jesse	Onsl 1770
GARVES, Job	Surr 1771	John Jr.	Norh 1762
GARVIN, Alexander	Casw 1777	John Sr.	NorH 1762
Daniel	Casw 1777	Thomas	Bute 1771
David	Casw 1777	Thomas	FWV 1771
Jesse	Casw 1777	Wm	NewH 1755
John	Casw 1777	Wm	NewH 1762
Joseph	Pitt 1764	Wm	NewH 1763
Matthew	Blad 1763	Wm	NewH 1775
Seythe	Casw 1777	GAYLER, Thomas	Hyde 1764
GASKINS, Cattarn	Pasq 1754	GAYTON	Blad 1763
David	Bert 1769	GAZIABLERK, John	Beau 1741
John	Oran 1755	GEAN, Philip	NorH 1762
Levin	Curr 1755	GEANEY, Thomas	Chow 1721
Thomas	Crav 1769	GEARIN, Joseph	Rand 1779
Thomas 3 slaves	Pasq 1769	GEDIONS, Benjamin	NewH 1762
GASSAWAY, Thomas	Surr 1772	GEE, Charles	NewH 1762
GASTON, Alexander	Crav 1769	John	Cumb 1767
Henry	Cumb 1767	Philip	Gran 1755
GATES, Dovet	Gran 1769	GEER, John's	
Lovet	Oran 1755	Estate	Gran 1769
Lovet	Gran 1784	GELLOW, Peter	N.C. 1701
Peter	Blad 1763	GENERETT, Elias	NewH 1762
Wm	Rand 1779	Elias' Estate	NewH 1763
GATEWOOD, Ambrose	Casw 1777	John	Brun 1772
Dudley	Casw 1777	GENET, Abraham	Perq 1740
GATHANS, Benjamin	Oran 1755	GENNINGER, George	Cumb 1767
Philip	Bute 1771	GENNY, Wm	Gran 1784
Philip	FWV 1771	GENTRY, Allen	Casw 1777
Wm	Oran 1755	Allen	Surr 1772
GATLIN, David	Crav 1769	Elkanah	Onsl 1769
Edward	Crav 1769	Elkanah	Onsl 1770
Edward 4 slaves		Mezhi	Surr 1772
	Crav 1769	Nicholas	Surr 1772
Elizabeth	Crav 1769	Richard	Surr 1771
James 4 slaves		Richard	Surr 1772
	Crav 1769	Samuel	Casw 1777
John	Crav 1769	Samuel	Surr 1771

GENTRY, Samuel	Surr 1772		GIBSON, Isel	Casw 1777
Shadrack	Casw 1777		Jacob	Surr 1771
GEORGE, Daniel	FWV 1771		James	Anso 1763
David	Crav 1742		James	Casw 1777
David	Pasq 1769		James Jr.	Casw 1777
David dec. 1784	Ruth 1784		Jerdon	Anso 1763
David	Tryo 1776		Joel	Casw 1777
Jesse	Surr 1772		John	Perq 1720
Moses 1 slave	Rand 1779		John	Rand 1779
Nancy 1 slave	Crav 1769		Mager	Oran 1755
Susannah 1 slave			Major	Rand 1779
	Crav 1769		Robert	Onsl 1769
Wm 1 slave	Crav 1769		Thomas	Anso 1763
GERGANUS, Francis	Pitt 1763		Thomas	Oran 1755
Solomon	Pitt 1763		Valentine	Surr 1771
GERMAN, John	Dobb 1769		Valentine	Surr 1772
John Jr.	Dobb 1769		Walter	Anso 1763
Joseph	Dobb 1769		Walter	Cumb 1755
GERROD, John	Beau 1755		Walter	1767
John	Oran 1755		Wm	Edge 1734
GESKIN, Benjamin	Beau 1764		Wm	Onsl 1769
GESS, Wm	Surr 1771		Wm	Onsl 1770
GEST, Christopher	Cumb 1767		Wm 6 slaves	Pasq 1769
Joshua	Cumb 1767		Wm	Surr 1771
GETLING, John	Gate 1786		Wm	Surr 1772
GIBBLE, Frederick	Dobb 1769		GIDDINGS, Abraham	Beau 1755
GIBBONS, Henry	Bert 1757		Abraham	Onsl 1769
Henry	Bert 1769		Abraham	Pitt 1762
Henry	Crav 1744		Isaac	Pitt 1762
Henry	Onsl 1769		Isaac	Pitt 1763
Henry	Onsl 1770		Isaac Jr.	Pitt 1763
Jonathan	Onsl 1769		Isaac	Pitt 1764
Stephen	Curr 1755		Isaac	Pitt 1775
Stephen	Perq 1720		Jacob	Beau 1755
Wm	Gran 1755		Jacob	Beau 1764
GIBBS, Cornelius	Gran 1755		Jacob	Onsl 1770
George	Blad 1763		Jacob	Pitt 1762
George	NewH 1755		Jacob Jr.	Pitt 1762
Henry	Curr 1715		Jacob	Pitt 1763
Henry	Curr 1742		Jacob Jr.	Pitt 1763
John	Bert 1757		Jacob	Pitt 1764
John	Gran 1755		Jacob Jr.	Pitt 1764
John Constable	Gran 1755		James	Pitt 1762
John	NewH 1755		James	Pitt 1763
John	NewH 1762		Thomas	Pitt 1762
John	NewH 1763		Thomas	Pitt 1763
Richard	Dobb 1769		Thomas	Pitt 1764
Richard	Oran 1755		Wm	Pitt 1762
GIBSON, Alexander	Brun 1772		Wm	Pitt 1763
Andrew	Casw 1777		GIDEONS, Thomas	NewH 1767
Ann	Gate 1786		GIELDINGS, Thomas	Beau 1742
Charles	Oran 1755		GILBERT, Benjamin	Beau 1764
David	Rand 1779		Benjamin	Crav 1769
Edw.	Roan 1720		Benjamin	Pasq 1769
Edward	Chow 1721		Francis	Beau 1755
Elijah	Anso 1763		Francis	Beau 1764
George	Oran 1755		Gideon	Cumb 1755
George	Rand 1779		Jeremiah 2 slaves	
Henry	Curr 1715			Pasq 1769
Hubbard Jr.	Chow 1721		Joel	Pasq 1769
Hubbard Jr.	Roan 1720		John	Crav 1769
Hubbard Sr.	Roan 1720		John	NewH 1762
Humphrey	Surr 1771		John	NewH 1763
Humphrey	Surr 1772		John	NewH 1767
Isaac	Onsl 1769		John	Pasq 1754

GILBERT, John	Pasq	1769		GILLS, Thomas	Surr	1771
John Jr.	Pasq	1769		GILLSON, David	Casw	1777
John	Surr	1771		Samuel	Casw	1777
John	Surr	1772		GILLYARD, Samuel	Crav	1742
Joseph	Chow	1717		GILMAN, James	Bert	1757
Joseph	Chow	1721		GILMORE, Hugh	Cumb	1755
Joseph	Crav	1769		Hugh	Cumb	1767
Josiah	Perq	1740		John	Cumb	1755
Nicholas	Tyrr	1755		John Sr.	Cumb	1767
Thomas 1 slave				Stephen	Cumb	1755
	Pasq	1769		Stephen	Cumb	1767
Thomas	Perq	1740		GILREATH, John	Bute	1771
Wm	Crav	1769		Wm	Bute	1771
Wm	Dobb	1779		GILSTRAP, Idolet	Crav	1769
Wm	Gate	1786		Peter	Crav	1769
GILCUT, John	Bert	1757		GIMMALIAN, Christian		
GILDINGS, Wm	Hyde	1744			Dobb	1779
GILES, Bowers	Gran	1755		GINKINS, David	Rowa	1759
Crispin	Rand	1779		Henry	Pitt	1762
John	Anso	1763		Henry	Pitt	1763
John	Crav	1745		John	Pitt	1762
Wm	Rowa	1759		John	Pitt	1764
GILFORD, Andrew	Beau	1755		Thomas	Rowa	1759
Demsey	Pasq	1769		GINN, George	Rowa	1759
Isaac	Pasq	1769		Hardy	Dobb	1769
Jacob	Pasq	1769		Jacob	Dobb	1769
Joseph	Pasq	1754		John	Rowa	1759
Joseph	Pasq	1769		Moses	Oran	1755
Wm	Pasq	1769		Wm	Chow	1721
GILGOE, Wm	Crav	1769		GINNIT, Jabin	Curr	1755
GILL, James	Gran	1755		GIOR, John	Perq	1740
Jonas	Gran	1755		GIPSON, James	Perq	1740
Joseph	Gran	1769		Robert	Curr	1755
Joseph	Gran	1784		GIRGAMUS, Francis	Pitt	1762
Levi	Crav	1769		Francis	Pitt	1764
Wm	Gran	1784		GIRKING, Joshua	Tyrr	1755
GILLAM, Charles	Gran	1769		Zachia	Tyrr	1755
Harris	Gran	1755		GIRKINS, Zackery	Chow	1721
Harris	Gran	1769		GISEN, John	Pasq	1769
Harris	Gran	1784		GIST, Nathaniel	Cumb	1767
Jesse	Bute	1771		GLANGER, Calope	NewH	1755
Jesse	FWV	1771		Joshua	NewH	1755
Robert	Gran	1769		GLANN, Henry	Onsl	1770
Wm	Gran	1769		GLASGOW, Daniel		
Wm Jr.	Gran	1769		Jr.	Curr	1715
GILLESPIE, Archibald				Daniel Sr.	Curr	1715
	Onsl	1770		Daniel	Curr	1755
Elijah	Surr	1772		James		1779
James	Casw	1777		Richard	Gran	1784
Robert	Gran	1784		Thomas	Curr	1755
GILLETT, Alexander	Onsl	1769		GLASS, Levey	Blad	1763
Alexander	Onsl	1770		Wm	Gran	1784
Anderson	Onsl	1769		GLASSCOCK, Lemuel	Curr	1755
Anderson	Onsl	1770		GLAUGHAN, Edward	Bert	1769
John	Cart	1752		John	Bert	1769
Patterson	Dobb	1769		GLAZE, Benjamin	Gran	1769
GILLEY, Robert	Gran	1755		Catherine	Gran	1784
Wm	Gran	1755		Joseph	Gran	1769
GILLIAM, John	Gran	1784		Thomas	Gran	1784
Wm	Gran	1784		GLENN, George	Surr	1772
GILLIAN, James	Cumb	1755		Hugh	Onsl	1769
GILLICAN, Thomas	Crav	1720		James	Surr	1771
GILLISPIE, Lydia	Onsl	1769		James	Surr	1772
Matthew	Rowa	1759		John	Anso	1763
Thomas	Rowa	1759		Richard	Chow	1721

GLENN, Tyree	Surr 1771	GODFREY, Joseph Sr.	
Tyree	Surr 1772		Pasq 1769
Wm	Casw 1777	Thomas	Perq 1740
Wm	Rowa 1759	Wm	Brun 1772
GLIDEWELL, Robert	Gran 1755	Wm 300 acres	Perq 1720
GLINN, Robert	Casw 1777	Wm s. of Wm	Perq 1720
GLISSON, Abraham	Beau 1755	GODLEY, Nathan	Beau 1755
Abraham	Pitt 1762	NATHAN	Pitt 1762
Abraham	Pitt 1763	Nathan	Pitt 1764
Abraham	Pitt 1764	Thomas	Onsl 1769
Daniel	Bert 1757	Thomas	Onsl 1770
Daniel	Bert 1769	GODSON, Ben	Chow 1717
Dennis	Beau 1755	GOEPFERT, George	Surr 1771
Dennis	Tyrr 1741	GOFF, Gregory	Dobb 1769
Isaac s. of		Henry Sr.	Oran 1755
Dennis	Beau 1755	John	NewH 1755
Isaac	Beau 1755	Nathaniel	Oran 1755
Jacob s. of		Thomas	Pitt 1762
Dennis	Beau 1755	Thomas	Pitt 1763
James	Beau 1755	Thomas	Pitt 1764
James	Bert 1757	Thomas	Pitt 1775
James	Bert 1769	GOFFORD, Andrew	Pitt 1762
James	Pitt 1762	Andrew	Pitt 1763
Joseph	Beau 1755	GOFORTH, Miles	Casw 1777
Joseph	Pitt 1762	Miles	Oran 1755
GLITON, Joseph	Dobb 1779	GOINE, Edward	FWV 1771
GLOVER, Cha.	Chow 1717	GOING, Joseph s.	
Daniel	Gran 1784	of Wm	Gran 1755
Elisha	Onsl 1769	Thomas	Gran 1755
Elisha	Onsl 1770	Wm	Gran 1755
George	Gran 1755	GOINS, Wm	Cumb 1767
Henry	Bute 1771	GOLD, Ephraim	Casw 1777
Henry	FWV 1771	Joseph	Casw 1777
Jacob	Gran 1784	GOLDEN, John	Bute 1771
John	Gran 1784	John Jr.	Bute 1771
John	Pasq 1769	John	Chow 1717
Joseph	Gran 1755	John & s.	
Joseph	Gran 1769	Richard	FWV 1771
Lowry s. of Wm	Gran 1755	John Jr.	FWV 1771
Thomas	Bute 1771	Wm	FWV 1771
Thomas	FWV 1771	GOLDINE, John	FWV 1771
Wm	Bert 1741	John Jr.	FWV 1771
Wm	Gran 1755	John	Gran 1755
Wm	Gran 1784	John Jr.	Gran 1755
Zach	Onsl 1769	Wm	FWV 1771
GOANS, Richard	Oran 1755	Goldsborough, Thomas	
GOBER, George	Gran 1784		Beau 1755
GODBEY, Nathan	Beau 1755	GOLDSBY, Danny	Rand 1779
Nathan	Pitt 1763	Drury	Rand 1779
GODDAM, Josiah	Bert 1769	GOLDSMITH, Daniel	Chow 1753
GODETT, Nancy	Crav 1769	GOLDWIN, Ann	Brun 1772
Nathan	Pitt 1762	Joseph 3 slaves	
Wm	Crav 1769		Brun 1769
GODFREY, David	Pasq 1769	Joseph	Brun 1772
Francis	Onsl 1770	GOLLIN, John	Dobb 1769
Isaac	Surr 1771	GOLLOHAN, John	NewH 1767
Jacob	Pasq 1754	GOLSON, Charles	Rand 1779
Jacob	Pasq 1769	GOOCH, Gideon	Gran 1784
James	Crav 1769	Joseph	Gran 1784
James	Gran 1784	Rowland	Gran 1784
Jesse	Pasq 1769	Wm Sr.	Casw 1777
John s. of Wm	Perq 1720	Wm	Casw 1777
Joseph	Pasq 1754	GOOD, Joseph	Crav 1769
Joseph Jr.	Pasq 1754	Peter	Gran 1769
Joseph Jr.	Pasq 1769	Richard	Surr 1771

GOOD, Richard	Surr	1772	GOODWIN, John	Gran	1784
Thomas	Edge	1742	Lucy	Bute	1771
Thomas	Surr	1771	Lucy	FWV	1771
Thomas	Surr	1772	Peter	Bute	1771
Timothy	Rand	1779	Peter	FWV	1771
GOODE, John	Gran	1769	Samuel	Gran	1784
GOODEN, Drury	Pitt	1764	Theophilus Jr.	Bute	1771
Richard Sr.	Cumb	1767	Theophilus Sr.	Bute	1771
Wm	Dobb	1779	Theophilus	Edge	1741
GOODIN, Henry s. of			Theophilus Jr.	Fwv	1771
Theophilis	Gran	1755	Theophilus Sr.	FWV	1771
Theophilis s. of			Thomas	Bute	1771
Theophilis	Gran	1755	Thomas & s.		
Theophilis	Gran	1755	Matthew	FWV	1771
GOODINE, Nelson	Gran	1755	Thomas & brother		
Vinson	Gran	1755	Mark	FWV	1771
GOODING, Aaron	Crav	1769	Thomas	Gran	1755
John	Chow	1717	GOOFE, Wm	Oran	1755
John	Chow	1721	GORBY, James	Casw	1777
John	Chow	1753	GORDON, Alexander		
John	Crav	1769	Esq.	Anso	1763
Joseph	Chow	1753	Benjamin	Gate	1786
GOODLOE, Robert	Bute	1771	David	Surr	1772
Robert	FWV	1771	George	Perq	1720
Robert	Gran	1784	George	Perq	1740
GOODMAN, Benjamin	Gran	1769	Isaac	Gran	1784
Charles & wife			Jacob	Gate	1786
Jane	FWV	1771	John	Chow	1753
Henry	Chow	1753	John	Gate	1786
Henry	Gate	1786	John	NorH	1763
Jacob	Curr	1755	John Esq.	Oran	1755
James	Dobb	1779	John	Perq	1740
Joel's Estate	Gate	1786	Patrick 5 slaves	Crav	1769
John	Gate	1786	Wm	Pasq	1769
Overton	Casw	1777	GORE, Wm	Brun	1772
Samuel	Blad	1743	GORHAM, Alexander	Chow	1721
Samuel	Blad	1763	John	Chow	1717
Timothy	Dobb	1769	GORJARD, Hardy	Pitt	1763
Wm	Chow	1753	GORMAN, John	Surr	1771
Wm	Dobb	1779	GORSORT, Wm	Oran	1755
Wm	Gate	1786	GORST, John	Pitt	1764
GOODRICH, Benjamin	Cumb	1755	GOSS, Frederick	Rowa	1759
Matthew	FWV	1771	Sherman	Gran	1784
Wm	Bute	1771	Thomas	Casw	1777
Wm & s. Lewis	FWV	1771	Thomas	Gran	1755
GOODRIDGE, Jeremiah			Thomas	Gran	1769
(Cpt.)	N.C.	1701	Thomas	Gran	1784
Walter	N.C.	1701	GOSS, Wm	NewH	1762
GOODSMAN, Henry	Dobb	1769	Wm	NewH	1763
GOODSON, John	Dobb	1769	Wm	Oran	1755
GOODVINE, Wm	Onsl	1769	Zachariah	Gran	1769
Wm	Onsl	1770	GOSSETT, Henry	Rand	1779
GOODWELL, John	Beau	1755	Wm	Rand	1779
GOODWIN, Alexander	Bute	1771	GOSSICK, Joseph	Bute	1771
Alexander	FWV	1771	Joseph	FWV	1771
Charles	Bute	1771	GOSWICK, Joseph	Bute	1771
George	Bute	1771	Joseph	FWV	1771
George	FWV	1771	GOUFF, John	Bert	1757
James	FWV	1771	GOUGH, Gregory	Chow	1753
James	Gate	1786	Magdalen	NewH	1762
James	Rand	1779	Wm	Bert	1769
John	Bute	1771	GOULD, Daniel	Oran	1755
John	Chow	1717	Elizabeth	Bert	1757
John 640 acres	Chow	1721	Ephraim	Oran	1755
John	FWV	1771	Henry	Oran	1755

GOULD, Joseph	Oran	1755	GRANDY, Absalom	Pasq	1769
GOULDSBOROUGH, James			Arnon	Pasq	1769
	NewH	1763	Caleb	Pasq	1754
GOWEN, Edward	Gran	1755	Caleb Jr.	Pasq	1769
Edward	Gran	1769	Charles	Pasq	1769
Edward	Gran	1784	Solomon 1 slave	Pasq	1769
John	Gran	1784	Thomas	Pasq	1769
Joseph	Gran	1755	Thomas	Pasq	1769
Michael	Gran	1755	GRANGE, John		
Moses	Gran	1769	49 slaves	Blad	1763
Thomas	Gran	1769	John Jr.		
Thomas	Gran	1784	38 slaves	Blad	1763
GOWIN, Jesse	Casw	1777	John 60 slaves	Brun	1769
Wm	Gran	1769	John	Brun	1769
GOWINE, Edward & w.	FWV	1771	GRANGER, Caleb	NewH	1755
Michael, wife s.			Caleb	NewH	1762
Michael David &			John	Dobb	1769
Elizabeth, dau			John	Dobb	1779
	FWV	1771	Joshua	NewH	1755
GOWING, Edward			Joshua	NewH	1762
black	Bute	1771	Thomas	Dobb	1769
Michael (black)	FWV	1771	Thomas	Pitt	1775
GRABBS, Gottfried	Surr	1771	GRANT, Daniel	Gran	1769
Gottfried	Surr	1772	Daniel	Gran	1784
GRACE, James	Dobb	1779	James	Curr	1755
Luke	Crav	1769	James	Onsl	1769
Rebecca	Perq	1720	James	Onsl	1770
Thomas	Dobb	1769	John	Dobb	1769
Thomas	Dobb	1779	Solomon	Onsl	1769
GRACEY, Patrick	Rowa	1759	Solomon	Onsl	1770
GRADY, John	Dobb	1769	Stephen	Onsl	1769
Wm	Chow	1717	Thomas	Gran	1784
Wm 1,200 acres	Chow	1721	Wm	Dobb	1769
Wm	Dobb	1769	Wm	Tryo	1776
Wm	Dobb	1779	GRANTHAM, Edward	Dobb	1769
GRAGG, Wm	Gran	1769	James	Dobb	1769
GRAHAM, Andrew	Blad	1763	John	Dobb	1769
Fergus	Rowa	1759	John s. of John	Dobb	1769
James	Rowa	1759	Joshua	Dobb	1769
John	Cumb	1767	Joshua	Dobb	1779
John	Rowa	1759	Thomas	Dobb	1769
Neil	Cumb	1755	Wm s. of John	Dobb	1769
Neil	Cumb	1767	GRAROT, Jonathan	Pasq	1754
Peter	Crav	1769	GRASSIT, George	NewH	1755
Richard	Rand	1779	GRATEHOUSE, Jacob	Anso	1763
Richard	Rowa	1759	GRATLEY, Wm	Casw	1777
Robert	Blad	1781	GRAVES, Henry	Gran	1769
Robert	Cumb	1755	Henry	Gran	1784
GRAINGER, Caleb	NewH	1763	James	Casw	1777
Caleb	NewH	1765	James	Pasq	1754
Caleb's Estate	NewH	1767	James	Pasq	1769
Catherine	NewH	1763	James	Rand	1779
Catherine	NewH	1765	John (Cpt.)	Casw	1777
Catherine	NewH	1767	John Sr.	Casw	1777
John	Crav	1769	John	Gran	1769
Joshua	NewH	1741	John	Gran	1784
Mary	NewH	1767	John	Rand	1779
Wm	NewH	1767	Joseph	Surr	1771
GRAMBREL, Martin	Surr	1771	Joseph	Surr	1772
GRANADE, John	Crav	1744	Richard Esq.		
GRANBURY, Josiah	Chow	1753	12 slaves	Crav	1769
Josiah	Gate	1786	Robert	Anso	1763
Wm	Bert	1769	Sarah	Rand	1779
GRANDEY, Ann	Pasq	1754	Thomas	Casw	1777
GRANDY, Abigail	Pasq	1769			

GRAVES, Thomas	Crav 1744		GRAYSON, Wm	Onsl 1770
Thomas 9 slaves	Crav 1769		GREADY, John	Blad 1741
Vincent	Rand 1779		GREAR, John	Onsl 1769
Wm	Cumb 1767		Robert	Rand 1779
Wm	Gran 1769		Wm	Rand 1779
Wm	Gran 1784		GREATHOUSE, Jacob	Anso 1763
GRAY, Abraham	NewH 1767		GREAVES, James	Pasq 1769
Ann	Bert 1757		GREEN, Abraham	Bute 1771
Ann	Bert 1769		Abraham	Cumb 1767
Charles	Rand 1779		Abraham	Edge 1741
Clifton s. of			Abraham	FWV 1771
James	Onsl 1769		Abraham	Gate 1786
Daniel	Bert 1757		Abraham	Gran 1755
Henry	Tyrr 1755		Anne	Casw 1777
Israel	Onsl 1769		Aquilla	Surr 1771
Israel	Onsl 1770		Aquilla	Surr 1772
Jacob	Gran 1755		Bartolet	Casw 1777
James	Bute 1771		Benjamin	Rand 1779
James s. George	FWV 1771		Benjamin	Surr 1771
James	Onsl 1769		Benjamin	Surr 1772
James	Onsl 1770		David	Cumb 1767
James	Surr 1771		David	Pitt 1762
James	Surr 1772		David	Pitt 1763
John	Bert 1741		David	Pitt 1764
John	Dobb 1769		Edward	Bute 1771
John	Dobb 1779		Edward s. Obed	FWV 1771
John	Onsl 1769		Ezekiel	Pitt 1763
John	Onsl 1770		Ezekiel	Pitt 1764
John	Oran 1755		Farn 1,400 acres	
John Sr.	Pasq 1754			Crav 1720
John Jr.	Pasq 1769		Farnifold	
John Sr. 7 slaves			19 slaves	Crav 1769
	Pasq 1769		Francis	Crav 1720
John	Rand 1779		Frank	Crav 1720
Joseph	Crav 1769		Frederick	Surr 1771
Joshua	Pasq 1769		Frederick	Surr 1772
Lodowick	Dobb 1769		Henry	Gran 1784
Lodowick	Pasq 1754		Isaac	NewH 1755
Mathias	Gran 1755		James Sr.	
Nathaniel	Pasq 1754		17 slaves	Crav 1769
Nathaniel			James (Neuce R.)	
1 slave	Pasq 1769			Crav 1769
Peter	Chow 1717		James of Trent	Crav 1769
Peter	Chow 1721		James	NewH 1762
Richard	Perq 1720		James	NewH 1763
Robert	Pasq 1769		James	NewH 1767
Robert	Rand 1779		James	Onsl 1742
Robert	Rowa 1759		James	Rowa 1759
Silvanus	Dobb 1769		James	Surr 1772
Thomas	Bute 1771		Jehoda	Gate 1786
Thomas	Crav 1769		Jeremiah	Rowa 1759
Thomas	Dobb 1779		Job	Gran 1784
Thomas	Pasq 1754		John	Bert 1757
Thomas	Perq 1720		John	Blad 1763
Thomas	Perq 1740		John	Chow 1753
Wm	Bert 1757		John Jr.	Chow 1753
Wm Esq.	Bert 1769		John, merchant	Crav 1769
Wm	Gran 1755		John, schoolmaster	
Wm	Rand 1779			Crav 1769
Wm	Rowa 1759		John	Bute 1771
Wm	Tyrr 1755		John	FWV 1771
GRAYHAM, Edward	Casw 1777		John s. of Abra	Gran 1755
Isaac	Casw 1777		John	Gran 1784
Wm	Casw 1777		John	NorH 1762
Wm Sr.	Casw 1777		John	Onsl 1769

GREEN, John	Onsl	1770	GREENSTREET, Peter	Surr	1772
John	Oran	1755	GREENWOOD, Thomas	NewH	1744
John	Perq	1740	GREER, Aquilla	Surr	1772
John	Roan	1720	Bartlett	Gran	1784
John	Surr	1772	Benjamin	Surr	1772
Jonathan	NewH	1767	John hunter	Blad	1763
Joseph	Bert	1757	John	Onsl	1769
Joseph	Bute	1771	John	Surr	1772
Joseph	Dobb	1769	Joshua	Surr	1772
Joseph s. Josiah			Robert	Rand	1779
	FWV	1771	Thomas Jr.	Blad	1763
Joseph	Gran	1755	Thomas Sr.	Blad	1763
Joshua	Surr	1772	Wm	Rand	1779
Malachi	Chow	1753	GREESON, Isaac	Oran	1755
Margaret	Gate	1786	GREFFEN, Benjamin	Dobb	1769
Matthew	Onsl	1769	GREGG, Frederick	NewH	1755
Matthew	Onsl	1770	Frederick	NewH	1762
Mathias	Gate	1786	Frederick	NewH	1763
Morsharp	Pasq	1769	Frederick	NewH	1765
Moses	Crav	1769	Frederick	NewH	1767
Peter	Bute	1771	Jacob	Rand	1779
Peter s. Wm			Lodowick	NewH	1755
Isham	FWV	1771	Wm	NewH	1755
Peter	Gran	1755	GREGORY, Aaron	NorH	1762
Richard	Anso	1763	Alexander	Cumb	1767
Richard	Cumb	1767	Caleb	Pasq	1754
Richard	Gate	1786	Caleb 2 slaves	Pasq	1769
Richard	Rowa	1759	Charles	Pasq	1754
Samuel	Beau	1755	Dempsey		
Samuel	Bute	1771	3 slaves	Pasq	1769
Samuel	FWV	1771	Francis	Crav	1769
Samuel	NewH	1741	Hardy	Onsl	1769
Samuel	NewH	1755	Hardy	Onsl	1770
Samuel	NewH	1762	Isaac	Pasq	1769
Samuel	NewH	1763	Jacob	Pasq	1754
Samuel	NewH	1765	James	Casw	1777
Samuel	NewH	1767	James	Gate	1786
Samuel	Pitt	1762	James	Pasq	1754
Samuel	Pitt	1763	Jesse	Onsl	1769
Samuel	Pitt	1764	Jesse	Pasq	1769
Solomon	Chow	1753	Job	Pasq	1754
Stephen	Cumb	1767	John	Onsl	1769
Thomas	Bert	1757	John	Onsl	1770
Thomas Jr.	Bert	1757	Luke	Chow	1744
Thomas	Bute	1771	Matthew	Onsl	1770
Thomas	Chow	1753	Richard	Pasq	1769
Thomas	Crav	1720	Samson	Pasq	1754
Thomas	Cumb	1767	Samson	Pasq	1769
Thomas	FWV	1771	Samuel	Chow	1753
Thomas	Gran	1755	Samuel	Pasq	1769
Wm	Bute	1771	Theophilus	Pasq	1754
Wm overseer	Bute	1771	Wm	NewH	1767
Wm	Casw	1777	GREGSON, George	Oran	1755
Wm 1,200 acres	Chow	1721	GRENADE, John	Crav	1744
Wm	Crav	1769	John 3 slaves	Crav	1769
Wm, Neuce R.	Cumb	1767	John Jr. 2 slaves		
Wm overseer	FWV	1771		Crav	1769
Wm	Gate	1786	Joseph	Crav	1769
Wm	NewH	1755	GRESSETT, George	Brun	1769
Wm	Onsl	1770	George 4 slaves		
Wm	Roan	1720		Brun	1772
Zachariah	Casw	1777	Wm 6 slaves	Brun	1769
Zachrie	Cumb	1767	Wm	Brun	1772
GREENAWAY, Thomas	NewH	1763	GREY, James	Surr	1772
GREENSTREET, Peter	Surr	1771	Peter	Chow	1721

GREY, Thomas	Perq	1720
Wm	Pitt	1763
Wm	Pitt	1764
GRICE, Francis	Crav	1720
Wm	Bert	1757
GRIEST, Richard	Pitt	1764
GRIFFIN, Andrew	Casw	1777
Andrew	Cumb	1767
Andrew	Tyrr	1755
Ann	Gran	1784
Benjamin	Crav	1769
Benjamin	Dobb	1779
Edmund	NorH	1762
Edward	Bert	1769
Ephenetus Jr.	Tyrr	1755
Ephenetus Sr.	Tyrr	1755
Ephraim	Gate	1786
Evan	Dobb	1779
Henry	Beau	1764
Henry	Gate	1786
James	Chow	1753
James	Onsl	1769
James	Onsl	1770
John	Beau	1764
John	Blad	1763
John	Crav	1769
John	Edge	1734
John	Pasq	1769
John	Perq	1740
John	Pitt	1764
John	Rand	1779
John	Roan	1720
John	Tyrr	1741
John	Tyrr	1755
Jonas 3 slaves	Crav	1769
Joseph	Chow	1753
Joseph	Gate	1786
Joshua	Oran	1755
Major	Dobb	1769
Matthew	Tyrr	1755
Michael	Bert	1757
Peter	Gran	1784
Samson	Edge	1734
Samuel	Oran	1755
Samuel	Rowa	1759
Simon	Dobb	1769
Simon	Dobb	1779
Solomon	Crav	1769
Thomas	Casw	1777
Wm	Bert	1769
Wm	Chow	1721
Wm	Cumb	1767
Wm	Pasq	1754
Wm	Pasq	1769
Wm	Tyrr	1755
GRIFFIS, Samuel	Crav	1769
GRIFFITH, James	Chow	1721
John	Surr	1771
John	Surr	1772
Richard	Bert	1757
Samuel	Crav	1743
Thomas	Bert	1757
GRIFFITHS, Benjamin	Anso	1763
Samuel	Onsl	1770
Zekeal	Anso	1763
GRIGGS, Daniel	Anso	1763
John overseer	Bute	1771
John	Gran	1784
John	NorH	1762
Minus	Gran	1755
GRIGORY, Griffith	Curr	1755
Richard	Curr	1755
GRILS, Richard	Chow	1721
GRIM, Samuel	Casw	1777
GRIMES, Absalom	Pasq	1754
Benjamin	Cumb	1767
George	Cumb	1767
George	Dobb	1769
George	Oran	1755
John Jr.	Cumb	1767
Michael	Rand	1779
Robert	Crav	1769
Samuel	Bert	1769
Wm	Oran	1755
Wm	Pitt	1762
Wm	Rand	1779
GRIMMEN, Robert	Pitt	1764
GRIMMER, Robert	Pitt	1762
GRIMMIN, Robert	Pitt	1763
GRIMS, John	Oran	1755
GRIMSLEY, Sherrod	Dobb	1769
GRINAWAY, Thomas	Gran	1769
GRISE, Jacob	Dobb	1769
Luke	Crav	1769
GRISHAM, Benjamin	Gran	1784
Edward	Gran	1784
Henry	Gran	1784
Richard	Gran	1784
Stephen	Gran	1784
GRISSOM, Benjamin	Gran	1769
Wm	Onsl	1769
GRISSARD, Hardy	Dobb	1779
Hardy	Pitt	1762
Joseph	Dobb	1779
GRISSETT, George	NewH	1762
George	NewH	1763
Wm	NewH	1762
Wm	NewH	1763
GRIST, John	Beau	1755
John	Pitt	1762
John	Pitt	1763
Richard	Beau	1755
Richard	Pitt	1762
Richard	Pitt	1763
Wm	Pitt	1762
Wm	Pitt	1763
Wm	Pitt	1764
GRIZARD, Henry	Pitt	1764
GROANE, Samuel	Perq	1740
Samuel Jr.	Perq	1740
GROGAN, Bartholomew	Rand	1779
Bartholomew	Surr	1771
GROINENDEYK, Cornelius	Crav	1769
GROOMS, John	NewH	1762
John	NewH	1763
GROVE, Susuannah	Cumb	1767
GROVER, Savin	Bert	1769
GROVES, Joseph	Brun	1769
Joseph	Brun	1772

GROZED, Thomas	Dobb 1769	HACKENWALDER, Christian	
GRYMES, Wm	Pitt 1764		Surr 1771
GRYNER, John	Surr 1771	HACKETT, Daniel	Rowa 1759
GRYSON, Wm	Onsl 1770	Michael (Dr.)	Crav 1769
GUEST, Elias	Gran 1769	HACKNEY, Joseph	Bute 1771
Elias	Gran 1784	Joseph s. Joseph	
John	Gran 1784	John	FWV 1771
GUILLAM, Robert	Gran 1755	Joseph	Gran 1755
GUILLFORD,	Crav 1720	Samuel	NorH 1743
GUIN, Christopher	Anso 1763	HACOS, Henry	Casw 1777
Christopher	Beau 1744	HADDER, Warren	Beau 1764
Henry	Crav 1769	HADDOCK, John	Beau 1755
Henry	Gran 1755	John	Pitt 1762
John	Gran 1755	John Jr.	Pitt 1762
GULLICK, Daniel	Surr 1771	John	Pitt 1764
Daniel	Surr 1772	John Jr.	Pitt 1764
GUMPLEY, James	Crav 1745	John	Pitt 1775
GUMS, Abraham	Chow 1753	Wm	Pitt 1764
Matthew	Chow 1721	Wm Jr.	Pitt 1764
Matthew	Chow 1753	HADLEY, Simon	Surr 1771
GUNFOIL, George	NewH 1755	Simon	Surr 1772
GUNHAM, George	Cumb 1755	Thomas	Cumb 1767
John	Cumb 1755	HADNOT, Rachel	Onsl 1769
GUNN, John	Casw 1777	Stephen	Onsl 1769
John	Gran 1755	Stephen	Onsl 1770
GUNTER, John	Gran 1769	Whitehurst	Onsl 1769
Wm	Gran 1769	Whitehurst	Onsl 1770
GUPTON, James	Bute 1771	Wm	Cart 1743
James	FWV 1771	Wm	Onsl 1769
Stephen	Bute 1771	HADRICK, John	Pitt 1775
Stephen	FWV 1771	HAGAN, Charles	Oran 1755
GURGANUS, Francis	Tyrr 1755	Henry	Pitt 1762
GURLEY, Benjamin	NewH 1755	Henry	Pitt 1764
Benjamin	NewH 1762	HAGATY, Patrick	Gate 1786
Benjamin	NewH 1763	HAGGARD, Edmund	Casw 1777
Benjamin	NewH 1765	Richard	Bute 1771
Benjamin	NewH 1767	Samuel	Bute 1771
Joel	Dobb 1779	HAGGERT, Richard	FWV 1771
GURNEY, Wm	Edge 1743	Samuel	FWV 1771
GURREL, Wm	Edge 1743	HAGGIN, John	Rowa 1759
GUTEN, Joseph	Beau 1764	HAILS, John	Cumb 1767
GUTHRIE, Garrett	Casw 1777	Joshua	Pitt 1764
John	Casw 1777	HAINES, Priscilla	Bute 1771
Wm	Gran 1784	Priscilla grands.	
GUY, Benjamin	Gran 1784	John	FWV 1771
Wm	NewH 1755	Samuel	Surr 1771
GWALTNEY, Thomas	Beau 1755	Samuel	Surr 1772
Thomas Jr.	Pitt 1762	HAINEY, Charles	Casw 1777
Thomas Sr.	Pitt 1762	Pridgeon	Casw 1777
Thomas Jr.	Pitt 1763	Wm	Casw 1777
Thomas Sr.	Pitt 1763	HAIR, Bryan	Bert 1757
Thomas Jr.	Pitt 1764	Bryan Jr.	Bert 1757
Thomas Sr.	Pitt 1764	Edward	Chow 1753
Wm 3 slaves	Crav 1769	James	Bert 1757
Wm	Pitt 1762	John	Bert 1757
Wm	Pitt 1764	Joseph	Crav 1745
GWANN, Sam	NewH 1767	Joseph	Cumb 1755
GWATNEY, Thomas	Beau 1755	Moses	Chow 1753
GWINN, Christooher	Anso 1763	Thomas	Bert 1757
Daniel	Casw 1777	HAIRMAN, Robert	Perq 1740
Daniel	Gate 1786	HAISLEP, Laban	Gran 1784
Hugh	Rand 1779	HAIST, Nancy	Bert 1769
Wm	Gate 1786	HAKINS, Edward	Bert 1757
GYE, Wm	FWV 1771	Joseph	Surr 1771
GYTON, Jacob	Blad 1781	HALBERT, John	Surr 1771

HALBERT, Wm	Surr	1771
HALBROOK, Wm	Surr	1771
Wm	Surr	1772
HALCOMB, Wm	Bute	1771
Wm	Casw	1777
Wm	FWV	1771
HALCUM, John	Gran	1755
Joseph	Gran	1755
Richard	Gran	1755
HALE, Benjamin	Dobb	1769
Edward	Dobb	1769
Hall s. of Thomas		
	Dobb	1769
John	Chow	1717
John	NewH	1755
Samuel	Chow	1753
Thomas Esq.		
24 slaves	Blad	1763
Thomas	Dobb	1769
Wm	Tryo	1776
HALES, John		
Constable	Chow	1721
Wm	Beau	1764
Wm	Crav	1769
HALEY, Richard	Gran	1784
Thomas	Chow	1717
Wm	Anso	1763
HALIBURTON, Charles		
	Casw	1777
HALL, Adam	Rowa	1759
Ann	Perq	1740
Benjamin	Bute	1771
Benjamin 2 slaves		
	Crav	1769
Benjamin	FWV	1771
Burrell	Dobb	1779
Burwell	Dobb	1769
Clem (Rev.)	Chow	1753
Clement 2 slaves		
	Pasq	1769
David	Bute	1771
David	Casw	1777
David	FWV	1771
Edward	NewH	1755
Elihu 1 slave		
	Crav	1769
Futral	Gran	1784
Henry	Anso	1763
Henry	Pasq	1769
Isaac	Bert	1757
James	Dobb	1769
James	Gran	1784
James	NewH	1763
James	NewH	1765
James	NewH	1767
Jethro	Cumb	1767
Job	N.C.	1701
John s. of Joseph		
	Anso	1763
John	Crav	1769
John	Dobb	1769
John	Edge	1734
John	Edge	1743
John	Gate	1786
John	Gran	1755

HALL, John	Gran	1784
John	Pasq	1769
John	Roan	1720
Joseph	Anso	1763
Joseph 2 slaves	Crav	1769
Joseph	Cumb	1767
Joseph	Edge	1734
Joseph	Edge	1743
Joshua	Crav	1769
Laurence	Perq	1740
Major	NewH	1767
Major	Onsl	1769
Margaret	Edge	1743
Mary	Perq	1740
Naomi	Bert	1757
Nathaniel	Bute	1771
Nathaniel	FWV	1771
Pool	Dobb	1769
Richard	Crav	1769
Richard	FWV	1771
Robert 3 slaves	Pasq	1769
Robert	Perq	1740
Samuel	Beau	1764
Samuel	Perq	1740
Stephen	Bert	1757
Stephen	Pasq	1754
Thomas	Bert	1757
Thomas	Brun	1769
Thomas	Brun	1772
Thomas	Crav	1769
Thomas	Edge	1741
Thomas	Onsl	1743
Thomas	Surr	1771
Wm s. of Joseph	Anso	1763
Wm	Crav	1769
Wm	Cumb	1755
Wm	Edge	1743
Wm	FWV	1771
Wm	Gran	1755
Wm	NewH	1763
Wm 540 acres	Perq	1720
Wm (Smith)		
313 a.	Perq	1720
Wm	Rowa	1759
Wm	Surr	1771
Wm	Surr	1772
HALLAWAY, David	Pitt	1764
HALLEY, Edward	Cumb	1755
Wm	Bute	1771
Wm	FWV	1771
Wm	Pasq	1754
HALLIBEE, James	Pasq	1769
HALLIER, Ann	NewH	1765
HALLIMON, Edward	FWV	1771
Nathan s. Jacob	FWV	1771
HALLOM, John	Bert	1757
Thomas	Perq	1720
HALLOWAY, David Sr.		
	Beau	1755
HALLOWELL, Luke	Perq	1720
HALSEY, Daniel	Chow	1717
Edward	Chow	1753
John	Chow	1744
John Esq.	Chow	1753
John	Chow	1753

HALSEY, Mary	Chow 1721	HAMMER, John Jr.	Anso 1763
Miles	Chow 1753	Wm	Anso 1763
Wm	Chow 1721	HAMMET, Hugh	Surr 1772
Wm	Perq 1740	HAMMOCK, Benedict	Onsl 1769
HALSTEAD, Drew	Pasq 1769	Benedict	Onsl 1770
Lemuel	Curr 1755	Charles	Gran 1784
HALTON, Jesse	Beau 1764	David	Gran 1769
Jesse Jr. s. of		Hugh	Surr 1771
Jesse	Beau 1764	Wm	Onsl 1769
John	Anso 1763	Wm	Onsl 1770
John	Pitt 1764	HAMMOND, Abraham	Rand 1779
Robert	NewH 1742	Boaz	Pasq 1769
Wm	Anso 1763	Edward	Onsl 1769
HAMBLETON, Andrew	Chow 1753	Edward	Onsl 1770
James	Beau 1755	Job	Gran 1784
John	Beau 1755	John Sr.	Pasq 1769
John	Dobb 1779	Joseph	Curr 1755
Moses	Chow 1753	Martin	Onsl 1769
Samuel	Beau 1755	Martin	Onsl 1770
HAMDEN, David	Casw 1777	Moses	Rand 1779
HAMILTON, Archibald	NewH 1741	Philip	Pasq 1769
Archibald	Rowa 1759	Rawley	Gran 1784
Charles	Cumb 1755	Samuel	Bute 1771
George	Rowa 1759	Samuel s. Job	
Guy	Dobb 1769	Samuel	FWV 1771
James	Beau 1743	Samuel	Gran 1769
John	Beau 1764	Samuel	Gran 1784
John	Blad 1763	Samuel Jr.	Gran 1784
John	Chow 1721	HAMMONS, Abs.	Casw 1777
John 1 slave	Crav 1769	Absalom	Casw 1777
John	Surr 1771	Archelaus	Onsl 1770
John	Surr 1772	HAMMONTREE, Reuben	Beau 1755
Joseph	Crav 1720	Reuben	Crav 1769
Malatiah	NewH 1762	HAMPTON, Andrew	Gran 1755
Malatiah	NewH 1763	Andrew	Tryo 1776
Malatiah	NewH 1767	Anthony	Rowa 1759
Malcomb	Rowa 1759	Anthony	Surr 1772
Morrison	Rand 1779	Ephraim s. of	
Moses	Rand 1779	Andrew	Gran 1755
Ninian	Rand 1779	Ezekiel	Gran 1769
Robert	Bert 1757	James	Surr 1771
Robert	Dobb 1769	James	Surr 1772
Thomas	Rand 1779	John	Gran 1769
Thomas	Rowa 1759	John	Rowa 1759
Wm	Rand 1779	Thomas	Rand 1779
HAMLET, Charles	Surr 1771	Thomas	Surr 1772
HAMLIN, Thomas	Bute 1771	Wm	Curr 1715
Thomas	Pasq 1754	Wm	Rowa 1759
HAMM, Henry	Dobb 1769	HAMRICK, Beach	Casw 1777
Henry s. of Wm		Samuel	Casw 1777
Jr.	Dobb 1769	HANCOCK, Benjamin	Gran 1769
Henry	Dobb 1779	Col.	Crav 1720
Richard	Bute 1771	David	Bert 1757
Richard	Dobb 1779	Henry	Beau 1764
Richard s. Elisha		John	Blad 1742
	FWV 1771	John	Cumb 1767
Richard	Gran 1755	John	Gran 1769
Wm	Beau 1744	Joseph	Rand 1779
Wm	Dobb 1769	Joshua	Cumb 1767
Wm s. of Henry	Dobb 1769	Lewis	NewH 1765
Wm Jr.	Dobb 1769	Martin	Gran 1784
Wm Sr.	Dobb 1779	Nathaniel	Onsl 1769
HAMMER, Elisha	Rand 1779	Nathaniel	Onsl 1770
John	Anso 1750	Samuel	Bute 1771
John	Anso 1763	Samuel	FWV 1771

HANCOCK, Simon bro.			HANLEY, Joseph	Pasq	1769
Wm	FWV	1771	Mary	Pasq	1754
Simon	Gran	1784	Wm	Gran	1769
Wm (Cpt.)	Crav	1721	HANNAH, John	Curr	1755
Wm & bro. Simon	FWV	1771	Jonathan	Curr	1755
HANCHEW, Edward	Pitt	1775	Joseph	Curr	1755
HAND, Elizabeth	NewH	1767	Thomas	Rand	1779
Henry	Surr	1771	Wm	Rand	1779
Henry	Surr	1772	HANSELL, Peter	Pitt	1775
Jeremiah	NewH	1762	Wm Constable	Bute	1771
Jeremiah	NewH	1763	Wm Constable	FWV	1771
Jeremiah	NewH	1765	HANSHEY, Jacob	NewH	1742
Wm	Rand	1779	HANSLEY, John	Onsl	1769
HANDCOCK, James	Crav	1769	HANSON, Adolphus	Curr	1715
James	Pitt	1762	Wm	Rand	1779
Major	Crav	1720	HANSUCKER, Abraham	Cumb	1767
Wm	Beau	1764	John	Cumb	1767
Wm	Casw	1777	HANTON, John	Beau	1764
Wm	Pitt	1775	HANUALT, Graff	Oran	1755
HANDES, Ceal	Pitt	1763	HAPELL, Julius	Pasq	1754
HANDIN, Isum	Blad	1763	HARBERT, Wm	Crav	1769
Josiah	Blad	1763	Wm	Tyrr	1743
Wm	Blad	1763	HARBORD, John Sr.	Anso	1763
HANDLEY, Jesse	Dobb	1779	HARD, Wm s. of Wm	Bert	1769
John	Cumb	1767	HARDEE, Andrew	Beau	1755
John	Dobb	1769	Andrew	Pitt	1762
John	Dobb	1779	Andrew	Pitt	1764
HANELION, Andrew	Casw	1777	Andrew	Pitt	1775
Elijah	Casw	1777	Isaac	Beau	1755
Elkanah	Casw	1777	Isaac	Pitt	1775
Ezekiel	Casw	1777	John	Beau	1755
Jean	Casw	1777	John Esq.	Pitt	1762
Major	Casw	1777	John Jr.	Pitt	1762
Miriam	Casw	1777	John	Pitt	1764
Nathaniel	Casw	1777	John	Pitt	1775
Paul	Casw	1777	Joseph	Pitt	1775
Thomas	Casw	1777	Josiah	Pitt	1762
Vincent	Casw	1777	Nelson	Pitt	1775
HANES, John	Dobb	1769	Robert	Beau	1755
HANEY, Abraham	Onsl	1769	Robert	Pitt	1762
Benjamin	Onsl	1769	Robert Jr.	Pitt	1762
Robert	Rand	1779	Robert	Pitt	1764
HANGLIN, John	Oran	1755	Robert Jr.	Pitt	1764
HANING, Philip	Tyrr	1755	Robert	Pitt	1775
HANKINS, Gideon	Onsl	1770	Thomas	Beau	1755
James	Onsl	1770	Thomas	Pitt	1762
Stephen	Onsl	1770	Thomas Jr.	Pitt	1762
Wm	Onsl	1770	Thomas	Pitt	1764
HANKS, Argil	Gran	1784	Thomas	Pitt	1775
Elijah	Gran	1769	HARDEN, Isaac	Pitt	1764
Epaphroditus	Dobb	1769	Sterling	Gran	1784
John Jr.	Dobb	1769	HARDESON, Jasper	Tyrr	1755
John Sr.	Dobb	1779	Joseph	Tyrr	1755
Mot	Dobb	1769	Richard	Tyrr	1755
Wm	Gran	1769	HARDETT, Enoch	Crav	1720
Wm	Gran	1784	HARDGROVES, Francis	Surr	1771
Wm	Onsl	1770	Francis	Surr	1772
HANLEY, James	Dobb	1769	Nathaneil	Bert	1757
Jesse	Pasq	1754	HARDICK, Wm	Anso	1763
John	Cumb	1767	HARDIN, Gabriel	Cumb	1767
John	Dobb	1769	HARDING, Abe	Rand	1779
John	Onsl	1770	James	Pitt	1762
John 3 slaves	Pasq	1769	John	Dobb	1769
John	Rowa	1759	John	Pitt	1762
Joseph	Gran	1769	Mark	Pitt	1762

HARDING, Richard	Perq	1740	HARGIS, Abraham	Casw	1777
Samuel	Crav	1743	HARGIS, John	Casw	1777
Stephen	Pitt	1762	John Sr.	Casw	1777
Stephen	Pitt	1764	Richard	Casw	1777
Sterling	Bute	1771	Shadrack	Casw	1777
Sterling	FWV	1771	Thomas	Casw	1777
Thomas	Beau	1755	HARGOOD, Hezekiah	Gran	1784
Wm	Surr	1772	HARGRAVES, Bray	Cumb	1755
HARDISON, Charles	Onsl	1770	Howell	Cumb	1755
Frederick	Bert	1769	John	Gran	1784
John	NewH	1742	Richard	Gran	1784
HARDLE, Wm	Gate	1786	HARGROVE, George	Gate	1786
HARDMON, Robert	Rowa	1759	John s. of		
HARDON, Wm	Casw	1777	Richard	Gran	1755
HARDWICK, Aaron	Bute	1771	John	Gran	1769
Aaron	FWV	1771	Richard	Bert	1742
James	Bute	1771	Richard	Gran	1755
James	FWV	1771	Richard s.		
HARDY, Benjamin	Dobb	1769	Richard	Gran	1755
Charles	Bert	1757	Richard	Gran	1769
Edward	Bert	1769	Robert	Rand	1779
Emanuel	Dobb	1769	Sam	Edge	1734
Humphrey	Bert	1769	Stephen	Bute	1771
Jacob	Chow	1717	Stephen	FWV	1771
Jesse	Bert	1769	Stephen	Gran	1784
Jno.	Chow	1717	Wm	Surr	1771
John	Beau	1744	HARION, Wm	Rand	1779
John	Bert	1769	HARKER, Henry	NewH	1762
John & s. Wm	Bert	1757	Henry	NewH	1763
John estate			Henry	Newh	1765
deceased	Chow	1721	HARLE, Adam Jr.	Bert	1757
John	Edge	1741	John	Bert	1757
John	Surr	1772	Thomas	Bert	1757
Joseph	Bert	1757	Wm	Bert	1757
Lemuel	Dobb	1779	HARLIN, Stephen	Cumb	1767
Robert	Bert	1757	HARLING, Aaron	Oran	1755
Thomas	Chow	1721	HARLON, Enoch	Rand	1779
Thomas	Dobb	1769	Stephen	Rand	1779
Thomas	Dobb	1779	HARLOW, Daniel	Cumb	1755
Thomas	Pitt	1775	John	Chow	1721
Wm Sr.	Bert	1757	John	Chow	1753
Wm s. of Samuel	Bert	1769	Wm	Chow	1753
Wm	Chow	1721	HARMER, James	Anso	1750
HARE, Bryan	Bert	1757	HARMON, Cutleff	Rand	1779
Bryan Jr.	Bert	1757	George	Rand	1779
Edward	Chow	1753	John	Perq	1740
James	Bert	1757	Leonard	Rand	1779
John	Bert	1757	Matthias	Rand	1779
Joseph	Crav	1745	Widow 92 acres	Perq	1720
Joseph	Gate	1786	HARNAGE, Jacob	NewH	1762
Moses	Chow	1753	Jacob	NewH	1763
Moses	Gate	1786	HARNETT, Cornelius	Chow	1721
Moses Jr.	Gate	1786	Cornelius	NewH	1741
Thomas	Bert	1757	Cornelius	NewH	1755
HARESON, James	Tyrr	1755	Cornelius	NewH	1762
John	Tyrr	1755	Cornelius	NewH	1763
Stephen	Tyrr	1755	Cornelius	NewH	1765
Thomas	Tyrr	1755	Cornelius	NewH	1767
HARFORD, Mark	Crav	1769	HARP, John	Gran	1784
HARGET, Frederick	Beau	1755	Thomas	Gran	1769
HARGET,	Crav	1769	Thomas	Gran	1784
Henry	Anso	1763	HARPER, Alexander	Dobb	1769
John	Pitt	1764	Blaine	Dobb	1779
Peter	Dobb	1769	Francis	Dobb	1769
Peter	Pitt	1762	George	Dobb	1769

HARPER, Jesse	Gran	1769	HARRELL, Jesse	Gate	1786
Jesse	Gran	1784	Jethro	Chow	1753
John	Blad	1763	John Sr.	Bert	1757
John	Crav	1769	John s. of		
John	Dobb	1779	Abraham	Bert	1757
Peter	Crav	1769	John	Bert	1769
Thomas	Beau	1755	John s. of		
Thomas	Pitt	1762	Abraham	Bert	1769
Thomas	Pitt	1764	John marshes	Bert	1769
Travis	FWV	1771	John	Dobb	1769
Wm	Dobb	1769	John	Dobb	1779
Wm	Dobb	1779	John	Gate	1786
Wm s. of			John Jr.	Gate	1786
Alexander	Dobb	1769	Jonathan	Surr	1772
HARRELL, Aaron	Gate	1786	Joseph	Bert	1757
Abner	Dobb	1779	Joseph	Bert	1769
Abraham	Bert	1769	Joseph	Dobb	1769
Abraham deceased	Bert	1769	Joshua	Bert	1757
Abraham	Gate	1786	Joshua	Bert	1769
Absalom	Bert	1757	Josiah	Bert	1757
Absalom	Bert	1769	Josiah	Bert	1769
Adam	Bert	1769	Josiah	Gate	1786
Adam Jr.	Bert	1757	Mary widow of		
Adam Sr.	Bert	1757	John	Bert	1757
Adan Jr.	Bert	1769	Mary widow of		
Adam Sr.	Bert	1769	Abraham	Bert	1757
Amos	Bert	1769	Mary	Bert	1769
Ann	Bert	1757	Millry	Gate	1786
Ann widow	Bert	1769	Moses	Bert	1757
Arthur	Bert	1769	Moses	Bert	1769
Balis	Bert	1769	Nancy	Bert	1769
Benjamin	Bert	1769	Noah	Gate	1786
Benjamin	Gate	1786	Peter	Gate	1786
Charity	Bert	1769	Richard	Bert	1757
Christopher	Bert	1769	Samuel	Bert	1757
David	Bert	1757	Samuel	Bert	1769
David	Bert	1769	Samuel	Chow	1753
Demsey	Bert	1769	Samuel	Dobb	1779
Demsey	Gate	1786	Samuel	Gate	1786
Ed s. of Thomas	Bert	1769	Shadrack	Bert	1769
Edward	Bert	1757	Stephen	Gate	1786
Edward	Bert	1769	Thomas	Bert	1757
Elijah	Bert	1757	Thomas s. of		
Elijah	Bert	1769	Edward	Bert	1757
Elijah	Chow	1753	Thomas	Bert	1769
Elisha	Bert	1769	Thomas Jr.	Chow	1753
Elisha	Gate	1786	Thomas Sr.	Chow	1753
Ezekiel	Bert	1757	Wm	Bert	1769
Francis	Bert	1757	Wm	Chow	1753
Francis	Bert	1769	Willis	Bert	1769
George	Bert	1757	Zachariah	Bert	1769
George	Bert	1769	HARRELSON, Paul	Oran	1755
Gilbert	Curr	1755	Joseph	Anso	1763
Henry	Bert	1757	Nathaniel	Oran	1755
Henry	Bert	1769	HARRIMAN, David	Surr	1771
Henry	Gate	1786	HARRINGTON, Charles	Anso	1763
Ignatius	Surr	1771	Thomas	Bute	1771
Isaac	Bert	1757	Thomas	Dobb	1769
Isaac	Chow	1753	Thomas & s.		
Isaac	Gate	1786	John	FWV	1771
Jacob	Bert	1769	Whipmall	Anso	1763
James	Bert	1757	HARRIS, Amos	FWV	1771
James	Bert	1769	Ann 100 acres	Perq	1720
Jesse	Bert	1757	Benjamin	Pitt	1764
Jesse	Bert	1769	Brittain	Bute	1771

HARRIS, Brittain	FWV	1771	HARRIS, John		Pasq	1769
Charles	Bute	1771	John Sr.		Pasq	1769
Charles s. Frederick			John 100 acres		Perq	1720
& Simon	FWV	1771	John		Perq	1740
Charles m. Sarah			John		Pitt	1764
Allen	Gran	1769	Jordan		Bute	1771
Charles	Gran	1784	Jordan		FWV	1771
Christopher	Gran	1755	Joseph		Bute	1771
Christopher	Gran	1769	Joseph		Chow	1753
Christopher	Gran	1784	Joseph		Dobb	1769
Claiborn	Gran	1755	Joseph		FWV	1771
Claiborn	Gran	1769	Joseph & s.			
Clayborn	Gran	1784	Howard		FWV	1771
Daniel	Gran	1755	Joseph		Gran	1755
Darwin	Gran	1784	Joseph		Pasq	1769
David	Gran	1769	Major		Beau	1755
David	Gran	1784	Major Constable		Pitt	1762
Edmond	Bute	1771	Matthew		Bute	1771
Edmund	FWV	1771	Matthew		FWV	1771
Edmund	Gran	1755	Michael		Bute	1771
Edmund s. of			Michael		FWV	1771
Robert	Gran	1755	Moses		Bute	1771
Edward	Beau	1755	Moses		FWV	1771
Edward	FWV	1771	Nathaniel		Gran	1755
Edward	Gran	1755	Newit		Bute	1771
Edward	Gran	1761	Newit		FWV	1771
Edward	Gran	1784	Richard		Beau	1755
Edward	Pitt	1764	Richard		Gran	1755
Edward	Pitt	1764	Richard		Gran	1769
Elijah			Richard m. Mary			
Elijah			Gwinn			1777
Elisha	Gate	1786			Gran	1769
Elizabeth 100 acres			Richard Jr. m.			
	Perq	1720	Elizabeth Phillips			
Evan	Rand	1779			Gran	1784
George	Beau	1755	Richard Sr.		Gran	1784
George	FWV	1771	Robert		Bute	1771
George	Gran	1784	Robert		Curr	1755
George	Pitt	1762	Robert		Edge	1743
George	Pitt	1764	Robert s.			
Gideon	Gran	1784	Burrell		FWV	1771
Gillam	Gran	1784	Robert		Gran	1755
Howard Esq.	Bran	1769	Robert Jr.		Gran	1769
Isaac	NewH	1767	Robert Esq.		Gran	1784
Isham	Gran	1769	Robert Jr.		Gran	1784
Jacob	Beau	1755	Samuel		Gran	1784
Jacob	Beau	1764	Samuel		Pitt	1764
James	Bute	1771	Sarah		Gran	1784
James	Chow	1753	Sarah 100 acres		Perq	1720
James	Dobb	1769	Sharrod s. of			
James	FWV	1771	Robert		Gran	1755
James	Gran	1755	Sherwood		Gran	1769
Job	Chow	1753	Sherwood Jr.		Gran	1769
Joel	Bute	1771	Sherwood m. Rebecca			
Joel	FWV	1771	Wilkins		Gran	1784
John	Beau	1755	Sterling		FWV	1771
John	Bute	1771	Thomas		Casw	1777
John	Crav	1769	Thomas		Crav	1769
John 3 slaves	Crav	1769	Thomas Constable		Crav	1769
John	Curr	1715	Thomas		Curr	1755
John & s. John	FWV	1771	Thomas		Gran	1755
John	Gate	1786	Thomas		Gran	1769
John	Gran	1755	Thomas		NorH	1762
John	Gran	1769	Thomas		Oran	1755
John	Gran	1784	Thomas		Pitt	1762
John	Oran	1755				

HARRIS, Thomas	Pitt 1764	HARRISON, Thomas	Bert 1769
Timothy	Beau 1744	Thomas	Chow 1721
Timothy	Beau 1755	Thomas	Gran 1769
Timothy	Pitt 1762	Thomas	Pasq 1769
Timothy	Pitt 1764	Wm 2 slaves	Crav 1769
Timothy	Pitt 1775	Wm Jr. 2 slaves	Crav 1769
Turner	Bute 1771	Wm	FWV 1771
Turner	FWV 1771	Wm	Pasq 1754
W.	N.C. 1701	Wm	Pasq 1769
West	Bute 1771	Wm	Surr 1771
West & s. Ethelred		Wm	Surr 1772
& Roland	FWV 1771	HARROD, James	Casw 1777
Wm	Beau 1755	HARS, Thomas	Bert 1769
Wm Jr.	Beau 1755	HARSKINS, James	Gran 1784
Wm	Chow 1717	HART, Aaron	Anso 1763
Wm	Chow 1721	Abigail	
Wm (Cpt.)	Gate 1786	3 slaves	Brun 1769
Wm	Gran 1769	Abigail	Brun 1772
Wm	Pitt 1762	David (Maj.)	Casw 1777
Wm Jr.	Pitt 1762	Henry	Gran 1769
Wm	Pitt 1764	James	Oran 1755
Wm Jr.	Pitt 1764	John	Dobb 1779
Wright	Gran 1755	John	Gran 1769
HARRISON, Abner	Pasq 1769	John	Gran 1784
Benjamin	Pasq 1754	John	NorH 1741
Benjamin	Gran 1769	Joseph	Gran 1784
Bessaiah	Surr 1771	Josiah	Oran 1755
Charles 32 slaves		Miles	Pitt 1775
	NewH 1742	Philip	Gran 1769
Charles	NewH 1755	Pleasant	Gran 1769
Charles	NewH 1762	Richard	Crav 1744
Dan.	Chow 1717	Richard	Dobb 1769
Daniel	Chow 1721	Richard	Dobb 1779
Edward Jr.	Blad 1763	Thomas	Gran 1769
Edward Sr.	Blad 1763	Wm	Gran 1769
Essiah	Surr 1772	Wm	Gran 1784
Isham	Gran 1784	Wm	NewH 1762
Jacob	Cumb 1767	Wm	Pitt 1775
James	FWV 1771	HARTER, Wm	Oran 1755
James	Gran 1784	HARTLEY, Francis	Rowa 1759
John	Beau 1764	Henry	Tyrr 1755
John	Blad 1763	Leonard	Cumb 1767
John	Blad 1781	Wm	Crav 1769
John 1300 acres	Chow 1721	Wm	Tyrr 1755
John	Dobb 1769	HARTMAN, Abigail	
John	Surr 1771	Adam	Rowa 1759
Joseph	FWV 1771	Adam Jr.	Rowa 1759
Joseph	Gate 1786	George	Rowa 1759
Joseph	NewH 1762	Harmon	Rowa 1759
Joseph	Pasq 1754	Henry	Rowa 1759
Joshua	Pasq 1754	Joseph	Rowa 1759
Josiah	Rowa 1759	Robert	Rowa 1759
Mary widow	Pasq 1769	Thomas	Rowa 1759
Milley	Gran 1784	HARTON, Thomas	Bute 1771
Okey	Dobb 1769	Thomas s. Thomas	
Paul	Pitt 1764	& Howell	FWV 1771
Peter	FWV 1771	HARTSFIELD, Andrew	
Richard	Blad 1763		Gran 1755
Richard	Blad 1781	Jacob	Bute 1771
Robert	Gran 1769	Jacob	FWV 1771
Robert	Pasq 1754	Jacob	Gran 1755
Robert Jr.	Pasq 1769	John	Dobb 1769
Robert Sr.	Pasq 1769	John	Dobb 1779
Sarah	Gran 1769	Paul	Dobb 1769
Tho.	Chow 1717	HARVEY, Ann	Blad 1781

HARVEY, Francis	NewH	1767	HASTINGS, Thomas	Pasq	1754
James	Beau	1755	HATCH, Anthony	Perq	1720
James	Beau	1764	Anthony 1233 acres		
John	Beau	1764		Perq	1740
Michael	Rand	1779	Edmond	Crav	1769
Richard	Beau	1764	John	Onsl	1769
Thomas	Beau	1755	John	Onsl	1770
Thomas	Beau	1764	Lemuel 22 slaves		
Thomas 1880 acres				Crav	1769
	Perq	1720	Lemuel	Onsl	1769
Thomas	Perq	1740	Lemuel	Onsl	1770
Wm	Beau	1755	HATCHER, John	Gran	1784
Wm Jr.	Rand	1779	HATHER, Robert	Bald	1763
Wm Sr.	Rand	1779	HATLE, John	Oran	1755
HARVIL, John	Cumb	1755	HATTAWAY, David	Pitt	1762
HARYS, Thomas	Bert	1769	David Sr.	Pitt	1762
Thomas	Crav	1720	David	Pitt	1764
HASE, Jack	NewH	1762	Edmond	Pitt	1762
John	Tyrr	1755	Edmond	Pitt	1764
HASELL, Abraham	Tyrr	1755	Francis	Pitt	1762
Edward	Tyrr	1755	Francis	Pitt	1764
Edward Jr.	Tyrr	1755	George	Beau	1755
Hasel	Tyrr	1755	Thomas	Pitt	1762
Jabez	Tyrr	1755	Thomas	Pitt	1763
James 28 slaves	Brun	1769	Thomas	Pitt	1764
James Jr.			HATTON, John	Pitt	1762
19 slaves	Brun	1779	HAUGHTON, Geo.	Chow	1717
James	Brun	1772	Henry	Pasq	1769
James Jr.	Brun	1772	Thomas	Chow	1717
James	NewH	1741	Wm	Chow	1717
James Jr.	NewH	1762	Wm	Chow	1721
James Sr.	NewH	1762	HAUSER, George	Surr	1771
James Jr.	NewH	1763	Martin	Surr	1771
James Sr.	NewH	1763	Michael	Surr	1771
John	Chow	1717	Peter	Surr	1771
John	Chow	1721	Rudolph	Surr	1771
John	Tyrr	1755	HAVARD, Thomas	Pasq	1769
Philip	Gran	1755	HAW, Moses	Beau	1764
Rachel	Tyrr	1755	HAWDING, Josiah	Blad	1781
Susannah	Brun	1772	HAWKE, Thomas	Crav	1769
Wm	Tyrr	1755	HAWKINS, Alexander	Surr	1772
HASELWOOD, George	FWV	1771	Benjamin	Beau	1755
George	Gran	1755	Benjamin	Beau	1764
Randol	Gran	1755	Benjamin	Casw	1777
Randolph	FWV	1771	Benjamin	FWV	1771
Thomas	FWV	1771	Br.	Beau	1755
HASEY, Isum	Anso	1763	Edward	Bert	1757
HASH, Nathaniel			Edward	Bert	1769
(Cpt.)	Casw	1777	George	Gran	1755
HASKETT, Abraham	Rand	1779	Gideon	Onsl	1769
Anthony 300 acres			Gideon	Onsl	1770
	Perq	1720	J.	Beau	1755
John	Rand	1779	James	Chow	1717
HASKINS, John	Pasq	1754	James	Chow	1721
Thomas	Onsl	1769	James	Onsl	1770
Thomas	Onsl	1770	John	Bert	1769
Wm Jr.	Onsl	1769	John Jr.	Bute	1771
Wm	Onsl	1770	John Sr.	Bute	1771
Wm Jr.	Onsl	1770	John Jr.	FWV	1771
HASKINSON, Moses	Beau	1755	John Sr. s.		
Samuel	Beau	1755	Philip	FWV	1771
HASLETT, Mary	Gate	1786	John	Gran	1755
HASLIN, Thomas	Crav	1769	John	Gran	1784
HASTE, Henry	Bert	1757	John	NewH	1741
HASTINGS, John	Pasq	1769	John	Perq	1740

HAWKINS, Joseph	Onsl	1769	HAYES, Joseph	Rowa	1759
Joseph	Surr	1771	Joshua	Blad	1763
Joseph	Surr	1772	Joshua	Blad	1781
Major	Bute	1771	Joshua	Gran	1769
Matthew	Gran	1784	Joshua	Gran	1784
Phil. (Col.)	Bute	1771	Joshua	NorH	1762
Philemon & s.			Patrick	Rowa	1759
Philemon	FWV	1771	Richard	Bert	1769
Philemon	Gran	1755	Robert	Crav	1744
Philemon	Gran	1769	Samuel	Bute	1771
Philemon Esq.	Gran	1784	Samuel	FWV	1771
Solomon	Bert	1769	Sarah	Gran	1784
Stephen	Onsl	1769	Suthew	Blad	1763
Stephen	Onsl	1770	Suthew	Blad	1781
Thomas	Bert	1757	Thomas	Bert	1769
Thomas	Bert	1769	Thomas	Bute	1771
Thomas	Chow	1717	Thomas	FWV	1771
Thomas	Chow	1721	Wm	Chow	1753
Thomas	Tyrr	1755	Wright	Gate	1786
Wm	Anso	1763	HAYMORE, John	Bute	1771
Wm	Beau	1764	John	FWV	1771
Wm	Brun	1772	HAYNES, John	Cumb	1767
Wm	Casw	1777	John	Gran	1784
Wm	Onsl	1770	Joseph	Rowa	1759
Wyatt	Bute	1771	Margaret	NewH	1743
Wyatt	FWV	1771	Margaret	NewH	1763
HAWKS, John			Margaret	NewH	1765
1 slave	Crav	1769	Priscilla	Bute	1771
HAWLEY, Benjamin	NorH	1762	Priscilla & g.son		
Jacob	Gran	1784	John	FWV	1771
Joseph	Gran	1784	Samuel	Surr	1771
HAWN, Wm	FWV	1771	Samuel	Surr	1772
HAWS, Arthur	NewH	1763	Thomas	Blad	1763
Charles	Onsl	1770	Thomas	Blad	1781
Edmund	Blad	1763	Thomas & bro		
Job	NewH	1763	John	FWV	1771
John	NewH	1762	HAYWOOD, Francis	Bute	1771
John	NewH	1763	John	Edge	1741
John	NewH	1767	Sherrard	Gran	1755
John	Onsl	1769	HAZEBURY, George	Casw	1777
John	Onsl	1770	HAZELWOOD, George	Bute	1771
HAWTHORN, John	Blad	1781	Randolph	Bute	1771
HAY, Alexander	Gran	1755	Thomas	Bute	1771
HAYCRAFT, John	Pitt	1764	HAZEWELL, Sampson	Bute	1771
HAYES, Abraham	Dobb	1769	HEAD, George	Gran	1769
Alexander	Casw	1777	James	Gran	1769
Benjamin	Gran	1784	Richard	Gran	1784
Daniel	Gate	1786	Richard	NorH	1762
George s. of			Wm	Bute	1771
Abraham	Dobb	1769	Wm	FWV	1771
Hardy	Bert	1769	Wm	Gran	1769
Henry	Casw	1777	HEADY, Daniel	Crav	1769
Henry	Gate	1786	HEARING, Jonathan	Pasq	1769
Henry Jr.	Gran	1784	HEARN, Wm	Pitt	1763
Henry Sr.	Gran	1784	HEARNE, Elisha	Onsl	1769
Henry	Tryo	1776	Thomas	Onsl	1769
Jacob	Gate	1786	Thomas	Onsl	1770
James	Gate	1786	HEARON, Samuel	Dobb	1769
Jesse	Dobb	1779	HEART, John	Pitt	1762
John	Bert	1757	Micager	Pitt	1762
John	Bert	1769	Micager	Pitt	1764
John	Casw	1777	Michael	Cumb	1767
John	Pasq	1743	Wm	Oran	1755
Joseph	Gran	1769	HEARTS, John	Beau	1755
Joseph	Gran	1784	HEASE, John	Tyrr	1742

HEASWELL, Sampson		
& s. Richard	FWV	1771
HEATH, Henry	Crav	1769
James	Crav	1769
Mark	Dobb	1779
Robert	Curr	1715
Robert	Curr	1755
Tho.	Chow	1717
Thomas	Chow	1721
Wm 2 slaves	Crav	1769
HEATON, Henry	Crav	1744
HECKLEFIELD, John	Perq	1720
HEDGEPETH, Carter	Gran	1755
Carter	Gran	1784
Daniel	Dobb	1769
Daniel	Dobb	1779
George s. of		
Ralph	Gran	1755
Giles	Gran	1755
James	Bert	1757
James	Bert	1769
Peter	Casw	1777
Ralph	Gran	1755
HEDGES, Elias	Beau	1745
HEDLEBERG, John	Onsl	1769
John	Onsl	1770
HEETH, George	Gran	1755
HEFLIN, Charles	Gran	1784
Fielding	Gran	1784
James	Gran	1769
James Jr.	Gran	1784
John	Gran	1769
John	Gran	1784
Wm	Gran	1784
HEIDELBURG, John	Onsl	1769
John	Onsl	1770
HEGE, Balzer	Surr	1771
Balzer	Surr	1772
HEIGH, James	Pasq	1754
HELDER, Peter	Surr	1772
HELLER, Henry	Rowa	1759
HELLIER, Ann	NewH	1762
Ann	NewH	1763
Richard	NewH	1741
HELMS, George	Anso	1763
Jonathan	Anso	1763
Tilman	Anso	1763
Walter	Oran	1755
Wm	Oran	1755
HELSENPEC, Frederick		
	Surr	1771
HELTON, James	Surr	1772
John	Surr	1771
Thomas	Surr	1771
HEMMON, Abraham	Rand	1779
Arche.	Onsl	1769
James	Onsl	1769
James	Onsl	1770
HEMPHILL, Hugh	Casw	1777
Samuel	Rand	1779
HENBY, James	Perq	1720
James Jr.	Perq	1740
James Sr.	Perq	1740
John	Perq	1720
John	Perq	1740

HENDERSON, Argulus	Oran	1755
Barnaby	Onsl	1769
Barnaby	Onsl	1770
Charles	Onsl	1769
Da.	Chow	1717
David	Chow	1721
Elizabeth	Gran	1784
Francis	Oran	1755
James	Gran	1769
James Constable	NewH	1762
James	NewH	1763
James	Pitt	1775
John	Dobb	1769
John	Rand	1779
John	Surr	1772
Nathaniel	Bute	1771
Nathaniel	FWV	1771
Nathaniel	Gran	1755
Nathaniel s. of		
Samuel	Gran	1755
Nathaniel	Gran	1784
Richard s. of		
Nathaniel	Gran	1755
Richard s. of		
Samuel	Gran	1755
Richard	Gran	1769
Richard Esq.	Gran	1784
Richard	Oran	1755
Rin	Anso	1763
Samuel	Casw	1777
Samuel	Edge	1742
Samuel	Gran	1755
Samuel	Gran	1769
Thomas	NewH	1762
Thomas	NewH	1763
Thomas	NewH	1765
Thomas	NewH	1767
Wm	Crav	1741
Wm	Oran	1755
HENDRICKS, Abraham	Perq	1720
Benjamin	Gran	1769
Daniel	Bert	1757
Edward	Rand	1779
Elizabeth	Bert	1769
Elizabeth	Perq	1720
Fran.	Crav	1720
Garrett	Surr	1771
Garrett	Surr	1772
James	Edge	1744
James	Oran	1755
James s. of Wm	Gran	1755
Jeremiah	Perq	1720
Joab	Perq	1720
John	Crav	1720
John	Curr	1715
John	Oran	1755
Joseph	Rand	1779
Nathan	Perq	1720
Samuel	Crav	1769
Solomon	Perq	1720
Thomas	Casw	1777
Wm	Gran	1755
HENDRICKSON, Abraham		
	Pasq	1754
Henry	Crav	1769

HENDRICKSON, John	Crav	1769	HERN, Wm s. of		
Jonathan	Bert	1769	Mason	Beau	1755
HENEGAN, Darby	NewH	1762	HERNDON, Humphrey	Gran	1769
HENESY, James	NewH	1762	Philip	Anso	1763
James	NewH	1763	Pumfrett	Gran	1769
John	NewH	1762	HERON, Arnwell	Dobb	1769
John	NewH	1763	Benjamin	NewH	1762
Widow	NewH	1762	Benjamin	NewH	1763
HENLEY, Darby	Casw	1777	Benjamin	NewH	1767
Elmore	Bute	1771	HERREN, Jacob	Dobb	1779
Elmore	FWV	1771	John		1743
James	Casw	1777	John	Dobb	1779
James	Dobb	1779	Joseph	Chow	1721
Jesse	Rand	1779	Lenny	Surr	1771
John	Casw	1777	Lenny	Surr	1772
John	Pasq	1769	Moses	Surr	1771
Joseph	Pasq	1769	HERRICK, Samuel	Pitt	1764
Wm	Gran	1769	HERRIMAN, David	Surr	1772
Wm	Gran	1784	George	Dobb	1769
HENNIN, Matthew	Rowa	1759	HERRING, Abraham	Bert	1743
HENNINGTON, John	Pitt	1762	Ann	Dobb	1769
John	Pitt	1764	Anthony	Bert	1742
Jonathan	Pitt	1764	Anthony	Crav	1742
HENNON, Wm	Gran	1784	Arthur	Dobb	1769
HENNONTON, John	Beau	1755	Benjamin	Dobb	1769
HENRY, Duncan	NewH	1767	Benjamin	Dobb	1779
Edward	Bert	1757	Edward	Surr	1772
Francis	Crav	1769	Frederick	Dobb	1769
Gabriel	Crav	1769	Frederick	Dobb	1779
J.	Chow	1721	Jacob	Dobb	1769
James	NewH	1767	James	Cumb	1755
John	Oran	1755	James	Dobb	1769
No.	Chow	1717	John	Chow	1721
Richard	NewH	1767	John	Crav	1743
Stephen	Crav	1769	John	Dobb	1769
Wm	Beau	1764	John	Dobb	1779
Wm	Edge	1734	John	NewH	1762
Wm	Edge	1743	John	NewH	1763
Wm	NewH	1767	John	NewH	1767
HENSLEY, Benjamin	Surr	1771	Joseph	Dobb	1769
Benjamin	Surr	1772	Joshua	Dobb	1769
James	Surr	1771	Matthew	Dobb	1769
John	Casw	1777	Michael	Dobb	1769
John	Onsl	1769	Michael	Dobb	1779
Maxfield	Casw	1777	Richard	NewH	1762
HENSON, Bartlett	Anso	1763	Richard	NewH	1763
Benjamin	Anso	1763	Sam	Chow	1717
Isum	Anso	1763	Samuel	Chow	1721
Philip Jr.	Anso	1763	Samuel	Crav	1742
Philip Sr.	Anso	1763	Simon 6 whites		
HERALD, Jonathan	Rowa	1759	4 blacks	Crav	1745
Pritchard	Perq	1740	Simon	Dobb	1769
HERBERT, James	Dobb	1769	Simon	Dobb	1779
HERBINE, John	Casw	1777	Solomon	Dobb	1769
HERD, Richard	Dobb	1769	Solomon	Dobb	1779
HEREL, Wm	Casw	1777	Thomas	Dobb	1769
HERENDEEN, Matthew	Pasq	1754	Wm	Cumb	1755
HERENTON, John	Beau	1743	Wm	Edge	1743
HERFORT, Mark	Beau	1755	HERRINGTON, Charles	Beau	1764
HERFTEE, Benjamin	Surr	1772	Jacob	Beau	1764
HERITAGE, Elizabeth	Dobb	1769	James	Beau	1755
John	Dobb	1769	John	Beau	1755
HERMAN, James	Dobb	1769	John	Beau	1764
HERN, John	Anso	1763	Paul	Beau	1755
Mason	Beau	1755	Paul	Pitt	1762

HERRITAGE, Hennage	Crav	1769	HEWS, Gabriel	Casw	1777
John	Dobb	1779	James	Casw	1777
Wm	Chow	1717	John	Casw	1777
Wm	Crav	1742	HIATT, Reuben	Gate	1786
HERRON, Anthony	Dobb	1769	Thomas	Gate	1786
HERVEY, Thomas	Perq	1740	HICKMAN, Benjamin	Crav	1769
HESTER, Benjamin	Gran	1784	Benjamin Jr.	Crav	1769
David	Gran	1769	Corbin	Gran	1784
Francis	Gran	1784	John	Brun	1769
Henry	Gran	1784	John	Brun	1772
James	Gran	1769	John	NewH	1755
James	Gran	1784	John	NewH	1762
John	Gran	1769	John	NewH	1763
Joseph	Gran	1784	Joseph	Pitt	1764
Robert	Gran	1784	Wm	Edge	1741
Thomas	Blad	1763	Wm	Gran	1769
Wm	Blad	1742	HICKS, Absalom	Gran	1769
Wm	Gran	1769	Billy	Dobb	1779
Wm	Gran	1784	Bishop	Gran	1784
Zachariah	Gran	1769	David	Chow	1717
Zachariah	Gran	1784	David	Chow	1721
HESTRIDGE, Ephraim	Bute	1771	Frederick	Surr	1771
Ephraim & s. Wm	FWV	1771	Frederick	Surr	1772
John	Bute	1771	Gilbert	Beau	1755
John	FWV	1771	Gilliard	Cumb	1767
Thomas	Bute	1771	Harrid	Gran	1784
Thomas	FWV	1771	Henry	Casw	1777
HEWBANK, Richard	Pitt	1762	James	Casw	1777
Richard	Pitt	1764	John	Anso	1763
HEWES, Sarah	Gate	1786	John	Bute	1771
HEWINS, James	Perq	1720	John Jr.	Bute	1771
HEWITT, Charles	Rand	1779	John	Cart	1744
Ebenezer	Brun	1769	John	Chow	1753
Ebenezer Jr.	Brun	1769	John	FWV	1771
Ebenezer	Brun	1772	John Jr.	FWV	1771
Ebenezer Jr.	Brun	1772	John	Pasq	1769
Ebenezer	NewH	1763	Patrick	Chow	1753
Ebenezer	Rand	1779	Rt. (Robert)	Chow	1717
Elisha	Brun	1769	Robert	Gran	1755
Elisha	Brun	1772	Robert	Gran	1769
Hezekiah	Brun	1772	Robert Jr.	Gran	1784
Jacob	Brun	1769	Samuel	Chow	1753
Jacob	Brun	1772	Samuel	Gran	1769
John	Gran	1769	Samuel	Gran	1784
John	Onsl	1769	Samuel	Pitt	1764
John	Onsl	1770	Stephen	Gran	1769
Joseph	Brun	1772	Thomas	Chow	1717
Joseph	NewH	1762	Thomas	Edge	1734
Joseph	NewH	1763	Thomas	FWV	1771
Philip	Brun	1769	Wm	Anso	1763
Philip	Brun	1772	Wm	Dobb	1769
Randall	Brun	1769	Wm Constable	Gran	1755
Randall Jr.	Brun	1769	Wm	Gran	1769
Randall	Brun	1772	Wm	Gran	1784
Randall Jr.	Brun	1772	HICKSON, Timothy	Pasq	1769
Randolph Sr.	NewH	1762	Timothy s.		
Randolph	NewH	1763	Timothy	Pasq	1769
Richard	Brun	1769	HIDE, Benjamin	Oran	1755
Richard	Brun	1772	Benjamin	Surr	1771
Richard	NewH	1763	George	Oran	1755
Wm	Gran	1769	Richard	NorH	1762
Wm	Gran	1784	Stephen	Surr	1771
HEWLITT, Eli	Bert	1769	HIDER, Ben	Ruth	1790
HEWS, Charles	Casw	1777	Benj.	Tryo	1776
Edward	Rand	1779	HIGDON, Leonard	Anso	1763

HIGGIE, Wm	Gran	1784	HILL, George	Brun	1772
HIGGINS, Charles	Oran	1755	George	NewH	1763
James	Anso	1763	Green	Bute	1771
Jephtha	Blad	1763	Green	FWV	1771
John	Anso	1763	Guy	Chow	1753
Michael	Crav	1750	Guy	Gate	1786
Michael	NewH	1741	Harmon	NorH	1762
Michael	Onsl	1769	Henry	Bert	1757
Michael	Onsl	1770	Henry	Bute	1771
Richard	Pitt	1764	Henry	Chow	1753
Wm	Anso	1763	Henry	FWV	1771
Wm	Crav	1769	Henry	Gate	1786
HIGGS, Abraham	Bert	1769	Himbrick	Gate	1786
Isaac	Bert	1769	Isaac	Blad	1763
John	Bert	1757	Isaac	Chow	1721
John	Bert	1769	Isaac	Cumb	1767
Leonard	Gran	1784	Isaac	Dobb	1779
Wm	Bert	1757	Jacob	Chow	1717
Zachariah Esq.	Gran	1784	Jacob	Perq	1720
HIGH, Samuel	Bute	1771	James	Cumb	1767
Samuel	FWV	1771	James	Edge	1734
HIGHACRE, James	Pitt	1764	James	Gran	1784
HIGHFIELD, Judith	Gran	1784	James	Pitt	1762
HIGHSMITH, Daneil	NewH	1763	Jane	Chow	1753
Daniel	NewH	1765	Jane	Gate	1786
Daniel	NewH	1767	John	Bert	1757
HIGHT, Herbert	Bute	1771	John Jr.	Bute	1771
Herbert	FWV	1771	John	Casw	1777
John	Bute	1771	John	Chow	1717
John	FWV	1771	John	Chow	1721
Richard	FWV	1771	John	Crav	1769
Samuel	Pitt	1775	John	Dobb	1779
Solomon	Chow	1753	John	Gran	1784
HIGHTOWER, Charnal	Bute	1771	John	NewH	1762
Charnal	FWV	1771	John	Rand	1779
John	Anso	1763	Joseph	Gran	1769
Thomas	Anso	1763	Joseph	Rand	1779
HILBURN, John	Beau	1764	Joshua	Pitt	1763
Vaughn	Dobb	1769	Joshua	Pitt	1764
HILDRETH, David	Anso	1763	Kean	Gate	1786
HILEY, Jethro	Dobb	1779	Major	Onsl	1770
HILL, Aaron	Pasq	1743	Mary	Crav	1719
Aaron	Pasq	1754	Michael	Bert	1757
Abraham	Chow	1721	Moses	Bert	1757
Abraham	Chow	1753	Moses	Chow	1717
Abraham	Pitt	1762	Moses	Chow	1721
Amos	Bute	1771	Moses	Gate	1786
Amos	FWV	1771	Nicholas	Bute	1771
Benjamin	Bert	1741	Nicholas s.		
Benjamin	FWV	1771	Richard	FWV	1771
Braggs	Dobb	1779	Richard	Crav	1720
Carmen	Beau	1764	Richard	Crav	1769
Charles	Anso	1763	Richard	Cumb	1767
Charles	Surr	1771	Robert	Bute	1771
Clement	Gate	1786	Robert	Dobb	1769
David	Gate	1786	Robert	Edge	1734
Edward	Dobb	1769	Robert	FWV	1771
Edward	NewH	1755	Robert	Pasq	1769
Ephraim	Bute	1771	Robert	Surr	1771
Ephraim	FWV	1771	Robert	Surr	1772
Francis			Samuel 4 slaves	Crav	1769
Constable	Crav	1720	Solomon	Bert	1757
Francis	Dobb	1769	Stephen	Crav	1769
George	Beau	1755	Thomas	Bute	1771
George	Brun	1769	Thomas Jr.	Bute	1771

HILL, Thomas Jr.   FWV 1771
   Thomas   Gran 1755
   Thomas   NewH 1741
   Thomas   Rand 1779
   Thomas   Tyrr 1755
   Widow   Beau 1755
   Wm   Blad 1763
   Wm   Brun 1769
   Wm   Brun 1772
   Wm Sr.   Bute 1771
   Wm   Bute 1771
   Wm   Chow 1717
   Wm   Chow 1721
   Wm   Chow 1743
   Wm   Dobb 1769
   Wm   FWV 1771
   Wm Jr.   FWV 1771
   Wm   NewH 1762
   Wm   NewH 1763
   Wm   Onsl 1770
   Wm   Pasq 1769
   Wm   Rand 1779
   Wm   Surr 1771
   Wm   Surr 1772
HILLEN, Nathaniel   Anso 1763
HILLIARD, Francis   Dobb 1769
   Jeremiah   Gran 1755
   John   Blad 1781
   John   NorH 1762
   Philemon   Gran 1784
HILLS, Bundy   Pasq 1769
HILLSMAN, Bennett   Bute 1771
   Bennett & s.
   James   FWV 1771
   Hind   Bute 1771
   Hind   FWV 1771
HILLYARD, James   Brun 1772
   Jesse   Brun 1769
   Jesse   Brun 1772
   John   Crav 1743
   Thomas   Beau 1745
   Thomas   Chow 1721
   Wm   NorH 1744
HILTON, James   Oran 1755
   Nathaniel   Anso 1763
   Peter   Oran 1755
   Peter Jr.   Oran 1755
   Richard   Oran 1755
HIMAN, Michael   Crav 1769
   Peter   Crav 1769
HINAWORTH, Wm   Cumb 1767
HINES, Cader   Dobb 1779
   Charles   Dobb 1769
   Charles   Dobb 1779
   Daniel   Brun 1772
   George   Dobb 1779
   Isaac   Dobb 1769
   James   Dobb 1769
   John   Bert 1757
   John   Rand 1779
   Jonas   Brun 1772
   Joseph   Rand 1779
   Joseph Jr.   Rand 1779
   Levi   Rand 1779
   Lewis   Bert 1757

HINES, Moses   Gate 1786
   Reuben   Dobb 1769
   Reuben   Dobb 1779
   Solomon   Dobb 1769
   Thomas   Rowa 1759
   Wm   Dobb 1769
HINNIN, David   NewH 1755
HINSHAW, Absalom Jr.
                    Rand 1779
   Absalom Sr.   Rand 1779
   Ezra   Rand 1779
   Jacob   Rand 1779
   Jacob Jr.   Rand 1779
   John   Rand 1779
   Joseph   Rand 1779
   Thomas   Rand 1779
   Wm Jr.   Rand 1779
   Wm Sr.   Rand 1779
HINSON, Aaron   Dobb 1769
   Jesse   Dobb 1769
   Joseph   Dobb 1769
   Moses   Dobb 1769
HINT, John   Chow 1721
HINTON, Amos   Bert 1757
   Elizabeth   Chow 1753
   Hardy   Edge 1743
   Jacob   Chow 1753
   James   Chow 1753
   John   Bert 1757
   John   Bert 1769
   John   Chow 1721
   John   Chow 1753
   John   Edge 1742
   Jonas   Bert 1757
   Jonas   Chow 1753
   Jonas   Gate 1786
   Kedar   Gate 1786
   Martha   Bert 1769
   Noah   Bert 1769
   Surbrook   Gate 1786
   Wm   Chow 1721
   Wm   Edge 1742
   Wm   Gate 1786
HISE, Joseph   Rand 1779
   Thomas   Bert 1769
HISS, Daniel   NewH 1755
   Smith   NewH 1755
HITT, Aaron   Rand 1779
HIX, Samuel   Beau 1755
HIXON, Wm   Pasq 1743
HOAG, Archibald   Casw 1777
HOARNE, Wm   Pitt 1762
HOBBA, Jesse   Bert 1769
HOBBS, Aaron   Gate 1786
   Amos   Chow 1753
   Amos   Gate 1786
   Edmund   Gate 1786
   Elisha   Rand 1779
   Hannibal   Crav 1769
   Henry   Gate 1786
   Jacob   Gate 1786
   James   Gran 1755
   James   Onsl 1769
   John   Chow 1753
   John   Dobb 1769

HOBBS, John	Onsl	1769
John	Onsl	1770
Mary	Chow	1753
Moses	Gate	1786
Patience	Gate	1786
Reubin	Gate	1786
Simon	Onsl	1769
Simon	Onsl	1770
Simon Jr.	Onsl	1770
Thomas	Chow	1721
Wm	Gran	1755
HOBBY, Laur.	Chow	1717
Laurence	Chow	1721
Wm	NorH	1742
HOBERN, Adam	Pasq	1769
HOBGOOD, Hezekiah	Gran	1769
HOBIE, George	Rand	1779
HOBSON, Fra.	Chow	1717
Francis	Beau	1755
Francis	Bert	1757
Francis	Chow	1721
Francis	Pitt	1762
Francis	Pitt	1764
Francis	Tyrr	1755
HOCOT, Edward	Pitt	1762
Edward	Pitt	1764
HODGE, James	Cumb	1767
John Sr.	Beau	1755
John	Casw	1777
Thomas	Cumb	1767
Thomas	Tyrr	1755
Wm	Cumb	1767
HODGES, Benjamin	Beau	1755
Cat.	Edge	1734
Elias	Bert	1757
Ellis	Pitt	1762
Francis	Crav	1745
Francis Sr.	Dobb	1769
Francis	Dobb	1769
Francis	Dobb	1779
Henry	Beau	1755
Henry	Pitt	1762
Henry	Pitt	1764
Howell	Pitt	1762
Howell	Pitt	1764
Isom Jr.	Pitt	1764
John	Beau	1755
John	Dobb	1769
John Sr.	Pitt	1762
John	Pitt	1762
Joseph	Gran	1769
Joshua	Dobb	1769
Joshua	Dobb	1779
Matthew	Bert	1769
Matthew	Pitt	1762
Matthew	Pitt	1764
Richard	Dobb	1769
Richard	Dobb	1779
Robert	Beau	1755
Robert	Pitt	1762
Robert	Pitt	1764
Roger	Beau	1744
Wm	Anso	1763
HODGIN, Robert	Rand	1779
HODGION, James	Beau	1764
HODGSON, Edward	Bert	1757
HOFFHEINB, Daniel	Surr	1771
HOFFLER, Thomas	Gate	1786
HOFFMAN, Fred.	Chow	1717
HOFLER, Hance	Chow	1753
HOGAN, Edward	Tryo	1776
Griffin	Oran	1755
John	Gran	1769
Joshua	Gran	1755
HOGANS, Juxon	NewH	1767
Shadrack	Anso	1763
HOGG, Gideon Jr.	Casw	1777
Gideon Sr.	Casw	1777
James	N.C.	1701
Thomas	Crav	1720
Wm	Casw	1777
HOGER, Thomas	N.C.	1701
HOGGARD, Patrick	Bert	1757
Patrick	Bert	1769
HOGGART, John	Rand	1779
HOGGETT, Anthony	Rowa	1759
Philip	Rowa	1759
Wm	Rowa	1759
HOGGINS, Samuel	NewH	1765
Simon	NewH	1763
Wm	Anso	1763
HOGWOOD, Francis s.		
Reuben Wm	FWV	1771
James	Oran	1755
John	Oran	1755
HOLADAY, Elizabeth	Tyrr	1755
Thomas	Tyrr	1755
HOLAN, David	NewH	1755
HOLBERT, Wm	Surr	1772
HOLBROOK, George	Surr	1772
John	Chow	1717
John 1400 acres	Chow	1721
Wm	Rowa	1759
HOLCOMB, Grimes	Cumb	1767
Wm	Oran	1755
HOLDEN, Arthur	Pitt	1762
Arthur	Pitt	1764
Benjamin	Brun	1772
Benjamin s. of		
David	Dobb	1769
David	Dobb	1769
Jesse	Casw	1777
Thomas	Oran	1755
HOLDER, Joseph	Surr	1771
Joseph	Surr	1772
Thomas	Bert	1757
Wm	Surr	1771
HOLDING, Benjamin	Brun	1769
Benjamin	Brun	1772
Joshua	Brun	1769
Joshua	Brun	1772
HOLDMAN, Isaac	Rowa	1759
HOLEPECT, Frederick	Surr	1772
HOLIDAY, Henry	Oran	1755
Robert	Bert	1769
Samuel	Dobb	1779
HOLIMAN, Richard	Casw	1777
HOLIONBACK, David	Casw	1777
John	Casw	1777
HOLLAMAN, Jean	Bert	1769

HOLLAND, Apshee	Pitt	1762	HOLLINGSWORTH,		
Daniel	NewH	1755	Stephen	NewH	1745
Daniel	NewH	1762	Valentine	Oran	1755
Daniel	NewH	1763	HOLLINSWORTH, John	NewH	1762
Dempsey	Bert	1757	John	NewH	1763
Edward	Cumb	1767	John	NewH	1765
Elisha	Dobb	1769	John	NewH	1767
Ezekiel	Dobb	1779	Samuel	Rand	1779
Henry	Bert	1757	HOLLIS, James	Crav	1769
Henry s. of John	Dobb	1769	Malcomb	Crav	1769
James	Dobb	1769	Moses	Oran	1755
James	Tyrr	1755	Nottby	Oran	1755
John	Beau	1755	Wm	Crav	1769
John	Dobb	1769	HOLLOWAY, James	Bute	1771
John	NewH	1763	James	FWV	1771
Joseph	Bert	1757	John	Casw	1777
Joseph	Bert	1769	John	Crav	1746
Joseph	Gate	1786	Stephany	Surr	1772
Moses	Dobb	1769	Stephany	Surr	1772
Otho	Curr	1755	Thomas	Perq	1720
Richard	Beau	1755	Thomas	Perq	1740
Richard	Edge	1743	Wm	Bert	1757
Richard	Pitt	1764	HOLLOWELL, Elizabeth		
Sewell	Bert	1769		Bert	1769
Squire	Pitt	1764	John	Perq	1740
Theophilis	Bert	1757	Thomas	Perq	1740
Thomas s. of			HOLLY, Joseph	Gran	1755
John	Dobb	1769	Nathaniel	Roan	1720
Wm	Bert	1757	Pat, w. of Jos.	Gran	1755
Wm	Bert	1769	Wm	Gran	1755
HOLLANDIN, Mark	Pitt	1764	HOLLYMAN, Edward	Gran	1755
HOLLAWAY, John	Crav	1769	Wm	Gran	1755
Wm	Crav	1769	HOLMAN, John	Dobb	1779
HOLLEY, Francis	Beau	1755	Richard	N.C.	1701
James	Bert	1757	Wm	N.C.	1701
James	Bert	1769	HOLMES, Archibald	Cumb	1767
James Jr.	Bert	1769	Charles	Dobb	1769
John	Chow	1721	Charles Jr.	Dobb	1769
Nathaniel	Bert	1757	Charles	Dobb	1779
Nathaniel	Bert	1769	Ebenezer	Onsl	1741
Nathaniel	Chow	1721	Edmund	Brun	1772
Richard	Bert	1743	Edward	Bert	1742
Thomas	Beau	1755	Edward	Brun	1769
HOLLOMAN, Christopher			Edward	Brun	1772
	Bert	1757	Edward s. of		
Christopher	Dobb	1779	Timothy	Dobb	1769
Edward or Edmund	Bert	1757	Frederick	Dobb	1779
Edward s. Thomas	Bert	1757	Frederick	Edge	1744
Edward	Bute	1771	Hamma	FWV	1771
Harmon	Bert	1757	Hammer	Bute	1771
Jeremiah	Dobb	1779	James	Bert	1757
Nathan	Dobb	1779	James	Dobb	1769
Samuel	Bert	1757	James	Dobb	1779
Samuel	Dobb	1769	John	Chow	1721
Solomon	Bert	1757	John	Crav	1769
HOLLINGSWORTH, Henry			John	Dobb	1769
	NewH	1741	John	Dobb	1779
Jacob	Rand	1779	Richard 2 slaves		
John	Blad	1763		Brun	1769
John	Blad	1781	Samuel	Gran	1769
Samuel	Blad	1743	Samuel	Gran	1784
Samuel	Blad	1763	Simon	Bert	1742
Samuel	Blad	1781	Simon Jr.	Dobb	1769
Stephen	Blad	1763	Simon	Dobb	1779
Stephen	Blad	1781	Timothy	Dobb	1769

HOLMES, Timothy	Dobb	1779	HOOTEN, Wm	Bert	1769
Wm	Bert	1757	HOOVER, Andrew	Rand	1779
Wm	Chow	1753	Henry	Crav	1769
HOLSHOES,	Beau	1755	Jonas	Rand	1779
HOLT, Charles	Gran	1784	Samuel	Crav	1769
Edward	Surr	1772	HOPKINS, Aaron	Dobb	1779
John	Gran	1769	Ainot	Pitt	1764
John	Gran	1784	Alexander	Tyrr	1755
Martin	Cumb	1767	Andre w	Dobb	1769
Obadiah	NewH	1762	Ann	Gran	1784
Obadiah	NewH	1765	Arnold	Chow	1717
Obadiah	NewH	1767	Arnold	Chow	1721
Thomas	Chow	1753	Arnoll	Pitt	1762
HOLTON, Alexander	Surr	1771	Charles	Rand	1779
Alexander	Surr	1772	Dennis	Rand	1779
George	Crav	1769	Isaac	Gran	1784
Jesse	Beau	1755	James	Dobb	1769
Jesse Jr.	Beau	1755	James	Oran	1755
Jesse	Crav	1769	John	Bert	1757
Nathaniel	Cumb	1767	John	Bert	1769
Sam	Cumb	1755	John	Chow	1753
Tuck	Beau	1764	John	Oran	1755
Wm	Oran	1755	Joseph	Rand	1779
HOLYFIELD, Gideon	Oran	1755	Lambeth	Anso	1763
HOMBEY, Samuel	Anso	1763	Nathaniel	Cumb	1767
HOMER, Walter	Anso	1763	Robert	Dobb	1769
HONGLEY, James			Samuel	Chow	1721
HOOD, Edward	Dobb	1779	Thomas	Gran	1784
John	Casw	1777	Wm	Oran	1755
Robert	Pitt	1762	Wm	Pitt	1764
Thomas	Pitt	1764	Wm	Pitt	1775
Wm	Dobb	1769	HOPPER, Charles	Rand	1779
HOODSON, Wm	N.C.	1701	George	Rand	1779
HOOKE, Thomas	Dobb	1769	James	Casw	1777
HOOKER, Benjamin	Bert	1757	James	Gran	1769
Benjamin	Bert	1769	John	Casw	1777
Godfrey	Chow	1721	Thomas Jr.	Casw	1777
Hamrick	Dobb	1769	Thomas Sr.	Casw	1777
Heymrick	Dobb	1779	HOPTON, Charles Jr.	Dobb	1769
James	Bert	1757	Charles Sr.	Dobb	1769
John	Gran	1769	Charles	N.C.	1701
John	Gran	1784	HORAH, Henry	Powa	1759
John Jr.	Gran	1784	HORD, Peter	Chow	1717
John Esq.	Tyrr	1755	HORLEY, Henry	Casw	1777
Robert	Surr	1771	John	Casw	1777
Wm	Bert	1757	HORNBECK, John	Blad	1745
Wm Jr.	Chow	1717	HORNBEY, Samuel	Anso	1763
Wm	Dobb	1769	HORNBUCK, John	Anso	1763
Wm	Dobb	1779	HORNE, Charles	Bert	1757
Wm	Surr	1771	John	Edge	1743
HOOKS, Jacob	Dobb	1769	Moses	Bert	1744
Robert	Dobb	1779	Nathaniel	Gran	1755
Thomas	Bert	1757	Richard	Chow	1717
Thomas	Bert	1769	Richard	Chow	1721
Wm	Bert	1757	Richard	Surr	1772
Wm	Dobb	1769	Sion	Cumb	1767
HOOMES, Handy	Rand	1779	Thomas	Chow	1721
HOOPER, James	Chow	1721	Thomas	NorH	1742
Thomas	Rowa	1758	HORNEDAY, John	Oran	1755
Thomas	Rowa	1759	HORNER, James	Rand	1779
Thomas	Surr	1771	Wm	Rand	1779
Thomas	Surr	1772	HORNSBY, Wm	Gran	1769
HOOTEN, John	Cumb	1767	Wm	Gran	1784
John Jr.	Cumb	1767	HORNSTON, Edmond	Perq	1740
Wm	Bert	1757	HORSENDS, Richard	Beau	1755

HORSENDS, Richard	Crav	1769
HORTON, David	Bert	1757
Hugh	Bert	1757
James	Oran	1755
Parmenas		
11 slaves	Crav	1769
Samuel	Bute	1771
Samuel	FWV	1771
Samuel Jr.	FWV	1771
Wm	Bert	1757
HOSA, Wm	Bert	1757
HOSE, Robert	Perq	1720
Robert	Perq	1740
HOSEA, Abram	Pasq	1769
John	Pasq	1754
John 5 slaves	Pasq	1769
Joseph	Pasq	1769
Robert 3 slaves	Pasq	1754
Robert	Pasq	1769
Thomas	Pasq	1769
HOSKINS, Thomas	Chow	1717
Thomas	Chow	1721
Thomas	Chow	1753
Thomas Jr.	Chow	1753
Wm	Chow	1753
HOSMER, Urian	Onsl	1770
HOSTAIN, Nicholas	Gran	1755
HOSTUN, Nicholas	Gran	1769
HOTERING, Wm	Casw	1777
HOTSON, John	Dobb	1769
John, s. of John	Dobb	1769
HOUGH, Hezekiah	NorH	1762
HOUGHKINS, Alexander		
	Surr	1771
HOUGHMAN, Barnett	Rand	1779
Daniel	Rand	1779
HOUGHTON, Charles	Chow	1753
David	Chow	1753
HOUK, James	Onsl	1770
HOULDER, James	Bert	1769
Thomas Jr.	Bert	1769
HOULT, Thomas	Chow	1753
HOUSE, Everett	Dobb	1779
George Jr.	Bert	1757
George Sr.	Bert	1757
George Sr.	Bert	1769
George	Bert	1769
Gentle	Bute	1771
Isaac	Bute	1771
Isaac overseer	FWV	1771
James	Bute	1771
James	FWV	1771
John	FWV	1771
John	NewH	1755
John	Oran	1755
Joshua	Dobb	1769
Thomas	Bert	1757
Thomas	Bert	1769
Thomas	Bute	1771
Thomas	FWV	1771
Wm	Bute	1771
Wm s. James		
& John	FWV	1771
Wm	Gran	1755
HOUSER, George	Surr	1772

Houser, Jacob	Surr	1772
John	Surr	1772
Martin	Surr	1772
Michael	Surr	1772
Peter	Surr	1772
HOUSTIN, Samuel	Blad	1763
HOUSTON, Wm	Dobb	1769
HOW, Alexander	Bert	1769
James	Bert	1769
Robert	Blad	1763
Robert Esq.	Blad	1763
Robert	NewH	1763
Wm	Blad	1763
HOWARD, Abraham	Surr	1771
Abraham	Surr	1772
Annol	Cumb	1767
Ashburne	Blad	1763
Benjamin	Blad	1763
Charles	Beau	1755
Ed.	Chow	1717
Edward	Bert	1757
Edward	Chow	1721
Edward	Gran	1784
Edward	Onsl	1769
Francis	Gran	1769
George	Curr	1755
Groves	Gran	1784
Hezekiah	Blad	1763
Hezekiah	Blad	1781
James	Anso	1763
James	Bert	1757
James	Cumb	1755
James	NewH	1762
James	NewH	1763
James	NewH	1765
James	NewH	1767
James Esq.	Onsl	1769
James Esq.	Onsl	1770
Jetus	Rowa	1759
John	Blad	1763
John	Crav	1769
John	Gran	1755
John	Gran	1769
John	Gran	1784
John	NewH	1741
John	Onsl	1742
John	Onsl	1769
John	Onsl	1770
John	Rowa	1759
John	Surr	1771
John Sr.	Surr	1772
Joseph	Blad	1763
Joseph	NewH	1762
Joseph	Onsl	1741
Julius	Bute	1771
Julius	FWV	1771
Lyman	NewH	1755
Nathan	Rand	1779
Parmenus	Blad	1781
Peter	Gran	1769
Philip Sr.	Rowa	1759
Robert	Cumb	1755
Samuel	Bert	1757
Samuel	Cumb	1755
Samuel	Dobb	1769

HOWARD, Seth	Crav 1769	HOWELL, Joseph	Edge 1742
Simon	NewH 1762	Joshua	Dobb 1769
Solomon	Bert 1757	Joshua	Dobb 1779
Solomon	Gran 1769	Lewis	Anso 1763
Stephen	Chow 1721	Lewis	Oran 1755
Stephen	Onsl 1741	Major	Dobb 1779
Stephen	Onsl 1747	Osborne	Dobb 1769
Stephen	Oran 1755	Robert	Bert 1743
Thomas	Bert 1757	Robert	Bert 1757
Thomas	Bute 1771	Thomas	Bert 1757
Thomas	FWV 1771	Thomas	Bert 1769
Widow	Rowa 1759	Thomas	Dobb 1769
Wm	Blad 1763	Thomas	Gran 1755
Wm	Cumb 1767	Thomas	Gran 1769
Wm	Curr 1755	Thomas	Gran 1784
Wm	Gran 1769	Watson	Gate 1786
Wm	NewH 1755	Wm	Bute 1771
Wm	Onsl 1769	Wm	Casw 1777
Wm	Onsl 1770	Wm	Dobb 1769
Wm	Oran 1755	Wm	Dobb 1779
Wm	Surr 1771	Wm & bro.	
Wm	Surr 1772	Samuel	FWV 1771
HOWCOTT, Ed.	Chow 1717	Wm	Gran 1769
Edward	Chow 1721	HOWEN, John	Dobb 1779
Gentle	Chow	HOWER, Wm	Gran 1769
Isaac		HOWET, Richard	Tyrr 1755
James		Wm	Chow 1721
John	Chow 1721	Wm	Tyrr 1755
John		Wm Jr.	Tyrr 1755
Nathaniel	Chow 1753	HOWLAND, Gershom	Cart 1741
Thomas		HOWLETT, Wm	Rand 1779
HOWE, Arthur	NewH 1762	HOWSE, James	Onsl 1769
Arthur	NewH 1767	HOZ, John	Surr 1771
Clifford	Crav 1769	Samuel	Surr 1771
Edmund	NewH 1767	HUBBARD, James	Bert 1757
Job	NewH 1762	James	Chow 1753
Job	NewH 1765	James	Crav 1769
Job	NewH 1767	John	Bert 1757
John	NewH 1755	John	Surr 1772
Robert Esq.		Matthew	Bert 1757
13 slaves	Blad 1763	Thomas	Chow 1753
Robert	Brun 1769	Wm	Casw 1777
Robert	Brun 1772	HUBERT, Benjamin	
Thomas	Crav 1769	Jr.	Casw 1777
Thomas	NewH 1762	Benjamin Sr.	Casw 1777
Wm	Blad 1763	James	Casw 1777
HOWELL, Adimal	Dobb 1779	Matthew	Casw 1777
Alexander	Blad 1763	HUCKABY, James	Bute 1771
Archelaus	Dobb 1779	James	FWV 1771
Caleb	Beau 1742	John	Bute 1771
Daniel	Dobb 1769	John	FWV 1771
Edmund	NorH 1762	Samuel	Gran 1769
Edward Sr.	Gate 1786	Thomas	Bute 1771
Griffith	Beau 1755	Thomas	FWV 1771
Hopkin	Anso 1763	Thomas	Gran 1769
James	Rowa 1759	HUCKER, Wm	Rand 1779
John	Bert 1743	HUCKILL, Harmon	Crav 1769
John	Bert 1757	HUDDLESTON, John	Gran 1784
John	Crav 1744	Wm	Gran 1769
John	Cumb 1767	HUDE, Stephen	Surr 1772
John	Dobb 1769	HUDGEON, Joseph	Casw 1777
John s. of		HUDGINS, Humphrey	Gate 1786
Joshua	Dobb 1769	HUDLAY, John	Perq 1720
John Sr.	Dobb 1779	HUDLER, Joseph	Crav 1769
Jonathan	Pasq 1754	HUDLES, John	Dobb 1769

HUDNALL, Robert	Edge	1741	HUGGINS, Jacob		Onsl	1770
HUDSON, Chamberlain	Bute	1771	Jacob Jr.		Onsl	1770
Chamberlain s.			James		Rowa	1759
Chamberlain	FWV	1771	John		Onsl	1742
Chamberlain	Gran	1755	John		Rowa	1759
Cuthbert	Gran	1769	Luke		Crav	1769
Henry	Bute	1771	HUGH, John		Pasq	1769
Henry	FWV	1771	John s. of John		Pasq	1769
Isaac	Bute	1771	Thomas		Pasq	1769
Isaac & s.			HUGHES, Demsey		Cumb	1767
John	FWV	1771	Edward		Blad	1763
Job	NewH	1762	Edward		Chow	1721
Job	NewH	1763	Edward		Rowa	1759
John	Bute	1771	Gabriel		Casw	1777
John	FWV	1771	John		Anso	1763
John	Perq	1720	John		Casw	1777
John	Perq	1740	John		Curr	1755
Jos.	Chow	1717	John		Tyrr	1755
Joseph	Chow	1721	Samuel		Blad	1763
Joseph	Pitt	1762	Samuel		Oran	1755
Joseph	Tyrr	1755	Solomon		Blad	1742
Joshua	Casw	1777	Thomas		Bert	1757
Lewis	Beau	1755	Thomas		Bert	1769
Lewis	Pitt	1762	Thomas		Dobb	1769
Robert	Casw	1777	Wm		Bert	1757
Wm	Bute	1777	Wm		Bert	1769
Wm	FWV	1771	Wm Jr.		Chow	1753
Wm	NewH	1762	Wm Sr.		Chow	1753
HUDSPETH, Carter	Gran	1769	Wm		Pasq	1769
Carter	Gran	1784	HUINS, John		Gran	1755
George	Gran	1769	HULES, Charles		Surr	1771
Jiles	Gran	1769	HULL, John		Chow	1743
Oris	Gran	1769	John		Chow	1753
Ralph	Edge	1742	Wm		Onsl	1769
HUELETT, Abraham	Pasq	1769	Wm		Onsl	1770
HUES, John	Pasq	1769	HULLEY, Charles		Surr	1771
Thomas	Oran	1755	HULLFORT, Wm		Crav	1720
HUFF, Daniel	Surr	1771	HULLSON, Robert		Crav	1720
Daniel	Oran	1755	HUMAN, Basil		Casw	1777
Daniel	Surr	1772	HUMPHREY, Benjamin		Blad	1781
Joseph	Cumb	1767	Chambers		Dobb	1769
Joseph	Oran	1755	Daniel		Onsl	1769
Richard	NewH	1741	Daniel		Onsl	1770
Wm	FWV	1771	Eustice		Onsl	1769
HUFFEIN, Solomon	NewH	1755	Eustice		Onsl	1770
HUFFERN, Solomon	NewH	1755	Jacob		Onsl	1769
HUFFHAM, Richard	NewH	1767	Jacob		Onsl	1770
Solomon Jr.	NewH	1767	John		Onsl	1769
Solomon Sr.	NewH	1767	Robert		Roan	1720
HUFFIND, Daniel	Surr	1772	Thomas		Onsl	1769
HUFFINS, Luke	Casw	1769	Wm		Bert	1757
HUFFMAN, George	Surr	1771	Wm		Brun	1769
George	Surr	1772	Wm		Brun	1772
Jacob	Cumb	1767	Wm		Onsl	1769
HUFFOM, John	NewH	1765	Wm		Onsl	1770
Richard	NewH	1765	HUMPHREYS, Adam		Pasq	1769
Solomon Jr.	NewH	1765	Felts		Perq	1720
Solomon Sr.	NewH	1765	Groffen		Oran	1755
HUFFON, Solomon	NewH	1755	John		Gran	1784
HUFTON, David	Perq	1740	Jonathan			
John	NewH	1762	1 slave		Pasq	1769
John	Perq	1740	Joseph		Blad	1763
HUGBURY, John	Anso	1763	Joseph		Crav	1769
HUGE, Thomas	Pasq	1769	Thomas 1 slave		Pasq	1769
HUGGINS, Jacob	Onsl	1769	Wm		Brun	1772

HUMPHREYS, Wm Jr.	Pasq	1769
HUNNICUTT, Augustine		
	Gran	1755
Hartwell	Cumb	1767
John	Cumb	1767
John	Gran	1755
Mansday	Cumb	1767
Meredith	Brun	1769
HUNT, Christopher	Gran	1769
Epectus	Onsl	1769
George	FWV	1771
George	Gran	1784
Gershom	Rowa	1759
Hardy	Bute	1771
Hardy	FWV	1771
Henry	Bute	1771
Henry	FWV	1771
James	Bute	1771
James	FWV	1771
James	Gran	1769
James	Gran	1784
John	Gran	1769
John	Gran	1784
John	Rowa	1759
Jonathan	Rowa	1759
Momucan	Gran	1769
Mourning	Gran	1769
Nathaniel	Bute	1771
Nathaniel	FWV	1771
Onesiphorus	Onsl	1769
Samuel	Gran	1784
Thomas	Bute	1771
Thomas	FWV	1771
Thomas	Gran	1755
Thomas	Gran	1769
Thomas	Rowa	1759
Wm	Bert	1769
Wm	Gran	1769
Wm Jr.	Gran	1784
Wm Sr.	Gran	1784
HUNTER, Abraham	Gran	1784
Allen	Pasq	1769
Charles	Rowa	1759
Daniel	Gran	1784
Elisha	Bute	1771
Elisha	Chow	1742
Elisha	Chow	1753
Elisha	Cumb	1767
Elisha	FWV	1771
Elisha	Gate	1786
Elizabeth	Onsl	1769
Elizabeth	Onsl	1770
Ephraim	Bert	1757
Ezekiel	Onsl	1769
Hardy	Bert	1757
Hardy	Bert	1769
Hartwell	Rand	1779
Henry	Bert	1757
Henry	Bert	1769
Henry	Rowa	1759
Isaac	Bute	1771
Isaac	Chow	1744
Isaac	Gate	1786
Jacob	Chow	1753
Jacob	Rowa	1759

HUNTER, Jesse	Bert	1757
Jesse	Bute	1771
Jesse	Chow	1753
Jesse	FWV	1771
John	Bert	1757
John, orphan	Gate	1786
John	Oran	1755
John	Pasq	1769
John (Cpt.)	Rowa	1759
Meshucah	Gran	1784
Patty	Bert	1757
Robert	NewH	1762
Samuel	Tryo	1776
Sarah	Bert	1769
Sarah	Chow	1753
Theophilis	Gate	1786
Thomas	Bert	1769
Thomas	Gate	1786
Wm	Chow	1753
Wm	Gate	1786
Wm	Oran	1755
Wm	Rand	1779
HURD, Charles	Cumb	1755
HURDLE, Abraham	Gate	1786
Hardin	Chow	1753
Joseph	Gate	1786
Sarah	Chow	1753
Thomas	Chow	1753
Thomas	Gate	1786
HURLEY, John	Oran	1755
John	Pitt	1762
Moses	Crav	1769
HURST, John	Bert	1757
John	Cumb	1755
Thomas	Bert	1757
Wm	Gran	1755
HURT, Solomon	NewH	1762
Susannah	Gran	1784
HUSBANDS, John	Anso	1763
Loamy	Surr	1772
Robert	Surr	1771
Robert	Surr	1772
HUSK, Wm	Bute	1771
Wm	FWV	1771
HUSKEE, Allen	Pasq	1769
Wm	Pasq	1769
HUSKETH, John Jr.	Gran	1784
John Sr.	Gran	1784
HUSSEY, Samuel	Pitt	1763
Simeon	Onsl	1769
Simon	NorH	1762
Stephen	Rand	1779
Wm	Rand	1779
HUST, John	Cumb	1767
Solomon	NewH	1767
HUSTON, Christopher	Casw	1777
George	Casw	1777
Robert	Casw	1777
Solomon Jr.	NewH	1762
Solomon Sr.	NewH	1762
HUTCHENS, John	FWV	1771
John	Surr	1771
John	Surr	1772
Joseph	NewH	1741
Wm	Gran	1755

HUTCHERN, Thomas	NewH 1755		INGRAM, John		NorH 1762
HUTCHINGS, Francis	Gran 1769		John		Rand 1779
Frederick	Gran 1769		Joshua		Bute 1771
Thomas	NewH 1762		Joshua		FWV 1771
Thomas	NewH 1763		Wm		Rand 1779
HUTCHINS, Anthony	Anso 1763		INMAN, George		Bert 1757
James	Anso 1763		James		Blad 1763
Miles	Dobb 1769		Robert		Edge 1734
Robert	Dobb 1769		INNES, Col.		NewH 1752
Thomas	NewH 1755		INSON, John		Pasq 1754
Thomas	NewH 1765		Joseph		Surr 1771
HUTCHINSON, James	Chow 1721		Joseph		Surr 1772
John	Beau 1755		Lemuel		Pasq 1754
HUTCHISON, Peter	Casw 1777		Wm		Rand 1779
HUTSON, Henry	Gran 1755		INYARD, Abraham		Surr 1771
John	Perq 1720		John		Surr 1771
John	Perq 1740		IPOCK, Christian		Crav 1742
Lewis	Pitt 1764		Christian		Crav 1769
Wm	Crav 1720		Felton		Dobb 1779
HUTTECALF, David	Beau 1755		Jacob		Crav 1742
HUTTON, Wm	Rowa 1759		Jacob		Crav 1769
HUZRY, Samuel	Pitt 1775		Peter		Crav 1769
HYATT, George	Rowa 1759		IRBY, Henry		NewH 1762
Jesse	Gate 1786		Henry		NewH 1763
John	Rowa 1759		IRELAND, Arthur		NewH 1767
Joseph	Rowa 1759		IRVIN, George		Oran 1755
Joseph	Surr 1771		James		Anso 1763
Joseph	Surr 1772		ISAAC, Elijah		Rand 1779
Wm	Surr 1771		Elisha		Rowa 1758
Wm	Surr 1772		Elisha		Rowa 1759
HYDE, Hartwell	Gran 1784		John		Blad 1763
HYMAN, John	Bert 1757		ISBELL, Zachariah		Surr 1771
Mary s. Wm			Zachariah		Surr 1772
Hardy	Bert 1757		ISLAND, Elizabeth		Curr 1755
Thomas	Bert 1757		ISLER, Frederick		
HYME, John	NewH 1755		14 slaves		Crav 1769
HYNMAN, Hugh	Bert 1769		John 4 slaves		Crav 1769
John	Bert 1769		Wm 8 slaves		Crav 1769
HYRNE, Benjamin	NewH 1762		IVES, Job		Beau 1755
Edward 32 persons			Job		Crav 1769
	NewH 1741		John		Crav 1769
Henry	NewH 1762		John		Curr 1715
Henry	NewH 1763		Timothy Jr.		Curr 1755
Henry	NewH 1765		Timothy Sr.		Curr 1755
Henry	NewH 1767		Wm		Crav 1769
John	NewH 1755		Wm		Curr 1755
Richard	NewH 1755		IVEY, Charles		Bute 1771
Sarah	NewH 1763		Charles s. Anthony		
Sarah	NewH 1765		Charles		FWV 1771
HYROM, Henry	NewH 1755		Charles		Gran 1755
HYRONE, Richard	NewH 1755		Henry		Gran 1755
			James		Anso 1763
			James		Pasq 1754
			James		Pasq 1769
IGNER, John	NewH 1762		Joel		Cumb 1767
INGEMON, Wm	Casw 1777		John		Curr 1715
INGER, Esau	Pasq 1754		John		Edge 1744
INGMAN, Wm	Rand 1779		John 5 slaves		Pasq 1769
INGOLD, Peter	Oran 1755		Robert		Dobb 1779
INGRAM, Benjamin	Casw 1777		Thomas		Blad 1763
Charles	Dobb 1779		Wm		Gran 1755
Jacob	Dobb 1769		IZARD, Edmond		Cumb 1767
Jacob	Dobb 1779				
James	Casw 1777				
James	Dobb 1779				

JACK, Wm	Oran 1755	JACKSON, Tillington	s.		
JACKSON, Aaron	Pasq 1754	of David	Pasq 1769		
Absalom	Rand 1779	Wm	Bute 1771		
Andrew	Rand 1779	Wm	Chow 1753		
Asa	Pasq 1769	Wm	FWV 1771		
Bailey	Pasq 1754	Wm & s. John	FWV 1771		
Bailey	Pasq 1769	Wm	Gran 1755		
Benjamin	Anso 1763	Wm	Pasq 1754		
Benjamin	Oran 1755	Wm	Pasq 1769		
Daniel	Pasq 1754	Wm s. Wm			
David	Pasq 1769	David	Perq 1720		
David s. of		Wm Jr.	Perq 1720		
David	Pasq 1769	Wm	Tyrr 1755		
David	Rand 1779	Zachariah	Pasq 1769		
Demsey	Pasq 1769	JACOBS, Benjamin	Casw 1777		
Drury	Bute 1771	Esther	NewH 1765		
Drury	FWV 1771	Jacob	NewH 1765		
Edward	Pasq 1754	James	NewH 1762		
Edward	Rand 1779	John	NewH 1762		
George	Onsl 1769	John	NewH 1763		
George	Pitt 1764	John	NewH 1765		
Henry	Bute 1771	Matthew	NewH 1762		
Henry	Cumb 1767	Matthew	NewH 1765		
Henry overseer	FWV 1771	Paul	Anso 1750		
Henry bro James	FWV 1771	Richard	Casw 1777		
Isaac	Oran 1755	Wm	Cumb 1755		
James	Onsl 1769	Wm 10 blacks	Dupl 1752		
James	Rand 1779	Wm	Gran 1769		
James	Rowa 1759	Wm	Gran 1784		
Joab	Pasq 1754	Zachariah	Brun 1772		
Joab	Pasq 1769	Zachariah	NewH 1762		
John Jr.	Anso 1763	JAMERSON, David	NewH 1742		
John Sr.	Anso 1763	JAMES, Absalom	Pitt 1762		
John	Bute 1771	Absalom	Pitt 1764		
John & s. James	FWV 1771	Benjamin	Bert 1769		
John	Oran 1755	Benjamin	NewH 1762		
John	Rand 1779	Charles	Crav 1769		
John	Tyrr 1755	Charles	FWV 1771		
Joseph	Bert 1757	Daniel	Rowa 1759		
Joseph	Crav 1769	David	Beau 1755		
Joseph	Rand 1779	David	Casw 1777		
Joshua	Pasq 1754	David	NewH 1767		
Joshua	Pasq 1769	Edward	Casw 1777		
Keas	Pasq 1769	Francis	Cumb 1767		
Mordica s. of		Francis	Perq 1740		
Moses	Pasq 1769	Frank	Chow 1753		
Moses	Pasq 1754	George	Anso 1763		
Moses	Pasq 1769	Henry	Pitt 1762		
Nathan	Gran 1784	Henry	Pitt 1764		
Nathan	Rowa 1759	Horatio	Onsl 1769		
Peter	Bute 1771	Horatio	Onsl 1770		
Peter	FWV 1771	Jacob	NewH 1762		
Robert	Pasq 1769	Jacob	NewH 1763		
Robert	Rand 1779	Jacob	NewH 1765		
Samuel	Cumb 1767	Jacob	NewH 1767		
Samuel	Dobb 1769	Jacob	Pasq 1754		
Samuel	Gran 1784	Jeremiah	Crav 1769		
Simeon	Pasq 1769	John	Casw 1777		
Simeon	Rand 1779	John Jr.	Casw 1777		
Stephen	Anso 1763	John	NewH 1755		
Thomas	Blad 1763	John	NewH 1762		
Thomas	Bute 1771	John	NewH 1763		
Thomas	FWV 1771	John	NewH 1765		
Thomas	Oran 1755	John	NewH 1767		
		John	N.C. 1701		

JAMES, John	Pitt 1762	JEAN, Matthew	Casw 1777
Joseph	Crav 1769	Wm	Bute 1771
Joseph	NewH 1755	Wm & s. Edmond	FWV 1771
Joshua	NewH 1755	JEFFRIES, Henry	Casw 1777
Josiah	Pasq 1754	James	Cumb 1767
Lanck	Pitt 1762	James	Casw 1777
Launce	Pitt 1764	John	Anso 1763
Lemuel	Beau 1755	John	Bute 1771
Richard	Anso 1763	John	Casw 1777
Richard	Dupl 1752	John	FWV 1771
Richard	NewH 1741	John	Gran 1755
Samuel	Onsl 1741	Henry	Casw 1777
Samuel	Pitt 1762	Osborne (Col.)	Bute 1771
Samuel	Pitt 1764	Osborne Jr.	Casw 1777
Solomon	Beau 1755	Osborne S. Simom	FWV 1771
Solomon	Pitt 1764	Osborne	Gran 1755
Solomon Jr.	Pitt 1764	Osborne	NorH 1742
Thomas	Anso 1763	Osborne	NorH 1743
Thomas	NewH 1755	Osborne	NorH 1745
Thomas	NewH 1762	Sarg.	Crav 1720
Thomas' estate	NewH 1763	Simon 1280 acres	Chow 1721
Thomas' estate	NewH 1765	Simon 600 acres	Chow 1721
Thomas	NewH 1765	Thomas	FWV 1771
Thomas	NewH 1767	Widow	Bute 1771
Thomas	Pasq 1754	Widow & s. Wm	FWV 1771
Thomas	Pasq 1769	Wm	Gran 1784
Thomas	Pitt 1762	JEMISON, John	
Thomas	Pitt 1764	5 w 5 b	Bert 1743
Wm	Crav 1769	JEMPSON, Elizabeth	Pasq 1769
Wm Jr.	Onsl 1770	Richardson	Pasq 1754
Wm	Pasq 1769	JENENING, Joshua	Pasq 1754
Wm	Rowa 1759	JENKINS, Benjamin	Bute 1771
Wm	Surr 1771	Benjamin	FWV 1771
Wm	Surr 1772	Cader	Bert 1769
JAMESON, James	Chow 1753	Charles Jr.	Bert 1757
Wm	Onsl 1770	Charles Sr.	Bert 1757
JANE, Philip	Bute 1771	Charles	Chow 1743
Philip	FWV 1771	Elizabeth s.	
JARANSKY, Charles	Bert 1769	Lewis	Bert 1757
JARMON, John	Onsl 1770	George	Onsl 1769
Mary	Onsl 1770	George	Onsl 1770
Thomas	Onsl 1770	Henry	Bert 1757
JARNIGAN, Arthur	Dobb 1779	Henry	Onsl 1769
David	Dobb 1779	Henry	Onsl 1770
David Sr.	Dobb 1779	James	Bert 1757
Frederick	Dobb 1779	James	Curr 1755
Gardner	Dobb 1779	James	Edge 1734
JAROCKS, Jonathan	Bert 1769	James	NewH 1755
JARRELL, Henry		Jeremiah	Bute 1771
Sr.	Crav 1769	Jeremiah	FWV 1771
Wm	Crav 1769	Jesse	Bute 1771
JARRETT, Abraham	Onsl 1769	Jesse	FWV 1771
Abraham	Onsl 1770	John	Anso 1763
Isaac	Onsl 1769	John	Beau 1755
James	Onsl 1770	John	Bert 1757
John	Onsl 1769	John	Bert 1769
Richard	Onsl 1770	John	Bute 1771
JARVIS, Jarvis	Surr 1771	John	Edge 1742
John	Blad 1763	John	FWV 1771
Jonathan	Curr 1755	John	Rand 1779
Samuel	Curr 1755	Jonathan	Onsl 1770
Wm	Curr 1755	Lewis	Bert 1769
JAUNT, Wm	Beau 1755	Lewis	Onsl 1742
JAY, James	Casw 1777	Lewis	Onsl 1769
Wm	Oran 1755	Lewis	Onsl 1770

JENKINS, Nathan	Dobb	1779		JESPER, Samuel	NorH	1742
Thomas	Bute	1771		Thomas	Beau	1755
Thomas	Chow	1721		JESSUP, Isaac	Cumb	1767
Thomas	FWV	1771		Joseph 700 acres		
Thomas	Onsl	1769			Perq	1720
Thomas	Onsl	1770		Thomas Jr.	Perq	1740
Thomas	Rand	1779		Thomas Sr.	Perq	1740
Timothy	Bert	1757		JETT, James	Gran	1784
Wm	Bert	1757		Stephen	Gran	1769
Wm	Onsl	1769		JETUN, Abraham	Rowa	1759
Wm	Onsl	1770		JEWELL, Fran.		
JENNETT, Abraham	Perq	1720		widow	Beau	1755
Abraham	Tyrr	1755		Thomas	Beau	1755
John	Chow	1717		Thomas	Beau	1764
John Jr.	Chow	1721		Wm	NewH	1762
Wm	Tyrr	1755		Wm	NewH	1763
JENNINGS, Arthur	Pasq	1769		Wm	NewH	1765
Ben s. of Benj.	Pasq	1769		Wm	NewH	1767
Benjamin	Pasq	1769		JIN, Joseph	Anso	1763
Demsey 2 slaves	Pasq	1769		JINKINS, James	Gran	1784
Henry	Gran	1755		Mansfield	Gran	1784
Isaac	Pasq	1754		Thomas	Gran	1784
Isaac 2 slaves	Pasq	1769		JOANUS, John	Oran	1755
Jabez	Pasq	1769		JOHN, Bray	Gate	1786
Jesse	Pasq	1769		David	Gate	1786
Thomas	NewH	1741		Demsey	Gate	1786
Thomas	NewH	1762		Ezekiel	Gate	1786
Thomas	NewH	1765		James	Dobb	1769
Thomas	NewH	1767		James	Gate	1786
Thomas	Pasq	1754		John	Gate	1786
JENSEN, John	Oran	1755		Joseph	Gate	1786
JENTRY, Nicholas	Surr	1771		Lewis	Gate	1786
JEPP, John	N.C.	1701		Moses	Gate	1786
JERMAN, Mary	Onsl	1769		Moses Jr.	Gate	1786
Thomas	Onsl	1769		JOHNS, Daniel	Rand	1779
JERNIGAN, Benjamin	Bert	1769		James	Dobb	1769
David	Bert	1757		James	Pitt	1764
David Jr.	Bert	1769		John	NewH	1767
David	Dobb	1769		Moses	Anso	1763
Davis s. of				Moses	Dobb	1769
David	Dobb	1769		Obadiah	Casw	1777
George	Bert	1757		Rachel, widow	Beau	1764
George	Bert	1769		Thomas	Crav	1720
George	Dobb	1779		Wm	Crav	1720
Isabel	Dobb	1769		JOHNSON, Abel	Chow	1717
Jacob	Bert	1743		Abel	Chow	1721
Jacob	Bert	1757		Abraham	Beau	1755
Jacob Jr.	Bert	1769		Arthur	Crav	1744
Jacob Sr.	Bert	1769		Benjamin	Onsl	1770
James	Bert	1769		Benjamin	Surr	1771
Jesse	Bert	1757		Burrell	Bert	1769
Jesse	Bert	1769		Edward	Rowa	1759
Jesse	Dobb	1769		Ezekiel	NewH	1767
Jesse	Dobb	1779		Francis	Bute	1771
Jesse Jr.	Dobb	1779		Francis	FWV	1771
John	Chow	1721		Francis	Gran	1755
Joshua	Dobb	1769		Francis	Rowa	1759
Stephen	Bert	1769		Henry	Oran	1755
Thomas	Chow	1717		Isaac	Beau	1755
Thomas	Dobb	1769		Isaac	Bert	1757
Wm	Bert	1769		Isaac	Gran	1755
JERRELL, John F.	FWV	1771		Isaiah	Dobb	1769
JERVIS, Foster	Curr	1715		Jacob	Crav	1720
Francis	Curr	1715		Jacob	Dobb	1769
JESPER, John Const.	Beau	1755		James	Beau	1755

JOHNSON, James	Crav 1769	JOHNSON, Wm	Gran 1755
James s. of		Wm	Onsl 1741
Mary	Dobb 1769	Wm	Rowa 1759
James	Rand 1779	Wm	Surr 1771
James	Rowa 1759	Wm	Surr 1772
Jeffrey	Surr 1771	JOHNSTON, Aaron	Cumb 1767
Jeffrey	Surr 1772	Abraham	Beau 1755
Jesse	Onsl 1770	Abraham	Beau 1764
John	Beau 1755	Alexander	Casw 1777
John	Beau 1764	Arthur 7 slaves	Crav 1769
John Jr.	Bert 1757	Ben	Surr 1771
John Sr.	Bert 1757	Benjamin	Casw 1777
John	Curr 1755	Benjamin	Gran 1769
John	Dobb 1769	Benjamin	Gran 1784
John s. of		Benjamin	Onsl 1769
Josep	Dobb 1769	Benjamin	Onsl 1770
John	FWV 1771	Benoni	Pitt 1764
John	Onsl 1770	Charles	Blad 1781
John	Oran 1755	Charles	Crav 1769
John	Perq 1720	Charles s. of	
John	Perq 1740	Garrett	Onsl 1770
John	Pitt 1775	Crosley	Beau 1764
John Jr.	Rand 1779	Daniel	Casw 1777
John Sr.	Rand 1779	Ezekiel	NewH 1755
John	Rand 1779	Ezekiel	NewH 1762
John	Rowa 1759	Ezekiel	NewH 1765
John Sr.	Surr 1772	Gabriel (Esq.)	
John	Tyrr 1742	(Gov.)	Crav 1742
Jonathan	Bute 1771	Garrett	Onsl 1769
Jonathan	FWV 1771	Garrett	Onsl 1770
Jonathan	Gran 1755	George	Casw 1777
Joseph	Dobb 1769	Gideon	Gran 1784
Joseph	NorH 1762	Griggers	Beau 1752
Joseph Jr.	NorH 1762	Henry	Anso 1763
Joseph	Onsl 1770	Henry	NewH 1762
Joseph	Rand 1779	Henry	Oran 1755
Joseph	Surr 1772	Isaac	Anso 1763
Larkin	Gran 1784	Isham	Gran 1784
Mary	Dobb 1769	Jacob	Dobb 1779
Matthew	NewH 1763	James	Beau 1764
Moses	Bert 1757	James	Blad 1781
Moses	Surr 1771	James	Cart 1744
Peter	Crav 1720	James	Casw 1777
Peter	NorH 1762	James	Dobb 1779
Philip	FWV 1771	James	Gran 1784
Rebecca	Bute 1771	James Sr.	Pitt 1762
Rebecca	FWV 1771	James	Pitt 1764
Richard	Crav 1720	James Sr.	Pitt 1775
Robert	Rowa 1759	James	Pitt 1775
Sarah (Mrs.)	Bute 1771	Jeffrey	Surr 1771
Stephen	Crav 1720	Jesse	Beau 1764
Stephen	NewH 1767	John	Beau 1764
Susan	Chow 1717	John	Bert 1743
Thomas	Chow 1717	John	Bert 1769
Thomas	Crav 1720	John	Blad 1763
Thomas	Gran 1755	John	Brun 1769
Thomas	Onsl 1770	John	Brun 1772
Wm s. of James	Beau 1755	John	Bute 1771
Wm (Col.)	Bute 1771	John	Casw 1777
Wm (Col.)	FWV 1771	John	Cumb 1767
Wm	Crav 1720	John	Dobb 1779
Wm	Crav 1744	John	Gran 1769
Wm	Edge 1743	John	Onsl 1769
Wm s. Benjamin		John	Surr 1771
James	FWV 1771	John Jr.	Surr 1771

JOHNSTON, Jonathan	Gran	1784	JOHNSTON, Wm	NewH	1767
Joseph	Casw	1777	Wm	Onsl	1743
Joseph	Gran	1769	Wm	Onsl	1770
Joseph	Gran	1784	Wm	Oran	1755
Joseph	NewH	1763	Wm	Surr	1771
Joseph	NewH	1765	Wm	Surr	1772
Joshua	Casw	1777	Zillah	Blad	1781
Joshua	Onsl	1769	JOINER, Abraham	Pitt	1764
Joshua	Onsl	1770	Israel	Dobb	1769
Joshua	Tyrr	1755	Israel	Pitt	1764
Josiah	Bert	1757	John	Pitt	1764
Josiah	Bert	1769	Nehemiah	Edge	1743
Lancelot	Casw	1777	Wm	Pitt	1764
Larkin	Gran	1769	JOLLES, Wm	Pitt	1764
Lazarus	Blad	1763	JOLLEY, Jesse	Pitt	1762
Lazarus	Blad	1781	Jesse	Pitt	1764
Lewis	NewH	1755	John	Pitt	1762
Luke	Anso	1763	John	Pitt	1764
Martin Jr.	Cumb	1767	Jonathan	Pitt	1762
Martin Sr.	Cumb	1767	Jonathan	Pitt	1764
Martin	Dobb	1769	Joseph Jr.	Beau	1755
Martin	Dobb	1779	Joseph Sr.	Pitt	1762
Matthew	NewH	1765	Joseph	Pitt	1762
Matthew	NewH	1767	Joseph	Pitt	1764
Nathan	Beau	1764	Peter	Pitt	1764
Nathan	Pitt	1762	Wm	Pitt	1762
Noel	Gran	1784	Wm	Pitt	1764
Peter	Beau	1764	JOLSON, Charles	Rand	1779
Philip	FWV	1771	JONAS, Park	Gran	1755
Randal	Tyrr	1755	JONE, L.	Beau	1755
Richard	Crav	1742	JONES, Aaron	Oran	1755
Richard	Curr	1715	Abigail	Gran	1755
Robert Esq.			Abner s. of		
11 slaves	Blad	1763	James	Pasq	1769
Robert	Casw	1777	Abraham or Allen	Bute	1771
Robert	Dobb	1779	Abraham	FWV	1771
Robert	Gran	1784	Abraham	Gran	1784
Samson	Cumb	1767	Abraham	NewH	1762
Samuel	Blad	1781	Abraham	NewH	1763
Samuel	Casw	1777	Abraham	NewH	1765
Samuel	Gran	1784	Abraham	Oran	1755
Samuel	Onsl	1742	Abraham	Surr	1771
Sarah (Mrs.)	Bute	1771	Abraham	Surr	1772
Sarah (Mrs.)	FWV	1771	Adam	Beau	1755
Solomon	Cumb	1755	Ambrose	Gran	1769
Stephen	NewH	1762	Ambrose	Gran	1784
Stephen	NewH	1765	Ambrose	Pitt	1762
Stephenson	NewH	1755	Ann widow	Beau	1764
Thomas	Anso	1763	Aquilla	Rand	1779
Thomas 1 slave	Blad	1763	Benjamin	Bute	1771
Thomas	Curr	1715	Benjamin s. Adam		
Thomas	Onsl	1769	Thomas	FWV	1771
Thomas	Oran	1755	Brereton	Gran	1784
Thomas	Surr	1771	Burrell	FWV	1771
Truitt	Beau	1764	Caleb	Pasq	1769
Wm	Anso	1763	Charles	Bert	1757
Wm	Beau	1764	Charles	Chow	1717
Wm	Blad	1781	Charles 900 acres		
Wm	Casw	1777		Chow	1721
Wm Jr.	Casw	1777	Charles	Crav	1769
Wm	Cumb	1767	Charles Jr.	Cumb	1767
Wm	Curr	1715	Charles Sr.	Cumb	1767
Wm	Dobb	1779	Charles	Gran	1784
Wm	Edge	1743	Charles	Rand	1779
Wm	Gran	1784			

JONES, Col.	17,260			JONES, Griffith		
Acres	Chow	1721		2 slaves	Pasq	1769
Daniel	FWV	1771		Hardy	Dobb	1769
David	Beau	1764		Hardy	Dobb	1779
David	Chow	1717		Harwood	NorH	1762
David	Chow	1721		Haymilla	Rand	1779
David	Chow	1753		Henry 640 acres	Chow	1721
David Jr.	Curr	1715		Henry	Crav	1769
David Sr.	Curr	1715		Henry	Pitt	1764
David	Curr	1755		Henry	Surr	1772
David	Dobb	1769		Hezekiah	Anso	1763
David	Gate	1786		Hezekiah	Gate	1786
David	NewH	1755		Hosea	Pasq	1769
David	NewH	1767		Isaac	Beau	1755
David	Onsl	1769		Isaac 5w 1b	Blad	1750
David	Onsl	1770		Isaac Esq.		
David	Pasq	1754		5 slaves	Blad	1763
David Jr.	Pasq	1769		Isaac Jr.	Blad	1781
David Sr.	Pasq	1769		Isaac	Curr	1715
Demcy	Onsl	1769		Isaac	Pasq	1754
Demcy	Onsl	1770		Isaac 2 slaves	Pasq	1769
Dinkler	Gran	1784		Jacob	Beau	1764
Drury	FWV	1771		Jacob	Bute	1771
Edmond	Bute	1771		Jacob	Crav	1769
Edmond	Casw	1777		Jacob	FWV	1771
Edmond	FWV	1771		James	Beau	1764
Edward	Blad	1781		James	Bert	1757
Edward	Bute	1771		James Esq.	Blad	1781
Edward	Curr	1715		James	Bute	1771
Edward	Edge	1743		James	Casw	1777
Edward	FWV	1771		James	Crav	1769
Edward	Gran	1784		James	Dobb	1769
Elizabeth	Chow	1721		James	FWV	1771
Elizabeth	Curr	1755		James	Edge	1734
Elizabeth	Perq	1720		James	Edge	1742
Emanuel	Onsl	1769		James s. of		
Emanuel	Onsl	1770		David Sr.	Gate	1786
Epaphroditus	Chow	1753		James	NewH	1767
Ephraim	Beau	1755		James	Pasq	1769
Evan	Crav	1743		James s. of		
Evan	Curr	1755		David	Pasq	1769
Evan	NewH	1741		James	Pitt	1762
Evan	NewH	1743		James	Pitt	1764
Evan	NewH	1755		Jason Sr.		
Evan Jr.	NewH	1755		8 slaves	Pasq	1769
Evan	NewH	1762		Jesse	Casw	1777
Evan	NewH	1763		Jesse school-		
Evan 2 slaves	Pasq	1769		mastr	Dobb	1769
Evan Jr.	Pasq	1769		Jesse	Gate	1786
Evan	Tyrr	1755		John	Anso	1763
Foaley	Tyrr	1755		John	Beau	1755
Fowler	Gran	1784		John	Beau	1764
Francis	Beau	1755		John	Bert	1757
Francis	Beau	1764		John s. Charles	Bert	1757
Francis	Cumb	1755		John	Bert	1769
Francis	Oran	1755		John	Blad	1763
Fred.	Chow	1717		John	Bute	1771
Frederick	Dobb	1769		John	Casw	1777
Frederick	Dobb	1779		John Jr.	Chow	1717
Frederick	NewH	1765		John Sr.	Chow	1717
Frederick	NewH	1767		John Jr.	Chow	1721
George	Curr	1755		John Sr.	Chow	1721
George	Oran	1755		John Jr.	Chow	1753
Griffin	Dobb	1769		John Sr.	Chow	1753
Griffith	Pasq	1754		John Jr.	Cumb	1755

JONES, John Sr.	Cumb	1755	JONES, Nathaniel	Onsl	1769
John Jr.	Curr	1715	Nathaniel	Onsl	1770
John Sr.	Curr	1715	Nehemiah	Pasq	1769
John	Curr	1755	Nehemiah		
John	Dobb	1769	5 slaves	Pasq	1769
John	Dobb	1779	Owen	Onsl	1742
John	Edge	1743	Owen	Onsl	1769
John	Edge	1744	Owen	Onsl	1770
John	FWV	1771	Patrick	Curr	1755
John s. Adam			Peter	Bert	1757
Benj.	FWV	1771	Peter & w.		
John	Gran	1769	Elizabeth	Bert	1757
John	Gran	1784	Peter s. of Thos	Gran	1755
John	NewH	1762	Peter	Gran	1769
John	NewH	1763	Peter 760 acres	Perq	1720
John	NewH	1765	Peter Jr.	Perq	1720
John	NewH	1767	Peter Jr.	Perq	1740
John	Oran	1755	Peter Sr.	Perq	1740
John	Pasq	1754	Philip	Brun	1769
John 4 slaves	Pasq	1769	Philip	Brun	1772
John	Pitt	1764	Philip	NorH	1762
Joseph	Bert	1757	Porter & s.		
Joseph s. Abraham			Charles	Bert	1757
	Bert	1757	Rachel	Perq	1720
Joseph	Blad	1763	Randell	Curr	1755
Joseph	Chow	1721	Richard	Bute	1771
Joseph	Chow	1753	Richard	Casw	1777
Joseph	NewH	1742	Richard Jr.	Casw	1777
Joseph	Oran	1755	Richard	Curr	1715
Joseph	Pasq	1754	Richard	Curr	1755
Joseph 11 slaves			Richard	Dobb	1769
	Pasq	1769	Richard	Dobb	1779
Joseph Jr.	Pasq	1769	Richard	Edge	1743
Joseph	Surr	1771	Richard	FWV	1771
Joseph	Surr	1772	Richard	Gran	1755
Josiah	Beau	1742	Richard	Gran	1769
Josiah	Beau	1755	Richard	Surr	1771
Kilmany	Chow	1717	Robert	Bute	1771
Lancelot	Beau	1755	Robert	Chow	1743
Levy	Surr	1771	Robert	Crav	1769
Levy	Surr	1772	Robert	FWV	1771
Lewelling	Bute	1771	Robert	Gran	1769
Lewhalling s. John			Roger	Bute	1771
Richard	FWV	1771	Roger	Crav	1769
Lewis	Chow	1753	Roger	FWV	1771
Lloyd	Curr	1755	Samuel	Blad	1763
Lovick	Crav	1769	Samuel	Bute	1771
Margaret	Beau	1755	Samuel	Crav	1720
Margaret	Crav	1769	Samuel	Crav	1769
Margaret	Pitt	1762	Samuel	Curr	1715
Margaret	Pitt	1764	Samuel	Curr	1755
Marmaduke Esq.			Samuel	Dobb	1769
19 s	Blad	1763	Samuel	FWV	1771
Marmaduke	NewH	1755	Samuel s. Henry	FWV	1771
Marmaduke	NewH	1762	Samuel	Gran	1784
Marmaduke	NewH	1765	Samuel	Rand	1779
Martha	NewH	1763	Savel	Curr	1755
Martha	NewH	1765	Simon	Beau	1755
Mary	Gran	1769	Simon	Beau	
Mary	Tyrr	1755	Simon	NorH	1762
Matthew	NewH	1765	Simon	Pitt	1762
Nathan	Onsl	1770	Simon	Pitt	1764
Nathan Jr.	Onsl	1770	Solomon	Bert	1757
Nathaniel s. of			Solomon s. of		
Thomas	Gran	1755	James	Pasq	1769

JONES, Stephen	Surr	1772	JONES, Wm	NewH	1765
Stoux	Pitt	1764	Wm	NewH	1767
Sugar	Gran	1755	Wm	Onsl	1769
Theophilus	Dobb	1769	Wm	Onsl	1770
Tho.	Chow	1717	Wm	Oran	1755
Thomas	Beau	1755	Wm	Pasq	1754
Thomas	Beau	1764	Wm	Pasq	1769
Thomas	Blad	1763	Wm	Perq	1740
Thomas	Blad		Wm	Pitt	1763
Thomas	Bute	1771	Wm	Roan	1720
Thomas Jr.	Bute	1771	Wm	Surr	1771
Thomas	Casw	1777	Willie	Bute	1771
Thomas	Chow	1721	Willis	Dobb	1779
Thomas Jr.	Chow	1753	Winkler	Gran	1769
Thomas	Cumb	1755	JONETT, Matthew		
Thomas	FWV	1771	(Cpt.)	Casw	1777
Thomas Jr.	FWV	1771	JORDAN, Abraham	Bert	1757
Thomas over the			Abraham	Bert	1769
R	FWV	1771	Arthur	Gran	1769
Thomas	Gran	1755	Arthur	Gran	1784
Thomas	Gran	1784	Charles	Chow	1753
Thomas	NewH	1743	Charles	Dobb	1769
Thomas	NewH	1762	Charles	Dobb	1779
Thomas	NewH	1763	Charles	NorH	1744
Thomas	NewH	1765	Charles	NorH	1762
Thomas	NewH	1767	Francis	Anso	1763
Thomas	Onsl	1770	Frederick	Dobb	1769
Thomas	Oran	1755	Frederick	Dobb	1779
Thomas	Pasq	1754	George	Gran	1755
Thomas	Rand	1779	George Jr.	Gran	1755
Thomas	Surr	1771	George	Gran	1769
Thomas	Surr	1772	George	Gran	1784
Thomas	Tyrr	1755	George	NorH	1742
Timothy	Pasq	1769	George	NorH	1762
Uriah	Dobb	1779	Henry	Gran	1755
Vinson	Gran	1755	Henry	Pasq	1769
Walter	Beau	1755	Isaac	Bert	1769
Walter	Beau	1764	Isabel widow	Anso	1763
Walter	Bert	1757	Jacob	Chow	1753
Walter	Crav	1769	James	Dobb	1769
Widow (Wo.)	Chow	1717	James Sr.	Dobb	1779
Widow	NewH	1762	James	Dobb	1779
Wm	Beau	1764	Jeremiah	Gate	1786
Wm	Bert	1757	John	Chow	1717
Wm	Bute	1771	John	Chow	1721
Wm	Casw	1777	John Jr.	Chow	1721
Wm (Serjt.)	Chow	1717	John Sr.	Chow	1753
Wm	Chow	1721	John	Chow	1753
Wm	Chow	1753	John s. of Chas.	Chow	1753
Wm (Wm s. of			John	Dobb	1769
Henry)	Chow	1753	John	NorH	1762
Wm (Wm s. of			John	Pitt	1762
Henry)	Crav	1720	John	Pitt	1764
Wm	Crav	1769	John	Tyrr	1755
Wm	Cumb	1767	Joseph s. Isaac		
Wm	Dobb	1769	Wm	Bert	1757
Wm	Dobb	1779	Joseph	Bert	1769
Wm	Edge	1741	Joseph Jr.	Bert	1769
Wm	FWV	1771	Joseph	Chow	1753
Wm Esq.	FWV	1771	Joseph	Dobb	1769
Wm s. Brereton	FWV	1771	Joseph	Pasq	1754
Wm	Gran	1755	Katherine deceased		
Wm	Gran	1769		Chow	1721
Wm s. Brereton	Gran	1784	Lewis	Chow	1753
Wm	NewH	1763	Mathias	Pasq	1754

JORDAN, Orr	NorH 1762	KASCO, Wm	Bert 1757
Reuben	Anso 1763	KATCHEM, Joseph	Onsl 1769
Robert 5 slaves	Pasq 1769	Joseph	Onsl 1770
Rowland	Gran 1769	KAY, Jonathan	Onsl 1770
Solomon	Chow 1717	KEA, Thomas	Chow 1721
Thomas	Crav 1769	KEAGLE, Henry	Onsl 1770
Thomas	NorH 1762	John	Onsl 1770
Wm	Bert 1757	KEARNEY, Thomas	Edge 1743
Wm	Bert 1769	KEATLEY, John	Dobb 1769
Wm Jr.	Bert 1769	John	Dobb 1779
Wm	Gran 1755	Jonathan	Dobb 1779
JOSEPH, Nathaniel	Beau 1764	Leonard	Cumb 1767
JOURDIN, John		Richard	Dobb 1779
11 slaves	Blad 1763	KEATON, Hillary	Curr 1755
JOYCE, John	Surr 1771	KEATS, James	Chow 1721
John	Surr 1772	KEE, Thomas	Beau 1764
Michael	Oran 1755	KEEFE, John	Bert 1757
JOYLES, Thomas	Surr 1772	Treadle	Chow 1721
JOYNER, Abraham	Pitt 1762	Wm	Bert 1757
Israel	Beau 1755	KEEHN, James	Gate 1786
Israel	Pitt 1762	John	Onsl 1769
John	Beau 1755	Lemuel	Gate 1786
John	Pitt 1762	Peter	Rowa 1759
Moses	Bute 1771	KEELE, Hardy	Pitt 1762
Moses	FWV 1771	Jacob	Bert 1757
Wm	Beau 1755	John	Chow 1721
Wm	Pitt 1762	Samuel	Bute 1771
JOYS, George	Oran 1755	Samuel	FWV 1771
JUDKINS, Thomas	Pitt 1762	Thomas	Chow 1721
Thomas	Pitt 1764	Wm	Chow 1717
Wm	Pitt 1762	Wm	Pitt 1762
Wm	Pitt 1764	KEELING, George	Gran 1755
JUDD, Roland	Surr 1771	KEEN, James	Gate 1786
Roland	Surr 1772	John	NewH 1743
JULIAN, George	Rand 1779	John	Onsl 1769
Isaac Jr.	Rand 1779	KEENAN, Jeremiah	NewH 1762
Isaac Sr.	Rand 1779	Jeremiah	NewH 1765
Reyney	Rand 1779	Jeremiah	NewH 1767
JUMP, Wm	Crav 1769	KEETER, Charles	Brun 1769
JUNER, Cornelius	Rowa 1759	Charles	Brun 1772
JUNKESON, Walter	Brun 1769	Wm	Bert 1757
Walter	Brun 1772	KEETING, Charles	Brun 1769
Wm	Bert 1769	Charles	Brun 1772
JURGEN, James Sr.	Dobb 1779	Jacob	Pasq 1769
JURMAN, Thomas	Crav 1741	Joseph Jr.	Pasq 1769
JURNIGAN, Benjamin s.		Joseph Sr.	Pasq 1769
of George	Onsl 1769	Zachariah	
George	Onsl 1769	3 slaves	Pasq 1769
JUSTICE, Barbara	Crav 1769	KEETON, Joseph	Pasq 1754
Elias	Crav 1769	Zack	Pasq 1754
Silvanus	Crav 1769	Zebulon	Pasq 1754
		KEETOR, Charles	NewH 1763
		John	Pasq 1769
		KEIGHT, John	Pasq 1769
KADE, Drury	Bute 1771	Zachariah	Pasq 1769
Drury	FWV 1771	KEITCH, John	Beau 1755
KAILE, Amos	Bert 1769	KEITH, Edmund	Crav 1741
John	Bert 1769	George	Gran 1769
Mary	Bert 1769	James	Crav 1720
KALEIGH, James	Oran 1755	John	FWV 1771
KAPP, Jacob	Surr 1771	KELLAM, Elijah	Cumb 1767
Jacob	Surr 1772	KELLEN, Thomas	Cumb 1767
KARR, Robert	Bute 1771	KELLET, Wm	Onsl 1743
Robert	FWV 1771	KELLEY, Edward	Gate 1786
Thomas	Surr 1771	Francis	Gran 1769

KELLEY, Francis	Gran 1784	KENNON, Thomas	Bute 1771
George	Cumb 1767	Thomas bro.	
Hugh	Casw 1777	Archib.	FWV 1771
James overseer	Bute 1771	KENT, Thomas	Crav 1769
James	Gran 1769	KENWORTHY, David	Rand 1779
James	1743	Joshua	Rand 1779
John	Beau 1755	KENYON, Roger	Perq 1740
John	Chow 1721	KEOUGH, Michael	NewH 1767
John	Curr 1755	KERBY, James	Edge 1734
John	NewH 1762	Thomas	Edge 1742
John	NewH 1763	Wm	Gate 1786
John	NewH 1765	KERKSEY, Richard	Oran 1755
John	Oran 1755	KERN, Leonard	Rowa 1759
John	Pasq 1769	KERNEGY, George	Crav 1742
John	Rowa 1720	John Jr.	Crav 1769
Joseph	Dobb 1769	KERNER, Joseph	Dobb 1779
Matthew	Blad 1763	KERNEY, John	Crav 1769
Patrick	Pasq 1769	Micajah	Gran 1755
Patrick	Rand 1779	Shemuel	Bute 1771
Samuel	Casw 1777	Shemuel	FWV 1771
Walter	NorH 1744	KERR, Alexander	Casw 1777
Wm overseer	Bute 1771	Gilbert	Dobb 1769
Wm	Casw 1777	James	Blad 1763
Wm overseer	FWV 1771	John	Casw 1777
Wm	Gate 1786	John	Rand 1779
KEMMY, Thomas	Onsl 1769	Joseph	Gran 1784
KEMP, Isaac	Crav 1769	Joseph	Rand 1779
James	Crav 1769	Moses	Dobb 1769
Job	Curr 1755	Nathaniel	Rand 1779
Joseph	Blad 1763	Robert	Rand 1779
Wm	Blad 1745	KERSEY, John	Blad 1763
Zebulon	Pasq 1769	John	Casw 1777
KENAN, Thomas	NewH 1743	Peter	Blad 1763
KENDALL, Benjamin	Rand 1779	Randolph	Tryo 1776
Thomas	Rand 1779	KERSHNER, Christopher	
KENDRICK, Wm	Bute 1771		Surr 1771
Wm	Edge 1744	KERVIN, Laurence	Pitt 1775
Wm s. Jones	FWV 1771	KESABLE, Michael	Crav 1720
KENEY, Lazarus	Onsl 1742	KESNER, Anthony	Surr 1772
KENLOW, Thomas	Blad 1763	KETCHERSON, James	Casw 1777
KENNAN, John	Gran 1784	KETTER, Charles	NewH 1762
KENNEDY, David	Bert 1757	KEY, Henry	Oran 1755
David	Crav 1769	Jonathan	Onsl 1769
David	Oran 1755	Thomas	Gran 1769
Edmund	Pitt 1762	Thomas	Gran 1784
Francis Esq.	Tyrr 1755	KEYS, John	Cumb 1767
George	Crav 1769	Wm	Cumb 1767
James	Bert 1757	KIBBLE, James	Onsl 1769
James	Casw 1777	James	Onsl 1770
James	NewH 1763	KIBIT, Peter	Rand 1779
James	Onsl 1769	KICKER, John	Bute 1771
James	Onsl 1770	John	FWV 1771
James	Oran 1755	KIEL, Hardee	Pitt 1764
Jesse	Pitt 1762	Wm	Pitt 1764
Jesse	Pitt 1764	KIFF, Wm	Bert 1757
John	Beau 1755	Wm	Onsl 1769
John	Crav 1769	KILBURN, Amos	Surr 1772
John	Dobb 1769	Isaac	
John	Pitt 1762	John	
John	Pitt 1764	KILGORE, Charles	Casw 1777
Wm	Cumb 1767	James	Curr 1755
Wm Esq.	Tyrr 1755	Robert	Oran 1755
KENNEL, Moses		Thomas	Casw 1777
s. Fred	FWV 1771	KILLEGREW, John	Crav 1769
KENNON, Joel	Gran 1755	KILLEM, Adam	Cumb 1767

KILLEROLL, Jonathan	Gran	1769
Samuel	Gran	1769
KILLET, Andrew	Dobb	1769
Wm	Cumb	1767
Wm s. of Andrew	Dobb	1769
KILLEY, John	Pitt	1762
Wm	Pitt	1762
KILLINGSWORTH,		
Nathaniel	Beau	1755
Richard	Chow	1721
Wm	Roan	1720
KILLONHOOK	Rowa	1759
KILPATRICK,		
Alexander	Dobb	1750
Esler	Dobb	1750
Wm	Dobb	1769
KIMBALL,		
Bartholomew	Bute	1771
Bartholomew	FWV	1771
Bartholomew	Gran	1784
Benjamin	Bute	1771
Benjamin	Edge	1743
Ben s. Davie		
James	FWV	1771
Benjamin	Gran	1755
Buckner	Bute	1771
Buckner overseer	FWV	1771
Charles	Bute	1771
Charles	FWV	1771
Charles	Gran	1755
Drury	Gran	1769
Drury	Gran	1784
Joseph	Bute	1771
Joseph 4 whites	Edge	1743
Joseph s. Lewis	FWV	1771
Joseph Sr.	Gran	1755
Joseph	Gran	1755
Joseph	Gran	1769
Peter	Bute	1771
Peter s.		
Nathaniel	FWV	1771
Peter	Gran	1755
Wm 10 whites	Edge	1743
Wm	Gran	1769
KIMBER, Ann	NewH	1762
Mary	NewH	1762
KINBRIE, Wm	FWV	1771
KINBROUGH, Marmaduke		
	Rowa	1759
Nathaniel	Oran	1755
Wm	Bute	1771
Wm	FWV	1771
KIMSEY, Thomas s.		
Thomas	Bert	1757
KINCHEN, Wm	NorH	1743
KINDALL, Benjamin	Rand	1779
John	Gran	1755
Thomas	Rand	1779
KINEAR, Thomas	NewH	1767
KINEER, Thomas	NewH	1765
KINEST, Christopher	Surr	1771
KING, Abraham	Blad	1763
Arrington	Crav	1769
Austin	FWV	1771
Benajah	Rowa	1759

KING, Benjamin	Oran	1755
Benjamin	Surr	1772
Benjamin	Surr	1772
Britton s. of Wm	Beau	1755
Britton	Pitt	1762
Britton	Pitt	1764
Cader	Bert	1769
Charles	Bert	1757
Charles	Bert	1769
Charles (Cpt.)	Chow	1753
Charles	Dobb	1779
Charles	Gran	1755
Daniel	Blad	1763
Daniel	Gran	1755
David	Bert	1769
David	Bute	1771
Davis s. Wood	FWV	1771
Edward	Rowa	1759
Ethelred	Pitt	1762
Francis	Gran	1755
Francis	Gran	1769
George	Gran	1755
Henry	Bute	1771
Henry	Chow	1753
Henry	FWV	1771
Henry	Gate	1786
Henry	Rowa	1759
Henry	Surr	1772
Higerson	Tyrr	1755
James	FWV	1771
James	Rand	1779
James	Rowa	1759
James	Surr	1772
Jesse	Pitt	1762
John	Blad	1781
John	Bute	1771
John 2,000 acres	Chow	1721
John	Gran	1755
John	Onsl	1769
John	Onsl	1770
John	Oran	1755
John	Rowa	1759
Johnson Jr.	Rand	1779
Johnson Sr.	Rand	1779
Johnson	Rowa	1759
Joseph	Edge	1744
Julian	Bute	1771
Julian	FWV	1771
Mary	Bute	1771
Mary	Crav	1769
Mary s. Charles		
John Philip	FWV	1771
Michael	Beau	1755
Michael	Bert	1769
Michael	Chow	1721
Michael 5w 5b	Dupl	1752
Miles	Gran	1784
Nathaniel	Casw	1777
Nicholas	Chow	1753
Pasw	FWV	1771
Peter	Rand	1779
Peter	Rowa	1759
Richard	FWV	1771
Richard	Rowa	1759
Robert	Bute	1771

KING, Robert	Casw	1777	KIRKPATRICK, Wm	Blad	1781
Robert	FWV	1771	KIRKWOOD, John	NewH	1767
Robert	Gran	1755	KIRSCHNER, Christian		
Robert	Rowa	1759		Rowa	1759
Roper	Bute	1771	KIRSH, Joseph	Bert	1769
Samuel	Crav	1769	KIRTLAND, John	Gran	1755
Sarah	Pitt	1762	KISKERD, John	Gran	1755
Solomon	Chow	1753	KISS, Nathaniel	Rand	1779
Solomon	Gate	1786	Robert	Casw	1777
Susannah	N.C.	1701	Thomas	Casw	1777
Thomas	Gran	1755	KITCHENS, Anthony	FWV	1771
Thomas s. of			KITCHIN, Anthony	Bute	1771
Thomas	Gran	1755	KITCHING, Wm		
Thomas	Gran	1769	820 acres	Perq	1720
Thomas	Onsl	1769	KITE, Amos	Curr	1755
Thomas	Onsl	1770	Samuel	Pitt	1762
Thomas	Rand	1779	Willey	Pasq	1769
Wm	Beau	1755	KITELY, Samuel	Pasq	1754
Wm	Bert	1769	KITLEY, Christopher	Gran	1784
Wm	Bute	1771	KITTED, Jonathan		
Wm Jr.	Bute	1771	Jr.	Gran	1784
Wm	Cumb	1767	KITTERLIN, Absalom	Beau	1764
Wm	FWV	1771	KITTRELL, George	Bert	1769
Wm Jr.	FWV	1771	Isaac	Gran	1784
Wm	Gate	1786	Jethro	Bert	1769
Wm	Gran	1755	John	Bert	1757
Wm s. of Wm	Gran	1755	John	Chow	1753
Wm	NewH	1767	John	Gran	1784
Wm	Onsl	1770	Jonathan	Bert	1743
Wm	Pitt	1764	Jonathan Jr.	Bert	1757
Wm	Pitt	1775	Jonathan	Gran	1784
Wm	Rand	1779	Joshua	Gran	1784
Zachariah	Casw	1777	Moses	Gate	1786
KINGHAM, Robert	Perq	1740	Samuel	Gran	1784
KINGSTON, Wm	Bert	1769	KITTS, John	Curr	1715
KINNAHAN, Samuel	NewH	1755	KLOCKMAN, Peter	Surr	1772
Thomas	NewH	1755	KNEE, John	Cumb	1755
KINNARD, Nathaniel	Dobb	1779	KNIGHT, Abel	Rowa	1759
KINNEDY, Anthony	Pitt	1764	Cader	Onsl	1769
KINEER, Thomas	NewH	1765	David	Oran	1755
KINNEY, Thomas	Dobb	1769	Dukell	Onsl	1769
KINSBROUGH, Graves	Casw	1777	Elizabeth	N.C.	1701
John	Casw	1777	Emanuel	Pasq	1754
Robert	Casw	1777	James	Gate	1786
Thomas	Casw	1777	James	Surr	1772
Thomas Jr.	Casw	1777	John	Chow	1753
Wm	Casw	1777	Jonathan	Gran	1769
KINSEY, Absalom	Crav	1769	Jonathan	Gran	1784
John	Crav	1720	Lewis	Pasq	1769
John	Crav	1769	Martha s. John		
Joseph	Crav	1769	Wm	Bert	1757
Priscilla 297			Matthew	Bert	1757
acres	Perq	1720	Robert	Chow	1753
Samuel	Dobb	1769	Robert	Onsl	1769
KIPPS, Francis	Crav	1769	Robert	Onsl	1770
KIRBY, Humphrey	Dobb	1769	Thomas	Rand	1779
KIRK, George	Bute	1771	Wm	Bert	1757
George	FWV	1771	Wm	Gran	1784
George	Gran	1755	Wm	Pasq	1754
Joseph	Gran	1755	KNIGHTING, Wm	Bert	1757
Lewis	Bute	1771	KNOP, Robert	Bert	1769
Lewis	FWV	1771	KNOTT, David	Gran	1784
Thomas	Chow	1717	James	Gran	1755
KIRKMAN, Wm	Beau	1764	James	Gran	1769
KIRKPATRICK, Samuel	NewH	1755	John	Crav	1769

KNOTT, John s. of		
James	Gran	1755
John	Gran	1769
John s. of		
James	Gran	1784
Joseph	Bert	1757
Joseph	Bert	1769
Nathaniel	Bert	1757
Wm	Bert	1757
Wm	Bert	1769
KNOWIS, John	Beau	1755
John	Pitt	1762
John Jr.	Pitt	1762
John Jr.	Pitt	1764
John Sr.	Pitt	1764
KNOWLEN, Howard	Gran	1769
Peter	Gran	1769
KNOWLES, George	Brun	1769
George	Brun	1772
James	Blad	1781
Laurence	Bute	1771
Laurence	FWV	1771
Robert	NewH	1744
Wm	Bute	1771
Wm	FWV	1771
KNOX, David	Pitt	1764
Isaac	Pitt	1762
John	Crav	1769
Josiah	Pitt	1762
Mark	Crav	1769
Robert	Pitt	1762
Robert	Pitt	1764
Wm	Crav	1769
Wm	Pitt	1762
KOFFLER, Adam	Surr	1771
KOGLE, John	Oran	1755
KONDRED, Jor	N.C.	1701
KOON, Caleb	Pasq	1769
Daniel	Pasq	1769
KOONCE, George	Crav	1769
Jacob	Crav	1769
John	Crav	1769
Michael Constable		
	Crav	1769
KRAMER, Adam	Surr	1771
Andrew	Surr	1771
KROSE, Wm	Gran	1755
KUHNAST, Christopher		
	Surr	1771
KURZE, George	Bert	1769
KYLE, John	Onsl	1769
John	Onsl	1770
LACEY, John	Perq	1740
LACKELUR, Henry	Blad	1763
LACKEY, Henry	Beau	1764
John	Anso	1763
John	Casw	1777
Richard	Bert	1769
LACKSTON, Thomas	Surr	1771
LADD, Enus	Surr	1771
Noble	Rowa	1759
Noble	Surr	1771

LADD, Noble	Surr	1772
LAFEE, Lewis	Cumb	1767
LAFIELD, Thomas	Bert	1769
LAFTEN, James	Bert	1757
Wm	Bert	1757
LAGALL, George	Rowa	1759
LAKE, Wm	Surr	1771
Wm	Surr	1772
LAKERS, Widow		
297 acres	Perq	1720
LAKEY, John	Bert	1757
Richard	Bert	1757
Wm	Bert	1757
LALEY, Jemru	Curr	1715
LAMB, Abraham	Blad	1763
Abraham	Dobb	1769
Arthur	Blad	1763
Esau	Pasq	1769
Esau	Rand	1779
Hardy s. of		
Jacob	Dobb	1769
Hardy	Dobb	1779
Henry	Perq	1740
Isaac	Blad	1763
Isaac	Gate	1786
Jacob	Dobb	1769
Jacob	Rand	1779
Jesse	Bert	1769
John	FWV	1771
John	Rand	1779
John	Rowa	1759
Joseph	NewH	1755
Joseph	Rand	1779
Joseph	Surr	1772
Joshua	Rand	1779
Josiah	Rand	1779
Luke 1 slave	Pasq	1769
Manasseh	Brun	1772
Peter	NewH	1755
Peter	NewH	1762
Peter	NewH	1765
Peter	NewH	1767
Reuben	Rand	1779
Robert	Brun	1772
Robert	Rowa	1758
Thomas	Blad	1763
Thomas	NewH	1763
Thomas	Rand	1779
Wm	Rand	1779
LAMBERT, Aaron	Pasq	1769
Benjamin	Blad	1763
Enoch	Onsl	1770
Israel	Pasq	1741
Jacob	Pasq	1769
James	Pasq	1769
John	Blad	1763
John	Onsl	1770
John	Oran	1755
Joseph	Oran	1755
Joseph	Pasq	1769
LAMBERTSON, James	Pasq	1769
Uriah	Beau	1755
Uriah	Crav	1769
LAMBKIN, George	Gran	1755
Samson	Bute	1771

LAMBKIN, Samson | FWV 1771
LAMMON, Leonard | Casw 1777
LANCASTER, Aaron s.
   of Laurence | FWV 1771
  Absalom | Bute 1771
  Absalom | FWV 1771
  John | Bute 1771
  John | Crav 1769
  John s. Joel | FWV 1771
  John | Gran 1755
  John 10 male
    slaves | Pasq 1769
  Joseph | Onsl 1770
  Laurence | Bute 1771
  Laurence s. John
    Moses | FWV 1771
  Laurence Jr. | FWV 1771
  Laurence | Gran 1755
  Moses s. of
    Laurence | FWV 1771
  Richard | Crav 1769
  Samuel | Bute 1771
  Samuel | FWV 1771
LAND, James | Rand 1779
  Robert | Beau 1755
LANDERS, John | Gran 1755
  John s. of
    John | Gran 1755
  Luke | Gran 1769
  Thomas | Rowa 1759
LANDES, John | Gran 1769
  Joseph | Gran 1769
LANDFORD, Henry | Gran 1784
  Jesse | Gran 1784
  John | Gran 1784
  Moses | Gran 1784
  Parish | Gran 1784
LANDING, Ellis | Onsl 1770
  James | Gate 1786
  Wm | Onsl 1770
LANDISH, John | Gran 1784
  Joseph | Gran 1784
LANDMAN, James | Casw 1777
LANDRUM, John Sr. | Oran 1755
LANE, Benjamin | NewH 1755
  Benjamin | NewH 1762
  Benjamin | NewH 1763
  Benjamin | NewH 1765
  Benjamin | Roan 1720
  Elizabeth | Pasq 1769
  Ephraim | Crav 1769
  George 4 slaves | Crav 1769
  Isham | Dobb 1779
  Isom | Dobb 1769
  Isom | Dobb 1779
  Israel | Crav 1769
  James | Bert 1769
  Jethro | Dobb 1769
  John | Chow 1721
  John | Crav 1769
  John | Edge 1743
  John | Rand 1779
  John | Roan 1720
  Joseph Sr.
    300 acres | Chow 1721

LANE, Joseph
    500 acres | Chow 1721
  Joseph | Edge 1742
  Joseph | Rand 1779
  Joseph | Roan 1720
  Levin 9 slaves | Crav 1769
  Richard | Rowa 1759
  Samuel | NewH 1762
  Samuel | NewH 1763
  Samuel | NewH 1765
  Thomas 500 a. | Chow 1721
  Thomas | Dobb 1769
  Thomas | Dobb 1779
  Thomas | Edge 1743
  Thomas | Perq 1740
  Tidance | Rand 1779
  Walter | Crav 1743
  Wm | Pasq 1754
  Wm s. of
    Elizabeth | Pasq 1769
LANEAR, James | Pitt 1762
  Wm | Pitt 1762
LANEMORE, George | Gran 1784
LANGE, James | Gate 1786
  James | Oran 1755
  Joshua | Bert 1757
  Judith | Chow 1753
  Robert
    616 acres | Chow 1721
  Wm | Chow 1753
LANGFORD, James | Surr 1771
  James | Surr 1772
  John | Surr 1771
  John | Surr 1772
LANGLEY, James | Dobb 1779
  Roganiah | Beau 1764
  Thomas | Casw 1777
  Thomas | Oran 1755
  Wm | Rowa 1758
LANGSDALE, John | Blad 1781
LANGSTON, Absalom s.
    of Jacob | Dobb 1769
  Absalom | Gran 1769
  Demsey | Gate 1786
  George | Dobb 1769
  Isaac | Gate 1786
  Jacob | Dobb 1769
  James s. of John | Gran 1755
  James | Gran 1769
  John | Edge 1744
  John | Gran 1755
  Joseph s. of
    John | Gran 1755
  Joseph | Gran 1769
  Laurence | Chow 1753
  Leonard | Bert 1741
  Leonard | Bert 1757
  Leonard | Chow 1753
  Luke | Bert 1757
  Mace s. of Jacob | Dobb 1769
  Moses | Chow 1753
  Mr. 100 acres | Chow 1721
  Solomon s. of
    John | Gran 1755
  Solomon | Gran 1769

LANGSTON, Thomas	Chow	1753
Thomas	Gate	1786
Uriah	Dobb	1779
Wm	Bert	1757
Wm	Chow	1753
LANGWORTHY, Jonathan		
	Pasq	1754
LANHERN, James	Gran	1769
LANIEN, James	Pitt	1764
John	Pitt	1764
Wm	Pitt	1764
LANIER, Alexander	FWV	1771
James	Pitt	1764
Nathaniel	Pitt	1775
Robert (Rt.)	Chow	1717
Robert 1,700 a.	Chow	1721
Thomas	Gran	1769
Thomas	Gran	1784
Wm	Beau	1743
Wm	Beau	1755
LANSTHALL, Benjamin	Blad	1781
LANSTON, Francis	Dobb	1769
LAPETER, Jacob	Bert	1769
LAPHAM, John	Cumb	1767
LAPSLY, Thomas	Oran	1755
LAREY, Darby	Bert	1757
James	Bert	1757
LARIMORE, Edward	Cumb	1755
LARIMOUNT, Richard	Hyde	1741
LARKINS, James	NewH	1762
James	NewH	1763
James	NewH	1765
James	NewH	1767
John	NewH	1755
John	NewH	1762
John	NewH	1763
John	NewH	1765
John	NewH	1767
Wm	NewH	1755
Wm	NewH	1762
Wm	NewH	1763
Wm	NewH	1765
Wm	NewH	1767
LARRY, Darby	Bert	1769
Darby	Onsl	1769
Darby	Onsl	1770
Evan	Pasq	1754
Jeremiah	Onsl	1769
Jeremiah	Onsl	1770
Larry	Onsl	1769
Larry	Onsl	1770
LASCOMB, John	Bert	1757
LASEY, Parker	Pitt	1762
LASHLEY, Patrick	Gran	1755
LASKY, Elisha	Rand	1779
LASLKFORD, John	Gran	1784
LASSEY, James	Pasq	1754
LASSITER, Aaron	Chow	1753
George	Chow	1717
George	Chow	1753
Jacob	Bert	1757
James	Bert	1769
James	Chow	1753
Jesse	NorH	1762
John	Chow	1753

LASSITER, Joseph	NorH	1762
Moses Jr.	Chow	1753
Moses Sr.	Chow	1753
Nathan	Dobb	1779
Rt.	Chow	1717
Robert	Chow	1753
Sarah	Rand	1779
Tobias	Chow	1753
Wm	Gran	1755
Wm	Gran	1784
LASWELL, Othneil	Pasq	1769
Wm	Surr	1771
LATER, Mathew	Pitt	1775
LATHAM, Cornelius		
Jr.	Rand	1779
Cornelius Sr.	Rand	1779
James	Beau	1755
James	Pitt	1762
James	Rand	1779
John	Rand	1779
Whin.	Beau	1755
LATHERS, James	Gran	1769
LATHRUM, Wm	Gran	1784
LATTA, James	Oran	1755
LATTERMORE, Wm		
Esq.	Chow	1721
LAUGHAN, James	Gran	1784
John	Beau	1755
John	Crav	1769
LAUGHINGHOUSE,		
Thomas	Beau	1755
Thomas	Pitt	1762
Thomas	Pitt	1764
LAUGHLAN, Hugh	Oran	1755
LAVENDER, John	Crav	1769
Wm	Crav	1769
LAVERMAN, George	Bert	1757
LAW, John	Bert	1769
LAWKEN, James	Dobb	1769
John	Dobb	1769
LAWLEY, Elisha	Rand	1779
Jemru	Curr	1715
Pat	Chow	1717
Thomas	Crav	1769
Wm	Crav	1769
LAWRENCE, Cornelius	NewH	1762
Dibman	Gran	1784
Griffin	Gran	1784
Humphrey	Bert	1769
Humphrey	Crav	1744
Jacob	Bert	1769
John	Bert	1757
John	Bert	1769
John	Gran	1755
John	Rand	1779
Joshua	Bert	1769
Michael	Gate	1786
Robert	Bert	1769
Thomas	Bert	1757
Wm	Gran	1755
Wm	Gran	1784
LAWS, Abram	Onsl	1770
George	Oran	1755
James	Oran	1755
Wm	Onsl	1769

LAWSON, David	Cumb 1767	LEACKEY, Wm	Oran 1755
James	Dobb 1769	LEACY, Wm	Oran 1755
James s. of		LEADAM, Wm	Gran 1755
James	Dobb 1769	LEADON, Jacob	Oran 1755
James	Dobb 1779	LEAFORD, John	Rand 1779
James	Surr 1772	John Jr.	Rand 1779
John	Casw 1777	Peter	Rand 1779
John	Dobb 1769	Wm	Rand 1779
John s. of		LEAK, Francis	Pasq 1754
James	Dobb 1769	Jeremiah	Pasq 1769
John	Dobb 1779	John	Pasq 1769
Reuben	Gran 1755	Thomas s. of	
Samuel	Crav 1769	Jeremiah	Pasq 1769
Thomas	Beau 1764	LEAKE, Wm Jr.	Casw 1777
Thomas	Pasq 1769	Wm Sr.	Casw 1777
LAWTER, Henry	Gran 1755	LEANEY, Totter	Oran 1755
James	Bute	LEARY, Cornelius	Chow 1753
James	FWV 1771	Cornelius	NewH 1741
John	Bute 1771	Johannes	Tyrr 1755
John	FWV 1771	John	Tyrr 1755
LAWTON, James Jr.	Bert 1769	Richard	Tyrr 1755
John	Dobb 1769	Thomas	Tyrr 1755
Thomas	Rowa 1759	Wm	Curr 1715
LAXTON, Thomas	Oran 1755	LEATH, Thomas	Bert 1769
LAY, Enos	Brun 1769	LEATHERS, James	Gran 1784
Enos	Brun 1772	LEDBETTER, Daniel	Casw 1777
John	Brun 1769	Henry	Casw 1777
John	Brun 1772	Isel	Casw 1777
John	Casw 1777	LEDFORD, Nicholas	Rowa 1759
John	NewH 1762	Wm	Pasq 1754
John Sr.	NewH 1762	LEE, Abel	Cumb 1767
LAYDEN, Wm	Perq 1740	Arthur	Dobb 1769
LAYFORE, James	Tyrr 1755	Brant	NewH 1767
LAYTON, Francis	Perq 1720	Bryan	NewH 1762
James	Casw 1777	Bryan	NewH 1763
John	Casw 1777	Bryan	NewH 1765
John Jr.	Casw 1777	Burrell	Blad 1763
John	Gran 1769	Burton	Crav 1769
Joseph		Daniel	Curr 1755
Wm	Blad 1741	David	Dobb 1769
LEA, Barnett	Casw 1777	Francis	Bert 1757
Burton	Crav 1769	Francis	Bert 1769
Edmund	Casw 1777	Francis	Pasq 1754
Enos	NewH 1763	Godfrey	Bert 1742
James Sr.	Casw 1777	Henry	Bert 1769
James	Casw 1777	Henry	Gate 1786
James	Oran 1755	Jacob	Crav 1769
John Jr.	Casw 1777	James s. of	
John Sr.	Casw 1777	Timothy	Dobb 1769
John Esq.	Casw 1777	James	NewH 1755
John	Casw 1777	John	Beau 1755
John	NewH 1763	John	Beau 1764
John	Oran 1755	John	Blad 1763
Mary	Casw 1777	John	Chow 1753
Richard	Casw 1777	John	Edge 1742
Thomas	Casw 1777	John Jr.	Onsl 1769
Wm Jr.	Casw 1777	John Sr.	Onsl 1769
Wm Sr.	Casw 1777	John Jr.	Onsl 1770
Wm	Casw 1777	John Sr.	Onsl 1770
Zachariah	Casw 1777	John	Roan 1720
LEACH, John	Beau 1764	Joseph	NewH 1763
Thomas	Gran 1769	Joshua	Bert 1757
Wm	Rand 1779	Joshua	Edge 1741
LEACHFIELD, Edward	Curr 1755	Joshua	NewH 1755
LEACKEY, Alexander	Oran 1755	Joshua	NewH 1762

LEE, Joshua	NewH 1767	
Lazarus	Dobb 1769	
Lazarus	NewH 1767	
Levi	Beau 1755	
Levi	Gate 1786	
Luke	Surr 1771	
Luke	Surr 1772	
Needham	Dobb 1769	
Robert	Cumb 1767	
Samuel	Curr 1755	
Sevin	Beau 1764	
Stephen		
27 slaves	Onsl 1769	
Stephen	Onsl 1770	
Stephen	Tyrr 1743	
Thomas 14,381 a.	Chow 1717	
Thomas' orphans	Chow 1721	
Thomas	Crav 1769	
Thomas	N.C. 1701	
Timothy	Dobb 1769	
Wm	Cumb 1755	
Wm	Curr 1755	
Wm	Perq 1740	
LEECH, Hugh	Rand 1779	
Joseph	Crav 1769	
Wm	Rand 1779	
LEETHE, Samson	Crav 1769	
LEGARE, Charlton	Rowa 1759	
LEGGETT, Abner	Curr 1755	
Absalom	Bert 1757	
Absalom	Curr 1755	
Benjamin	Bert 1757	
James	Bert 1757	
James Jr.	Bert 1757	
Titus	Bert 1757	
LEINBECK, Ludwick	Surr 1771	
Ludwick	Surr 1772	
LEKE, John	Pasq 1769	
LEMAN, Henry	Oran 1755	
LEMER, Christian	Rowa 1759	
LEMMOND, Arthur	Curr 1755	
LEMMONN, Henry	Cumb 1767	
LEMONS, John	Oran 1755	
N. 410 acres	N.C. 1701	
LENEAR, John	Beau 1744	
John	FWV 1771	
LENNON, Ephraim	Blad 1763	
John	Blad 1743	
John	Blad 1781	
LENTERMAN, Henry	Rand 1779	
Henry Jr.	Rand 1779	
John	Rand 1779	
LEONARD, Edward	Cumb 1767	
Henry	Brun 1769	
Henry	Brun 1772	
Henry Jr.	Brun 1772	
Jacob	Brun 1769	
Jacob	Brun 1772	
John	Brun 1769	
John	Brun 1772	
John	Chow 1721	
John	Gran 1755	
Samuel	Brun 1772	
Samuel Jr.	Brun 1772	
Samuel Sr.	NewH 1762	

LEONARD, Samuel Jr.	NewH 1763	
Samuel Sr.	NewH 1763	
Theophilis	Pasq 1754	
LEPARD, Peter	Casw 1777	
LEPTROT, James	Cumb 1767	
LERICKFIELD, John	Beau 1742	
LESLY, Joel	Oran 1755	
LESSLIE, John	Pitt 1775	
LESTER, Bannister	Onsl 1770	
Elizabeth	Pasq 1769	
Wm	Onsl 1770	
LETCHER, Frederick	Rowa 1759	
LETCHWORTH, Joseph		
Jr.	Crav 1769	
Joseph Sr.	Crav 1769	
LETMAN, Samuel	Oran 1755	
LEUTS, Henry	NorH 1762	
LEVESTON, George	Gran 1784	
LEVINGTON, Wm	Cumb 1767	
LEVY, Alexander	NorH 1762	
LEWALLEN, Wm	Rand 1779	
LEWALLING, Wm	Anso 1763	
LEWING, Joseph	Curr 1755	
LEWIS, Anthony	Chow 1721	
Anthony Jr.		
640 a.	Chow 1721	
Anthony	Dobb 1769	
Anthony		
14 persons	Onsl 1741	
Creesey	Pitt 1764	
Daniel	Rowa 1759	
David	Crav 1769	
David	Gate 1786	
David	Rand 1779	
Edmond	Casw 1777	
Enoch	Oran 1755	
Fielding	Casw 1777	
Francis	Gran 1784	
George	Rand 1779	
Hanson	Blad 1763	
Henry	Surr 1771	
Henry	Surr 1772	
Howell	Gran 1769	
Howell Jr.	Gran 1784	
Isaac	Bert 1757	
Isaac 650 acres	Chow 1721	
Jacob	Beau 1755	
Jacob	Brun 1772	
Jacob	Chow 1717	
Jacob	Chow 1721	
Jacob	Crav 1769	
Jacob	Dobb 1769	
Jacob	Gran 1755	
Jacob	NewH 1762	
Jacob	NewH 1763	
Jacob	NewH 1765	
Jacob	NewH 1767	
Jacob	Rand 1779	
James	Blad 1763	
James	Dobb 1769	
James	Dobb 1779	
James	Gran 1784	
James	NorH 1762	
Jean	Beau 1755	
Jeremiah	Gran 1769	

LEWIS, John	Beau 1755	LILES, Wm		Chow 1753
John	Beau 1764	LILLINGTON, Alexander		
John	Bert 1757		NewH 1762	
John	Blad 1741	Alexander	NewH 1763	
John (Col.)	Casw 1777	Alexander	NewH 1765	
John Esq.	Chow 1753	Alexander	NewH 1767	
John	Chow 1753	Ann	Chow 1717	
John	Gate 1786	LILLY, Elisha	Cumb 1767	
John	Onsl 1769	John	Perq 1740	
John	Rand 1779	John	Perq 1745	
John	Roan 1758	Sarah widow	Perq 1740	
Joseph	Beau 1755	Thomas 650 acres	Perq 1720	
Joseph	Crav 1769	Thomas	Perq 1740	
Josiah	Blad 1763	Timothy	Chow 1753	
Kenton	Pitt 1764	LILLYBRIDGE, James	Onsl 1769	
Mary	Beau 1755	James	Onsl 1770	
Mary	Pitt 1762	Joseph	Onsl 1770	
Mary	Pitt 1764	LIMLING, Moses	Cumb 1755	
Mills	Gate 1786	LINBARGAIN, John	Rowa 1759	
Norval	Gran 1784	LINDLEY, James	Oran 1755	
Peter	Beau 1755	Thomas	Oran 1755	
Peter	Crav 1769	LINDSAY, James	Dobb 1769	
Peter	FWV 1771	John	Dobb 1769	
Philip	Gate 1786	Joshua	Crav 1769	
Philip	Gran 1769	Joshua	Dobb 1769	
Philip	Gran 1784	LINDSEY, Joseph	Gran 1769	
Richard (Rd.)	Chow 1717	Joseph		
Robert	Gran 1769	2 slaves	Pasq 1769	
Robert	Gran 1784	LINKFIELD, Francis	Crav 1742	
Robert deceased	Gran 1784	John 7 w	Beau 1744	
Samuel	Bert 1769	John 2w 6b	Crav 1750	
Samuel	NewH 1755	LINN, John	Surr 1772	
Samuel	Rand 1779	LINSEY, Benjamin	Curr 1755	
Stephen s. of		Daniel	Curr 1715	
Jacob	Dobb 1769	Daniel	Curr 1755	
Stephen	Rand 1779	Dennis	Gran 1755	
Sweten	Gate 1786	Elisha	Gran 1784	
Thomas	Cart 1743	John	Curr 1755	
Thomas	Crav 1720	Joseph	Curr 1755	
Thomas	Crav 1743	Leonard	Gran 1755	
Thomas	Tyrr 1742	Leonard	Gran 1784	
Wm s. of John	Beau 1764	Wm	Gran 1755	
Wm	Blad 1763	LINTON, Bernard	Pasq 1769	
Wm	Chow 1753	Cattron	Curr 1755	
Wm	Crav 1769	Hezekiah	Pasq 1769	
Wm	Curr 1755	Jehu s. of		
Wm	FWV 1771	Hezekiah	Pasq 1769	
Wm	Gate 1786	John	Dobb 1769	
Wm	Pitt 1762	Moses	Curr 1715	
Wm	Pitt 1764	Silas	Pasq 1769	
LEWISTON, George	Gran 1769	Wm	Crav 1720	
LIGARDERE, Elias		LINVILLE, Aaron	Surr 1771	
9 b	Crav 1750	Aaron	Surr 1772	
LIGGITT, Benjamin	Pitt 1764	Daniel	Rowa 1759	
David	Curr 1715	David	Rowa 1759	
Elizabeth	Bert 1769	David	Surr 1772	
John	Curr 1715	John	Rowa 1759	
LIKENS, Hans	Rowa 1759	Moses	Surr 1772	
Hans	Surr 1771	Richard	Rowa 1759	
Hans	Surr 1772	Richard	Surr 1771	
Jacob	Rowa 1759	Richard	Surr 1772	
LILES, Benjamin	Brun 1772	Thomas	Rowa 1759	
George	Chow 1753	Thomas Jr.	Rowa 1759	
Henry	Chow 1721	Thomas	Surr 1771	
John	Cumb 1755	Thomas	Surr 1772	

LINVILLE, Wm Jr.	Rowa	1759
Wm Sr.	Rowa	1759
LION, John	NewH	1755
LIPSEY, Arthur	Crav	1769
James	Crav	1769
John 10 persons	Onsl	1741
Wm	Crav	1769
LIPSCOMB, John	Bert	1769
LIPSON, Wm	Onsl	1741
LIRMANY, Edward	Pitt	1775
LISLE, John	Edge	1742
LISTER, John	Pasq	1754
Willis	Bert	1769
LITFORD, Frederick	Rowa	1759
John	Rowa	1759
Wm	Rowa	1759
LITHERY, Richard	Crav	1720
LITTGOW, Mary	NewH	1742
LITTLE, Abraham	Beau	1755
Abraham	Crav	1769
George	Pitt	1764
Isaac	Dobb	1769
Isaac	Pitt	1762
Isaac	Pitt	1764
James	Beau	1755
James	Crav	1769
James	Dobb	1769
James	Pitt	1762
James	Pitt	1764
John	Beau	1755
John	Pitt	1762
John	Pitt	1764
John	Tyrr	1742
John	Tyrr	1755
Joseph	Pitt	1762
Joseph	Pitt	1764
Josiah	Pitt	1764
Leah	Crav	1769
Robert	Pitt	1762
Sarah	Crav	1769
Thomas	Beau	1755
Thomas	Dobb	1769
Thomas	Pitt	1764
Thomas	Tyrr	1755
Wm	Beau	1755
LITTLEDELL, Jonathan		
	Bert	1757
LITTLETON, Edmund	Crav	1769
Southey	Onsl	1770
Thomas	Crav	1769
LITTLEWOOD, Jacob	N.C.	1701
LIVELY, Henry	Rowa	1759
Mark	Surr	1771
Mark	Surr	1772
Wm	Surr	1771
LIVERMAN, John	Bert	1769
LIVINGSTONE, Joseph	Cumb	1755
LLOYD, David	Blad	1781
Edward	Gran	1769
Griffin	Beau	1741
Henry	Bert	1757
James	Onsl	1770
Joseph	Bert	1757
Joseph	Onsl	1769
Thomas	Dobb	1779

LLOYD, Thomas s.		
of Joseph	Onsl	1769
Thomas	Onsl	1770
Wm	Onsl	1770
LOAGET, Benjamin	Pitt	1762
LOCK, Benjamin	Blad	1781
David	Blad	1763
David	Blad	1781
Elizabeth	Blad	1781
Francis	Rowa	1759
George	Rowa	1759
Jacob	Rowa	1759
John ferryman	Blad	1763
John	Blad	1781
John	Gran	1784
Joseph	Blad	1763
Joseph	Blad	1781
Leonard	Blad	1763
Leonard Sr.	Blad	1781
Leonard	Cumb	1767
Matthew	Rowa	1759
Thomas	Blad	1781
Wm	Gran	1769
Wm	Gran	1784
Wm	Rowa	1759
LOCKALEER, John	Cumb	1755
Major	Cumb	1755
Thomas	Gran	1784
LOCKEY, Henry	Beau	1764
LOCKHART, Elizabeth	Bert	1769
George	Bert	1757
George	Bert	1769
James	Pitt	1775
Lillington	Bert	1757
Lillington	Bert	1769
LOCKS, John	Blad	1750
LOCKSTON, Thomas	Surr	1772
LOCKWOOD, Joseph	Brun	1772
LOCUS, Valentine	Gran	1784
LODWICK, Peter	Surr	1772
LOFLY, Daniel	Dobb	1769
LOFTON, Bennie	Dobb	1769
Col.	Crav	1720
Cornelius	Crav	1720
Cornelius	Cumb	1767
Elkanah Constable		
	Dobb	1769
Francis s. of		
Bennie	Dobb	1769
John	Dobb	1769
Joseph	Crav	1769
Len	Crav	1720
Leonard	Crav	1720
Leonard	Crav	1743
Leonard	Crav	1769
LOGAN, George	NewH	1762
James	Gran	1755
Patrick	Surr	1771
Wm	Surr	1771
Wm	Surr	1772
LOLAR, John	Rand	1779
LOMAIN, Osborne	Rand	1779
LONDON, John	NewH	1767
Mark	Oran	1755
LONER, John	NewH	1763

LONER, Michael	NewH	1763
Peter	NewH	1763
Thomas	NewH	1763
LONG, Ambrose	Casw	1777
Andrew	Tyrr	1755
Benjamin	Casw	1777
Charles	Gran	1784
Drury	Bute	1771
Drury	FWV	1771
Elizabeth	Chow	1721
George	Gran	1784
George	Rowa	1759
Giles Esq.	Oran	1755
James	Casw	1777
James	Chow	1717
James	NewH	1745
James 200 acres	N.C.	1701
James	Tyrr	1755
John	Bute	1771
John	FWV	1771
John	Gran	1755
John	Tyrr	1755
Jonathan	Bert	1769
Joshua	Perq	1740
Mary	Chow	1721
Matthew	Rowa	1759
Nicholas	Bert	1769
Richard	Gran	1784
Richard	Rand	1779
Robert	Casw	1777
Solomon	Rand	1779
Thomas	Chow	1717
Thomas	Chow	1721
Thomas	Crav	1742
Thomas	Crav	1743
Thomas	Perq	1740
Wo. (widow)	Chow	1717
Wm 500 acres	Perq	1720
Wm	Perq	1740
LONGBOTTOM, Thomas	Gran	1784
LONGMIRE, Wm	Gran	1784
LONSDALE, Christopher		
	Curr	1715
LOOD, Lor d	Casw	1777
LOOSABLE, Michael	Crav	1720
LOPER, John	NewH	1762
John	NewH	1767
Michael Jr.	NewH	1755
Michael Sr.	NewH	1755
Michael	NewH	1762
Peter	NewH	1765
Peter	NewH	1767
Thomas	NewH	1762
Thomas	NewH	1765
Thomas	NewH	1767
LORANCE, David	Rowa	1759
John	Rowa	1759
Peter	Rowa	1759
LORD, Peter Esq.	Blad	1763
Wm	Blad	1781
Wm 15 slaves	Brun	1769
Wm	Brun	1772
Wm	NewH	1755
Wm	NewH	1762
Wm	NewH	1763

LOSETALLY, Simeon	Casw	1777
LOSSITER, Aaron	Gate	1786
Abisthai	Gate	1786
Amos	Gate	1786
George	Gate	1786
George Jr.	Gate	1786
James	Gate	1786
Jeremiah	Gate	1786
Jonathan	Gate	1786
Josiah	Gate	1786
Michael	Gate	1786
Reuben	Gate	1786
Timothy	Gate	1786
LOTT, John	Edge	1742
Mark	Cumb	1755
LOUDERMILK, Jacob	Rand	1779
LOUPER, Richard	NewH	1767
LOURTON, John	Beau	1764
LOVE, Amos	Onsl	1769
Amos	Onsl	1770
Edmond	Dobb	1779
Isom	Casw	1777
James	Cumb	1767
John	Curr	1755
Jonathan	Casw	1777
Rachel	Casw	1777
Ralph	Curr	1715
Richard	Curr	1755
Robert	Cumb	1755
Robert	Cumb	1767
Samuel	Casw	1777
Thomas	Curr	1755
Wm	Rand	1779
LOVELATTY, Thomas		
Jr.	Oran	1755
Thomas Sr.	Oran	1755
LOVEN, Wm	Surr	1771
LOVETT, David	Dobb	1769
David	Dobb	1779
John Jr.	Dobb	1769
Lancaster	Tyrr	1755
Moses	Dobb	1769
Thomas 2 slaves	Crav	1769
LOVEWELL, Peter	Pasq	1754
LOVICK, Carteret		
Esq.	Chow	1721
Carteret	Crav	1750
George		
27 slaves	Crav	1769
John	Crav	1750
Richard		
11 persons	Crav	1741
Thomas	Cart	1742
LOVING, Arthur	Casw	1777
John	Surr	1772
Wm	Bert	1757
LOWBER, John	NewH	1765
LOWDEN, Alex	Pasq	1754
LOWDIN, John	Pitt	1764
Thomas	Pitt	1764
LOWE, Aaron	Pasq	1769
Barney	Pasq	1769
Caleb	Surr	1772
Conrad	Oran	1755
Ebenezer	Blad	1763

LOWE, Elizabeth	Pasq	1754
Gabriel	Casw	1777
George	Pasq	1754
George	Pasq	1769
Hannah	Pasq	1769
Isaac	Surr	1771
Isaac	Surr	1772
Jehu	Pitt	1775
John	Casw	1777
John	Chow	1721
John	Pasq	1754
John Jr.	Rand	1779
John Sr.	Rand	1779
John	Roan	1720
John	Surr	1772
Ralph	Rand	1779
Samuel	Rand	1779
Stephen	Bute	1771
Stephen	FWV	1771
Thomas	Crav	1743
Thomas	Gran	1755
Thomas	Oran	1755
Thomas Jr.	Oran	1755
Thomas	Pasq	1754
Thomas	Rand	1779
Thomas Jr.	Rand	1779
Thomas	Surr	1772
Wm	Casw	1777
Wm	NorH	1762
Wm	Pasq	1754
Wm	Pasq	1769
Wm	Rand	1779
Wm	Roan	1720
Wm	Surr	1771
Wm	Surr	1772
LOWELL, John	Dobb	1779
LOWIST, John	Curr	1715
LOWRY, Benjamin	Pasq	1769
James	Blad	1781
Jeremiah	Pasq	1769
John	Dobb	1779
John	Gran	1769
John	Pasq	1769
Noah	Pasq	1769
Thomas	Pasq	1754
Wm	Pasq	1754
LOWMAN, Samuel	Pasq	1754
LOWTHER, Charles	Beau	1755
Thomas	Curr	1742
Tristrim	Bert	1757
Wm Esq.	Bert	1769
LOYD, Ebenezer	Gran	1784
Edward	Gran	1755
Edward	Gran	1769
Edward	Gran	1784
Henry	Bert	1769
Isaac	Bert	1757
Isaac	Gran	1784
John	Dobb	1779
John	Rowa	1759
Joseph	Pasq	1769
Nicholas	Gran	1784
Thomas	Oran	1755
Wm	Gran	1784
LUCAS, George	Rand	1779

LUCAS, Henry	Beau	1755
John 10 slaves	Blad	1763
Samuel	Beau	1764
LUCKEY, George	Rowa	1759
Henry	Beau	1764
John	Rowa	1759
John Jr.	Rowa	1759
Joseph	Rowa	1759
Robert	Rowa	1759
LUCY, Isham	Bute	1771
Isham	FWV	1771
LUDDING, Abraham	NewH	1767
LUDFORD, Thomas (Cpt.)	Tyrr	1755
LUDLAM, Isaac	Brun	1769
Isaac	Brun	1772
Isaac Sr.	NewH	1762
Jeremiah	Brun	1769
Jeremiah	Brun	1772
Jeremiah	NewH	1762
John	NewH	1763
Joshua	Brun	1772
LUDWICK, Peter	Surr	1771
Peter	Surr	1772
LUERTON, John	Beau	1755
LUFFMAN, Wm	Curr	1715
Wm	Pasq	1769
LUIDER, John	Casw	1777
LUMAX, Wm	Cumb	1755
LUNG, Jacob	Surr	1771
LUNSFORD, Benjamin	Gran	1769
James	Gran	1769
James	Rand	1779
John	Gran	1769
Joseph	FWV	1771
Lyman	Bute	1771
Lyman	FWV	1771
Wm	Gran	1769
LURRY, Evan	Pasq	1769
Evan s. of Evan	Pasq	1769
Evan Jr.	Pasq	1769
LURRY, John	Curr	1755
John	Pasq	1769
Thomas	Pasq	1769
Wm	Pasq	1769
LUTTON, Constable	Chow	1717
Constable	Chow	1721
James	Chow	1753
John	Chow	1753
Thomas Jr.	Chow	1717
Thomas Sr.	Chow	1717
Thomas	Chow	1721
Thomas Jr.	Chow	1721
Thomas Esq.	Chow	1753
Thomas Jr.	Chow	1753
Wm	Chow	1753
LUTTRELL, John (Col.)	Casw	1777
LYLES, Benjamin	Brun	1769
Benjamin	Brun	1772
Charles	Bute	1771
Charles	FWV	1771
Henry	Chow	1717
Henry	N.C.	1701
Jeffrey	Chow	1717

LYLES, Wm	Gran	1784	MACKENDON, Simon	Dobb	1769
LYNAUGH, Francis	NewH	1762	MACKENZIE, Kinnett	Dobb	1769
Francis	NewH	1765	MACKERTY, Charles	FWV	1771
Francis	NewH	1767	MACKEY, Arthur	Brun	1772
LYNCH, Bryan	Dobb	1779	Joseph	Pasq	1769
Cornelius	Dobb	1769	Thomas	Pasq	1743
Daniel	Gran	1784	Thomas	Pasq	1769
Frederick	Gran	1784	Wm	Tyrr	1755
James	Bute	1771	MACKIE, Michael	Gran	1755
James	Dobb	1779	Wm	Curr	1755
John Jr.	Bute	1771	MACKELWAIN, James	Crav	1742
John Sr.	Bute	1771	John	Dobb	1769
John	Edge	1744	MACKLE, George	Casw	1777
Joshua	Dobb	1779	John	Casw	1777
LYNN, Thomas	Rowa	1759	MACKLEJOHN, George	Casw	1777
Wm	Rowa	1759	MACKLENDON, Thomas	Crav	1741
LYNICK, Francis	NewH	1767	MACKLEWAIN, James	Crav	1742
LYON, Henry	Gran	1784	MACKLING, Robert	Perq	1740
John	NewH	1762	MACREE, Robert	NewH	1763
John	NewH	1763	MACKSIMMONS, John	Dobb	1769
John	NewH	1765	MACON, Gideon	Gran	1755
John	NewH	1767	James	FWV	1771
Redmon 2 slaves	Crav	1769	John	Edge	1743
Richard Esq.	Cumb	1767	Thomas	Bute	1771
LYTLE, Robert	Oran	1755	Thomas	FWV	1771
			Wm	FWV	1771
			MADDOCK, Joseph	Oran	1755
			MADEWELL, James	Rand	1779
MABIN, Wm	Rowa	1759	MADISON, Abraham	Casw	1777
Wm	Surr	1771	MADKINS, Richard	Pasq	1769
MABRY, Francis Jr.	Bute	1771	MADLINE, Henry	FWV	1771
Francis Sr.	Bute	1771	Taylor	FWV	1771
Francis Jr.	FWV	1771	MADREN, Jacob	Pasq	1769
Francis Sr.	FWV	1771	John	Pasq	1769
Francis	Gran	1755	Robert	Pasq	1769
Isaac	Gran	1755	Wm	Pasq	1769
Jesse	FWV	1771	MADRY, James	Gran	1755
John	FWV	1771	John	Bert	1769
John	Gran	1784	Richard	Gran	1755
Richard	Bute	1771	MAGEE, Daniel	Chow	1717
Richard	FWV	1771	Daniel 100 acres	Chow	1721
Wm	FWV	1771	Daniel	Dobb	1769
MABSON, Arthur	NewH	1755	James	Beau	1755
Arthur	NewH	1762	MAGER, Michael	Gran	1755
Arthur	NewH	1763	MAGOFFER, Nathaniel	NewH	1755
Arthur	NewH	1765	MAGOONE, George	Rowa	1759
Arthur	NewH	1767	MAGOT, Mark	Cumb	1767
MACE, John	Rand	1779	MAGUE, Laurence	Chow	1717
Wm	Beau	1741	Laurence	Chow	1721
Wm	Beau	1755	MAHAINS, Stephen	Crav	1769
Wm Jr.	Beau	1755	MAHOON, James	Tyrr	1755
Wm	Pitt	1764	MAHOW, Silvanus	Pasq	1769
MACHEN, Thomas	FWV	1771	Thomas	Pasq	1769
MACKAM, Robert	Dobb	1769	MAILAND, David	Dobb	1769
MACKAY, Arthur	Brun	1769	MAILER, David	Blad	1763
MACKELAM, Daniel	Tyrr	1755	MAINER, John	Chow	1721
MACKELDON, Dennis	Crav	1741	Joseph	Chow	1721
Thomas	Crav	1741	MAINES, Robert	Dobb	1769
MACKELROY, Archibald			MAINS, James	NewH	1755
	Crav	1743	Matthew	Casw	1777
John	Crav	1743	MAIRS, James	Cumb	1767
MACKENBALE, Benjamin			MAISON, Caleb	NewH	1755
	FWV	1771	MAJOR, John	Gran	1784
Jonah	FWV	1771	MAJORS, John	Surr	1771
Wm	FWV	1771	John	Surr	1772

MAJORS, Joseph	Perq	1740	MANLEY, Absalom	Rand	1779
Nicholas	Surr	1771	Gabriel	Bert	1757
MALLARD, Daniel	Crav	1769	Henry	Dobb	1779
George	Crav	1769	James	Dobb	1779
John	Crav	1769	Moses	Bert	1757
John	Gran	1755	Solomon	Bert	1757
John overseer	Gran	1769	MANN, Absalom	NorH	1762
Peter	Crav	1769	Arnold	Gran	1784
MALLET, Wm	Cumb	1767	James	Curr	1715
MALLORY, Wm	Gran	1784	John	Casw	1777
MALLOW, Wm	Gran	1755	John	Curr	1715
MALONE, David	Gran	1769	John	John	1750
George	Gran	1784	Thomas	Chow	1717
Henry	Gran	1769	Thomas	Edge	1742
Isham	Gran	1769	Thomas	Surr	1771
John	Bute	1771	Thomas	Surr	1772
John Sr. & s.			Wm	Casw	1777
Frederick	Bute	1771	Wm	Curr	1755
John Sr. & s.			Wm	Perq	1720
Frederick	FWV	1771	Wm	Perq	1740
Robert	Gran	1784	MANNAMAD, Joel	Crav	1720
Simon	Gran	1769	MANNDEW, Henry	Surr	1771
Wood	Bute	1771	Henry Constable	Surr	1772
Wood	FWV	1771	Thomas	Chow	1717
MALPASS, Ed.	Chow	1717	MANNERING, Wm	Edge	1743
MALSBEY, John	NewH	1755	MANNING, Benjamin	Bert	1757
MALONEY, Jacob s.			Benjamin	Bert	1769
of Moses	Onsl	1769	David	Beau	1755
Moses	Onsl	1769	George	Pasq	1769
MALPUS, John	NewH	1763	John	Bert	1742
John	NewH	1765	John	Bert	1757
Richard	NewH	1763	Moses	Dobb	1769
Richard	NewH	1765	Moses	Dobb	1779
MALTSBY, John	Blad	1781	Reuben	Pitt	1775
MAN, John	Pasq	1754	Samuel	Crav	1769
MANCER, James	Pitt	1764	Samuel	Gran	1784
Roger	Pitt	1764	MANOR, Christopher	Surr	1771
MANCRIEF, Thomas	Curr	1715	George	Surr	1771
Thomas	Curr	1755	George	Surr	1772
Wm	Curr	1755	Gibson	Surr	1771
MANDELY, Gabriel			Henry	Onsl	1769
Jr.	Bert	1757	Henry	Onsl	1770
MANDOWELL, John	Hyde	1741	Jacob	Onsl	1769
MANEN, John	Oran	1755	Jacob	Surr	1771
MANEON, James	Pitt	1762	Jacob	Surr	1772
Richard	Pitt	1762	Thomas	Dobb	1769
Robert	Pitt	1762	MANTANCY, Nicholas	Bert	1757
MANER, Christopher	Beau	1764	MANTON, Joseph	Pitt	1764
Henry	Bert	1757	MANTUS, James	Dobb	1769
Henry	Onsl	1770	MANUEL, Isaac	FWV	1771
John	Bert	1757	MAPEY, Richard	Rand	1779
MANES, Wm	Oran	1755	MAPP, Littleton	Gran	1769
MANFORD, Irvin	Beau	1764	MAPPLES, Thomas	Cumb	1767
MANGELY, Gabriel			Wm	Cumb	1767
Jr.	Bert	1757	MARCH, Bernard	Gate	1786
MANGHAM, Howell	Gran	1784	Daniel	Gate	1786
MANGRAM, John	Bert	1769	John	Beau	1764
MANGRUM, Joseph	Gran	1755	Thud	Rowa	1759
MANGUM, Howell	FWV	1771	MARCHANT, Caleb	Curr	1755
James s. of Wm	Gran	1755	Gideon	Curr	1755
Samuel	Gran	1755	John	Curr	1755
Wm	Gran	1755	Keador	Curr	1755
Wm s. of Wm	Gran	1755	Willoughby	Curr	1755
MANLEY, Abel & w.			MARCHMENT, Wm	Onsl	1769
Ann	Bert	1757	Wm	Onsl	1770

MARCHMENT, Wm	Onsl	1770	MARSHALL, John	Crav	1720
MARDAGN, John	Pasq	1754	John s. Dixon	FWV	1771
MARDREN, John	Pasq	1754	John	NewH	1741
MAREDITH, Nathan	Blad	1763	John	NewH	1755
MARION, Isaac	Brun	1769	John	NewH	1762
Isaac 10 slaves	Brun	1772	John	NewH	1763
Wm	Rand	1779	John	NewH	1765
MARISDIN, Alis	NewH	1755	John	NewH	1767
MARISTON, Alexander	NewH	1755	Joseph	Dobb	1769
MARIX, Job	Blad	1750	Nicholas	Curr	1715
MARKET, John			Samuel	NewH	1762
1 slave	Crav	1769	Samuel	NewH	1763
MARKHAM, Anthony	Pasq	1754	Samuel	NewH	1765
Anthony	Pasq	1769	Samuel	NewH	1767
Charles	Dobb	1769	Thomas	Bute	1771
Charles	Dobb	1769	Thomas overseer	FWV	1771
Charles	Dobb	1779	Wm	Curr	1755
Charles	Pasq	1754	Wm	Oran	1755
Charles	Pasq	1769	Wm	Rand	1779
Joshua			Willis	Pasq	1769
4 m slaves	Pasq	1769	MARSHBURN, Benjamin	Onsl	1769
MARKLAND, Charles	Dobb	1769	Benjamin	Onsl	1770
Charles	Dobb	1779	Daniel	Onsl	1769
MARKS, James	Surr	1772	Daniel	Onsl	1770
Wm	FWV	1771	Edward	Onsl	1769
MARKUS, Wm	FWV	1771	Edward	Onsl	1770
MARLEY, Wm	Rand	1779	MARTIN, Aaron	Dobb	1779
MARLIN, Aaron s.			Abel	Chow	1753
of Richard	Dobb	1779	Abraham	Surr	1771
Richard	Dobb	1779	Abraham	Surr	1772
MARLING, John	NewH	1755	Alexander	Surr	1772
MARLOR, Charles	Gran	1769	Anthony	Casw	1777
Thomas	Surr	1771	Benjamin	Hyde	1741
MARLOW, Archibald	NewH	1755	Benjamin 6w 2b	Hyde	1745
James	Brun	1769	Benjamin 1w	Hyde	1752
James	Brun	1772	Clement	Onsl	1770
James	NewH	1762	Collen	Rand	1779
James Sr.	NewH	1763	David	Surr	1771
John	Brun	1772	David	Surr	1772
Nathaniel	Surr	1771	Elizabeth	N.C.	1701
Wm Jr.	Brun	1769	Francis	Pasq	1754
Wm Jr.	Brun	1772	Francis	Pitt	1762
MARNAN, Thomas	Brun	1769	Gabriel	Gate	1786
Thomas	Brun	1772	George	Bute	1771
MARNS, Wm	Edge	1744	George	FWV	1771
MARQUIS, Elias	Bute	1771	George	Oran	1755
Elias s. John	FWV	1771	Higlety	Dobb	1769
MARRETT, Stephen	Oran	1755	James	Anso	1763
MARRIOTT, Benjamin			James	Bute	1771
Jr.	Casw	1777	James	Curr	1715
Benjamin Sr.	Casw	1777	James	FWV	1771
MARSBY, John	NewH	1755	James	Pasq	1754
MARSDEN, Alice's			James	Surr	1771
est.	NewH	1762	James	Surr	1772
Rufus	NewH	1741	Joel	Beau	1755
MARSH, John	Oran	1755	John	Beau	1755
Katharine	Rand	1779	John	Bert	1769
Wm Jr.	Oran	1755	John	Bute	1771
Wm Sr.	Oran	1755	John	Chow	1753
MARSHALL, Charles	Casw	1777	John	Crav	1769
Frederick	Surr	1771	John	Edge	1743
George	Dobb	1769	John	FWV	1771
Humphrey	Dobb	1769	John	Gran	1755
Job	Crav	1720	John	NorH	1762
John	Bute	1771	John	Pitt	1762

MARTIN, Johnson	Surr	1771
Johnson	Surr	1772
Joseph	Blad	1763
Joseph s. of		
John	Gran	1755
Levi	Rand	1779
Lewis	Rand	1779
Lodowick	N.C.	1701
Lodowick Jr.	N.C.	1701
Lodwick	Beau	1742
Lodwick	Beau	1755
Lodwick	Beau	1764
Mary	N.C.	1701
Moses	Rowa	1759
Moses	Surr	1771
Moses	Surr	1772
Nathaniel	Pasq	1742
Obadiah	Casw	1777
Paul	Dobb	1769
Peter	Onsl	1770
Peter	Oran	1755
Richard	Beau	1755
Robert	N.C.	1701
Samuel	Crav	1743
Thomas	Bert	1769
Thomas	Cart	1743
Thomas	Crav	1769
Thomas	Cumb	1767
Thomas	Dobb	1769
Thomas	Edge	1742
Thomas	Pasq	1754
Wm	Beau	1741
Wm	Beau	1742
Wm	Beau	1755
Wm	Beau	1764
Wm s. of John	Gran	1755
Wm	Gran	1784
Wm	Hyde	1741
Wm	N.C.	1701
Wm	Oran	1755
Wm	Pasq	1754
Wm	Rand	1779
Zachariah	Oran	1755
MARTINLEER, John	Cumb	1767
MARTINS, Godfrey	Gran	1755
MASBORN, Daniel	Onsl	1743
MASHBURN, Edward	Crav	1769
MASKINS, Edward	Dobb	1769
MASON, Alexander	Onsl	1769
Caleb	NewH	1762
Caleb	NewH	1763
Caleb	NewH	1765
Caleb	NewH	1767
David	Gran	1784
Edward s. of		
Alex.	Onsl	1769
Elijah	Casw	1777
Elizabeth	Crav	1769
Foster	Chow	1721
Foster	Roan	1720
James	Surr	1771
John	Casw	1777
John	Curr	1715
Joseph	Onsl	1769
Joseph	Onsl	1770

MASON, Matthew	Dobb	1769
Matthew	Onsl	1769
Matthew	Onsl	1770
Miles	Bert	1757
Miles Sr.	Bert	1769
Ralph 350 acres	Chow	1721
Ralph	Edge	1743
Ralph Jr.	Roan	1720
Ralph Sr.	Roan	1720
Richard	NewH	1767
Roger	Hyde	1741
Ross	Edge	1734
Sally	Curr	1755
Scilly 1 slave	Pasq	1769
Solly	Pasq	1769
Thomas	Bert	1769
Thomas	Casw	1777
Thomas	Edge	1744
Wm	Anso	1763
Wm	NewH	1767
MASSAGEE, Abraham	Pasq	1769
Ann	Pasq	1769
Benjamin	Pasq	1754
Benjamin	Pasq	1769
MASSEY, Hezekiah	Gran	1755
James	Gran	1755
John	Bute	1771
John Jr.	Bute	1771
John	FWV	1771
John Jr.	FWV	1771
John	Gran	1755
Richard	Bute	1771
Richard & bro.		
John	FWV	1771
Richard	Rand	1779
Wm	Bute	1771
Wm s. Drury Wm	FWV	1771
Wm	Rand	1779
MASTERS, John Const	Crav	1769
Joseph	Crav	1743
Samuel	Crav	1769
Sarah	Crav	1769
Thomas	Crav	1769
MASTERSON, Edward	Dobb	1769
MATCHET, Edward	Beau	1741
Edward	NewH	1743
John	NewH	1741
John	NewH	1746
Thomas	Crav	1745
MATENLFO, Francis	Rand	1779
MATHERS, Edward	Beau	1741
MATHES, Andrew	Chow	1753
Mesheck	Dobb	1769
MATHIAS, Wm	Gate	1786
MATHIS, Alexander	Dobb	1769
Alexander s. of		
Alexander	Dobb	1769
Shadrack	Dobb	1769
Wm	Bute	1771
Wm	Dobb	1769
Wm	FWV	1771
MATHISON, Wm		
(Doc.)	Crav	1769
MATHUS, Richard	NewH	1767
MATTESS, Matthew	Oran	1755

MATTHEWS, Alexander	Dobb	1779	MAY, Peter	Pitt	1764
Anthony	Gate	1786	Tho.	Chow	1717
Hugh	Rand	1779	Tom	Edge	1734
James	Bute	1771	Wm	Bute	1771
James	Dobb	1779	Wm sons John		
James	Edge	1741	Wm	FWV	1771
James	FWV	1771	MAYBEN, Wm	Rowa	1759
James	Rowa	1759	Wm	Surr	1771
John	Bute	1771	MAYER, Jacob	Surr	1771
John	Crav	1743	John	Surr	1772
John	Cumb	1767	Peter	Surr	1771
John	FWV	1771	Philip Sr.	Oran	1755
John	Gran	1784	MAYES, Drury	Surr	1771
John	NewH	1767	Matthew	Surr	1771
Josiah	Dobb	1779	Matthew	Surr	1772
Reuben	Surr	1771	Tom	Edge	1734
Reuben	Surr	1772	MAYFIELD, A. B.	FWV	1771
Scott	Rand	1779	Ab	Bute	1771
Thomas	Chow	1721	Abe	Gran	1784
Thomas	Cumb	1755	Abraham	Bute	1771
Thomas	Cumb	1767	Abram	FWV	1771
Wm	Gate	1786	John	FWV	1771
MATTIS, Matthew	Oran	1755	Robert	Bute	1771
Richard	Rand	1779	Robert s.		
Wm	Rand	1779	Abraham	FWV	1771
MATTSON, Robert	Crav	1720	Stephen	Bute	1771
MAUBLEY, Wm	Gran	1769	Stephen	FWV	1771
MAUBRON, Nicholas	Bert	1769	Thomas	Bute	1771
MAUDLIN, Edward	Perq	1720	Thomas	FWV	1771
Edward	Perq	1740	Valentine	Bute	1771
Ezekiel	Perq	1720	Valentine overs	FWV	1771
Hannah	Perq	1720	Valentine	Gran	1784
John	Perq	1740	MAYHAB, Robert	Surr	1771
MAULDING, John Jr.	Cumb	1767	MAYNOR, Henry	Oran	1755
John Sr.	Cumb	1767	Wm	Onsl	1743
Robert	Cumb	1767	MAYO, Benjamin	Pitt	1764
MAULE, John	Beau	1755	Henry	Beau	1764
Wm	Chow	1717	James	Beau	1755
Wm (Col.)			James	Pitt	1762
9,000 a.	Chow	1721	James	Pitt	1764
MAULTSBY, Samuel	Blad	1781	James Jr.	Pitt	1764
Wm	Blad	1763	James Sr.	Pitt	1775
Wm	Cumb	1767	James	Pitt	1775
MAXWELL, Edward	Casw	1777	John	Beau	1742
James	Rand	1779	John	Beau	1755
John	Dobb	1769	John	Beau	1764
Mary	Casw	1777	John	Pitt	1762
Robert	Dobb	1769	John	Pitt	1763
Wm	Casw	1777	John	Pitt	1764
MAY, Benjamin	Pitt	1762	Mary	Beau	1755
Benjamin	Pitt	1775	Mary (widow)	Pitt	1764
Daniel	Oran	1755	Nathan	Beau	1755
George	Dobb	1769	Nathan	Pitt	1762
James	Beau	1755	Nathan	Pitt	1764
James	Pitt	1762	Peter	Pitt	1762
James	Pitt	1764	Peter	Pitt	1764
James	Pitt	1775	Peter	Pitt	1775
John	Beau	1745	Richard	Beau	1755
John	Bute	1771	Richard	Pitt	1762
John	Cumb	1767	Thomas	Beau	1755
John	FWV	1771	Thomas	Beau	1764
John Jr.	Oran	1755	Wm Jr.	Beau	1755
John	Pitt	1762	Wm Sr.	Beau	1755
John	Pitt	1763	Wm	Pitt	1762
John	Pitt	1775	Wm	Pitt	1764

MAYO, Wm	Pitt	1775	McCLENDEN, Deborah	Perq	1720
MAYS, Richard	Pitt	1764	Dennis	Chow	1721
MAZLING, Thomas	Crav	1720	Francis	Chow	1717
McADAM, James	Gran	1755	Francis	Chow	1721
McADDEN, Hugh	Casw	1777	Francis	Crav	1743
McADOO, John	Rowa	1759	Francis	Cumb	1767
McAFEE, Ezekiel	Pitt	1775	Thomas	Chow	1717
Eziolian	Pitt	1775	Thomas	Chow	1721
McALEXANDER, Alexand			Thomas	Crav	1742
	NewH	1762	Thomas	Cumb	1767
Alexander	NewH	1763	McCLENEN, Samuel	Pasq	1769
Alexander	NewH	1765	McCLENING, Samuel	Pasq	1769
Alexander	NewH	1741	McCLINTOCK, John	Rowa	1759
Hugh	NewH	1741	McCLOUD, Wm	Gran	1769
McALLEY, Laughlin	Casw	1777	McCLURE, John	Tryo	1776
Patrick	Casw	1777	Thomas	Rowa	1759
McALLISTER, Alexand			McCOBBINS, Samuel	Crav	1743
	Cumb	1767	McCOLLAM, Jonathan	Rand	1779
Alexander	NewH	1755	McCOLLEY, Wm	Surr	1771
Hector	Blad	1741	McCOLLUM, Duncan	Rand	1779
Hector	Cumb	1755	Isaac	Rand	1779
James	Oran	1755	James	Rand	1779
John	Cumb	1767	John	Casw	1777
Neil	Casw	1777	Thomas	Crav	1720
McANALLEY, Charles	Surr	1771	McCOMB, John	Oran	1755
Charles	Surr	1772	McCOMISH, David	Oran	1755
McBAY, Edward	Cumb	1767	McCONKEY, Alexander	Blad	1763
McBEAT, Wm	Gran	1755	Patrick		
McBEE, Wm	Bute	1771	2 slaves	Blad	1763
Wm	FWV	1771	Robert	Blad	1763
Wm	Gran	1755	Samuel	Casw	1777
McBOYD, Patrick	FWV	1771	McCONNELL, John	Bert	1769
Thomas	FWV	1771	John	Rowa	1759
McBRIDE, Elisha	Pasq	1769	Robert	Oran	1755
Joseph	Pasq	1769	Samuel	NewH	1765
McBURNEY, Charles	Rowa	1759	McCONOUGH, Samuel	Bute	1771
McCARROL, Nathan	Surr	1771	McCORKLE, Alexander	Rowa	1759
McCARTNEY, James	Gran	1769	Margaret	NewH	1762
McCARTY, Bailey	Hyde	1744	Margaret	NewH	1763
Charles	Bute	1771	Simeon	Rowa	1759
Darby	Hyde	1744	McCORKLEM, Wm	Casw	1777
Timo.	Chow	1717	McCORMICK, Wm	Pasq	1769
McCASLIN, John	Blad	1741	McCOULSKEY, Arch	Blad	1763
McCASTLETON, Samuel	Curr	1755	Neil	Blad	1763
McCAY, Daniel	Curr	1715	McCOY, Abel	Crav	1769
McCAYOE, Wm	Onsl	1769	Alexander	NewH	1755
McCLAIN, Bryant	Brun	1772	Daniel	Pasq	1769
Solomon	Dobb	1779	Elijah	Gran	1755
McCLAMEY, Oney	NewH	1763	Iver	Blad	1763
Oney	NewH	1767	James	Rowa	1759
Thomas	NewH	1763	John	Blad	1745
Wm	NewH	1763	John	Pasq	1769
McCLAMMY, Mark	NewH	1767	Joshua s. of		
Thomas	NewH	1755	John	Pasq	1769
Thomas	NewH	1767	Nancy	Casw	1777
Wm	NewH	1767	Neil	Blad	1763
McCLANDEL, John	Blad	1763	Neil	Oran	1755
McCLARN, John	NewH	1755	Wm	Blad	1745
McCLARNEY, Paul	Casw	1777	Wm	Casw	1777
Thomas	NewH	1762	Wm	Crav	1769
Wm	NewH	1762	Willis	Crav	1769
McCLELAND, Andrew	Blad	1763	McCRAKEN, Alexander	Oran	1755
McCLENDEL, Jacob	Cumb	1767	McCRAIN, Hugh	Cumb	1755
Joel	Cumb	1767	McCRANEY, Daniel	Cumb	1767
John	Blad	1763	Hugh	Cumb	1767

McCREAM, Daniel	Cumb	1755
McCREERY, Daniel	Rowa	1759
John	Rowa	1759
McCREY, Adam	Beau	1755
Thomas s. of		
Adam	Beau	1755
Wm	Beau	1755
McCUISTON, Benjamin	Casw	1777
Thomas	Rowa	1759
McCULLEN, Bryan	Dobb	1779
McCULLERS, Charles	Edge	1742
McCULLEY, Wm	Surr	1771
Wm	Surr	1772
McCULLOCH, Eustace	Gran	1769
Patrick	Oran	1755
Robert	Gate	1785
McCULLOM, Daniel	Oran	1755
McCUN, Joseph	Curr	1755
McCURY, John	Rowa	1759
McDADE, Barney	Rand	1779
John	Rand	1779
McDANIEL, Absalom	Oran	1755
Absalom	Rand	1779
Archibald	Cumb	1767
Caleb	Pasq	1754
Caleb	Pasq	1769
Daniel	Oran	1755
Daniel	Rand	1779
Isaac	Rand	1779
James	Bert	1757
James	Blad	1763
James	Crav	1769
James	Pasq	1754
James	Pasq	1769
James s. of		
James	Pasq	1769
John	Crav	1769
John	Pasq	1769
John s. of John	Pasq	1769
John	Rand	1779
John	Rowa	1759
Joseph	Gran	1769
Joshua	Pasq	1754
Joshua 1 slave	Pasq	1769
Josiah s. of		
John	Pasq	1769
Miley	Pasq	1754
Peter s. of		
Caleb	Pasq	1769
Risdon	Crav	1769
Wm	Blad	1781
Wm	Casw	1777
Wm	Pasq	1769
McDEED, Wm	Beau	1755
Wm	Cumb	1755
McDOLE, Wm	Rowa	1759
McDONALD, Alex	Tryo	1776
Duncan	Casw	1777
James	Bert	1769
James	Crav	1769
James	Gran	1784
Joseph	Gran	1784
Owen	Chow	1717
Wm	Casw	1777
McDONOUGH, Andrew	Beau	1755

McDONOUGH, Samuel	FWV	1771
McDOUGALL, Alexander		
	Blad	1763
Duncan	Cumb	1767
Hugh	Cumb	1767
McDOWELL, James		1744
Wm	NewH	1755
Wm	NewH	1762
Wm	NewH	1763
Wm	NewH	1765
McDUEL, Peter	Curr	1755
McDUFFEY, Archibald	Cumb	1767
Daniel	Cumb	1767
Duncan	Cumb	1767
John	Blad	1763
John	Cumb	1767
McDUMMICK, Andrew	Beau	1764
McDUNACH, Andrew	Beau	1755
McEACHEM, John	Cumb	1767
McELROY, James	Crav	1744
Wm	Crav	1744
McENTIRE, John	Oran	1755
McEWEN, Hugh	Rowa	1759
James	Rowa	1759
James	Surr	1771
James	Surr	1772
John	Blad	1763
Thomas	Rowa	1759
McFADDEN, Elias	Tryo	1776
James	Tryo	1776
John	Tryo	1776
John Sr.	Tryo	1776
McFALL, John	Cumb	1755
McFARLAND, Daniel	Casw	1777
John	Casw	1777
Robert	Casw	1777
McFARLIN, Daniel	NewH	1755
John	Cumb	1755
Sarah (widow)	NewH	1762
McFARLING, Wm	Bert	1769
McFARSON, Daniel	Crav	1769
Daniel	Pasq	1769
Jonathan	Crav	1769
Joseph	Pasq	1769
Joshua s. of		
Josep	Pasq	1769
Moses	Pasq	1769
Moses s. of		
Moses	Pasq	1769
McFATER, Arch	Blad	1763
Archibald	NewH	1741
McFEE, Duncan	Cumb	1755
Wm	Surr	1771
McFEETERS, Daniel	Rowa	1759
James	Rand	1779
McFERSON, Alexander	Cumb	1755
Daniel	Pasq	1769
John	Cumb	1755
Joseph	Pasq	1769
McFITRICH, Matthew	Rand	1779
McGEE, Benjamin	Gran	1769
Charles	Gran	1769
John	Gran	1769
John	NewH	1767
John	Oran	1755

McGEE, Joseph	Bute	1771	McINTOSH, Wm	Beau	1764
Joseph	FWV	1771	Wm	Casw	1777
Nathan	Gran	1769	McINTOY, Thomas	Blad	1763
Patrick	Dobb	1779	McINTHEM, John	Cumb	1767
Wm	Edge	1744	McKAIN,	NewH	1742
McGEEHEE, Benjamin	Gran	1784	McKAY, Alexander	Cumb	1767
James	Gran	1784	Anguish	Cumb	1767
Nathan	Gran	1784	Archibald	Cumb	1755
McGEHE, Mumford	Casw	1777	Archibald	Cumb	1767
McGERALD, Alexander	NewH	1767	Daniel	Cumb	1767
McGILL, Daniel	Cumb	1767	Evor	Cumb	1755
Daniel	Pitt	1764	Henry	NewH	1762
McGINNIS, John	NewH	1744	Henry	NewH	1763
McGLAHON, John	Beau	1755	Henry	NewH	1765
McGLAUGHAN, Edmund	Bert	1757	McKEE, Wm	Rand	1779
James	Bert	1757	McKEEL, Edward	Beau	1755
McGLAWHON, Adam	Pitt	1762	John	Beau	1755
McGLOCKLIN, Richard	Chow	1721	John	Pasq	1769
McGOONE, John	Rowa	1759	Thomas	Beau	1755
McGOWAN, Wm	NewH	1755	Thomas	Pasq	1754
Wm	NewH	1762	McKEEN, Hugh	Casw	1777
Wm	NewH	1763	McKEITHEN, Daniel	Blad	1763
Wm	NewH	1765	Duncan	Blad	1763
McGOWEN, George	Pitt	1775	McKELLUP, Ephraim	Oran	1755
McGOWING, John	Onsl	1769	McKIKIAN, Daniel	NewH	1741
McGOWN, Andrew	Pasq	1769	Duncan	NewH	1741
George	Beau	1764	McKILDO, John	Chow	1721
James Jr.	Oran	1755	McKINNEY, Bar	Roan	1720
James Sr.	Oran	1755	Garrett	Gran	1755
McGRAHAM, Robert	NewH	1762	John	Dobb	1779
McGRAIN, John	Onsl	1769	John	Onsl	1769
McGRANAHAN, Robert	NewH	1763	John	Onsl	1770
Robert	NewH	1765	Mill	Roan	1720
McGRANE, John	Onsl	1770	Richard	Dobb	1779
McGREGOR, Wm	Bute	1771	Wm	Dobb	1769
Wm	FWV	1771	Wm Jr.	Dobb	1769
McGRENE, John	Onsl	1770	Wm	Dobb	1779
McGUFFEY, Ephraim	Bute	1771	Wm	Pitt	1762
Ephraim s. John	FWV	1771	McKINNICK, John	Onsl	1770
McGUFFORD, James	NewH	1762	McKINZEY estate	Bert	1769
James	NewH	1763	McKISSICK, Archibald		
James	NewH	1765		Blad	1763
James	NewH	1767	Archibald	Cumb	1755
Nath	NewH	1744	John	Bute	1771
Nathaniel	NewH	1762	John Jr.	Bute	1771
Nathaniel	NewH	1763	John & s.		
Nathaniel	NewH	1767	Robert	FWV	1771
McGUIRE, Edward	Rowa	1759	John Jr.	FWV	1771
Philip	Chow	1717	John	Gran	1755
Philip	Chow	1721	McKITCHEN, James	Cumb	1755
Thomas	NewH	1762	McKNIGHT, George	Rowa	1759
McGUMRAY, James	Bert	1769	James	Casw	1777
McHENRY, Wm	Pitt	1764	John	Rowa	1759
McHORTON, Archibald	Rand	1779	Thomas	Pasq	1769
McILHENNY, James	Brun	1772	McKOWN, James	Surr	1771
McILVALE, James	Bute	1771	McLANE, Arch	NewH	1755
Joanna	Bute	1771	Archibald	NewH	1762
McINN, Wm	Pitt	1775	Charles	Pitt	1762
McINTIRE, James	Oran	1755	David	Pitt	1762
John	Oran	1755	John	Cumb	1767
McINTOSH, Alexander	Casw	1777	Robert	Rand	1779
Eneas	Crav	1743	Wm	Surr	1772
John	Casw	1777	McLAREN, Duncan	Cumb	1755
Thomas	Casw	1777	Duncan	Cumb	1767
Wm	Beau	1755	John	Cumb	1767

McLEAN, Archibald	Cumb 1767	McNORTON, Neil	Blad 1763
Hugh	Cumb 1755	McPEAK, James	Surr 1772
John	Tryo 1775	McPERCHIN, Angus	Cumb 1755
McLEMORE, Adkin	Bute 1771	McPHAIL, Douglas	Cumb 1767
Adkin	FWV 1771	McPHALE, John	Cumb 1767
Atkin	Gran 1755	McPHERSON, Alexander	
James	Gran 1769		Cumb 1767
James	Gran 1784	Andrew	Curr 1715
John	Gran 1784	Andrew	Curr 1755
Lawrence	Pitt 1762	Daniel	Curr 1715
Young	Bite 1771	Daniel	Curr 1755
Young	FWV 1771	Daniel	Dobb 1779
McLAUGHLIN, James	Crav 1769	John	Curr 1755
McLELLEN, Duncan	Cumb 1755	Jonathan	Dobb 1769
McLEROY, James	Beau 1755	Robert	Rowa 1759
McLEWAIN, James	Crav 1741	Wm	Oran 1755
McLIN, Thomas		McQUILLIN, John	NewH 1767
24 slaves	Crav 1769	Philip	Crav 1769
McLOCHLAN, Hugh	Cumb 1755	Wm	NewH 1762
McMAHON, Bryan	Beau 1764	Wm	NewH 1763
McMANUS, James	Crav 1742	Wm	NewH 1765
James	Crav 1748	Wm	NewH 1767
McMASTER, Rachel	Blad 1781	McQUISTON, James	Rowa 1759
Wm	Blad 1763	Thomas	Rowa 1759
McMICHAEL, John	Surr 1771	McREE, Robert	Dupl 1752
John	Surr 1772	Samuel	Blad 1763
McMILLEN, Henry	FWV 1771	Wm	Blad 1763
Stephen	Oran 1755	Wm	NewH 1741
Wm	Oran 1755	McREYNOLDS, Robert	Casw 1777
McMULLEN, Henry	Casw 1777	Rowland	Casw 1777
Torrence	Gran 1755	McSCARBROUGH,	
McMUNN, James	Casw 1777	Solomon	Perq 1740
McMUNNAMY, John	Casw 1777	McSHEY, Isaac	Crav 1769
McMURRY, John	Casw 1777	McSIMMONS, John	Dobb 1769
Samuel	Casw 1777	McTEACHY, Wm	Oran 1755
McMURTER, Andrew	Pasq 1769	McTHEEL, Edmond	Beau 1764
McNAIR, Archibald	Cumb 1767	John	Beau 1764
McNEAL, George	Casw 1777	McUGLIN, James	Beau 1755
Daniel	Pasq 1769	McVAILY, Thomas	Gran 1784
Henry	Casw 1777	McVEY, Hugh	Casw 1777
Joseph	Pasq 1769	McWHORTER, John	Rowa 1759
Thomas	Casw 1777	McWILLIAMS, James	Casw 1777
McNEELY, James	Tryo 1776	MEA, Joseph	Rand 1779
McNEIL, Archibald	Cumb 1755	MEADE, Benjamin	
Archibald	Cumb 1767	1 b	Pasq 1769
Daniel	Cumb 1767	David	Bert 1757
Duncan	Cumb 1755	Joseph	Pasq 1769
Duncan	Cumb 1767	MEADOWS, Daniel	Bute 1771
Hector	Cumb 1755	Daniel	FWV 1771
Hector	Cumb 1767	Isham	Bute 1771
James	Cumb 1755	Isham	FWV 1771
John Constable	Cumb 1767	James	Gran 1755
Lochlan	Cumb 1755	James	Gran 1769
Neil	Blad 1742	James	Gran 1784
Neil	Cumb 1755	Jesse	Gran 1784
Neil weaver	Cumb 1767	John	Bute 1771
Neil	NewH 1741	John	FWV 1771
Norton	Cumb 1767	Wm	Gran 1755
Roger	Cumb 1767	MEADS, Benjamin	Pasq 1754
Torquil	Cumb 1755	John	Pasq 1754
McNEMAN	Pitt 1764	Quarter	Gran 1769
McNEMAR, Francis	Pitt 1762	Susannah	Pasq 1754
Francis	Pitt 1764	Thomas	Pasq 1769
McNESS, Isaiah	Dobb 1769	MEANS, Andrew	Rand 1779
McNORTON, Archibald	Rand 1779	Benjamin	Rand 1777

MEADS, John	Pasq	1754
Quarter	Gran	1769
Susannah	Pasq	1754
Thomas	Pasq	1769
MEANS, Andrew	Rand	1779
Benjamin	Rand	1777
Samuel	Oran	1755
Wm	Oran	1755
MEARCY, John	Rand	1779
MEARS, Abraham	Bert	1769
Anthony s. of		
Sarah	Dobb	1769
George	NewH	1762
George	NewH	1763
John	Dobb	1779
Mark	Dobb	1769
Mark	Dobb	1779
Nathan Jr.	Bert	1769
Nathan Sr.	Bert	1769
Sarah	Dobb	1769
Thomas	Rowa	1759
Thomas	Surr	1771
Thomas	Surr	1772
MEASEY, John	Rand	1779
MECES, Solomon	Blad	1763
MEAZELL, Luke	Chow	1717
Luke Esq.		
1180 a.	Chow	1721
Wm	Chow	1717
Wm	Chow	1721
MEBANE, Alexander		
Esq.	Oran	1755
Wm	Rowa	1759
Wm	Surr	1771
MECHAM, Henry	NorH	1762
MECK, George	Dobb	1769
MECKINGS, Isaac	Tyrr	1755
MECON, Harrison	FWV	1771
MEDDERAH, John	Chow	1753
MEDFORD, Joel	Cumb	1767
MEDLIN, Bryan	Dobb	1769
Nicholas	Dobb	1779
Owen	Surr	1771
Real	Bute	1771
Real	FWV	1771
Wm	Bute	1771
Wm s. Shead	FWV	1771
Wm	Surr	1771
MEDLOCK, John	Gran	1769
Nicholas	Gran	1769
MEDONEL, Joseph	Rowa	1758
MEEK, James	Beau	1755
John	Beau	1755
Joseph	Casw	1777
MEEKENS, Wm	Curr	1755
MEEKLEJOHN, Geo.		
(Rev.)	Gran	1784
MEEKS, Francis	Pitt	1762
Francis	Pitt	1764
James	Pitt	1762
James	Pitt	1764
John Constable	Pitt	1762
John	Pitt	1764
Nathan	Pitt	1762
Nathaniel	Pitt	1764

MEEKS, Robert	Pitt	1775
Thomas	Pitt	1762
Thomas	Pitt	1764
Walter	Pitt	1762
Walter	Pitt	1764
MEES, Stephen	Crav	1720
MEGARY, Hugh	Surr	1771
MEGGS, John	Casw	1777
MEIRE, Joseph	Pitt	1762
Joshua	Pitt	1762
MELTEAR, Jethro	Gate	1786
MELTON, Barnaba	NorH	1762
Berriday		
620 acre	Chow	1721
Berry	Roan	1720
Edward	Onsl	1769
Edward	Onsl	1770
Elizabeth 150 a.	Chow	1721
James	Onsl	1769
James	Onsl	1770
John	Chow	1721
John	NorH	1762
John	Onsl	1769
John	Onsl	1770
Joseph	Onsl	1770
Michael	Bute	1771
Richard	NewH	1762
Richard	Roan	1720
Robert	Onsl	1770
Wm	Casw	1777
Wm	Onsl	1770
MELVIN, Daniel	Blad	1763
MENDENHALL, Elisha	Rand	1779
John	Rand	1779
Mordecai	Rowa	1759
Richard	Rowa	1759
MENSHAW, Bond	Gate	1786
Isaac s. of		
Martha	Dobb	1769
Jacob	Bert	1757
Jacob	Dobb	1769
Martha	Dobb	1769
Maximillian	Gate	1786
Wm	Bute	1771
Wm	Dobb	1769
Wm	FWV	1771
MENUS, Wm Jr.	Cumb	1767
MERCER, Christopher	Dobb	1769
Coy	Pasq	1769
Henry	Blad	1763
Jacob	Pitt	1764
James	Casw	1777
James	Curr	1755
James	Pasq	1769
Jeremiah	Curr	1755
Joseph	Beau	1755
Joseph	Pasq	1769
Joseph Jr.		
1 slave	Pasq	1769
Peter	Cumb	1767
Shadrack	Dobb	1779
Stephen	Pasq	1769
Thomas	Crav	1743
Thomas	Curr	1755

MERCER, Thomas s. of		
Christopher	Dobb	1769
Thomas	Pitt	1764
Wm	Pasq	1769
MERCHANT, Capt.		
MEREDITH, Elizabeth		
	NewH	1752
James	Surr	1771
James Jr.	Surr	1772
James Sr.	Surr	1772
John	Surr	1772
Joseph	NewH	1741
Joseph	NewH	1742
Wm	Surr	1771
Wm	Surr	1772
MERKLE, Christopher	Surr	1771
James	Surr	1771
MERRICK, Eleanor	NewH	1765
Elizabeth	NewH	1767
Francis s. John	FWV	1771
George	NewH	1755
George	NewH	1762
George	NewH	1763
George	NewH	1765
George	NewH	1767
Grace	NewH	1742
Thomas	NewH	1762
Thomas	NewH	1763
Thomas	NewH	1765
MERRILL, Benjamin	Rowa	1759
Daniel	Rand	1779
John	Pasq	1754
John	Rand	1779
Thomas	Pasq	1769
Wm	Pasq	1769
Wm	Rand	1779
Wm	Rowa	1759
MERRIMAN, Allen	Pitt	1764
Charles	Bute	1771
Charles s.		
Benjamin Wm	FWV	1771
Charles	Gran	1784
MERRITT, Ephraim	Gran	1755
Hezekiah	Dobb	1769
Hezekiah	Pitt	1764
James overseer	FWV	1771
Joseph	Bute	1771
Joseph s. John		
Joseph Lloyd	FWV	1771
Nathaniel	Roan	1720
Reuben	Bute	1771
Reuben	FWV	1771
Silvanus	Bute	1771
Silvanus	FWV	1771
Stephen	Gran	1784
Thomas	Edge	1744
Wm	Bute	1771
Wm	Chow	1721
Wm	Edge	1743
Wm	FWV	1771
MERRONEY, Henry	Gate	1786
MESHAC, John	Cumb	1767
MESLINGER, John	Beau	1764
MESSER, Christian	Surr	1771
Coy	Pasq	1754

MESSER, Joseph	Blad	1763
Joseph	Pasq	1754
Joseph	Tyrr	1742
Noah	Crav	1769
Robert	Crav	1769
MESSEY, Joseph	Rand	1779
MESSICK, Jacob	Blad	1781
METCALF, Anthony	Tryo	1776
Colen	Crav	1720
Francis	Rand	1779
Isaac	Tryo	1776
Thomas	Chow	1721
Wm	Pasq	1769
METTS, George	Crav	1769
MEW, Philip	Crav	1743
Philip	Crav	1769
MEWBERN, George	Bert	1757
John	Bert	1757
John	Bert	1769
Mary	Dobb	1769
Thomas	Bert	1769
Thomas	Chow	1721
MEZELL, James	Pitt	1762
John	Bert	1757
Wm	Pitt	1762
MICARS, Thomas	Bert	1769
MICHAEL, Barnet	Rowa	1759
Conrad	Rowa	1759
George	Crav	1741
George	Rowa	1759
Thomas	Anso	1763
Wm	Surr	1771
Wolf	Crav	1741
MICKES, Pratley	Surr	1771
MIDDLEBROOKS, Anne	Casw	1777
John	Casw	1777
MIDDLETON, Henry	Chow	1721
James	Cumb	1767
James	HewH	1767
John	Gran	1755
Martha	Onsl	1769
Stephen s. of		
Martha	Onsl	1769
Stephen s. of		
Martha	Onsl	1770
Wm	Casw	1777
MIDGETT, Joseph Jr.	Curr	1755
Joseph Sr.	Curr	1755
Joseph	Curr	1755
Samuel	Curr	1755
Thomas	Curr	1755
MIDOWS, Edward	Cumb	1767
MIERS, Nathan	Bert	1757
Thomas	Bert	1757
Wm	Oran	1755
MILES, Abraham	Casw	1777
Alexander	Casw	1777
David	Dobb	1769
David	Dobb	1779
Hannah	Casw	1777
Jacob Jr.	Casw	1777
Jacob Sr.	Casw	1777
James s. of		
David	Dobb	1769
James	Dobb	1779

MILES, John s. of		
David	Dobb	1769
John	Bert	1769
Thomas	Bert	1757
Thomas	Dobb	1769
Wm s. of David	Dobb	1769
Wm	Dobb	1779
MILL, James	Crav	1769
Wm	Crav	1769
MILLAM, Adam	Bute	1771
Adam s. Lewis	FWV	1771
MILLARD, Kno.	Beau	1755
MILLEN, James	Casw	1777
MILLER, Daniel	Crav	1769
Elizabeth	Curr	1755
Evan	Curr	1715
Evan	Curr	1755
George	Cumb	1767
George	Dobb	1769
George	Dobb	1779
George	Rowa	1759
Gustrod s. of Wm	Dobb	1769
Haman	Rand	1779
Harmon	Surr	1771
Hayman	Rand	1779
Henry s. of Wm	Dobb	1769
Henry	Rowa	1759
Isaac	Curr	1755
Jacob 800 acres	Crav	1720
Jacob	NewH	1762
Jacob	NewH	1763
Jacob	Surr	1772
James	Bert	1769
James	Tryo	1776
Jesse	Gran	1755
Johanah	Curr	1755
John	Crav	1769
John	Gate	1786
John	Gran	1755
John	NewH	1742
John taylor	Pasq	1769
John	Rowa	1759
John	Surr	1771
John	Surr	1772
Jonathan	Bert	1769
Joseph	Gran	1769
Joseph	Surr	1771
Joshua	Blad	1769
Joshua	Dobb	1769
Joshua	Dobb	1779
Leonard	Rowa	1759
Michael	Rowa	1759
Monas	Surr	1771
Monas	Surr	1772
Nathaniel	Beau	1764
Nicholas	Beau	1764
Philip	Crav	1743
Philip	Dobb	1769
Ralph Esq.		
3 slaves	Blad	1763
Ralph	Blad	1781
Randolph	Dobb	1769
Richard	Dupl	1752
Richard	Rand	1779
Stephen	Dobb	1769

MILLER, Stephen	Gran	1769
Stephen	Surr	1771
Thomas	Bute	1771
Thomas	Curr	1715
Thomas	Curr	1755
Thomas & s.		
Thomas	FWV	1771
Tobias 1 slave	Crav	1769
Ventle	Rowa	1759
Wm Jr.	Curr	1755
Wm Sr.	Curr	1755
Wm (Rev.)	Dobb	1769
Wm	Dobb	1769
Wm	Dobb	1779
Wm	Pitt	1764
Wm	Rand	1779
Wm	Rowa	1759
MILLERFIELD, Jacob	Crav	1720
MILLIKIN, Benjamin	Rand	1779
Samuel	Rand	1779
Wm	Rand	1779
Wm Jr.	Rand	1779
Wm	Rowa	1759
MILLINER, James	Gran	1784
MILLS, Anthony	Crav	1769
Anthony	Pitt	1762
Anthony	Pitt	1764
David	Blad	1743
David	Pitt	1775
Edward	Brun	1769
Edward	Brun	1772
Fred	Pitt	1775
Henry	Rowa	1759
Hurr	Rowa	1759
Isaac	Pitt	1762
Isaac	Pitt	1764
Isaac	Pitt	1775
James	Bute	1771
James	FWV	1771
James Jr.	Onsl	1770
Joan	Oran	1755
John	Beau	1741
John	Beau	1755
John Jr.	Beau	1755
John 7w 2b	Crav	1745
John	Crav	1769
John	Curr	1715
John s. of Wm	Onsl	1769
John Jr.	Pitt	1762
John Sr.	Pitt	1762
John	Pitt	1762
John	Pitt	1764
John Jr.	Pitt	1775
John Sr.	Pitt	1775
John	Pitt	1775
John	Rowa	1759
John Jr.	Rowa	1759
Jonathan	NewH	1755
Nasbey	Pitt	1762
Nasbey Jr.	Pitt	1762
Nasbey	Pitt	1764
Nasbey Jr.	Pitt	1764
Nasbey	Pitt	1775
Nasbey Jr.	Pitt	1775
Robert Jr.	Gran	1769

MILLS, Robert	Gran	1784	MILTON, Merida	Surr	1772
Simon	Crav	1769	MINYARD, Israel	Gate	1786
Thomas	Crav	1750	Thomas	Blad	1741
Wm	Brun	1769	MIRES, David	Oran	1755
Wm	Brun	1772	MISSER, Wm	Onsl	1770
Wm	Gran	1769	MITCALF, Caleb	Crav	1720
Wm	Gran	1784	MITCHELL, Abraham	Gran	1784
Wm	Onsl	1741	Abraham	Onsl	1741
Wm Jr.	Onsl	1769	Adam	Rowa	1759
Wm Sr.	Onsl	1769	Adam	Surr	1772
Wm Jr.	Onsl	1770	Andrew Esq.	Oran	1755
Wm Sr.	Onsl	1770	Ann	Bert	1757
Wm	Oran	1755	Archibald	Gran	1784
Wm	Pasq	1769	Arthur	Casw	1777
MILLSAPS, Robert	Rowa	1759	Catherine	Gran	1755
Thomas	Rand	1779	David	Bert	1757
Thomas	Rowa	1759	David	Casw	1777
MILNER, Benjamin	Rowa	1759	David Jr.	Casw	1777
James	Gran	1784	David	Gran	1755
John	Bute	1771	David	Gran	1769
John	FWV	1771	David	Gran	1784
Patewells	Bute	1771	David	Oran	1755
Patewells	FWV	1771	Elijah	Gran	1784
MILOM, Lewis	Gran	1784	Francis	Pasq	1769
MILTON, Henry	Gran	1784	Francis s. of		
Michael s. Wm			Francis	Pasq	1769
Richd.	FWV	1771	George	Bert	1769
Richard	Brun	1769	George	Edge	1744
Richard	Brun	1772	Henry	Pasq	1755
Robert	Oran	1755	Henry s. of		
Robert	Rand	1779	Francis	Pasq	1769
Wm	Brun	1772	Isaac	Bert	1757
MILVAIL, James			Isaac	Bert	1769
overseer	FWV	1771	Isaac	Gran	1769
MIMS, David	Brun	1772	Isham	Gran	1784
David	Bute	1771	Jacob	Crav	1769
David	FWV	1771	Jacob 59 slaves	Crav	1769
George	Blad	1763	Jacob	Gran	1784
George	Brun	1769	Jacob	Pasq	1754
George	Brun	1772	James	Bert	1757
James	Brun	1772	James	Bert	1769
Joseph	Edge	1742	James	Edge	1742
Thomas	Blad	1763	James	Gran	1755
MING, James			James Sr.	Gran	1769
530 acres	Perq	1720	James	Gran	1769
John	Gran	1755	James	Surr	1772
Joseph	Chow	1753	Jeremiah	Bert	1769
Nathaniel	Chow	1753	John	Bert	1757
Rachel	Chow	1753	John	Bert	1769
Thomas	Chow	1753	John	Casw	1777
Thomas	Perq	1740	John	Chow	1721
MINOR, John	Gran	1784	John 2 slaves	Crav	1769
MINSHEW, Boz	Chow	1753	John	Dobb	1769
Isaac	Dobb	1779	John	Gran	1769
John	Chow	1753	John	Gran	1784
Maximilian	Chow	1753	John	Rowa	1759
Nathan	Dobb	1779	Joseph	NewH	1763
Richard Jr.	Chow	1753	Josiah	Gran	1755
Richard Sr.	Chow	1753	Josiah	Gran	1769
MINTER, Joseph	Gran	1769	Josiah	Gran	1784
MINTON, James	Bert	1757	Major	Gran	1784
James	Bert	1769	Matthew	Bert	1769
Joseph Jr.	Bert	1757	Rachel	Pasq	1769
Joseph Sr.	Bert	1757	Robert	Casw	1777
Joseph Jr.	Bert	1769	Robert	Edge	1742

MITCHELL, Robert	Edge	1742	MONEY, John	Gran	1755
Robert	Gran	1755	Joseph	Oran	1755
Robert	Gran	1769	Robert	Gran	1755
Sarah	Pasq	1769	MONGER, Jethro	Bute	1771
Thomas	Edge	1741	Jethro	FWV	1771
Wm	Beau	1755	Robert	NorH	1743
Wm Jr.	Beau	1755	Samson	FWV	1771
Wm	Bert	1769	MONK, John	Crav	1741
Wm	Casw	1777	Minan	Dobb	1779
Wm	Curr	1755	Timothy	Beau	1755
Wm	NorH	1762	MONROE, Patrick	Cumb	1767
Wm	Pitt	1764	Wm	Onsl	1769
Wm	Surr	1772	Wm	Onsl	1770
MITCHENER, Jeremiah	Chow	1753	MONTAGUE, Harvey	Gran	1784
MIXCAN, John	Beau	1764	Latena	Gran	1784
MIXON, Salathiel	Beau	1755	Tho. 133 acres	Perq	1720
MIZE, Henry	Gran	1784	Thomas	Perq	1740
MIZELL, Aaron	Chow	1753	MONTFORD, Joseph		
James	Tyrr	1755	(Col.)	Bute	1771
Luke	Bert	1757	Joseph Esq.	FWV	1771
Luke	Tyrr	1755	MONTGOMERY, Elizabeth		
Margaret	Chow	1753		N.C.	1701
Mark	Tyrr	1755	George	N.C.	1701
Moses	Chow	1753	Hugh	Cumb	1767
Timothy	Chow	1753	Hugh	Gran	1755
Wm	Tyrr	1755	Hugh	Surr	1771
MOAT, David	Oran	1755	Humphrey	Rowa	1759
Robert	Surr	1772	James	Casw	1777
MOBERLY, Middleton	Pitt	1764	John Esq.	Chow	1741
Wm	Pitt	1764	John	N.C.	1701
MOBLEY, Burrell	Tyrr	1755	Mary	Casw	1777
MOCAN, John	Tyrr	1755	Michael	Casw	1777
MOCHERN, Henry	NorH	1762	MONTJOY, Allen	Bute	1771
MOCK, Dewault	Rowa	1759	Allen	FWV	1771
George	Cumb	1767	Allen	Gran	1755
MODBY, Cath.	Chow	1717	MOODY, Dinah w. of		
MODLIN, Edward	Chow	1753	Gabriel	Pitt	1764
MODOC, John	Gran	1755	Gabriel	Pitt	1764
MOFFITT, Adam	Cumb	1767	Humphrey	Bute	1771
Adam	Rand	1779	Humphrey s. Wm	FWV	1771
Charles	Cumb	1767	James	Pitt	1764
George 200 acres	Crav	1720	John	Bute	1771
James	Rand	1779	John	FWV	1771
Robert	Rand	1779	John	Gran	1755
Wm	Rand	1779	Thomas	NewH	1767
MOFORD, Solomon	Crav	1743	Wm	Anso	1763
MOGLIN, John	Gran	1755	MOON, Joseph	Rand	1779
MOHURT, Hezekiah	Bert	1769	Richard	Rowa	1759
MOLESES, John	Oran	1755	MOORE, Aaron	Bert	1757
MOLIN, John	Dobb	1769	Abraham	Beau	1755
MOLINRUIK, Joshua	Bert	1769	Abraham	Pitt	1762
MOLINS, Thomas	Rand	1779	Abraham	Pitt	1764
MOLLAHAN, Thomas	Crav	1720	Abram	Crav	1769
MOLLIN, John	Dobb	1769	Adam	Crav	1719
MOLLISTON, Job	Crav	1769	Adam	Crav	1744
John	Crav	1769	Alexander		
MOLLUS, Israel	Pitt	1764	ferryman	Blad	1763
MOLOR, John	Rand	1779	Andrew	Surr	1772
MOLPUS, John	NewH	1755	Anthony	Crav	1769
John	NewH	1767	Anthony	NorH	1762
Richard	NewH	1755	Arthur	Bert	1757
Richard	NewH	1762	Arthur	Casw	1777
MOLTON, John	Dobb	1779	Arthur	Pitt	1762
Thomas	Dobb	1769	Arthur	Pitt	1764
MONCRIEF, John	Pasq	1769	Arthur Jr.	Pitt	1764

MOORE, Arthur	Pitt 1775		MOORE, James	Gran 1769
Arthur Jr.	Pitt 1775		James	FWV 1771
Arthur	Casw 1777		James	NewH 1762
Azariah	Dobb 1779		James' estate	NewH 1762
Benjamin	Blad 1763		James	NewH 1763
Benjamin	Gran 1784		James Jr.	NewH 1763
Benton	Bert 1757		James Jr.	NewH 1765
Berr Esq.			Jesse	Pitt 1762
22 slaves	Blad 1763		Jesse	Pitt 1775
Brittain	Dobb 1769		John	Beau 1755
Brittain	Dobb 1779		John	Beau 1764
Britton	Pitt 1762		John	Bert 1741
Britton	Pitt 1764		John	Bert 1757
Carter	Chow 1721		John	Bert 1769
Charles	Gran 1769		John	Blad 1763
Charles	Gran 1784		John	Casw 1777
Contie	Rand 1779		John	Chow 1753
Curtis	Rand 1779		John	Crav 1743
David	Bute 1771		John	Crav 1769
David	FWV 1771		John 2 slaves	Crav 1769
David	Onsl 1769		John	Gran 1784
David	Onsl 1770		John	NewH 1755
Dennis	NewH 1755		John's estate	NewH 1762
Dennis	NewH 1762		John	Perq 1740
Dennis	NewH 1763		John	Pitt 1762
Dennis	NewH 1765		John	Pitt 1764
Dennis	NewH 1767		John	Rand 1779
Edmund	Onsl 1769		Joseph	Casw 1777
Edmund	Onsl 1770		Joseph	Cumb 1755
Edward	Beau 1755		Joseph	Gran 1755
Edward	Chow 1717		Joseph	Gran 1784
Edward	Chow 1721		Juan	NewH 1765
Edward	Gran 1755		Keziah	Beau 1755
Edward	Gran 1769		Keziah	Beau 1764
Edward	Pitt 1762		Keziah	Crav 1769
Edward	Pitt 1764		Kuffee (free	
Elizabeth	Bert 1757		negro)	Crav 1769
Elizabeth	NewH 1755		Lemuel	Dobb 1779
Epaphroditis	Bert 1742		Levi	Pitt 1764
George	Beau 1755		Margaret (widow)	NewH 1755
George	Blad 1744		Margaret	NewH 1762
George	Brun 1769		Margaret	NewH 1763
George	Brun 1772		Margaret	NewH 1767
George Esq.	Casw 1777		Miriam	Casw 1777
George	NewH 1755		Mark	Pitt 1762
George	NewH 1762		Mark	Pitt 1764
George	NewH 1763		Mark	Pitt 1775
George	NewH 1765		Mary	Beau 1755
George	NewH 1767		Mary	Bert 1757
George	Pitt 1762		Mary	NewH 1755
George	Pitt 1764		Mathias	Pitt 1762
Henry	NewH 1755		Mathias	Pitt 1764
Henry	Pitt 1762		Mathus	Beau 1755
Henry	Pitt 1763		Maurice	
Henry	Pitt 1764		67 slaves	Brun 1769
Jacob	Beau 1755		Maurice	Brun 1772
Jacob	Pitt 1762		Maurice (Col.)	
Jacob	Pitt 1764		64 b	NewH 1741
Jacob Jr.	Pitt 1764		Maurice	NewH 1755
James	Beau 1755		Maurice	NewH 1762
James	Beau 1764		Maurice' estate	NewH 1762
James	Bert 1757		Moody	Crav 1769
James	Blad 1781		Morris	NewH 1755
James	Bute 1771		Moses	Beau 1755
James	Crav 1769		Moses	Bert 1769

MOORE, Moses	Casw	1777	MOORE, Wm		Oran	1755
Nathan	Chow	1717	Wm 1,397 acres		Perq	1720
Nathan	Pitt	1762	Wm		Perq	1740
Nathan	Pitt	1764	Wm		Pitt	1762
Nathaniel	Pitt	1762	Wm		Pitt	1764
Nathaniel	Pitt	1764	Wm		Rowa	1759
Pettigrew	NewH	1765	Wood		Pitt	1762
Richard	Casw	1777	MOOREFIELD, James		Gran	1755
Richard	Chow	1717	MOOREHEAD, James		Blad	1781
Richard	FWV	1771	Wm		Blad	1781
Richard s. of Wm	Gran	1755	MOORING, John		Pitt	1764
Robert	Casw	1777	MOORS, George		NorH	1744
Robert	Gran	1755	James		Bert	1769
Robert	NewH	1755	John		NewH	1743
Robert	Perq	1720	MOOT, Joseph		NewH	1755
Robert	Perq	1740	MORAH, Nottingham		Bert	1769
Rober's estate	Blad	1763	MORAN, James		NewH	1762
Roger	NewH	1741	James		NewH	1763
Roger Esq.	NewH	1744	James		NewH	1765
Roger	NewH	1762	James		NewH	1767
Samuel	Beau	1755	John		Gate	1786
Samuel & bro			MORDICA, Norman		Pitt	1764
John	Bert	1757	MORDLIN, John		Cumb	1767
Samuel	Dobb	1769	MORDOCK, James		Oran	1755
Samuel	Onsl	1741	MORDY, Daniel		Gran	1755
Samuel	Perq	1740	MORE, Morris		Tyrr	1755
Samuel	Pitt	1762	MOREFIELD, James		Gran	1755
Samuel	Pitt	1764	MORGAN, Abraham		Gate	1786
Schencking	Blad	1781	Andrew		Crav	1744
Schencking			Anthony		Surr	1771
37 slaves	Brun	1759	Anthony Jr.		Surr	1771
Schencking	Brun	1772	Anthony		Surr	1772
Schencking	NewH	1762	Asa		Pasq	1769
Schencking	NewH	1763	Benjamin		Gran	1784
Shadrack	Pitt	1762	Benjamin		NewH	1762
Shadrack	Pitt	1775	Benjamin		NewH	1763
Simon	Crav	1769	Benjamin		NewH	1765
Stephen Esq.	Casw	1777	Benjamin		Pasq	1769
Susan	Beau	1755	Claudius		Pasq	1769
Tatum	Casw	1777	Daniel		NewH	1762
Thomas	Crav	1769	Daniel		NewH	1763
Thomas	Pitt	1762	Daniel		NewH	1765
Thomas	Pitt	1764	David 9 persons		NewH	1741
Truman	Perq	1740	David		NewH	1752
Truman	Perq	1741	David		NewH	1755
Wm	Beau	1755	David		Rowa	1759
Wm	Bert	1741	Ezekiel		NewH	1762
Wm	Blad	1763	Ezekiel		NewH	1763
Wm	Blad	1781	Ezekiel		NewH	1765
Wm	Bute	1771	George		Crav	1769
Wm	Casw	1777	George		Oran	1755
Wm 550 acres	Chow	1721	Henry		Chow	1753
Wm	Cumb	1755	James		Cumb	1767
Wm	Cumb	1767	James		NewH	1762
Wm	Dobb	1769	James		NewH	1763
Wm	Dobb	1779	James		Pasq	1754
Wm	Gran	1755	James Sr.			
Wm s. of Wm	Gran	1755	3 slaves		Pasq	1769
Wm Sr.	Gran	1769	James		Pasq	1769
Wm	Gran	1769	James 200 acres		Perq	1720
Wm	Gran	1784	James		Perq	1740
Wm	NewH	1755	James		Rand	1779
Wm	NorH	1762	Jane		Perq	1740
Wm	Onsl	1769	Jarvis		Rand	1779
Wm	Onsl	1770	Joab		Pasq	1769

MORGAN, John	Bert	1769	MORR, Wm		Dobb	1769
John	Cumb	1767	Zachariah s. of			
John	Gate	1786	Ephraim		Dobb	1769
John	Gran	1769	MORRELL, Wm		Pasq	1769
John	Gran	1784	MORRIFET, Peter		Curr	1755
John	NewH	1762	MORRIS, Aaron		Pasq	1754
John	NewH	1763	Aaron Sr.		Pasq	1769
John	Onsl	1769	Aaron s. of			
John	Onsl	1770	Aaron Sr.		Pasq	1769
John Sr.	Pasq	1754	Aaron s. of			
John 200 Acres	Perq	1720	John Jr.		Pasq	1769
John Jr.	Perq	1740	Aaron s. of			
Joseph	Cumb	1755	Joseph Sr.		Pasq	1769
Joseph	Onsl	1746	Abraham		Bert	1769
Joseph	Onsl	1769	Arthur		Pasq	1769
Joseph	Onsl	1770	Benjamin		Pasq	1754
Joseph	Pasq	1754	Benjamin		Pasq	1769
Joseph 4 slaves	Pasq	1769	Charity		Gate	1786
Joseph	Perq	1740	Charles		Gate	1786
Lambeth	Casw	1777	Christian		Oran	1755
Lambeth	Gran	1769	Christian		Rand	1779
Lewis	Rand	1779	Edward		Onsl	1770
Luke	Onsl	1769	Edward		Tyrr	1755
Luke	Onsl	1770	Elizabeth		NewH	1762
Mack	Pasq	1769	Elizabeth		NewH	1763
Mark	Blad	1744	Ephraim		Gate	1786
Mark	Oran	1755	Floyd		Gran	1784
Mathias	Gate	1786	Frederick		Cumb	1767
Menton	Rand	1779	George		Surr	1771
Michael	Cumb	1767	Hannah 200 acres	Perq	1720
Morgan	NewH	1741	Henry		Crav	1743
Morgan	Rand	1779	Isaac		Pasq	1754
Philip	FWV	1771	James		FWV	1771
Philip	Pasq	1769	James		NewH	1755
Robert	Bute	1771	James		Tryo	1776
Robert & s. Ben	FWV	1771	John		Bert	1757
Robert	Gran	1755	John		Bert	1769
Robert	Pasq	1754	John		Crav	1769
Robert	Pasq	1769	John		Gran	1769
Ruddy	Rand	1779	John		Gran	1784
Samuel	Casw	1777	John		NewH	1762
Samuel	Surr	1771	John		NewH	1763
Samuel	Surr	1772	John Jr.		Pasq	1769
Solomon	NewH	1762	John Sr.			
Wm	Casw	1777	3 slaves		Pasq	1769
Wm	Cumb	1755	John s. of			
Wm	Gran	1769	Joseph Sr.		Pasq	1769
Wm	NewH	1765	John		Pasq	1769
Wm	Onsl	1769	John		Rand	1779
Wm	Onsl	1770	John		Tryo	1776
Wm 500 acres	Perq	1720	Joseph		Bert	1769
Wm	Perq	1720	Joseph		Pasq	1743
Wm	Rowa	1759	Joseph Jr.		Pasq	1754
MORING, Boothes	Dobb	1769	Joseph Sr.		Pasq	1769
Burrel s. of			Joseph		Pasq	1769
John	Dobb	1769	Joshua		Pasq	1754
John	Dobb	1769	Lodowick		Crav	1769
MORLEY, Richard	Rowa	1759	Mauries		NewH	1763
MORMON, George	Gran	1784	Merriman		Gran	1784
MORNING, John	Tyrr	1755	Moses, s. of			
MOROUGH, Thomas	Casw	1777	Joseph Sr.		Pasq	1769
MORPUS, John	NewH	1755	Richard		Surr	1771
Richard	NewH	1755	Richard		Surr	1772
MORPUS, Widow	NewH	1762	Robert		Pasq	1769
MORR, Ephraim	Dobb	1769	Solomon		NewH	1762

MORRIS, Solomon	NewH 1763	MOSELEY, Jacob	Bute 1771
Solomon	NewH 1765	Jacob	FWV 1771
Solomon	NewH 1767	Jacob	Oran 1755
Thomas	Bert 1769	James	Bute 1771
Thomas	Crav 1769	James	FWV 1771
Thomas	Curr 1755	James	Gran 1755
Thomas	Gran 1755	James	NewH 1765
Thomas	NewH 1755	John	Beau 1755
Thomas	NewH 1762	John	Bute 1771
Thomas	NewH 1763	John	FWV 1771
Thomas	NewH 1765	John & s. Ben	FWV 1771
Thomas	Onsl 1769	John s. of James	Gran 1755
Thomas	Onsl 1770	John	Gran 1784
Thomas	Pasq 1769	John	NewH 1762
Thomas	Tryo 1776	John	NewH 1763
Wm	Bert 1769	John	NewH 1765
Wm	Chow 1721	John	NewH 1767
Wm	Crav 1769	Samson	NewH 1762
Wm	Cumb 1767	Samson	NewH 1763
Wm	Gate 1786	Samson	NewH 1767
Wm	NewH 1755	Thomas	Bute 1771
Wm	NewH 1762	Thomas	Dobb 1769
Wm	NewH 1763	Thomas	FWV 1771
Wm	NewH 1765	Wm Jr.	Beau 1755
Wm	NewH 1767	Wm Sr.	Beau 1755
Wm	Pasq 1769	Wm	Bute 1771
Wm	Rowa 1759	Wm s. Thomas Wm	FWV 1771
Wm	Tryo 1776	MOSEN, Wm	Bert 1757
MORRISON, James	Dobb 1769	MOSER, Christian	Surr 1772
John	Oran 1755	MOSES, Abraham	Bert 1769
Nathaniel	Surr 1771	John	Anso 1763
Nathaniel	Surr 1772	Michael	Pitt 1764
Samuel	Rowa 1759	MOSHERLAND, John	Casw 1777
Wm	Oran 1755	MOSIER, Tobias	Rand 1779
MORROW, James	Casw 1777	MOSS, Abraham	Gran 1769
Robert	Casw 1777	Henry	Gran 1769
Wm	Casw 1777	Henry	NorH 1762
MORSE, Howell	Gran 1784	James	Oran 1755
Reuben	Gran 1784	John	Pitt 1764
Samuel	Gran 1784	John	Rand 1779
MORTIMER, John	NewH 1762	Joshua	Gran 1755
John	NewH 1763	Mary (widow)	Pitt 1764
John	NewH 1765	Michael	Pitt 1762
MORTON, Joseph	Onsl 1769	Michael	Pitt 1763
Joseph	Onsl 1770	Michael	Pitt 1775
Joshua	Onsl 1769	Peter	Pitt 1762
Peter	Onsl 1769	Peter	Pitt 1763
Peter	Onsl 1770	Peter	Pitt 1775
Richard	Curr 1715	Reuben	Gran 1769
Richard	Onsl 1769	Robert	Chow 1721
Richard	Onsl 1770	Samuel	Gran 1769
MOSELEY, Ann	NewH 1762	Sarah	Tyrr 1755
Ann	NewH 1763	Wm	Gran 1755
Ann (Miss)	NewH 1767	MOSSFORD, Robert	
Benjamin	Bute 1771	(deceased)	Gran 1784
Benjamin	FWV 1771	MOTHERSHEAD,	
Edward (Col.)	Chow 1717	Christopher	Bute 1771
Edward (Col.)		Christopher	FWV 1771
6,065 acres	Chow 1721	MOTLOW, John	Gran 1755
Edward (Col.)		MOTT, Benjamin	NewH 1767
11 w 90 b	NewH 1744	John	NewH 1741
Edward's estate	NewH 1762	John	NewH 1762
Edward's estate	NewH 1763	John	NewH 1763
Edward	NewH 1765	John	NewH 1755
Edward's estate	NewH 1765	Joseph	NewH 1762

MOTT, Joseph	NewH	1763	MULLINS, Thomas	Gran	1755
Joseph	NewH	1765	MULPHERD, Ephem	Blad	1763
Wm	NewH	1763	MUMFORD, Jehu	Onsl	1769
Wm	NewH	1767	Jehu	Onsl	1770
MOTTEN, Wm	Bert	1757	MUNCREF, Thomas	Curr	1715
MOUAT, Wm	NewH	1767	Wm	Curr	1715
MOUATT, Wm	NewH	1763	MUNDAY, Benjamin	Perq	1720
MOULTON, John Jr.	Chow	1721	MUNDEN, Stephen	Beau	1755
MOUNCEY, John Jr.	Rowa	1759	MUNDINE, John	Pitt	1763
John Sr.	Rowa	1759	John	Pitt	1764
MOUNTS, Jeremiah	Pitt	1764	Stephen	Pitt	1762
Jonathan	Pitt	1762	Stephen	Pitt	1764
Jonathan	Pitt	1764	MUNGER, Samuel	NorH	1762
John 1w 1b	Crav	1744	Simson	Bute	1771
John 5w	Crav	1744	Wm	NorH	1762
MOY, Elizabeth			MUNROE, Daniel	Cumb	1755
400 acres	Chow	1721	Daniel	Cumb	1767
George	Beau	1755	Dugal	Cumb	1755
George Jr.	Beau	1755	Hugh	Brun	1772
John	Beau	1755	John	Cumb	1755
John Jr.	Beau	1755	Lewis	Cumb	1767
John	Crav	1769	Malcomb	Cumb	1755
MOYE, George Esq.	Pitt	1762	Pat	Cumb	1755
George	Pitt	1764	Revelle	NewH	1762
George	Pitt	1775	Revelle	NewH	1763
John Jr.	Pitt	1762	Wm	Onsl	1770
John Sr.	Pitt	1762	MUNS, Jacob	Blad	1763
Mary	Pitt	1762	Thomas	Chow	1717
Richard	Pitt	1764	Thomas	Chow	1753
MOYERS, Andrew			MURDOCK, John	Oran	1755
1 slave	Crav	1769	John	Rand	1779
MOYR, Matthias	Gran	1755	MURDEN, Isaac	Pasq	1769
MOZEL, John	Bert	1769	MURDIVANT, Matthew	Pitt	1775
MOZINGO, Boothe,	Dobb	1779	MURKET, Thomas	Pitt	1764
George	Dobb	1779	MURPHY, Alexander	Casw	1777
MUCKE, Johannes	Surr	1771	Archibald Esq.	Casw	1777
John	Surr	1772	Arthur	Bute	1771
MUCKELROY, Adam	Beau	1764	Arthur s. James	FWV	1771
James	Beau	1764	Benjamin	Bute	1771
Thomas	Beau	1764	Benjamin	FWV	1771
MUIRHEAD, Henry	FWV	1771	Benjamin	Gran	1755
MUKES, Prelly	Surr	1772	Daniel	Bert	1757
MULFORD, Thomas	Brun	1769	Darby	Blad	1763
Thomas	Brun	1772	Edmond	Crav	1769
Wm	NewH	1763	Gabriel	Casw	1777
MULHOLLAND, Charles	Rand	1779	James	Blad	1763
MULKEY, James	Surr	1771	James	Rowa	1759
James	Surr	1772	John	Beau	1755
MULLEN, Daniel	Rand	1779	John 1w 1b	Crav	1744
MULLENS, Abraham	Perq	1720	John 5w	Crav	1744
Abraham Jr.	Perq	1740	MUSGROVE, Caleb	Dobb	1769
Abraham Sr.	Perq	1740	Caleb	Dobb	1779
Isaac	Perq	1740	James	Dobb	1769
Jacob	Perq	1740	James	Dobb	1779
John	Bute	1771	Moses	Dobb	1769
John	FWV	1771	Moses	Dobb	1779
Patrick	Rowa	1759	Thomas	Dobb	1769
Thomas	Bute	1771	Thomas	Dobb	1779
Thomas	FWV	1771	MUSICK, Ambrose	Dobb	1769
MULLER, John	Surr	1771	Joel s. of		
Thomas	Gran	1769	Ambrose	Dobb	1769
MULLIN, Charles	Rand	1779	John	Dobb	1769
MULLING, Joseph	Crav	1769	MUSCLEWHITE, Jesse	Blad	1763
MULLINGS, Joseph	Crav	1769	Thomas	Blad	1763
MULLINGTON, Richard	Blad	1763	MUTTER, Thomas	Gran	1784

MUTTON, Wm	Surr 1772	NEALE, Abner Jr.		
MYARS, Mathias	Gran 1769	2 slaves	Crav	1769
MYERS, John	Rand 1779	Abner Sr.		
Michael	Rowa 1759	6 slaves	Crav	1769
Peter	Surr 1772	Christopher		
MYRICK, Francis	Bute 1771	7 slaves	Crav	1769
Francis Sr.	FWV 1771	Richard 1 slave		
James	Bute 1771		Crav	1769
James	FWV 1771	Samuel	Brun	1769
John	Bute 1771	Thomas	Brun	1769
John	FWV 1771	Wm	Brun	1769
Matthew	Bute 1771	NEALEY, Thomas	Casw	1777
Matthew	FWV 1771	NEALY, Wm	Casw	1777
Wm	Bute 1771	NEARN, Jesse	Bert	1769
		John	Roan	1720
		NEASE, Francis	Rowa	1759
		NEEDHAM, Bailey	Pasq	1769
NAIBBY, John	Gran 1784	Gideon 1 m		
NAIL, Jacob	NewH 1755	slave	Pasq	1754
Samuel	NewH 1755	Gideon 1 f		
NAILING, Wm	Gran 1784	slave	Pasq	1769
NAILOR, Charles	Cumb 1767	John	Pasq	1769
NAIRNE, John		John	Rand	1779
1280 acres	Chow 1717	Joseph	Pasq	1769
NALL, John	Cumb 1767	Thomas	Pasq	1769
Wm	Surr 1772	Thomas	Rand	1779
NALLEYBOY, James	Edge 1744	Wm	Onsl	1770
NANBLY, Richard	N.C. 1701	Wm	Rand	1779
NANCE, Richard	Gran 1784	NEEL, Christopher	Curr	1755
Sherwood	Casw 1777	NEELY, Richard	Rowa	1759
Thomas	Casw 1777	Samuel	Casw	1777
NANSON, Richard	NewH 1762	NEELE, Wm	Oran	1755
Richard	NewH 1763	NEIL, Benjamin	NewH	1767
NAPKIN, Magdalen	N.C. 1701	James	NewH	1755
NASERY, Wm	Rowa 1759	James	Oran	1755
NASH, Edward	Casw 1777	Samuel	NewH	1755
Francis	Casw 1777	NEILL, James	Cumb	1767
Francis 2 slaves	Crav 1769	NELMS, Presley	Bute	1771
Josiah	Pasq 1769	Presley	FWV	1771
NATION, Christopher	Rand 1779	NELSON, Aaron	N.C.	1701
Christopher	Rowa 1759	Alexander	NewH	1763
John	Rand 1779	Alexander	NewH	1767
John	Rowa 1758	Alexander	Rowa	1759
John	Rowa 1759	Berry	Cart	1744
Joseph	Rand 1779	Berry	Crav	1769
Thomas	Rand 1779	Eleazer	Crav	1769
NAZARA, Wm	Crav 1769	Elizabeth	N.C.	1701
NEADELTON, Wm	Edge 1734	Elliott	N.C.	1701
NEAL, Daniel	Dobb 1769	George	Rowa	1759
Elisha	Dobb 1769	John	Bute	1771
Hugh	Rand 1779	John	Chow	1721
Joseph	Gran 1784	John Esq.	Crav	1720
Margaret	Brun 1772	John	Crav	1742
Ralph	Gran 1784	John	Crav	1769
Ralph Jr.	Gran 1784	John	FWV	1771
Reuben	Gran 1784	John	Gran	1769
Samuel	Brun 1772	John	N.C.	1701
Thomas	Bert 1757	John	Tryo	1776
Thomas	Brun 1772	Jonas	Surr	1771
Thomas	NewH 1762	Jonas	Surr	1772
Thomas	NewH 1763	Jone w. of		
Wm	Brun 1772	John Sr.	N.C.	1701
Wm	Bute 1771	Joseph	Surr	1771
Wm Constable s.		Joseph	Surr	1772
Wm Older	FWV 1771	Martin	Beau	1755

NELSON, Martin Jr.	Beau	1755	NEWBY, Samuel	Rand	1779
Martin Sr.	Pitt	1762	Thomas	Gran	1755
Martin	Pitt	1762	Thomas	Gran	1769
Mary	N.C.	1701	Thomas	Gran	1784
Morgan	NewH	1755	Thomas	Pasq	1754
Peter	Pitt	1762	Thomas	Pasq	1769
Samuel	Oran	1755	Wm	Rand	1779
Samuel	Rowa	1759	NEWCOM, Edward	Onsl	1770
Thomas	Crav	1769	NEWFIELD, John	Blad	1763
Thomas	Oran	1755	NEWIL, John	Dobb	1779
Wm	Crav	1769	NEWLIN, Daniel	Gran	1755
Wm	Oran	1755	Wm	Gran	1769
NESFIELD, John	Blad	1763	NEWMAN, George	Bute	1771
NETHERY, John	Oran	1755	George	FWV	1771
NETTLES, Shadrack	Ruth	1790	John	Beau	1755
Shadrack	Tryo	1776	John	Beau	1764
NEVIL, Abe	Beau	1764	John	Bute	1771
Jacob	Beau	1755	John	FWV	1771
Jacob Jr.	Beau	1755	Richard	Beau	1755
John	Beau	1764	Richard	Beau	1764
John	Gran	1755	Thomas	Bute	1771
Moses	Beau	1755	Thomas	FWV	1771
Moses	Beau	1764	NEWPORT, Lovina	Gran	1784
NEVIN, Maurice	NewH	1755	NEWSON, David	Dobb	1769
Maurice	NewH	1762	Hardy	Dobb	1779
Maurice	NewH	1763	Joel	Dobb	1769
Wm	Crav	1741	NEWTON, Daniel	Onsl	1769
NEW, Wm	Dobb	1769	Elizabeth	Onsl	1769
Wm	Gran	1784	George	NewH	1762
NEWALL, Robert	Beau	1764	George	NewH	1765
Samuel	Beau	1764	George	NewH	1767
NEWBERRY, Jesse	Cumb	1755	Henry	NewH	1765
John Sr.	Blad	1763	Isaac	NewH	1762
John Sr.	Blad	1781	Isaac	NewH	1765
John	Cumb	1755	Jacob	NewH	1765
NEWBOLD, Thomas	Onsl	1769	Jesse	Bert	1769
Thomas	Onsl	1770	John	Gran	1769
NEWBY, Ann			John	Onsl	1769
200 acres	Perq	1720	John	Onsl	1770
Benjamin	Pasq	1754	Joseph	NewH	1762
Benjamin	Pasq	1769	Joseph	NewH	1765
Edward 400 acres	Perq	1720	Joseph	NewH	1767
Francis			Richlew	Casw	1777
300 acres	Perq	1720	Wm	Dobb	1769
Francis s.			NICHOLAS, Alexander	Crav	1720
Robert	Perq	1740	David	Pasq	1769
Gabriel s.			John	Onsl	1769
Jesse	Perq	1720	Mathias	Bert	1757
Jacob	Pasq	1754	Richard	Bert	1757
Jacob	Pasq	1769	Willis	Bert	1757
James Sr.	Pasq	1754	Wm	Pitt	1762
James	Pasq	1769	Wm	Pitt	1764
Jesse	Perq	1740	NICHOLS, Andrew	NewH	1762
Joseph	Pasq	1754	Andrew	NewH	1763
Joseph	Pasq	1769	Andrew	NewH	1767
Joseph 300 acres			Anthony	Pasq	1769
	Perq	1720	Caleb	NewH	1763
Joseph s.			Caleb	Pasq	1769
Joseph	Perq	1740	Charles	Bute	1771
Mary	Brun	1772	Charles	FWV	1771
Mordica	Pasq	1769	Daniel	Pasq	1769
Nathan	Perq	1720	David	Pasq	1769
Samuel	Pasq	1754	Edward	Pasq	1769
Samuel Jr.	Pasq	1769	Francis	Beau	1755
Samuel Sr.	Pasq	1769	George	Bute	1771

NICHOLAS, George s.			NICHOLSON, Samuel s.		
of Wm	Gran	1755	of Benjamin	Gran	1755
Henry	Bute	1771	Samuel 350 acres	Perq	1720
Henry & s.			Thomas 7w 1b	Pasq	1743
Shadrack	FWV	1771	NICKELSON, James	Oran	1755
Henry	Pasq	1769	NICKEN, James & w.		
Humphrey	Bert	1757	Margaret	Bert	1757
Humphrey	Bert	1769	NICKERSON, Henry	Surr	1771
Jacob	Surr	1772	NICKSON, Benjamin	Onsl	1769
James	NewH	1763	Benjamin	Onsl	1770
James	NewH	1767	Richard 6 slaves	Crav	1769
James	Onsl	1769	Robert	Onsl	1769
James	Onsl	1770	Robert	Onsl	1770
Jeremiah	Pasq	1769	NICLOES, George	NewH	1755
Joel	Pitt	1775	Wm	NewH	1755
John	Bert	1757	NIEDAN, Nicholas	Cumb	1767
John	Bert	1769	NIGHTSMALL, John	Onsl	1770
John	Bute	1771	NILER, Starkey	Crav	1769
John	FWV	1771	Wm	Crav	1769
John	NewH	1762	NILLY, Bennett	Casw	1777
John	NewH	1763	NILSON, John	Pitt	1764
John	NewH	1767	Martin	Pitt	1764
John	Tyrr	1755	Martin Jr.	Pitt	1764
Jonathan	Gate	1786	Nathan	Pitt	1764
Joseph	Pasq	1769	Peter	Pitt	1764
Julius	Bute	1771	NIX, John	Rowa	1759
Julius	FWV	1771	NIXON, Andrew	NewH	1767
Lemuel	Pasq	1769	Barnaby	Pasq	1754
Nathan	Pasq	1769	Elizabeth		
Robert	NewH	1767	(widow)	Perq	1740
Thomas s. of			Henry	Dobb	1779
Henry	Pasq	1769	Henry	Surr	1772
Thomas	Perq	1720	John	Perq	1740
Timothy	Beau	1755	Joshua	NewH	1762
Willis	Casw	1777	Joshua	NewH	1763
Willis	Pasq	1769	Morgan	NewH	1755
Wm	Beau	1755	Peter	Gate	1786
Wm	Curr	1715	Phineas	Perq	1740
Wm	Gran	1755	Robert	NewH	1755
Wm	Pasq	1754	Robert	NewH	1762
Wm Jr.	Pasq	1769	Robert	NewH	1763
Wm	Pitt	1775	Robert	NewH	1767
Wm	Surr	1771	Thomas	NewH	1755
NICHOLSON, Benjamin	Gran	1755	Thomas Jr.	NewH	1755
Christopher	Pasq	1754	Thomas	NewH	1767
Christopher			Thomas	Rand	1779
688 acres	Perq	1720	Zachariah		
George	Edge	1743	780 acres	Perq	1720
George	Gran	1784	Zachariah	Perq	1740
James	Bute	1771	NOBLE, George	Dobb	1769
James s. Arch			Isaac	Pitt	1762
James	FWV	1771	Isaac	Pitt	1764
James	Gran	1755	Isaac Jr.	Pitt	1764
John	Bute	1771	Isaac	Pitt	1775
John	Curr	1755	John	Pitt	1762
John s.			Mark	Beau	1764
Alexander	FWV	1771	Nathaniel	Pitt	1762
Nathaniel	Bute	1771	Nathaniel	Pitt	1764
Nathaniel	FWV	1771	Philemon	Dobb	1769
Nathaniel s. of			Thomas	Pitt	1762
James	Gran	1755	Thomas	Pitt	1764
Nathaniel			Wm	Pitt	1764
100 acres	Perq	1720	NOBLES, John	Beau	1755
Nicholas	Curr	1755	Nicholas	Oran	1755
			NOBLIN, John	Edge	1741

NOBLIN, Luke	Perq	1720	NORTON, Jonathan	Curr	1755
NODDER, John	FWV	1771	Joseph	Crav	1769
NOKES, George	Casw	1777	Messer	Rand	1779
NOLAND, Edward	Gran	1784	Mr	Blad	1741
James	Gran	1784	Wm	Anso	1763
Wm	Rowa	1759	Wm	Pasq	1769
NOLES, Adam	Perq	1740	Wm	Rand	1779
Thomas	Perq	1720	NORVEL, Benjamin	Bert	1757
Wm	Perq	1720	Edmund	Casw	1777
NORAND, Thomas	Pitt	1762	Ephraim	Casw	1777
NORCOM, John			James	Casw	1777
200 acres	Perq	1720	James	Gran	1784
Thomas	Perq	1720	Solomon	Bert	1757
Thomas Jr.	Perq	1740	NORWOOD, Benjamin	Gran	1784
Thomas Sr.	Perq	1740	Gillam	Gran	1769
Widow 300 acres	Perq	1720	Gillam	Gran	1784
NORFLEET, Abraham	Chow	1753	John	Bert	1769
Elisha	Gate	1786	John	Bute	1771
Eliza	Chow	1753	John	FWV	1771
Elizabeth	Gate	1786	John	Gran	1755
James	Gate	1786	Jordan	Gran	1784
Joseph	Gate	1786	Nathaniel	Gran	1769
Marmaduke	Perq	1740	Nathaniel	NorH	1744
Marmaduke			Samuel	NorH	1762
5w 19b	Perq	1743	Thomas	Pitt	1764
Mary (Mrs.)	Perq	1740	Wm	NorH	1762
Reuben	Bert	1757	NOSBETT, Wm	N.C.	1701
Reuben	Bert	1769	NOTGRASS, James	Gran	1784
NORKET, Wm	Pitt	1762	NOTTS, John	Dobb	1769
NORMAN, Jeremiah	Tyrr	1755	NOW, Jesse	Perq	1720
John	Onsl	1770	NOWELL, Demsey	Bert	1757
Joseph	Tyrr	1755	James	Bert	1757
Nehemiah	Tyrr	1755	James	Chow	1721
Samuel	Tyrr	1755	NOWLIN, Charles	Gran	1784
NORMENT, Stokes	Crav	1769	John	Surr	1771
NORMAN, Eli	Surr	1771	NOZLING, Thomas	Crav	1720
Eli	Surr	1772	NUGENT, Edmond	Brun	1769
Henry	Chow	1721	Edmund	Brun	1772
NORRIS, Daniel	Oran	1755	NULL, James	FWV	1771
George	Crav	1742	NUNN, Francis	Dobb	1769
James	Crav	1741	John	Dobb	1769
John	Beau	1755	Wm	Oran	1755
John	Pitt	1762	NUNNERY, Joseph	FWV	1771
John	Pitt	1764	NUSHAM, Wm	Rand	1779
John	Surr	1771			
John	Surr	1772			
Joseph	Bute	1771			
Joseph	FWV	1771	OAKES, John	Casw	1777
Theophilis	Crav	1720	OAKFORD, Edmund	Casw	1777
Thomas	Chow	1753	OAKLEY, Joseph	Gran	1769
Thomas	Pasq	1769	Joseph Jr.	Gran	1784
Wm	Onsl	1769	Sobourn	Gran	1784
Wm	Onsl	1770	Thomas	Gran	1769
Wm 2 slaves	Pasq	1769	Wm	Gran	1769
NORTHCUT, Wm	Pitt	1764	Wm	Gran	1784
NORTHERN, Benjamin	Curr	1755	OALY, Jesse	Rand	1779
John	Curr	1715	OASES, John	NewH	1742
Philip	Curr	1755	OATES, James	John	1750
NORTHON, Solomon	Crav	1769	OATS, Joseph	Perq	1720
Wm	Crav	1769	OBANION, Wm	Bute	1771
NORTIN, Daniel	Blad	1763	Wm	FWV	1771
NORTON, Edward	Rand	1779	O'BARR, Daniel	Surr	1771
Isom	Casw	1777	Daniel	Surr	1772
Jacob	Blad	1763	Michael	Casw	1777
John	Rand	1779	Michael	Surr	1772

OBODYFORD, Green	Bert	1769
O'BRYAN, Dennis	Gran	1784
Patrick	Gran	1769
Patrick	Gran	1784
OCELLEHAM, John	Pitt	1764
ODAM, Aaron	Blad	1763
Aaron	Chow	1753
Abraham	Crav	1742
Abraham	Edge	1742
Benjamin	Blad	1763
Isaac	Anso	1750
Isaac	Cumb	1755
Jacob	Chow	1753
Jacob s. of		
Moses	Chow	1753
Jacob	Dobb	1769
Jacob	Dobb	1779
John	Chow	1717
John 500 acres	Chow	1721
John	Chow	1753
Moses	Chow	1753
Moses Jr.	Chow	1753
Thomas	Bert	1744
Thomas	Blad	1763
ODELL, Thomas	Cumb	1767
ODEM, John	Blad	1781
ODEON, Charles	Beau	1755
Eliza (widow)	Beau	1764
John	Beau	1755
Richard	Beau	1755
ODLE, Joseph	Surr	1772
Nehemiah	Rand	1779
ODOM, Demsey	Gate	1786
Elisha	Gate	1786
Jacob	Dobb	1769
John	Gate	1786
Mills	Gate	1786
Wm	Blad	1781
Wm	Gate	1786
ODOWDEY, James	Curr	1755
John	Curr	1755
Joseph	Curr	1755
Joshua	Curr	1755
Thomas	Curr	1755
OENMEDLEN, Wm	Surr	1772
OFFIL, Wm	Oran	1755
OGDEN, Isaac	NewH	1755
Isaac	NewH	1762
Isaac	NewH	1763
Isaac	NewH	1767
Richard	NewH	1741
Richard	NewH	1755
Solomon	NewH	1762
Solomon	NewH	1763
Solomon	NewH	1765
Solomon	NewH	1767
Wm	Brun	1769
Wm	Brun	1772
OGGS, John	Pasq	1769
OGILVIE, Harris	Gran	1784
Kimbrell	Gran	1784
Wm	Gran	1755
Wm	Gran	1769
Wm	Gran	1784
OGLESBY, Bathena	Pitt	1775

OGLESBY, James	Beau	1755
Wm	Beau	1755
OGLETHORP, Richard	Surr	1772
OGLETREE, John	Casw	1777
OGUINE, John	Blad	1781
Tarlon	Blad	1781
Tarlon Sr.	Blad	1781
OLDERTHIGHS,		
Richard	Surr	1771
OLDFIELD, Richard	Onsl	1769
Richard	Onsl	1770
Wm	Onsl	1752
OLDHAM, George	Casw	1777
Jesse	Casw	1777
John	Casw	1777
Moses	Casw	1777
Richard	Casw	1777
Wm Jr.	Surr	1771
OLDS, Arthur	Pitt	1775
John	Perq	1720
OLIPHANT, Wm	Blad	1763
Wm	Blad	1781
OLIVE, John	Brun	1769
OLIVER, Aaron	Bert	1757
Aaron 1,100		
acres	Chow	1721
Aaron	Cumb	1767
Andrew	Tyrr	1755
James	Onsl	1770
John	Bert	1757
John	Bert	1769
John	Brun	1772
John 8 slaves	Crav	1769
John	Crav	1769
John	Gran	1769
Mary	Gran	1784
Moses	Chow	1717
Moses	Cumb	1767
Peter	Gran	1769
Peter	Gran	1784
Samuel	Crav	1769
OMACK, John	Rand	1779
Peter	Rand	1779
OMARK, Filis	Rand	1779
Nicholas	Rand	1779
Omack	Rand	1779
OMERY, Richard	Beau	1755
Richard	Beau	1764
ONCAT, Thomas	Cumb	1755
O'NEAL, Arthur	NorH	1762
John	Curr	1715
John	Curr	1755
John	Edge	1742
Margaret	N.C.	1701
Michael Sr.	Curr	1715
Michael	Curr	1755
Richard	Beau	1755
Richard	Pitt	1762
Robert	N.C.	1701
Samson	Anso	1763
ONLY, Penelope	Gate	1786
OPLEY, George	Bert	1769
John	Bert	1769
O'QUINN, Alexander	Bert	1757
Daniel	NorH	1762

Name	Place	Year	Name	Place	Year
O'QUINN, Martha	Bert	1757	OSTEN, Thomas Sr.	Surr	1772
Tarlor	Edge	1743	Valentine	Surr	1772
ORELL, John	Onsl	1770	Valentine	Surr	1772
Thomas	Onsl	1770	OTTERY, Alexander	Oran	1755
ORMAND, Henry	Beau	1764	James	Pitt	1764
Roger	Beau	1764	John	Pitt	1764
Wm	Beau	1755	John	Rowa	1759
Wm	Beau	1764	Wm	Pitt	1764
Wm	Dobb	1769	OTTEY, Elizabeth	NewH	1742
Wy	Beau	1755	OULEY, John	Rand	1779
Wy	Beau	1764	OUTLAW, Edward	Bert	1741
Wyngatt	Beau	1764	Edward	Bert	1757
Wyriot	Beau	1742	Edward	Bert	1769
ORME, Deborah			Edward	Chow	1721
8 slaves	Crav	1769	George	Gate	1786
ORMSBY, George			Jacob	Gate	1786
2 slaves	Crav	1769	John	Bert	1757
Luke	Oran	1755	John	Bert	1769
ORRELL, John	Onsl	1769	Josiah	Bert	1769
John	Onsl	1770	Levis	Gate	1786
Thomas	Onsl	1769	Lewis	Bert	1769
Thomas	Onsl	1770	Lewis	Chow	1753
ORRENDALL, Ed	Chow	1721	Ralph	Bert	1757
Edward	Chow	1753	Ralph	Bert	1769
ORRICK, John	Rand	1779	Ralph	Chow	1753
Samuel	Rand	1779	Thomas	Bert	1757
Wm	Rand	1779	Thomas	Bert	1769
OSBORNE, Alexander	Rowa	1759	Wm	Bert	1744
Caleb	Rowa	1759	Wm	Bert	1757
Christopher	Gran	1755	Wm	Bert	1769
Ephraim	Rowa	1759	Wm Jr.	Bert	1769
James	Bute	1771	OVELAR, John	Cumb	1767
James	Chow	1753	OVERHISON, Paul	NewH	1762
James	FWV	1771	Paul	NewH	1763
James	NorH	1762	Paul	NewH	1767
Jeffrey	Gran	1755	OVERMAN, Benjamin		
John	Rowa	1759	2 slaves	Pasq	1754
John	Surr	1771	Benjamin	Pasq	1769
Jonathan	Rowa	1759	Benjamin Jr.	Pasq	1769
Jonathan	Surr	1771	Charles	Pasq	1754
Joseph	Rowa	1759	Charles	Perq	1740
Matthew	Rand	1779	Enoch 4m		
Matthew	Rowa	1759	slaves	Pasq	1769
Samuel	Bute	1771	Ephraim	Pasq	1754
Samuel	FWV	1771	Ephraim	Pasq	1769
Samuel	Rand	1779	Is	Pasq	1769
Samuel	Rowa	1758	Jacob	Perq	1740
Samuel	Rowa	1759	James	Pasq	1769
Stephen Jr.	Rowa	1759	James s. of		
Stephen Sr.	Rowa	1759	Benjamin	Pasq	1769
Stephen	Surr	1771	John	Pasq	1754
Stephen	Surr	1772	John 3m		
Wm	Pitt	1764	slaves	Pasq	1769
Wm	Pitt	1775	John s. of		
OSHEAL, Daniel	Gran	1755	Samuel	Pasq	1769
OSMER, James	Anso	1763	Joseph	Pasq	1754
OSMORE, Uriah	Onsl	1769	Joseph	Pasq	1769
OSTEEN, John	Crav	1769	Joseph s. of		
Samuel	Crav	1769	Samuel	Pasq	1769
Wm	Crav	1769	Joshua	Pasq	1769
OSTEN, John	Dobb	1769	Nathan	Pasq	1754
John (Constable)	Surr	1771	Nathan	Pasq	1769
John (Constable)	Surr	1772	Reuben s. of		
Thomas	Surr	1771	Samuel	Pasq	1769
Thomas Jr.	Surr	1772	Samuel	Pasq	1754

OVERMAN, Samuel		OWENS, Thomas	
3 slaves	Pasq 1769	2 slaves	Blad 1763
Thomas Sr.	Pasq 1754	Thomas 1 slave	Blad 1763
Thomas Jr.	Pasq 1769	Wm	Oran 1755
Thomas Sr. 3m		Wm	Surr 1772
slaves	Pasq 1769	OWINGS, Richard	Gran 1755
Thomas tailor	Pasq 1769	OWRAM, Timothy	Brun 1769
Thomas	Perq 1740	Timothy	Brun 1772
Wm 3 slaves	Pasq 1769	OXLEY, George	Dobb 1779
OVERSTREET, Henry	Cumb 1755	John s. George	Bert 1757
John	Casw 1777	W.	Chow 1721
John	Cumb 1755	OZELL, Thomas	Beau 1775
OVERTON, Aaron	Bute 1771		
Aaron	Bute 1771		
David s. of Wm	Pasq 1769		
James	Bert 1757	PACE, George	Chow 1721
John	Cumb 1767	James	Edge 1744
John	Pasq 1769	James Constable	Gran 1755
Joseph	Pasq 1769	John 1,000 acres	Chow 1721
Joshua	Pasq 1769	John	NorH 1762
Malachi s. of Wm	Pasq 1769	Richard	NorH 1741
Peter	Pasq 1769	Stephen	Bute 1771
Richard	Pasq 1769	Stephen	FWV 1771
Titus	Blad 1763	Thomas	NorH 1762
Titus	Cumb 1767	Wm s. of James	Gran 1755
Willis s. of		Wm Jr.	NorH 1762
Wm Jr.	Pasq 1769	Wm Sr.	NorH 1762
Wm Jr.	Pasq 1769	PACKER, Micajah	Dobb 1779
Wm Sr.	Pasq 1769	PACKET, John	NewH 1755
OWEN, Ephraim	Cumb 1767	PADEMON, Thomas	Pasq 1769
Frederick	Gran 1784	PADGETT, Abraham	Surr 1772
Henry	Rand 1779	Edward	Chow 1717
Jacob	Gran 1784	Edward	Chow 1721
James	Gran 1769	James	Dobb 1769
James	Gran 1784	James	NewH 1762
John deceased	Blad 1781	James	NewH 1763
John	Cumb 1755	James	Perq 1720
John	Gran 1769	James	Perq 1740
John Sr.	Gran 1784	Samuel	Chow 1717
John	Gran 1784	Samuel	Chow 1721
John	NewH 1767	Wm	Chow 1717
Moses	NorH 1762	Wm 900 acres	Chow 1721
Richardson	Gran 1769	PADRICK, Benjamin	Pasq 1769
Stephen	Rand 1779	Benjamin	
Thomas	Blad 1781	2 slaves	Pasq 1769
Thomas	Gran 1769	Benjamin Jr.	Pasq 1769
Thomas	Gran 1784	John	Pasq 1769
Wm	Gran 1769	PAGE, Benjamin	Gran 1784
Wm Sr.	Gran 1784	Henry s. of	
Wm	Gran 1784	Thomas	Dobb 1769
Wm S. of James	Gran 1784	Humphrey	Rowa 1759
OWENS, Ann	Tyrr 1755	James	Chow 1721
Branath	Beau 1764	John	Bert 1757
Daniel	NewH 1763	John	Chow 1721
Ephraim Constable		John	Pitt 1775
	Blad 1763	Joseph	Casw 1777
Esther	Crav 1769	Nathan	Bert 1769
James	Surr 1772	Samuel	Bert 1757
John	Blad 1763	Samuel	Bert 1769
John	Bute 1771	Samuel Jr.	Bert 1769
John	FWV 1771	Thomas	Bert 1757
Owen	Crav 1769	Thomas	Bert 1769
Owen Jr.	Crav 1769	Thomas	Dobb 1769
Shellaman	Bert 1769	Thomas	NorH 1742
Solomon	Crav 1769	Tom	Crav 1720

PAGE, Wm	Gran	1784	PARDUE, Joseph	Bute	1771
PAGETHET, John	Tyrr	1755	PARHAM, Avery	Gran	1769
PAGETT, Joab	Onsl	1770	Henry	Gran	1769
Solomon	Tyrr	1755	Isham	Gran	1769
PAGGET, John	Tyrr	1755	John	Gran	1769
PAGIT, James	NewH	1762	Richard	FWV	1771
PAIGHT, Joseph	Onsl	1770	Wm	Gran	1769
PAINE, James	Bute	1771	Wm	Gran	1784
James (Cpt.)	FWV	1771	Wm	NorH	1762
James	Gran	1755	PARIS, John	Chow	1753
John	NewH	1762	PARIT, Lewis	NewH	1755
John	NewH	1763	PARK, Joseph	Casw	1777
Samuel	Crav	1769	Joseph	Gran	1769
Samuel	Curr	1755	Robert	Crav	1744
Thomas	Curr	1755	Wm	Bute	1771
Wm	Cumb	1767	Wm	FWV	1771
PAINTER, Richard	Casw	1777	Wm	Gran	1769
PAISLEY, David	Rowa	1759	PARKER, Aaron	Casw	1777
PALE, John Jr.	Dobb	1769	Amos	Chow	1752
Joseph s. of			Ann	Chow	1753
John	Dobb	1769	Ann	Gate	1786
PALIN, Henry	Pasq	1754	Azaricam Jr.	Curr	1755
Henry 2 slaves	Pasq	1769	Azaricam Sr.	Curr	1755
John 5 slaves	Pasq	1769	Azricom	Curr	1715
Thomas	Pasq	1769	Benjamin	Bert	1769
PALLESTEEL, John	Pasq	1769	Benjamin	Chow	1753
Pearce	Pasq	1769	Benjamin	Dobb	1779
PALMER, Benjamin			Benjamin	Gate	1786
(Cpt.)	Pasq	1754	Daniel	Casw	1777
David	Pasq	1769	Daniel	Chow	1753
Isaiah	Pitt	1764	Daniel	Onsl	1769
Jacob	Pitt	1762	Daniel	Onsl	1770
Joanna	Perq	1740	David	Beau	1755
John	Casw	1777	David	Dobb	1769
Malachi	Pasq	1769	Demsey	Chow	1753
Martin	Bert	1769	Demsey	Gate	1786
Paul	Perq	1720	Elisha	Chow	1753
Robert	Beau	1755	Elisha	Gate	1786
Robert	Beau	1764	Elisha	Pasq	1769
Robert	Curr	1755	Elizabeth	Onsl	1769
Robert 3 slaves	Pasq	1754	Francis	Chow	1753
Robert	Pasq	1769	Francis	Edge	1734
Thomas	Casw	1777	Francis	Edge	1742
Thomas	Dobb	1769	Francis	Gate	1786
Thomas	Pasq	1754	Francis	Onsl	1769
Thomas Jr.	Pasq	1769	Francis	Onsl	1770
Wm	Bute	1771	Francis	Perq	1740
Wm (Col.)	FWV	1771	George	Cumb	1767
Wm & s. George	FWV	1771	George	Dobb	1769
Wm	Gran	1784	George	NewH	1762
PANDER, Morgan	Casw	1777	George	NewH	1763
PANEL, Benjamin	Surr	1772	George	NorH	1762
PARADISE, Wm	NewH	1755	Hardy	NewH	1767
Wm	NewH	1762	Isaac	Beau	1755
PARAMOORE, Ezekiel	Pitt	1762	Isaac	Bert	1769
Ezekiel	Pitt	1764	Isaac	Dobb	1779
James	Beau	1755	Isaac	Gate	1786
James	Pitt	1762	Isaac	Pasq	1754
James Jr.	Pitt	1762	Jacob	Bert	1769
James	Pitt	1764	James	Bert	1757
James Jr.	Pitt	1764	James 370 acres	Chow	1721
Matthew	Pitt	1762	James	Chow	1753
Matthew	Pitt	1764	James	Curr	1755
PARCE, John	Roan	1720	James	Dobb	1769
PARDUE, John	Bute	1771	James	Gate	1786

PARKER, James	Roan 1720	PARKER, Simon	Chow 1753
Jane	Chow 1717	Simon	Dobb 1769
Jephthah	Gran 1784	Solomon	Onsl 1769
Jeremiah Esq.	Casw 1777	Solomon	Onsl 1770
Jesse	Gran 1769	Stephen	Gate 1786
John	Beau 1755	Thomas	Casw 1777
John	Chow 1753	Thomas	Chow 1753
John s. of		Thomas	Curr 1755
George	Dobb 1769	Thomas	Edge 1741
John	Dobb 1779	Thomas	Gate 1786
John	Gate 1786	Thomas	Gran 1755
John	NewH 1767	Thomas Sr.	NewH 1762
John	Pasq 1754	Thomas	NewH 1762
John	Pitt 1762	Thomas	NewH 1763
John	Pitt 1764	Thomas Jr.	NewH 1767
John	Surr 1772	Thomas Sr.	NewH 1767
Jonas	Gran 1755	Thomas	NorH 1762
Jonathan		Thomas	Perq 1740
deceased	Casw 1777	Willis	Gate 1786
Jonathan	Chow 1743	Wm	Beau 1755
Jonathan	Gran 1755	Wm	Bert 1757
Jonathan	Gran 1784	Wm	Chow 1753
Joseph	Bert 1769	Wm	Curr 1715
Joseph	Gate 1786	Wm	Curr 1755
Joseph	Gran 1769	Wm s. of George	Dobb 1769
Joseph	Gran 1784	Wm	Gate 1786
Joseph	Perq 1740	Wm	Pasq 1769
Joshua	NewH 1755	Wm	Perq 1740
Josiah Sr.	Gate 1786	Zachariah	Gate 1786
Josiah	Gate 1786	Zenis	Dobb 1769
Kedar	Gate 1786	PARKHAM, Avery Jr.	Gran 1784
Mary	Gate 1786	Henry	Gran 1769
Meajah	Dobb 1769	Isham	Gran 1784
Miles	Gate 1786	John Sr.	Gran 1784
Miles	Oran 1755	Lewis	Gran 1784
Mills	Gate 1786	Thomas Jr.	Gran 1784
Moses	Chow 1753	Thomas Sr.	Gran 1784
Peter	Bert 1757	PARKINSON, John	Crav 1769
Peter	Bert 1769	PARKS, George	Rowa 1759
Peter	Chow 1717	Hugh	Rowa 1759
Peter Jr.	Chow 1717	James	NorH 1762
Peter 1,040		John	Surr 1771
acres	Chow 1721	John Jr.	Surr 1771
Peter Jr.		John	Surr 1772
110 acres	Chow 1721	John Jr.	Surr 1772
Peter 300 acres	Chow 1721	Linsfield	Surr 1772
Peter	Chow 1753	Noah	Rowa 1759
Peter	Curr 1715	Robert	Blad 1745
Peter	Gate 1786	Robert Esq.	Casw 1777
Peter	Onsl 1742	Robert	NorH 1762
Peter	Oran 1755	Samuel	Chow 1753
Rebecca (widow)	Casw 1777	Samuel	Oran 1755
Rebecca	Curr 1755	Samuel	Rand 1779
Richard	Chow 1753	Thomas	Surr 1771
Richard	Oran 1755	Thomas Jr.	Surr 1771
Robert	Anso 1763	Thomas Sr.	Surr 1772
Robert Jr.	Gate 1786	PARMER, Joseph	Dobb 1769
Robert Sr.	Gate 1786	Thomas	Gate 1786
Robert	Gate 1786	PARMON, Wm	Dobb 1779
Robert	Gran 1755	PARNALL, Isaac	Surr 1772
Ruth	Chow 1753	John	Cumb 1755
Samuel	Gate 1786	PARR, Wm Sr.	Casw 1777
Samuel	NorH 1762	Wm	Curr 1755
Samuel	Onsl 1769	PARREL, James	NewH 1755
Samuel	Onsl 1770	James	NewH 1762

PARRIS, George	Crav	1769	PASCHALL, Dennis	Gran	1784
PARRISH, Ancil	Gran	1769	Eleizer s. of		
Brepie	Gran	1769	Wm	Gran	1755
Briscoe	Gran	1784	Elisha	Gran	1784
Charles	Gran	1769	Isaiah s. of Wm	Gran	1755
Charles	Gran	1784	Isaiah s. of Wm	Gran	1769
Claibourn	Gran	1784	James	Bute	1771
David	Gran	1755	James	FWV	1771
David	Gran	1769	James s. of Wm	Gran	1755
David	Gran	1784	James	Gran	1784
Elijah	Gran	1769	John s. of Wm	Gran	1755
Elijah	Gran	1784	John	Gran	1769
Gideon	Blad	1763	Samuel	Bute	1771
Gideon	NewH	1762	Samuel	FWV	1771
Henry	Gran	1769	Samuel s. of Wm	Gran	1755
John	Bute	1771	Silas	Gran	1784
John	Edge	1734	Thomas	Bute	1771
John s. of			Thomas	FWV	1771
David	Gran	1755	Wm	Bute	1771
John	NewH	1762	Wm	Casw	1777
John 1,130 acres	Perq	1720	Wm	FWV	1771
John	Perq	1740	Wm s. of Wm	Gran	1755
John	Tyrr	1755	Wm	Gran	1784
Joseph	Gran	1769	PASHAM, Ephraim	Gran	1784
Joshua Jr.	Gran	1784	PATCHETT, Abraham	Cumb	1767
Joshua Sr.	Gran	1784	James	Perq	1720
Justin	Gran	1769	James	Perq	1740
Justin	Gran	1784	Wm	Chow	1717
Lennon	Blad	1763	PATE, Edmund Jr.	Crav	1769
Lewis	Gran	1784	Isaac	Dobb	1779
Sherwood	Gran	1784	Joseph	Dobb	1779
Thomas	Gran	1755	Theophilis	Cumb	1767
Thomas	Gran	1769	Thoroughgood	Cumb	1767
Thomas	Gran	1784	Wm	Dobb	1769
Wm	Gran	1769	Wm	Dobb	1779
Wm	Gran	1784	PATICUNCE, George	Blad	1763
Wm Jr.	Gran	1784	PATILLO, Henry		
PARROT, Ben s.			(Rev.)	FWV	1771
of John	Onsl	1769	PATRICK, Daniel	Blad	1763
John	Crav	1720	Joel	Dobb	1779
John	Dobb	1769	Samuel	Blad	1763
John	Dobb	1779	Samuel	NewH	1762
John	Onsl	1769	Zeakel	Anso	1763
Lewis	NewH	1755	PATRIDGE, John	Dobb	1779
Wm	Dobb	1769	PATT, Andrew	Cumb	1755
PARRY, John	Onsl	1769	Thomas	Cumb	1755
John	Onsl	1770	Wm	Cumb	1755
PARSONS, John	Crav	1769	PATTERSHALL,		
Nathan	Crav	1769	Elizabeth	Bute	1771
Samuel s.			Elizabeth & sons		
Samuel	Perq	1720	Thomas & Wm	FWV	1771
Thomas 1 slave	Crav	1769	PATTERSON, Alexand	Casw	1777
Thomas	Rowa	1759	Alexander	Rand	1779
PARTEE, Charles	Gran	1769	Andrew	Gran	1784
Mary	Gran	1769	Archibald	Cumb	1755
PARTILLO, Henry			Archibald	Cumb	1767
(Rev.)	Bute	1771	David	Bute	1771
PARTRICK, Daniel	Dobb	1769	David	FWV	1771
Joel	Dobb	1769	David	Gran	1755
Menan	Dobb	1769	David	Gran	1784
Mensak	Dobb	1769	Duncan	Cumb	1755
PARVESAL, Isaiah	Brun	1769	Duncan	Cumb	1767
Isaiah	Perq	1740	Francis	FWV	1771
PASCHALL, Dennis	Bute	1771	George	Bute	1771
Dennis	FWV	1771	George	FWV	1771

PATTERSON, Gideon	Casw 1777	PEACE, John Jr.	Gran 1784
Greenberry	Surr 1771	Joseph	Gran 1784
Greenberry	Surr 1772	PEACOCK, Abraham	Dobb 1779
James	Casw 1777	Frank s. of	
James	Gran 1769	Samuel	Dobb 1769
John	Bute 1771	Jesse	Dobb 1779
John Jr.	Cumb 1755	John	Blad 1763
John Sr.	Cumb 1755	John	Dobb 1769
John Jr.	Cumb 1767	John	NorH 1742
John Sr.	Cumb 1767	Richard	Blad 1763
John	Edge 1744	Samuel	Chow 1721
John s. King	FWV 1771	Samuel	Dobb 1769
John	Gran 1755	Samuel	NorH 1742
John Esq.	Oran 1755	Solomon	Dobb 1779
Lewis	Bute 1771	Wm	Pasq 1754
Lewis	FWV 1771	PEAK, James (Cpt.)	Chow 1721
Lewis	Gran 1755	Wm	Surr 1771
Mary	Edge 1742	PEALE, Daniel	Bert 1757
Robert	Chow 1717	John	Gran 1769
Robert	Oran 1755	Joseph	Gran 1769
Smith	Bute 1771	PEARCE, Arthur	1743
Smith s. Young	FWV 1771	Benjamin	Pitt 1762
Smith	Gran 1755	Edward	Beau 1755
Widow 1,867		Elisha	Surr 1771
acres	Chow 1721	Elizabeth	
Wm	Curr 1755	s. Philip	FWV 1771
Wm s. of John	Gran 1755	George	FWV 1771
PATTON, Elijah	Rowa 1759	George Jr.	FWV 1771
James	Rowa 1759	Hezekiah	Beau 1764
Robert	Bute 1771	Isaac	Bert 1757
Robert	FWV 1771	Jesse	Blad 1763
Robert	Rowa 1759	Jesse	Oran 1755
PAU, John	NorH 1762	John	Bert 1757
PAUCK, Jesse s.		John	Pitt 1764
of John	Dobb 1769	Joshua	Beau 1764
John	Dobb 1769	Lazarus	Beau 1755
Peter s. of		Lazarus	Pitt 1762
John	Dobb 1769	Lazarus	Pitt 1764
PAUL, Andrew	Rowa 1759	Samuel	Gran 1784
Ann (widow)	Beau 1764	Solomon	Gran 1784
George	Beau 1755	Thomas	Beau 1755
George	Crav 1769	Thomas	Tyrr 1755
George	Onsl 1743	Wm	Bert 1757
Jacob	Beau 1764	Wm Jr.	Bert 1757
James	Oran 1755	Wm	FWV 1771
John	Beau 1755	Wm	Surr 1771
John	Crav 1769	Windsor	Rand 1779
Samuel	Casw 1777	PEARCELL, Catherine	NewH 1763
Wm	Anso 1763	Edward	NewH 1755
PAVEY, Adam	Curr 1715	Edward's estate	NewH 1762
Dial	Oran 1755	PEARSEY, John	Bert 1757
Joshua	NewH 1755	Stephen	Rand 1779
Joshua	NewH 1767	Wm	Bert 1757
Samuel	Pasq 1754	Wm	FWV 1771
Webley	Pasq 1754	PEARSON, Christopher	
PAYNE, James	Casw 1777		Rand 1779
John (Maj.)	Casw 1777	Jacob	Casw 1777
John	Chow 1717	John	Bert 1757
John	Surr 1771	John	Bert 1769
Peter Esq.	Chow 1753	John	Onsl 1769
Robert (Cpt.)	Casw 1777	John	Onsl 1770
Wm	Casw 1777	Peter	Pasq 1769
PAYTON, Robert	Beau 1749	Peter	Perq 1740
PEABODY, Joseph	Brun 1769	Rachel	Perq 1740
Joseph	Brun 1772	Salisbury	Onsl 1770

PEARSON, Salisbury	Onsl	1770
PEAVY, Joseph	Oran	1755
Joshua	NewH	1762
Joshua	NewH	1763
PEAK, Frederick	Gran	1769
John comber	Gran	1769
John	Gran	1769
John	Gran	1784
Leonard	Gran	1769
PECONCTON, Thomas	Blad	1763
PEDRICK, Henry	Curr	1755
John	Curr	1755
Peter	Curr	1755
PEBBLES, David	Bute	1771
David overseer	FWV	1771
David	Pitt	1764
Nathaniel	Bute	1771
Nathaniel	FWV	1771
Wm	Pitt	1764
Wm	Pitt	1775
PEEL, Jesse	Chow	1753
Joseph	Gate	1786
PEELE, Francis	Curr	1755
James	Bert	1769
John	Bert	1769
Joshua	Bert	1769
PEGGS, John	Pasq	1754
PEGRIM, Daniel	Bute	1771
Daniel Jr.	FWV	1771
Daniel s.		
Edward	FWV	1771
George	Bute	1771
George	FWV	1771
PEIRSON, John	Crav	1769
PELL, John	Curr	1715
John	Curr	1755
Pellepool	Curr	1755
PELT, Van	Bert	1769
Wimon	Bert	1769
PELTON, Thomas	Pitt	1764
PEMBERTON, Margaret	Blad	1763
PENDER, Hezekiah	Bert	1769
Martin	Crav	1741
Paul	Bert	1757
Richard	Beau	1755
Solomon	Bert	1769
PENDERGRASS, David	Gran	1784
John	Bute	1771
John	Casw	1777
John	FWV	1771
John	Gran	1769
Luke	Casw	1777
Richard	Casw	1777
Spencer	Bute	1771
Spencer	FWV	1771
Wm	Bute	1771
Wm	FWV	1771
PENDLETON, Caleb		
3 slaves	Pasq	1769
George 1m		
slave	Pasq	1769
Henry 3m		
slaves	Pasq	1769
John	Pasq	1754
John 1m slave	Pasq	1769

PENDLETON, Joseph Jr.		
5m slaves	Pasq	1769
Joseph Sr.		
1m slave	Pasq	1769
Robert	Pasq	1769
Sarah	Pasq	1754
Timothy	Pasq	1769
PENEL, Thomas & s.		
Thomas	FWV	1771
PENNINGTON, Benajah		
	Rowa	1759
Edward	NorH	1762
Levi Jr.	Rand	1779
Levi Sr.	Rand	1779
Levy	Rowa	1759
Stephen	Onsl	1770
Thomas	Bert	1757
Wm	Brun	1769
Wm	Brun	1772
PENRICE, Eliz	Chow	1753
Francis	Chow	1753
Francis	Perq	1720
Francis	Perq	1740
Thomas 600 acres	Perq	1720
PEPINAN, Joseph	Surr	1772
PERAY, Wm	Rowa	1759
PERCH, Wm	Gran	1755
PERCY, Wm	Bute	1771
PERDOM, Jeremiah	Cumb	1755
John	Cumb	1755
PERDUE, Dennis	Crav	1769
John	Beau	1755
Richard	Beau	1764
Richard s. of		
Richard	Beau	1764
PERISHER, Joshua	Pasq	1769
PERKINS, Absana	Pitt	1764
Asa	Pasq	1769
David	Pitt	1762
David	Pitt	1767
George	Crav	1769
Henry	Curr	1755
James	Beau	1755
James	Casw	1777
James	Pitt	1764
John Jr.	Casw	1777
John Sr.	Casw	1777
John Jr.	Curr	1715
John Sr.	Curr	1715
John	Curr	1743
John Jr.	Curr	1755
John Sr.	Curr	1755
Jonathan	Beau	1755
Mary	Beau	1755
Thomas	Pasq	1769
Valentine	Surr	1771
Wm	Beau	1764
Wm	Casw	1777
PERKINSON, Drury	Gran	1784
Joel	Gran	1784
PERMENTER, James	Edge	1741
PERNALL, John	Blad	1781
PERRIGREW, Robert	Cumb	1767
PERRIMAN, Wm	Rand	1779
PERRIMORE, James	Cumb	1767

PERRISHOE, James &		
s. James	Perq	1720
James	Perq	1740
John	Perq	1740
Joseph	Perq	1740
PERRITT, John	Pitt	1764
PERRY, Abraham	Bert	1757
Abraham	Bert	1769
Benjamin	Bert	1757
Benjamin	Bert	1769
Benjamin	Bute	1771
Benjamin	FWV	1771
Benjamin	Perq	1740
Booth	Gran	1769
Burrell	Bute	1771
Burrell	FWV	1771
Daniel	Crav	1769
Ephraim	Bute	1771
Ephraim	FWV	1771
Francis	Gran	1755
Isaac	Bert	1757
Jacob	Gran	1755
Jacob	Perq	1740
James	Bert	1757
James	Bert	1769
James	Bute	1771
James	Dobb	1769
James	FWV	1771
Jenkins	NewH	1755
Jenkins	NewH	1767
Jeremiah	Bute	1771
Jeremiah	FWV	1771
Jeremiah	Gran	1755
Jesse	Blad	1763
John	Bert	1742
John	Bert	1757
John Jr.	Bert	1757
John	Bute	1771
John 400 acres	Chow	1721
John	Crav	1769
John	Gran	1755
John	Perq	1740
Joseph	Bert	1757
Joshua	Bute	1771
Joshua	FWV	1771
Joshua	Gran	1755
Josiah	Bert	1769
Lewis	Bert	1757
Linkin	NewH	1762
Micajah	Gran	1755
Mordecai	Gate	1786
Nathaniel	Bute	1771
Nathaniel	FWV	1771
Nathaniel	Gran	1755
Nicholas	Bert	1757
Peter	Bute	1771
Peter	FWV	1771
Philip	Perq	1740
Richard	Surr	1771
Richard	Surr	1772
Robert	Crav	1769
Samuel	Chow	1753
Samuel	Perq	1740
Simon	Bute	1771
Simon	FWV	1771

PERRY, Thomas	Bert	1769
Thomas	Perq	1740
Valentine	Gran	1769
Wm	Bert	1742
Wm	Bert	1769
Wm	Bute	1771
Wm	Dobb	1769
Wm s. John Wm	FWV	1771
Wm	Rowa	1759
PERSON, Anne	Bute	1771
Ann	FWV	1771
Benjamin	FWV	1771
Francis	FWV	1771
Jesse	Bute	1771
Jesse	FWV	1771
John	Bute	1771
John s. Josiah	FWV	1771
John	Gran	1755
Joseph	Bute	1771
Joseph s. Henry	FWV	1771
Peter	Surr	1771
Peter	Surr	1772
Samuel	Perq	1740
Solomon	Dobb	1769
Solomon	Dobb	1779
Thomas	Gran	1769
Thomas	Gran	1784
Wm (Cpt.)	Bute	1771
Wm	Edge	1741
Wm	FWV	1771
Wm	Gran	1755
PERTER, Samuel	Blad	1781
PETERKIN, Alexander	Cumb	1767
PETERS, Ethelred	Crav	1769
John	NewH	1755
Jonathan	Cumb	1755
Joseph	Crav	1769
Miles	NewH	1755
Robert	NewH	1755
PETERSON, James	Casw	1777
James	Rowa	1759
John	Casw	1777
John	Rowa	1759
PETPOOL, Abraham	Pitt	1762
PETTARD, John	Gran	1784
PETTIFOR, John		
120 acres	Perq	1720
PETTIFORD, Drury	Gran	1784
Elias	Gran	1784
George	Casw	1777
George	Gran	1769
Laurence	Gran	1755
Laurence	Gran	1769
Laurence	Gran	1784
Philip	Gran	1784
Wm	Gran	1784
PETTIGREW, Charles	Bute	1771
Charles	FWV	1771
PETTIPOOL, Abraham	Pitt	1764
Ephraim	Dobb	1769
Ephraim	Pitt	1764
John	Gran	1769
John	Gran	1784
Moses	Pitt	1764
Seth	Gran	1769

PETTIPOOL, Seth	Gran	1784	PHILLIPS, Benjamin	Perq	1754
PETTIT, Anne	Pitt	1775	Benjamin	Perq	1769
Benjamin	Rowa	1758	Charles bro. of		
Benjamin	Surr	1771	Wm	FWV	1771
Benjamin	Surr	1772	David	Edge	1742
Charles	Crav	1741	David	Oran	1755
George	Surr	1772	David Jr.	Oran	1755
Henry (Rev.)	Gran	1784	Demsey	Gate	1786
Thomas	Surr	1771	Elijah	Bute	1771
PETTY, George	Gran	1784	Elijah	FWV	1771
James	Gran	1755	James	Blad	1763
Thomas	Gran	1755	James	Bute	1771
PETTYGROVES, John	Chow	1753	James	Casw	1777
PEUGH, Stephen	Curr	1755	James	Cumb	1767
PEW, George	Curr	1755	James	Dobb	1769
Thomas	Curr	1755	James	FWV	1771
PEYLAND, Edward	Chow	1753	James	Gate	1786
George	Chow	1753	Jeremiah	Dobb	1769
James	Chow	1753	John	Cumb	1755
Thomas	Chow	1753	John Sr.	Cumb	1767
PEYTON, Benjamin			John	Cumb	1767
24b	Beau	1754	John	Edge	1734
Pettyford	Gran	1755	John	Onsl	1769
Robert	Beau	1755	John	Onsl	1770
Robert	Onsl	1769	John	Oran	1755
Robert	Onsl	1770	Joseph	Surr	1771
Wm 3w 7b	Beau	1744	Joseph Jr.	Surr	1771
Wm	Beau	1744	Joseph	Surr	1772
Wm	Beau	1764	Joseph Jr.	Surr	1772
PFEIFFER, Christian	Surr	1771	Mark	Crav	1745
Christian	Surr	1772	Mark	Cumb	1755
PFEIL, Frederick	Surr	1771	Mark	Dobb	1769
Frederick	Surr	1772	Mason	Dobb	1769
PHARROH, John	Casw	1777	Michael	Beau	1764
Joseph	Casw	1777	Michael	Curr	1755
Peter	Casw	1777	Michael	Onsl	1769
Thomas	Cumb	1767	Nehemiah	Cumb	1767
Wm	Casw	1777	Nehemiah	Rand	1779
PHELPS, Aaron	Dobb	1769	Paul	Chow	1721
Aquilla	Rowa	1759	Robert	Beau	1755
Cuth	Chow	1717	Robert	Bute	1771
Cuthbert	Chow	1721	Robert	Cumb	1767
Ed	Chow	1717	Robert	FWV	1771
Edward Sr.	Tyrr	1755	Samuel	NorH	1762
Edward s. of			Samuel	Pasq	1754
Edward	Tyrr	1755	Stephen	Cumb	1767
Edward s. of			Stephen	Oran	1755
James	Tyrr	1755	Stephen	Rowa	1759
Jacob	Brun	1772	Thomas	Chow	1753
James	Chow	1753	Wm	Beau	1764
John	Bert	1757	Wm	Blad	1781
John	Chow	1753	Wm	Bute	1771
John	FWV	1771	Wm bro Charles	FWV	1771
John	Perq	1740	Wm	Oran	1755
Jonathan 500 a	Perq	1720	PHILPOT, Thomas	Gran	1769
Jordan	FWV	1771	Thomas	Gran	1784
Joseph	Tyrr	1755	Wm	Gran	1784
Joshua	Tyrr	1755	PHILYAW, John		
Micajah	Gate	1786	3 slaves	Crav	1769
Samuel			PHIPPS, Isaiah	Gran	1769
1,097 acres	Perq	1720	Thomas	Pitt	1762
Thomas	Casw	1777	Thomas	Pitt	1764
Wm	Dobb	1769	Wm	Beau	1744
PHILLIPS, Anthony	FWV	1771	PHISOCK, John	Beau	1742
Arthur	Bert	1757	Peter	Crav	1769

PHOENIX, Mary	Bute 1771		PIGMAN, Mason	Oran 1755
Mary	FWV 1771		PIKE, Benjamin Jr.	Pasq 1769
PIANO, Joshua	Beau 1764		Benjamin Sr.	Pasq 1769
Rachel (widow)	Beau 1764		John	Dobb 1769
Thomas	Beau 1764		John	Dobb 1779
PICK, Nathaniel	Surr 1772		John	Pasq 1769
PICKETT, Cager	Oran 1755		Joseph	Pasq 1769
James	Bert 1757		Samuel	Pasq 1769
Ralph	Cumb 1755		Samuel Jr.	Pasq 1769
Wm	Bert 1757		PILAND, Ann	Gate 1786
Wm Jr.	Bert 1757		Edward	Gate 1786
PICKRELL, Benjamin	Bute 1771		George	Gate 1786
Benjamin	FWV 1771		James	Gate 1786
Henry	Rand 1779		Peter	Gate 1786
Richard	Chow 1721		Stephen	Gate 1786
Wm	Bute 1771		PILCHARD, Edward	Onsl 1769
Wm	FWV 1771		Edward	Onsl 1770
PICKREN, Gabriel	Crav 1769		PILFORD, John	Pitt 1762
Moses	Crav 1769		PILGRINE, Isaac	Beau 1755
Richard	Crav 1769		PILKINGTON, James	Beau 1755
PICKRING, Richard	Chow 1717		Sarah	Beau 1755
PICO, Daniel	Beau 1764		Sesh	Beau 1742
PIDCOCK, John	NewH 1741		Wm	FWV 1771
PIERCE, Abner	Gate 1786		PILLEY, John	Beau 1764
Abraham	Gate 1786		Thomas	Beau 1764
Christopher	Gate 1786		PILLSHER, Mary	Onsl 1770
Christopher	Perq 1740		PINCHER, Joseph	Rand 1779
Edmond	Beau 1741		Richard	Rand 1779
Edmund 2 slaves	Crav 1769		PINCOMB, Samuel	Pitt 1762
Elizabeth	Bute 1771		PINDAR, Ward	Dobb 1769
George	Bute 1771		PINDERGRASS, Robert	
George Jr.	Bute 1771			Oran 1755
George	Gran 1755		PINDLETON, Thomas	Chow 1743
George	Surr 1772		PINER, Arthur	Bert 1757
Isaac	Gate 1786		Edward	Beau 1755
Jacob	Gate 1786		Thomas	Onsl 1769
James	Bert 1769		Thomas	Onsl 1770
James 4 slaves	Crav 1769		PINES, Thomas	Onsl 1770
James	Perq 1740		PINEY, Wm	Pitt 1763
Jesse	Cumb 1767		PINION, John s.	
John 300 acre			of Richard	Oran 1755
pat	Perq 1720		Joshua s. of	
Philip	Tyrr 1755		Richard	Oran 1755
Potsful	Perq 1740		Richard	Oran 1755
Richard			PINK, John Esq.	Gran 1784
351 acres	Perq 1720		PINKERTON, David	Oran 1755
Richard	Perq 1740		PINCKETT, Daniel	Beat 1755
Thomas	Bert 1744		Daniel	Pitt 1762
Thomas	Bert 1769		Daniel	Pitt 1764
Thomas	Chow 1721		Eleanor	Beau 1755
Thomas 8w 13b	Chow 1743		Thomas	Beau 1755
Thomas	Chow 1753		Thomas	Pitt 1762
Thomas	Crav 1769		Thomas	Pitt 1764
Thomas 150 acres	Perq 1720		Wm	Beau 1755
Widow	Perq 1740		Zachariah	Pitt 1762
Wm	Bert 1757		Zack	Pitt 1764
Wm	Chow 1717		PINNELL, John	Bute 1771
Wm	Gate 1786		John	FWV 1771
PIERSON, James	Beau 1764		Richard	Bute 1771
Peter	Rowa 1759		Richard	FWV 1771
PIGFORD, Wm	NewH 1767		PINNER, Arthur	Onsl 1769
PIGG, Paul	Cumb 1755		PINSON, Aaron	Gran 1769
PIGGOTT, Benjamin	Oran 1755		Aaron	Oran 1755
Jeremiah	Oran 1755		Joseph	Oran 1755
Wm	Oran 1755		Thomas	NewH 1762

PINSON, Thomas	NewH	1762	PLUMMER, Jeremiah			
PIPER, Isaac	Bute	1771	Constable	Blad	1763
Nathaniel	Pasq	1769	John	Blad	1781
PIPES, Abner	Surr	1771	John	Curr	1755
John	Surr	1771	Joseph	Blad	1741
John	Surr	1772	Joseph	Blad	1763
Philip	Surr	1772	Laban 3w 9b		
PIPKIN, Arthur	Dobb	1769	slaves	Pasq	1743
Arthur	Dobb	1779	Moses	Blad	1741
Daniel	Dobb	1769	Wm	Blad	1763
Elisha s. of			Zachariah	Blad	1781
Joseph	Dobb	1769	POCOCK, Abel	Surr	1772
Elisha	Dobb	1779	POE, Benman	Rand	1779
Isaac	Chow	1753	Robert	Cumb	1767
Isaac	Gate	1786	POINDEXTER, David	Surr	1771
Jesse	Dobb	1769	Thomas	Surr	1772
Jesse s. of			POINER, Benjamin	Curr	1755
John	Dobb	1769	Humphrey	Curr	1755
Jesse	Dobb	1779	Joel	Curr	1755
John	Dobb	1769	Joell	Curr	1755
Joseph	Dobb	1769	Jonathan	Curr	1755
Luke	Dobb	1769	Joseph	Curr	1755
Luke	Dobb	1779	Peter	Curr	1755
Miller	Dobb	1769	Robert	Curr	1755
Philip	Dobb	1769	Samuel	Beau	1755
Stephen	Dobb	1779	POINTER, Aaron	Gran	1784
PIPPES, John	Casw	1777	John	Blad	1763
PIPPIN, Isaac	FWV	1771	John Sr.	Pasq	1769
PIRRES, John	Bert	1769	Samuel	Gran	1784
Thomas	Bert	1769	Samuel	Pasq	1769
PITMELL, John	Beau	1764	POLE, John		
PITT, John Jr.	Rand	1779	Constable	Dobb	1769
PITTARD, Samuel	Gran	1784	Thomas	Perq	1740
PITTMAN, John			POLING, John	Pasq	1769
1 slave	Crav	1769	POLLARD, Benjamin	Pitt	1762
Joseph	Cart	1743	Benjamin	Pitt	1764
Joseph 1 slave	Crav	1769	John	Pitt	1762
Michael	Crav	1742	John	Pitt	1764
Southey	Crav	1769	Thomas	Crav	1769
Thomas	Edge	1742	Wm	Pitt	1762
Wm Jr.	Oran	1755	POLLOCK, Col		
PITTS, Andrew	Rowa	1759	50,000 acres	Chow	1721
Benjamin	Onsl	1769	Cullen Esq.	Bert	1757
Ed	N.C.	1701	Cullen	Bert	1769
Thomas	Onsl	1769	John	Onsl	1769
Thomas s. of			John	Onsl	1770
Thomas	Onsl	1769	Thomas 30,964		
Thomas	Onsl	1770	acres	Chow	1717
Widow	Onsl	1769	POLLOD, Benjamin	Beau	1755
PIVEY, Amos	Cumb	1767	John	Beau	1755
PLATT, Nathaniel	Blad	1741	Matthew	Beau	1755
Thomas	Blad	1763	Wm	Beau	1755
PLAYER, Richard	NewH	1741	POLLOM, Cullen		
Richard	NewH	1762	Esq.	Bert	1757
Richard	NewH	1763	Cullen Esq.	Bert	1769
Richard	NewH	1767	POLSON, Andrew	Surr	1771
Stephen	NewH	1762	Caleb	Chow	1753
Stephen	NewH	1763	Caleb	Gate	1786
Stephen	NewH	1767	Edward	Gate	1786
Thomas	NewH	1762	John	Gate	1786
Thomas	NewH	1767	Sarah	Gate	1786
PLOWMAN, John	Chow	1717	Wm	Bert	1757
John	Chow	1721	POMPHREY, Silva	Beau	1755
PLUMMER, Aaron	Blad	1781	Silva Jr.	Beau	1755
Dr.	Chow	1753	POND, John	Bute	1771

POND, John s.			PORTER, Edward	NewH	1762
John Samuel	FWV	1771	Edward	NewH	1763
John	Surr	1772	George	Pitt	1762
PONE, Diana w.			Hugh	Surr	1771
of John	Gran	1755	John	NewH	1741
John	Gran	1755	John Esq.		
PONRELL, John	NorH	1762	8w 22b	NewH	1742
PONYMAN, Wm	Casw	1777	John	NewH	1762
POOLE, Aaron	Dobb	1769	John	NewH	1763
Barnaby s. of			John	NewH	1767
Joseph	Pasq	1769	Joseph	Casw	1777
Benjamin 1 slave	Pasq	1769	Joseph	Chow	1717
Grace	Pasq	1754	Joseph	Surr	1771
Jacob	Rowa	1759	Joseph	Surr	1772
James	Dobb	1769	Mary	Chow	1717
John	Pasq	1769	Wm	Bert	1757
Joseph	Pasq	1754	Wm	Bert	1769
Joseph Jr.	Pasq	1754	Wm	Crav	1769
Joseph	Pasq	1769	Wm	Surr	1771
Moses	Beau	1764	PORTERFIELD,		
Patrick	Pasq	1769	Matthew	Cumb	1767
Richard 1 slave	Pasq	1769	PORTIVINE, James	NewH	1755
Samuel	Dobb	1779	PORTIVINTE,		
Solomon	Pasq	1754	Margaret	NewH	1762
Solomon			PORTLOCK, Caleb	Pasq	1769
3 slaves	Pasq	1769	PORTWOOD, Gilbert	Curr	1755
Thomas	Gran	1755	Martin	Curr	1755
Thomas	Gran	1784	POSER, Robert	Beau	1755
Wm	Bert	1743	POSEY, Benjamin	Oran	1755
POOR, David	Blad	1763	John	Cumb	1767
John	Blad	1763	John	Surr	1772
Moses	Surr	1772	Nehemiah	Cumb	1767
Ned	Edge	1734	POST, Frank	Edge	1734
POPE, Charles	Bute	1771	POSTON, John	Oran	1755
Charles	FWV	1771	Thomas	Rowa	1759
Everett	Pitt	1764	POTEAT, John	Casw	1777
Jacob	Dobb	1769	POTTE, Abraham	Rowa	1759
Jacob	Dobb	1779	POTTER, Christian	Gran	1769
John	Dobb	1769	Daniel	Bute	1771
John	Dobb	1779	Daniel s. Daniel		
John 6w	Edge	1743	& John	FWV	1771
John 6w 20b	Edge	1744	Daniel	Gran	1755
John	Gran	1769	Ephraim	Oran	1755
John Esq.	Gran	1784	John	Gran	1769
John Jr.	Gran	1784	John	Gran	1784
John	Pitt	1764	Michael	Gran	1769
Matthew s. of			Miles	Brun	1772
Solomon	Dobb	1769	Miles	NewH	1763
Nathaniel	Casw	1777	Robert 4 slaves	Brun	1769
Pool	Dobb	1779	Robert	Brun	1772
Samuel	Dobb	1769	Robert	NewH	1741
Simon	Pitt	1764	Robert	NewH	1762
Solomon	Dobb	1769	Thomas	Surr	1771
POPWITH, Wm	Curr	1755	Virginia	Gran	1769
PORCH, Wm	Gran	1755	Wm	Dobb	1779
PORE, Andrew	Dobb	1769	Wm	Gran	1769
Edward	Cumb	1767	POTTS, Abraham	NewH	1762
PORSEL, Richard	Edge	1734	Andrew	Rowa	1759
PORTAVINT, Joseph	NewH	1755	John	Tryo	1776
PORTEOUS, George	Edge	1743	Ozwell	Bute	1771
PORTER, Alexander	Casw	1777	Ozwell	FWV	1771
Carpen	NewH	1741	Robert	Dobb	1769
Charles	Gran	1784	Stephen s. of		
David	Casw	1777	Robert	Dobb	1769
Edmund	Gran	1784	Stringer	Dobb	1769

POTTS, Stringer	Dobb	1779	POWELL, Wm	Beau	1755
Thomas	Anso	1750	Wm	Bert	1769
Thomas	Oran	1755	Wm	Bute	1771
POUBROOK, George	Casw	1755	Wm Jr.	Chow	1753
POUND, Billy	Onsl	1770	Wm Sr.	Chow	1753
James	Rand	1779	Wm	Curr	1715
John	Brun	1772	Wm	Dobb	1769
John	NewH	1763	Wm s. John		
John	Onsl	1769	Horatius	FWV	1771
John	Onsl	1770	Wm	Gate	1786
Jonathan	Onsl	1770	Wm	Pitt	1762
POUNDS, Isaac	NewH	1755	Wm	Pitt	1764
John	Brun	1769	POWERS, Charles	Bert	1769
John	Brun	1772	David	Beau	1755
John	NewH	1755	David	Pitt	1762
Wm	NewH	1755	David	Pitt	1764
POWELL, Aaron	Bert	1757	Isabella	Curr	1755
Charles	Beau	1755	James	Blad	1769
Elias	Oran	1755	James M. D.	FWV	1771
Elijah	Gran	1755	James	Rand	1779
Enoch	Bute	1771	John	Tyrr	1755
Enoch	FWV	1771	Mansfield	Tyrr	1755
George	Bert	1757	Samuel	Dobb	1779
George	Chow	1721	Sarah	Tyrr	1755
Hardy	Dobb	1779	Wm	Curr	1755
Hardy	NewH	1762	Wm	Edge	1734
Hardy	NewH	1763	Wm 3 slaves	Pasq	1769
Henry	Cumb	1767	POWK, Abel	Surr	1771
Henry	Rand	1779	POWNALL, John	Bute	1771
Isaiah	Cumb	1755	John & s. Henry	FWV	1771
Jacob	Bute	1771	John	NewH	1755
Jacob s. Jacob	FWV	1771	Wm	FWV	1771
Jacob	Gate	1786	POYNER, Edmond	Beau	1764
Jacob	Gran	1755	Edward	Curr	1715
Jacob	NewH	1762	Fetter	Curr	1715
Jacob	NorH	1762	James	Beau	1764
James	Bert	1757	James	Curr	1715
James	Bute	1771	Joseph	Curr	1715
James	FWV	1771	Samuel	Curr	1715
John	Chow	1721	Samuel	Pitt	1762
John	Edge	1743	Samuel	Pitt	1764
John	Gate	1786	Thomas	Curr	1715
John	NorH	1762	Widow	Curr	1715
John	Oran	1755	Wm	Curr	1715
John	Perq	1740	Wm	Surr	1772
Joseph	Gran	1755	POYNES, Wm	Surr	1772
Kador	Bert	1757	PRATT, David	Chow	1753
Lewis	Onsl	1750	Jeremiah 500 acres		
Margaret	Casw	1777		Perq	1720
Mark	Beau	1755	Jeremiah	Perq	1740
Mark	Pitt	1762	John	Perq	1740
Mark	Pitt	1764	Joshua s. of		
Nathan	Oran	1755	David	Chow	1753
Nathaniel	Edge	1742	Joshua	Perq	1740
Ozburn 3 slaves	Crav	1769	Wm	Casw	1777
Paul	Beau	1755	PERFECT, Benjamin	Curr	1755
Richard	Edge	1742	PRESCOTT, Aaron	Curr	1715
Robert	Chow	1753	Aaron	Dobb	1769
Samuel	NorH	1762	Aaron	Onsl	1769
Sarah	Gran	1755	Aaron	Onsl	1770
Shadrack	Chow	1753	Benjamin	Crav	1769
Stephen	Cumb	1767	Charles	Beau	1764
Stephen	Pitt	1762	John	Beau	1755
Stephen	Pitt	1764	John Jr.	Beau	1764
Thomas	Cumb	1767	John	Dobb	1769

PRESCOTT, John			PRICHARD, Benoni		
s. of Aaron	Onsl	1769	3m slaves	Pasq	1769
Moses	Beau	1755	David	Pasq	1769
Moses	Beau	1764	Davis s. of		
Moses	Dobb	1769	David	Pasq	1769
Moses	Onsl	1769	David s. of		
Moses	Onsl	1770	James	Pasq	1769
Simon	Pitt	1762	Elisha	Pasq	1769
Simon	Pitt	1764	Hugh	Pasq	1769
Thomas	Beau	1755	James 2m 2f		
Willis	Crav	1769	slaves	Pasq	1769
Wm	Beau	1755	Jesse s. of		
Wm Jr.	Dobb	1769	Thos Sr.	Pasq	1769
Wm Sr.	Dobb	1769	John	Pasq	1769
Wm	Onsl	1769	John Jr.	Pasq	1769
Wm	Onsl	1770	Joseph	Pasq	1769
Wm	Pitt	1764	Matthew 2 slaves		
PRESNALL, Daniel	Rand	1779		Pasq	1769
James	Rand	1779	Samuel	Pasq	1769
John	Rand	1779	Thomas Sr.	Pasq	1769
Stephen	Rand	1779	Thomas 9m		
Wm	Rand	1779	2f slaves	Pasq	1769
PRESSLEY, Alice wo	Pasq	1769	Thomas s. of		
Garret	Pasq	1769	Arthur	Pasq	1769
John	Bert	1757	PRICKET, George	Rand	1779
Nathan	Pasq	1769	Gideon	Blad	1781
PREVAT, Thomas	Crav	1769	PRIDDY, George	Gran	1769
PREW, Nicholas	Chow	1721	George	Gran	1784
PRICE, Absalom	Beau	1755	Harlow	Gran	1784
Bardan	Dobb	1769	Robert	Gran	1784
Charles	Pitt	1762	Thomas	Gran	1784
Charles	Pitt	1764	PRIDE, Morley	Casw	1777
Daniel	Dobb	1769	Thomas	Casw	1777
Edmond	NewH	1767	PRIDGEON, Francis	Chow	1717
Edward	Perq	1740	Francis	Chow	1721
Elisha	Surr	1772	Francis	Roan	1720
James	NewH	1762	Matthew	Blad	1781
James	NewH	1763	Thomas	Dobb	1769
John Sr.	Beau	1755	Thomas	Dobb	1779
John	Beau	1755	Wm	Dobb	1779
John	Beau	1764	PRIDGET, Abraham	Surr	1771
John 3w 5b	Crav	1745	PRIMM, Kitchen	Bute	1771
John	Dobb	1779	Kitchen	FWV	1771
John	Oran	1755	PRINCE, Daniel	Gran	1755
John	Perq	1720	Edward	FWV	1771
John	Pitt	1762	Gilbert	Bute	1771
John Jr.	Pitt	1762	Gilbert	FWV	1771
John Sr.	Pitt	1764	James	Bute	1771
John	Pitt	1764	James s. John	FWV	1771
Rice	Crav	1741	Moses	Casw	1777
Richard	NewH	1755	PRINGLE, John	Crav	1769
Thomas	Dobb	1769	PRIOR, Samuel	Crav	1769
Thomas Jr.	Dobb	1769	PRISTON, John	Oran	1755
Thomas	Dobb	1779	PRITCHARD, David	Pasq	1754
Thomas	Edge	1744	Herbert	Bert	1769
Thomas	NewH	1767	James	Bert	1769
Wm	Beau	1755	James	Pasq	1754
Wm	Beau	1764	John	Bert	1769
Wm Jr.	Beau	1764	Joseph	Pasq	1754
Wm	Blad	1763	Matthew	Pasq	1769
Wm	Dobb	1779	Richard	Pasq	1754
Wm	Perq	1740	Samuel	Pasq	1754
PRICHARD, Ann			Thomas Jr.	Pasq	1754
1m 1f	Pasq	1769	Wm	Bert	1757
Arthur	Pasq	1769	Wm	Bert	1769

PRITCHART, Jeremiah	Crav	1769
PRITCHETT, Jacob	Beau	1755
James	Beau	1755
James	Beau	1764
Joshua	Beau	1755
Joshua	Beau	1764
Margaret	Beau	1755
Peter	Beau	1755
Peter	Beau	1764
Philip	Beau	1755
Philip	Beau	1764
Philip	Gran	1755
Simon	Beau	1764
PRITLOW, John	Perq	1720
PRIVITT, Jacob	Chow	1753
John	Chow	1753
PROBEY, Wm		
1f slave	Pasq	1769
PROCK, Paul	Oran	1755
PROCTOR, Richard	Bute	1771
Wm	Beau	1755
Wm	Pitt	1762
PROG, John	Casw	1777
PROPHET, John	Surr	1772
PROUGH, Adam	Surr	1771
PROVO, Samuel	Casw	1777
PROWELL, Wm	Casw	1777
PRYOR, Ann	Casw	1777
Ann	Gran	1769
Anthony	Gran	1769
Haden	Gran	1769
Henry	Casw	1777
John	Casw	1777
John Esq.	Oran	1755
Margaret	Casw	1777
Philip	Gran	1755
Robert	Gran	1769
Seth	Brun	1772
Tabitha	Casw	1777
PUCKETT, Allan	Bute	1771
Gideon	Blad	1763
Shippe	Bute	1771
Shippe	FWV	1771
PUGH, Daniel		
(Cpt.)	Chow	1753
David	Bute	1771
David	FWV	1771
Francis	Bert	1757
Francis	Blad	1753
George	Curr	1755
Hugh 4m 4f		
slaves	Crav	1769
James	Rand	1779
John	Rand	1779
Samuel	Rand	1779
Thomas	Bert	1757
Thomas Esq.	Bert	1769
Thomas	Chow	1753
Thomas	Curr	1755
Thomas	Rand	1779
Wm	Blad	1752
PULLEN, John	Gran	1769
Thomas	Gran	1769
PULLING, Frederick	FWV	1771
Thomas	Bute	1771

PULLING, Thomas	FWV	1771
PUMPHREY, Nathan	Pitt	1764
Silvanus	Pitt	1764
PURCELL, David	NewH	1742
John	Chow	1717
PURDIE, Hugh Esq.	Blad	1763
PURDUE, Blackman	Gran	1784
John	FWV	1771
Joseph	FWV	1771
PURIFY, Nicholas	Crav	1743
PURKINS, Absalom	Pitt	1762
Elijah	Bert	1769
Haberhanah	Pasq	1754
John	Anso	1763
PURSE, Henry	Crav	1769
PURSELL, Edward	Curr	1755
PURSER, Richard	Beau	1755
PURVER, Robert	Beau	1764
PURVIANCE, Wm	NewH	1762
Wm	NewH	1763
Wm	NewH	1767
PURVICE, George	Bert	1757
PURVIS, James	Bert	1769
PURYEAR, Absalom	Gran	1784
John	Gran	1784
Robert	Gran	1784
Wm	Gran	1784
Wm Jr.	Gran	1784
PUSSELL, James	Beau	1755
James	Beau	1764
James	Pitt	1762
PUTMAN, Benjamin	Bute	1771
Benjamin	FWV	1771
Benjamin	Gran	1784
Thomas	Bute	1771
Thomas s. John	FWV	1771
PUTNAL, Joshus	Pitt	1763
Joshua	Pitt	1764
Joshua	Pitt	1775
PUTNAM, Thomas	Gran	1755
PUTTESON, Thomas	Bert	1769
PYBUS, Henry	Crav	1769
PYRENT, Wm	Casw	1777
PYSON, Charles	Casw	1777
QUARLES, Moses	Gran	1755
QUARTERMUSS, James	Pitt	1775
QUEEN, Henson	Anso	1763
Timotny	Anso	1763
Wm Constable	Anso	1763
QUIBLIN, Togge	Oran	1755
QUICK, Thomas	Bert	1757
QUILLEN, Daniel	Crav	1769
QUINCE, John	NewH	1762
John	NewH	1767
Parker 16m		
5f slaves	Brun	1769
Parker 16 m		
5f slaves	Brun	1772
Richard 66m		
43f slaves	Brun	1772
Richard Jr.	Brun	1772
Richard	NewH	1755

QUINCE, Richard	NewH	1762	RAIFORD, Robert	Crav	1742
Richard Sr.	NewH	1763	RAILEY, Andrew	Bute	1771
Richard	NewH	1767	Maurice	Bute	1771
QUINN, Benjamin	Casw	1777	RAINBOLT, Joseph	Cumb	1767
Henry	Casw	1777	RAINE, Joseph	Bute	1771
James	Chow	1753	RAINES, Anthony	Dobb	1769
Wm Jr.	Casw	1777	Anthony	Rand	1779
Wm Sr.	Casw	1777	George	Rand	1779
Wm	Casw	1777	Ishmael	Rand	1779
QUINNEY, Sutton	Crav	1769	James	Rand	1779
Wm	Crav	1769	John	Bert	1769
QUOMONE	Tyrr	1755	John	Gran	1769
QUOTURMUS, Isaac	Pitt	1764	John	Gran	1784
James	Pitt	1762	John Sr.	Rand	1779
James	Pitt	1764	Laurence	Rand	1779
Josiah	Pitt	1762	Leonard	Rand	1779
Patrick	Pitt	1762	Luke	Bert	1769
Patrick Jr.	Pitt	1762	Richard	Bert	1769
Patrick	Pitt	1764	Robert	Rand	1779
Thomas	Pitt	1762	Wm	Gran	1755
			RAINSEY, Samuel	Onsl	1742
			RAINWATER, James s.		
			of John	Gran	1755
RABON, George	Blad	1763	James	Surr	1772
John	Blad	1763	John	Gran	1755
RABORN, Richard	Gran	1755	John Jr.	Surr	1771
Wm	Gran	1755	John Sr.	Surr	1772
RABY, Adam	Bert	1757	RALEY, John	Anso	1763
Edward	NewH	1755	RALLS, Marmaduke	Dobb	1769
John	NewH	1755	RALSTON, Samuel	Rand	1779
RACKLEY, Anthony	Gran	1755	RAMBO, Laurence	Oran	1755
John	Gran	1755	RAMEY, John	Casw	1777
John	NorH	1743	RAMM, Michael	Crav	1742
Joseph	FWV	1771	RAMSEY, Daniel	Casw	1777
Joshua	Gran	1755	David	Crav	1769
Miles	Bute	1771	Elizabeth	Onsl	1769
Miles	FWV	1771	James	Brun	1769
Mills	Gran	1755	James	Brun	1772
Parson	Bute	1771	Moses	Curr	1755
Parson s. John			Randal	NewH	1763
& Frederick	FWV	1771	Randell	NewH	1767
Parson	Gran	1755	Randolph	NewH	1762
Saul	Gran	1755	Robert	Crav	1720
RAD, John	Bert	1757	Thomas	Dobb	1769
RADFORD, Wm	Dobb	1769	Wm	Onsl	1770
Wm	Dobb	1779	RANCH, Michael	Surr	1772
RAE, Hugh	Cumb	1767	RAND, John Jr.	Rand	1779
RAGAIN, James	Gran	1769	John Sr.	Rand	1779
John	Gran	1769	RANDALL, John		
Wm	Rand	1779	Const	Dobb	1769
RAGLAND, Amey	Gran	1784	RANDEL, Jacob	Rowa	1759
Benjamin	Gran	1769	RANDOLPH, James Jr.	Casw	1777
Evan	Gran	1769	James Sr.	Casw	1777
George	NorH	1762	Nehemiah	Crav	1769
Wm	Gran	1769	Wm 1m 1f slave	Crav	1769
Wm	Gran	1784	RANK, John	Surr	1771
RAGON, John	Gran	1755	John	Surr	1772
RAGSDALE, Thomas	Casw	1777	Michael	Surr	1771
Wm	Casw	1777	RANKHORN, Elizabeth	Pasq	1754
RAGUN, Gabriel	Cumb	1755	Joseph	Pasq	1754
RAHM, Jeremiah	Pitt	1764	Wm	Pasq	1754
RAIFORD, Matthew	Anso	1763	RANKIN, James	Casw	1777
Matthew Jr.	Cumb	1755	Robert	Rowa	1759
Matthew Sr.	Cumb	1755	Wm	Casw	1777
Philip	Roan	1720	RANN, John	Gran	1755

RANSOM, George	Onsl	1770	RATLIFF, Richard		
James Jr.	Bute	1771	133 acres	Perq	1720
James Sr.	Bute	1771	Wm	Pasq	1769
James Sr. & s.			RATTER, Wm	Gate	1786
Richard	FWV	1771	RAUS, Laurence	Surr	1771
John	Gran	1769	RAVEN, John	Gran	1769
RAPER, Cornelius	Pasq	1769	RAVENSCROFT, Thomas	Bute	1771
Henry	Pasq	1754	Thomas	FWV	1771
Henry	Perq	1740	RAWLANDS, Joseph	Dobb	1769
John	Pasq	1769	RAWLES, Henry	Bert	1769
Josiah	Pasq	1754	Wm	Bert	1769
RASBERRY, Abraham	Onsl	1769	RAWLINGS, James	Blad	1781
Abraham	Onsl	1770	James	Onsl	1769
Absalom	Onsl	1769	Richard	Gate	1786
Absalom	Onsl	1770	RAWLINS, John	NorH	1742
Horace s. of			Thomas	Crav	1743
John	Dobb	1769	RAWLS, Absalom	Bert	1757
James	Bert	1757	Duke	Chow	1753
John	Bert	1742	Henry	Bert	1757
John	Chow	1721	James	Casw	1777
John	Dobb	1769	John	Bert	1757
John s. of			Wm	Bert	1757
John	Dobb	1769	RAWSON, Samuel	Crav	1720
Joseph	Dobb	1769	RAY, Alexander s.		
Joseph	Dobb	1779	James John Wm	Bert	1757
Philip	Onsl	1769	Ambrose, s.		
Philip	Onsl	1770	of John	Gran	1755
Thomas	Bert	1757	Amelia	Blad	1781
Wm s. Ben John			Anguish	Cumb	1767
Philip	Bert	1757	Ann	Bute	1771
Wm Jr.	Bert	1757	Ann	FWV	1771
Wm	Onsl	1769	Christmas	Gran	1755
Wm	Onsl	1770	Gabriel	Bute	1771
RASCO, Daniel	Bert	1757	Gabriel	FWV	1771
Wm	Bert	1757	Horel	Casw	1777
RASHER, Benjamin s. of			Isaac	Blad	1763
John	Dobb	1769	James	Bert	1769
John	Dobb	1769	James	Casw	1777
John s. of John	Dobb	1769	James	Oran	1755
Thomas s. of			John	Bert	1769
John	Dobb	1769	John	Cumb	1767
RASOR, Edward	Bert	1757	John	Edge	1744
Edward Esq.	Bert	1769	John	Gran	1755
Fred. 800 acres			Joseph	Blad	1763
	Chow	1721	Joseph	Cumb	1767
Martin	Chow	1717	Mary	Tyrr	1755
Martin	Chow	1721	Mayandop	Bert	1769
RATCLIFF, Isaiah s.			Neill	Cumb	1767
of Joseph	Dobb	1769	Robert	Onsl	1769
John Sr.	Crav	1738	Samuel	Anso	1763
John Jr.	Dobb	1769	Thomas	Casw	1777
John Sr. 450			Wm	Edge	1734
acres	Dobb	1769	Wm s. of John	Gran	1755
Joseph s. of			Wm	Tyrr	1755
John Sr.	Dobb	1769	RAYBURN, John	Surr	1771
Moses s. of			John Jr.	Surr	1771
John Sr.	Dobb	1769	RAYFIELD, Wm	Tyrr	1755
Samuel	Anso	1763	RAYFORD, Philip	Cumb	1767
Samuel	Anso	1784	Wm	Dobb	1769
Thomas s. of			RAYLY, Charles	Oran	1755
John Jr.	Dobb	1769	RAYNER, John	Bert	1757
Thomas	Dobb	1769	Richard	Bert	1757
Wm s. of Joseph	Dobb	1769	REA, John	Cumb	1755
Wm	Dobb	1769	READ, Charles	Tyrr	1755
RATLIFF, Joseph	Perq	1740	John	Gran	1784

READ, John	Oran	1755	REE, Wm Esq.	Blad	1781
Wm	Anso	1763	Wm Jr.	Blad	1781
READOCK, John Jr.	Rand	1779	REECE, Travis	Bute	1771
Joseph	Rand	1779	Travis	FWV	1771
READY, Daniel	Crav	1769	Wm	Casw	1777
James	NewH	1763	REED, Andrew		
Thomas	NewH	1762	755 acres	Perq	1720
Thomas	NewH	1763	Benjamin	Crav	1769
REALY, Andrew	FWV	1771	Christian	Pasq	1769
John	NewH	1755	Christopher	Perq	1740
Morris s. John	FWV	1771	George	Cart	1742
REAMY, John	Casw	1777	George	FWV	1771
REAPER, Wm	Rowa	1759	Hardy	Gate	1786
REARDON, Henry	Gran	1769	Isaac	Crav	1769
REASONOVER, Joseph	Crav	1769	Isaac	Gate	1786
REASONS, Ann	Bert	1769	James	Crav	1769
Thomas	Bert	1757	James on Neuce	Crav	1769
REAVES, Peter	Pitt	1762	James	Gran	1769
Peter	Pitt	1764	John	Bert	1757
Richard	Pitt	1762	John	N.C.	1701
Richard	Pitt	1764	John	Surr	1771
Timothy	Dobb	1769	John	Surr	1772
Wm	Dobb	1769	Joseph	Pasq	1754
REBBIL, George	Bert	1757	Joseph	Perq	1740
REDDEN, Joseph	Perq	1740	Joseph	Rowa	1759
REDDETT,			Lambert	Cumb	1767
Constantine	Bert	1769	Madas	Surr	1771
REDDICK, John s.			Nathaniel	Oran	1755
of Wm Sr.	Dobb	1769	Nathan	Rowa	1758
John	Tyrr	1755	Owen	Oran	1755
Joseph	Perq	1740	Roger	Gran	1755
Robert	Perq	1740	Samuel Jr.	Rowa	1759
Thomas	Tyrr	1755	Susannah	Bute	1771
Wm	Bute	1771	Susannah	FWV	1771
Wm	Chow	1717	Thomas	Bute	1771
Wm	Chow	1753	Thomas	FWV	1771
Wm	Crav	1745	Thomas	NewH	1755
Wm Sr.	Dobb	1769	Wm	Bute	1771
Wm Jr. s.			Wm	Chow	1721
of Wm Sr.	Dobb	1769	Wm (Col.)	Curr	1715
Wm	Dobb	1769	Wm	FWV	1771
Wm	Pasq	1769	Wm	Gran	1755
REDDING, Benjamin	Pasq	1769	Wm	Oran	1755
David	Pasq	1769	Wm	Pasq	1769
Joseph	Pasq	1754	Wm	Rowa	1759
Joseph 2m			REEL, James 1m		
2f slaves	Pasq	1769	3f slaves	Crav	1769
Lionel	Curr	1715	Peter 1f		
Rachel 1f slave	Pasq	1769	slave	Crav	1769
Richard	Blad	1781	REES, Abraham	Surr	1772
Samuel	Pasq	1754	John	Gran	1769
Thomas	Pasq	1754	REESE, Abraham	Rand	1779
Thomas 2m 1f			Charles	Casw	1777
slave	Pasq	1769	REEVES, Allen	Gran	1784
Trimagain 2f			Burgess	Bute	1771
slaves	Pasq	1769	Burgess	FWV	1771
REDDITT, Josiah	Bert	1769	Burgess	Gran	1784
Peter	Bert	1769	Edward	Blad	1763
REDDIX, John	Rowa	1759	Frederick	Gran	1784
REDFERN, Isaac	Rand	1779	Isaac	Casw	1777
REDFORD, Matthew	Crav	1720	Jesse	Blad	1763
REDMAN, Thomas	Casw	1777	Jonathan	Gran	1784
REDWINE, Lodowick	Gran	1769	Malachi	Gran	1769
Michael	Gran	1769	Malachiah	Gran	1784
REE, Robert	Blad	1781	Robert	Blad	1742

REEVES, Samuel	Gran	1784
Wm 130 acres	Chow	1721
Wm	Dobb	1779
Wm	Gran	1769
Wm	Gran	1784
Wm	Oran	1755
Wm	Surr	1771
REGAN, Francis	Gran	1755
Isaac	Pitt	1775
John	Gran	1755
Joseph	Blad	1763
Richard	Blad	1781
REID, Aaron	Gran	1769
Arthur	Gran	1769
Arthur	Rand	1779
Christian		
5m slaves	Pasq	1769
Field	Gran	1784
Jacob	Casw	1777
John	Casw	1777
John	Gran	1784
John Jr.	Oran	1755
John Sr.	Oran	1755
Lambert	Gran	1784
Lambert	Rand	1779
Robert	Gran	1769
Robert	Gran	1784
Wm	Gran	1784
Wm 2m 2f		
slaves	Pasq	1769
Wm Jr.	Rand	1779
Wm Sr.	Rand	1779
Wm	Rand	1779
REILLY, James	Oran	1755
RELFE, Enoch	Pasq	1769
John 1f		
slave	Pasq	1769
Robert	Pasq	1769
Thomas Jr.	Pasq	1769
Thomas Sr.		
4m 4f slaves	Pasq	1769
Wm 2m 2f		
slaves	Pasq	1769
Wm Jr.	Pasq	1769
REMCY, Wm	Bute	1771
REMICK, Jacob	NewH	1762
Jacob	NewH	1763
RENN, Francis	Gran	1755
James	Gran	1755
John	Bute	1771
John	FWV	1771
Joseph	FWV	1771
RENNALS, George	Oran	1755
Nathaniel	Oran	1755
RENNER, George	Surr	1771
George	Surr	1772
RENNICK, George	Anso	1750
RENRELL, Samuel	NorH	1762
RENTFROW, Enoch	Gran	1755
Jacob	Dobb	1769
Jacob	Dobb	1779
James	Dobb	1769
Neal	Dobb	1769
Wm	Dobb	1769
Wm	Dobb	1779

RENTLEMAN,		
Christopher	Rowa	1759
RETTER, Thomas	Chow	1753
REUTER, Gotleib	Surr	1771
REVELL, Edmond	Dobb	1769
Edmund	Dobb	1779
John	Dobb	1779
Joseph	Dobb	1769
Josiah s. of		
Joseph	Dobb	1769
Randall s. of		
Joseph	Dobb	1769
Randall	Dobb	1779
REVIS, Nat	Blad	1781
Zah.	Blad	1781
REW, Beverly 2m		
4f slaves	Crav	1769
Charles 1f		
slave	Crav	1769
REYNOLDS,		
Christopher	Dobb	1779
Francis	Surr	1772
Hamilton	Casw	1777
Henry	Rand	1779
Hugh	Casw	1777
James	Surr	1772
Jeremiah	Rand	1779
Jeremiah	Rowa	1758
Jeremiah	Rowa	1759
John	Curr	1715
John	Edge	1743
John	Rand	1779
Joseph	Bert	1757
Nathaniel	Oran	1755
Robert	Dobb	1769
Samuel	Rand	1779
Sharp s. of		
Christopher	Dobb	1769
Wm	Bute	1771
Wm	Dobb	1769
Wm	FWV	1771
Wm Jr.	Onsl	1769
Wm	Rowa	1758
Wm	Rowa	1759
RHEM, Jacob		
1f slave	Crav	1769
Peter	Crav	1769
RHOADS, George	Gran	1755
John	Tyrr	1755
Wm	Tyrr	1755
RHODES, Christopher	Oran	1755
Henry	Onsl	1769
Henry	Onsl	1770
James	Bert	1757
James	Dobb	1769
John	Bert	1743
John	Bute	1771
John & s. Wm	FWV	1771
Solomon	Dobb	1779
Thomas	NewH	1741
Wm	Oran	1755
RHOODS, Wm	Pasq	1754
RICE, Abraham	Casw	1777
Aeajah	Dobb	1769
Benjamin	Gran	1755

RICE, Cleverly	Beau	1755	RICHARDS, Wm	Rand	1779
Cleverly	Crav	1769	RICHARDSON,		
David	Gate	1786	Benjamin	Pasq	1769
Ephraim	Crav	1769	Drury	Cumb	1767
Evan	Beau	1755	Edward	Bute	1771
Evan	Crav	1769	Edward	FWV	1771
Gideon	Crav	1769	Evan	Pasq	1769
Harness	FWV	1771	James	Blad	1781
Harness	Gran	1784	James	Casw	1777
Hezekiah (Cpt.)	Casw	1777	James	Pasq	1769
James	Beau	1755	John	Onsl	1742
James Esq.	Casw	1777	John s. of		
James	Crav	1769	Tobias	Pasq	1769
James	NewH	1755	John	Pasq	1769
Jephtha	Casw	1777	Joseph	Dobb	1769
John	Casw	1777	Joseph Jr.	Pasq	1769
John Sr.	Casw	1777	Joseph Sr.	Pasq	1769
John	Chow	1721	Josiah	Pasq	1769
John	Crav	1745	Laurence Jr.	Casw	1777
John Jr. 4m			Laurence Sr.	Casw	1777
4f slaves	Crav	1769	Moses	Casw	1777
John Sr.	Crav	1769	Nathaniel	Beau	1755
John	Gate	1786	Owen	Rand	1779
John	Gran	1784	Peter	Rand	1779
John	Onsl	1770	Robert	Blad	1763
Micajah	Dobb	1769	Samuel	Blad	1781
Nathan	Casw	1777	Stephen Jr.	Pasq	1769
Nathaniel	Casw	1777	Stephen Sr.	Pasq	1769
Nathaniel	NewH	1741	Tobias	Pasq	1769
Nathaniel 8w			Tobias s. of		
17b slaves	NewH	1745	Tobias	Pasq	1769
Stephen	NewH	1763	Wm	Bute	1771
Thomas	Casw	1777	Wm	Cumb	1767
Thomas Esq.	Casw	1777	Wm	FWV	1771
Thomas	Gran	1769	Wm	Gran	1755
Thomas	Gran	1784	Wm	Pasq	1769
Wm Constable	Bert	1757	RICHETSON, Gordias	Crav	1769
Wm	Casw	1777	RICHEY, Anthony	NewH	1763
Wm 2,370 acres			Wm	Rowa	1759
	Chow	1721	RICHINARD, George	NewH	1763
Wm	Chow	1753	RICHMOND, James	Casw	1777
Zebulon	Crav	1769	John Jr.	Casw	1777
Zorable	Gran	1784	John Sr.	Casw	1777
RICH, Deliverance	Pasq	1754	Matthew	Casw	1777
John Jr.	Rand	1779	Wm	Casw	1777
John Sr.	Rand	1779	RICHTER, John	Surr	1771
Obadiah	Curr	1715	John	Surr	1772
RICHARDS, Amos	Rowa	1759	RICKETTS, Charles	Chow	1717
Evan	Rowa	1759	Charles	Chow	1721
George	Bute	1771	RICKS, Benjamin	Chow	1717
George	FWV	1771	Isaac	Edge	1742
John	Bute	1771	Sarah 300 acres	Chow	1721
John	Curr	1755	Thomas	Gran	1769
John	Edge	1744	Thomas	Gran	1784
John s. John			Timothy	Gran	1769
Wm	FWV	1771	Wm 2,370 acres	Chow	1721
Laurence	Casw	1777	Wm	NorH	1742
Ralph	Beau	1755	RIDANCE, John	Surr	1772
Ralph	Pitt	1762	Wm	Surr	1771
Ralph	Pitt	1764	Wm	Surr	1772
Thomas	Beau	1755	RIDDICK, Abraham	Gate	1786
Thomas	Pitt	1762	Christopher	Gate	1786
Thomas	Pitt	1764	Job	Gate	1786
Wm	Bute	1771	John	Gate	1786
Wm & s. Major	FWV	1771	John	Perq	1740

RIDDICK, Joseph	Gate	1786	RIGGS, James s.		
Micajah	Gate	1786	of John	Beau	1764
Sarah	Gate	1786	John	Beau	1755
Seth	Gate	1786	John	Beau	1764
RIDDLE, Stephen	Rowa	1759	John	Crav	1769
RIDGE, Godfrey	Rand	1779	John	Pitt	1762
Wm	Surr	1771	Reuben	Surr	1771
RIDGEHILL, John	Blad	1763	Samuel	Surr	1771
Richard	Blad	1763	Samuel	Surr	1772
RIDGEON, Wm	Dobb	1769	Wm	Surr	1772
RIDGEWAY, James	Onsl	1741	RIGHT, Henry	Curr	1755
Josiah 1m			Solomon	Dobb	1769
2f slaves	Crav	1769	Wm	Pitt	1764
RIDING, David	Pasq	1769	RIGNEY, James	Beau	1741
John	Surr	1771	RILEY, Edward	NewH	1762
Wm	Surr	1771	Edward	NewH	1763
Wm Jr.	Surr	1771	James	Casw	1777
Wm Jr.	Surr	1772	John	NewH	1762
Wm Sr.	Surr	1772	John	NewH	1763
RIDINGS, Wm	Gran	1755	John	NewH	1767
RIDLEY, Bromfield	Gran	1784	Richard	Brun	1772
Mary	Oran	1755	Richard	NewH	1763
Moses	Oran	1755	Thomas	Casw	1777
RIELEY, Richard	Brun	1769	Wm	NewH	1741
RIESSET, John Esq.	Chow	1753	Wm	NewH	1762
RIEVES, James	Gran	1755	RILLO, Moses	Dobb	1769
John	Gran	1755	RIMER, Wm Hon	Rowa	1759
Malachi	Gran	1755	RIMY, Wm	FWV	1771
Malachi s. of			RING, Peter	Surr	1772
James	Gran	1755	Thomas	Gran	1769
Thomas s. of			Wm	Casw	1777
John	Gran	1755	RIS, John	Brun	1772
Wm	Gran	1755	RISBE, Richard	Bert	1757
Wm	Rand	1779	RISPES, Richard	Bert	1757
RIGBY, John	Rand	1779	Thomas	Bert	1757
RIGDON, Enoch	Rowa	1758	RITESMAN, Christian	Rand	1779
RIGEN, John	Blad	1781	RIVENBARK, Philip	NewH	1767
Joseph	Blad	1781	RIVERS, Jesse	NewH	1762
Ralph	Blad	1781	ROACH, Charles	Crav	1769
Regan	Cumb	1755	David	Crav	1769
RIGGAN, Charles	Bute	1771	Francis	Dobb	1769
Charles s.			John	Dobb	1769
Jesse	FWV	1771	Patrick	Brun	1772
Francis	Bute	1771	Solomon	Dobb	1769
Francis	FWV	1771	Wm	Dobb	1779
Jesse	FWV	1771	ROADES, Mary	NewH	1762
John	Bute	1771	ROADS, Henry	Bert	1757
John	FWV	1771	Henry	Bert	1769
Jonathan	Bute	1771	Henry	Dobb	1769
Jonathan	FWV	1771	Henry	Onsl	1742
Peter	Bute	1771	Jacob	Bert	1769
Peter	FWV	1771	Jacob	Dobb	1769
Powell	FWV	1771	James	Bert	1757
Wm	FWV	1771	James	Bert	1769
RIGGS, Abraham			James	Dobb	1769
miller	Pasq	1754	John	Bert	1757
Abraham	Perq	1720	John of Sandy		
Abraham	Perq	1740	Run	Bert	1757
David	Surr	1771	John	Bert	1769
David	Surr	1772	Levant s. of		
Edward	Surr	1771	Thomas	Pasq	1769
Edward	Surr	1772	Robert	Bert	1757
Giles	Crav	1769	Robert	Bert	1769
Jacob	Pasq	1769	Thomas	Bert	1757
			Thomas	Bert	1769

ROADS, Thomas	Chow	1721
Thomas	Pasq	1754
Thomas	Pasq	1769
Thomas	Roan	1720
Wm	Bert	1769
Wm	Dobb	1769
ROAN, James	Casw	1777
ROB, Thomas	Curr	1755
Thomas Sr.	Curr	1755
ROBARDS, Philip	Cumb	1755
Wm	Cumb	1755
ROBBINS, Arthur	Brun	1769
Arthur	Brun	1772
Christopher	Rand	1779
Isaac	Rand	1779
Jacob	Rand	1779
James	Rand	1779
Jethro	Brun	1769
Jethro	Brun	1772
John Jr.	Gate	1786
John Sr.	Gate	1786
John	Rand	1779
John	Rowa	1759
Joseph	Rand	1779
Joseph	Rowa	1758
Josiah	Rowa	1759
Matthew	Rowa	1759
Michael	Rand	1779
Richard	Rand	1779
Richard Jr.	Rowa	1758
Richard	Rowa	1759
Richman	Rand	1779
Thomas	Bute	1771
Thomas	FWV	1771
Wm	Rand	1779
Wm Jr.	Rand	1779
Wm	Rowa	1758
Wm	Rowa	1759
ROBENSON, Wm	Oran	1755
ROBERSON, Christopher		
	FWV	1771
Daniel	Tyrr	1755
David	Gran	1755
Henry	Tyrr	1755
Henry Sr.	Tyrr	1755
Israel	Gran	1755
John	Dobb	1779
John	Gran	1755
John	Gran	1769
John	Tyrr	1755
Marmaduke	Tyrr	1755
Mary	Tyrr	1755
Matthew	Gran	1755
Nicholas	Gran	1769
Robert Jr.	Gran	1769
ROBERTS, Abraham	Casw	1777
Absalom	Casw	1777
Andrew	Crav	1720
Asil	Casw	1777
Asil Jr.	Casw	1777
Charles	Bert	1757
Charles	Chow	1753
David	Casw	1777
Edmund	Casw	1777
Edward	Bert	1742

ROBERTS, Edward	Gran	1755
Edward	Onsl	1769
Edward	Onsl	1770
George	Cumb	1767
George	Gran	1755
Henry	Crav	1743
James	Casw	1777
James	Chow	1721
James	Dobb	1769
James	Gran	1755
James	Onsl	1750
James	Rand	1779
John	Casw	1777
John	Crav	1743
John	Dobb	1769
John	Dobb	1779
John	Gran	1784
John	Onsl	1750
Jonathan	Gran	1784
Joseph	Crav	1769
Joseph	Gran	1769
Joseph	Gran	1784
Moses	Surr	1772
Owen	Bert	1757
Richard	Gran	1755
Richard	Gran	1769
Samuel	Casw	1777
Samuel	Crav	1769
Sarah	Perq	1740
Shadrack	Gran	1784
Thomas	Bute	1771
Thomas	FWV	1771
Thomas	Gran	1769
Thomas	Gran	1784
Thomas	Perq	1720
Willis	Gran	1784
Wm	Blad	1742
Wm	Curr	1755
Wm	Gran	1769
Wm	Gran	1784
Wm	Rand	1779
Wm Jr.	Rand	1779
Wm Sr.	Rand	1779
Wm	Surr	1772
Wm	Surr	1779
ROBERTSON,		
Christopher	FWV	1771
Israel	Dobb	1769
James	Bute	1771
John	Bert	1757
John	Bute	1771
John	Chow	1721
John	Curr	1715
John	Curr	1755
John	FWV	1771
John	Onsl	1769
John	Oran	1755
John	Perq	1740
Jonathan	Bert	1757
Joseph	Perq	1740
Malachi	Pasq	1769
Matthew	Bute	1771
Matthew s. Daniel		
George Moses	FWV	1771
Robert	Gran	1769

ROBERTSON, Samuel	Casw 1777	ROBINSON, Wm	Rand 1779
Thomas	Gate 1786	ROBISON, Edward	Cumb 1767
Wm	Bert 1757	Edward Jr.	Cumb 1767
Wm	Rand 1779	Henry	Tyrr 1742
Wm	Surr 1771	James	NewH 1762
ROBESON, Benjamin	Rowa 1759	James	NewH 1763
George	Rowa 1759	John	Cumb 1767
Jacob	Rowa 1759	John	NewH 1762
John	NewH 1763	John Jr.	NewH 1762
John	Rowa 1759	John	Surr 1772
Peter	Blad 1781	Thomas Jr.	Blad 1763
Richard	Rowa 1759	Thomas Sr.	Blad 1763
Thomas	Blad 1781	Thomas	Cumb 1767
Wm	Rowa 1759	Wm	Cumb 1767
ROBINS, John	Anso 1763	Wm	Surr 1772
Joseph	Crav 1720	ROBSON, Solomon	Beau 1755
Thomas	NewH 1767	Wm	Beau 1755
ROBINSON, Alexander		ROCH, John	Dobb 1769
	Casw 1777	ROCHELLE, George	Tyrr 1744
Buckner	Gran 1784	ROCKE, Edmund	Blad 1763
Burwell	Bute 1771	RODEFORD, Patrick	Oran 1755
Burwell	FWV 1771	RODGER, Joseph	Gran 1769
Charles	Anso 1763	RODGERS, James	NewH 1763
Christopher	Bute 1771	John	NewH 1762
Christopher	FWV 1771	John	NewH 1763
Cornelius	Anso 1763	Joseph	N.C. 1701
Edward	Casw 1777	Mary	N.C. 1701
Edward Jr.	Casw 1777	Robert	Chow 1753
Humphrey	1743	Stephen	Chow 1753
James	Casw 1777	Thomas	NewH 1763
James	NewH 1755	Wm	Chow 1753
James	NewH 1767	RODIWALT, Samuel	Chow 1717
Jean 200 acres	Perq 1720	RODWELL, John	FWV 1771
John	Beau 1764	RODY, Louis	Edge 1734
John	Bert 1769	ROE, Coleman	Beau 1755
John	Brun 1769	James	Curr 1715
John	Brun 1772	James	NewH 1762
John	Casw 1777	James	NewH 1763
John	Chow 1717	John	Beau 1755
John	Chow 1753	John	Beau 1764
John	Onsl 1770	John	NewH 1762
John	Pitt 1762	John	NewH 1763
John	Pitt 1764	John	NewH 1767
John	Pitt 1775	Joseph	NorH 1762
Jonathan	Bert 1769	Joshua	Beau 1750
Lovereign	Pitt 1764	Joshua	Beau 1755
Mary	Gran 1784	Joshua	Beau 1764
Nathaniel	Gran 1769	Luke	Crav 1769
Nicholas	Gran 1769	Sarah (widow)	Beau 1764
Nicholas	Gran 1784	Thomas Constable	Crav 1769
Solomon	Pitt 1762	ROEBUCK, Benjamin	Casw 1777
Solomon	Pitt 1764	George	Casw 1777
Sovereign	Pitt 1764	ROGERMAN, Thomas	Crav 1744
Terry	Anso 1763	ROGERS, Absalom	Pitt 1762
Thomas	Blad 1743	Absalom	Pitt 1764
Thomas	Bute 1771	Benjamin	Bert 1769
Thomas	Casw 1777	Daniel	Bert 1757
Thomas	Chow 1753	Daniel	Pitt 1764
Thomas	FWV 1771	Emanuel	Chow 1721
Thomas	Gran 1755	Enos	Gate 1786
Wm	Curr 1755	George	Surr 1772
Wm	NewH 1755	Hinson	Dobb 1769
Wm	NewH 1767	Isaac	Pitt 1762
Wm	Pitt 1762	Isaac	Pitt 1764
Wm	Pitt 1764	Jacob	Chow 1753

ROGERS, Jacob	Cumb 1767		ROOK, James	Cart 1742
Jacob	Edge 1742		Thomas	Dobb 1779
James	NewH 1767		ROOKE, Bartholomew	Crav 1769
Jethro	Onsl 1769		ROOKES, Jacob	Bert 1769
Job	NewH 1767		James	Beau 1764
John	Brun 1769		ROOKS, Buckner	Gran 1784
John	Brun 1772		Demsey	Chow 1753
John	Chow 1721		Henry	NewH 1762
John	Chow 1753		Jacob	Chow 1753
John	Crav 1745		Joseph	Chow 1753
John	Edge 1734		Joseph Jr.	Gate 1786
John	Gran 1784		Joseph Sr.	Gate 1786
John	NewH 1762		Thomas	Chow 1753
John	NewH 1767		ROOTS, John	
John	Oran 1755		1m 1f slave	Brun 1769
John	Rand 1779		John	Brun 1772
Joseph	Gran 1784		ROPER, David Jr.	Casw 1777
Joseph	Pitt 1764		David Sr.	Casw 1777
Mary s. Thomas	Bert 1757		James	Casw 1777
Milley	Gate 1786		Thomas	Chow 1721
Minute	Bert 1769		Wm	Casw 1777
Nathaniel	Casw 1777		ROSE, Alexander	Casw 1777
Nathaniel	Cumb 1767		Amey	Gran 1769
Philip	Gate 1786		Frederick	Gran 1784
Richard	Brun 1772		George	Bute 1771
Richard	Chow 1753		George	FWV 1771
Robert	Pitt 1762		John	Bert 1757
Robert	Pitt 1764		John	Crav 1745
Robert	Tyrr 1755		John	Gran 1769
Samuel	Curr 1755		John	Onsl 1770
Stephen	Gran 1784		John	Pasq 1769
Thomas	Bert 1757		Ralph	Pasq 1754
Thomas Jr.	Bert 1757		Richard	Chow 1717
Thomas	Bert 1769		Samuel	Anso 1763
Thomas	Chow 1717		Thomas	Gran 1755
Thomas	Chow 1721		Thomas	Gran 1769
Thomas	NewH 1755		Wm	Bute 1771
Thomas	NewH 1767		Wm	Curr 1715
Thomas	Surr 1771		Wm s. Richard	
Thomas	Surr 1772		& Thomas	FWV 1771
Timothy	Gate 1786		Wm	Gran 1784
Wm	Bert 1757		ROSELAND, Richard	Gran 1784
Wm	Crav 1769		ROSEUR, David	Blad 1763
Wm	Gran 1784		ROSITER, Wm	Gran 1784
Wm	Pitt 1762		ROSS, Abel	Pasq 1754
Wm	Pitt 1764		Abel 1m 2f	
Zilpha	Gate 1786		slaves	Pasq 1769
ROGGONSON, Daniel	Perq 1740		Alexander	NewH 1762
ROLAND, Augustus	Anso 1763		Alexander	NewH 1763
Jesse	Bute 1771		Ann	NewH 1762
John	Anso 1763		Ann	NewH 1763
John	Blad 1781		Ann	NewH 1767
Jordan	Bute 1771		Archibald	NewH 1762
Philip	Pitt 1764		Bennett	Surr 1772
Thomas	Blad 1781		David	Crav 1769
Wm	Bute 1771		Edward	Crav 1769
Wm Jr.	Bute 1771		James	Bute 1771
Wm	N.C. 1701		James Sr.	
ROLLINS, Agnes	Rand 1779		Constable	Bute 1771
ROLLIS, Wm	Surr 1772		James	FWV 1771
ROLOWAND, Jesse	Gran 1755		James Sr.	
RONE, Henry	Brun 1772		Constable	FWV 1771
Henry Jr.	Brun 1772		James	Gran 1755
Peter	Brun 1772		John	Tyrr 1755
RONEY, James	Oran 1755		Laurence	Surr 1772

ROSS, Nathan	Gran	1784	ROWAN, Matthew Esq.		
Reuben	Crav	1769	26b slaves	NewH	1745
Roman	Crav	1720	Matthew	NewH	1755
Solomon	Gate	1786	Robert	NewH	1762
Stephen	NewH	1762	ROWDTEW, Wm	Curr	1755
Wm	NewH	1755	ROWE, Christopher	Onsl	1769
Wm	Surr	1771	Hezekiah s. of		
Wm	Tyrr	1755	Christopher	Onsl	1769
ROSSER, John	FWV	1771	James	NewH	1767
King	FWV	1771	ROWELL, Benjamin	Dobb	1779
Thomas	FWV	1771	John	Dobb	1769
ROTCHELL, John	NewH	1767	John	Dobb	1779
ROTHWELL, Richard	FWV	1771	ROWLAND, Cornelius	Surr	1772
ROTTENBURY, Richard	Anso	1763	Jesse	Bute	1771
Wm	Anso	1763	Jesse & s. Jesse		
ROUGATON, John			Frederick	FWV	1771
Esq.	Tyrr	1755	John	Gran	1755
ROUNDTREE, Francis	Beau	1755	Jordan	Bute	1771
Jesse	Beau	1755	Jordan	FWV	1771
ROUNSEVAL, Benjamin	Brun	1772	Thomas	Gran	1769
David	Brun	1772	Thomas	Gran	1784
Josiah	Brun	1772	Wm	Bute	1771
Uriah	Brun	1772	Wm Jr.	Bute	1771
ROUNTREE, Cader	Dobb	1769	Wm	FWV	1771
Charles	Chow	1753	Wm Jr.	FWV	1771
Charles	Gate	1786	ROWLIN, George	Curr	1755
Fra.	Chow	1717	Robert	Curr	1755
Francis	Chow	1721	ROWTHAN, John s.		
Francis	Pitt	1762	of Robert	Beau	1764
Francis	Pitt	1764	Robert	Beau	1764
Jesse	Pitt	1762	ROYAL, Edmund	Anso	1763
Jesse	Pitt	1764	John	Anso	1763
Jethro	Gran	1755	Joseph	Anso	1763
Livinia	Gate	1786	Samuel	Onsl	1770
Mark	Pitt	1764	Thomas	Anso	1763
Obed	Pitt	1762	Thomas	Crav	1769
Obed	Pitt	1764	Timothy	Curr	1715
Peninah	Gate	1786	Wm	Pasq	1754
Priscilla	Gate	1786	ROYSTER, Wm	Gran	1784
Rachel	Gate	1786	RUDLEY, James	NewH	1767
Tho.	Chow	1717	RUDOLPH, Andrew	Surr	1771
Thomas	Chow	1721	Andrew	Surr	1772
Thomas	Chow	1753	RUFF, Daniel	Dobb	1779
ROUSE, Jesse	Dobb	1769	Keziah	Pitt	1764
Jesse	Dobb	1779	RUFFIN, Ethelred	Dobb	1779
John	Dobb	1769	Samuel	Edge	1743
John	Dobb	1779	RUFKIN, Robert	NorH	1741
John Jr.	Dobb	1779	RUFLIN, Jeffrey	Dobb	1769
Mary	Dobb	1769	Samuel	Dobb	1769
Simon	Dobb	1769	RUGSDALE, John	Cumb	1767
Simon	Dobb	1779	RUNNELDS, Francis	Surr	1771
Solomon	Crav	1769	RUNNELLS, Dudley	Casw	1777
Solomon	Dobb	1769	Wm	Onsl	1770
Thomas	Brun	1772	RUSE, Roger	Casw	1777
ROUSHAM, John	Chow	1753	RUSH, Benjamin	Bute	1771
ROUTLEDGE, Charles	NewH	1763	Benjamin & s.		
Thomas	NewH	1763	Wm	FWV	1771
ROW, John	NewH	1755	Benjamin	NewH	1767
John	Oran	1755	Benjamin	Onsl	1770
ROWAN, John 19m			Benjamin	Rand	1779
11f slaves	Brun	1769	Crawford	Rand	1779
John	Brun	1772	Crawford	Rowa	1759
John	NewH	1762	Isaac	Rand	1779
John	NewH	1763	Jacob	Rand	1779
Matthew	NewH	1743	James	Rand	1779

RUSHELL, Richard		
Esq.	Crav	1720
RUSHIN, Matthew	Chow	1721
RUSKIN, Wm	Anso	1763
RUSS, David	Blad	1763
David	Blad	1781
Hezekiah	Anso	1763
John Jr.	Blad	1763
John Sr.	Blad	1763
John	Blad	1763
John	Brun	1769
John	Brun	1772
Jonadab	Blad	1763
Joseph	Blad	1763
Joseph	Blad	1781
Joseph	Brun	1769
Joseph	Brun	1772
Mary	Blad	1763
Thomas	Anso	1763
Thomas	Blad	1763
Thomas Jr.	Blad	1763
Thomas	Brun	1769
Thomas	Brun	1772
Wm	Blad	1763
RUSSELL, Ed.	Chow	1717
George	Gate	1786
George	Surr	1771
George	Surr	1772
George	Tryo	1776
James	Bute	1771
James	Casw	1777
James	FWV	1771
John	Bute	1771
John	Crav	1745
John & s. Wm	FWV	1771
John	Gran	1755
John	Gran	1784
John	Rowa	1759
John	Surr	1771
John	Tryo	1776
Luke 1m		
1f slave	Crav	1769
Major	Blad	1763
Peter	Gran	1769
Richard Esq.	Crav	1720
Robert	Rowa	1759
Thomas	Crav	1769
Thomas	Curr	1755
Twitty	Bute	1771
Twitty	FWV	1771
Wm	Bute	1771
Wm 1m 1f		
slave	Crav	1769
Wm	Curr	1715
RUST, George	Gran	1784
John	Gran	1784
Nathan	Beau	1755
Samuel	Gran	1784
RUTH, Jacob	Rand	1779
Jacob Bear		
Creek	Rand	1779
James	Rand	1779
Jeremiah	Rowa	1759
Joseph	Rand	1779
Zachariah	Rowa	1759

RUTHERFORD, Griffith		
	Rowa	1759
James	Casw	1777
James	Cumb	1767
John	NewH	1755
John	NewH	1762
John	NewH	1763
Wm	Casw	1777
Wm	Onsl	1769
RUTLAND, Charity	Bert	1769
James	Chow	1717
RUTLEDGE, Thomas	NewH	1752
Wm	Crav	1742
Wm	Rowa	1759
Wm	Surr	1771
RUTTER, Jasper	Dobb	1769
RYALL, Charles	Onsl	1741
Charles	Onsl	1750
Charles	Onsl	1769
Charles	Onsl	1770
David	Bert	1757
Edmund	Anso	1763
John	Anso	1763
John s. of		
Charles	Onsl	1769
Samuel	NewH	1767
RYAN, Benjamin	Gran	1755
Darby	Surr	1771
Edward	Rowa	1759
George	Bert	1769
James	Bert	1769
John	Rand	1779
RYLAND, Philip	Pitt	1762
Philip	Pitt	1763
Philip	Pitt	1775
RYLE, John	Rowa	1759
Joshua	Rowa	1759
RYLEY, Cornelius	Crav	1769
Widow	Rowa	1759
SADLER, Eleanor		
Wm's mother	Chow	1717
Richard	Chow	1753
Wm	Chow	1717
SAGE, Robert	NewH	1762
Robert	Onsl	1769
Robert	Onsl	1770
SAGERS, Joseph	Dobb	1769
SAIL, Cornelius	Surr	1771
SAILEN, Edward Jr.	Pitt	1764
SAILS, Thomas	Gran	1755
SAINSING, Charles	FWV	1771
James	Bute	1771
James	FWV	1771
Peter	Bute	1771
Peter	FWV	1771
SALLER, Michael	Surr	1771
SALLERWHITE, Thomas		
	Gran	1784
SALLISBURY, Joseph	Rand	1779
SALMON, Daniel	Bert	1757
Jonathan	Bute	1771
Jonathan	FWV	1771

SALSER, Benjamin	Dobb 1769	SANDERS, James	Anso 1763
John	Dobb 1769	James	Bert 1744
Wm	Dobb 1769	James (Col.)	Casw 1777
Wm Jr.	Dobb 1769	James	Casw 1777
SALTER, Edward	Beau 1755	James	Cumb 1767
Edward	Pitt 1762	James	Dobb 1769
Edward Jr.	Pitt 1762	James	Edge 1734
Edward	Pitt 1764	James	Gran 1784
Edward Jr.	Pitt 1764	Jesse	Gran 1769
James	Beau 1741	Joel	Cumb 1767
Richard	Blad 1763	John	Bute 1771
Richard	Blad 1781	John	FWV 1771
Robert	Pitt 1762	John	Onsl 1770
Robert	Pitt 1764	John	Pasq 1754
Thomas	Onsl 1769	Joseph	Rand 1779
Thomas	Pitt 1764	Luke	Gran 1784
Wm	Blad 1763	Moses	Onsl 1743
SALYAR, John	Onsl 1769	Nahum	Gran 1769
SALYER, Samuel	Curr 1755	Patrick	Anso 1763
SAMFORD, Samuel Jr.	Dobb 1769	Richard	Casw 1777
SAMOSELL, Lazarus	Bert 1769	Richard	Pasq 1754
SAMOZELL, Joseph	Bert 1769	Richard	Pasq 1769
SAMPLES, Charles	Surr 1771	Richard	Perq 1740
SAMPSON, James	Cumb 1767	Robert	Gran 1755
Jeremiah	Brun 1769	Robert	Pitt 1764
Jeremiah	Brun 1772	Robert	Surr 1771
Jeremiah	NewH 1767	Robert	Surr 1772
Jerry	NewH 1763	Sarah	Bert 1757
John	NewH 1767	Simon	Pitt 1764
Joshua	Pasq 1769	Thomas	Bert 1757
Samuel	Anso 1763	Thomas	Bute 1771
SAMS, James	Surr 1771	Thomas	Dobb 1769
James	Surr 1772	Thomas & bro	
SAMSON, Free	Pasq 1754	Alexander	FWV 1771
John	NewH 1755	Wm	Bute 1771
SAMUEL, Anthony	Casw 1777	Wm Jr.	Casw 1777
Foster	Surr 1771	Wm Sr.	Casw 1777
Foster	Surr 1772	Wm	Chow 1753
George	Casw 1777	Wm	FWV 1771
John	Surr 1772	Wm	Oran 1755
SANDERLIN,		Wm	Perq 1740
Collingsworth	Pasq 1754	SANDERSON, Joseph	Curr 1715
Devotion	Pasq 1769	Joseph	Curr 1755
Ezekiel	Pasq 1769	Richard Esq.	Curr 1715
James	Pasq 1754	Richard	Perq 1720
James	Pasq 1769	Thomas	Curr 1755
John	Pasq 1754	SANDFORD, Robert	Gran 1769
John Jr.	Pasq 1769	Robert	Gran 1784
Maxey	Pasq 1769	SANDFUR, Joseph	Dobb 1769
Robert	Pasq 1754	SANDLAND, John	Bert 1757
SANDERS, Abraham	Perq 1720	John	Gran 1755
Abraham	Perq 1740	John Jr.	Gran 1755
Adam (Cpt.)	Casw 1777	SANDLEY, Jeremiah	Gran 1784
Alexander & bro		SANDLIN, Elizabeth	Bute 1771
Thomas	FWV 1771	Elizabeth	FWV 1771
Ambrose	Pitt 1764	John	Bute 1771
Benjamin	Perq 1720	John & s. Wm	FWV 1771
Benjamin	Perq 1740	SANDY, Jeremiah	Bute 1771
Benjamin	Pitt 1762	Jeremiah	FWV 1771
Benjamin	Tyrr 1741	SANFORD, James	Casw 1777
Daniel	Casw 1777	Jesse	Casw 1777
Daniel	Rowa 1759	Samuel	Beau 1741
Francis	Beau 1755	SAPP, Elijah	Blad 1763
Francis	Chow 1753	Henry	Blad 1763
Isaac	Bert 1757	Jesse	Blad 1763

RUSHELL, Richard			RUTHERFORD, Griffith		
Esq.	Crav	1720		Rowa	1759
RUSHIN, Matthew	Chow	1721	James	Casw	1777
RUSKIN, Wm	Anso	1763	James	Cumb	1767
RUSS, David	Blad	1763	John	NewH	1755
David	Blad	1781	John	NewH	1762
Hezekiah	Anso	1763	John	NewH	1763
John Jr.	Blad	1763	Wm	Casw	1777
John Sr.	Blad	1763	Wm	Onsl	1769
John	Blad	1763	RUTLAND, Charity	Bert	1769
John	Brun	1769	James	Chow	1717
John	Brun	1772	RUTLEDGE, Thomas	NewH	1752
Jonadab	Blad	1763	Wm	Crav	1742
Joseph	Blad	1763	Wm	Rowa	1759
Joseph	Blad	1781	Wm	Surr	1771
Joseph	Brun	1769	RUTTER, Jasper	Dobb	1769
Joseph	Brun	1772	RYALL, Charles	Onsl	1741
Mary	Blad	1763	Charles	Onsl	1750
Thomas	Anso	1763	Charles	Onsl	1769
Thomas	Blad	1763	Charles	Onsl	1770
Thomas Jr.	Blad	1763	David	Bert	1757
Thomas	Brun	1769	Edmund	Anso	1763
Thomas	Brun	1772	John	Anso	1763
Wm	Blad	1763	John s. of		
RUSSELL, Ed.	Chow	1717	Charles	Onsl	1769
George	Gate	1786	Samuel	NewH	1767
George	Surr	1771	RYAN, Benjamin	Gran	1755
George	Surr	1772	Darby	Surr	1771
George	Tryo	1776	Edward	Rowa	1759
James	Bute	1771	George	Bert	1769
James	Casw	1777	James	Bert	1769
James	FWV	1771	John	Rand	1779
John	Bute	1771	RYLAND, Philip	Pitt	1762
John	Crav	1745	Philip	Pitt	1763
John & s. Wm	FWV	1771	Philip	Pitt	1775
John	Gran	1755	RYLE, John	Rowa	1759
John	Gran	1784	Joshua	Rowa	1759
John	Rowa	1759	RYLEY, Cornelius	Crav	1769
John	Surr	1771	Widow	Rowa	1759
John	Tryo	1776			
Luke 1m					
1f slave	Crav	1769	SADLER, Eleanor		
Major	Blad	1763	Wm's mother	Chow	1717
Peter	Gran	1769	Richard	Chow	1753
Richard Esq.	Crav	1720	Wm	Chow	1717
Robert	Rowa	1759	SAGE, Robert	NewH	1762
Thomas	Crav	1769	Robert	Onsl	1769
Thomas	Curr	1755	Robert	Onsl	1770
Twitty	Bute	1771	SAGERS, Joseph	Dobb	1769
Twitty	FWV	1771	SAIL, Cornelius	Surr	1771
Wm	Bute	1771	SAILEN, Edward Jr.	Pitt	1764
Wm 1m 1f			SAILS, Thomas	Gran	1755
slave	Crav	1769	SAINSING, Charles	FWV	1771
Wm	Curr	1715	James	Bute	1771
RUST, George	Gran	1784	James	FWV	1771
John	Gran	1784	Peter	Bute	1771
Nathan	Beau	1755	Peter	FWV	1771
Samuel	Gran	1784	SALLER, Michael	Surr	1771
RUTH, Jacob	Rand	1779	SALLERWHITE, Thomas		
Jacob Bear				Gran	1784
Creek	Rand	1779	SALLISBURY, Joseph	Rand	1779
James	Rand	1779	SALMON, Daniel	Bert	1757
Jeremiah	Rowa	1759	Jonathan	Bute	1771
Joseph	Rand	1779	Jonathan	FWV	1771
Zachariah	Rowa	1759			

SALSER, Benjamin	Dobb	1769	SANDERS, James	Anso	1763
John	Dobb	1769	James	Bert	1744
Wm	Dobb	1769	James (Col.)	Casw	1777
Wm Jr.	Dobb	1769	James	Casw	1777
SALTER, Edward	Beau	1755	James	Cumb	1767
Edward	Pitt	1762	James	Dobb	1769
Edward Jr.	Pitt	1762	James	Edge	1734
Edward	Pitt	1764	James	Gran	1784
Edward Jr.	Pitt	1764	Jesse	Gran	1769
James	Beau	1741	Joel	Cumb	1767
Richard	Blad	1763	John	Bute	1771
Richard	Blad	1781	John	FWV	1771
Robert	Pitt	1762	John	Onsl	1770
Robert	Pitt	1764	John	Pasq	1754
Thomas	Onsl	1769	Joseph	Rand	1779
Thomas	Pitt	1764	Luke	Gran	1784
Wm	Blad	1763	Moses	Onsl	1743
SALYAR, John	Onsl	1769	Nahum	Gran	1769
SALYER, Samuel	Curr	1755	Patrick	Anso	1763
SAMFORD, Samuel Jr.	Dobb	1769	Richard	Casw	1777
SAMOSELL, Lazarus	Bert	1769	Richard	Pasq	1754
SAMOZELL, Joseph	Bert	1769	Richard	Pasq	1769
SAMPLES, Charles	Surr	1771	Richard	Perq	1740
SAMPSON, James	Cumb	1767	Robert	Gran	1755
Jeremiah	Brun	1769	Robert	Pitt	1764
Jeremiah	Brun	1772	Robert	Surr	1771
Jeremiah	NewH	1767	Robert	Surr	1772
Jerry	NewH	1763	Sarah	Bert	1757
John	NewH	1767	Simon	Pitt	1764
Joshua	Pasq	1769	Thomas	Bert	1757
Samuel	Anso	1763	Thomas	Bute	1771
SAMS, James	Surr	1771	Thomas	Dobb	1769
James	Surr	1772	Thomas & bro		
SAMSON, Free	Pasq	1754	Alexander	FWV	1771
John	NewH	1755	Wm	Bute	1771
SAMUEL, Anthony	Casw	1777	Wm Jr.	Casw	1777
Foster	Surr	1771	Wm Sr.	Casw	1777
Foster	Surr	1772	Wm	Chow	1753
George	Casw	1777	Wm	FWV	1771
John	Surr	1772	Wm	Oran	1755
SANDERLIN,			Wm	Perq	1740
Collingsworth	Pasq	1754	SANDERSON, Joseph	Curr	1715
Devotion	Pasq	1769	Joseph	Curr	1755
Ezekiel	Pasq	1769	Richard Esq.	Curr	1715
James	Pasq	1754	Richard	Perq	1720
James	Pasq	1769	Thomas	Curr	1755
John	Pasq	1754	SANDFORD, Robert	Gran	1769
John Jr.	Pasq	1769	Robert	Gran	1784
Maxey	Pasq	1769	SANDFUR, Joseph	Dobb	1769
Robert	Pasq	1754	SANDLAND, John	Bert	1757
SANDERS, Abraham	Perq	1720	John	Gran	1755
Abraham	Perq	1740	John Jr.	Gran	1755
Adam (Cpt.)	Casw	1777	SANDLEY, Jeremiah	Gran	1784
Alexander & bro			SANDLIN, Elizabeth	Bute	1771
Thomas	FWV	1771	Elizabeth	FWV	1771
Ambrose	Pitt	1764	John	Bute	1771
Benjamin	Perq	1720	John & s. Wm	FWV	1771
Benjamin	Perq	1740	SANDY, Jeremiah	Bute	1771
Benjamin	Pitt	1762	Jeremiah	FWV	1771
Benjamin	Tyrr	1741	SANFORD, James	Casw	1777
Daniel	Casw	1777	Jesse	Casw	1777
Daniel	Rowa	1759	Samuel	Beau	1741
Francis	Beau	1755	SAPP, Elijah	Blad	1763
Francis	Chow	1753	Henry	Blad	1763
Isaac	Bert	1757	Jesse	Blad	1763

SAPP, John	Blad	1763	SAUNDERS, Joseph	Onsl	1769
SARCENET, Joshua	Crav	1745	Joshua	Bert	1769
SARGENT, James	Casw	1777	Morgan	Crav	1769
Joseph	Casw	1777	Moses	Dobb	1769
Richard	Dobb	1769	Richard	Dobb	1769
Stephen	Casw	1777	Robert	Dobb	1769
Thomas	Casw	1777	Sarah	Gate	1786
Wm	Casw	1777	Thomas	Blad	1763
Wm	Dobb	1769	Wm	NewH	1767
Wm	Edge	1742	SAUNDERSON, Benjamin		
Wm	Oran	1755		Crav	1769
SARLS, Wm	Dobb	1769	Jonathan	Crav	1769
SARRAT, Samuel	Oran	1755	Joseph 1m		
SARSNUTT, Joseph	Crav	1743	3f slaves	Crav	1769
Joshua	Crav	1745	Wm	Crav	1769
Richard	John	1750	SAVAGE, Andrew	Dobb	1769
SARTEN, Widow	Bute	1771	Benjamin	Bute	1771
Widow	FWV	1771	Benjamin	FWV	1771
SARTINOT, Thomas	Gran	1784	Francis	Brun	1772
SARVER, Andrew	NorH	1762	George	Bert	1757
Samuel	NorH	1762	John	Bert	1757
Thomas	NorH	1762	Joshua	NorH	1762
SASSER, James	Crav	1769	Randolph	Bute	1771
Stephen	Dobb	1779	Randolph	FWV	1771
Thomas	Crav	1741	Robert	Crav	1744
Wm	Dobb	1779	Thomas	Bert	1757
Wm	Edge	1743	Thomas	Rand	1779
SATCHWEL, Rebecca	Beau	1755	SAVEL, Daniel	Curr	1715
SATTERFIELD, Bidwell			SAVELY, Marmaduke	Curr	1755
	Casw	1777	SAWRY, Wm	Dobb	1769
James	Casw	1777	SAWYERS, Alexander	Pasq	1769
James	Gran	1784	Aliz.	Pasq	1754
James	Oran	1755	Benjamin	Pasq	1769
John	Casw	1777	Caleb	Pasq	1754
John Jr.	Casw	1777	Caleb	Pasq	1769
John Jr.	Oran	1755	Caleb Jr.	Pasq	1769
John Sr.	Oran	1755	Charles	Pasq	1754
SATTERWHITE, John	Gran	1769	Charles	Pasq	1769
Joseph	Hyde	1744	Climond	Pasq	1769
Michael	Gran	1769	Coston	Pasq	1769
Michael	Gran	1784	David	Pasq	1769
Thomas	Gran	1784	Dempsey 2m		
SAUBER, Christian	Surr	1772	1f slave	Pasq	1769
SAUL, Benjamin	NorH	1762	Elisha	Pasq	1769
Edward	NewH	1762	Evan	Pasq	1769
Edward	NewH	1763	Ezekiel	Pasq	1754
Edward	NewH	1767	Isaac	Pasq	1754
John	Cumb	1767	James Jr.	Pasq	1769
Lewis	Cumb	1767	Job	Pasq	1769
Wm	Gran	1755	Jobe	Pasq	1769
SAULS, James	Dobb	1779	Joel	Pasq	1769
Ramon	Dobb	1779	John	Pasq	1754
SAUNDERLIN, John	Bert	1769	John 1m 3f		
SAUNDERS, Abraham	Gate	1786	slaves	Pasq	1769
Benjamin	Gate	1786	Jonathan	Pasq	1769
Charity	Gate	1786	Joseph	Pasq	1754
Charles	Chow	1753	Joseph 1f		
Charles	Crav	1769	slave	Pasq	1769
Henry	Gate	1786	Joshua	Pasq	1754
Jesse	Gate	1786	Joshua	Pasq	1769
John	Crav	1769	Lemuel	Pasq	1769
John Blair's			Lewis	Pasq	1769
Over	Crav	1769	Margaret 2m		
John	Gate	1786	2f slave	Pasq	1769
Joseph	Gate	1786	Nathaniel	NewH	1755

SAWYERS, Richard	Pasq	1754	SCOTT, Daniel	Rand	1779
Richard s. of			James	Casw	1777
Thomas	Pasq	1754	James	Chow	1753
Robert	Pasq	1754	James	Gate	1786
Silvanus 2m			James	Oran	1755
1f slave	Pasq	1769	James	Perq	1740
Solomon	Pasq	1754	James	Rowa	1759
Solomon	Pasq	1769	John	Bute	1771
Stephen 1f slave	Pasq	1769	John	Casw	1777
Thomas	Pasq	1754	John	FWV	1771
Thomas 1m			John	Gran	1784
1f slave	Pasq	1769	John s. of Wm	Onsl	1769
Truman	Pasq	1769	John	Rand	1779
Wm s. of Joseph	Pasq	1769	John	Roan	1720
SAYER, Robert	Onsl	1769	John	Rowa	1759
Robert	Onsl	1770	Joseph	Bert	1757
SAYLOR, Michael	Surr	1771	Joseph Sr.	Pasq	1754
Michael	Surr	1772	Joseph Jr.	Pasq	1769
SCARBROUGH, Austin	Curr	1755	Joseph Sr.	Pasq	1769
Austin	Pasq	1754	Joshua	Pasq	1754
Benjamin	Dobb	1769	Levan	Onsl	1769
Edward	Bute	1771	Levan	Onsl	1770
Edward s. Peter	FWV	1771	Mary 1f slave	Pasq	1769
Edward	Gran	1755	Matthew	Rand	1779
Frederick	Dobb	1779	Richard	NewH	1741
George	Curr	1715	Richard	NewH	1755
George	Curr	1755	Samuel 7m slaves	Pasq	1769
John Jr.	Curr	1755	Samuel Jr.	Pasq	1769
John Sr.	Curr	1755	Stephen		
John	Pasq	1754	2f slaves	Pasq	1769
John Jr.	Pasq	1754	Thomas	Dobb	1769
John	Pasq	1769	Wm	Curr	1715
Macrora		1743	Wm	Curr	1755
Nathaniel	Crav	1769	Wm	Onsl	1769
Wm	Pitt	1764	Wm	Onsl	1770
SCARF, Edward	Pasq	1754	SCOTTAN, Thomas	Bert	1769
James	Pasq	1754	SCOTTIN, John	Rand	1779
John	Pasq	1754	SCREECH, Joseph	Curr	1715
Jonathan	Pasq	1754	SCREWS, Benjamin	Onsl	1769
SCARLETT, John	Rand	1779	SCRITCHFIELD, John	Surr	1771
SCHAFF, Jeremiah	Surr	1771	Nathaniel	Surr	1771
SCHAUB, Jonathan	Surr	1771	Nathaniel	Surr	1772
SCHAUP, Johannes	Surr	1772	Samuel	Surr	1771
SCHAUS, Philip	Surr	1771	Samuel	Surr	1772
SCHEMEL, John	Surr	1772	SCRIVIN, Thomas	Blad	1781
SCHMIDT, Christopher			SCURRY, Jesse	Gran	1784
	Surr	1772	SEABREE, Wm	Dobb	1769
SCHNERT, Peter Sr.	Surr	1771	SEAGRAVE, John	FWV	1771
Peter	Surr	1772	Wm	Bute	1771
SCHOOL, Russ	Blad	1763	Wm	FWV	1771
SCHORE, Henry	Surr	1771	SEAGRAVES, Wm	NorH	1762
Henry	Surr	1772	SEAL, Charles	Cumb	1755
SCHULTZ, George	Surr	1771	SEALES, Wm	Bert	1769
George	Surr	1772	SEALS, Charles	Cumb	1767
SCIBNA, Dorothy	Gran	1784	Thomas	Cumb	1767
SCLATER, John	Oran	1755	Wm	Bert	1757
SCOGGIN, Nathan	Casw	1777	Wm	Cumb	1767
SCOTTIN, Earl	Rand	1779	SEARCY, Bartlett	Gran	1784
John	Rand	1779	Berthal	Gran	1769
SCOLLAY, Elizabeth	Bert	1757	John Jr.	Gran	1769
SCOTT, Aaron	Bert	1757	John Sr.	Gran	1769
Alexander			Reuben	Gran	1769
1m 1f slave	Pasq	1769	Reuben	Gran	1784
Caleb	Pasq	1754	Richard	Gran	1784
Daniel	Gran	1784	Samuel	Gran	1784

SEARCY, Wm	Gran 1784		SENSING, James	Gran 1755
SEARS, Ebron	Gate 1786		SEOULS, Joseph	NorH 1762
John	Gran 1784		SERIVAN, Isaac	Dobb 1769
Joseph	Curr 1755		SERRY, Henry	NorH 1762
Wm	Gran 1784		SERTAIN, Josiah	Surr 1772
SEARSEY, Wm	Rand 1779		SESEY, Wm	Oran 1755
SEARSY, Bartlett s.			SESHORE, Jarvis	Pasq 1754
of John	Gran 1755		SESSION, John	Pitt 1764
John	Gran 1755		Walter	Pitt 1762
John Jr.	Gran 1755		Walter	Pitt 1764
Reuben	Gran 1755		SESSIONS, Cullen	Bert 1757
Richard s.			Culmer	Bert 1757
of John	Gran 1755		John	Bert 1757
Timothy s.			John	Chow 1717
of John	Gran 1755		John	Chow 1721
SEAVERN, James	Crav 1769		Joseph	Dobb 1779
SEAY, James	Bert 1755		Nicholas	
James	Crav 1769		700 acres	Chow 1721
Matthew	Bert 1757		Richard	Dobb 1779
SEBURN, John	Pasq 1754		Samuel	Cumb 1767
SECREST, Jacob	Rowa 1759		Thomas	Brun 1769
SEDBY, Williamson	NorH 1762		Thomas	Brun 1772
SEDDBY, Billiason	NorH 1762		Walter	Beau 1755
James	NorH 1762		Waltson	Beau 1755
SEEGAR, Christopher	Bert 1757		SESSONS, Absalom s.	
John	Bert 1757		of John	Dobb 1769
SEEGUL, Christopher	Bert 1757		John	Dobb 1769
SEEMORE, Thomas	Cumb 1755		SEVILLE, John	Pasq 1769
SEEMS, Henry	Roan 1720		Wm	Crav 1769
Joseph	Roan 1720		SEVRIN, Job	Bert 1769
Robert	Roan 1720		SEWAL, Alexander	Pitt 1764
SEERS, James			SEWARD, Mary	Chow 1753
2m 1f slaves	Crav 1769		SEWELL, Joseph	Bute 1771
SEEVI, Hugh	Rand 1779		Joseph	FWV 1771
SEGIER, John	Bert 1769		SEXTON, Jeremiah	Pasq 1754
SEGLER, Henry	Rand 1779		Jeremiah	Pasq 1769
SEIZ, Michael	Surr 1771		John	Beau 1755
Michael	Surr 1772		Josiah	Pasq 1754
SELF, Job	Bute 1771		Wm	Pasq 1754
Job	FWV 1771		Wm	Pasq 1769
Willoughby	FWV 1771		SEYERS, Henry	NewH 1762
SELLER, Jacob s.			SEYMORE, Adam	Pasq 1769
of Judith	Beau 1755		Jarvis	Pasq 1769
SELLERS, Benjamin	Brun 1769		John Jr.	Pasq 1754
Benjamin	Brun 1772		John Sr.	Pasq 1754
Elisha	Brun 1769		SEYMOUR, Benjamin	Perq 1720
Elisha	Brun 1772		Richard Jr.	
Elisha	Pitt 1764		170 acres	Perq 1720
George	Bert 1757		SEYNARD, Jonathan	Casw 1777
Jaconias	Brun 1769		SHABROUGH, Jonathan	Pasq 1769
Jaconias	Brun 1772		SHACKLEFORD, Francis	
James	Brun 1769			Casw 1777
James	Brun 1772		Francis	Onsl 1769
Joel	Brun 1769		Francis	Onsl 1770
Joes	Brun 1772		James	Crav 1720
John	Crav 1742		John	Casw 1777
Martha	Brun 1772		John	Crav 1720
Matthew	Brun 1769		John	Onsl 1769
Matthew	Brun 1772		John	Onsl 1770
Matthew	Chow 1721		Ned	Onsl 1769
Michael	Surr 1771		Willoughby	Dobb 1779
Simon	Brun 1769		Wm	Onsl 1769
Simon	Brun 1772		SHADDER, James	Casw 1777
Thomas	Oran 1755		SHADDOCK, Benjamin	Rand 1779
SEMORE, Edward	Pitt 1764		Henry	Blad 1742

SHADDOCK, James	Dobb	1779	SHEARIN, John Jr.	FWV	1771
SHAKELFORD, Willoughby			John Sr.	FWV	1771
	Dobb	1769	John	Gran	1755
Willoughby	Dobb	1779	Joseph	Bute	1771
SHALLER, John	Bert	1757	Joseph s. Henry		
John	Chow	1717	& Joseph	FWV	1771
Wm	Bert	1757	Wm	Bute	1771
SHALLONGER, James	Chow	1753	Wm	FWV	1771
SHALLOWELL, Ben	Rowa	1759	Wm s. of John	Gran	1755
John	Rowa	1759	SHEARING, Charles	Gran	1769
SHANEWOLF, Charles	Crav	1769	SHEARMAN, John	Gran	1755
SHANKLE, George	Anso	1763	SHEARS, John	Gran	1769
SHANNAGER, Peter	Cumb	1767	Wm	Gran	1769
SHANNON, Ann			SHECKAN, John	Bert	1769
(widow)	Pitt	1764	SHEETS, Jacob Esq.	Crav	1720
John	Pitt	1762	Jacob	Crav	1741
Michael	Beau	1755	SHEETZ, Caton	Rand	1779
Wm	Rowa	1759	SHEFFIELD, John	Cumb	1767
SHANNONHOUSE, James	Pasq	1769	Robert	Bute	1771
SHARBER, Thomas	Perq	1740	Robert s.		
SHARBO, Thomas	Perq	1740	Zachariah	FWV	1771
SHALLIANS, Moses	Bert	1757	Wm	Cumb	1767
SHARP, Edward	Rand	1779	SHEILS, Thomas	Oran	1755
Richard	Dobb	1769	SHEITS, Martin	Rand	1779
Thomas	Oran	1755	SHELL, Stephen	Bute	1771
Wm	Chow	1717	Stephen Jr.	Bute	1771
SHARPLEY, John	Crav	1769	Stephen	FWV	1771
SHARROD, Benjamin	Dobb	1779	Stephen Jr.	FWV	1771
Benjamin	Onsl	1770	SHELLE, Philip	Surr	1771
Capt.	FWV	1771	Philip	Surr	1772
John	Dobb	1779	SHELLER, John	Surr	1772
John	NorH	1742	SHELTON, David Esq.	Casw	1777
Jonathan	Perq	1740	John	Casw	1777
Robert	Chow	1717	John	Surr	1771
Robert	Dobb	1779	John	Surr	1772
Robert	FWV	1771	Ralph	Surr	1771
Robert	Tyrr	1755	Ralph	Surr	1772
Thomas			Stephen	Casw	1777
Constable	FWV	1771	SHENGLETTO, Hannah	Dobb	1769
SHAVER, Dorothy	Blad	1763	Spyer s. of		
Peter	Blad	1763	Hannah	Dobb	1769
SHAW, Amos	Casw	1777	SHENNEL, John	Surr	1772
Archibald	Blad	1763	SHEPHERD, Andrew		
Catherine	Cumb	1767	Esq.	Cumb	1767
Collin	Cumb	1767	David	Crav	1720
Daniel	Blad	1763	John	Crav	1720
Daniel	Cumb	1767	John	Cumb	1767
Duncan	Cumb	1755	John	Gate	1786
Duncan	Cumb	1767	Joseph	Pasq	1769
Duske	Cumb	1755	Martha	Cumb	1767
Gabriel	Gran	1784	Mary	Blad	1781
John	Blad	1763	Stephen	Blad	1763
Mathias	Beau	1755	Thomas	NorH	1762
Neal	Blad	1742	SHEPPARD, Abraham		
Neal	Blad	1763	Sr.	Dobb	1769
Neal	Blad	1781	Abram	Dobb	1779
Neil	Cumb	1767	Benjamin s. of		
Ralph	Casw	1777	Abraham	Dobb	1769
Samuel	Surr	1771	Benjamin	Dobb	1779
Samuel	Surr	1772	Benjamin	Onsl	1769
SHEAR, Christian	Rand	1779	Benjamin	Onsl	1770
SHEARER, Samuel	Perq	1720	Charles	Rand	1779
Wm	Perq	1740	David	Cart	1742
SHEARIN, John Jr.	Bute	1771	George	Onsl	1769
John Sr.	Bute	1771	George	Onsl	1770

SHEPPARD, Jacob	Anso 1763	SHIPPER, Barnaba	Anso 1763
Jacob 1m		Benjamin	Anso 1763
2f slaves	Crav 1769	George	Anso 1763
Jacob	Dobb 1769	SHIRLEY, David	Dobb 1769
Jacob	Rand 1779	David	Dobb 1779
James	Anso 1763	Michael	Dobb 1769
James	Dobb 1769	Michael	Dobb 1779
James	Surr 1771	SHIRLOE, Daniel	Onsl 1741
John	Crav 1720	SHIVERS, John	Chow 1717
John	Dobb 1779	Wm	Bert 1757
John	Gran 1769	SHOELY, David	Gran 1755
John	NorH 1762	SHOEMAKER, Francis	Oran 1755
John Jr.	Onsl 1769	Josiah	Casw 1777
John Sr.	Onsl 1769	SHOLAR, Thomas	Bert 1757
John Jr.	Onsl 1770	SHOLLAR, John	Bert 1769
John Sr.	Onsl 1770	Thomas	Bert 1769
John	Rand 1779	Wm	Bert 1769
Peter	Rand 1779	SHOOTS, Jacob	Crav 1720
Smith	Onsl 1769	SHORES, Reuben	Surr 1771
Smith	Onsl 1770	Reuben	Surr 1772
Stephen	Chow 1753	Wm	Surr 1771
Thomas	NorH 1762	SHORT, Aaron	Rowa 1759
Thomas	Onsl 1743	Daniel	Anso 1763
Wm	Dobb 1779	Jacob	Crav 1720
Wm	Onsl 1770	James	Anso 1763
Wm	Surr 1771	James	Surr 1771
Wm	Surr 1772	James	Surr 1772
SHERED, Benjamin s.		John	Bute 1771
of John	Dobb 1769	John	FWV 1771
John	Dobb 1769	John	NorH 1762
John s. of John	Dobb 1769	Moses	Rowa 1759
SHERMAN, John	Gran 1769	Wm	NorH 1762
John	Gran 1784	SHOULDER, John	Bert 1757
SHERMER, Peter	Surr 1771	Wm Jr.	Bert 1757
Peter	Surr 1772	SHOUS, Henry	Surr 1772
SHERRARD, Aaron	Gran 1755	SHUALDEN, Charles	Gran 1769
SHERREL, Philus	Anso 1762	SHUTE, Philip	Beau 1755
Wm	Anso 1763	SHY, John	Casw 1777
SHERROD, Robert	Dobb 1769	SIBORN, Wm	Pasq 1754
Robert	NorH 1762	SICKES, Abel	Curr 1755
Simon	Dobb 1769	SIDES, Anthony	Rowa 1759
SHERWOOD, Alex.	Chow 1717	SIDWELL, John	Oran 1755
David 200 acres	Perq 1720	Richard	Oran 1755
David	Perq 1740	SIGLER, Henry	Rand 1779
Jonathan	Perq 1740	SIGLEY, Aaron	Beau 1755
Robert	Chow 1717	Aaron	Onsl 1770
SHIBOW, Lewis	NewH 1763	Curtis	Beau 1755
SHIELDS, Wm	Pitt 1762	SIKELS, Wm	NorH 1762
SHILES, John	Onsl 1770	SIKES, Asa	Pasq 1769
SHIN, Cornelius	Anso 1763	Caleb	Curr 1755
Matthew	Rowa 1759	James	Pasq 1769
Samuel	Rowa 1759	John	NewH 1763
Samuel	Surr 1772	John	NewH 1767
Silas	Rowa 1759	John	Pasq 1754
SHINE, Daniel		Joshua	NewH 1767
2m 2f slaves	Crav 1769	Josiah	NewH 1767
Thomas	Crav 1769	Maximillian	Pasq 1769
SHINES, James s.		Thomas	NorH 1762
of John	Dobb 1769	Wm	Pasq 1769
John	Dobb 1769	SILVERS, Patrick	Rowa 1759
SHINGLETON, Wm	Beau 1755	Wm	Rowa 1759
Wm	Pitt 1762	SILVESTER, Augustine	
Wm	Pitt 1764		Beau 1755
SHIP, Willis	Crav 1769	Richard	Hyde 1743
SHIPMAN, Daniel	Blad 1763	Richard	1743

SILVESTER, Wm		1743	SIMMS, Edward	Bute	1771
SILVEY, Edward	Gran	1769	Edward	FWV	1771
SIMMONDS, Isaac	Brun	1769	Henry	Blad	1742
Isaac	Brun	1772	Henry 200 acres	Chow	1721
John	Brun	1769	Joseph	Chow	1721
John	Brun	1772	Joseph	Edge	1742
SIMMONS, Abraham	Casw	1777	Robert Constable	Chow	1721
Abraham	Crav	1769	Robert	Dobb	1779
Andrew	Beau	1742	Shadrack	Dobb	1779
Argyle	Chow	1753	SIMON, Jefferson	Chow	1721
Asa	NewH	1767	John	Pasq	1769
Bullock	Curr	1742	Thomas	Beau	1764
Edward	Onsl	1770	Wm	Beau	1764
Elizabeth	Perq	1720	SIMONS, Edward	Onsl	1769
George	Onsl	1770	Henry Jr.	Onsl	1769
Henry	Blad	1742	Henry Sr.	Onsl	1769
Henry 5w 32b	NewH	1744	Wm	Tyrr	1755
Henry Jr.	Onsl	1769	SIMONTON, Wm	Rowa	1759
Henry Sr.	Onsl	1769	SIMPKINS, Joseph	Crav	1769
Henry Jr.	Onsl	1770	Timothy	Crav	1769
Henry Sr.	Onsl	1770	SIMPSON, Abraham	Onsl	1769
Hillary	Curr	1755	Abraham	Onsl	1770
Isaac	Crav	1769	Benjamin	Chow	1717
Isaac	NewH	1762	Benjamin	Perq	1740
Isaac Jr.	NewH	1763	Edward	Onsl	1769
Isaac Sr.	NewH	1763	Edward	Onsl	1770
Isaac	Oran	1755	Gilbert	Anso	1763
James	Onsl	1769	Joab s. of		
James Jr.	Onsl	1770	Ruth	Pasq	1769
Jesse	Dobb	1779	John	Beau	1755
John	Anso	1763	John	Cart	1744
John	Beau	1755	John	Chow	1753
John	Bute	1771	John	Crav	1720
John	Chow	1753	John	NewH	1752
John 2m 3f			John	NewH	1755
slaves	Crav	1769	John	NewH	1762
John	Curr	1755	John	NewH	1763
John 9w 1b			John	NewH	1767
slaves	Edge	1743	John	Onsl	1769
John	FWV	1771	John	Onsl	1770
John	Gran	1755	John	Perq	1720
John	Gran	1769	John	Pitt	1762
John	Gran	1784	John	Pitt	1764
John	NewH	1755	John	Pitt	1775
John	NewH	1762	John	Surr	1771
John	NewH	1763	John	Surr	1772
John	Rand	1779	Richard (Cpt.)	Casw	1777
Melborn	Onsl	1769	Richard	Casw	1777
Melborn	Onsl	1770	Richard	Oran	1755
Robert	Curr	1755	Richard	Rowa	1759
Samuel	Curr	1715	Robert	Crav	1720
Samuel	Curr	1742	Robert	Onsl	1770
Samuel	Curr	1755	Robert 2m		
Thomas	Casw	1777	1f slave	Pasq	1769
Thomas	Crav	1769	Robert s. of Wm	Pasq	1769
Thomas	Curr	1715	Samuel	Anso	1763
Thomas	Curr	1755	Thomas	Anso	1763
Wm	Bute	1771	Thomas Jr.	Onsl	1769
Wm	FWV	1771	Thomas Sr.	Onsl	1769
Wm Sr.	Gran	1755	Thomas Jr.	Onsl	1770
Wm	Gran	1755	Thomas Sr.	Onsl	1770
Wm	Gran	1769	Wm 2m 3f slaves	Brun	1769
Wm	Perq	1740	Wm Jr.	Brun	1772
SIMMS, Bartain	Dobb	1769	Wm Sr.	Brun	1772
Brittain	Dobb	1779	Wm	NewH	1763

SIMPSON, Wm	Pasq 1754	SKETTLETHORPE, Thomas	
Wm	Pasq 1769		Chow 1753
SIMS, Elisha	Gran 1769	SKIBBOE, Henry	NewH 1750
Elisha	Gran 1784	Henry	NewH 1755
James Jr.	Blad 1763	Henry	Onsl 1741
James Sr.	Blad 1763	Henry	Onsl 1750
Leonard	Gran 1769	Wm	NewH 1745
Leonard	Gran 1784	SKIDMORE, Elisha	Rowa 1759
Sherwood	Gran 1769	Henry	Rowa 1759
Sherwood Jr.	Gran 1784	SKILES, Benjamin	Bert 1757
Sherwood Sr.	Gran 1784	Benjamin	Bert 1769
Thomas	Gran 1784	John	Bert 1769
Wm	Gran 1784	Nicholas	Bert 1757
SIMSON, James	Curr 1755	SKINNER, Anne	Chow 1753
Sarah	Curr 1755	Benjamin	Dobb 1769
Thomas	Blad 1763	James	Gate 1786
Walter	NewH 1755	James	Perq 1740
Wm	Curr 1755	John	Bert 1757
SINCLAIR, David	FWV 1771	John	Bert 1769
Peter	Bute 1771	John s.	
Peter	FWV 1771	of John	Chow 1753
Samuel	Hyde 1743	John	Chow 1753
SINES, John Sr.	Rand 1779	Louis	Perq 1720
SINGER, Wm	Onsl 1769	Mills	Gate 1786
SINGLETARRY, Benjamin		Richard Sr.	Perq 1720
	Blad 1763	Richard Jr.	Perq 1740
Ithamer	Blad 1763	Richard Sr.	Perq 1740
John	Blad 1763	Samuel	Perq 1740
Richard	Blad 1763	Wm	Dobb 1769
Wm	Blad 1763	Wm	NorH 1762
SINGLETERRY, James	Blad 1781	SKIPPER, Barnaba	Anso 1763
James Jr.	Blad 1781	Benjamin	Anso 1763
James Sr.	Blad 1781	Clemonds	Brun 1772
John	Blad 1781	Fred	Blad 1763
Joseph	Blad 1781	George Sr.	Anso 1763
Richard Jr.	Blad 1781	George 160 acres	Chow 1721
Thomas	Blad 1781	Hardy	Blad 1763
Wm	Blad 1781	Jacob	Dobb 1779
SINGLETON, James	Chow 1717	James	Roan 1720
James	Crav 1769	Joseph	Blad 1763
John	Crav 1769	Joseph	Onsl 1769
SINGLEY, Aaron	Onsl 1769	Moses	Brun 1772
Curtis	Onsl 1769	Robert	Chow 1721
SINK, Jacob	Rowa 1759	Thomas	Roan 1720
SINQUA, Charles	Curr 1715	SKOYLES, Wm	Chow 1717
SINTON, Robert	Bert 1769	SKUTT, Edward	Bert 1757
SISCO, John	Anso 1763	SLADE, Henry	Curr 1715
SISSIL, Wm	Cumb 1755	Henry Jr.	N.C. 1701
SISSON, Martin 2m		Henry	Tyrr 1755
slaves	Crav 1769	John	Beau 1755
Wm	Gran 1755	Joseph	Beau 1755
SITGRAVES, Thomas	Crav 1769	Joseph 4w 1b	
SITTERSON, James &		slaves	John 1752
s. James	Perq 1740	Samuel	Beau 1741
SIZEMORE, Samuel	Chow 1721	Samuel 6m	
SKEEN., Alexander	Dobb 1769	1f slaves	Crav 1769
Jacob	Rand 1779	Thomas Jr.	Casw 1777
Jonathan	Casw 1777	Thomas Sr.	Casw 1777
Peter	Casw 1777	SLATTINGS, Josiah	Bert 1769
SKEETO, Edward	Chow 1753	SLATTON, George	Surr 1772
SKEGGS, Aaron	Oran 1755	John	Surr 1771
SKELTON, John	Edge 1743	John	Surr 1772
SKETTLETHORPE, Joseph		Major	Surr 1772
	Chow 1717	SLAUGHTER, Alexander	
Joseph 100 acres	Chow 1721		Bert 1757

SLAUGHTER, Benjamin	Beau	1755
Jacob	Gran	1769
Jacob	Gran	1784
Jacob Jr.	Gran	1784
James	Bert	1769
John	Beau	1745
John	Beau	1755
John Jr.	Beau	1755
John	Pitt	1762
John Jr.	Pitt	1762
John Jr.	Pitt	1764
John Sr.	Pitt	1764
Luke	Bert	1742
Luke	NewH	1767
Mandred	NorH	1762
Mary	Bert	1769
Owen	Anso	1763
Owen	Bert	1757
Sampson	Pitt	1775
Thomas	Bert	1769
Wm	Pitt	1775
SLAVIN, John	Gate	1786
SLEDGE, Daniel	Bute	1771
Daniel s. James		
& Arthur	FWV	1771
SLEVIN, Wm	Rowa	1759
SLOAN, Allen	NewH	1755
Allen	NewH	1762
Allen	NewH	1763
Allen	NewH	1767
George	Rowa	1759
Henry & s.		
James	Rowa	1759
Wm	Onsl	1770
SLOCUM, Ezekiel	Dobb	1779
J. C.	Crav	1720
John Esq.	Crav	1720
John	Crav	1720
John	Crav	1741
John	Dobb	1769
Joseph	Crav	1720
Joseph	Dobb	1779
SLUSY, Joseph	Gran	1784
SMALL, David	Gate	1786
Dick	Blad	1763
Dick	Pasq	1769
James	Casw	1777
James	Gate	1786
John	Blad	1763
John	Pasq	1769
Joseph	Chow	1753
Joshua	Chow	1753
Joshua	Gate	1786
Obadiah	Pasq	1769
Thomas	Perq	1740
SMALLAGE, John	Onsl	1769
John	Onsl	1770
SMALLEY, Joshua	Cumb	1767
Matthew	Cumb	1767
SMALLWOOD, Elijah	Surr	1771
Ignatius		1743
Mary	Gran	1769
SMART, John	Bute	1771
John	FWV	1771
John	Gran	1755

SMART, Joseph	Rand	1779
Joseph	Surr	1771
Matthew	FWV	1771
Peter	Bute	1771
Peter	FWV	1771
Peter	Gran	1755
SMAW, Henry	Bert	1757
Henry Jr.	Bert	1757
SMEETH, David	Brun	1769
David	Brun	1772
David	NewH	1762
David	NewH	1763
SMELLY, John	NorH	1743
SMITH, Abel s.		
of David	Dobb	1769
Abraham	Bert	1757
Abraham	Bute	1771
Abraham & s.		
Abraham	FWV	1771
Adam	Gran	1784
Alexander	Rand	1779
Amos	Gate	1786
Anderson	Gran	1784
Andrew	Rowa	1759
Ann	Beau	1764
Ann	Blad	1745
Anne	Casw	1777
Arthur	Dobb	1769
Arthur	Dobb	1779
Arthur	Rand	1779
Basil	Crav	1769
Benjamin	Anso	1763
Benjamin	Dobb	1769
Benjamin	Gran	1784
Benjamin	Pitt	1764
Benjamin	Pitt	1775
Benjamin	Surr	1772
Bennett	NewH	1767
Caleb	Dobb	1769
Captain	N.C.	1701
Casper	Rowa	1759
Charles	Anso	1763
Charles	Dobb	1769
Charles	Gran	1786
Christopher	Pitt	1762
Christopher	Pitt	1764
Christopher	Surr	1771
Colonel	Crav	1769
Conrad	Gran	1769
Daniel	Brun	1772
Daniel	Crav	1769
Daniel	Cumb	1755
Daniel	Onsl	1769
Daniel	Onsl	1770
Daniel	Perq	1740
Daniel Jr.	Rand	1779
Daniel Sr.	Rand	1779
David	Beau	1755
David	Blad	1763
David	Brun	1769
David	Brun	1772
David 1m 2f		
Slaves	Crav	1769
David	Cumb	1755
David	Cumb	1767

SMITH, David	Dobb	1769	SMITH, James	Crav	1752
David Jr. s.			James	Crav	1769
of David	Dobb	1769	James Constable		
David	Gran	1784		Crav	1769
David	Pitt	1764	James s.		
David Jr.	Rand	1779	of David	Dobb	1769
David Sr.	Rand	1779	James	FWV	1771
David	Rowa	1759	James	Gran	1755
David	Surr	1771	James	Gran	1784
Drury s.			James	Onsl	1770
of James	Gran	1755	James	Pasq	1769
Drury s.			James 290 acres	Perq	1720
of James	Gran	1784	James	Perq	1740
Edward	Anso	1763	James	Tyrr	1741
Edward	Blad	1763	James	Tyrr	1755
Edward	Gran	1784	Jarvis	Beau	1755
Edward	Oran	1755	Jarvis	Beau	1764
Ephraim	Bert	1769	Jer.	Beau	1755
Ezekiel	Pasq	1769	Jeremiah	Curr	1715
Finley	NewH	1755	Jerry	Onsl	1770
Francis	Chow	1717	Jesse	Dobb	1769
Francis	Chow	1721	Jesse	Pitt	1764
Frederick	Rowa	1759	Job	Onsl	1769
Garvis	Beau	1764	Job	Onsl	1770
George	Beau	1755	John	Anso	1763
George	Beau	1764	John High	Beau	1755
George	Blad	1763	John	Bert	1757
George 700 acres	Chow	1721	John	Bert	1769
George	Crav	1769	John Esq.	Blad	1763
George s.			John	Blad	1763
of David	Dobb	1769	John	Blad	1781
George	Oran	1755	John's estate	Blad	1781
George	Roan	1720	John 7m		
Guilelma	Gran	1769	7f slaves	Brun	1769
Guilelmus	Gran	1784	John	Brun	1772
Guy	Gran	1769	John	Bute	1771
H.	Beau	1755	John	Casw	1777
Harry	Pitt	1775	John 640 acres	Chow	1721
Henry	Beau	1744	John	Chow	1753
Henry	Chow	1753	John	Crav	1741
Henry	Crav	1769	John	Crav	1769
Henry	Cumb	1767	John Brice's		
Henry	Dobb	1779	Creek	Crav	1769
Henry	Gran	1755	John at Mrs.		
Henry	Gran	1784	Powell	Crav	1769
Henry (Cpt.)	N.C.	1701	John	Cumb	1755
Henry	Surr	1771	John	Cumb	1767
Henry	Surr	1772	John Little	Cumb	1767
Holloman	Crav	1769	John free negro	Curr	1715
Houghton s.			John	Dobb	1769
of David	Dobb	1769	John	Dobb	1779
Hugh	Cumb	1755	John s. Ben		
Humphrey	Crav	1769	John	FWV	1771
Isaiah	Rand	1779	John	Gran	1755
Jacob	Curr	1755	John	Gran	1769
Jacob	Onsl	1770	John Jr.	Gran	1784
Jacob	Rowa	1759	John Sr.	Gran	1784
James	Beau	1764	John	Gran	1784
James	Bert	1757	John	Hyde	1741
James	Brun	1772	John	Hyde	1742
James	Bute	1771	John	Hyde	1743
James	Casw	1777	John	Hyde	1744
James	Chow	1717	John	NewH	1767
James	Chow	1721	John the		
James	Chow	1753	cooper	Onsl	1769

SMITH, John s.			SMITH, Peter	Rowa 1759
of Widow	Onsl	1769	Purley	Casw 1777
John	Onsl	1770	Ransom	Gran 1784
John	Pasq	1769	Reuben	FWV 1771
John 2m			Reuben	Gran 1784
slaves	Pasq	1769	Richard	Bute 1771
John	Pitt	1762	Richard	Casw 1777
John	Pitt	1764	Richard	Chow 1753
John	Rand	1779	Richard	Crav 1769
John miller	Rand	1779	Richard 1 slave	Crav 1769
John s. James	Rowa	1759	Richard	Curr 1715
John	Surr	1771	Richard	Dobb 1769
John	Surr	1772	Richard	Dobb 1779
John	Tyrr	1755	Richard	FWV 1771
John in			Richard	Gran 1755
Allegator	Tyrr	1755	Richard	Onsl 1769
Jonathan	Gate	1786	Richard	Rowa 1759
Joseph	Dobb	1779	Robert	Bute 1771
Joseph	Gran	1769	Robert	Casw 1777
Joseph	Onsl	1769	Robert	Chow 1721
Joseph	Perq	1720	Robert	Crav 1720
Joseph	Perq	1740	Robert	Crav 1741
Joseph	Pitt	1764	Robert	Cumb 1755
Joseph	Rand	1779	Robert	Cumb 1767
Joshua	Pitt	1762	Robert	FWV 1771
Josiah	Bert	1769	Ruskin	Casw 1777
Laurence	Dobb	1769	Samuel	Chow 1721
Laurence	Surr	1771	Samuel	Crav 1742
Laurence	Surr	1772	Samuel	Crav 1769
Lazarus	Pitt	1764	Samuel	Gate 1786
Leonard	Gran	1784	Samuel	Gran 1755
Lewis	Dobb	1769	Samuel	Gran 1769
Lewis	Pitt	1762	Samuel	Gran 1784
Luke	Oran	1755	Samuel	Onsl 1770
Mace	Casw	1777	Samuel	Pitt 1762
Malcomb	Cumb	1755	Samuel	Rand 1779
Malcomb	Cumb	1767	Sarah	Curr 1715
Maloom	NewH	1755	Sarah	Curr 1755
Mark	Dobb	1779	Sarah	Gran 1769
Matthew	Pasq	1769	Simon	Blad 1781
Meanas	Curr	1755	Solomon	Crav 1720
Meenay	Curr	1755	Solomon	Curr 1755
Mordicai	Pasq	1769	Solomon	Pasq 1754
Nathan	Onsl	1770	Stephen	Casw 1777
Nathaniel	Cumb	1767	Stephen	Gran 1755
Nathaniel	Gran	1755	Temperance	Onsl 1770
Nathaniel	Onsl	1769	Thomas	Beau 1755
Nathaniel	Onsl	1770	Thomas	Bert 1757
Nathaniel	Perq	1740	Thomas	Bute 1771
Neal	Beau	1755	Thomas	Chow 1753
Neil	Pitt	1764	Thomas	Crav 1741
Nicholas	Dobb	1769	Thomas	Crav 1745
Nicholas	NewH	1767	Thomas 1m slave	Crav 1769
Oliver	N.C.	1701	Thomas	Dobb 1769
Owen	Cumb	1767	Thomas	Edge 1742
Peter	Bert	1757	Thomas s. Philip	
Peter	Bert	1769	& Wm	FWV 1771
Peter	Casw	1777	Thomas	Gate 1786
Peter Jr.	Casw	1777	Thomas	Gran 1755
Peter	Crav	1769	Thomas	Gran 1769
Peter	Cumb	1767	Thomas	Gran 1784
Peter	Gran	1755	Thomas	NewH 1743
Peter	NorH	1762	Thomas	Onsl 1769
Peter	Perq	1740	Thomas	Onsl 1770
Peter	Rand	1779	Thomas	Oran 1755

SMITH, Thomas	Pasq	1754	SMYTHE, Wm Jr.		Pitt	1762
Thomas 1f			SMYTHICK, Edmond		Pitt	1764
slave	Pasq	1754	SNAP, Laurence		Rowa	1759
Thomas	Pasq	1769	SNEAD, David		Anso	1763
Thomas	Perq	1740	Henly		Anso	1763
Thomas	Pitt	1764	Isaiah		Anso	1763
Thomas	Pitt	1775	Israel		Anso	1763
Thomas	Surr	1771	Robert 4 slaves		Onsl	1769
Thomas	Surr	1772	Robert		Onsl	1770
Widow	Chow	1717	Samuel		Anso	1763
Widow	Onsl	1769	Solt		Anso	1763
Wm	Anso	1763	Wm		Anso	1763
Wm	Beau	1755	SNEDLING, Aquillar		Gran	1755
Wm	Bert	1769	SNEED, Aubley		Gran	1784
Wm	Blad	1763	John		Casw	1777
Wm	Bute	1771	Samuel		Gran	1784
Wm	Casw	1777	Stephen		Gran	1784
Wm	Chow	1721	SNELL, Roger		Chow	1721
Wm	Chow	1753	Roger		Tyrr	1755
Wm	Crav	1720	SNELLING, Alexander		Gran	1769
Wm	Cumb	1767	Aquilla		Gran	1755
Wm Jr.	Cumb	1767	Aquilla		Gran	1769
Wm	Edge	1742	Barnett		Gran	1784
Wm	Edge	1744	Hugh		Gran	1784
Wm	Gran	1755	Lottice		Gran	1784
Wm	Pasq	1769	Richard		Casw	1777
Wm	Pitt	1762	SNIPE, Nathaniel		Gran	1769
Wm Jr.	Pitt	1762	SNIPER, Nathaniel		Gran	1784
Wm	Pitt	1764	SNIPES, John		NorH	1762
Wm	Rand	1779	SNIPS, Robert		Anso	1763
Zachariah	Anso	1763	SNOAD, Elizabeth		Beau	1744
Zachariah	Blad	1763	Henry		Beau	1743
SMITHART, John	Blad	1763	Henry		Beau	1750
SMITHER, Moses	Oran	1755	John		Beau	1742
SMITHSON, John	Pasq	1754	SNORD, Esau		Pasq	1769
John	Pasq	1769	SNOW, Esau		Pasq	1769
Joseph	Pasq	1754	Henry		Surr	1771
Reuben	Pasq	1769	Henry		Surr	1772
SMITHWICK, Asia	Chow	1717	Robert 14m			
Ed Jr.	Chow	1717	6f slaves		Brun	1769
Edmond	Bert	1757	Robert		NewH	1755
Edmond	Chow	1717	Robert		NewH	1762
Edmund	Chow	1721	Robert		NewH	1763
Edmund	Tyrr	1741	SNOWDEN, Elizabeth		Perq	1740
Edmund Esq.	Tyrr	1755	George		Perq	1740
Edmund s.			John		Perq	1740
of Edmund	Tyrr	1755	Joseph		Perq	1740
John	Bert	1757	Samuel		Pasq	1769
John	Chow	1717	Thomas		Perq	1720
John of Chinkapin			Wm Jr.		Curr	1755
	Chow	1717	Wm		Perq	1740
John	Chow	1743	SNYDER, Anthony		NewH	1767
John	Tyrr	1755	SOALS, Gideon		Brun	1769
John Jr.	Tyrr	1755	Gideon		Brun	1772
Samuel	Chow	1721	Joseph		Brun	1769
Samuel	Tyrr	1743	Joseph		Brun	1772
Samuel	Tyrr	1755	Silvanus		Brun	1769
Sarah	Bert	1769	Silvanus		Brun	1772
Wm s. of John			SOLAR, John		Rand	1779
& Edmond bro.	Bert	1757	SOLE, Joseph		NewH	1762
SMYTHE, Christopher	Pitt	1762	Silvanus		NewH	1762
Josh	Pitt	1762	SOLLEY, John		Pasq	1754
Samuel	Crav	1769	Joseph		Pasq	1754
Samuel	Pitt	1762	SOLOMON, John		Bute	1771
Wm	Pitt	1762	John		FWV	1771

SOLOMON, Peter	Bute	1771
Peter	FWV	1771
Richard	Beau	1764
Wm	Beau	1764
Wm	Bute	1771
Wm	FWV	1771
SOLSBERRY, George	Curr	1715
SOMERVIL, John	Gran	1784
SONAW, John	Beau	1764
SONES, Wm	Tyrr	1755
SORER, Philip	Rowa	1759
SORRELL, George	Surr	1771
Robert	Gran	1769
Simon	Gran	1769
Thomas	Bert	1757
SORRILL, John	Ruth	1790
John Jr.	Ruth	1790
John	Tryo	1776
SORRY, Henry	NorH	1762
SOSEBERRY, Allen	FWV	1771
SOULE, John	Rand	1779
SOUTH, Benjamin	Casw	1777
SOUTHARD, Wm	Casw	1777
SOUTHERLAND, Sanders		
	Casw	1777
Wm	Edge	1744
SOUTHWELL, Richard	Oran	1755
SOWBRIDGE, Wm	Crav	1720
SOWELL, Charles	Bert	1769
Francis	Bert	1769
Isaac	Bert	1757
James	Bert	1757
James	Bert	1769
Mary	Bute	1771
Mary s. Clayton		
& Samuel	FWV	1771
Obadiah	Bert	1757
Obadiah Jr.	Bert	1757
Richard	Bert	1757
Richard	Bert	1769
Richard	Chow	1717
Richard	Chow	1721
SPACH, Adam	Rowa	1759
SPAIN, Drury	Pitt	1762
Drury	Pitt	1764
SPANN, Griffith	Pitt	1764
John Jr.	Dobb	1769
John Sr.	Dobb	1769
John s. of		
John Jr.	Dobb	1769
John	Dobb	1779
Moses	Gran	1769
Wm	Dobb	1769
SPAREMAN, Andrew	NewH	1755
SPARKMAN, Edmund	Bert	1769
James	Bert	1757
James	Chow	1753
Jesse	Bert	1769
Jesse	Tyrr	1755
John	Chow	1753
Lewis	Gate	1786
Reuben	Gate	1786
Thomas	Chow	1753
Willis	Gate	1786
Wm & s. Edward	Bert	1757

SPARKMAN, Wm	Bert	1769
Wm	Chow	1753
SPARKS, Augustine	Gran	1755
Jonas	Rowa	1759
Solomon	Rowa	1759
Solomon	Surr	1771
Solomon	Surr	1772
Wm	Surr	1771
SPARROW, Robert	Crav	1720
Smith 1m		
1f slave	Crav	1769
SPEAR, James	Pitt	1762
Joseph	Pitt	1762
SPEARMAN, Abraham	Crav	1769
Andrew	NewH	1763
Edward	NewH	1762
Edward	NewH	1763
John	Onsl	1770
Samuel	Onsl	1770
SPEARPOINT, Joseph	Surr	1771
Joseph	Surr	1772
SPEARS, John	Tyrr	1755
Levi	Casw	1777
Philip	Gran	1784
Wm	Gran	1769
Wm Jr.	Gran	1784
Wm Sr.	Gran	1784
Wm	NewH	1762
Wm	NewH	1763
SPEDDY, Caleb	Pitt	1764
SPEERS, Absalom	Bert	1757
Andrew	Surr	1771
Andrew	Surr	1772
James	Edge	1734
James	Edge	1743
John	Pitt	1762
John Jr.	Pitt	1762
Wm	Edge	1734
Wm	Pitt	1762
SPEIGHT, Ann	Gate	1786
Francis	Chow	1742
Francis	Chow	1743
Francis	Dobb	1779
Francis	Gate	1786
G. 600 acres	Chow	1721
Henry	Chow	1753
Henry	Gate	1786
Isaac	Perq	1740
Jeremiah	Gate	1786
John	Dobb	1769
John	Dobb	1779
Joseph	Chow	1753
Joseph	Dobb	1769
Joseph	Gate	1786
Mary	Chow	1753
Moses	Chow	1753
Moses	Dobb	1769
Moses	Gate	1786
Samuel	Dobb	1779
Seth	Dobb	1779
Simon 1m 2f		
slaves	Crav	1769
Thomas 1,170		
acres	Perq	1720
Wm	Chow	1753

SPEIGHT, Wm 1m		
2f slaves	Crav	1769
Wm Jr.	Dobb	1769
Wm Sr.	Dobb	1769
Wm	Dobb	1769
Wm Esq.	Dobb	1779
SPEIN, John	Pitt	1764
Wm	Pitt	1764
SPEIRS, Solomon	Pitt	1775
SPELLAR, Henry	Bert	1769
SPENCE, Aliz.	Pasq	1754
Ann	Pasq	1754
Charles	Onsl	1769
David	Pasq	1754
David	Pasq	1769
Greaves	Pasq	1769
James	Pasq	1769
Jeremiah	Pasq	1754
Jeremiah	Pasq	1769
Job	Pasq	1769
John	NewH	1767
Joseph	Pasq	1754
Joseph Jr.	Pasq	1769
Joseph Sr.	Pasq	1769
Lemuel	Pasq	1769
Rancher s. of		
Joseph Sr.	Pasq	1769
Robert	Pasq	1754
Thomas	Pasq	1769
Timothy	NewH	1767
Truman	Pasq	1754
Wm	Crav	1769
SPENCER, Benjamin	Casw	1777
Charles	Onsl	1769
Charles	Onsl	1770
John	Casw	1777
John	Surr	1771
Stanton	Onsl	1770
Thomas	Bert	1757
Thomas	Casw	1777
Thomas	Curr	1715
Thomas	Surr	1772
SPENGLER, Peter	Rowa	1759
SPENHAUR, Henry	Surr	1771
Henry	Surr	1772
Werner	Surr	1771
Werner	Surr	1772
SPERRY, Joab	Dobb	1769
SPICER, John	Onsl	1769
John s. of John	Onsl	1769
John	Onsl	1770
SPIER, James s.		
of John	Beau	1755
Jesse s. of John	Beau	1755
John	Beau	1755
Wm	Beau	1755
SPIGHT, Henry	Bert	1769
SPILLER, Hen.	Chow	1717
Henry	Chow	1721
SPINGLE, George	Beau	1764
SPINKS, Amey	Rand	1779
Enoch	Oran	1755
John	Rand	1779
SPIRE, Caleb	Beau	1755
SPIRES, Absalom	Bert	1757

SPIRES, James		1743
John	Crav	1769
Robert	Surr	1772
Thomas	Chow	1721
SPIVEY, Abraham	Chow	1721
Abraham	Gate	1786
Benjamin	Chow	1717
Benjamin	Chow	1721
Benjamin	Chow	1753
Bligy	Chow	1753
Caleb	Pitt	1762
Elizabeth	Bert	1757
Elizabeth	Chow	1753
Ephraim	Dobb	1779
Francis	Bert	1757
George	Bert	1757
George	Chow	1717
Jacob	Chow	1717
Jacob	Chow	1721
Jacob	Chow	1753
Jacob	Gate	1786
Jesse	Gate	1786
Joab	Dobb	1779
John	Bert	1757
Jonathan	Bert	1757
Joshua	Bert	1769
Lydia	Gate	1786
Moses	Bert	1757
Moses	Bert	1769
Moses	Chow	1753
Nathaniel	Chow	1753
Nathaniel	Gate	1786
Thomas Sr.	Chow	1717
Thomas	Chow	1721
Thomas Jr.	Chow	1721
SPIVY, Littleton	Gran	1755
SPOONER, Jabez	Onsl	1741
SPRADLING, Charles	Anso	1763
SPRICE, Wm	Rowa	1759
SPRING, Aaron	Beau	1742
Aaron	Beau	1755
Aaron Jr.	Beau	1755
Aaron	Beau	1764
John	Bert	1757
John	Tyrr	1755
Joseph	Tyrr	1755
Robert	Beau	1755
Wm	Beau	1764
SPRINGER, George	Rowa	1759
SPRINGLE, George	Beau	1764
George	Surr	1771
George	Surr	1772
Wm	Beau	1755
SPRINGS, Christian	NewH	1767
John	NewH	1762
John	NewH	1763
SPROCK, George	Rowa	1759
SPROOLE, Joseph	Tyrr	1755
Samuel Sr.	Tyrr	1755
SPROW, Robert	Crav	1720
SPROWL, Wm	Cumb	1767
SPRUELL, Elizabeth	Bert	1769
Godfrey	Bert	1769
Godfrey	Tyrr	1755
Jasper	Bert	1769

SPRUELL, Jasper	Tyrr	1755
Jeremiah	Bert	1769
Jeremiah	Tyrr	1755
Joseph Jr.	Tyrr	1755
Joseph Sr.	Tyrr	1755
SPRUILL, Godfrey	Chow	1717
Godfrey	Chow	1721
Joseph	Chow	1721
Samuel	Chow	1717
Samuel	Chow	1721
SPRUNT, Wm	Bute	1771
Wm	FWV	1771
Wm	Gran	1755
SPRY, Francis	N.C.	1701
SPURGEON, Samuel	Rowa	1759
Wm	Rowa	1759
SPURLOCK, John	Surr	1772
SQUIRES, Amos	Beau	1755
Amos	Crav	1769
Appleton	Beau	1764
Boaz	Crav	1769
John	NewH	1762
John	NewH	1763
John 1m 1f		
slave	Pasq	1754
John	Pasq	1769
Roger	Beau	1755
Roger	Casw	1777
Roger	Pasq	1754
Roger 2m 1f		
slaves	Pasq	1769
Thomas	NewH	1767
Thomas	Pasq	1769
ST. GEORGE, George	NewH	1762
George	NewH	1763
ST. JOHN, Wm	Bute	1771
Wm	FWV	1771
STACY, Benjamin	Surr	1771
Benjamin	Surr	1772
Charles	Chow	1717
Charles	Chow	1721
Thomas	Chow	1717
Thomas	Chow	1721
STAFFORD, David	Crav	1720
Edward	Curr	1715
Edward Esq.	Pitt	1762
Edward	Pitt	1764
John	Pasq	1769
Laban	Casw	1777
Richard	Pitt	1762
Samuel	Pasq	1769
Samuel	Pitt	1775
Stephen	Pasq	1769
Thomas	Perq	1720
Thomas	Perq	1740
Wm	Beau	1742
Wm	Curr	1715
Wm	NewH	1762
Wm	NewH	1763
Wm	Onsl	1769
Wm	Onsl	1770
Wm	Pitt	1762
Wm Jr.	Pitt	1762
Wm	Pitt	1764
Wm Jr.	Pitt	1764

STAFFORD, Wm	Rowa	1759
Wm	Surr	1771
Wm	Surr	1772
STAGG, Wm	Oran	1755
STAGNER, Barnett	Rowa	1759
STAINBACK, Thomas	Bert	1769
STAKES, Thomas	Pasq	1769
STALEY, Jacob	Rand	1779
STALFORD, Edward	Beau	1755
Joshua	Beau	1755
Wm	Beau	1755
STALLINGS, Elias	Bert	1742
Elias Jr.	Bert	1757
Elias Sr.	Bert	1757
Elias	Bute	1771
Elias	FWV	1771
Elias	Perq	1740
Isaac	Bert	1757
Isaac	Perq	1740
Jesse	Bert	1757
Josiah	Bert	1757
Lot	Perq	1740
Moses	Bert	1757
Moses	Bute	1771
Moses	Chow	1753
Moses s. Josiah	FWV	1771
Nicholas	Perq	1740
Reuben	Bute	1771
Reuben	FWV	1771
Samuel	Chow	1753
Simon	Perq	1740
STAMPER, Henry	Oran	1755
James	Rand	1779
Jonathan	Surr	1771
Jonathan	Surr	1772
STANALAND, Gershom	Brun	1769
Gershom	Brun	1772
John 1m 1f		
slave	Brun	1769
John	Brun	1772
John	Crav	1743
Samuel	Brun	1772
Thomas	Brun	1769
Thomas	Brun	1772
STANBURY, Wm	Brun	1769
Wm	Brun	1772
STANCEL, John	Chow	1717
John	Chow	1721
John	Dobb	1769
John	Dobb	1779
Wm	Beau	1755
Wm Jr.	Beau	1755
Wm Jr.	Beau	1764
STANCER, John	Dobb	1769
STANDAM, John	Cumb	1767
STANDING, Edward	Chow	1721
Edward	Chow	1753
Henderson	Chow	1753
Samuel	Perq	1740
STANDARD, Thomas	Bute	1771
Thomas	FWV	1771
STANDLEY, David	Bert	1769
Edmond	Bert	1769
Gershom	Crav	1769
Isaac	Dobb	1769

STANDLEY, Isaac	Dobb	1779		STARKEY, John	Onsl	1769
James	Crav	1769		John 26 slaves	Onsl	1770
Jonathan	Bert	1757		Jonathan	Casw	1777
Jonathan	Bert	1769		Peter	Onsl	1769
Moses	Dobb	1769		Peter 15 slaves	Onsl	1770
Moses	Dobb	1779		STARLING, Wm	Dobb	1769
Sands	Dobb	1769		STARNS, Isaac	Rand	1779
Sands	Dobb	1779		Peter	Oran	1755
Shadrack	Dobb	1779		STARR, Ann (widow)	Beau	1764
Wm	Bert	1769		STARRETT, Benjamin	Rowa	1759
Wm	Crav	1769		STATLINGS, John	Gate	1786
STANFIELD, John	Cumb	1767		Josiah	Gate	1786
John	Gran	1755		Richard	Gate	1786
John	Oran	1755		Seth	Gate	1786
John	Rand	1779		Simon	Gate	1786
STANFILLS, Godfrey	Pitt	1775		STAUGHTON, Henry	Pasq	1754
STANFORD, James	Rand	1779		STAUP, Francis	Surr	1771
Thomas	Bute	1771		Franz	Surr	1772
Thomas	FWV	1771		STEAD, John Jr.	Rand	1779
Wm	Bute	1771		John Sr.	Rand	1779
Wm	FWV	1771		Joshua	Rand	1779
STANLEY, George	Bert	1757		STEADFORD, Richard	Rand	1779
James	NewH	1767		STEALEY, Conrod	Rand	1779
Jonathan	Chow	1717		Jacob	Rand	1779
Jonathan	Chow	1721		Martin	Rand	1779
Joseph Jr.	Surr	1771		STEALY, Wm Sr.	Tyrr	1755
Joseph Sr.	Surr	1771		Wm	Tyrr	1755
Joseph Jr.	Surr	1772		STEDON, John	Oran	1755
Joseph Sr.	Surr	1772		STEEL, David	Oran	1755
Richard	Curr	1755		James	Crav	1769
Sizely	Surr	1772		Peter	Crav	1769
Wm	John	1750		STEELY, Jacob	Cumb	1767
Wm	Surr	1771		Thomas	Chow	1717
Wm	Surr	1772		Wm	Chow	1717
Zedekiah	Bert	1769		Wm	Chow	1721
STANSELL, Edrew	Pitt	1764		STEFFINS, Isens	Rowa	1759
Godfrey	Pitt	1762		STEINBECK, John	Gran	1769
John	Pitt	1762		STEP, John	Gran	1769
John	Pitt	1764		John	Surr	1771
John	Tyrr	1755		John	Surr	1772
Peter	Pitt	1762		STEPHEN, John	Cumb	1755
Samuel	Pitt	1764		STEPHENS, Absalom	Dobb	1769
Samuel	Tyrr	1755		Ann	N.C.	1701
Wm	Pitt	1762		Barnabas	Blad	1763
Wm Jr.	Pitt	1762		Ben	Onsl	1769
Wm	Pitt	1764		Ben	Onsl	1770
Wm Jr.	Pitt	1764		Charles	Blad	1763
STANTON, Benjamin	Pasq	1769		David	Oran	1755
Edward	Chow	1717		Ebenezer	Pasq	1769
Edward	Chow	1721		Edward	Crav	1743
James	NorH	1762		Evan	Rowa	1759
John	Brun	1772		Gabriel	Dobb	1779
John	Crav	1769		George	Bute	1771
Margaret	Perq	1740		George	FWV	1771
Samuel	Rand	1779		James	Beau	1755
Wm	NewH	1755		Jeremiah	Curr	1755
STAPLER, David	Oran	1755		Joseph	Pitt	1764
STARK, James	Gran	1784		Joseph	Pitt	1775
STARKE, Wm	NewH	1767		Joshua	Bert	1757
STARKEY, Edward	Onsl	1769		Josiah	Blad	1763
Edward	Onsl	1770		Nehemiah	Blad	1763
John	Cart	1741		Wm	Bert	1757
John	Cart	1751		Wm	Gran	1769
John	Onsl	1744		Wm s. of Ebenezer		
John	Onsl	1751			Pasq	1769

STEPHENSON, James	Crav 1769		STEWART, John	Pitt 1762
James	Dobb 1779		John	Pitt 1764
John	Cumb 1767		John	Roan 1720
Matthew	Crav 1769		John	Rowa 1759
Robert	Rand 1779		John Jr.	Surr 1771
Wm	FWV 1771		John Sr.	Surr 1771
Wm	NewH 1763		John	Surr 1772
STEPNEY, John	Perq 1720		Joseph	Perq 1740
John	Perq 1740		Joseph	Surr 1771
STERLING, John	Cumb 1767		Joseph	Surr 1772
STEVENS, Alexander	Brun 1772		Patrick	Blad 1763
Benjamin	Onsl 1769		Patrick	NewH 1741
Caleb	Chow 1721		Patrick	NewH 1750
Charles	Brun 1769		Peter	NorH 1762
Charles	Brun 1772		Robert 1m slave	Brun 1769
Charles	Casw 1777		Robert	Brun 1772
Charles 160			Samuel	Pitt 1764
acres	Chow 1721		Samuel	Rowa 1759
Charles	NorH 1743		Wm	Blad 1763
George 1w 5b			Wm	Chow 1717
slaves	Edge 1744		Wm	Crav 1769
Henry	Bert 1769		Wm	Surr 1771
James	Cumb 1767		Wm	Surr 1772
James Jr.	Cumb 1767		STIBBINS, Gideon	NewH 1762
James	Gran 1755		STIDWELL, John	Rowa 1759
John	Chow 1721		STILES, James	Bute 1771
John	Curr 1755		James	Gran 1755
John	Perq 1740		John	Casw 1777
John	Rowa 1759		Samuel	FWV 1771
Moab	Blad 1781		STILL, O'Neill	NewH 1755
Phineas	Onsl 1742		Robert	Curr 1755
Richard	Onsl 1769		STILLWELL, Daniel	Oran 1755
Richard	Onsl 1770		STIMSON, Richard	NewH 1762
Thomas	Casw 1777		Richard	NewH 1763
Thomas	Crav 1769		STOCKLEY, Isaac	Pasq 1754
Wm	Crav 1742		Jacob	NewH 1767
Wm	NewH 1762		Joseph	Pasq 1769
Wm	Perq 1720		Thomas	NewH 1755
STEVENSON, Charles	NorH 1743		STODGEHILL, John	Edge 1741
George	NorH 1743		STOKES, Arthur	Crav 1769
STEWART, Al. (Rev.)	Beau 1755		David	Casw 1777
Alexander	Beau 1755		David 1m slave	Crav 1769
Alexander	Beau 1764		Henry	Anso 1763
Alexander	Brun 1769		Isaac	Beau 1755
Alexander	Pitt 1762		Isaac	Pitt 1762
Alexander	Tyrr 1755		Isaac	Pitt 1764
Benjamin	Surr 1771		Isaac	Pitt 1775
Benjamin	Surr 1772		John	Beau 1755
Charles	Cumb 1767		John Jr.	Pitt 1762
Charles	Rand 1779		John Sr.	Pitt 1762
Daniel	Beau 1755		John	Pitt 1764
Daniel	Pitt 1762		John Jr.	Pitt 1775
David	Rowa 1759		John Sr.	Pitt 1775
George	Beau 1764		Nathaniel s.	
Gordon	Pitt 1775		of John	Beau 1755
Hugh	Blad 1763		Samuel	Beau 1755
James	Blad 1763		Samuel	Pitt 1762
James Jr.	Casw 1777		Samuel	Pitt 1764
James Sr.	Casw 1777		Wm	Casw 1777
James	Oran 1755		Wm	Crav 1769
James	Surr 1771		Wm	Pitt 1762
John 620 acres	Chow 1721		Wm	Pitt 1764
John	Cumb 1755		STONE, Austin s.	
John	Cumb 1767		of Philip	Dobb 1769
John	Onsl 1741		Benjamin	Bert 1757

STONE, Benjamin	Bert	1769	STOVAL, Joseph	Gran	1784
Benjamin	Brun	1769	Josiah	Gran	1769
Benjamin	Brun	1772	Wm	Gran	1769
Benjamin	Casw	1777	Wm	Gran	1784
Benjamin	NewH	1762	STOW, Samuel	Curr	1755
Benjamin	NewH	1763	STRADER, Conrad	Casw	1777
Edward	Oran	1755	STRADLER, Mark	Dobb	1769
Elias	Brun	1769	STRAHON, David	Gran	1755
Elias	Brun	1772	STRAIDER, Conrad	Oran	1755
Hezekiah	Gran	1784	STRAITE, Wm	Oran	1755
Indian	Crav	1720	STRANGE, John	Crav	1769
James	Blad	1781	Maatlier	Onsl	1769
John	Blad	1763	STRATER, Benjamin	Bert	1757
John	Blad	1781	STRAUB, John	Surr	1771
John Constable			Johannes	Surr	1772
s. Jonathan	Bute	1771	STRAUGHAN, David	Blad	1763
John	Casw	1777	George	Bert	1757
John s. Jonathan	FWV	1771	Othneil	Blad	1763
John	Gran	1769	Thomas	Beau	1764
John	Onsl	1769	Thomas	Crav	1769
John	Onsl	1770	STRAUTHER, Francis	Gran	1755
John	Perq	1740	STREET, Anthony	Bute	1771
John	Surr	1771	Anthony	FWV	1771
Marble	Surr	1772	Moses	Casw	1777
Martin	Dobb	1769	STREIN, Thomas	Oran	1755
Philip	Dobb	1769	STRETTON, Joseph	Oran	1755
Richard	Pitt	1762	STRIBLING, Francis	Cumb	1767
Thomas	Surr	1771	STRIDLEY, Nimrod	Dobb	1779
Wm	Blad	1742	Samuel	Dobb	1779
Wm	Casw	1777	STRINGER, Edward	Casw	1777
Wm	Gran	1769	Francis	Crav	1742
Wm	Surr	1771	James	Casw	1777
Wm	Surr	1772	Jane	Crav	1769
STONEHAM, Thomas	Roan	1720	STRINGFELLOW, Enoch	Bute	1771
STONEHOUSE, Thomas	Curr	1715	Enoch	FWV	1771
STORER, Henry	Anso	1763	Enoch	Onsl	1769
Pritchett	Cumb	1767	Enoch	Onsl	1770
STORM, John	Blad	1781	STRINGFIELD, James	Oran	1755
Mary	Blad	1781	Richard	Cumb	1767
Windol	Blad	1763	Richard	Oran	1755
STORY, James	Bute	1771	STRODER, Samson	Cumb	1767
James	FWV	1771	STROTHER, Christopher		
John	Gran	1769		Bute	1771
Richard	Pitt	1764	Christopher	FWV	1771
STOTT, Francis	Roan	1720	Francis	Bute	1771
Jacob	Surr	1772	Francis	FWV	1771
John	Surr	1772	John	Bute	1771
Peter	Surr	1771	John	FWV	1771
STOUDER, Mark	Rand	1779	Richard	FWV	1771
STOUT, Charles Jr.	Onsl	1769	STROUD, Abraham	Rand	1779
Charles Sr.	Onsl	1769	Jesse	Rand	1779
Charles Jr.	Onsl	1770	John	Gran	1755
Jacob	Onsl	1769	John	Oran	1755
Jacob	Onsl	1770	John Sr.	Oran	1755
Samuel	Rand	1779	Joshua s. of		
STOVAL, Bartholomew	Gran	1769	John	Oran	1755
Bartholomew	Gran	1784	Wm	Oran	1755
Benjamin	Gran	1784	Yarby	Bute	1771
Darius	Gran	1784	Yarby	FWV	1771
Drewry	Gran	1784	STROWHORNE, Moses	Pitt	1775
Drury	Gran	1784	STRUDWICK, Samuel	NewH	1767
John	Gran	1755	STUART, James	Cumb	1755
John Jr.	Gran	1769	John	Oran	1755
John Sr.	Gran	1769	John	Roan	1720
John	Gran	1784	Samuel	Oran	1755

STUBBLEFIELD, Wyatt	Casw	1777
STUBBS, John	Blad	1763
Wm	Beau	1755
STUBS, Everett	Tyrr	1755
John	Tyrr	1755
Thomas	Tyrr	1755
STUCKEY, Wm	NewH	1762
Wm	NewH	1767
STUDEFANT, Matthew	Pitt	1764
STUKN, Israel	Dobb	1769
STULL, Robert	Bert	1769
STUMP, Thomas	Pasq	1754
STURGIS, Jonathan	Brun	1772
Jonathan	NewH	1762
Jonathan	NewH	1763
Thomas	Chow	1721
STUTLEY, Sherly	Anso	1763
Shurly	Oran	1755
Wm	Anso	1763
Wm	Oran	1755
STUTSMAN, Jacob	Rand	1779
STYLES, John	Onsl	1769
STYMER, George	NewH	1762
George Jr.	NewH	1762
George	NewH	1763
George Jr.	NewH	1763
STYYRING, George	Beau	1741
SUAFORD, Anthony	Oran	1755
James	Oran	1755
SUDBURY, George	NewH	1767
Moses	NewH	1762
Moses	NewH	1763
Moses	NewH	1767
Stockley	NewH	1767
SUDMAN, Willis	Pasq	1754
SUETTEN, Elisha	Anso	1763
SUGGIN, Francis	Casw	1777
SUGGS, Absalom	Dobb	1769
Absalom	Dobb	1779
Allen	Pitt	1762
Allen	Pitt	1764
Allen	Pitt	1775
George	Anso	1763
George	Beau	1755
George	Cumb	1755
Joel	Pitt	1762
Joel	Pitt	1764
Joel	Pitt	1775
John	Dobb	1769
John	Dobb	1779
Leonard	Gran	1755
Rasha	Anso	1763
Thomas	Anso	1763
Thomas Jr.	Anso	1763
SULF, Job	Oran	1755
SULLIVAN, Abraham	Bert	1769
Darby	Pitt	1762
Darby	Pitt	1764
John s. of		
Lambeth	Dobb	1769
Joseph	Pitt	1762
Joseph	Pitt	1764
Lambeth	Dobb	1769
Owen	Oran	1755
SULMON, Daniel	Dobb	1769
SUMARAN, Wm	Anso	1763
SUMERAL, Griffin	Bert	1757
John	Bert	1757
Lazarus	Bert	1757
SUMMERLIN, Edward	Pitt	1764
Flowers	Pitt	1764
Griffin	Bert	1757
Jacob	Pitt	1764
Jesse	Pitt	1764
John	Bert	1757
Thomas Sr.	Beau	1755
SUMMERS, George	Casw	1777
Jacob	Oran	1755
John	Rand	1779
John	Rowa	1759
John	Surr	1771
John	Surr	1772
Robert	Surr	1771
Thomas	Rand	1779
Thomas	Rowa	1759
Waitman	Surr	1772
Wm	Rand	1779
SUMNER, Abraham	Gate	1786
Demsey	Chow	1753
Demsey	Gate	1786
Edwin	Gate	1786
Francis	Onsl	1743
George	Onsl	1770
Hezekiah	Cumb	1767
James	Chow	1753
James	Gate	1786
James	Perq	1740
Jethro	Bute	1771
Jethro	FWV	1771
Jethro	Gate	1786
John	Chow	1753
John	Gate	1786
Joseph	Gate	1786
Luke	Chow	1753
Martha	Gate	1786
Richard	NorH	1743
Robert	Bert	1757
Robert	Rowa	1759
Robert	Surr	1771
Robert	Surr	1772
Wm	Surr	1772
SUMOSELL, Joseph	Bert	1769
Lazarus	Bert	1769
SUMRELL, Edward	Pitt	1762
Flowers	Pitt	1762
Flowers	Pitt	1764
Jacob	Pitt	1762
Jacob	Pitt	1764
Jesse	Pitt	1762
Jesse	Pitt	1764
Thomas Jr.	Pitt	1762
Thomas Sr.	Pitt	1762
Thomas	Pitt	1764
SUMTER, Thomas	Anso	1763
SUNDERLAND, James	Bert	1743
SURESBURY, Samson	FWV	1771
SURLS, Edward	Dobb	1769
SURMON, Edward	Pitt	1762
Joseph	Pitt	1762
SUTHERLAND, Daniel	NewH	1762

SUTHERLAND, Daniel	NewH	1762
Daniel	NewH	1767
SUTTLE, Basham	Casw	1777
Joseph	Casw	1777
SUTTON, Betty	Beau	1755
Christopher	Perq	1740
David	Crav	1769
Ethelred	Casw	1777
George	Bert	1757
George 314 acres	Perq	1720
Hannah	Rand	1779
Hannaim	Rand	1779
Henry	Blad	1763
James	Gran	1755
John Jr.	Casw	1777
John Sr.	Casw	1777
John	Dobb	1769
John	Gran	1784
Joseph Esq.	Perq	1740
Joseph Jr. 510 acres	Perq	1720
Joseph Sr. 300 acres	Perq	1720
Joseph	Rand	1779
Joshua	NewH	1763
Nathaniel 257 acres	Perq	1720
Richard 451 acres	Perq	1720
Sarah	Chow	1717
Solomon	Beau	1755
Solomon	Pitt	1762
Solomon	Pitt	1764
Thomas	Chow	1721
Thomas	Crav	1745
Thomas	Dobb	1779
SWAFFER, Thomas	Crav	1769
SWAFFORD, Thomas	Oran	1755
SWAIMER, John	Chow	1717
Matthew	Chow	1717
SWAIN, Arthur	Brun	1769
Arthur	Brun	1772
David	Brun	1769
David	Brun	1772
David Constable	NewH	1762
David	NewH	1763
James	Tyrr	1743
James	Tyrr	1755
Jeremiah	Tyrr	1743
John	Chow	1717
John 436 acres	Chow	1721
John South Shores	Chow	1721
John	Surr	1771
John	Surr	1772
John Jr.	Tyrr	1755
Jonathan 3m 4f slaves	Brun	1769
Jonathan	Brun	1772
Jonathan	NewH	1755
Jonathan	NewH	1762
Joshua	Tyrr	1755
Judah 1m slave	Brun	1769
Judah	Brun	1772
Judith	NewH	1762

SWAIN, Levi	NewH	1762
Rebecca	Brun	1772
Richard s. John	Bert	1757
Samuel	NewH	1755
Stephen	Bert	1757
Tidammes	Rand	1779
Wm	Bert	1757
Wm	Bert	1769
Wm	Rand	1779
SWAMP, Loosing	Bert	1757
SWANN, Ann	NewH	1762
Aquilla	Casw	1777
Evan	Crav	1769
John	Crav	1769
John	Gate	1786
John 27 persons	NewH	1741
John	NewH	1755
Joseph	Casw	1777
Samuel Jr. 900 acres	Chow	1721
Samuel 38 persons	NewH	1741
Samuel 6w 39b slaves	NewH	1742
Samuel	NewH	1763
Samuel	NewH	1767
Thomas	Casw	1777
Thomas	Curr	1715
Wm	Curr	1715
Wm	NewH	1755
Wm	NewH	1762
Wm	Pasq	1769
SWANNER, Wm	Tyrr	1755
SWANSON, Samuel	Surr	1771
SWARE, Mary	Tyrr	1755
SWAY, Isaac	Anso	1763
John	Anso	1763
SWEARINGHAM, Thomas	Beau	1755
SWEENEY, Daniel	Curr	1755
Joseph	Oran	1755
SWEM, Michael	Rowa	1758
SWETT, George	FWV	1771
SWETTMAN, Stephen	N.C.	1701
SWIFT, Ebenezer	Onsl	1769
John	Casw	1777
Thomas	Rand	1779
Wm Esq.	Casw	1777
SWINCE, John	Casw	1777
SWINDALE, Parker	Curr	1755
SWINDOLL, John	Curr	1715
John	Curr	1742
SWING, Lodwick	Oran	1755
SWINNEY, Daniel	Rowa	1759
Morgan	Perq	1720
Thomas	FWV	1771
Thomas	Gran	1784
Wm	Gran	1784
SWINSON, John Jr.	Beau	1755
John	Chow	1717
John	Perq	1720
John	Pitt	1762
John	Pitt	1764
John Jr.	Pitt	1764
Levi	Pitt	1762
Levi	Pitt	1764

SWINSON, Richard	Chow	1717	TANNER, Jennings	FWV	1771
Richard	Chow	1721	Jennings	Gran	1784
Wm	Chow	1717	John	Bute	1771
SWORFORD, Wm	Rand	1779	John	FWV	1771
SYKES, Jacob	Crav	1769	Joseph	Surr	1772
John	Blad	1763	Lodowick	Edge	1741
John	NewH	1762	Margaret	Pitt	1775
John Jr.	NewH	1762	Wm	Chow	1717
Joshua	Blad	1763	Wm	Gran	1784
Thomas	NorH	1762	TANSELL, John	Bute	1771
SYMMONDS, George	Onsl	1769	John	FWV	1771
SYMONS, Abraham			TANT, Wm	Beau	1764
1m 1f slave	Pasq	1769	Wm	Bute	1771
Abram 2m slaves	Pasq	1769	Wm	FWV	1771
Jehosaphat	Pasq	1754	Wm	Gran	1755
Jeremiah 2m			TANWAY, John	FWV	1771
slaves	Pasq	1754	TAPLEY, Hosea	Anso	1763
John	Pasq	1754	TAPMAN, Wm	Onsl	1770
John Jr. 1m			TAPP, Wm	Casw	1777
1f slave	Pasq	1769	TARKINGTON, Benjamin		
John Sr. 1m				Tyrr	1755
1f slave	Pasq	1769	John	Tyrr	1755
Joseph	Pasq	1754	Joshua	Tyrr	1755
Nathan	Pasq	1769	Wm	Chow	1717
Peter	Pasq	1754	TARRANS, John	Dobb	1769
Samuel 1m slave	Pasq	1769	Thomas	Dobb	1769
Thomas	Beau	1755	TART, Jonathan	Dobb	1769
Thomas	Pasq	1754	Michsel	Beau	1755
Wm	Pasq	1754	TARVER, Jacob	Dobb	1779
SYMS, George	Casw	1777	Samuel	Dobb	1779
			TATE, Enos	FWV	1771
			Joseph	Rowa	1759
			Robert	Rowa	1759
TABB, Wm	Bute	1771	Wodd (Cpt.)	Casw	1777
Wm	FWV	1771	TATERMAN, John	Tyrr	1755
TABOR, James	Casw	1777	TATOM, Bernard	Gran	1784
John	Bute	1771	John	Gran	1769
John	FWV	1771	John	Gran	1784
Timothy	Anso	1763	John Jr.	Gran	1784
TABOURN, Wm	Gran	1784	Samuel	Gran	1784
TADLOCK, Edward	Pasq	1769	Thomas	Curr	1755
James	Pasq	1769	Wm	Gran	1784
Thomas	NorH	1762	TATUM, Peter	Bute	1771
TAFF, John	Surr	1771	Peter	FWV	1771
TALBERT, John	Bert	1757	TAUGA, Michael	Surr	1771
Samuel	Bute	1771	TAUNT, John	Pitt	1762
TALBOT, Francis	Casw	1777	John	Pitt	1764
James	Casw	1777	Simon	Pitt	1764
John	Casw	1777	Thomas	Crav	1769
Joseph	Casw	1777	Thomas	Pitt	1762
TALER, John	Anso	1763	Thomas	Pitt	1764
Thomas	Dobb	1769	Wm	Pitt	1762
TALL, Isaac	Dobb	1769	Wm	Pitt	1764
John s. of Isaac	Dobb	1769	TAYLOR, Aaron	Crav	1769
TALLANT, Aaron	Anso	1763	Abraham	Bert	1769
John	Anso	1763	Abraham Jr.	Dobb	1769
Moses	Anso	1763	Abraham Sr.	Dobb	1769
Thomas	Anso	1763	Absalom	Crav	1769
TALLERMAN, Josh.	Onsl	1769	Andrew	NorH	1741
TALLEY, Nicholas	Gran	1784	Ann	NewH	1763
Reuben	Gran	1784	Arthur	Cumb	1767
TALLMAN, Joseph	Onsl	1770	Benjamin	Curr	1755
TALOM, John	Gran	1769	Benjamin	Onsl	1769
TALORTON, Wm	Tyrr	1755	Caleb	NorH	1762
TANNER, James	NorH	1762	Caleb	Tryo	1776

TAYLOR, Charles	Casw	1777	TAYLOR, Jonathan	NewH	1767
Charles	Pasq	1754	Jonathan 184		
Charles Jr.	Pasq	1769	acres	Perq	1720
Charles	Pitt	1775	Jonathan	Pitt	1764
Christopher	Dobb	1769	Jonathan	Pitt	1775
Cornelius	Dobb	1769	Jonathan	Tyrr	1755
Daniel	Dobb	1779	Joseph	Chow	1753
Daniel	Pasq	1769	Joseph Jr.	Dobb	1769
David	Perq	1740	Joseph Sr.	Dobb	1769
Drury	Surr	1771	Joseph	Gran	1769
Ebenezer	Curr	1755	Joseph Esq.	Gran	1784
Edmund	Dobb	1769	Joseph	Pasq	1769
Edmund	Gran	1784	Joshua	Crav	1769
Edmund Jr.	Gran	1784	Joshua	Curr	1755
Edward	Chow	1717	Joshua	FWV	1771
Elizabeth	Chow	1753	Joshua	Tryo	1776
Evan s. of Jacob	Pasq	1769	Lemuel	Perq	1720
Gabriel	Pasq	1769	Lewis	Gran	1784
George	Cumb	1767	Maccabeus s.		
George	Gran	1769	of Wm	Pasq	1769
George	Gran	1784	Moses	Crav	1769
Henry	Blad	1781	Moses s. of		
Henry	Bute	1771	Abraham	Dobb	1769
Henry	Dobb	1769	Philip	Bute	1771
Henry	FWV	1771	Philip	Crav	1769
Hugh	Oran	1755	Philip	FWV	1771
Isaac	Dobb	1769	Reuben	Casw	1777
Jacob	Beau	1755	Reuben	Cumb	1767
Jacob Jr.	Beau	1755	Robert	Bute	1771
Jacob	Crav	1742	Robert	Chow	1753
Jacob	Pasq	1769	Robert	Crav	1769
Jacob	Pitt	1762	Robert	Dobb	1779
James	Crav	1769	Robert	FWV	1771
James	Dobb	1769	Robert	Gate	1786
James	Dobb	1779	Robert	Onsl	1769
James	Gran	1784	Robert	Tryo	1776
James	Oran	1755	Samuel	Beau	1755
James	Pasq	1769	Samuel	Beau	1764
James	Surr	1771	Samuel	Crav	1769
James	Surr	1772	Samuel 6w		
Jeremiah	Pasq	1769	6b slaves	Edge	1743
John	Beau	1755	Samuel	Gate	1786
John	Beau	1764	Samuel	Tyrr	1755
John	Bute	1771	Simon	Beau	1755
John	Casw	1777	Simon	Pitt	1762
John	Chow	1753	Thomas	Beau	1755
John	Crav	1769	Thomas Jr.	Chow	1715
John Jr.	Crav	1769	Thomas Sr.	Chow	1715
John	Curr	1755	Thomas	Chow	1753
John	Dobb	1769	Thomas Jr.	Curr	1715
John	Edge	1742	Thomas Sr.	Curr	1715
John	FWV	1771	Thomas	Curr	1755
John	Gran	1769	Thomas	Dobb	1769
John	Gran	1784	Thomas Sr. 6m		
John	NewH	1755	6f slaves	Pasq	1754
John	NewH	1762	Thomas	Pitt	1764
John	NewH	1763	Widow	Perq	1720
John	NewH	1767	Wm	Beau	1744
John	Pasq	1769	Wm	Beau	1752
John	Pitt	1762	Wm	Beau	1755
John	Pitt	1764	Wm	Bute	1771
John	Pitt	1775	Wm	Crav	1743
Jonas	Gate	1786	Wm	Curr	1755
Jonathan	Bert	1743	Wm	Dobb	1769
Jonathan	Dobb	1779	Wm	Dobb	1779

TAYLOR, Wm	FWV	1771	TERRILL, Robert	Blad	1763
Wm	Gran	1769	TERRY, George	Anso	1763
Wm	NewH	1767	James	Anso	1763
Wm	Onsl	1769	James	Casw	1777
Wm	Onsl	1770	James	Edge	1741
Wm	Oran	1755	James	FWV	1771
Wm Jr.	Pasq	1769	James	Gran	1769
Wm Sr.	Pasq	1779	James	Gran	1784
Wm 1 slave	Pasq	1769	James Jr.	Gran	1784
Wm Jr.	Pitt	1762	John	Anso	1763
Wm Sr.	Pitt	1762	John	Gran	1784
Wm	Pitt	1762	Olive	Casw	1777
Wm Jr.	Pitt	1764	Peter	Gran	1784
Wm Sr.	Pitt	1764	Robert	Casw	1777
Wm	Pitt	1764	Rowland	Gran	1769
Wm	Pitt	1775	Rowland	Gran	1784
TEAGUE, Wm	Brun	1769	Stephen	Gran	1784
Wm	Brun	1772	Wm	Anso	1763
Wm	Rand	1779	TETTERTON, John	Dobb	1779
Wm (preacher)	Rand	1779	John	Perq	1720
TEAKEL, Patrick	Anso	1763	Wm 480 acre		
TEAL, Edward	NewH	1762	patent	Perq	1720
Edward	NewH	1763	THACKERSON, Thomas	Casw	1777
Emmanuel	Beau	1755	THACKERY, John	Chow	1721
Thomas	Pitt	1764	John Jr.	Pasq	1769
Wm Jr.	Beau	1755	Joseph	Pasq	1769
Wm	Pitt	1764	THAIN, James	Pitt	1762
TEALL, John	Gran	1784	THAINE, James	Pitt	1764
TEAN, Wm	Pitt	1764	THARP, Samuel	Brun	1769
TEAT, Robert	Oran	1755	Samuel	Brun	1772
TEATER, Jacob	Rowa	1759	Samuel	NewH	1755
TICKLE, Richard	Brun	1769	Samuel	NewH	1762
Richard	Brun	1772	THARPE, Theophilus	NorH	1762
TEDDER, Benjamin	Beau	1755	THARWIN, Thomas	Bert	1757
George Jr.	Dobb	1769	THEACH, Valentine	Casw	1777
George	Dobb	1779	THEMAL, Wm	Anso	1763
TEDFORD, Joseph	Rand	1779	THIGPEN, James Jr.	Perq	1720
Temple	Rand	1779	Joab	Dobb	1779
TEDRICK, John	Blad	1763	Sipherand	Dobb	1779
John	Cumb	1767	Travis	Dobb	1779
Thomas	Blad	1763	THIGPIN, Jonathan	Dobb	1769
TEEL, Emanuel	Pitt	1762	Joshua	Dobb	1769
Joseph	Pitt	1762	Sol s. of		
Wm	Pitt	1762	Joshua	Dobb	1769
TEMPLE, James	Gran	1784	THIMES, Isaac	Blad	1781
Joseph	Pasq	1769	Joseph	Blad	1781
Solomon	Pasq	1754	Martha	Blad	1781
Thomas	Pasq	1754	Wm	Blad	1781
Thomas	Pasq	1769	THOMAS, Abel	Pitt	1775
TEMPLES, Frederick	Anso	1763	Andrew	Rand	1779
Samuel	Oran	1755	Barnaby	NorH	1762
TENNANT, Cairns	Oran	1755	Benjamin	Bute	1771
John	Oran	1755	Benjamin	FWV	1771
TENNING, Thomas	Gran	1755	Benjamin Jr.	FWV	1771
TENNISON, James	Gran	1755	Benjamin	Gran	1784
TERRELL, Hezekiah	Gran	1755	Christian	Gran	1784
Joel	Bute	1771	Daniel	Pitt	1763
Joel	FWV	1771	David	Gran	1769
John	Bute	1771	David	Pitt	1763
John	FWV	1771	David Jr.	Pitt	1763
John	Gran	1755	Edward	Gran	1755
Obadiah	Anso	1763	Evan	Blad	1763
Obadiah	Oran	1755	Francis	Bert	1757
Timothy	FWV	1771	Francis	NewH	1744
Timothy	Oran	1755	George	Blad	1763

THOMAS, Gwaltney	Pitt	1763	THOMAS, Wm	Onsl	1770
Isaac	Rowa	1759	THOMASON, John	Gran	1755
Isaac	Surr	1771	THOMASSON, John	Gran	1784
James	Bert	1757	THOMLINSON, John		
James	Bert	1769	3f slaves	Crav	1779
James	Gate	1786	John S. River		
James	NewH	1755	4m 3f slaves	Crav	1769
James	NewH	1762	THOMPSON, Ann	Curr	1715
James	NewH	1763	Azariah	Dobb	1769
James	NewH	1767	Benjamin	Bute	1771
John	Blad	1763	Benjamin	Edge	1743
John	Blad	1781	Benjamin	FWV	1771
John	Brun	1769	Benjamin	Gran	1755
John	Brun	1772	Charles	Anso	1763
John	Casw	1777	Charles	Crav	1769
John	Crav	1743	Charles	Onsl	1769
John	Crav	1769	Charles	Oran	1755
John	Cumb	1755	Drury	Bute	1771
John	Cumb	1767	Drury	FWV	1771
John	NewH	1755	Elizabeth	Bute	1771
John	NewH	1762	Elizabeth & s.		
Jonathan	Bert	1757	Gideon & Shem	FWV	1771
Jonathan	Bert	1769	George	Gran	1769
Joseph	Bert	1757	Henry	Onsl	1769
Joseph	Cumb	1767	Henry	Onsl	1770
Joseph 5w			Hezekiah	Bert	1769
5b slaves	Edge	1743	Hugh	Onsl	1769
Joseph	Surr	1771	Hugh	Onsl	1770
Josiah	Bert	1769	James	Bute	1771
Lazarus	Chow	1717	James	Chow	1753
Lazarus	Chow	1721	James Constable	FWV	1771
Lazarus	Crav	1769	James	Gran	1755
Lemuel	Gate	1786	James Jr.	Onsl	1769
Lewis	Beau	1764	James Sr.	Onsl	1769
Lewis	Bert	1769	James Jr.	Onsl	1770
Lewis	Crav	1720	James Sr.	Onsl	1770
Louis	Bert	1757	James	Surr	1772
Louis	Crav	1720	Jennings	Gran	1755
Mary	Chow	1753	John	Beau	1764
Matthew	Bute	1771	John	Bute	1771
Matthew s. James	FWV	1771	John	Chow	1753
Nathan	Bute	1771	John	Dobb	1779
Nathan	FWV	1771	John	FWV	1771
Nathan	Gran	1755	John	Gran	1755
Philip	Cumb	1767	John s. of		
Richard	Crav	1720	Benjamin	Gran	1755
Richard	Perq	1720	John	Onsl	1769
Robert	Anso	1763	John	Onsl	1770
Robert	Chow	1753	John	Rand	1779
Samuel	Bert	1757	Joseph	Chow	1721
Samuel	Crav	1741	Joseph	FWV	1771
Samuel	Gate	1786	Joseph	Gate	1786
Samuel	Onsl	1769	Joseph	Rand	1779
Solomon s.			Laurence	Oran	1755
of Thomas	Dobb	1769	Mary	Rand	1779
Solomon	Dobb	1779	Richard	Gran	1784
Spight	Bert	1769	Robert	Beau	1755
Stephen	Gate	1786	Robert	Bert	1757
Thomas	Dobb	1769	Robert	Bute	1771
Widow	Gran	1755	Robert	Dobb	1769
Wm	Beau	1755	Robert	FWV	1771
Wm	Bert	1757	Robert	Rowa	1759
Wm	Chow	1753	Samuel	Beau	1764
Wm	Crav	1743	Samuel	Bute	1771
Wm	Onsl	1769	Samuel	FWV	1771

THOMPSON, Samuel	Gran	1755
Sarah (Mrs.)	Bute	1771
Sarah (Mrs.)	FWV	1771
Sarah	Gran	1755
Simon	Gate	1786
Thomas	Cumb	1767
Thomas	Dobb	1779
Thomas	Gran	1784
Thomas	Oran	1755
Wm & w.		
Elizabeth	Bert	1757
Wm	Chow	1717
Wm	Chow	1721
Wm s. of		
Benjamin	Gran	1755
Wm	Gran	1784
Wm	NewH	1767
Zachariah	Bute	1771
Zachariah	FWV	1771
THOMSON, Andrew	Rand	1779
James	Rand	1779
Jesse	Casw	1777
John	Casw	1777
THORN, Merriman	Gran	1784
Presley	Gran	1784
Richard	Cumb	1755
Solomon	Gran	1784
THORNBOROUGH, Edward		
	Rand	1779
Edward Jr.	Rand	1779
Edward Sr.	Rand	1779
Edward	Rowa	1758
Edward	Rowa	1759
George	Rand	1779
Joseph	Rowa	1759
Thomas	Rowa	1759
Walter	Rowa	1759
Wm	Rowa	1758
Wm	Rowa	1759
Wm	Rowa	1759
THORNE, Merriman	Gran	1769
THORNTON, Francis	FWV	1771
Henry	Gran	1755
James	Cumb	1755
Joel	Bute	1771
Joel	FWV	1771
John	Bute	1771
John	Cumb	1767
John s. Wm John		
& Samuel	FWV	1771
John	Gran	1755
Mark	Bute	1771
Mark Sr. & s.		
Dozer	FWV	1771
Mark	FWV	1771
Roger	Gran	1755
Roger	Gran	1784
Samuel	Rowa	1759
Sarah	Gran	1755
Thomas	Bute	1771
Thomas	Crav	1769
Thomas	FWV	1771
Wm	Bert	1757
Wm	Gran	1784
THORNWELL, Wm	Anso	1763

THOROWGOOD, Henry	Pasq	1769
THORP, James	Tyrr	1755
John	Gran	1784
Paul	Tyrr	1755
THRALL, Joseph	Dobb	1769
THRASH, Jacob	Casw	1777
THRASHER, John	Oran	1755
THRIFT, John	Casw	1777
Nathaniel	Crav	1769
THURMAN, John	Anso	1763
THURRELL, Moses	Onsl	1770
THURSTON, Benjamin	Gran	1784
TIDWELL, John	Rowa	1759
TIGNOR, Tolson	Crav	1769
TILDESLEY, Thomas	Beau	1755
Thomas	Pitt	1762
Thomas	Pitt	1764
TILER, John	Brun	1769
TILGHMAN, John Jr. s.		
of John Sr.	Dobb	1769
John Sr.	Dobb	1769
John	Dobb	1769
Joseph	Dobb	1769
Moses	Dobb	1769
TILLA, Lazarus	Surr	1772
TILLET, Giles	Oran	1755
TILLETT, John	Pasq	1754
John	Pasq	1769
Malachi	Pasq	1769
Wm	Pasq	1769
TILLEY, John	Gran	1769
Stephen	Surr	1771
TILLIT, Edward	Curr	1755
John	Curr	1755
TILLIS, Richard	Cumb	1767
TILLMAN, George	Gran	1769
John	Crav	1769
John	Gran	1755
John	Gran	1769
Moses	Crav	1743
TILTON, John	Dobb	1769
TIMBERLAKE, Richard	Dobb	1779
TIMBERMAN, Casper	Crav	1719
TIMMONS, Moses	Onsl	1770
TIMMS, Cornelius	Blad	1752
TINDALE, Charles	Crav	1769
Charles	Pitt	1764
John	Beau	1742
John	Beau	1755
John Jr.	Dobb	1769
John Sr.	Dobb	1769
Samuel	Beau	1744
Samuel	Onsl	1769
Samuel	Pitt	1762
TINER, James	Dobb	1769
John	Dobb	1769
Nicholas Jr.	Dobb	1769
Nicholas Sr.	Dobb	1769
Nicholas	NorH	1742
Wm	Bert	1757
Wm	Dobb	1769
TINGLE, Esau	Beau	1755
Esau	Crav	1769
Gideon 2m slaves	Crav	1769
Hugh	Beau	1755

TINGLE, Jacob	Beau	1755		TOMES, Francis	Perq	1720
James	Beau	1755		Francis	Perq	1740
James	Crav	1769		Joshua 692 acre		
Joseph	Beau	1755		patent	Perq	1720
Joseph	Crav	1769		TOMLIN, Wm	Oran	1755
Mary 1m 1f				Wm 288 acre		
slave	Crav	1769		patent	Perq	1720
Solomon	Beau	1755		Wm	Perq	1740
Solomon	Crav	1769		TOMLINSON, John	Crav	1769
TINHALLS, John	Beau	1764		Wm Sr.	Cumb	1767
TIPPIN, Perry	Beau	1764		TOMMEE, Henry	Blad	1763
TIPPINS, Henry	Anso	1763		Joseph	Blad	1763
Henry	Brun	1769		TOMMY, Dennis	Rand	1779
Henry	Brun	1772		Henry	Cumb	1767
Thomas	Brun	1769		Joseph Constable	Cumb	1767
Thomas	Brun	1772		TOMPSON, Jacob	Dobb	1769
TIPPIT, John	Crav	1769		John	Dobb	1769
John	Gran	1784		John Jr. s.		
TIRE, John	Surr	1772		of John	Dobb	1769
TISDALE, Antipas				Thomas	Dobb	1769
1m slave	Crav	1769		TOMSON, George	Gran	1755
Wm 1f slave	Crav	1769		John	Curr	1755
TITTERTON, John	Crav	1769		John	Gran	1755
TODD, Elizabeth				Major	Dobb	1769
1m 2f slaves	Pasq	1769		Wm	Curr	1755
Hardy	Bert	1769		TOOGOOD, Elizabeth	N.C.	1701
John	Bert	1769		TOOLE, David	Bert	1769
John	Onsl	1741		Edward	Bert	1757
John	Rowa	1759		Edward	Bert	1769
Nathan	Rowa	1759		Jonathan	Bert	1769
Thomas	Bert	1757		TOOLEY, Adam	Beau	1764
Thomas	Bert	1769		Adam	Crav	1769
Thomas s. of Wm	Bert	1769		TOOMER, Henry	NewH	1762
Thomas	Brun	1769		Henry	NewH	1767
Thomas	Brun	1772		Joshua	NewH	1762
Thomas	Rowa	1759		Sophia	NewH	1767
Wm	Bert	1757		TOOTLE, Thomas	Crav	1769
Wm Jr.	Bert	1769		TOP, Roger	Gran	1755
Wm Sr.	Bert	1769		TOPLEY, Adam	Cumb	1767
Wm s. of Tom	Bert	1769		Elona	Casw	1777
Wm	Brun	1769		TORCHLAND, Thomas	Pasq	1754
Wm	Brun	1772		TORKSEY, Benjamin Jr.		
Wm	Gran	1769		1f slave	Pasq	1769
Wm	Gran	1784		Benjamin Sr.	Pasq	1769
TOLBARD, John	Oran	1755		John (boatswain)	Pasq	1769
TOLBERT, Samuel	FWV	1771		Philip	Pasq	1769
TOLER, Demcey	Dobb	1769		Thomas	Pasq	1769
Mathias	Beau	1755		TOTEN, Pearlon	Pitt	1775
Mathias	Crav	1769		TOTWINE, Winder	Dobb	1779
Nehemiah	Dobb	1769		TOUCHSTONE, Caleb	Anso	1763
Nehemiah	Dobb	1779		Daniel	Anso	1763
Robert	Dobb	1769		Stephen	Anso	1763
Robert	Dobb	1779		TOUGH, Josh	Onsl	1769
Thomas Jr.	Dobb	1779		TOWERS, Mary		
Wm	Dobb	1769		(widow)	Anso	1763
Wm Jr.	Dobb	1769		Thomas	Anso	1763
TOLLIVER, John	Surr	1771		Wm	Anso	1763
John	Surr	1772		TOWLER, James	Curr	1755
Wm	Surr	1771		TOWNING, Glomaw	NewH	1755
Wm	Surr	1772		Solomon	NewH	1755
TOLLOHY, Wm	Bert	1769		Solomon	NewH	1762
TOLSON, Benjamin	Crav	1769		TOWNLEY, Wm	NewH	1767
Tignor	Crav	1769		TOWNS, David	Bute	1771
TOMALIN, John	Oran	1755		David & s. John		
TOMES, Foster	Perq	1740		& David	FWV	1771

TOWNS, Richard	Bute	1771
Richard	FWV	1771
TOWNSEND, Joshua	Dobb	1769
Thomas	Blad	1763
Thomas	Blad	1781
Wm	Blad	1781
Wm	Perq	1740
TOWRY, George	Rowa	1759
TRACEY, John	Crav	1769
TRADER, John	Gate	1786
TRAGIN, George	Cumb	1755
TRAINHAM, John	Gran	1784
TRANSAW, Philip	Surr	1771
Philip	Surr	1772
TRANTHAM, David	Cumb	1755
Martin	Cumb	1755
Martin Jr.	Cumb	1755
TRAP, John	Cumb	1767
Wm	Cumb	1755
TRAVILIAN, James	Gran	1755
TRAVIS, Charles	Bute	1771
Charles	FWV	1771
John	Anso	1763
John	Oran	1755
Thomas	Gate	1786
Thomas	Pitt	1762
Thomas	Pitt	1764
Wm	Beau	1755
Wm	Pitt	1762
Wm	Pitt	1764
TRAWICKS, Robert	Onsl	1769
TRAYWICKS, Robert	Onsl	1770
TRAYLOR, Wm	Bute	1771
Wm	FWV	1771
TREADAWAY, Richard	Cumb	1767
TREADWELL, Adoniram	Newh	1755
Adoniram Jr.	NewH	1762
Adoniram Sr.	NewH	1762
John	NewH	1762
Stephen	Onsl	1769
TRENTHAM, Martin	Cumb	1767
TREWHIT, Henry	Crav	1769
Levi	Crav	1769
Levi Jr.	Crav	1769
Wm	Crav	1769
TRICKEY, Giles	Casw	1777
TRIGGE, Samuel	Bert	1769
TRIM, Charles	Casw	1777
TRIPLER, John	Oran	1755
TRIPLETT, Daniel	Casw	1777
Francis	Casw	1777
John	Casw	1777
TRIPP, Cales	Dobb	1769
Henry	Beau	1764
John Jr.	Beau	1755
John	Beau	1764
Nevill	Beau	1764
Robert	Beau	1764
Wm	Beau	1764
TROGDON, Wm	Oran	1755
Wm	Rand	1779
TROLINGER, Adam	Oran	1755
TROTMAN, Amos	Gate	1786
Demsey	Gate	1786
Edward	Chow	1753

TROTMAN, Ezekiel	Gate	1786
Thomas	Gate	1786
TROTT, Adam	Onsl	1769
Lewis Jr.	Onsl	1770
TROTTER, James		
2w 11b slaves	Chow	1743
James	Chow	1753
Joseph	Oran	1755
TROUBERFIELD, Francis		
	Roan	1720
John	Chow	1721
John	Roan	1720
Wm	Chow	1721
Wm	Roan	1720
TROUT, Henry	Linc	1790
Henry	Tryo	1776
TROWELL, Joseph	Chow	1721
Joseph 400 acres	Chow	1721
Joseph	Cumb	1755
TRUEBLOOD, Abel	Pasq	1754
Abel 1m slave	Pasq	1769
Amos	Pasq	1754
Caleb	Pasq	1754
Caleb 7m slaves	Pasq	1769
Daniel 2m slaves	Pasq	1769
Fisher 1m 1f		
slaves	Pasq	1769
Joshua	Pasq	1754
Josiah	Pasq	1754
Josiah	Pasq	1769
Thomas	Pasq	1754
TRUELOVE, Timothy	Chow	1717
Timothy	Chow	1721
Wm	FWV	1771
TRUETT, Abraham	Beau	1764
Abraham	NewH	1767
John	Brun	1769
John	Brun	1772
John	Dobb	1769
Levi	Dobb	1769
Levy	Crav	1743
Lodwick	Beau	1764
Wm	Dobb	1769
TRULOS, Samuel	Pitt	1775
TRULUCK, George	Crav	1769
TRUMBLE, Thomas		
175 acres	Perq	1720
TRUSS, Samuel	Pitt	1762
TRYON, Wm (Gov.)		
8m 2f slaves	Brun	1769
Wm (Gov.)	Brun	1772
TRUS, Samuel	Pitt	1764
TUB, Wm	Oran	1755
TUCKER, Daniel	Onsl	1769
Edward	Gran	1755
Edward	Rowa	1759
George	Bute	1771
George	Rand	1779
George	Rowa	1759
John	Bute	1771
John	Dobb	1769
John	FWV	1771
John & s. David	FWV	1771
John	Gran	1755
John	Surr	1772

TUCKER, Joshua	Pitt	1762	TURNER, Henry	Dobb	1769
Joshua	Pitt	1764	Jacob	FWV	1771
Nathaniel	Rand	1779	James	Brun	1769
Robert	Curr	1715	James	Casw	1777
Robert	Rand	1779	James	Crav	1769
Roger Jr.	Rowa	1759	James	Dobb	1769
Samuel	Surr	1772	James	NorH	1762
Thomas	Onsl	1769	James	Perq	1740
Thomas	Onsl	1770	John Esq.	Blad	1763
Thomas	Rowa	1759	John	Blad	1781
Wm	Bute	1771	John	Chow	1717
Wm	FWV	1771	John	Crav	1769
Wm	Rand	1779	John 4m 1f		
TUDAR, Elizabeth	Gran	1784	slaves	Crav	1769
Valentine	Gran	1784	John	Pasq	1754
TUDER, George	Beau	1755	Josa	Chow	1721
George s. of			Joseph	FWV	1771
George	Beau	1755	Joseph	Pasq	1754
John	Gran	1769	Mary	Rand	1779
Thomas s of Geo.	Beau	1755	Matthew	Bert	1757
TUDOR, Henry	Gran	1784	Matthew	Bert	1769
John	Gran	1784	Nedem	Pitt	1762
TUGGAL, Griffin	Gran	1784	Nedum	Pitt	1764
TUGGEL, John	Gran	1784	Samuel	Onsl	1769
TUGWELL, James	Gate	1786	Samuel	Onsl	1770
TUINS, Amos	Gran	1784	Stephen	Gran	1784
Hollis	Gran	1784	Thomas	Bert	1757
TUIT, Jacob	Gran	1784	Thomas	Bert	1769
John	Gran	1784	Thomas	Bute	1771
TULL, Benjamin	Curr	1715	Thomas Esq.	FWV	1771
Charles	Dobb	1779	Thomas	FWV	1771
Edward	NewH	1767	Thomas	Gran	1755
Isaac Jr.	Dobb	1779	Thomas	Onsl	1770
John	Dobb	1779	Thomas	Surr	1771
Wm	Dobb	1779	Wilkerson	Oran	1755
TULLY, Wm	Cumb	1767	Wm	Bert	1757
TUMBLES, Samuel	Pasq	1769	Wm	Bert	1769
TUMERES, Jesse	Pitt	1775	Wm	Bute	1771
TUNNEN, Thomas	Anso	1763	Wm	FWV	1771
TRUMAN, Thomas	Beau	1755	Wm	Gran	1784
TURNAGE, Charity	Pitt	1775	Wm	Pitt	1762
George	Chow	1717	Wm	Pitt	1764
George	Dobb	1779	TURNIFIELD, Ned	Dobb	1769
James	Dobb	1779	TURPIN, Henry	FWV	1771
John	Pitt	1764	Thomas & s.		
Luke	Pitt	1775	Hugh	FWV	1771
Sarah	Pitt	1775	Wm	Surr	1771
Wm	Bert	1769	TURTON, Joseph	Beau	1755
Wm	Pitt	1764	Thomas	Curr	1755
Wm	Pitt	1775	TUTAN, Absalom	Crav	1769
TURNER, Abraham	Blad	1763	TUTON, Thomas	Pitt	1775
Benjamin	Onsl	1769	TUTTLE, John	Dobb	1769
Benjamin	Onsl	1770	Wm	Dobb	1769
Berryman	Casw	1777	TWITTY, John	Bute	1771
Charles	Gran	1769	John	FWV	1771
Charles	Gran	1784	Peter	Bute	1771
Daniel	Blad	1763	Peter	FWV	1771
Daniel	Pasq	1769	Susannah	Tryo	1776
David	Onsl	1769	Wm (deceased)	Tryo	1776
David	Onsl	1770	TYER, James	Pitt	1762
Edward	Perq	1740	Thomas	NewH	1762
Elias	Onsl	1769	Thomas	NewH	1767
Elias	Onsl	1770	Wm	NewH	1762
Ezekiel	FWV	1771	Wm	NewH	1767
Henry	Casw	1777	TYLER, Absalom	Cumb	1767

TYLER, Adam	Cumb 1767		TYSON, Thomas	Pitt 1775
John	Bert 1757		Wm s. of Edmund	Pitt 1764
John	Brun 1772		Wm	Pitt 1775
Sarah	Blad 1763			
Thomas	Pitt 1775			
Wm	Bert 1757			
Wm	Dobb 1769		UMFLEET, David	Gate 1786
TYLOR, Bartlett	Gran 1769		Job	Gate 1786
Berthal	Gran 1784		Wm	Chow 1753
TYNER, Asa (black)	Bute 1771		Wm Jr.	Chow 1753
Asa (black)	FWV 1771		UMFREE, Wm	Bert 1757
Nicholas	Dobb 1779		UNDERDOWN, Stephen	Casw 1777
TYRE, Wm	Beau 1755		UNDERHILL, James	Crav 1769
Wm 1m 2f slaves	Crav 1769		UNDERWOOD, Daniel	Gran 1755
TYREE, Harris	Casw 1777		Daniel s. of	
TYRRELL, John	Edge 1742		Daniel	Gran 1755
TYSON, Aaron	Beau 1755		George	FWV 1771
Aaron	Pitt 1762		George	Gran 1755
Aaron	Pitt 1764		Henry	Gran 1755
Aaron	Pitt 1775		James s. of	
Abraham	Beau 1755		George	Gran 1755
Abraham Esq.	Pitt 1762		John	Bute 1771
Abraham	Pitt 1764		John	FWV 1771
Abraham Esq.	Pitt 1775		Richard	Gran 1769
Ann	Pitt 1775		UNTHANK, Joseph	Rowa 1759
Cornelius	Cumb 1755		UPCHURCH, Richard	Gran 1755
Cornelius	Cumb 1767		Wm	Gran 1755
Edmund	Beau 1755		Wm	Gran 1769
Edmund	Pitt 1762		Wm Jr.	Gran 1769
Edmund	Pitt 1764		UPTON, Amos	Pasq 1769
Edmund Jr.	Pitt 1764		Christian	Pasq 1754
Edmund	Pitt 1775		Edward	Casw 1777
George	Beau 1755		Josiah	Pasq 1769
George	Pitt 1762		Richard	Cumb 1767
George	Pitt 1764		Thomas	Pasq 1769
George	Pitt 1775		Willis 1f slave	Pasq 1769
Jehu	Pitt 1762		USSERY, John	Anso 1763
Jehu	Pitt 1775		Wm	Anso 1763
John	Beau 1755		USUARY, John	Casw 1777
John Jr.	Beau 1755		UXFORD, Samuel	Crav 1750
John	Pitt 1762		UZZELL, Elisha	Dobb 1769
John the Baptist	Pitt 1762		Elisha	Dobb 1779
John	Pitt 1764		Thomas	Dobb 1769
Jonathan	Beau 1755			
Jonathan	Pitt 1762			
Jonathan	Pitt 1764			
Jonathan	Pitt 1775		VAHAN, Benjamin	Anso 1763
Major	Beau 1755		VAIL, Edward	Chow 1753
Mathias	Beau 1755		Jeremiah 1,548	
Mathias	Hyde 1742		acres	Chow 1717
Mathias	Pitt 1762		Jeremiah	Crav 1750
Mathias	Pitt 1764		Jeremiah 14b	
Moses	Beau 1755		slaves	NewH 1742
Moses Jr.	Pitt 1762		John	Chow 1753
Moses Sr.	Pitt 1762		Margaret 5m	
Moses	Pitt 1764		7f slaves	Crav 1769
Moses Jr.	Pitt 1764		Wm	NewH 1755
Moses	Pitt 1775		VALENTINE, Alexander	
Patience	Pitt 1775			Bert 1757
Sabra	Beau 1755		Christopher	Pasq 1754
Samuel	Pitt 1762		David	Bert 1757
Samuel 2 slaves	Pitt 1762		Edward	Tyrr 1755
Samuel	Pitt 1764		Henry	Bert 1757
Thomas	Pitt 1762		Henry	Curr 1755
Thomas	Pitt 1764		John	Crav 1720

VALENTINE, Rowe	Pasq 1754	VANPELT, Henry	Crav 1769
Malachi	Bert 1757	Jacob	NorH 1742
VAN, Edward	NewH 1755	Johannas	Bert 1757
VANCE, John	Crav 1769	John	Bert 1757
John	Pitt 1764	Simon	Bert 1757
VANDERFORD, John	Rand 1779	VANUPSTALL, Garrot	Bert 1757
Michael	Bert 1757	Gerard	Bert 1757
VANDERMULLEN, Thomas		VANDELL, John	Bert 1757
	Curr 1715	VARDIN, Bryan	Curr 1755
VANDERPOOL, Abraham	Surr 1771	Silvester	Curr 1755
Abraham	Surr 1772	VARNELL, John	Gate 1786
Jacob	Surr 1772	Richard	Surr 1771
John	Surr 1772	VARNER, Adam	Rand 1779
Whynant	Surr 1771	John	Gran 1769
Winyard	Surr 1772	VARNUM, John	Onsl 1741
VANDUCE, John	Chow 1753	VARSER, Jesse	Bute 1771
VANDYKE, Henry	Gran 1755	Jesse	FWV 1771
John	Gran 1784	Wm	Bute 1771
Lydia	Gran 1769	Wm	FWV 1771
VANHOOK, Aaron	Casw 1777	VASSAR, John	Dobb 1779
David	Casw 1777	VASSER, Robert	Gran 1755
Isaac	Casw 1777	VASTON, Robert	Cumb 1767
Laurence	Casw 1777	VAUGHAN, Benjamin	Anso 1763
Lloyd	Casw 1777	Hilburn	Dobb 1769
VANHOOSER, Jacob	Anso 1763	John	Bert 1757
John	Anso 1763	Vincent	NorH 1762
John Jr.	Anso 1763	Wm	NorH 1762
VANHOUCKS, Aaron	Oran 1755	VAUGHN, Azariah	Pasq 1769
VANHOUSER, John	Surr 1771	Richard	Gran 1769
Valentine	Surr 1771	Wm	Crav 1769
Valentine	Surr 1772	VAUN, Azariah	Pasq 1769
VANLANDINGHAM, Dawson		VAUSE, Thomas	Dobb 1769
	Bute 1771	VEAZEY, Edward	Gran 1769
Dawson	FWV 1771	James	Gran 1769
John	Gran 1769	James	Gran 1784
Wm	Gran 1784	Thomas	Gran 1769
VANLUVEN, Christopher		Thomas	Gran 1784
	Chow 1717	Zebulon	Gran 1784
Christopher	Chow 1721	VEMIER, Frederick	Rand 1779
VANN, Charles'		Randolph	Rand 1779
estate	Gate 1786	VENABLE, Wm	Surr 1771
Darius	Gate 1786	Wm	Surr 1772
Dempsey	Bert 1769	VENCELNER, Wm	Rowa 1759
Edward	Bert 1757	VENDRICK, Daniel	Crav 1769
Edward Jr.	Bert 1757	John	Crav 1769
Edward	Bert 1769	John Jr.	Crav 1769
Edward	Chow 1753	John The Younger	Crav 1769
Edward	Gate 1786	VENOY, Andrew	
George	Chow 1753	(Cpt.)	Casw 1777
Jesse	Gate 1786	Andrew	Casw 1777
John	Gate 1786	VENTERS, Absalom	NewH 1762
Mary	Chow 1753	David 1m slave	Crav 1769
Wm	Bert 1769	David 1f slave	Crav 1769
VANOY, Andrew	Surr 1771	Moses	Onsl 1770
Andrew	Surr 1772	Pharaoh	Rand 1779
Francis	Surr 1771	VENTRESS, Pharaoh	Pasq 1769
Francis	Surr 1772	VENTURES, Daniel	Bert 1769
John	Rowa 1759	VERDEN, Thomas	Pasq 1769
John	Surr 1771	VERGEN, George	Dobb 1779
John	Surr 1772	James	Chow 1753
VANPELT, Anthony	Dobb 1769	VERNAL, Richard	Surr 1771
Anthony	Dobb 1779	Richard	Surr 1772
Daniel	Bert 1742	Thomas	Bert 1757
Daniel & s. John	Bert 1757	Wm	Oran 1755
Harmon	Bert 1757	Wm	Surr 1771

VERNAL, Wm	Surr	1772	VINSON, Levin	Dobb	1779
VERNON, Ephraim	NewH	1742	Peter	Gran	1755
Ephraim's estate	NewH	1755	Thomas	Chow	1721
Ephraim's estate	NewH	1762	Thomas	FWV	1771
Estate 11m			Wm	Chow	1721
11f slaves	Brun	1769	Wm & s. Thomas	FWV	1771
Estate	Brun	1772	Wm	Gran	1755
John	Dobb	1769	VINSTEAD, Samuel	Casw	1777
Thomas	Blad	1763	VIRGIN, George	Dobb	1779
Wm	Brun	1772	James	Chow	1753
VERSIE, Edward	Gran	1755	Wm	Bert	1769
VESTAL, James	Oran	1755	VIRMILLION, Jesse	Casw	1777
Thomas	Oran	1755	Wilson	Casw	1777
Wm	Oran	1755	VIZE, Elizabeth &		
VICE, John	Casw	1777	s. John	Bert	1757
VICKARS, John			VOLLOWAY, Jonathan	Chow	1717
6m 6f slaves	Crav	1769	John	Chow	1721
VICKERS, George	NewH	1767	VORHES	NewH	1767
VICKERY, Ezekiel	Anso	1763	VOSE, Ishmael	Beau	1755
James	Anso	1763	Thomas	Beau	1755
John	Rowa	1759	VOSHEN, Peter		
Marmaduke	Rowa	1758	5m slaves	Pasq	1769
Marmaduke	Rowa	1759	VOSS, James	Beau	1764
VICKORY, Christopher			John	Casw	1777
	Rand	1779	Joseph	Casw	1777
James	Rand	1779	Joseph Jr.	Casw	1777
John	Rand	1779	Thomas	Beau	1764
Marmaduke	Rand	1779	VOUSE, Joseph	Oran	1755
Wm	Gran	1769			
VINCE, Humphrey	Curr	1715			
Thomas	Blad	1742			
Thomas	Blad	1763	WADE, Amey	Gran	1784
Thomas	Curr	1715	Andrew	Gran	1784
VINCENT, Alexander	Gran	1784	Benjamin	Gran	1769
David Constable	Bute	1771	Charles	Gran	1769
David	Bute	1771	Charles	Gran	1784
Isaac	Gran	1784	James	Bute	1771
Jacob	Gran	1784	James	Dobb	1769
Jesse	Bute	1771	James	Dobb	1779
Joshua	FWV	1771	James & s.		
Peter	Gran	1769	Andrew & John	FWV	1771
Peter	Gran	1784	James	Gran	1755
Thomas	Bute	1771	James	Gran	1784
Wm	Bute	1771	John	Edge	1741
VINES, John	Beau	1755	John	NorH	1744
John	Brun	1772	John	NorH	1762
Samuel	Beau	1745	Joseph	Gran	1769
Samuel	Beau	1755	Joseph	Rand	1779
Samuel	Beau	1764	Robert	Gran	1784
Wm	Beau	1755	Robert	Gran	1784
Wm	Beau	1764	Samuel	Dobb	1769
VINING, Frederick	Dobb	1769	WADDELL, Charles	Surr	1771
John	Dobb	1769	Hughes Esq.	Blad	1763
Wm	Dobb	1769	Humphrey Esq.	Blad	1763
Wm	Dobb	1779	Jacob	Bute	1771
VINSON, David			James	Tyrr	1755
Constable	FWV	1771	WADSWORTH, Ignatius	Crav	1769
Drury s. of			James	Cumb	1767
David	FWV	1771	Jason	Cumb	1767
James	NorH	1762	John	Cumb	1767
Jesse	Bert	1769	Thomas	Cumb	1767
Jesse	FWV	1771	WAGGONER, Joseph	Surr	1772
John	Bert	1769	Samuel	Surr	1771
John	Dobb	1769	Samuel	Surr	1772
Joseph	Dobb	1769	Susannah, widow	Beau	1764

WAGGONER, Wm	Beau	1755	WALKER, James s.		
Wm	Surr	1771	of James	Gran	1755
Wm	Surr	1772	James	Gran	1769
WAGNER, Jesse	Dobb	1769	Jesse	Bute	1771
WAGSTAFF, Wm	Gran	1755	Jesse	FWV	1771
WAHABB, James	Curr	1755	Joel	Bute	1771
WAIDE, Joseph	Oran	1755	Joel	FWV	1771
WAILS, Robert	NewH	1762	John	Beau	1764
WAIN, Wm	Crav	1769	John	Brun	1769
WAINRIGHT, Wm	NewH	1762	John	Brun	1772
WAIRE, Wm Sr.	Casw	1777	John	Bute	1771
WAIT, John	Bert	1757	John	Casw	1777
WAKLEY, Robert	NewH	1755	John 1,220 acres	Chow	1721
WALBURTON, John	Bert	1757	John	Crav	1769
Robert	Chow	1717	John	Cumb	1767
Robert 450 acres	Chow	1721	John	Curr	1755
WALDEN, Benjamin	Dobb	1779	John	FWV	1771
Wm	Gran	1784	John	Gran	1755
WALDO, John	Dobb	1769	John	Gran	1769
WALDRIDGE, Richard	Surr	1771	John	NewH	1755
WALDRON, Charles	Pitt	1775	John	NewH	1762
Isaac 7m			John	Onsl	1769
8f slaves	Brun	1769	John	Rand	1779
Isaac	Brun	1772	John	Rowa	1759
Isaac	NewH	1762	Jonathan	Oran	1755
John	Dobb	1769	Joseph	Blad	1763
John	Onsl	1769	Joseph	Oran	1755
John	Onsl	1770	Mary	Gran	1784
Wm	Onsl	1769	Moses	Casw	1777
Wm	Onsl	1770	Peter	Bute	1771
WALDROP, James	Gran	1769	Peter	Gran	1755
John s. of Luke	Gran	1755	Robert	NewH	1741
John	Gran	1769	Robert	NewH	1744
Joseph	Gran	1769	Robert	Surr	1771
Luke	Gran	1755	Robert Jr.	Surr	1772
WALKER, Ann	NewH	1755	Robert Sr.	Surr	1772
Ann	NewH	1767	Samuel	Bert	1757
Benjamin	Tyrr	1755	Samuel	Bute	1771
Capt. 1,500 acres			Samuel	Casw	1777
	N.C.	1701	Samuel	FWV	1771
Daniel	Beau	1764	Samuel	Gran	1769
David Constable	Bute	1771	Samuel	Gran	1784
David Constable	FWV	1771	Samuel	Rand	1779
David	Surr	1771	Solomon	Gran	1755
David	Surr	1772	Solomon	Gran	1769
Edward	Tyrr	1755	Stephen	Rand	1779
Francis	Cumb	1767	Thomas	Beau	1755
Francis	Gran	1755	Thomas	Beau	1764
Francis s. of			Thomas	Bert	1757
Francis	Gran	1755	Thomas & S.		
George	Beau	1764	George & Wm	Bert	1757
George	Bute	1771	Thomas	Blad	1741
George	Dobb	1769	Thomas	Gran	1755
George	FWV	1771	Thomas	Surr	1771
Hardidge	Bute	1771	Thomas	Surr	1772
Hardwitch	FWV	1771	Thomas	Tyrr	1755
Hatton	Bert	1757	Usley	Bute	1771
Hawtree	FWV	1771	Usley & her s.		
Henry	Edge	1734	Thomas	FWV	1771
Henry	Surr	1772	Wm	Bute	1771
Homer	Anso	1763	Wm Jr.	Bute	1771
James	Casw	1777	Wm	Dobb	1769
James Jr.	Casw	1777	Wm	Edge	1743
James	Dobb	1779	Wm	FWV	1771
James	Gran	1755	Wm Jr.	FWV	1771

WALKER, Wm	Dobb	1769	WALLER, Henry	Surr	1771
Wm	Edge	1743	James	Beau	1764
Wm	FWV	1771	Jesse	Bert	1757
Wm Jr.	FWV	1771	Jesse	Pitt	1762
Wm & bro James	FWV	1771	Michael	Rowa	1759
Wm & s. James	FWV	1771	Zephaniah	Gran	1784
Wm	Gran	1784	WALLICKS, Martin	Rowa	1759
Wm	NewH	1755	WALLS, John	Pitt	1764
Wm	NewH	1762	Joshua	Curr	1755
Wm 2m 3f slaves	Pasq	1769	WALSH, John	Chow	1717
Wm	Rand	1779	John	Cumb	1767
Wm	Surr	1772	John Jr.	Cumb	1767
WALL, Arthur	NorH	1762	Thomas	Cumb	1767
Benjamin	Edge	1743	WALSTON, George	Beau	1755
Edward	Blad	1763	George	Pitt	1762
Elizabeth	Pitt	1762	George	Pitt	1764
Esse	Edge	1734	John	Dobb	1779
Garrett	Edge	1734	John	Pitt	1762
Garrett	Edge	1743	Jonathan	Dobb	1779
Howell	Pitt	1764	Philip	Bert	1757
Jeremiah	Dobb	1769	Philip	Bert	1769
Josa.	Chow	1721	Philip Jr.	Bert	1769
Joseph Jr.	Beau	1755	Phil.	Chow	1717
Joseph	Edge	1734	Phil.	Chow	1721
Joseph Constable	Pitt	1762	Thomas	Dobb	1769
Thomas	Beau	1755	Thomas	Pitt	1762
Thomas	NorH	1741	Wm	Chow	1717
Walter	Edge	1734	Wm	Chow	1721
Wm	Pitt	1764	Wm	Dobb	1769
WALLACE, Aaron	Dobb	1769	Wm	Dobb	1779
Adam	Crav	1769	Wm	Pitt	1762
Andrew	Crav	1743	WALTERS, Abimelech s.		
Ann	Gate	1786	of John	Dobb	1769
Benjamin	Crav	1769	Armstrong	Dobb	1769
Caleb	Beau	1755	Isaac	Gate	1786
Caleb	Pitt	1762	Jacob	Gate	1786
Caleb	Pitt	1764	John	Dobb	1769
Elias	Casw	1777	John s. of John	Dobb	1769
Francis	Rand	1779	John	NewH	1755
James	Chow	1753	Jude	Dobb	1769
James	Gran	1769	Wm	Chow	1753
John	Beau	1743	Wm	Dobb	1769
John	Beau	1755	Wm	Gate	1786
John	Beau	1764	Wm	Gran	1755
John	Casw	1777	WALTHENS, Henry	Surr	1772
John Jr.	Casw	1777	WALTON, Ann	Gate	1786
John	Chow	1721	Henderson	Rowa	1759
John	Chow	1753	Henry	Gate	1786
John	Pitt	1762	Henry	Rowa	1758
Jonathan	Chow	1753	Henry	Rowa	1759
Mark	Crav	1769	James	Gate	1786
Michael	Cumb	1767	James	Onsl	1769
Richard 7m			Jesse	Surr	1771
5f slaves	Crav	1769	John B.	Gate	1786
Richard 5w			John	Rand	1779
6b slaves	Onsl	1751	Lewis	Gate	1786
Robert 2m slaves	Crav	1769	Priscilla	Gate	1786
Robert	Dobb	1779	Robert	Surr	1772
Stephen	Crav	1769	Thomas	Chow	1742
Thomas	Beau	1755	Thomas	Chow	1753
Wm	Beau	1755	Thomas	Gate	1786
Wm	Beau	1764	Timothy	Chow	1753
Wm	Chow	1753	Wm	Chow	1753
Wm	Gate	1786	Wm Sr.	Chow	1753
Wm	Gran	1769	WAMMOTH, John	Gran	1769

WANEW, Joseph	Bert	1769		WARD, Luke	Bert	1769
WANTLAND, James	Onsl	1741		Mary	Onsl	1769
WAPPING, Andrew	3m			Mary	Onsl	1770
1f slaves	Pasq	1769		Melton	Onsl	1769
WARBUTTON, John	Bert	1757		Michael Jr.	Bert	1757
John (Walburton?)				Michael	Pitt	1762
	Chow	1753		Michael Jr.	Pitt	1762
John	Onsl	1770		Michael	Pitt	1764
Robert	Chow	1717		Nathan	Dobb	1769
Robert 450 acres	Chow	1721		Notty	Bert	1769
Wm	Dobb	1779		Paul	Onsl	1769
WARD, Anthony	NewH	1755		Philb.	Chow	1717
Anthony	NewH	1762		Philb.	Chow	1721
Benjamin	Bute	1771		Philip	Bert	1757
Benjamin & s.				Philip	Bert	1769
Joseph	FWV	1771		Rhoser	Surr	1771
Benjamin	Gran	1755		Rhoser	Surr	1772
Benjamin	Gran	1769		Richard	Bert	1757
Bridgett	Bert	1769		Richard	Bute	1771
Catherine	Chow	1753		Richard	FWV	1771
Christian	Chow	1753		Richard	Gate	1786
Daniel	Dobb	1779		Richard	Onsl	1769
David	Dobb	1769		Richard	Onsl	1770
David	Onsl	1769		Richard	Rand	1779
David	Oran	1755		Robert	Bute	1771
David	Rowa	1759		Robert & s.		
Edward	Beau	1755		Henry	FWV	1771
Edward	Crav	1720		Robert	Gate	1786
Edward	Onsl	1743		Robert	Pitt	1762
Edward	Onsl	1769		Robert	Pitt	1764
Edward	Onsl	1770		Samuel	Beau	1755
Edward	Pitt	1764		Samuel	Pitt	1762
Elizabeth	Onsl	1769		Samuel Jr.	Pitt	1762
Ezekiel	Dobb	1769		Samuel	Pitt	1764
Ezekiel	Dobb	1779		Seth	Onsl	1769
Francis	Pitt	1764		Seth	Onsl	1770
Francis	Tyrr	1755		Simon	Onsl	1769
Henry	Cumb	1767		Simon	Onsl	1770
Hugh 5m				Solomon	Dobb	1769
2f slaves	Crav	1769		Solomon s. of		
James	Bert	1757		Solomon	Dobb	1769
James	Bert	1769		Solomon	Onsl	1769
James	Chow	1717		Thomas	Anso	1763
James	Chow	1753		Thomas	Bert	1769
James	Pasq	1754		Thomas	Brun	1769
James	Rand	1779		Thomas	Brun	1772
Jeremiah	Gran	1769		Thomas Jr.	Chow	1753
Jesse	Gate	1786		Thomas Sr.	Chow	1753
John (Wood?)	Anso	1763		Thomas	Chow	1753
John	Beau	1755		Thomas	Pasq	1769
John	Bert	1769		Thomas	Pitt	1762
John	Brun	1743		Thomas	Rand	1779
John	Brun	1772		Wm	Bute	1771
John	Chow	1717		Wm	Oran	1755
John	Chow	1721		Wm	Rand	1779
John Jr.	Chow	1721		Wm	Tyrr	1755
John	Chow	1753		WARDEN, Wm	Curr	1755
John	Dobb	1769		WARDIN, Daniel	Casw	1777
John	FWV	1771		WARDSWORTH, Edward	Pasq	1754
John	Onsl	1769		WARE, Henry	Gate	1786
John	Pitt	1762		WARNER, Benjamin	Pitt	1762
John	Pitt	1763		Francis	Beau	1755
John	Pitt	1764		John	Beau	1755
Joseph	Chow	1753		John	NewH	1742
Luke	Bert	1757		Richard	Beau	1755

WARNER, Richard	Beau	1764	WASHINGTON, Richard		
Wm	Beau	1742	Constable	Chow	1717
WARNOCK, Matthew	Surr	1772	Richard 300 acres		
Robert	Surr	1771		Chow	1721
Robert	Surr	1772	Wm	Gran	1755
WARR, Jane	Chow	1721	Wm	Gran	1769
John	Chow	1717	WATERFIELD, Michael	Curr	1755
Thomas	Chow	1717	WATERON, Jacob	NewH	1762
Thomas	Chow	1721	WATERS, Amos	Beau	1755
Thomas	NorH	1762	Amos	Beau	1764
Wm	Rand	1779	Elizabeth	Bute	1771
WARRELL, David	Dobb	1769	Elizabeth s. Ben	FWV	1771
John Jr. s.			Elizabeth	NewH	1762
of John	Dobb	1769	Gab.	Onsl	1770
John Sr.	Dobb	1769	Gabriel	Onsl	1769
Richard	Dobb	1769	John	Beau	1764
Wm	Dobb	1769	John	Chow	1753
WARREN, Abraham			John	NewH	1755
1m 1f slave	Crav	1769	John	Onsl	1769
Ann	Bert	1757	Joseph's estate	Brun	1772
Benjamin	Bert	1757	Joseph's	NewH	1755
Benjamin Jr.	Bert	1757	Joseph's	NewH	1762
Benjamin	Crav	1769	Pauley	Gran	1769
Edward	Bert	1757	Raleigh	Surr	1772
Edward	Chow	1753	Samuel 23m 18f		
Edward Jr.	Chow	1753	slaves	Brun	1769
Edward	Gate	1786	Samuel	Brun	1772
Goodlow	Casw	1777	Samuel	NewH	1762
Hackey	Oran	1755	Sarah	NewH	1755
Henchy	Onsl	1769	Seth	Onsl	1770
Henchy	Onsl	1770	Southey	Onsl	1769
Hincher	Onsl	1769	Thomas	Beau	1755
Hincher	Onsl	1770	Thomas	Casw	1777
Horsington	Crav	1769	Thomas	Dobb	1769
James	Casw	1777	Thomas	Gran	1769
James	Oran	1755	Will	Onsl	1769
John	Casw	1777	Wm's estate	Brun	1772
John Sr.	Casw	1777	Wm	Dobb	1779
John	Curr	1715	Wm	Onsl	1769
John	Curr	1721	Wm	Onsl	1770
John	Gate	1786	WATES, John	Beau	1755
Joseph	Casw	1777	WATFORD, Joseph	Bert	1769
Joseph	Gate	1786	WATKINS, Henry	Chow	1753
Robert	Bert	1757	Henry	Rowa	1759
Robert	Edge	1742	Henry	Surr	1771
Robert	Gate	1786	Isaiah	Gran	1755
Robert	NorH	1743	James	Rowa	1759
Samuel	Casw	1777	John	Beau	1755
Wm	Bert	1757	John	Bute	1771
Wm	Bert	1769	John	Casw	1777
Wm	Gate	1786	John	FWV	1771
WARROW, Wm	Bert	1769	John	Pitt	1762
WARTELE, John	Surr	1771	John	Pitt	1764
WARTON, David	Bert	1757	Wm	Anso	1763
WARWESTON, James	Bert	1769	Wm 8w 4b		
WARWICK, Andrew	Casw	1777	slaves	Beau	1745
WASDEN, Joseph	Surr	1771	Wm	Dobb	1779
Joseph	Surr	1772	Wm Jr.	Pitt	1762
Thomas	Surr	1771	Wm Sr.	Pitt	1762
Thomas	Surr	1772	Wm	Pitt	1764
WASHBURN, James	Blad	1781	Wm Jr.	Pitt	1764
Richard	Casw	1777	WATLEY, John s.		
WASHINGTON, Ephraim	Gran	1784	of Shirley	Gran	1755
John	Pitt	1762	Shirley	Gran	1755
John	Pitt	1764	Richard	FWV	1771

WATLEY, Shirley s.			WEAVER, Edward	Gran	1769
Willis	FWV	1771	WEAVER, Edward	Gran	1784
Wilson	FWV	1771	Frederick	Gran	1769
Wm	FWV	1771	Henry	FWV	1771
Wm s. of Shirley	Gran	1755	Henry	Gran	1755
WATSFORD, John	Bert	1757	James	Bute	1771
Joseph	Bert	1757	James	Curr	1755
WATSON, Alexander	Cumb	1767	James	FWV	1771
Alexander	Pasq	1754	James	Gran	1784
Arthur	Gran	1755	John	Dobb	1769
Benjamin	Dobb	1769	John	Gran	1755
Benjamin	Surr	1771	John	Gran	1769
Benjamin	Surr	1772	John	Gran	1784
David	Gate	1786	Manus	Gran	1784
Isaac	Surr	1772	Stephen s. of		
Isom	Dobb	1779	John	Dobb	1769
James 2m			Susannah 2m		
1f slaves	Crav	1769	3f slaves	Brun	1769
James	Oran	1755	Susannah	Brun	1772
James	Rowa	1759	Wm w. Elizabeth		
John	Bert	1757	s. James	Bert	1757
John Jr.	Bert	1769	Wm	Cumb	1767
John Sr.	Bert	1769	Wm	Gran	1784
John	Bute	1771	WEBB, Aaron	Dobb	1769
John	Chow	1717	Anthony	Bert	1741
John	Chow	1753	Charles	Beau	1764
John	Edge	1742	Col.	N.C.	1701
John	Gran	1755	David	Dobb	1769
John	NewH	1741	Demsey	Onsl	1769
John	NewH	1755	Ethelred	Bert	1769
Joseph	NewH	1755	Ethelred	NorH	1762
Nathaniel	Surr	1771	George	FWV	1771
Neale 1f slave	Crav	1769	George	Onsl	1769
Samuel	Dobb	1769	George	Onsl	1770
Wm	Chow	1717	Henry	Oran	1755
Wm	Pasq	1769	Jacob	Blad	1763
Wm	Perq	1720	James	Gran	1769
Wm	Rowa	1759	James	Gran	1784
WATT, Samuel	Oran	1755	James	Rowa	1758
WATTS, Andrew	Crav	1769	James	Surr	1771
Berryman	Blad	1763	Jeremiah	Gran	1769
John	Anso	1763	Jessy s. of		
John	Oran	1755	Wm Sr.	Onsl	1769
Richard	Gran	1784	John	Anso	1763
Thomas	Oran	1755	John	FWV	1771
Wm	Casw	1777	John	Gran	1784
Wm	Gran	1755	John	NorH	1762
WAUCHOP, John	Pasq	1769	Joseph	Rand	1779
WAVER, Marion	NewH	1762	Martin	Surr	1771
Sue	NewH	1762	Martin	Surr	1772
WAYMAN, Charity	Pasq	1769	Richard	Chow	1753
George	Oran	1755	Richard	FWV	1753
Henry	Oran	1755	Richard	Oran	1755
Thomas	Blad	1763	Robert	Casw	1777
Thomas	Brun	1769	Samuel	Onsl	1769
Thomas	Brun	1772	Samuel	Onsl	1770
Wm s. of Charity	Pasq	1769	Thomas	Bert	1769
WEAK, Thomas	Anso	1763	Thomas	Bute	1771
Wm	Anso	1763	Thomas s. Thomas	FWV	1771
WEAKS, Thomas	Anso	1763	Thomas	Onsl	1769
WEAN, John	Crav	1744	Thomas	Onsl	1770
WEATHERLY, John	Gate	1786	Wm	Bute	1771
WEATHERS, James	Gran	1784	Wm s. of Aaron	Dobb	1769
WEATHERSPOON, John	Surr	1771	Wm	Dobb	1779
John	Surr	1772	Wm	FWV	1771

WEBB, Wm & s.		
Stephen	FWV	1771
Wm	Gran	1784
Wm	NorH	1762
Wm Jr.	Onsl	1769
Wm Sr.	Onsl	1769
Wm Jr.	Onsl	1770
Wm Sr.	Onsl	1770
WEBBER, Edward	Beau	1741
WEBLIN, Wm	Crav	1769
WEBSTER, John	Cart	1741
Wm	Hyde	1741
WEEDON, John	FWV	1771
WEEKS, Benjamin	Cart	1741
Benjamin	Onsl	1769
Benjamin	Onsl	1770
Elias	Surr	1772
Joseph	Onsl	1769
Morris	Onsl	1769
Theophilis	Onsl	1742
Theos.	Onsl	1769
Thomas	Cumb	1755
Thomas	Onsl	1769
Thomas	Onsl	1770
Thomas	Perq	1740
WEGG, Benjamin	Dobb	1769
WEIGHT, Joseph	Oran	1755
Mary	NewH	1762
WEIR, Robert	Blad	1763
WEIRE, George	Blad	1781
WELCH, James	Anso	1763
John ?	Chow	1721
John	Gran	1784
Matthew	Beau	1764
Michael	Chow	1753
Nathaniel	Perq	1740
Wm	Beau	1764
WELDEN, Abraham	Pasq	1754
WELL, Joseph	Pitt	1764
WELLBANK, Robert	NewH	1755
WELLING, Wm	Bert	1757
WELLES, Benjamin	Blad	1763
Corbett	Blad	1763
Daniel	Blad	1763
WELLS, Daniel	Rowa	1759
Francis	N.C.	1701
Francis	Perq	1720
Jane	Chow	1753
John	Bert	1742
John	Rowa	1759
Joseph	Onsl	1769
Joseph Jr.	Oran	1755
Joseph Sr.	Oran	1755
Martin	Rowa	1759
Matthew	FWV	1771
Nathaniel	Onsl	1769
Nathaniel	Onsl	1770
Robert	Anso	1763
Robert	Brun	1772
Samuel	Bute	1771
Samuel	Chow	1753
Samuel	FWV	1771
Wm	Curr	1715
WERRY, Anthony	Crav	1769
WESON, Wm	Rowa	1759

WEST, Alexander	Oran	1755
Arthur	Brun	1769
Arthur	Brun	1772
Charles	Pasq	1769
Christian	Gran	1784
Cornelius	Surr	1772
Elizabeth	Bert	1757
Ephraim	Oran	1755
Henry	Chow	1721
Henry	Edge	1734
James	Blad	1763
James	Brun	1769
James	Brun	1772
James	Crav	1769
James	FWV	1771
James	Gran	1784
John	Bute	1771
John	Crav	1769
John s. John		
George	FWV	1771
John Sr.	Oran	1755
John	Oran	1755
John	Pasq	1769
Lemuel	Pasq	1754
Lemuel 8m		
slaves	Pasq	1769
Martha	Chow	1721
Meredith	Brun	1772
Nathaniel	Curr	1755
Peter	Bert	1742
Peter	Bert	1757
Peter	Bert	1769
Peter 800 acres	Chow	1721
Peter	Chow	1721
Peter	Edge	1734
Richard s. of		
Thomas	Gran	1755
Robert (Col.)	Bert	1757
Robert	Bert	1757
Robert	Bert	1769
Robert	Brun	1769
Robert	Brun	1772
Robert	Chow	1717
Robert	Chow	1721
Robert	Edge	1734
Robert	Roan	1720
Samson	Bute	1771
Samson	FWV	1771
Samuel	Crav	1769
Samuel	Tyrr	1755
Solomon	Oran	1755
Thomas	Brun	1769
Thomas	Chow	1717
Thomas	Gran	1755
Wm 1,610 acres	Chow	1721
Wm	Crav	1769
Wm Jr.	Crav	1769
Wm	Edge	1742
Wm	Surr	1771
WESTBROOK, James	Dobb	1769
James	Dobb	1779
John	Dobb	1779
Moses	Dobb	1769
Wm	Dobb	1779
WESTMORELAND, Isham	Surr	1771

WESTON, Ephraim	Bert	1757
Ephraim	Bert	1769
John	Bert	1757
John	Bert	1757
Malachi	Chow	1753
Wm	Chow	1753
WETHERING, Cleverly	Dobb	1769
John Jr.	Dobb	1769
John Sr.	Dobb	1769
Robert	Dobb	1769
WEATHERINGTON, Thomas		
	Dobb	1769
WEHE, Joseph	Beau	1764
WHALEBONE, Duke	Casw	1777
WHALEY, John	Dobb	1769
Rachel	Curr	1755
WHARBURTON, John	Onsl	1769
WHARTON, David	Crav	1769
Edward Sr.	Pasq	1754
Isaac 1f slave	Pasq	1769
James 1m		
1f slave	Crav	1769
John	NewH	1741
Willis	Pasq	1769
Wm	Gran	1769
WHARTONS, Constable	Onsl	1769
WHEATLEY, Arthur	Beau	1764
George	Surr	1771
James	Bute	1771
James	FWV	1771
John	Bute	1771
John	FWV	1771
Mary	NewH	1762
Richard	Bute	1771
Samuel	Chow	1721
Shirley	Bute	1771
Solomon	Beau	1764
Wilson	Bute	1771
Wm	Bute	1771
WHEDBE, John	Curr	1715
John	Perq	1740
Richard	Perq	1720
Richard	Perq	1740
WHEELER, Ann	Gran	1784
Benjamin	Gran	1784
Henry	Chow	1717
Henry 440 acres	Chow	1721
Henry	NorH	1762
Henry	Roan	1720
Ignatius	Surr	1771
Ignatius	Surr	1772
James	Surr	1772
John	Bert	1757
John	Pitt	1762
Martin	Oran	1755
Samuel	Casw	1777
Samuel	Gran	1769
Thomas	Bute	1771
Thomas s. Samuel	FWV	1771
Thomas	Gran	1755
Wm	Bert	1757
Wm	Bert	1769
Wm	Gran	1755
Wm	NorH	1762
Wm	Onsl	1769

WHEELER, Wm	Onsl	1770
WHEELTON, Levin	Crav	1769
WHERRY, Anthony		
6w 1b slaves	Beau	1744
Wm	Crav	1769
WHICHURCH, Wm	Gran	1784
WHICKARD, John	Pitt	1762
John	Pitt	1763
John	Pitt	1764
Solomon	Pitt	1762
Solomon	Pitt	1764
WHILLIN, Samuel	Pitt	1775
WHISTLEHUNT, Adam	Rowa	1759
WHITAKER, Benjamin	Crav	1769
John	Pitt	1764
Joshua	Rowa	1759
Mark	Rowa	1759
Robert	Gran	1755
Wm	Rowa	1759
WHITBEY, John	Curr	1755
WHITCHOVES, Batson	Pitt	1762
WHITE, Abraham	Pasq	1769
Ann	Pasq	1754
Arnold	Pasq	1769
Arnold	Perq	1740
Arthur	Beau	1755
Benjamin	Bute	1771
Benjamin	Crav	1769
Benjamin	FWV	1771
Benjamin	Pasq	1754
Benjamin	Pasq	1769
Benjamin 1m 1f		
slaves	Pasq	1769
Burgess	Gran	1769
Charles	Tyrr	1755
David	Blad	1763
David L.	Blad	1781
David	Gran	1781
Davis	Anso	1763
Easter	Curr	1755
Evan	Gran	1755
Francis	NewH	1755
George	Chow	1717
George 510 acres	Chow	1721
George	Chow	1753
George	Gran	1784
George Sr.	Surr	1772
Hane	Bert	1769
Henry	Curr	1755
Henry s. of		
Jonathan	Gran	1755
Henry	Gran	1769
Henry	Gran	1784
Hillary	Curr	1755
Isaac	Gran	1769
Jacob	Beau	1764
Jacob	Pitt	1762
James	Brun	1772
James	Gran	1755
James	NewH	1755
James	Pasq	1769
Jesse	FWV	1771
John	Bert	1769
John 5 slaves	Blad	1763
John Jr.	Chow	1717

WHITE, John Sr.	Chow 1717
John Jr.	Chow 1721
John Sr.	Chow 1721
John Constable	Gran 1755
John	Gran 1769
John	Oran 1755
John	Pitt 1764
John	Rand 1779
Jonathan	Edge 1742
Jonathan	Gran 1755
Jonathan s. of	
/ Jonathan	Gran 1755
Jonathan	Gran 1769
Jonathan Jr.	Gran 1769
Jonathan	Gran 1784
Jonathan	Pasq 1754
Joseph Jr.	Anso 1763
Joseph	Blad 1781
Joseph	Pasq 1754
Joseph	Pasq 1769
Joshua	Curr 1755
Joshua 2m	
slaves	Pasq 1769
Joshua	Pasq 1769
Josiah	Curr 1715
Little Berry	FWV 1771
Luke Jr.	Bert 1757
Luke	Bert 1769
Luke	Chow 1717
Luke	Chow 1721
Luke	Chow 1753
Luke	Curr 1715
Luke	Curr 1755
Malachi orphan of	
Malachi	Curr 1715
Margaret	Curr 1755
Mark	Gran 1784
Mary	Blad 1781
Mathias	Rand 1779
Matthew	Blad 1781
Micajah	Bute 1771
Micajah	FWV 1771
Mordica	Bert 1769
Mordica Jr.	Bert 1769
Moses Constable	Rowa 1759
Nicholas	Anso 1763
Nicholas	Rand 1779
Paul	Chow 1753
Peter	Blad 1750
Philemon	Gran 1784
Raglan	Gran 1755
Richard	Bute 1771
Richard s. John	FWV 1771
Robert	Bert 1757
Robert	Dobb 1769
Robert	Pasq 1754
Robert	Pasq 1769
Samuel	Casw 1777
Samuel	Crav 1769
Samuel 1m slave	Pasq 1769
Shadrack	Bute 1771
Shadrack	FWV 1771
Solomon	Bert 1757
Solomon	Chow 1753
Stephen	Bert 1757

WHITE, Stephen	Bert 1769
Stephen	Blad 1763
Thomas	Blad 1763
Thomas	Chow 1753
Thomas	Gate 1786
Thomas	Gran 1784
Thomas	Pasq 1754
Thomas	Rand 1779
Thomas	Rowa 1759
Thomas	Surr 1771
Thomas	Surr 1772
Timothy	Casw 1777
Valentine	Gran 1755
Valentine	Gran 1784
Vinson	Curr 1755
Willis	Pasq 1769
Wm	Blad 1763
Wm trader	Blad 1763
Wm	Bute 1771
Wm	Casw 1777
Wm	Chow 1721
Wm	Curr 1755
Wm	Dobb 1769
Wm	FWV 1771
Wm s. Dempsey	
Wm & Gardner	FWV 1771
Wm	Gran 1755
Wm	Gran 1759
Wm	Gran 1784
Wm	Perq 1740
Wm	Rand 1779
Zachariah 1f	
slave	Pasq 1769
WHITEACRE, John	Beau 1755
John	Pitt 1762
WHITEBREAD, Sacheveral	
	Crav 1769
WHITECAR, Edward	Bert 1769
WHITEHALL, Robert	Curr 1755
Thomas	Curr 1755
WHITEHEAD, Benjamin	Gran 1769
Joshua	Rowa 1759
Robert	Oran 1755
Samuel	Gran 1769
Wm 1,040 acres	Chow 1721
Wm	Dobb 1769
Wm	Gran 1769
Wm	Roan 1720
WHITEHURST, Arthur	Bute 1771
Arthur	FWV 1771
Charles	Pasq 1769
Gideon	Curr 1755
John	Pasq 1769
Jonathan	Pasq 1769
WHITEKER, Samuel	Gran 1784
WHITELY, Joseph	Dobb 1769
Solomon	Blad 1763
Wm	Dobb 1769
WHITENER, Lewis	Rowa 1759
WHITFIELD, Constantine	
	Dobb 1769
Elisha	Bert 1757
Elisha	Bert 1769
John	Gran 1784
Joseph	Pitt 1762

WHITFIELD, Joshua	Tyrr	1755
Luke	Onsl	1743
Matthew	Onsl	1750
Needham	Dobb	1779
Wm	Bert	1741
Wm	Chow	1721
Wm	Dobb	1769
Wm Jr.	Dobb	1769
Wm Sr.	Dobb	1779
Wm	Dobb	1779
WHITFILLS, Henry	Oran	1755
WHITFORD, Bastin	Crav	1769
Boston	Onsl	1770
John 1m slave	Crav	1769
Martin	Crav	1769
Thomas	Crav	1769
Wm	Crav	1769
WHITHOUSE, Richard	Crav	1720
WHITIET, John	Casw	1777
WHITINGTON, Edward	Cumb	1767
WHITLEY, Josiah	Dobb	1779
Wm	Dobb	1769
WHITLOCK, James	Bert	1769
Nathaniel	Surr	1772
Robert	Casw	1777
WHITLOW, John	Gran	1769
John	Gran	1784
Nathan	Gran	1784
Solomon	Gran	1784
Thomas	Pitt	1775
WHITMAN, Thomas	Chow	1721
WHITMELL, Thomas		
(Col.)	Bert	1757
Thomas	Bert	1769
Thomas Jr.	Bert	1769
Thomas	Roan	1720
WHITNEY, Ebenezer	Rand	1779
WHITSON, Michael	Bert	1757
Wm Jr.	Bert	1757
WHITTLE, Wm	Cumb	1755
WHITTON, George	Casw	1777
Wm	Casw	1777
WHITUS, Batson	Pitt	1775
WHORTON, Caleb	Pasq	1769
WIATT, James	Edge	1734
John 883 acres	Perq	1720
Samuel 790 acres		
	Perq	1720
Samuel	Perq	1740
Solomon	Perq	1740
Thomas 286 acres		
	Perq	1720
Wm	Perq	1740
WIBB, Daniel	NewH	1767
Jacob	NewH	1767
WICHER, Lott	Onsl	1769
WICKER, Benjamin	Gran	1769
Elizabeth	Curr	1755
James	Gran	1769
John	Gran	1769
Joseph	Curr	1715
Richard	Curr	1755
Thomas	Gran	1769
Thomas	Gran	1784
Wm	Gran	1784

WICKLIEF, Wm		
3m 3f slaves	Crav	1769
WICKS, Ez.	Beau	1755
Zachariah	NewH	1755
WIDEMAN, Henry	Gran	1769
WIGGINS, Caleb	Crav	1769
Charles	Bert	1769
Edward	Bert	1769
Ezekiel	Gran	1769
Frederick	Gran	1784
George	Dobb	1769
Gershom	Dobb	1769
James	Chow	1753
James	Crav	1769
John Jr.	Bute	1771
John Sr.	Bute	1771
John	Chow	1721
John	Crav	1769
John Jr.	FWV	1771
John Sr.	FWV	1771
Malachi	Bert	1757
Malachi	Bert	1769
Margaret	Dobb	1769
Matthew	Bert	1769
Mick	Dobb	1779
Richard 6w		
3b slaves	Crav	1743
Samson	FWV	1771
Samuel	Bert	1757
Samuel	Crav	1769
Thomas	Chow	1753
Thomas	Dobb	1779
Thomas	Gran	1755
Thomas	Gran	1769
Thomas	Gran	1784
Thomas	Perq	1740
WIGGS, Benjamin	Dobb	1779
Henry	Dobb	1769
Henry	Dobb	1779
John	Dobb	1769
John	Dobb	1779
WIGGINTON, George	Cumb	1755
WILAND, Philip	Beau	1755
WILBOURN, John	Gran	1784
Zachariah	Gran	1784
WILBURN, Esther	Rand	1779
John	Rand	1779
Robert	Anso	1763
Wm	Rand	1779
WILCOX, Isaac	Rowa	1759
James cooper	Crav	1769
James	Crav	1769
James Jr.	Crav	1769
John	Cumb	1767
John	Perq	1740
John	Perq	1743
Stephen	Pasq	1769
Wm	Crav	1769
Wm	Rand	1779
WILCOXEN, John	Rowa	1759
WILDER, Hopkins	Edge	1734
Hopkins 4w		
2b slaves	Edge	1744
Hopkins	Onsl	1769
Jacob	Surr	1771

WILDER, Jacob	Surr 1772	WILKINSON, Wm	Perq 1740
Job	Edge 1743	WILKS, Daniel	Blad 1781
John	Onsl 1770	James	Bert 1757
Nathaniel	Dobb 1769	James	Bert 1769
Stephen	Onsl 1770	Matthew	Crav 1769
Wm		WILLARD, John	Beau 1755
WILDMAN, Elias	Rand 1779	John	Tyrr 1741
WILEY, Alexander	Casw 1777	WILLBURN, Isaac	Rowa 1759
Jacob	Onsl 1769	WILLCOCK, James	Beau 1755
Jacob	Onsl 1770	Wm s. of James	Beau 1755
James	Tyrr 1742	WILLETTS, Hope	NewH 1744
James	Tyrr 1755	Hope	NewH 1763
John	Casw 1777	J.	Edge 1734
John	Onsl 1769	JoBuck	Brun 1769
Thomas	Casw 1777	JoBuck	Brun 1772
Thomas	Oran 1755	Mary	Brun 1772
Thomas	Tyrr 1755	Samuel	Brun 1769
WILFOUND, Joseph	Pitt 1764	Samuel	Brun 1772
WILFRED, Joseph	Rowa 1759	Samuel	NewH 1763
WILHIDE, Philip	Bute 1771	WILLEY, Hillary	Gate 1786
Philip s. Wm		Rachel	Gate 1786
Lewis	FWV 1771	WILLIAMS, Absalom	Dobb 1769
WILKERSON, Benjamin	Beau 1755	Alexander s. of	
Benjamin	Pitt 1762	Jonas Sr.	Dobb 1769
David	Gran 1769	Alexander	Dobb 1779
David	Gran 1784	Amos	Onsl 1769
Francis	Gran 1784	Amos	Onsl 1770
Hazelwood	Gran 1784	Amos	Rand 1779
John	Gran 1769	Anthony	Chow 1717
John	Gran 1784	Arthur	Beau 1755
Joshua	Beau 1755	Arthur	Bert 1757
Wm	Gran 1769	Arthur	Bert 1769
Wm	Gran 1784	Arthur	Chow 1717
Wyatt	Gran 1784	Arthur 1,200	
WILKINS, Benjamin	Beau 1764	acres	Chow 1721
Benjamin	Onsl 1769	Arthur	Dobb 1769
Charles	Chow 1721	Askenas	Bute 1771
James	Beau 1764	Askenas	FWV 1771
James	Onsl 1769	Benedict	Blad 1763
John	Chow 1753	Benedict	Brun 1772
John	Crav 1769	Benjamin	Bute 1771
John	Onsl 1750	Benjamin	Casw 1777
John	Onsl 1769	Benjamin	Crav 1743
John s. of John	Onsl 1769	Benjamin	Crav 1769
Jonathan	Anso 1763	Benjamin	Dobb 1769
Joseph	Anso 1763	Benjamin	FWV 1771
Norman	Onsl 1769	Benjamin	Onsl 1750
Richard	Gran 1784	Benjamin	Onsl 1769
Wm	Chow 1753	Benjamin	Onsl 1770
Wm	NewH 1755	Benjamin	Oran 1755
Wm	Onsl 1769	Benjamin	Pasq 1769
WILKINSON, Benjamin	Pitt 1764	Benjamin	Pitt 1775
James	Chow 1717	Betty	Bute 1771
James 900 acres	Chow 1721	Betty	FWV 1771
John 2 slaves	Blad 1763	Billy	Crav 1769
John 2m 1f		Billy	Rand 1779
slaves	Brun 1769	Browning	Bute 1771
John	Brun 1772	Browning John	
John	Chow 1743	Morgan	FWV 1771
John	Gate 1786	Browning	Gran 1755
John	NewH 1762	Charles	Curr 1755
John	N.C. 1701	Charles s. of	
John	Rand 1779	John	Gran 1755
Wm	Blad 1763	Charles	Gran 1769
Wm (Col.)	N.C. 1701	Charles	Gran 1784

WILLIAMS, Daniel	Gran	1769	WILLIAMS, James		Bert	1769
Daniel	Gran	1784	James		Chow	1721
Daniel	Pasq	1769	James		FWV	1771
David	Beau	1764	James		Gran	1769
David	Bute	1771	James		Oran	1755
David	Crav	1769	James		Pasq	1754
David	FWV	1771	James		Pitt	1762
David	Gran	1769	James		Pitt	1764
David	NewH	1741	James		Pitt	1775
David	NewH	1750	James		Rand	1779
David	Pasq	1769	James		Rowa	1759
David	Pitt	1762	Jane (widow)		Pitt	1762
David	Pitt	1764	Jane (widow)		Pitt	1764
David	Pitt	1775	Jean		Chow	1753
Demsey	Gate	1786	Jesse		Beau	1755
Dove	Beau	1755	Jesse		Onsl	1769
Dove	Pitt	1762	Jesse		Onsl	1770
Dove	Pitt	1764	Jesse		Pasq	1769
Edward	Beau	1755	Jesse		Pitt	1762
Edward	Bert	1757	Jesse		Pitt	1764
Edward	Chow	1717	John		Anso	1763
Edward	Crav	1742	John		Beau	1743
Edward	Dobb	1769	John		Beau	1755
Edward	Oran	1755	John		Bert	1757
Edward	Pasq	1754	John		Blad	1742
Edward	Pitt	1762	John		Bute	1771
Edward or Edmund	Pitt	1764	John		Cart	1743
Edward	Pitt	1775	John (Cpt.)		Casw	1777
Edward Sr.	Rand	1779	John		Casw	1777
Edward	Rand	1779	John		Chow	1717
Edward	Rowa	1759	John 1,620			
Edward	Surr	1772	acres		Chow	1721
Edward	Tyrr	1755	John Jr.			
Eli	NorH	1762	1,065 acres		Chow	1721
Elijah	Dobb	1769	John 500 acres		Chow	1721
Elizabeth	Curr	1715	John of			
Elizabeth	Dobb	1769	Chinkapin		Chow	1721
Elizabeth	Gran	1769	John		Chow	1753
Elkeney	Pasq	1769	John		Crav	1741
Evan	Dobb	1769	John 5w 14b			
Ezekiel	Bert	1757	slaves		Crav	1750
Floyd	Bute	1771	John		Crav	1769
Floyd s. Nathaniel			John		Cumb	1755
Charles	FWV	1771	John		Curr	1755
Francis	Gran	1769	John		Dobb	1769
George	Chow	1753	John		FWV	1771
George	Gate	1786	John		Gran	1755
George	Oran	1755	John Jr.		Gran	1755
George	Pitt	1775	John		Gran	1769
George Jr.	Roan	1720	John Jr.		Gran	1769
George Sr.	Roan	1720	John S. D.		Gran	1769
Giles	Tryo	1776	John Esq.		Gran	1784
Gillstop	Bert	1757	John		Gran	1784
Henry	Brun	1769	John		NewH	1755
Henry	Brun	1772	John		Onsl	1769
Henry	Casw	1777	John		Onsl	1770
Henry	Cumb	1767	John		Oran	1755
Henry	Gran	1784	John		Pasq	1769
Howard	Rowa	1759	John		Perq	1720
Humphrey	Dobb	1769	John		Pitt	1762
Humphrey	NorH	1762	John		Pitt	1764
Isaac	Chow	1753	John Jr.		Pitt	1764
Isaac	Edge	1742	John		Rand	1779
Jacob	Surr	1772	John		Surr	1771
James	Bert	1757	John		Surr	1772

WILLIAMS, Jonas Jr. s.		
of Jonas	Dobb	1769
Jonas Sr.	Dobb	1769
Jonas	Dobb	1779
Jonas	Tryo	1776
Jonathan	Gate	1786
Jonathan	Oran	1755
Jonathan	Rowa	1759
Joseph	Bert	1757
Joseph	Blad	1781
Joseph	Bute	1771
Joseph Jr.	Bute	1771
Joseph	Chow	1721
Joseph	Curr	1755
Joseph	Dobb	1769
Joseph	Dobb	1779
Joseph	Dupl	1754
Joseph	FWV	1771
Joseph s. John		
& Martin	FWV	1771
Joseph	Gran	1769
Joseph	Onsl	1770
Joseph	Pasq	1769
Joshua	Dobb	1769
Joshua	Onsl	1769
Joshua	Pitt	1762
Josiah	Cumb	1767
L.	Edge	1734
Laban	Onsl	1770
Laban	Pitt	1770
Leonard	Pasq	1769
Leonard	Pitt	1775
Lewis	Bert	1757
Lewis	Onsl	1769
Lewis	Onsl	1770
Lodwick	Pasq	1754
Lodwick	Pasq	1769
Lot	Crav	1769
Lucy	Bute	1771
Lucy	FWV	1771
Lydia orphan of		
Thomas	Curr	1715
Mary 140 acres	Chow	1721
Mary	Rand	1779
Matthew	Dobb	1769
McKinney	Blad	1763
Michael	Onsl	1769
Michael	Onsl	1770
Miles	FWV	1771
Miles	Gran	1769
Moses	Gate	1786
Nathan	Dobb	1769
Nathaniel	Anso	1763
Nathaniel s.		
of John	Gran	1755
Nathaniel	Gran	1769
Nathaniel	Gran	1784
Nehemiah	Rand	1779
Nicholas	Curr	1755
Nimrod overseer	Bute	1771
Nimrod	FWV	1771
Norman	Rand	1779
Obed	Onsl	1769
Obed	Onsl	1770
Parmenus	Bute	1771

WILLIAMS, Parmenus	FWV	1771
Parmenus	Gran	1784
Peter	Gran	1755
Philip	Rowa	1759
Pilgrim	Chow	1717
Raizer of Lot	Crav	1769
Richard	Bert	1757
Richard	Bute	1771
Richard	Crav	1769
Richard	FWV	1771
Richard	Pitt	1762
Richard	Pitt	1775
Robert	Beau	1755
Robert	Beau	1764
Robert	Bute	1771
Robert	Crav	1769
Robert Jr.	Dobb	1769
Robert Sr.	Dobb	1769
Robert s. George	FWV	1771
Robert s. Archelaus		
	FWV	1771
Robert	Onsl	1743
Robert	Pasq	1769
Robert	Pitt	1762
Robert	Pitt	1764
Robert	Pitt	1775
Roderick	Pitt	1762
Roderick	Pitt	1764
Roderick	Pitt	1775
Roger	Bute	1771
Roger	FWV	1771
Roland	Anso	1763
Roland	NorH	1741
Samson	Cumb	1755
Samson	Gran	1784
Samuel	Anso	1763
Samuel	Bert	1757
Samuel	Chow	1717
Samuel 320 acres	Chow	1721
Samuel 150 acres	Chow	1721
Samuel	Chow	1753
Samuel Jr.	Chow	1753
Samuel	Edge	1743
Samuel	FWV	1771
Samuel	Gate	1786
Samuel	Gran	1784
Samuel	Pasq	1754
Samuel	Roan	1720
Samuel	Rowa	1759
Shadrack	Pasq	1754
Shadrack	Pasq	1769
Shadrack	Pitt	1764
Simon	Gran	1769
Simon	Gran	1784
Simon	Rand	1779
Solomon	Bute	1771
Solomon	FWV	1771
Spencer	Pasq	1769
Stephen 600		
acres	Chow	1721
Stephen	Curr	1755
Stephen	Gran	1769
Stephen	Onsl	1743
Stephen	Onsl	1769
Stephen	Onsl	1770

WILLIAMS, Theo.	Chow	1717
Theodore 915		
acres	Chow	1721
Thomas	Anso	1763
Thomas	Beau	1741
Thomas	Beau	1755
Thomas Jr.	Beau	1755
Thomas	Bert	1757
Thomas	Blad	1763
Thomas 2 slaves	Blad	1763
Thomas school-		
master	Bute	1771
Thomas	Casw	1777
Thomas	Curr	1715
Thomas	Curr	1755
Thomas	Dobb	1769
Thomas	Dobb	1779
Thos school-		
master	FWV	1771
Thomas	Gran	1755
Thomas Jr.	Gran	1784
Thomas Sr.	Gran	1784
Thomas	NorH	1762
Thomas	Oran	1755
Thomas	Pasq	1769
Thomas	Pitt	1762
Thomas Jr.	Pitt	1762
Thomas Jr.	Pitt	1764
Thomas Sr.	Pitt	1764
Thomas	Pitt	1775
Thomas	Rand	1779
Timothy	Surr	1771
Tulle	Perq	1740
Tulle	Perq	1743
Uzy	Onsl	1769
Uzy	Onsl	1770
Vincent	Rowa	1759
Wallis	Beau	1755
West	Dobb	1769
Willis	Chow	1753
Willis	Pasq	1754
Willis	Pasq	1769
Willoughby	Dobb	1779
Wm	Bert	1757
Wm	Bert	1769
Wm	Casw	1777
Wm	Crav	1769
Wm	Curr	1715
Wm	Curr	1755
Wm of Trent	Dobb	1769
Wm	Dobb	1769
Wm Jr.	Dobb	1769
Wm Great	Dobb	1769
Wm Sr.	Dobb	1769
Wm	Edge	1734
Wm	Edge	1743
Wm	Gate	1786
Wm	Gran	1755
Wm	Gran	1769
Wm	Gran	1784
Wm	Onsl	1743
Wm	Oran	1755
Wm	Pasq	1754
Wm	Pitt	1762
Wm	Rand	1779

WILLIAMS, Wm	Rowa	1759
Wm	Tyrr	1755
Zorababel	Gran	1784
WILLIAMSON, Charles	Curr	1715
Hall	Casw	1777
Henry	Pasq	1769
Henry	Pitt	1764
James	Bert	1757
James	Bert	1769
James	Dobb	1769
James	Gran	1769
James 1,114 acres		
	Perq	1720
Jehu	Casw	1777
John	Blad	1763
John	Chow	1753
John	Cumb	1767
John	NewH	1762
Joseph	Dobb	1769
Joseph		
Martha	Bute	1771
Martha s. George		
& Wm	FWV	1771
Michael	Gran	1769
Nathan	Casw	1777
Richard	Crav	1720
Richard	Onsl	1769
Richard	Onsl	1770
Samson	Cumb	1767
Samuel	Casw	1777
Thomas	Curr	1715
Thomas	Gran	1784
Wm	Bert	1757
Wm	Blad	1763
Wm	Chow	1717
Wm	Chow	1721
Wm	Curr	1755
Wm	Edge	1742
Wm	Gran	1755
Zackary	FWV	1771
WILLIARD, Augustine	Gran	1784
Thomas	Gran	1784
WILLIFORD, Benjamin	Bert	1757
Britain	Bute	1771
Britain	FWV	1771
Burton	Bert	1769
John	Bert	1757
Richard	Bert	1742
Richard	Bert	1757
Richard	Bert	1769
Samuel	Bert	1757
Wm	Bert	1757
WILLINGHAM, John	Gran	1769
Thomas	Gran	1769
WILLIS, Agerton	Blad	1781
Agerton	NewH	1755
Benjamin	Blad	1781
Benjamin Jr.	Blad	1781
George	Blad	1781
George	NewH	1762
Henry	Casw	1777
Hope	NewH	1755
James 1m 1f		
slave	Crav	1769
James Jr.	Crav	1769

WILLIS, James	Gran	1769
John 1f slave	Crav	1769
Joseph	Casw	1777
Richard	Perq	1740
Thomas	Crav	1769
Thomas	Pitt	1762
Thomas	Pitt	1764
Wm	Beau	1755
Wm	Gran	1769
Wm	Pitt	1762
Wm	Pitt	1764
WILLISON, John	Cart	1743
Shadrack	Pitt	1775
WILLOUGHBY, Ann	Pasq	1754
John	Bert	1757
Mary	Perq	1720
Wm	Bert	1769
WILLS, Harry	Gate	1786
Jacob	NewH	1755
James	Gate	1786
John	Gate	1786
John	NewH	1755
Miles	Gran	1769
Miles	Gran	1784
WILRUNTUN, Joseph	Bert	1757
Wm	Bert	1757
WILSHIRE, Nathaniel	Rowa	1759
Wm	Anso	1763
WILSON, Benjamin	Pasq	1754
Benjamin 1f slave	Pasq	1769
Benjamin 580 acres	Perq	1720
Benjamin	Perq	1720
Benjamin	Surr	1771
Benjamin	Surr	1772
Charity	Dobb	1769
Charles	Rowa	1759
Daniel	Casw	1777
Daniel	Pitt	1762
Daniel	Pitt	1764
Daniel	Pitt	1775
Edward	Bert	1757
Edward	Bert	1769
Elias	FWV	1771
Francis	Curr	1755
Francis	Pasq	1769
George	Dobb	1769
George s. of Charity	Dobb	1769
George	Gran	1769
George	Rand	1779
George	Rowa	1759
George	Surr	1771
George Whitefield	Surr	1772
Henry	Gran	1784
Hosea	Dobb	1779
James	Bert	1757
James	Bert	1769
James	Bute	1771
James	Casw	1777
James	Chow	1753
James	Crav	1769
James	Dobb	1769

WILSON, James	Dobb	1769
James	Dobb	1779
James	FWV	1771
James	Rowa	1759
John	Bert	1757
John	Casw	1777
John Jr.	Casw	1777
John	Crav	1769
John	Cumb	1767
John	Dobb	1779
John	Gran	1769
John	Gran	1784
John	NewH	1767
John	Oran	1755
John	Perq	1740
John	Pitt	1762
John	Pitt	1764
John	Rand	1779
John	Rowa	1759
John	Surr	1771
John	Surr	1772
Jonathan	NewH	1767
Joseph	Rand	1779
Joseph	Surr	1771
Josiah Constable	Blad	1763
Michael	Gran	1769
Michael Constable	Gran	1769
Nathaniel	Pasq	1754
Richard 1m slave	Brun	1769
Richard	Brun	1772
Robert	Casw	1777
Robert	FWV	1771
Robert	Gran	1784
Robert	Perq	1740
Robert	Pitt	1764
Robert	Rowa	1759
Sarah	Curr	1755
Seasbrook	Gate	1786
Silvanus	Blad	1763
Silvanus	Cumb	1767
Silvanus	NewH	1755
Simon	Onsl	1741
Solomon	Dobb	1769
Thomas	Bert	1757
Thomas	Bert	1769
Thomas	Bute	1771
Thomas	Casw	1777
Thomas	Dobb	1769
Thomas	Dobb	1779
Thomas s. Richard & Thomas	FWV	1771
Thomas	Oran	1755
Thomas	Pitt	1762
Thomas	Pitt	1764
Thomas (4)	Rand	1779
Thomas	Surr	1771
Thomas	Surr	1772
Wm (black)	Bute	1771
Wm (2)	Casw	1777
Wm	Chow	1717
Wm	Chow	1753
Wm 83 persons	Crav	1741
Wm	Curr	1715

WILSON, Wm Jr.	Curr 1715	WINGET, Wm	Beau 1764
Wm (black)	FWV 1771	WINHAM, Wm	Chow 1753
Wm	Gran 1769	WINKFIELD, Wm	Dobb 1769
Wm	Oran 1755	WINKLES, Hester wo	Pitt 1764
Wm	Pasq 1754	John	Pitt 1764
Wm	Pitt 1764	WINLEY, Aaron	Beau 1764
Wm (3)	Rand 1779	Israel	Beau 1764
Wm	Rowa 1759	WINLOM, John	Beau 1755
Wm Jr.	Surr 1771	WINN, Dor	N.C. 1701
Wm Sr.	Surr 1771	Elizabetn	N.C. 1701
Wm Jr.	Surr 1772	Grace	N.C. 1701
Wm Sr.	Surr 1772	Lemuel	N.C. 1701
WIMAN, One	Beau 1755	Mary	N.C. 1701
WIMBERLY, Abraham	Bert 1757	Robert	FWV 1771
Abraham	Bert 1769	Samuel	Pitt 1775
Benjamin	Bert 1757	Wm	N.C. 1701
Benjamin	Bert 1769	Wm Jr.	N.C. 1701
Elizabeth	Bert 1757	WINNEHAM, Francis	Anso 1763
Ezekiel	Bert 1757	WINNINGHAM, James	Gran 1784
Ezekiel	Bert 1769	John	Gran 1784
Jacob	Bert 1757	Sherwood	Gran 1784
Joseph	Bert 1742	WINNS, 1,380 acres	Chow 1721
Joseph	Bert 1757	WINOOM, Benjamin	Pitt 1775
Joseph	Pasq 1743	John	Pitt 1775
Josiah	Bert 1769	Solomon	Pitt 1775
Levi	Bert 1769	WINSCOTT, Isaac	Surr 1772
WINBERRY, George	Pasq 1754	Richard	Rowa 1759
John	Pasq 1769	WINSETT, John	Dobb 1769
Newell	Pasq 1754	Robert	Dobb 1769
Nowal	Pasq 1769	WINSLOW, John	Perq 1720
Thomas	Pasq 1769	John	Perq 1740
Wm	Pasq 1769	John	Rand 1779
WINBON, Harding	Beau 1755	Joseph	Perq 1740
WINBORNE, Philip	Gate 1786	Joseph	Perq 1741
Philip	NorH 1762	Josiah 1m	
WINBURN, Henry	Bert 1757	slave	Pasq 1769
Isaac	Rowa 1759	Thomas	Perq 1720
WINCHESTER, Thomas	Oran 1755	Thomas	Perq 1740
WINDOM, Wm	Tyrr 1742	Thomas Sr.	Perq 1740
WINDHAM, Ben	Pitt 1764	Timothy 4w	
John	Pitt 1764	1b slaves	Perq 1743
WINDOM, John	Beau 1755	WINSTON, Anthony	Bute 1771
John Sr.	Pitt 1762	Anthony s. Isaac	
Wm	Beau 1755	& John	FWV 1771
Wm	Tyrr 1742	George Constable	FWV 1771
WINDSOR, John	Casw 1777	George	Gran 1755
WINE, Claret	Dobb 1779	Isaac	Gran 1755
John	Dobb 1769	Joseph	Gran 1769
WINFIELD, Edward s.		Wm	Bute 1771
of Joseph	Dobb 1769	Wm	FWV 1771
Joseph	Dobb 1769	Wm	Gran 1755
Joseph	Dobb 1779	WINTERS, George	Tryo 1776
Thomas	Crav 1769	John	Bute 1771
WINFREY, Isaac	Gran 1769	John	FWV 1771
James	Gran 1784	Michael	Curr 1715
WINGATE, Ed	Chow 1721	WIREMAN, Wm	Rand 1779
Edward 3m		WIRRELL, John	Chow 1721
1f slaves	Brun 1769	WISE, Isaac s.	
Edward	Brun 1772	of James	Dobb 1769
Edward	NewH 1755	James	Dobb 1769
Edward	NewH 1762	James	Dobb 1779
John 2m 4f		James s. of	
slaves	Brun 1769	Thomas	Dobb 1769
John	Brun 1772	John s. of	
Thomas	Crav 1769	Thomas	Dobb 1769

WISE, Ninian	Dobb 1769	WOOD, James	FWV 1771
Rubin s. of		Jesse	Bert 1757
Thomas	Dobb 1769	Jessy Jr.	Onsl 1769
Sarling s. of		Jessy Sr.	Onsl 1769
Thos	Dobb 1769	Jessy Jr.	Onsl 1770
Thomas	Dobb 1769	Jessy Sr.	Onsl 1770
WISEMAN, Wm	Casw 1777	John	Anso 1763
WITHERINGTON, Cleverly		John	Bute 1771
	Dobb 1779	John	Edge 1742
Joseph	Bert 1757	John	FWV 1771
Nathan	Dobb 1779	John (3)	Gran 1755
Stephen	Dobb 1779	John	Oran 1755
Wm	Bert 1757	John	Pasq 1769
Wm	Dobb 1779	John	Rand 1779
WITHERSPOON, John	Gran 1769	John Jr.	Rand 1779
John	Rowa 1759	Jonah	Onsl 1770
WITHERTON, John	Rand 1779	Jonathan	Onsl 1769
WITTEY, Robert	Oran 1755	Jonathan	Onsl 1770
Solomon	Oran 1755	Joseph	Blad 1781
WOLBANKS, John	Gran 1755	Lucy	Blad 1781
Wm	Gran 1755	Michael	FWV 1771
WOLFE, Charles	Dobb 1769	Moses	Gran 1784
Charles	Dobb 1779	Moses	Perq 1740
George	Dobb 1769	Penuel	Gran 1755
George	Dobb 1779	Peyton	Gran 1784
Thomas	Gran 1755	Richard Sr.	Perq 1740
Wm	Surr 1771	Robert	Bute 1771
Wm	Surr 1772	Robert	FWV 1771
WOLFINDEN, George	Pitt 1775	Robert	Gran 1755
WOLFORD, Nicholas	Anso 1763	Samson 2 slaves	Blad 1763
WOLLARD, John	Tyrr 1755	Wm	Bert 1757
WOMACK, Abraham	Casw 1777	Wm	Bert 1769
David	Casw 1777	Wm Sr.	Bute 1771
John	Casw 1777	Wm	Bute 1771
WOMBLE, Benjamin	Pitt 1762	Wm	Dobb 1769
Jordan	Pitt 1764	Wm	Dobb 1779
Mary	Pitt 1764	Wm Sr.	FWV 1771
Nathan	Beau 1755	Wm	FWV 1771
Nathan	Dobb 1769	Wm	Gran 1755
Wm	Beau 1755	Wm Jr.	Gran 1755
WOMICK, Abigail	Crav 1720	Wm	Perq 1740
WOMING, Abigail	Crav 1720	Wm	Surr 1771
WOMWELL, Nathan	Pitt 1762	Wm	Surr 1772
WOOD, Aaron	Perq 1740	Zebedee	Rand 1779
Abraham	Surr 1772	WOODALL, Jacob	Gran 1769
Adam	Crav 1720	Jacob	Gran 1784
Ann	Bute 1771	WOODARD, Isaac	Dobb 1779
Ann & s. John	FWV 1771	Jesse	Dobb 1779
Bennett	Bute 1771	Luke	Dobb 1779
Bennett	FWV 1771	Simon	Beau 1755
D.	Chow 1717	Wm	Gran 1755
Dempsey	Bert 1757	WOODCOCK, Joseph	NewH 1755
Drachet	Gran 1755	WOODEY, John	Chow 1717
Edward	Chow 1717	WOODHAM, Edward Jr.	Dobb 1769
Francis	Dobb 1769	Edward Sr.	Dobb 1769
Furnifold	Dobb 1779	WOODHOUSE, Henry	Curr 1715
Gershom	Crav 1769	Hezekiah	Curr 1755
Henry	Bute 1771	Horatio	Onsl 1742
Henry	FWV 1771	John	Curr 1715
Humphrey	Pasq 1769	John	Curr 1755
Isaiah	Crav 1769	John	Dobb 1779
James	Bert 1757	WOODIN, John	Gran 1755
James	Bert 1769	WOODLEY, Andrew	Perq 1740
James 350 acres	Chow 1717	Thomas	Bute 1771
James	Dobb 1769	Thomas & s. John	FWV 1771

WOODLEY, Wm	Pasq	1754
Wm 476 acres	Perq	1720
WOODLIEF, George	Gran	1755
John	Rand	1779
Littlebury		
Constable	Gran	1755
Thomas	Gran	1755
WOODRUFF, Nathaniel	Surr	1771
Nathaniel Jr.	Surr	1771
Nathaniel	Surr	1772
Thomas	Surr	1771
Thomas	Surr	1772
WOODS, John	Curr	1755
John	FWV	1771
Judith	N.C.	1701
Robert	Rowa	1759
Samuel	Casw	1777
Wm	FWV	1771
WOODSIDE, Robert	Brun	1772
WOODWARD, Abraham	Rand	1779
Edward	Chow	1753
Elisha	Dobb	1769
Isaac s. of		
Thomas Sr.	Dobb	1769
Luke s. of		
Thomas Sr.	Dobb	1769
Peter	Surr	1771
Peter	Surr	1772
Richard	Chow	1753
Samuel 2,050 acres		
	Chow	1717
Samuel	Chow	1721
Samuel	Chow	1753
Thomas s. of		
Thomas Sr.	Dobb	1769
Thomas Sr.	Dobb	1769
Wm	Bute	1771
Wm	FWV	1771
WOODY, John	Oran	1755
WOOLARD, Absalom	Beau	1764
Benjamin	Beau	1764
John	Beau	1764
Martin	Beau	1764
Michael	Beau	1764
Wm	Chow	1753
WOOLBANKS, Joseph	Bute	1771
Joseph	FWV	1771
Richard	Surr	1771
Wm	Bute	1771
Wm	FWV	1771
WOOLDRIDGE, John	Pasq	1769
WOOLFE, George	Dobb	1769
WOOLSON, Ebenezer	Rand	1779
WOOTEN, Daniel	Cumb	1755
George	Bute	1771
George	Cumb	1755
George & s.		
Moses	FWV	1771
James	Bute	1771
Jeremiah	Bute	1771
Jeremiah	FWV	1771
Jeremiah	Gran	1755
John	Cumb	1755
John	Pitt	1764
John	Pitt	1775

WOOTEN, Nehemiah	Pitt	1764
Thomas	Bute	1771
Thomas Jr.	Bute	1771
Thomas	FWV	1771
Thomas	Gran	1755
WOOTERS, John	Dobb	1769
WOOTINS, John	Gran	1784
WOOTON, Thomas	Pasq	1769
Widow	Pasq	1769
WORD, Thomas	Anso	1763
WORDEN, James	Chow	1753
WORKMAN, John	Rand	1779
WORLEY, Daniel	Bert	1757
Daniel	Bert	1769
John Esq. 1,900		
acres	Chow	1717
John	Chow	1717
Joshua 5w		
13b slaves	Tyrr	1743
Joshua	Tyrr	1755
Thomas	Bute	1771
Thomas	FWV	1771
WORMINGTON, John	N.C.	1701
WORRELL, Amos	Rand	1779
Benjamin s. of		
John Sr.	Dobb	1769
David	Dobb	1779
Isaiah	Dobb	1779
Jesse	Gate	1786
John Jr. s. of		
John Sr.	Dobb	1769
John Sr.	Dobb	1769
John	Dobb	1779
Nathan	Gran	1769
Richard	Dobb	1779
Wm	Bute	1771
Wm	FWV	1771
WORRIN, Joseph	Surr	1771
WORSLEY, John	Pitt	1762
John	Pitt	1764
John	Pitt	1775
Joseph 3m		
1f slaves	Crav	1769
Joseph	Pitt	1762
Joseph	Pitt	1764
Martin	Crav	1769
Stephen	Beau	1755
Stephen	Beau	1764
Thomas	Beau	1755
Thomas	Beau	1764
Wm	Beau	1764
WORTH, Jethro	Rand	1779
Joseph	Rand	1779
Thomas	Crav	1769
WORTHAM, Charles	Bute	1771
Charles	FWV	1771
John	FWV	1771
Wm	Bute	1771
Wm	FWV	1771
WORTTON, Wm	Pasq	1754
WOTEN, John	Pitt	1762
WOTTEN, Christopher	NewH	1762
WOTTON, Christopher	Brun	1769
WRAN, James	Tryo	1776
WRASLER, John	Pitt	1762

WRAY, Robert	Casw	1777
WRAYGON, David	Casw	1777
Jesse	Casw	1777
John Jr.	Casw	1777
John Sr.	Casw	1777
Nathan	Casw	1777
WRENFORD, Edmund 8m		
5f slaves	Crav	1769
WRIGHT, Abraham	Casw	1777
Augustine	Pasq	1769
Barnaby	Pasq	1769
Bartlett	Gran	1784
Benjamin	Rand	1779
Charles 1m		
1f slave	Pasq	1754
Charles	Pasq	1769
Clayborne	Casw	1777
Cornelius	Pasq	1769
George	Gran	1784
George	Rand	1779
Gideon	Surr	1772
Hezekiah	Surr	1772
Hynson 1m slave	Crav	1769
Jacob	Casw	1777
James	NewH	1755
James	Onsl	1741
John s. of		
Richard	Anso	1763
John	Anso	1763
John Jr.	Bute	1771
John Sr.	Bute	1771
John	Cumb	1767
John Jr.	FWV	1771
John Sr. & s.		
James & Jesse	FWV	1771
John 8w 9b		
slaves	NewH	1745
John 8w 9b		
slaves	NewH	1755
John Jr.	Oran	1755
John Sr.	Oran	1755
John	Oran	1755
John Jr.	Pasq	1754
John Sr.	Pasq	1754
John Jr.	Pasq	1769
John Sr. 1m		
6f slaves	Pasq	1769
John	Rand	1779
Joseph	Bute	1771
Joseph & s.		
Jesse	FWV	1771
Joseph	Gran	1755
Joseph s. of		
Joseph	Gran	1755
Levi	Pasq	1769
Moses	FWV	1771
Peter	Rand	1779
Philburt Jr.	Rand	1779
Philburt Sr.	Rand	1779
Ralph	Rand	1779
Richard	Casw	1777
Richard	Rand	1779
Samuel	Bute	1771
Samuel	FWV	1771
Samuel	Perq	1740

WRIGHT, Samuel	Surr	1771
Solomon	Beau	1755
Thomas	Bert	1757
Thomas	Casw	1777
Thomas	NewH	1762
Thomas	Pasq	1769
Willard	Rand	1779
Wm	Anso	1763
Wm	Bute	1771
Wm	Casw	1777
Wm	Chow	1753
Wm	Cumb	1767
Wm	FWV	1771
Wm	Gran	1784
Wm	Oran	1755
Wm	Pasq	1754
Wm Sr. 1m		
3f slaves	Pasq	1769
Wm	Pasq	1769
Wm	Rand	1779
WRITE, Solomon	Beau	1755
WROTTEN, Leven	Pitt	1762
Nehemiah	Pitt	1762
WYARS, Wm	Gran	1769
WYATT, John	Bert	1757
John	FWV	1771
Nathan	FWV	1771
WYLEY, Thomas	Chow	1717
WYMENTS, Peter	Bert	1769
WYNNE, Haskin	Bert	1769
James	Bert	1769
Jeremiah	Tyrr	1755
Peter	Tyrr	1755
Thomas	Casw	1777
Wm	Bert	1769
Wm	Casw	1777
WYNNS, Benjamin	Bert	1757
George	Bert	1757
John	Bert	1757
Joseph	Bert	1757
Pollasiah	Bert	1757
Wm	Bert	1757
WYSONG, Arthur	Bert	1757
YANAL, Thomas	Tyrr	1755
YANCEY, Bartlett s.		
of James	Gran	1755
James	Gran	1755
James	Gran	1769
Lewis	Gran	1755
Richard	Gran	1755
Richard	Gran	1769
Thornton s.		
of James	Gran	1755
Wm	Gran	1769
YARBOROUGH, Henry	Bute	1771
Henry Jr.	Bute	1771
Henry & s.		
Charles	FWV	1771
Henry Jr.	FWV	1771
Humphrey	Anso	1763
James	Bute	1771
James	FWV	1771

YARBOROUGH, Joel	Anso 1763	YATES, Wm	Rand 1779
John	Bute 1771	YEARGIN, Samuel	Bute 1771
John	Casw 1777	Samuel	FWV 1771
John	FWV 1771	YELVERTON, John	Chow 1717
John	Gran 1755	John	Roan 1720
John	Gran 1769	John	Roan 1720
Jonathan	Anso 1763	Noah s. of John	Dobb 1769
Joshua	Bute 1771	Noah	Dobb 1779
Joshua	FWV 1771	YEOMANS, Harris	Crav 1769
Joshua	Gran 1755	John	Crav 1769
Littleton	FWV 1771	YEW, Christopher	Crav 1741
Lucy	Casw 1777	Christopher	Cumb 1767
Maner s. of		YIELDING, Francis	Dobb 1769
Thomas	Gran 1755	YIEW, Christopher	Cumb 1755
Micajah	Bute 1771	YOPP, John	Onsl 1769
Micajah	FWV 1771	John	Onsl 1770
Richard	Bute 1771	YORK, Aaron	Rand 1779
Samuel	Casw 1777	Edmund	Rand 1779
Sarah	Casw 1777	Edward	Rand 1779
Thomas	Gran 1755	George Sr.	Rand 1779
Wm	Casw 1777	Henry	Oran 1755
Zachariah	Bute 1771	Henry	Rand 1779
Zachariah	FWV 1771	James	Rand 1779
YARNEL, Daniel	Rand 1779	Jeremiah	Rand 1779
YATES, Charles	Bert 1757	John	Oran 1755
Charles	Surr 1771	John	Rand 1779
Daniel	Bert 1757	John tailor	Rand 1779
Daniel	Crav 1769	John	Surr 1771
Daniel	Onsl 1769	Joseph	Rand 1779
Daniel	Onsl 1770	Mary 1m slave	Crav 1769
Edward	Blad 1781	Simon	Oran 1755
Francis	Cumb 1767	Simore	Oran 1755
George	Surr 1772	Thomas	Bute 1771
Henry	Cumb 1767	Thomas	Cumb 1755
James	Bert 1757	Thomas	FWV 1771
James	Bert 1769	Thomas	Rand 1779
James	Bute 1771	Wm s. of John	Rand 1779
James	Cart 1742	YOUELL, Mae	Pitt 1764
James	Onsl 1769	Thomas	Onsl 1769
James	Onsl 1770	YOUNG, Bartolet	Casw 1777
Jane	Blad 1781	Benjamin	Surr 1771
John	Bert 1757	Benjamin	Surr 1772
John	Bert 1769	Cecil	Surr 1772
John	Blad 1781	Charles	Gran 1784
John	Casw 1777	Daniel	Blad 1763
John	John 1746	David	Blad 1763
Peter	Bert 1757	David	Bute 1771
Peter	Bert 1769	David	FWV 1771
Peter	Blad 1781	Edward	Bute 1771
Robert	Bert 1757	Edward	FWV 1771
Thomas	Bert 1742	Edward	Gran 1755
Thomas	Bert 1757	George	Blad 1763
Thomas	Casw 1777	Grace	Dobb 1769
Thomas	Chow 1717	James	Casw 1777
Thomas	Chow 1721	James	Gran 1755
Thomas	Onsl 1769	James	Gran 1784
Thomas	Rand 1779	James	Surr 1772
Thomas	Rowa 1759	John	Bute 1771
Wm	Bert 1757	John s. of	
Wm	Bert 1769	Grace	Dobb 1769
Wm	Bute 1771	John & s. Wm	FWV 1771
Wm	Casw 1771	John	Gran 1755
Wm	Chow 1717	John	Gran 1769
Wm	Chow 1721	John	Gran 1784
Wm	FWV 1771	Joshua	Casw 1777

YOUNG, Lovick	Dobb	1769
Samuel	Rowa	1759
Thomas	Bute	1771
Thomas	FWV	1771
Wm	Casw	1777
Wm	Gran	1755
YOUNGBLOOD, Peter		
Jr.	Oran	1755
Peter Sr.	Oran	1755
Wm	Cumb	1755
YOUNGER, James	Oran	1755
Michael	Rowa	1759
YOURK, Seymore	Rand	1779
YOUSHAW, Wm	NewH	1762
YUNT, George Jr.	Rand	1779
George Sr.	Rand	1779
Henry	Rand	1779

ZACKARY, Thomas	Edge	1743
Thomas	Gran	1755
ZAHANDER, Isaac	Chow	1721
ZEISLOVE, George	Rowa	1759
ZELL, Edmund	FWV	1771
ZHEN, Christopher	Chow	1717
ZILMAN, Henry	Surr	1771
Isaac	Surr	1771
ZIMMERMAN, Christian		
	Rowa	1759
ZINK, George	Rand	1779
ZINOCK, Jacob	Rowa	1759
ZITTSWOOD, Isaac	Surr	1771
ZUCHRY, John	Cumb	1767